The Electronic Oracle

The Electronic Oracle

Computer Models and Social Decisions

D.H. Meadows

and

J.M. Robinson

Reprint with forewords by
Dennis Meadows and John Sterman

System Dynamics Society
Albany, New York

Originally published by John Wiley & Sons Ltd, 1985
(ISBN 0 471 90558 5)

Republished with forewords by Dennis Meadows and John Sterman
by the System Dynamics Society, 2007

Main text: Copyright © 2007 International Institute for
Applied Systems Analysis, 1985
Foreword by Dennis Meadows: Copyright © Dennis Meadows, 2007
Foreword by John Sterman: Copyright © John Sterman, 2007

All rights reserved.

No part of this book may be reproduced or transmitted
in any form or by any means, electronic or mechanical, including
photocopying, recording, or by any information storage or retrieval
system, without written permission of the publisher.

Library of Congress Cataloging-in-Publication Data

Meadows, Donella H.
  The electronic oracle : computer models and social decisions /
Donella H. Meadows and Jennifer M. Robinson. -- Reprint with
forewords by Dennis Meadows and John Sterman.
    p. cm.
"Originally published by John Wiley & Sons Ltd, 1985."
  Includes bibliographical references and index.

ISBN 978-0-9745329-6-7 (hardcover : alk. paper)
  1. Social sciences--Mathematical models. 2. Econometric models.
3. Mathematical models. 4. Computer simulation.   I. Robinson, J.
M. (Jenny M.)
II. Title.
H61.25.M4 2007
003'.3--dc22
                        2007015197

ISBN 978-0-9745329-6-7

Printed and bound in Troy, New York, United States of America.

1985
Dedication

To *Gerald O. Barney*
who got us started and kept us going
and to *Hugh J. Miser*
who pushed us through to completion.

2007
Acknowledgements

To *John Wiley & Sons*, publisher,
and *International Institute for Applied Systems Analysis*,
copyright holder, for granting permissions for this reprint.

Special thanks
to *Dennis Meadows* and *John Sterman*
for writing the forewords for this reprint.

And finally, thanks
to *Jane and Allen Boorstein* and *anonymous donors*
who contributed the seed money
that made this reprint project possible.

Contents

Foreword about Dana Meadows
by Dennis Meadows... xiii

Foreword about *The Electronic Oracle* Reprint
by John Sterman xvii

Prologue
by Donella H. Meadows xix

Part I. Introduction... 1

Chapter 1 The electronic oracle.. 5
   A. Computer models: the new oracles 5
   B. A comparative model survey 7
   C. The outline of this book 10
   D. Some definitions and conventions 11
   E. A personal statement 13

Part II. Modeling paradigms.. 17

Chapter 2 Models of modeling 19
   A. The concept of paradigm 19
   B. Preconceptions and purposes of modeling........................... 20
   C. The paradigms 26
      1. System dynamics 27
      2. Econometrics 42
      3. Input–output analysis 55
      4. Optimization 64
   D. Composite models 73
   E. An example of paradigm conflict: econometrics and
       system dynamics 75

F. Conclusion 86

Part III. Nine models **91**

Chapter 3 How to describe a model? **93**
    A. Checklist 93
    B. Boundary diagram 97
    C. Causal diagram 97
    D. Reference structure 100
    E. Tolerance 104

Chapter 4 SAHEL: The tragedy of the commons **106**
    A. Institutional setting 106
    B. Purpose 107
    C. Method 108
    D. Boundaries 108
    E. Structure 110
    F. Data 115
    G. Conclusions 115
    H. Testing 119
    I. Computer requirements 120
    J. Implementation 120
    K. Documentation 123

Chapter 5 RfF: Adding a combine to a tractor **125**
    A. Institutional setting 125
    B. Purpose 126
    C. Method 126
    D. Boundaries 130
    E. Structure 132
    F. Data 134
    G. Testing 136
    H. Conclusions 137
    I. Implementation 140
    J. Documentation 141

Chapter 6 SOS: The perfectly-adjusting society **144**
    A. Institutional setting 144
    B. Purpose 145
    C. Method 145
    D. Boundaries 147
    E. Structure 149
        1. Population 149

    2. Production 150
    3. Resources 151
    4. Adjustment set 153
  F. Data 155
  G. Testing 156
  H. Conclusions 157
  I. Implementation 159
  J. Computer requirements 160
  K. Documentation 160

Chapter 7 TEMPO: Educating the third world 162
  A. Institutional setting 162
  B. Purpose 163
  C. Method 163
  D. Boundaries 164
  E. Structure 165
  F. Data 170
  G. Conclusions 172
  H. Testing 174
  I. Implementation 175
  J. Computer requirements 177
  K. Documentation 177

Chapter 8 LTSM: The race between production and consumption 179
  A. Institutional setting 179
  B. Purpose 179
  C. Method 181
  D. Boundaries 182
  E. Structure 183
  F. Data 191
  G. Testing 191
  H. Conclusions 193
  I. Implementation 195
  J. Computer requirements 195
  K. Documentation 195

Chapter 9 BACHUE: A twenty-legged robot 198
  A. Institutional setting 198
  B. Purpose 199
  C. Method 200
  D. Boundaries 202
  E. Structure 205
  F. Data 216
  G. Testing 217

H.	Conclusions	219
I.	Implementation	221
J.	Computer requirements	222
K.	Documentation	222

Chapter 10 KASM: Not a puree but a stew 225
A.	Institutional setting	225
B.	Purpose	227
C.	Method	227
D.	Boundaries	228
E.	Structure	230
F.	Data	236
G.	Conclusions	237
H.	Testing	241
I.	Implementation	242
J.	Computer requirements	245
K.	Documentation	245

Chapter 11 *MexicoV*: Statistical patches 248
A.	Institutional setting	248
B.	Purpose	249
C.	Method	249
D.	Boundaries	252
E.	Structure	253
F.	Data	260
G.	Testing	260
H.	Conclusions	262
I.	Computer requirements	264
J.	Implementation	264
K.	Documentation	264

Chapter 12 CHAC: Optimizing Mexican agriculture 267
A.	Institutional setting	267
B.	Purpose	268
C.	Method	269
D.	Boundaries	273
E.	Structure	274
F.	Data	279
G.	Testing	279
H.	Conclusions	281
I.	Computer requirements	284
J.	Implementation	285
K.	Documentation	286

Part IV. The state of the art **289**

Chapter 13 Model content: The process of industrialization **291**
    A. Population growth 293
        1. Mental models 293
        2. Computer models 295
        3. Summary and commentary 302
    B. Production and allocation 305
        1. Mental models 305
        2. Computer models 307
        3. Summary and commentary 314
    C. Technological change 318
        1. Mental models 318
        2. Computer models 319
        3. Summary and commentary 329
    D. Migration and labor allocation 331
        1. Mental models 331
        2. Computer models 333
        3. Summary and commentary 342
    E. Environment and natural resources 344
        1. Mental models 344
        2. Computer models 345
        3. Summary and commentary 351
    F. Conclusion: Lessons about industrialization 352

Chapter 14 Model quality: Advantages of computer models **358**
    A. Rigor 358
    B. Comprehensiveness 362
    C. Logic 363
    D. Accessibility 366
    E. Testability 368
    F. Conclusion: Room for improvement 370

Chapter 15 Implementation: Changing the world **373**
    A. The evaluation of models and of policy: A necessary digression .. 374
        1. The modelers' and clients' and evaluators' goals 374
        2. The extent to which the goals were reached 376
        3. The cost of reaching whatever goals were reached 376
        4. The unintended, unforeseen impacts 376
    B. The implementation record - as we see it 378
    C. Some hypotheses 382
        1. Policymakers as boors 382

    2. Modelers as clowns... 383
    3. Supermodeler... 383
    4. The two cultures 384
    5. The learning curve 384
    6. No problem 384

Part V. Prescriptions.. **389**

  Chapter 16 An inventory of suggestions for improvement **391**
    A. Knowledge problems 392
    B. Institutional problems 395
    C. Practice problems.. 396
    D. Guidelines, for what they are worth 403

  Chapter 17 The transformation of modeling.. **414**
    A. The ultimate source of system structure................................... 417
    B. Computer modelers as scientists 419
    C. Computer modelers as policymakers 424
    D. Computer modelers as human beings 429

Epilogue **435**

Index... **439**

Foreword About Dana Meadows

The decision to reprint *The Electronic Oracle* was made during the 2001 annual meeting of the International System Dynamics Society, in Atlanta, Georgia. At that meeting John Sterman organized a panel of speakers to reflect on the nature and the importance of Donella Meadows' contributions to the field. Among her friends she was known as Dana. I spoke as a member of that panel and referred to Dana's many publications. I pointed out the unique role of this book and lamented that it was no longer available. It is still a unique resource for any serious student or practitioner who is eager to use mathematical models to gain insights that are relevant to the behavior of social and economic systems.

Dana came to our field after her formal education was completed. She already had a Ph.D. from Harvard University and an international reputation in biophysics. One night in June 1970, I brought home a copy of Jay Forrester's text, *Principles of Systems*. She read it through and decided to abandon a post doctoral fellowship in one of Harvard's most prestigious laboratories. She joined the team I was assembling for the Club of Rome to elaborate Jay Forrester's World2 global model. She was a central member of the team, formulated the demographic sector of our world model, and was the principal author of our most widely-known report, *The Limits to Growth*.

Dana and I moved to Dartmouth College in 1972. There she became that college's first tenured female professor and eventually Dartmouth's first female full professor. Along the way she was also selected one year as the most outstanding young woman faculty member in the entire United States.

She worked with me and others to create two new academic programs at Dartmouth. One was for undergraduates; the other for graduate students. Both emphasized systems analysis and policy design. She was a brilliant teacher—dedicated, creative, caring, and effective. She would have felt that her most important professional legacy was the group of students and colleagues that she informed and inspired. She challenged the ideas and raised the aspirations of almost everyone she worked with. Many of the senior professionals active in system dynamics today benefited from their association with her.

Despite her success as a professor, she became impatient with the demands of conventional academic life. She gave up her title and her tenure. This had never happened before at Dartmouth, and the College's administration was nonplussed. Finally she accepted an appointment as an adjunct professor. She kept an office, and she taught one course each year at Dartmouth in environmental journalism. She wanted to concentrate on her writing.

She was a prolific writer, producing hundreds of newspaper columns, many magazine articles, and numerous books including *The Electronic Oracle*. Even though she and Jennifer Robinson started their research for the book in 1975, over 30 years ago, this text remains a profoundly important resource for our field—for all of us, whether we labor as teachers, analysts, managers, consultants, or even as philosophers.

I have been building, teaching, and using system dynamics models for over 35 years, yet I still gain inspiration and insight from Dana's writings on the theoretical foundations of our field and on the standards of excellence for modeling. Her writing is a treasure chest for those of us trying to understand the field, increase our own mastery, teach our skills to others, or enhance our effectiveness in communicating our results to clients.

Meetings of the System Dynamics Society's Policy Council often address the issue of model quality. As Jay Forrester recently observed, "We do not have in the System Dynamics Society the culture of active critique that is found in some societies." But Dana came to system dynamics from biophysics, where intense scrutiny, criticism, and defense of one's work are essential for the field's progress. She brought that culture of active critique with her, and it was one of the central characteristics and preoccupations of her writing.

Many of Dana's articles offer sage pronouncements on the roles of models—their advantages and disadvantages. But the most profound treatment of these issues is in this book, which was published in 1985 by John Wiley & Sons.

Oracle offers an extremely detailed analysis of nine different models related to economic and social development—widely respected models that were elaborated using one or another of four different modeling paradigms—econometrics, input-output, system dynamics, and optimization. Typically for Dana, she not only read each model report thoroughly, she also studied many of the classic texts that lay behind the four paradigms. After critiquing the details of each model, Dana provided a set of chapters on modeling methodology. I do not know a more penetrating or useful discussion about what we modelers have actually accomplished and where we still have enormous, and profoundly important, work to do.

In *Oracle* (pp. 414–415), she wrote that social system problems:

> are persistent. They go on [and on] in spite of the most sophisticated scientific establishments, communication systems, satellites, models, and databases the world has ever known. And at the same time, [computer modeling], a field that has real promise of raising the global level of understanding and of giving human beings a perspective from which they might be able to untangle their self-tied knots, that field is persisting in its own perverse behavior:
>
> - It concentrates on easily-quantifiable parts of the system, not important parts.
> - It devotes tremendous labor...to achieving small increases in precision, meanwhile doing little effective testing for general accuracy.
> - It assumes and reinforces the social structure that is the cause of the destructive behaviors, rather than raising questions of long-term goals, meaningful social indicators, or system redesign.
> - It produces complicated black boxes that outsiders must take on faith—it does not share its learning effectively with users....
> - It rarely sets its sights high enough to demonstrate its unique contribution—its ability to focus attention on systems as wholes [not parts] and on long-term evolution [rather than short-term palliatives].
> - Many of its efforts are not credible, not used, and not even documented so that others can learn from our mistakes.

I know we all like to pat ourselves on the back and gloat that system dynamicists do not make those mistakes nearly as much as the econometricians or the linear programmers or the input-output analysts. Perhaps that is true. I hope it is true. But you all know that every one of those criticisms applies to most of what we do—and it does not need to.

Dana did not write her book merely to criticize; she wanted to inspire change in our practices and our goals. And she details the ways to do that.

As she wrote (*Oracle*, p. 415):

modelers themselves recognize and complain about [their own] underperformance. They describe the better ways they could all behave, to be more effective. Then they don't behave that way. Clearly there are systemic, structural reasons why they do not. But there the conversation stops.

Many of us are focused on defending our work; Dana was defending global society. She thought computer modeling is by far the most useful tool for clarifying the important problems of our time. But she recognized the shortcomings inherent in our techniques and the limitations in our canons of professional practice. She had infinite faith in our capacity to do better and profound hope that we would do better and thereby help the world move in more equitable, beautiful, and sustainable paths.

So let me finish with a brief parable that Dana liked very much. Dana was fascinated by the Sufi religion and especially by its oral traditions. Many of them involve stories about a lay religious teacher, Nasrudin. He was a simple man with profound insights about paradigms and social systems. Dana started one of her books with this Sufi parable:

A neighbor passing by saw Nasrudin searching for something on the ground in the road under the street lamp outside his house. "What have you lost, teacher?" he asked. "I have lost my key," said Nasrudin. So they both went down on their knees and looked for it. But after much effort they had no success.

After a time the man asked, "Where exactly did you drop your key?" "Oh," said Nasrudin, "I dropped it in my house." "Then why are you looking for it out here?" asked the neighbor. "Oh," said the mulla, "there is more light here than in my house."

Dana found Nasrudin's fruitless search to be a wonderful metaphor for most computer modeling efforts. She felt they are vain searches for solutions in areas where client interest or available data or public funds or political trends make it easy and professionally rewarding to look. Dana followed another path. She spent her professional life groping for important answers in the dark. And in the process she discovered and left us some important keys to the future of our discipline. Many of them are discussed in this book.

Dennis Meadows
Durham, New Hampshire, USA
January 2007

Foreword About *The Electronic Oracle* Reprint

Why reprint a book on computer modeling originally published in 1985 and reporting modeling work even older? Back then, computers were large, expensive mainframes available only to a technical elite with large budgets. There was no Internet. Data were scarce and unreliable. Systems analysis methods were comparatively new, and few members of the public had ever worked first-hand with a simulation. Today everything is different, right? *Plus ça change*.... Despite the enormous changes in technology, the ubiquity of computers, video games and simulations, the insights in this book are as fresh and relevant today as when originally published.

The Electronic Oracle investigates the practice and impact of systems analysis and computer modeling, particularly as applied to social policy. Dana and Jenny have not written a theoretical tract on how modeling ought to be done; they report how modeling is actually done. A report from the field, *Oracle* explores the nature of models, the biases and hidden assumptions of different modeling methods, the pragmatics of the modeling process, and the impact of modeling on the real world. They do so through detailed case studies of nine models designed to address issues of economic development, resources and the environment. The insights Dana and Jenny offer here are based on thousands of hours of painstaking work. For each model, they acquired all the available documentation and, where possible, the original code, along with reports, white papers, news accounts, and other archival data bearing on how the models were built, represented to the public and policymakers, and used. Thinking that modelers, as scientists, would adhere to proper scientific method, Dana and Jenny originally expected that the models would be fully documented, available, and easily examined. They quickly discovered that the documentation was incomplete and obscure, that many of the models could not be replicated, that modeling methods often drove the framing of the problem rather than being chosen to suit the purpose and needs of the client, and that most of the models had, at best, limited impact. I recall seeing large stacks of model documentation in Dana's office, stacks that lingered for years, each representing the material from one of the models. Each required months of difficult effort simply to generate a model boundary diagram showing which concepts were captured endogenously, which were exogenous, and which concepts important for the issue were excluded. Every modeler should have the experience of replicating and explicating someone else's model so as to learn firsthand the importance of clear, complete documentation, of replication, of transparent and forthright declaration of purpose, background, and motives.

So what are the results? The models Dana and Jenny examined spanned a range of methods including econometrics, linear programming, input/output analysis, and system dynamics. Although these models were "identified as 'better than average' " by the authors and by "other modelers, clients, and sponsors," Dana and Jenny found "mismatches of methods with purposes, sloppy documentation, absurd assumptions buried in over complex structures, conclusions that do not even follow from model output, and project management strategies that destroy the possibility of influencing actual policy." Despite many notable successes, the record today, in both social policy and in the world of business, is at least as dismal.

While the specific models explored in *Oracle* are no longer in use, the methods Dana and Jenny developed to expose hidden assumptions, to make undiscussable values and biases discussable, to highlight the dysfunctional practices that prevent clients—and modelers—from learning, remain central to anyone seeking to use modeling effectively or to have an impact on the real world. The book both anticipated and shaped important developments in the field of system dynamics, including the focus on modeling for learning, group model building, and the systems thinking and organizational learning movements. With characteristic passion, and not a little humor, Dana and Jenny show us how to be better modelers, scientists, communicators, advocates, and policymakers. Despite welcome advances in hardware, software, and modeling methods since the book was written, the practice of modeling lags behind. We have not yet realized the authors' vision of a world in which modelers are not only scientific and rigorous, but "compassionate, humble, open-minded, responsible, self-insightful, and committed."

John Sterman
Cambridge Massachusetts, USA
January 2007

Prologue

We started writing this book in 1974, and completed a first draft in 1980. Then the manuscript sat on my desk for three years, where it was likely to stay forever, holding up my clock, and blocking the view out of my window. The book was finally resurrected and brought into print, primarily because of the constant urging of Hugh Miser, who took an early interest in the book while he was head of publications at the International Institute of Applied Systems Analysis (IIASA), and whose encouragement never weakened, even after he left that position. Finally he used the one argument no author could possibly resist—he said that the book was too important to the field to remain unpublished. Whether or not that was true, the strategy worked. I did one more editing, added a final chapter, and the book is now off my desk and in your hands.

I should probably explain the long incubation process, the near-abandonment of the manuscript, and why I finally convinced myself that a book on the state of an art should be published, even though its examples come from the art of ten years ago. While we were writing the book Jenny Robinson and I were more involved in teaching and doing systems analysis than in surveying the state of the art. Except for the first year, when we were gathering data and reading descriptions of dozens of models, the book was a part-time and uncompensated activity for both of us. I was also farming, teaching at Dartmouth, doing my own policy-oriented systems studies, and working for the end of world hunger. Jenny was earning an M.S. in agricultural economics, working on the *Global 2000* study, making models at IIASA, and finally returning for her Ph.D. in geography at Santa Barbara. Somewhere in there she also designed and built her own house.

When the book was put on the shelf, we were finished with everything except a few parts we were most stuck on. We were frustrated trying to trace down the effects of the example models in the real world. We were not sure how to end the book. We were tired of the whole enterprise and deeply involved in starting new ventures. The parts of the book I liked best had already been published separately in various places. Since I have never believed in publishing simply to keep from perishing, but only in publishing when I have something I really want to communicate, I let the book fade in my attention.

Coming back to it now after three years, I am surprised and somewhat appalled at how much of it is still relevant. There are now more recent economic–demographic models we could include, but they are not significantly different in concept, method, content, or implementation effectiveness from the models described here. The list of complaints and suggestions for improvement from practitioners in the field has changed not at all over the years, and it is still true that virtually no one is following any of the suggestions. As far as I can tell, there are no exciting new methods, no more wisdom in matching method to problem, no more imagination in depicting society, and certainly no better standards of documentation. So the examples, literature references, and conclusions we cite here are, I believe, still representative. Adding more recent examples would neither contradict nor make more clear any of the points of the book.

There are, however, a few hints of change detectable now that we could not see during the 1970s. One is that social-system modeling seems to have become less visible. It is still going on, but at a slower pace, with much less fanfare and less ambitious expectations. Very few people are still worried that computer modelers are about to usurp political power. Some of this slowdown can be traced to the stagnant world economy and to new political regimes in several Western countries that are decidedly anti-analytical. But I think much of the eclipse of computer modeling comes from disillusionment on the part of both modelers and clients with what modeling can accomplish. Much of that disillusionment is appropriate, as this book demonstrates. The initial heyday and the exaggerated claims are gone; I hope that means that everyone is settling down to more professional practice, rather than no practice at all.

A second change now visible is the sudden presence of microcomputers in the lives of ordinary people. I think that familiarity with these computers will have a liberating effect on social-system modeling. There will be sufficient public understanding of the computer to disperse the remaining traces both of distrust and of unthinking acceptance of any advice coming from a computer. Computer models will be questioned more intelligently, modelers will be less able to hide behind jargon. It is also possible that widespread use of small computers will force the construction of simple models, which would be a good thing. Unfortunately, however, since more computing capacity is being packaged in smaller and cheaper compartments, reasonable constraints on the size of models may be too much to hope for.

The third change is one we mention in the epilogue. At the same time that users are becoming disillusioned with modeling, the field of modeling is reforming itself. There is more humility and humanity now in the way many modelers do their work. There is less hype and more wisdom, less mystery, more communication. The field is certainly a long way from the paradigm shift we call for in the last chapter, but the shift is visible within many individuals in the modeling community.

The reader may detect some inconsistencies in tone and emphasis between the early and late chapters of the book. We ourselves were undergoing a paradigm shift over the years we were compiling the book, similar to that described in Chapter 16. Having made the transition ourselves, we are confident of the ability of our colleagues to make it as well. We look forward to the exciting revelations awaiting them and us and the field as a whole, as more practitioners come to see the world from a different, and what looks to us like a more constructive, place.

We need to express our appreciation to the many people who helped us with this book, beginning with Gerald Barney, who suggested it, provided the funding to begin it, and was almost as insistent as Hugh Miser in keeping us at it. The makers of the models described in the book have been very patient with our requests for documentation, our blunt questions, and our delay in publication. Helpful reviewers of the book at various times have included Jay Forrester, John Richardson, Edward Quade, and Nino Majone. Dennis Meadows has tolerated the manuscript cluttering up his household for years, and he has also provided searching criticism of the text. Many of those just listed will find that we have not always followed their suggestions. We would like to assure them that we did hear and appreciate their advice, but that finally we had to say what we had to say.

DONELLA H. MEADOWS
Plainfield, New Hampshire
December 29, 1983

PART I

Introduction

> You may very appropriately want to ask me how we are going to resolve the ever-acceleratingly dangerous impasse of world-opposed politicians and ideological dogmas. I answer, it will be resolved by the computer. Man has ever-increasing confidence in the computer; witness his unconcerned landings as air transport passengers ... in the combined invisibility of fog and night. While no politician or political system can ever afford to yield to their adversaries and opposers, all politicians can and will yield enthusiastically to the computer's safe flight-controlling capabilities in bringing all of humanity in for a happy landing.
> R. Buckminster Fuller

> I can't understand it. I can't even understand the people who can understand it.
> Queen Juliana of the Netherlands,
> watching a demonstration of an electronic computer at Amsterdam

One of the most enduring problems of the human race is that each person must continually take actions that require knowledge of the future. A general decides whether to attack, a farmer chooses which crops to plant, a student selects a course of study and a career, a nation stockpiles grain or bombs. These decisions must be made under a discomforting ignorance of what the future will be like or how one's current decisions may affect it. Whatever one suspects about the future can only be derived from accumulated observations and generalizations from the past. And no one knows the past very well either. Human understanding of any event, even one witnessed directly, is obscured, warped, tainted by all sorts of unrecognized conceptual and perceptual biases. Hence the dilemma: one needs to foresee the future in order to make wise decisions, but one cannot even be very certain about the past or the present.

Decision makers have devised ingenious methods over the centuries to bridge the gap between imperfect knowledge of the past and necessary decisions about the future. At the Delphic oracle of ancient Greece a priestess delivered futuristic pronouncements from a trance induced by breathing sulfurous fumes. Royal courts in many countries and over many centuries maintained a corps of soothsayers, astrologers, Merlins, and Rasputins. Forecasting techniques in the Middle Ages included divination by the Bible (bibliomancy), by the entrails of sacrificed animals (hieromancy), by dots made at random on paper (geomancy), and by dropping melted wax into water (ceromancy). Human legend and history are filled with crystal balls, Cassandras, prophets and omens.

All these magical techniques are based on essentially two sources of information. One is chance; the working out of some complex process like the fall of dice or the swirling of tea leaves according to the laws of the gods, or as we would say nowadays, the laws of science. Even the chance-based methods of forecasting, however, depend also on the second source of information—human interpretation. Whether the human mind is used to read the tea leaves, decipher the messages of the stars, or deliver a straight prophecy without props, mental images and analogies, quirks and visions are and always will be the ultimate basis for human statements about the future.

This book is about *models*, by which we will mean any set of generalizations or assumptions about reality. Models are the tools—the only tools—that human beings use to link the prop to the prophecy; the past to the future. The most common models are in people's heads; we will call them *mental models*. Mental models are nebulous and imprecise, the unexpressed observations, abstractions, and intuitions that make up each person's image of the world. The human brain can store an amazing number and variety of observations, and combine them into extremely sophisticated generalizations. Mental models are not numerically exact, but they contain an immensely rich collection of information, much of it derived from direct experience. The vast majority of human decisions are based on individual, unverbalized, shifting mental models. These decisions seem to allow most people to function reasonably well, most of the time, in a complex and variable world.[1]

Organizational decision makers, whether they are heads of families, firms, or nations, deal with decisions so complex and far-reaching that the intuitions and experiences of a single person are clearly insufficient for the task. Therefore they seek expert advice, conduct opinion polls, read the literature on a subject, form a study committee, put the matter to a vote, or consult whatever sort of oracle is available. All these activities involve assessing several models and either choosing the single 'best' one or combining the assumptions and conclusions of several into a model that is intended to be more comprehensive, correct, or acceptable than any single person's could be.

Such joint decisions require communication of mental models. But models are not directly transferable from one mind to another. Their transmission can take place only through symbols, usually spoken or written words. Communication of a mental model through symbols is terribly difficult. One is usually only vaguely aware of one's own intuitions and assumptions. Mental models shift from moment to moment. They do not fit the linear, sequential format required by language. And words are inherently ambiguous, as are the images, thoughts, and hunches the words describe. Because of all these difficulties, verbal expression more often takes the form of advocating *what* one thinks should be done than of detailing all the semi-conscious urges that determine *why* one thinks it should be done.

Even in the modern age of science and industrialization social policy decisions are based on incompletely-communicated mental models. The assumptions and reasoning behind a decision are not really examinable, even to the decider. The logic, if there is any, leading to a social policy is unclear to most people affected by the policy. As far as the general public and even many policymakers themselves are concerned, today's vital decisions are about as understandable and accessible as if they had been handed down by a Delphic oracle.

NOTES AND REFERENCES

1. For some varied and detailed discussions of the development, strengths and weaknesses of mental models, see R. E. Ornstein, *The Psychology of Consciousness*, San Francisco, W. H. Freeman, 1972; and J. W. Forrester, 'Counterintuitive Behavior of Social Systems', *Technology Review* **73**, (**3**), January 1971.

CHAPTER 1

The Electronic Oracle

A. COMPUTER MODELS: THE NEW ORACLES

Just as mental models can be partially, approximately, expressed in words, they can also be partially, approximately, expressed in mathematical symbols. Mathematical symbols are much more precise and unambiguous, though less rich and varied, than words. Until this century the expression of models through mathematical equations was limited almost entirely to the physical sciences, where the relationships to be described were usually simple and precise enough to be fitted easily to mathematical notation. However, in the last few decades a new symbol-processing tool, the computer, has allowed mathematical symbols of all sorts to be stored and manipulated in quantities and at speeds orders of magnitude greater than were possible before. Computer models are nothing but mathematical models translated into the special, usually digital, languages that computers can read. Computer models of social as well as physical systems are increasing in number, complexity, and size as computers become cheaper and more widely accessible.

A 1974 study identified 650 mathematical models made for the U.S. non-defense federal agencies alone.[1] Virtually all of these were complex enough to be computerized. Computer models are used to decide how much pollution a new factory should be allowed to put into a river, whether aerosol cans should be banned, and what the price of natural gas should be. Computer-generated conclusions have been entered as evidence in court cases. Computer programs routinely churn out ordering decisions to manage inventories, work through the implications of alternate investment schemes, and tell the business community what rate of economic growth to expect. In federal governments computer models forecast future taxes and budget balances, decide on agricultural pricing schemes and, in centrally-planned economies, lay-out the details of the next five years' production. The Delphic oracle is gone, but the need for pronouncements about the future persists. Now there is a very sophisticated new way to meet that need.

Promoters of the computer as a forecasting tool claim that mathematical models contribute greatly to the effectiveness, utility and equity of social decision making. They claim that computer models have several potential advantages over even the best mental models:

1. *Rigor.* The assumptions in computer models must be specified explicitly, completely, and precisely; no ambiguities are possible. Every variable must be defined, and assumptions must be mutually consistent. Computer modelers often mention that the discipline required to formulate a mathematical model is helpful in organizing and clarifying their own mental models, even before any computer analysis takes place.
2. *Comprehensiveness.* A computer can manipulate more information than the human mind and can keep track of many more interrelationships at one time. It can combine observations from many mental models into a more comprehensive picture than could ever be contained in a single human head.
3. *Logic.* If programmed correctly, the computer can process even a very complicated set of assumptions to draw logical, error-free conclusions. The human mind is quite likely to make errors in logic, especially if the logical chain is complex. Different people may agree completely about a set of assumptions and still disagree about the conclusion to be drawn from them. A computer model should always reach the same conclusion from a single set of assumptions.
4. *Accessibility.* Because all the assumptions must be explicit, precise, and unambiguous in order to communicate them to the computer, critics can examine, assess, and alter computer models, whereas mental models are virtually unexaminable and uncriticizable.
5. *Flexibility.* Computer models can easily test a wide variety of different conditions and policies, providing a form of social experimentation that is much less costly and time-consuming than tests within the real social system.

Given these advantages, one would expect computer models to be welcomed and widely used. But in practice computer models have clarified and improved social decisions only in limited areas. They have been readily adopted to help make short-term, clearly-definable, operational decisions, such as how to allocate mail trucks among various delivery routes, how many beds a new hospital should have, or what the prime interest rate should be. When it comes to large-scale, far-reaching social decisions, where mental models may be weakest and computer models uniquely helpful, decisions about such things as energy policy, international trade, or design of new institutions, computer models are regularly viewed with suspicion. Millions of dollars and thousands of person-years of effort have been invested in such models, but they have yielded only a small return in terms of any recognizable impact on actual social decisions. Computer models of large, complex social systems are more often made than used, more often criticized than praised.[2]

Professional modelers are concerned by the mixed record of rapid growth and slow implementation of their efforts. Surveys and studies are appearing, assessing the state of the art and attempting to explain and promote the practice of computer modeling to the non-modeling world, especially to the policymaker.[3] Conferences and training sessions are held to bring modelers and policymakers together, to 'bridge the gap' between the world of analysis and the world of action.

The gap remains unbridged. Over and over in writing and in person, the modelers keep asking: 'Why don't you use our models?' The policymakers respond: 'Why don't you make models we can use?'

B. A COMPARATIVE MODEL SURVEY

In this book we attempt to answer these questions: Are computer models of large-scale social systems useful? Do they expand or enhance mental models and provide some help in managing human affairs in a complex world? If not, why not? And if so, why are computer models so seldom used as input to important decisions? Our goal is constructive; we would like to live in a society where decisions are based on the most accurate possible image of both the past and the future. Therefore, we would hope that any means to increase understanding of complicated, interconnected social systems would be encouraged and used.

When we began the work described here, we intended to demonstrate that:

1. Complex models based on dissimilar methods can be discussed within a common format, so that a non-technical audience can compare and evaluate them.
2. These models are capable of generating new insights into difficult current socioeconomic problems.
3. A few straightforward alterations of the process of model construction, the interaction with clients, and the reporting of results could strengthen the inherent advantages of computer models and allow policymakers to make more informed choices among the many policy options available to them.

It will become clear as we proceed that our message ended up being more complicated than that. We found that some computer models are so incongruent with either mental models or real-world processes that we despaired of finding ways to communicate them. Some very complicated models generate no insights beyond elaborate translations of the modelers' original assumptions. Others produce messages so antithetical to established thinking that they are rejected out of hand even though they may be correct. And the necessary changes in the practice of computer modelling may be major, not minor, and personal, not technical. But before we discuss these conclusions further, let us describe the process that led us to them.

We approached our task by taking as examples several major computer models that have been formulated as inputs to social policy. The stories of these models provide a number of useful lessons about the problems and potentials of modeling in social decision-making. The models all address a roughly similar set of broad and long-term issues—the formulation of national policy to deal with interacting processes of population growth, agricultural production, and economic development. We chose studies of both industrialized and non-industrialized nations, to assess the similarities and differences of models of various stages of the industrialization process. The models were constructed by different groups for different sponsors, using a number of different modeling techniques. The models, their formulators, sponsors, and study areas are summarized in Table 1.1.

We chose our sample according to the following criteria:

1. Each model should be sufficiently mature and documented to permit technical examination of its assumptions and conclusions. (This criterion alone eliminated many possible models from our survey.)
2. A wide variety of techniques and countries of application should be included to illustrate the scope of analytical possibilities.
3. The models should address development/food/population policy at the national, not the global or local, level, so that they deal with comparable problems and policy questions.
4. The models should be good examples of the current state of the modeling art, highly regarded by those familiar with the field. Each one was suggested to us as especially interesting or useful by its sponsor and/or by other modelers in the field.
5. The models should have been developed in consultation with or at the request of national policymakers. They should be concrete policy models rather than academic exercises.

We started with a large sample and gradually eliminated all but nine models. Each of the nine meets most of our original criteria.

We assembled the available documents for each model and in most cases directly interviewed the modelers and sponsors concerning unclear points or unfinished work. We prepared a verbal summary of each model and several diagrams of its boundaries and primary assumptions. Our summary of each model was reviewed by the modelling group and/or sponsor to correct misunderstandings or inaccuracies.

Although we are modelers ourselves, we are not expert at all the technical methods used, nor were we familiar with the details of any of these models before we began our study. We tried to approach the various models as a technically educated, concerned citizen or policymaker would, one who has no particular knowledge of any branch of modeling, but who wants to understand what the models say about the process of industrialization and the consequences of national policies. We tried to ask questions such a person might ask

Table 1.1 Models included in the survey

Model name (principal modelers) Modeling institution	Sponsor	Client	Region of Application
1. SAHEL (Picardi) Massachusetts Institute of Technology	United States Agency for International Development, Africa Bureau	USAID and Sahel national governments	Sahel
2. No model name (Ridker) Resources for the Future (RfF)	Commission on Population Growth and the American Future	United States Government	USA
3. SOS (House and Williams) United States Environmental Protection Agency	United States Environmental Protection Agency and modelers' private resources	National or regional governments	USA or regional
4. TEMPO II (Enke) General Electric Tempo	United States Agency for International Development, Office of Population	National governments	Peru, Venezuela, Chile, many others
5. LTSM (Martos, Lin) United Nations Food and Agriculture Organization	United Nations Fund for Population Activities	National governments	Egypt, Pakistan, non-industrialized countries with labor surplus
6. BACHUE (Rodgers, Wery, and Hopkins) United Nations International Labor Organization	United Nations Fund for Population Activities	National governments	Philippines, Brazil, Kenya and others
7. KASM (Johnson, Rossmiller, Abkin, Carroll, de Haen) Michigan State University	United States Agency for International Development, Technical Assistance Bureau	Korean Ministry of Agriculture and Fisheries	South Korea
8. MEXICOV (Beltran del Rio) Wharton Economic Forecasting Associates	Mexican private businesses	Mexican private businesses and government	Mexico
9. CHAC (Duloy, Norton) World Bank	World Bank, Bank of Mexico, Mexican government	World Bank, Mexican government	Mexico

about a model, questions focused on content, utility, and real-world relationships rather than mathematical elegance or computer technicalities.

As we worked, it became obvious that two factors beyond the available data and theory on development were significant in determining the final messages of the models. One was the underlying and usually unexpressed methodological assumptions of each different school of modeling. The other was the organizational situation of the model: the interrelationships, forms of communication, pressures, deadlines, and motivations that characterized each set of modelers and policymakers. Methodological assumptions and institutional settings were rarely described in the model documentation, but we found them so important that we had to delve fairly deeply into them before we could understand how the models came to be and why they took the forms they did. A large part of this report, therefore, is devoted to the modeling methods and the institutional settings within which modelers work.

C. THE OUTLINE OF THIS BOOK

Each school of modeling is based on a set of operational assumptions about what the world is like, what a model should be, what makes it valid, and what questions should be asked about it. To make sense of the modeling field, and especially to sort out the claims and counterclaims of the various schools, one must understand the method-based assumptions that shape the worlds of different kinds of modelers. In Part II we summarize the primary conceptual predispositions underlying each modeling method represented in this study.

Part III contains descriptions of each of the nine models in our survey. The institutional setting of each model and the results of its implementation, if any, are discussed, as well as its primary assumptions and conclusions. This Part is long and heavy for those not intrinsically interested in the gory and contorted innards of the models; it can be skipped by all but the most technically dedicated readers. Others can pick up the essence of the nine models in what we consider the heart of the book—Parts IV and V.

Part IV raises the evaluative questions. From these nine models, what can we conclude about the state of the modeling art? Are the models scientifically useful? Do they tell us anything about the world, especially about the process of development, we did not already know? We look at what the models have contributed to understanding of such aspects of the industrialization process as population growth, technical change, and use of natural resources. We consider how the models demonstrate the theoretical advantages of computer modeling and where they fall short. We also ask questions about implementation. Are computer models used? Have they in any sense changed the world? We review the implementation histories of some of the models, which indicate that the modeling process has obvious impact on the world, but not often the impact that was intended.

Finally, in Part V we turn from evaluation to prescription. We collect from the modelers themselves a list of suggestions for improvement, and we conclude with our own deeper list of improvements that we believe will lead both to more frequent implementation of models and to models that are more accessible and useful as inputs to public policy.

D. SOME DEFINITIONS AND CONVENTIONS

Some fairly common words and symbols have come to have subtly different meanings in the policy world and in the modeling world, and sometimes semantic misunderstandings even arise among different kinds of modelers. Since this report is intended to span those several worlds, we need to define carefully some of the basic terms and representational conventions we will use.

A *model* is any set of generalizations or assumptions about the world. A *mental model* is the set of assumptions in a single person's head; a *formal model* is written down, either in words, or in the case of the models in this book, in mathematical equations and computer language.

A *system* is any set of interrelated elements. Thus a system is composed of two kinds of entities; *elements*, which are generally visible or measurable objects or flows, and *relationships*, which are connections that are postulated to exist between these elements. For example a model might contain two elements, food *per capita* and death rate, and a postulated relationship indicating how different values of the element food *per capita* affect the element death rate.

A relationship will be defined as *causal* if it is necessarily sequential in time and incorporates some hypothesis about the mechanisms whereby one element directly influences another. Food *per capita* may influence death rate through the known biochemical effects of malnutrition on human health; this relationship is causal. We will represent causal relationships with a single-headed arrow pointing from the causal element to the affected element. A + sign near the arrow indicates that the first element causes the second to vary in the same direction; an increase in one causes an increase in the other, a decrease causes a decrease. A − sign indicates variation in the opposite direction Thus as food *per capita* increases, death rate decreases; as food *per capita* goes down, death rate goes up.

$$\text{food } per\ capita \xrightarrow{-} \text{death rate}$$

Causal relationships between two elements may go both directions; for example, a higher death rate will decrease population (all else equal), which will increase food *per capita* (as always when just one relationship in a system is being discussed, all else equal).

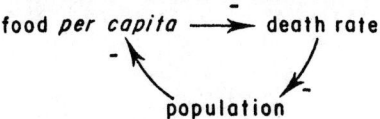

A closed chain of causal relations like this is called a *feedback loop*.

A relationship will be called *correlational* if a direct causation is not hypothesized but the two elements are presumed to vary together. For example, a correlational relationship might link food *per capita* and health services *per capita*. Neither of these elements is assumed to influence the other directly and causally, but for the purposes of a model they may be assumed to change simultaneously. Correlational relationships will be shown with a double-headed arrow. The sign on this arrow indicates whether the two elements are directly (+) or inversely (−) correlated. The notation below indicates that an increase in food *per capita* is assumed to be accompanied by, but not necessarily caused by, an increase in health services *per capita*.

$$\text{food per capita} \xleftrightarrow{+} \text{health services per capita}$$

We will distinguish between the *structure* of a model and its *parameters*. The structure is the general pattern of elements and interrelationships, the qualitative hypotheses about what is connected to what. The parameters are the exact numbers used to define the strengths of the connections. Thus in the simple causal model

$$\text{food per capita} \xrightarrow{-} \text{death rate}$$

the structural assumption is that food *per capita* negatively influences death rate. If the relationship is made precise by the equation:

$$\text{death rate} = 0.08 - 0.001 \,(\text{food per capita})$$

the numbers 0.08 and 0.001 are parameters that quantify that structural assumption.

Other model-related words we shall be using frequently and with special care are:

Accuracy—correctness, conformity to the real world, absence of error; does not necessarily imply precision or correctness to many significant digits. 'About 2' is an accurate (not precise) estimate of a real-world value of 2.00563.

Precision—exactness, expression to many significant digits, not necessarily accuracy. '2.97351' is a precise (not accurate) estimate of a real-world value of 2.00563.

Exogenous—determined outside the system, an independently-specified input to the model. An exogenous factor influences the model system but is not influenced by it. For example, solar energy is exogenous to the earth's ecosystem.

Endogenous—determined by the system, an output of the model. An endogenous factor is calculated from other factors in the model system. For example, the amount of industrial production per year is assumed to be endogenous in most of the models in our survey, varying with such factors as capital, labor, or consumer demand.

In addition to the terms we will use to describe models, elements, and relationships, we need a few definitions to clarify the environment within which policy-oriented models are made. We will refer to the individual or organization that contracted and paid for a model as the model's *sponsor*. The term *client* will be used to designate the individual or organization in the appropriate policymaking position to use the model conclusions in formulating actual programs or decisions. For some of our nine sample models, the modeling, sponsor, and client institutions are the same; more typically, all three are different. We will define the word *implementation* as any use of the model, direct or indirect, that changes the way policies or decisions are made.

E. A PERSONAL STATEMENT

This book is about the controversial interface between two controversial fields, computer modeling and politics. There is no neutral position from which to view this subject. Even supposedly objective modeling techniques and scientific disciplines endow their practitioners with subjective preferences and prejudices about how science should be carried out and how policy should be made. Like anyone who writes about these matters, we have biases. We feel that we should make them as clear as possible.

We are both Americans, steeped in the Western traditions of democracy, individuality, and scientific rationality. We are white, female and middle-class. Both of us were formally trained in the sciences, particularly biology and chemistry. The only sort of computer modeling we have personally practiced is system dynamics, and in the next chapter we take particular care to define the preconceptions that technique has given us. They are among the most important preconceptions that color this book. We have worked closely with people using other modeling methods, sometimes in joint projects. Some of our best friends are econometricians.

We have no direct experience in the world of policy; only the indirect experience of working with policymakers in the construction of our own models. Our political preferences are not easily defined along the traditional conservative/liberal spectrum; we sympathize with some important beliefs from each end of the spectrum and reject others. We have both lived in Asian countries and have found much to admire in the people, philosophies, and cultures we met there. We both have direct, dirty-hands experience in agriculture.

One of us was involved in the *Limits to Growth*[4] and the other in the *Global 2000*[5] modeling study, both of which caused controversy because they were accused of being biased by a pessimistic, Malthusian point of view. We are not personally pessimistic—in fact we are idealistic. We think both of these studies questioned current mental models, particularly models of the possible paths and goals of material progress, not in order to deny those paths and goals, but to point out even better ones.

As modelers we are, of course, pro-modeling. However, one of our main reasons for writing this book is a deep concern that the modeling profession is acquiring some attributes that will prevent it from contributing as much to social decision making as we believe it can contribute. The attributes we like and dislike will be apparent from our comments throughout the book. We value simplicity, transparency, and enduring general insights, and we are repelled by complexity, jargon, secrecy, and elitism.

We take quite seriously the criticisms commonly directed at our field. We worry that supercomplex computer models might be less open to critical evaluation than are mental models. That marvelous tools for error-free calculation might be worthless if they contain undetected errors in programming and typing. That people who work with computers create around them a mystical wall that excludes the uninitiated. If these criticisms are correct, we believe that the social decision maker will find all models—mental, verbal, and computer—unexaminable black boxes, differentiated primarily by the personal persuasiveness of the modelers. In that case, there is no more reason to rely on computer models than on mental models, unless the technocratic mystique of computers happens to appeal. And if a computer model comes to be accepted on the basis of personal persuasiveness and mystique instead of understanding, we feel that it can really claim no advantage over a crystal ball or Delphic oracle.

The political acceptance of black-box models, if it ever did happen, would be a strange, technocratic *coup d'état* in which modelers have gained the power to shape assumptions, perceptions, and conclusions of decision-makers in a way the decision-makers themselves do not quite understand.

> Previously, it seems to me, we have had two groups of persons in secret government: the circle of scientists who are knowledgeable about what is happening and which decisions must be made, and the larger circle of administrators and politicians to whom the scientists' findings have to be translated. My worry is that the introduction of the computer is going to lead to a smaller circle still ... we shall have a tiny circle of computer boys, a larger circle of scientists who are not familiar with the decision rules and are not versed in the new computer art, and then, again, the large circle of politicians and administrators ... I suspect that the chap standing next to the machine, who really knows how it makes decisons, and who has the machine under his command, is going to be in an excessively influential position.[6]

We conducted this study and wrote this book in order to confirm and communicate two very strong convictions that sound contradictory. First, we were, and are still, worried about 'excessively influential computer boys' (and even 'computer persons'). We would not like to live in a society run by an unaccountable elite of computer experts, even if these experts did really understand the society they were controlling. We are even more worried after conducting the study, because it has persuaded us that the computer persons, like everyone else, in fact understand very little. If there is anything more to be feared than technocratic rule, it is rule by technocrats who *do not know what they are doing*.

However, at the same time we believe that computer models can tell us things we need to know about the causes and cures of important social problems. We have personally learned useful lessons from our own models and from the ones described here, lessons that are far from total understanding but that are nevertheless worth learning and that could not be learned from mental models alone. And we know there are many more lessons still to be learned. We believe these lessons can be expressed in language any citizen can understand. Computer models could be tools of democracy instead of autocracy, and the people who make them could be valuable, sharing, inspiring partners in social evolution instead of remote, inaccessible authorities.

So the biases that underlie this book are the opposite poles of a duality, and we will often swing wildly from one side to the other. On the one hand, computer modeling is a dangerous technology likely to be misused as a source of unjustified power by people who look like they know what they are doing but actually do not. On the other hand, computer modeling is a wondrous new tool that is already producing exciting results and that should be more respected and accepted than it now is. Our job here is to maintain a balance between these two positions.

Computer modelers are human beings with human strengths and failures. To the extent that their work can be structured to bring out their strengths and correct for their failures, they can contribute immensely to human understanding of how the world works, to social decision-making, and to the shaping of the uncertain future.

NOTES AND REFERENCES

1. G. Fromm, W. L. Hamilton, and D. E. Hamilton, *Federally Supported Mathematical Models: Survey and Analysis*, RANN Division of Social Systems and Human Resources, Washington, U.S. Government Printing Office, 1974, p. 3.
2. For criticisms of computer modeling, see D. Lee, 'Requiem for Large-Scale Models', *Journal of the American Institute of Planners*, May 1973; G. Brewer, *Politicians, Bureaucrats, and the Consultant*, New York, Basic Books, 1973; I. R. Hoos, *Systems Analysis in Public Policy*, Berkeley, University of California Press, 1972; D. Berlinski, *On Systems Analysis*, Cambridge, Mass, MIT Press, 1976; B. Mar, 'Problems Encountered in Multidisciplinary Resources and Environmental Simulation Models Development', *Journal of Environmental Management*, 2, 83, 1974; R. L. Ackoff, 'The Future of Operational Research is Past', *Journal of the Operational Research Society*, 30, (2), 93–104, 1979.
3. See, for example, S. Cole, 'World Models, their Progress and Applicability', *Futures*, p. 201, June 1974; N. Carter, 'Population, Environment, and Natural Resources: a Critical Review of Recent Models', IBRD Working Paper No. 174, April 1974; M. Shubik and G. Brewer, *Models, Simulations and Games—a Survey*, Rand R-1060- ARPA/RC, May 1972; Subcommittee on Fisheries and Wildlife Conservation and the Environment, *Computer Simulation Methods to aid National Growth Policy*, Serial no. 95b, Washington, U.S. Government Printing Office, 1974; M. Greenberger, M. A. Crenson, and B. L. Crissey, *Models in the Policy Process*, New York, Russell Sage Foundation, 1976; K. F. Watt, 'Why Won't Anyone Believe Us?', *Simulation*, p. 1, January 1977.
4. D. H. Meadows, D. L. Meadows, J. Randers and W. L. Behrens, *The Limits to Growth*, New York, Universe Books, 1972.
5. G. O. Barney (ed.), *The Global 2000 Report to the President*, Washington, D.C., U.S. Government Printing Office, 1982.
6. C. P. Snow, in Martin Greenberger (ed.) *Management and the Computer of the Future*, Cambridge, Mass, MIT Press, pp. 10–11, 1962.

PART II

Modeling Paradigms

A man saw Nasrudin searching for something on the ground. 'What have you lost, Mulla?' he asked.
'My key,' said the Mulla.
'So the man went down on his knees too, and they both looked for it. After a time the other man asked, 'Where exactly did you drop it?'
'In my own house.'
'Then why are you looking here?'
'There is more light here than inside my own house.'

Ancient Sufi teaching story,
retold by Idries Shah

Although the field of computer modeling has only existed for a few decades, a number of distinct modeling methods have already appeared. They include linear programming, input–output analysis, econometrics, stochastic simulation, and system dynamics. These modeling schools share a number of common concepts about the properties of systems, the process of modeling, the use of the computer, and the role of models in decision making. In addition to these shared concepts, each methodological school also employs its own set of theories, mathematical techniques, languages, and accepted procedures for constructing and testing models. Every modeling discipline depends on unique underlying assumptions; that is, each modeling method is itself based on a model of how modeling should be done.

CHAPTER 2

Models of Modeling

A. THE CONCEPT OF A PARADIGM

Deep, implicit operating assumptions at the foundation of each modeling method are crucial to the practice and products of modeling. These assumptions are seldom stated or critically examined. Practitioners of each method absorb its operating assumptions indirectly, by imitation and experimentation, and thereafter they reflect on these assumptions only occasionally. Typically, the assumptions of each modeling school are part of the subconscious rather than conscious reasoning that goes into the making of models. Just as physicists rarely rethink the laws of algebra or the second law of thermodynamics as they work, practicing econometricians seldom question the use of statistics to measure model validity, and system dynamicists regularly use the principle of feedback control without stopping to wonder whether it is applicable to the problem at hand.

Such time-tested, constantly-used, and rarely-examined pre-conceptions seem to fit the concept of a *paradigm* as defined by Thomas S. Kuhn:

> Scientists work from models acquired through education and through subsequent exposure to the literature often without quite knowing or needing to know what characteristics have given these models the status of community paradigms ... Paradigms may be prior to, more binding, and more complete than any set of rules for research that could be unequivocally abstracted from them ... (Paradigms) are the source of the methods, problem-field, and standards of solution accepted by any mature scientific community at any time ... In learning a paradigm the scientist acquired theory, methods, and standards together, usually in an inextricable mixture. Therefore, when paradigms change, there are usually significant shifts in the criteria determining the legitimacy both of problems and of proposed solutions ... Paradigm changes ... cause scientists to see the world of their research-engage-

ment differently. In so far as their only recourse to that world is through what they see and do, we may want to say that after a (paradigm) revolution scientists are responding to a different world.[1]

Different modeling paradigms cause their practitioners to define different problems, follow different procedures, and use different criteria to evaluate the result. Paradigms deeply bias the way modelers see the world and thus influence the contents and shapes of models. As Abraham Maslow says: 'If the only tool you have is a hammer, you tend to treat everything as if it were a nail'.[2]

The selective blindness induced by any operational paradigm has both unfortunate and fortunate results. Unfortunately, it constrains thinking, and it often leads to sterile arguments across paradigms, each school criticizing the problems, assumptions, and standards of the other from the biased perspective of its own problems, assumptions, and standards. On the fortunate side, paradigms create a framework for discipline, coherence, and rigor. Paradigm-directed research seems to be not only psychologically necessary but exceptionally fruitful.

> Within those areas to which the paradigm directs the attention of the group, normal science leads to a detail of information and to a precision of the observation-theory match that could be achieved in no other way.[3]

Because of the pervasive effect of methodological paradigms on modelers' thoughts and perceptions, this comparison of models begins with a description of the underlying paradigms within which the models were made. In this chapter we summarize, insofar as it is possible to verbalize them, the paradigms of the four primary methods represented in our study: system dynamics, econometrics, input–output analysis, and optimization (linear programming). We will also discuss composite models, in which two or more of these methods are combined. Several other methods, such as stochastic simulation, are omitted here, not because they are unimportant, but because they were not used in any of the nine models in our survey. We conclude the chapter with an example of paradigm conflict, contrasting the world views inherent in system dynamics and econometrics, and illustrating why the twain shall probably never meet.

Before examining specific modeling schools, however, we should have an overview of the modeling field as a whole, the scientific paradigm shared by all modelers, the different ways of classifying models, and the various purposes for which models are intended to be used.

B. PRECONCEPTIONS AND PURPOSES OF MODELING

Although modelers may disagree vehemently about their specific methods or models, they are unified by some very basic assumptions that define the whole modeling approach to problem solving. First of all, social system modelers generally come from or were educated in a Western culture, where the rational, logical, scientific mode of thought is valued and emphasized. They believe that whatever happens is not totally senseless or random or unknowable; events have causes that can be understood and probably altered. One presumably can discover those causes through careful measurement, clever experimentation, and logical deduction. The source of understanding is observation and thinking, not intuition or meditating.

Furthermore, modelers share a basically managerial world view. Problems can be and should be actively confronted, not passively endured. One does not ride along with the process of social evolution, one strives to direct that evolution. The world is not only knowable but controllable. This managerial world view is generally shared not only by modelers, but by most engineers, businessmen, scientists, and politicians. It is not always shared by artists, theologians, other humanists, or by those educated in traditional Eastern cultures:

> By one Chinese view of time, the future is behind you, where you cannot see it. The past is before you, below you, where you can examine it. Man's position in time is that of a person sitting beside a river, facing always downstream as he watches the water flow past ...
> In America and other Western countries, the commonest view of abstract time seems to be the opposite of the old Chinese one. In this, man faces in the other direction, with his back to the past, which is sinking behind him, and his face is turned upward to the future, which is floating down upon him. Nor can this man be static: by our ambitious Western convention, he is supposed to be rising into the future under his own power, perhaps by his own direction. He is more like a man in a plane than a sitter by a river.[4]

Although computer modelers use historic observations to form their hypotheses, their faces are primarily turned upstream, toward the future.

Computer modelers differ from other managerial types primarily in their willingness to make entire organizational systems the subject of their analysis. Computer modelers use the computer as a tool not just for accounting, but for representing the complex of interactions among human decision-makers. They assume that human actions and purposes as well as the operations of the physical universe can be categorized, quantified, and represented by mathematical equations. This postulate does not necessarily imply, as many non-modelers believe it does, a belief that human beings or the systems they create are totally predictable. It does require a belief that they are predictable in the aggregate and on the average, however. As E. F. Schumacher says:

> In principle, everything which is immune to the intrusion of human freedom like the movements of the stars, is predictable, and everything subject to this intrusion is unpredictable. Does that mean that all human actions are unpredictable? No, because most people, most of the time, make no use of their freedom and act purely mechanically. Experience shows that when we are dealing with large numbers of people, many aspects of their behaviour are indeed predictable; for out of a large

number, at any one time, only a tiny minority are using their power of freedom, and they often do not significantly affect the total outcome.[5]

Most computer modelers, when confronted with the task of learning about a complex phenomenon such as the human body, the interdependent species living in a coral reef, or an industrial economy, supplement the reductionist approach of taking it apart and examining each of its pieces with the systems approach, focusing on the whole and on the pattern of interrelationships among the pieces. They are attuned to the ways that whole systems may exhibit properties that cannot be derived simply from the sum of their parts.

Systems analysts tend to see analogies between systems with different elements but similar relationships, analogies that would be missed by those who concentrate on elements alone. For example, an introductory systems textbook points out that the same simple first-order differential equation can be used to describe the depreciation of industrial capital, the decay of radioactive materials, the inventory-ordering policy of a beer distributor, or the cooling of a cup of hot coffee.[6]

Because they are concerned with the interconnections among real world entities, modelers tend to include a wide spectrum of indirectly-related elements in their explanations of events. They cross the boundaries of traditional disciplines regularly and with relative ease. Because they see complex interrelationships in the world, they need the computer to represent, to keep track of, and to help untangle their theories.

Upon the rock of these basic assumptions about rationality, the scientific method, the computer, and the systems approach, a number of different modeling schools (it is hard to resist the word 'churches' here) have been erected. Each was originally developed in response to a specific social need, each has evolved its own methods and languages, and each shapes the procedures and perceptions of its adherents in a distinct way.

The different kinds of modeling can be classified along a number of dimensions, some of which are partially overlapping and some of which are totally incommensurable. For example, modeling paradigms may be distinguished by their information bases. Some are designed to pull meaning from social statistics, some are derived from laboratory experiments, others depend on economic theory or ecological observations. Some modeling schools are eclectic and accommodate information from any source, including hunches or guesses or intuition.

Modeling paradigms also differ in the mathematical procedures they employ. Some express their assumptions in differential equations, which are then solved by the techniques of calculus to obtain an analytical expression for the behavior of the modeled system at any moment in time. Others use difference equations that step a system forward in time moment by moment in imitation of the real system's evolution. Other modelers habitually use simultaneous equation solution techniques to find a system's equilibrium or optimum points.

Modelers also distinguish their work by the nature of the model relationships they employ. For example, relationships may be:

Stochastic (elements are related by probabilistic statements) If A = 2, then there is a 20% chance that B = 3, a 60% chance that B = 4, and a 20% chance that B = 5, or
deterministic (elements are related by absolute statements) If A = 2, B = 4.
Continuous (the relationship contains no sudden steps, jumps, or breaks; it can be graphically represented by a smooth, unbroken line) A = 3.6 + 8.7B or A = B^2, or
discrete (the relationship is described by threshholds, discontinuities, or individual points rather than smooth curves) If A < 2, then B = 10; if A ⩾ 2, then B = 100.
Linear (the relationship can be graphed as a straight line; the marginal change in B in response to a given marginal change in A is constant) A = 2B + 6, or
non-linear (the relationship can be graphed as any sort of curved line; non-linear is usually also interpreted to mean continuous) A = B^2 or A = 23 + 56e^B − sin B^3 + (33lnB)/B^5.
Simultaneous (elements respond to each other fully within a time period so short as to be insignificant for purposes of the model) A = 2B, or
lagged (elements respond to each other only after some specified delay time). A (this year) = 1.3 + 7.2B (last year) + 0.5B (two years ago) or A (this year) = A (last year) + B (over the interval from last year to this year)

These properties of models are combined in practice into a limited number of consistent sets. For example, engineering models of physical systems tend to be based on information from controlled laboratory experiments, to be solved analytically, and to consist of linear, deterministic, continuous relationships. Econometric models are based on statistical data, they typically contain a mixture of simultaneous and lagged relationships, they are predominantly linear, and they are solved by iterative simultaneous equation techniques. Complex dynamic models with non-linear and lagged equations necessarily must be solved by simulation techniques (difference equations) because they are too mathematically complex to be solved analytically. Information base, disciplinary preconceptions, and mathematical necessity interact to form the philosophical view and the procedural rules that characterize each modeling paradigm.

The following discussion could be organized around any one of the properties of models listed above, but instead we shall choose as the primary point of distinction another property that is not very often mentioned in model classifications. That is the *use* to which the model is to be put. We are concerned here only with models that contribute to the understanding and management of social systems. Therefore, we shall classify models according to the stage of social decision-making at which they are most applicable.

When a social problem is first identified, there may be a need for *general understanding*. Things are happening that make no sense; old theories and old social structures are called into question. Important data may be missing, interconnections that had been considered absent or unimportant may suddenly appear significant, or new and unexpected behavior may need to be explained. Why has the grain price, which was stable for decades, started to fluctuate? If the carbon dioxide content of the atmosphere goes on increasing, what will happen to the climate? How can there be high inflation and high unemployment simultaneously?

This is typically the point where learned study commissions are established or research projects are funded. Current models, mental or otherwise, may need revision, updating, or complete overhaul before the problem can be tackled. Whole institutions or social systems may need to be designed or redesigned. Most global problem areas are still at the general-understanding stage today, including international monetary relations, energy, environmental degradation, economic development, and especially the interactions among all of these.

Models that can contribute to improved general understanding must allow the organization and communication of ideas and hypotheses. They must be easily understood. The path by which their assumptions lead to their conclusions should be clear, and they should provide structural insights about the working of some real-world system. Quantitative precision and excessive detail are unnecessary and probably unattainable at this point; it is difficult enough to decide what system elements are even qualitatively important and how they are related. Because no one is sure what the sources or consequences of the problem being addressed might be, the model must have very broad boundaries, usually crossing many disciplines. General-understanding modeling tends to be more *process-oriented* than product-oriented; that is, the very process of making the model, asking questions systematically, and defining new concepts may be more important than the calculations done with the final model. By the time a general-understanding computer model is completed, its concepts and conclusions may have been integrated into the mental models of both modelers and clients, so that the model itself looks obvious and is taken for granted.

If there is some agreement about the cause of the problem or the nature of the system generating it, then the second phase, which we will call *policy design*, begins. If a theory about the cause of the problem is accepted, suggestions about the general directions in which a cure might be found will follow naturally. Several broad policy choices are usually apparent, which must be evaluated and integrated to identify possible trade-offs or synergies. The questions to be answered by a model are still imprecise and generic at this stage, but the examination can be limited to those points in the system that have been identified as potential policy foci. Given that foreign aid will be sent to nation X, should the aid package emphasize family planning, health care, or armaments? Given a basic free-market theory of the agricultural system, what would happen if government control of domestic grain prices were imposed? Policy-design models produce conditional, imprecise information: if this general policy is followed, what will be the general results?

A model that can help in policy design should be able to reproduce the real system's behavior, at least roughly, under all the conditions and policies under consideration. It should be easily alterable to test a number of hypotheses and policies, and should also clarify why different policies lead to different results. Quantitative precision is more important here than at the level of general understanding, but the emphasis is still primarily qualitative and process-oriented.

When a basic policy direction has been formulated, a whole host of new questions arises concerning the *detailed implementation* required to carry out that policy. A decision to promote family planning engenders numerous further decisions about budgets, personnel training, geographic distribution, and educational techniques. A policy to stabilize grain prices by creating a buffer stock will require the creation of new organizations to establish and maintain the stock, a precise set of rules for buying and selling, and a plan linking markets, warehouses, transportation systems, and final consumers, so that the greatest stabilization can be realized at the least cost.

As these detailed-implementation decisions become complex and require the organization and processing of many pieces of information, computer models become very useful. These models must be detailed and accurate, but each one need represent only one basic policy direction so its boundary can be narrow. Detailed-implementation modeling schools are usually *product-oriented*. The process of constructing such models is often quite difficult and tedious, so the modelers aim to produce a model that can be used again and again to transform new input data into specific predictions or operating instructions. Once a model of an oil refinery and distribution system has been made, it need only be updated with recent figures for, say, this month's orders, stock levels, and prices, in order to turn out detailed instructions for least-cost operation. Product-oriented modelers rarely need to involve the client in the modeling process or try to make clear all the model's assumptions, since most of the assumptions are routine and uncontroversial. Most computer models now being made are directed to this stage of detailed decision making.

In short, different people sit at the various stages of the policy process, asking different sorts of questions requiring different kinds of models. Each of the methodological paradigms described in this chapter can be regarded as one useful tool in a tool box. Knowledge of all their properties is essential in deciding which is the best tool for a given specific purpose. It is possible to use each of these methods for several different purposes, and even by stretching things a bit, for all purposes. A saw could be used to pound in a nail, if necessary. But a hammer would do the job better and faster, and so an essential aspect of wisdom in making, sponsoring, criticizing, or using models is knowing when to put down the saw and pick up the hammer. Since modeling schools are more than tools, however, since they are also at least partially world views, a better metaphor might be picking up the microscope and putting down the telescope. Doing that usually means finding an appropriate group of modelers, rather than asking telescope experts to learn to see the world as if they were microscope experts. In order to match the tool to the policy question, one therefore must define the question carefully and must know something about the nature of the tools available.

C. THE PARADIGMS

Four modeling schools are described here, beginning with those best suited for the general-understanding phase of problem solving, and ending with those used mostly at the detailed-implementation stage. After a brief summary of the historical development of each field, a very basic sample model will be described as an example. Each sample model is, of necessity, extremely simple; it will illustrate the basic form and general techniques of the method but will not do justice to the subtleties or complexities that can be included in actual working models. The sample models are included primarily for those interested in the mathematical tools of the modeling schools and can be skipped by readers who are uninterested in technical details.

Following the sample model, the most important characteristics and assumptions of each modeling paradigm are discussed. Examples of actual policy applications of the technique are given. Finally, the most common pitfalls and limitations of the method as encountered in practice are described. These pitfalls are not necessarily present in all models within each method; in fact, the best models are often recognized as good because they have managed to avoid them. Nevertheless, every method has its characteristic traps, which students often fall into and which advanced modelers must continually guard against. Understanding these inherent limitations as well as the strengths of the various modeling paradigms may be one of the most effective steps toward better use of models.

Nearly every modeler who has reviewed this chapter has taken exception to the way his or her modeling school is represented, but has been satisfied with our depiction of the *other* schools. From this we can only conclude that modelers think of their own paradigms in ideal form, as described in the textbooks, but think of the other paradigms as they are actually experienced in practice. Since the textbooks already exist and can be referred to by anyone, practice is what we emphasize here.

Finally, we should re-emphasize that these methods can be contrasted and compared, their strengths and weaknesses can be discussed, but they cannot be ranked or evaluated according to any absolute standard of 'best' or 'worst'. Any such standard implies some sort of unidimensional criterion by which modeling methods might be measured. But since problem-solving required a broad range of models, addressed to many different kinds of questions and purposes, no such single dimension exists. It would be wrong to dismiss a general-understanding method for its lack of quantitative precision, and equally wrong to complain about a detailed-implementation method because of its narrow boundary. Different scientific approaches, like different tools, should not be promoted or castigated in themselves, without reference to the task they are to accomplish.

We repeat this warning as a reminder to ourselves as well as the reader. As modelers, our preference for one of the modeling schools should not blind us to the merits of the others. We are system dynamicists, and we will describe that method first, both because it is useful in the general-understanding phase of policy-making, and because we want to begin by alerting the reader to our own methodological biases.

1. System dynamics

We find that people perceive correctly their immediate environment. They know what they are trying to accomplish. They know the crises that will force certain actions. They are sensitive to the power structure of the organization, to traditions, and to their own personal goals and welfare. In general, ... people can usually state what they are doing and can give rational reasons for their actions ... People are usually trying in good conscience and to the best of their abilities to solve the major difficulties ... One can combine these policies into a computer model to show the consequences of how the policies interact with one another. In many instances it then emerges that the known policies describe a system that actually causes the troubles. In other words, the known and intended practices of the organization are fully sufficient to create the difficulty.[7]

a. Origin of system dynamics

System dynamics was developed at M.I.T. during the 1950s, primarily by Jay W. Forrester, who is by training an engineer and computer scientist. He brought together ideas from three fields that were then relatively new—control engineering (the concepts of feedback and system self-regulation), cybernetics (the nature of information and its role in control systems), and organizational theory (the structure of human organizations and the mechanisms of human decision-making). From these basic ideas Forrester developed a guiding philosophy and a set of representational techniques for simulating complex, non-linear, multiloop feedback systems. These techniques were originally applied to the management of industrial firms. The first system dynamics models addressed such common problems as inventory fluctuations, instability of labor force, and falling market share.[8]

The methods worked out by Forrester and his group have since been applied to a wide variety of social systems including cities, regions, and the entire world.[9] From the beginning the field has been dominated by engineers, industrial managers, and physical scientists. The literature of system dynamics is almost entirely pragmatic; it contains many more descriptions of actual models addressed to policy questions than theoretical discussions about modeling techniques.

System dynamics is a subset of the larger field of *simulation* modeling. Simulation modelers attempt to represent a real system by mimicking with the computer the actual (but simplified) forces, motivations, and influences that they believe make the system work. Simulation models are causal. They are made up of general rules describing how each element in the system will change in response to conceivable combinations of the other elements. When the model is run, each element is set at some specific initial value, and then the computer works out the response of each to each, according to the prespecified rules, moving forward through simulated time until the program tells it to stop.

For example, a very simple simulation model of population growth might consist of two equations. One could be a general rule stating that the population always increases by 10% of its current value each year.

population change each year = 0.1 * population

The second would simply update the model to the next year by adding the amount of annual population change to the current population.

population this year = population last year + population change last year

If the initial value of the population were set at 1000, the model would generate output as shown in Table 2.1.

Table 2.1

Year	Population	Population change
0	1000	100
1	1100	110
2	1210	121
3	1331	133.1
and so forth		

Simulation modeling is widely practiced in many traditional disciplines such as engineering, economics, and ecology. Since the formulation of differential equations to simulate the progression of systems through time is nearly a free-form exercise, with very few paradigmatic constraints, simulation modeling is usually shaped by the paradigm of discipline more than by the modeling technique. The concept of simulating a system is too general and unstructured to be in itself a paradigm that helps one organize questions and observations about the world.

System dynamics, however, includes not only the basic idea of simulation, but also a set of concepts, representational techniques, and beliefs that make it into a definite modeling paradigm. It shapes the world view of its practitioners in ways that will become clearer after we describe a sample model and the major characteristics of the system dynamics technique.

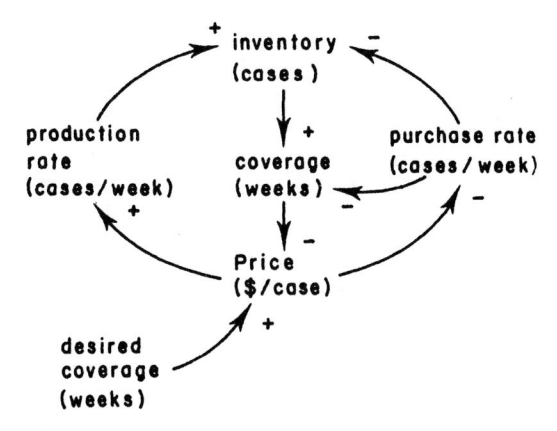

Figure 2.1 Causal diagram for simple system dynamics model

b. Sample system dynamics model

A very simple system dynamics model of a generic market system for a single economic commodity is illustrated in Figure 2.1. The relationships are causal and thus represented by single arrows.* Here the supply of the commodity on the market is represented by the current inventory of goods, which is increased by a flow of goods from production and decreased by purchases (sales). The decision process by which producers alter prices is modeled explicitly. It is assumed that producers are concerned with controlling the coverage time of their inventory—the amount of time the inventory on hand would supply the current purchase rate. If coverage is too high, there will be unacceptable storage or carrying costs. If it is too low, there are likely to be stockout costs—lost sales due to insufficient inventory.

Producers are assumed to adjust their actual coverage to achieve some desired coverage by changing the price, which then alters both the production and purchase rates. Higher prices are assumed to spur increased production and also to discourage purchases to some extent; lower prices do the reverse.

The system dynamics computer model that represents this hypothesis is shown in Figure 2.2a. It consists of twelve equations in the computer language DYNAMO, which reduce to six rather simple algebraic statements, as follows:

$$\text{inventory}_t = \text{inventory}_{t-1} + \text{production}_{t-1 \to t} - \text{purchases}_{t-1 \to t}$$

The inventory at any time (t) equals the inventory at the previous time ($t-1$) plus the amount of production that took place in the interval ($t-1 \to t$) and minus the number of purchases over the same interval. The DYNAMO

---
* See the discussion of causality and its representation in Chapter 1.

(a)

```
L  INV.K=INV.J+(DT)(PROD.JK-PURCH.JK)
N  INV=500
R  PROD.KL=TABLE(PRODT,PRICE.K,0,10,2)
T  PRODT=0/0/30/70/90/100
R  PURCH.KL=TABLE(PURCHT,PRICE.K,0,10,2)
T  PURCHT=100/90/70/30/10/0
A  COV.K=INV.K/PURCH.JK
C  DCOV=10
R  PCR.KL=PRICE.K*TABLE(PCRT,COV.K/DCOV,0,2,.4)
T  PCRT=.8/.4/.1/-.1/-.4/-.8
L  PRICE.K=PRICE.J+(DT)(PCR.JK)
N  PRICE=2
C  DT=.1
C  LENGTH=20
PLOT INV=I/PRICE=$/PURCH=D,PROD=S
```

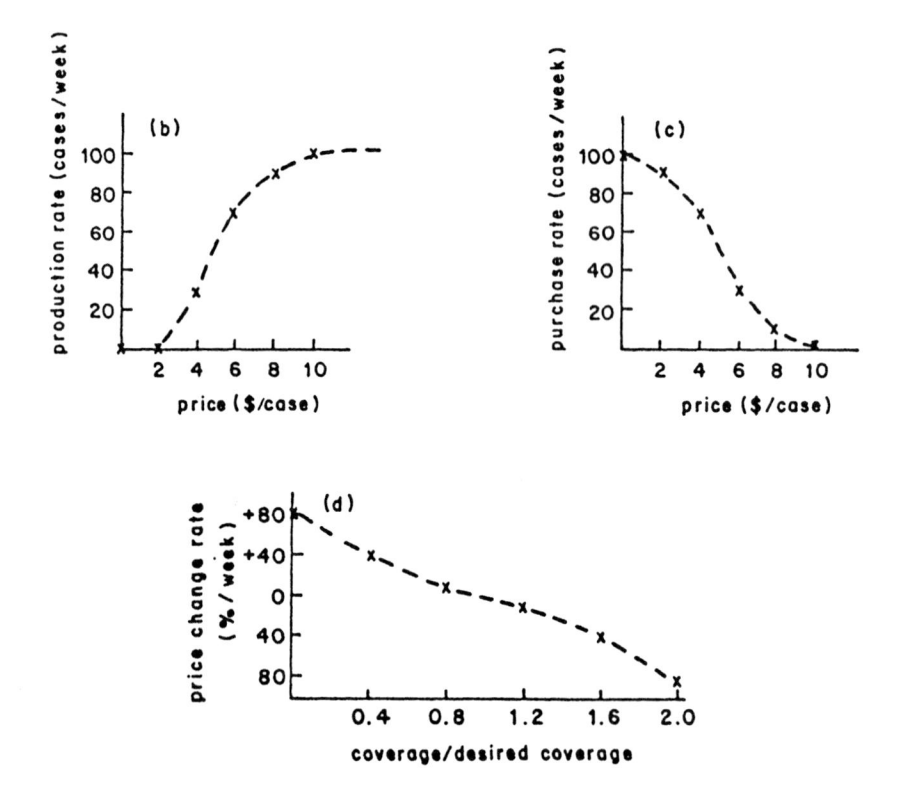

Figure 2.2 Simple system dynamics model of market system
(a) Dynamo equations.
(b) Response of supply to price.
(c) Response of demand to price.
(d) Response of price to supply/demand balance

equation labeled N simply gives the inventory an initial value of 500 cases to begin the simulation.

$$\text{production}_{t \to t+1} = f(\text{price}_t)$$

The quantity produced over any time interval is a non-linear function of the price at the beginning of that interval. This relationship is analogous to a short-term supply curve in economic theory. The non-linear function hypothesized for this particular model is shown in Figure 2.2b. Production capacity is limited to 100 cases per week, even at very high price, and production becomes so unprofitable at prices lower than $2 per case that no production takes place. Points from the graph in Figure 2.2b are read directly into the DYNAMO equations, to generate a piecewise-linear approximation to a continuous non-linear curve. This procedure allows a very simple and quick representation even of complex non-linear relationships.

$$\text{purchases}_{t \to t+1} = f'(\text{price}_t)$$

The quantity purchased is also a non-linear function of price, as in the demand curve of classical economic theory. The assumed relationship is shown in Figure 2.2c. Consumers cannot use more than 100 cases per week, even if the commodity is given away, and at the other extreme, no goods will be bought if the price exceeds $10 per case.

$$\text{coverage}_t = \text{inventory}_t/\text{purchases}_{t-1 \to t}$$

This equation defines the coverage as the ratio between inventory and purchase rate. It is assumed that producers aim to maintain a ten-week supply of the commodity, and that this goal does not vary over time (the actual number of cases necessary to meet this goal will vary with the purchase rate).

$$\text{price change rate}_{t \to t+1} = \text{price}_t * f''(\text{coverage}_t/\text{desired coverage})$$

The response of producers to inventories that are higher or lower than the desired level is summarized in this non-linear table function (illustrated in Figure 2.2d). If actual coverage is just equal to desired coverage (COV/DCOV=1), the price will not be changed. If actual coverage is higher than that desired (COV/DCOV>1), inventory is in excess and price will be decreased by a percentage that becomes larger as the situation deviates further from the ideal. If coverage is too low (COV/DCOV<1), price will be increased.

$$\text{price}_t = \text{price}_{t-1} + \text{price change rate}_{t-1 \to t}$$

The price at any time is equal to the price at the previous interval, plus (or minus since the price change rate can be negative) the change in price that took place over that interval. This formulation implies that price changes are continuous and incremental, that producers are reluctant to change price suddenly except under extreme conditions, and therefore that price does not immediately adjust to its equilibrium value. The initial value of the price at the beginning of the simulation is set at $2 per case.

The remaining equations in Figure 2.2a are simply instructions to the computer about the length of time the simulation should be run, the length of the incremental calculation period, and the form of output desired.

Three output graphs from this model are shown in Figure 2.3. The first (Figure 2.3a) illustrates the movement of price, supply, and demand over a 20-week period with the model parameters set as in Figure 2.2a. The system adjusts from an initial disequilibrium position to the equilibrium price, with a slight overshoot of price and a dip and then recovery of inventory. The second simulation, Figure 2.3b, shows the recovery from the same disequilibrium position when the elasticities of supply and demand are decreased—that is, when the responses of producers and consumers to price as illustrated in Figures 2.2b and 2.2c, become less sensitive. Under these conditions the system takes longer to settle into equilibrium and the variations in price and inventory are greater. The third simulation, Figure 2.3c, indicates the path toward equilibrium followed when elasticities are low, the desired coverage is changed from 10 weeks to four weeks, and the initial inventory is decreased from 500 units to 200. The lower inventory makes the system still more unstable, there are several oscillations on the approach to equilibrium. Note that these three different results, all of which are variations on a basic oscillatory behavior, are obtained by changing the *parameters* (specific numbers) in the model, not by changing its causal *structure*.

The model takes statements about the general behavior, decisions, and goals of the producers, consumers, and inventory-holders in the system, as well as simple physical statements (such as a produced good goes into inventory and stays there until it is sold), and generates the changes in the system element over time. The output indicates both the equilibrium point of the system and the dynamic approach to that point. Typically the model would be run from many different starting points and with many different sets of parameters, to produce an understanding of the dynamic characteristics of the system, such as the role of inventory as a stabilizing buffer, and the relationship between elasticities and time required to reach equlilibrium. For purposes of system *design* the model would be run with different formulations for the price-setting policy, until a policy is found that damps oscillations and keeps inventory within a desirable range.

A more rigorous system dynamics model of this system would contain more detailed representations of response mechanisms linking supply, demand, and price. Supply might be broken down into factory, distributor, and retailer inventories. Demand might be represented as a gap between consumers' actual stock of goods and their desired stock. Consumers' desired stock of goods might be influenced by changes in income and in advertising expenditures. The distinction between short-term and long-term supply would be included by an explicit level of production capacity, with account taken of the delays in acquiring new capacity. The pricing decision would include cost considerations.[10]

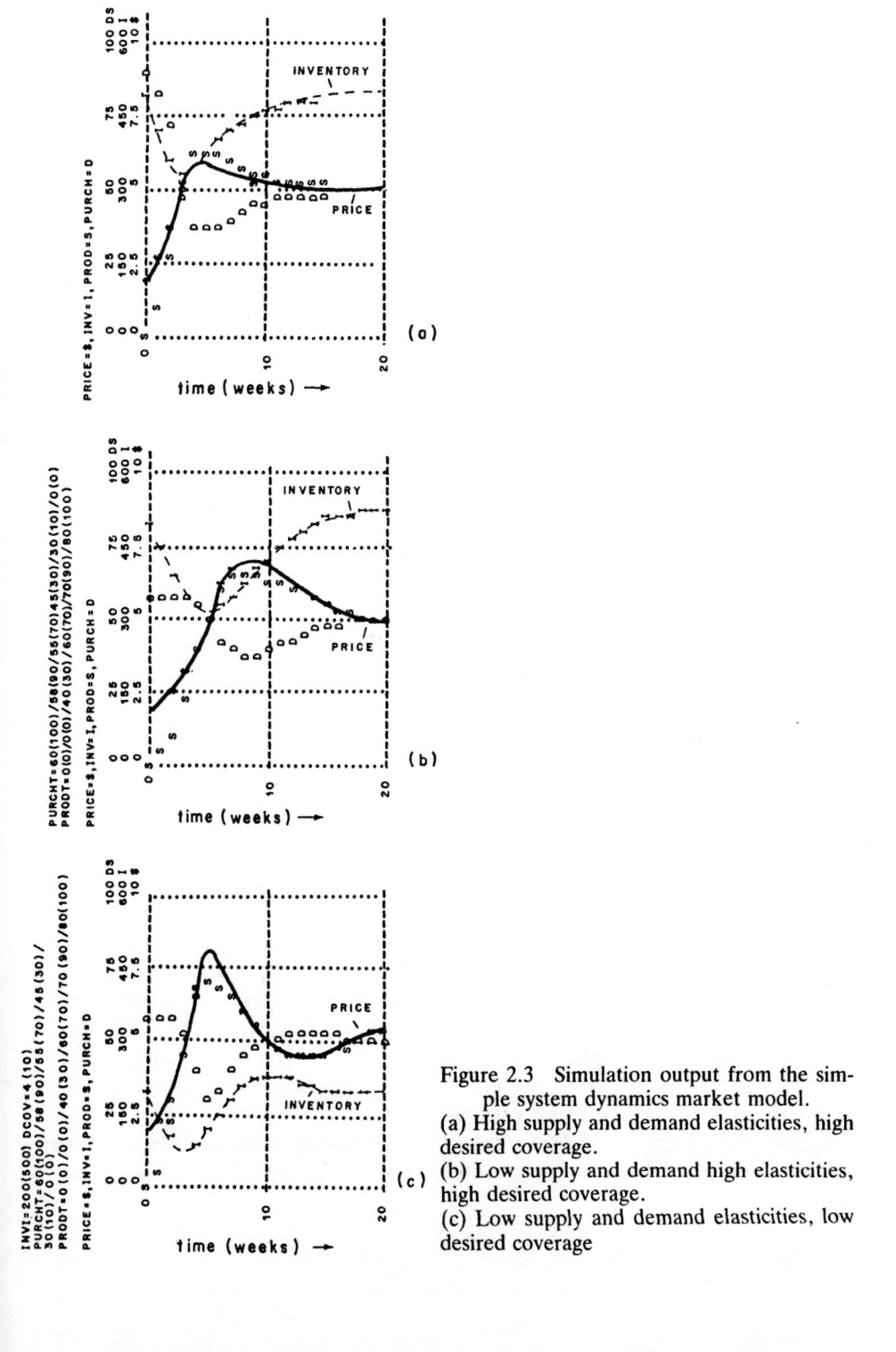

Figure 2.3 Simulation output from the simple system dynamics market model.
(a) High supply and demand elasticities, high desired coverage.
(b) Low supply and demand high elasticities, high desired coverage.
(c) Low supply and demand elasticities, low desired coverage

c. Characteristics of system dynamics

As its name implies, system dynamics is concerned with questions about the dynamic tendencies of complex systems—what kinds of behavioral patterns they generate over time. System dynamicists are not primarily concerned with forecasting specific values of system variables in specific years. They are much more interested in general dynamic tendencies; under what conditions the system as a whole is stable or unstable, oscillating, growing, declining, self-correcting, or in equilibrium. To explore these dynamic tendencies they include in their models the concepts from any discipline or field of thought, with special emphasis on the physical and biological sciences and some tendency to discount (or rediscover and rename) theories from the social sciences.

The primary assumption of the system dynamics paradigm is that the persistent dynamic tendencies of any complex social system arise from its internal causal structure—from the pattern of physical constraints and social goals, rewards, and pressures that cause people to behave the way they do and to generate cumulatively the dominant dynamic tendencies of the total system. A system dynamicist is likely to look for explanations of recurring long-term social problems within this internal structure rather than in external disturbances, small maladjustments, or random events. For example, a system dynamicist is led by his paradigm to explain the U.S. energy problem in terms of reserve depletion, internal pricing decisions, and rising material aspirations, rather than OPEC oil embargoes or bad weather. He is likely to look for a solution to the problem through changing the goals and the kinds of information that influence decisions, not through small numerical adjustments in taxes, research expenditures, environmental standards, or foreign policy. This basic assumption does not necessarily imply that all problems originate from faulty system structure; just that system dynamicists are more likely to see and become interested in the ones that do.

The central concept that system dynamicists use to understand system structure is the idea of two-way causation or feedback. It is assumed that social or individual decisions are made on the basis of information about the state of the system or environment surrounding the decision-makers. The decisions lead to actions that are intended to change (or maintain) the state of the system. New information about the system state then produces further decisions and changes (see Figure 2.4). Each such closed chain of causal relationships forms a feedback loop. System dynamics models are made up of many such loops linked together. They are basically closed-system representations; most of the variables occur in feedback relationships and are endogenous. When some factor is believed to influence the system from the outside without being influenced itself, however, it is represented as an exogenous variable in the model.

Feedback processes do not operate instantly; the timing of system behavior depends on the presence of system elements that create inertia or delays. These inertial elements are referred to as state variables or *levels*. Each level is an

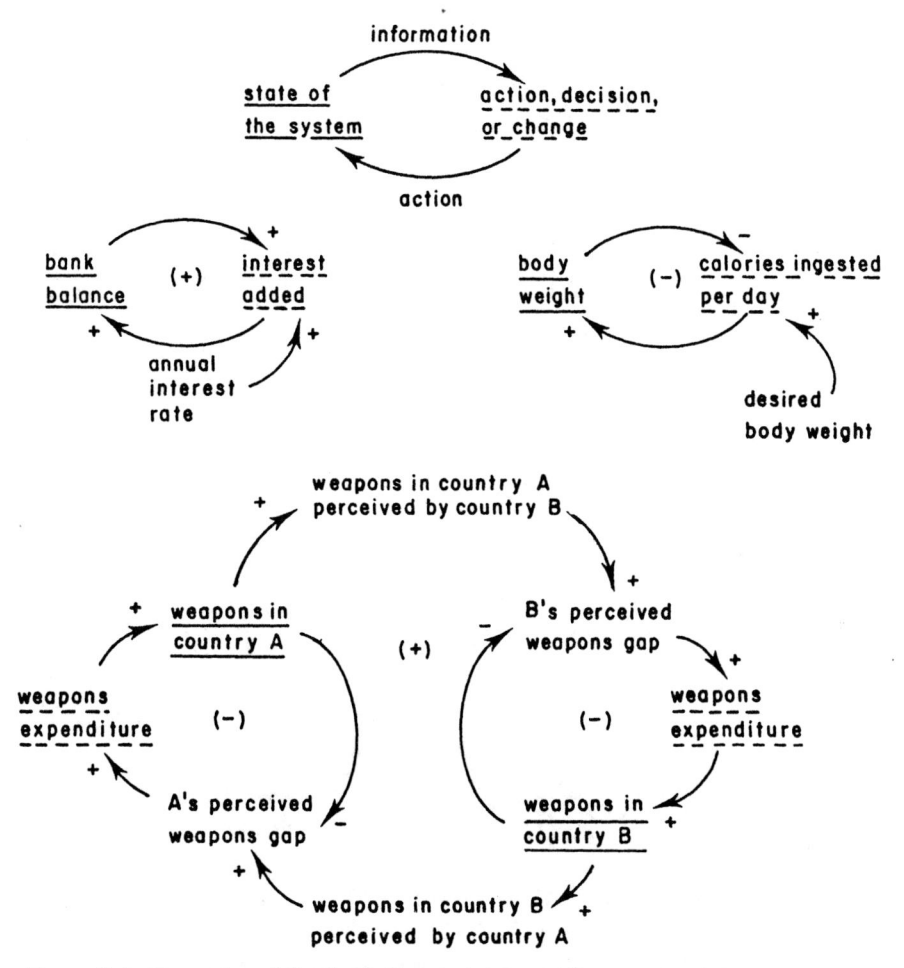

Figure 2.4 Examples of feedback loops. Arrows indicate causal influence. Positive loops are designated by (+) and negative loops by (−). Levels are underlined with a solid line (———), rates with a dashed line (----). Elements not underlined are goals, perceptions, or other information affecting rates

accumulation or stock of material or information. Typical levels are population, capital stock, inventories, and perceptions.

System elements representing the decision, action, or change in a level (often, but not always, induced by human decision-makers) is called a *rate*. A rate is a flow of material or information to or from a level. Examples are birth rate, death rate, investment rate, or rate of sales from inventory. Figure 2.4 illustrates several levels and rates and shows how they are causally linked into feedback loops.

The representation of a system by means of feedback, levels, and rates requires a careful distinction between stocks and flows of real physical quantities and of information. In the system dynamics paradigm physical flows are constrained to obey physical laws such as conservation of mass and energy. Information, on the other hand, need not be conserved, it may be at more than one place at the same time, it cannot be acted upon at the same moment it is being generated, and it may be systematically biased, delayed, amplified, or attenuated.

Two kinds of feedback loops are distinguished. Positive loops tend to amplify any disturbance and to produce exponential growth. Negative loops tend to counteract any disturbance and to move the system toward an equilibrium point or goal. Certain combinations of these two kinds of loops recur frequently and allow system dynamicists to formulate a number of useful generalizations or theorems relating the structure of a system (the pattern of interlocking feedback loops) to the system's dynamic behavioral tendencies. For example, an observation of exponential growth in the real system indicates the presence of some dominant positive feedback loop.

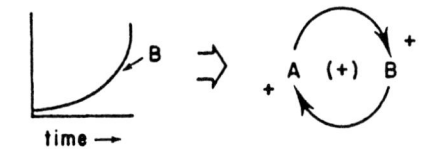

A tendency for a system to return to its original state after a disturbance indicates the presence of at least one strong negative feedback loop.

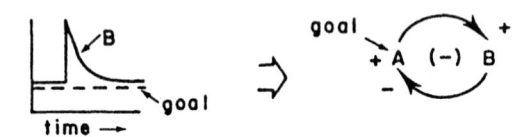

A single negative feedback loop with at least two levels in it can produce oscillatory behavior.

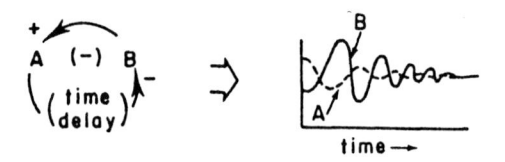

Sigmoid or S-shaped growth results from linked positive and negative loops that respond to each other non-linearly and with no significant time delays.

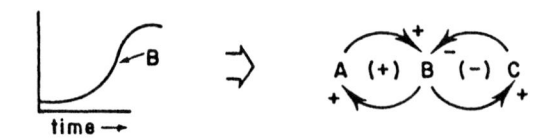

These and other structure-behavior theorems are the main intuitive guides that help a system dynamicist interpret the observed dynamic behavior of a real-world system, specify causal hypotheses about that behavior, and detect structural insufficiencies in a model. They permit identification of isomorphisms in very different systems that can be expected to have similar behavioral patterns. For example, to a system dynamicist, a population with birth and death rates is structurally and behaviorally the same as an industrial capital system with investment and depreciation rates. They look like this:

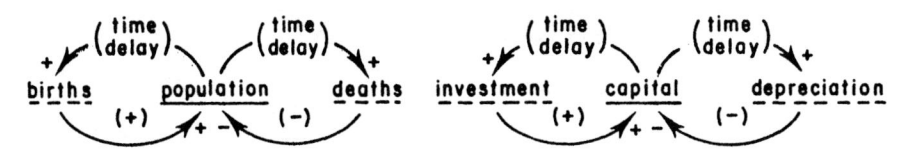

```
       (time)         (time)                    (time)         (time)
     +/ (delay)\     /(delay)\+               +/(delay)\     /(delay)\+
   births     population     deaths         investment    capital    depreciation
         \___(+)___/ +  -\___(-)___/              \___(+)___/ +  -\___(-)___/
```

and from their structure can be expected to grow exponentially, decline exponentially, or oscillate, but not to exhibit sigmoid growth (because of time delays).

As these examples illustrate, time delays can be crucial determinants of the dynamic behavior of a system. System dynamics theory emphasizes the characteristics and consequences of different types of delays, both in information and in physical flows. System dynamicists expect and look for lagged relationships in real systems, and represent such lags carefully in their models.

Non-linearities are also considered important in explaining system behavior. Non-linear relationships can cause feedback loops to vary in strength, depending on the state of the rest of the system. Linked non-linear feedback loops thus form patterns of shifting loop dominance—under some conditions one part of the system is very active, and under other conditions another set of relationships takes control and shifts the entire system behavior. A model composed of several feedback loops linked non-linearly can produce a wide variety of complex behavior patterns, and can represent an evolving or adapting system structure. System dynamicists are trained to be very sensitive to non-linearities and to expect that proper identification of them will help in understanding how a system works.

Non-linear, lagged feedback relationships are notoriously difficult to handle mathematically. Forrester and his associates developed a computer simulation language called DYNAMO[11] that allows non-linearities and time delays to be represented with great ease, even by persons with limited mathematical training. DYNAMO is widely used by system dynamicists because of its convenience, and therefore, it is often thought to be an identifying characteristic of a system dynamics model. But any system dynamics model can be written in a general-purpose language such as FORTRAN, or BASIC and, conversely, DYNAMO can be used to program linear, open-system models that are not philosophically system dynamics models at all.

A final distinguishing characteristic of the system dynamics paradigm is its emphasis on underlying causal mechanisms, whether directly observable or not, rather than on observed correlations. In social systems models, any representation of causation must include human motivations. System dynamicists are trained to be aware of and to include explicitly such factors as desires, expectations, perceptions, and goals. Information about these behavioral factors is gained from social and psychological theory, from interviews with decision-makers in the system being simulated, and from observation of the actual decisions made under a variety of external circumstances.

System dynamics models are usually intended for use at the general-understanding or policy-design stages of decision-making. Therefore, they tend to be process-oriented, fairly small, aggregated, and simple.* Most fall within the range of 20–200 endogenous variables. The individual model relationships are usually derived directly from mental models and thus are intuitive and easily understandable. The paradigm requires that every element and relationship in a model have a readily identifiable real-world counterpart; nothing should be added for mathematical convenience or historical fit. Thanks to the high standards initially set by Forrester, system dynamics models are usually well-documented and easy to reproduce.

d. Typical uses of system dynamics

The system dynamics paradigm assumes that the world is composed of closed, feedback-dominated, non-linear, time-delayed systems and thus the method must be most applicable to systems that do indeed possess these characteristics. In general, such systems will be characterized by distinctive dynamic patterns, long time horizons, and broad interdisciplinary boundaries.

For example, some questions that have been addressed with system dynamics models include:

Why have most American cities experienced a 100–200 year life cycle of growth, followed by stagnation and decay? What urban policies can restore economic vitality to stagnant urban centres?[12]

How do primitive slash-and-burn agricultural societies control their populations and their land use practices to ensure a stable pattern of life in an ecologically fragile environment?[13]

What causes short- and long-term economic cycles, and what national policies would ease the severity of economic downturns?

What has caused the decrease in the number of economically viable dairy farms in Vermont, and what policies might halt that decrease?[15]

There are some notable exceptions to this generalization, such as the National Economic Model, constructed by Jay Forrester and his colleagues at M.I.T., which contains over 2,000 endogenous variables.

What policies will help the United States energy system make a smooth transition from a petroleum base to other energy sources?[16]

All of these studies have a time horizon of 30 years or more, and all have purposes of general understanding and/or policy design.

e. Problems and limitations of system dynamics

The DYNAMO language associated with system dynamics is a mixed blessing. No special knowledge of computer science is required to use it, nor is knowledge of mathematics beyond algebra. The DYNAMO compiler automatically arranges equations in logical order, moves the simulation forward through time, generates output graphs, and detects common errors of format and logic. The modeler must supply knowledge and judgement about interconnections in the real-world system, but not extraordinary programming skill.

This well-developed software package has obvious advantages, but it also has several disadvantages. First, it makes modeling look so easy that beginners who know the language but not the underlying paradigm are likely to become overconfident about their skills and their models. Second, because alterations are readily made and analyzed within minutes, beginners and advanced modelers alike are tempted to play with endless model variations, rather than analyze carefully the experiments they have tried and the lessons they have learned. Finally, the mechanical simplicity of adding new elements and relationships to a model enhances the natural tendency of all modelers to create an overcomplex, opaque, incomprehensible structure.

The ease with which models can be overelaborated is a problem common to many modeling schools, but it is especially troublesome in system dynamics. Both the philosophy and the general-understanding purpose of the system dynamics method require simplicity and transparency, so that the reasons for the model's behavior can be understood. System dynamicists recognize the problem of overcomplex models and greatly emphasize, both in training and in publication, the necessity and difficulty of creating simple methods. System dynamicists tend instinctively to criticize complex models and to admire simple ones. But the pains that are taken to instill and reiterate the goal of model simplicity reflect the very real difficulties in achieving it.

The emphasis on simplicity in system dynamics is consistent with the purposes for which this technique is usually intended, but it has also limited its range of application, so far at least, primarily to questions that involve the behavior of aggregate quantities. Distribution of income, resources, opportunity, pollution, or any other quantity among people or over geographical space is represented in almost any modeling school by the 'brute force' method of disaggregation. Each class, person, or area concerned are represented explicitly, and the flows of goods and bads among them are accounted for. Disaggregation into even a few classes or levels can complicate a model tremendously. A modeler striving for clarity and simplicity will try to avoid disaggregation as much as possible, and thus may be likely to discount, avoid, or simply not perceive questions of distribution. This does not mean that system dynamicists are unable to deal with distribution questions, just that their paradigm gives them a certain reluctance to disaggregate. This relative neglect of distributional issues may disappear as the field grows and as the DYNAMO III compiler with matrix capabilities decreases the labor of disaggregation.

Three problems that recur in all modeling techniques are estimation of parameters, sensitivity testing, and assessment of model validity. Parameter estimation is of less concern in system dynamics than in other modeling schools, and statistical estimation procedures are used less, for several reasons. First, most system dynamics models are not aimed at problems of detailed implementation or precise prediction, but at problems of general understanding that do not require highly precise numbers. Second, because of the long-term nature of most system dynamics problem statements, parameters are likely to exceed historic ranges, so estimation based on statistical analysis of historic data is of limited usefulness. Third, the non-linear feedback structure of system dynamics models renders them less sensitive than open-loop models to precise refinements of parameter values. The presence of numerous negative feedback loops, each acting to maintain a system variable within a certain range of values, offsets small numerical changes or errors in any one loop by inducing opposing changes in other loops.

Thus feedback systems tend to be more numerically stable than open systems. This property does not allow parameter values in a model to be totally wrong or randomly chosen, but it does mean that the time and computer costs of rigorous estimation techniques are often not worth the benefit in terms of improved model utility. System dynamicists are often content to use parameters that are simply 'in the right ballpark'. There is nothing inherent in the method to prevent the use of statistical estimation methods, however, when the data are of sufficiently high quality and when the model purpose requires numerical precision.[17]

The numerical insensitivity of system dynamics models is partly a result of their feedback structure, but it is also partly due to the way sensitivity is defined in the system dynamics paradigm. Model output is read not for quantitative predictions of particular variables in particular years, but for qualitative behavioral characteristics (growth, decline, oscillation, stability, instability). A model is said to be sensitive to a given parameter only if a change in the numerical value of the parameter changes the entire behaviour of the model (from growth to decline, for example, or from damped oscillation to exploding oscillation) or if a change in parameter leads to a reversal of a policy conclusion. Sensitivity of this kind is rare, both in system dynamics models and in social systems, but it does occur. In fact, detection of a particularly sensitive parameter is an important result of the modeling process because it earmarks that parameter as one that must be estimated carefully and one that might be an effective site for inducing changes in the real system.

System dynamics lacks rigorous theory or procedures for performing sensitivity analysis, that is, for testing the full range of uncertain parameters to see what effect the uncertainty might have on policy conclusions. The informal structure-behavior theorems that characterize the paradigm sometimes do permit an experienced dynamicist to locate possibly sensitive parameters by inspection of the model structure and thus to eliminate the necessity of testing every possible parameter in the system. This intuitive approach to sensitivity testing is effective only for small models.

The system dynamics paradigm also handles the problem of model validity qualitatively and informally. System dynamicists use no precise, quantitative index to summarize the validity of a system dynamics model. Reference is usually made not to absolute validity, but to model *utility* or to building *confidence*—is the model sufficiently representative of the real system to answer the question it was designed to answer, and is its structure convincing enough to induce someone to act on its conclusions? It is assumed that every model is by definition not totally valid, but a simplification. Furthermore, statistical fit to historical data is so easy to achieve that it has little meaning.

A system dynamicist begins to have confidence in his model when it meets several conditions:

1. Every element and relationship in the model has identifiable real-world meaning and is consistent with whatever measurements or observations are available.
2. When the model is used to simulate historical periods, every variable exhibits the qualitative, and roughly quantitative, behavior that was observed in the real system. In particular, the model clearly generates the problem it was built to investigate.
3. When the model is simulated under extreme conditions, the model system's operation is plausible (physical quantities do not become negative or exceed feasible bounds, impossible behavior modes do not appear).
4. Parameters that are sensitive to numerical changes in the model are also sensitive to similar changes in the real system.

These standards are imprecise and do not lend themselves to quick evaluation. They are also quite difficult to achieve in practice. The issue of model validity is an unresolved one in every modeling field. System dynamics approaches it by admitting the indeterminacy of the very concept of validity and by establishing performance standards that are qualitative but demanding.

The most difficult problems in system dynamics appear in the process of modeler-client interaction. They may explain at least partially why this field is associated with political controversy.

First, the system dynamics paradigm leads analysts to adopt long time-horizons and wide boundaries, which are inconsistent with the very real short-term pressures and constraints felt by decision-makers. The result is often an impasse; the client cannot take the broad perspective of the modeler, and the modeler is convinced that no other perspective will lead to a solution of the client's problem.

If this problem is overcome, a worse one appears as the modeler works out his conclusions. Since system dynamicists assume that most problems, like most model elements, are endogenous to the system, they tend to look for, and often find, internal policies as a major cause of problems. Investigating the falling market share of a company, the modeler will concentrate on company policies as well as the behavior of consumers or competitors. He will assume that economic stagnation in a city is at least as likely to be caused by city policies as by those imposed by state or federal governments. Thus a system dynamics study is likely (but not certain) to lead to the conclusion that the problem is caused, at least partially and usually inadvertently, by the client. The recommended solution often requires structural change. This change may be as simple as bringing new information to bear on a decision, but it may also involve revision of goals, reward structures, or areas of authority. Needless to say, these recommendations are often politically unacceptable. The problem is intrinsic to the basic paradigm of system dynamics and the nature of public decision making.

f. Summary

When system dynamicists look at the world, their attention is caught by problems that can be expressed in terms of time trends or dynamic behavior patterns. In exploring a new problem, they look for feedback loops, stocks and flows, material and information. They expect that elements within any system will respond to each other in a non-linear fashion and with time delays. The principles they use to formulate a model include an awareness of the relationships between the feedback structure of a system and the system's behavior. And they are particularly interested in the decision points within a system, in the kinds of information available to decision makers, and in the constraints and motivations that cause decision-makers to transform information about a system into actions that control or alter the system.

System dynamics models are most effectively used for purposes of general understanding or broad policy-making and design for aggregate systems. They tend to be comparatively simple to understand, undetailed, and well-documented. They are likely to represent the broad, long-term context surrounding a problem and to suggest structural system changes as solutions.

2. Econometrics

Statistical models of the working of the economy are not proposed as magic formulas which divulge all the secrets of the complex real world in a single equation. The statistical models attempt to provide as much information about future or other unknown phenomena as can be gleaned from the historical records of observable and measurable facts. To the extent to which people maintain their past behavior patterns in the future, the statistical models provide information about the quantitative properties of economic variables in the future. ... The non-statistical economist has only qualitative information from which to make judgements. The statistical economist has this same qualitative information plus a thorough knowledge of historically developed behavior patterns.[18]

a. Origin of econometrics

Econometrics is the use of statistical methods to verify and quantify economic theory. An econometric model is a set of theoretical relationships that has been statistically quantified with historic data from a particular economic system. The model can be used for structural analysis, for policy design, or for forecasting.

The field of econometrics arose from the two older disciplines of economics and statistics. Therefore it shares aspects of those two paradigms as well as adding its own special perspectives to the world-view of its practitioners. The application of statistics to economics developed in the 1930s as a result of a rising interest in the quantitative behavior of national economic variables, especially aggregate consumption, which was postulated to be a major cause of the great depression. The journal *Econometrica* was begun in 1933. By the late 1930s Jan Tinbergen had constructed the first dynamic models of the Dutch, United States, and British economies.[19] Much theoretical and practical work had already been done by the 1950s, when the availability of the computer permitted a great expansion in the scope and complexity of econometric models.

Econometrics is now a widely-practiced modeling technique, with the journals, university chairs, and textbooks that signify the maturity of a scholarly discipline.[20] The greatest practical use of the technique has been in generating short-term forecasts of the performance of national economies.[21] However, many other types of econometric models exist, on both micro and macro scales, and for both academic and pragmatic purposes.

b. Sample econometric models

An econometrician interested in a market system similar to the one we illustrated in the system dynamics section might construct either a static or a dynamic model. A simple static supply-demand model for an agricultural commodity could consist of as few as three equations.[22] One would be a demand equation:

$$D = \beta_{10} + \beta_{11}P + \beta_{12}Y + E_1$$

where D is the quantity demanded, P is the price, Y is the consumer's income, and β_{10}, β_{11}, and β_{12} are constants called *structural coefficients*. E_1 is an expression of the variation in observed values of D not explained by the other terms of the equation (partly due to unsystematic variation in the system, partly to explanatory variables that have been omitted, and partly to measurement errors). An *error term* of this sort is added to every *behavioral equation*, that is, every equation that represents human decisions or responses, which are assumed to be partially uncertain and unpredictable.

The supply equation might be:

$$S = \beta_{20} + \beta_{21}P + \beta_{22}Z + E_2$$

where S is the quantity supplied, P is the price, Z is the amount of annual rainfall, β_{20}, β_{21}, and β_{22} are structural coefficients, and E_2 is another error term.

The third equation is the assumption of supply-demand equilibrium: to clear the market the quantity supplied must equal the quantity demanded. No error term is needed in this equation since it is an identity; it must always hold true by definition.

$$D = S = Q$$

Note that these equations are linear, and they are expressed in terms of directly observable variables. The equations for supply and demand are indirectly causal. They do not indicate explicitly the presumed underlying mechanisms that cause demand to change with price and income or supply to change with price and rainfall. But one can imagine what the hypothesized mechanisms must be. And the equations are not reversible; one would not invert them to determine income as a function of price and demand or to determine rainfall as a function of price and supply. The third equation is not causal but definitional. The amount sold must be equal to the amount bought.

This model is simple enough to solve analytically for the two endogenous variables Q (quantity) and P (price) in terms of the two exogenous variables Y (income) and Z (rainfall):

$$P = \frac{1}{\beta_{11} - \beta_{21}} (\beta_{20} - \beta_{10} + \beta_{22}Z - \beta_{12}Y + E_2 - E_1)$$

$$Q = \frac{1}{\beta_{11} - \beta_{21}} (\beta_{20}\beta_{11} - \beta_{21}\beta_{10} + \beta_{22}\beta_{11}Z - \beta_{21}\beta_{12}Y + \beta_{11}E_2 - \beta_{21}E_1)$$

The postulated system might be represented graphically as in Figure 2.5, where the double-headed arrows stand for the assumed mutual and simultaneous dependency of S, D, and P.

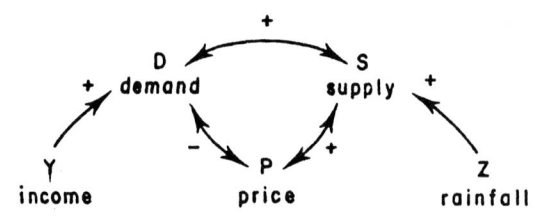

Figure 2.5 Relationships in static econometric market model

Having postulated this model or one like it, an econometrician will compare it to historical observations of P, Q, Z, and Y. A number of statistical techniques are at his disposal for this process, which will give him estimated values for all the structural coefficients (βs) in the model and indices of how well the estimated values explain the actual observed values of the model variables. If a set of structural coefficients can be found that bring the model into satisfactory agreement with real-world observations, the model, now estimated, can be used to give the equilibrium point of the market, given any specified rainfall and income, or to predict next year's supply and price, given assumptions about next year's rainfall and income. The individual structural coefficients can also provide useful information. For example, the coefficient β_{12}, which represents the income elasticity of demand, indicates how much consumer demand would change with an increase in income if price remained constant. Since the model is static, it provides no information about the dynamic path by which the market attains equilibrium.

A *dynamic* econometric model of the market for an agricultural product could consist of the following three equations:[23]

$$S_t = \beta_1 P_{t-1} + E_1$$

Supply at any time t is assumed to be a linear function of price in the previous year. (The time interval $t - 1 \to t$ in an econometric model is typically one accounting period, such as a year or a quarter, rather than a very small interval as in system dynamics.)

$$D_t = \beta_2 P_t + \beta_3 Y_t + E_2$$

Demand is a linear function of price and income in the current year.

$$P_t = \beta_4(D_{t-1} - S_t) + \beta_5 Y_t + E_3$$

Price is assumed to be set by producers on the basis of their expectation of what the excess of demand over supply is likely to be. This expectation comes from an accurate forecast of this year's supply and an assumption that this year's demand will be the same as last year's. An income term is also added because the average income is presumed to be related to production costs (labor). This third equation is now also a behavioral equation with an error term.

All of the equations in this model are (indirectly) causal and can be represented by single arrows as in Figure 2.6. The model consists of two negative feedback loops, as did the sample system dynamics model of the same system.

This model is now too complex to be solved analytically. Instead it is simulated through time. Once its structural coefficients have been estimated from historical data, and once initial values for P and D and a forecasted time trend for the exogenous variable Y have been decided upon, the model can generate the dynamic behavior of price, supply, and demand. An example of output from the model, estimated for the United States onion market from 1930–1950, is shown in Figure 2.7. The sharp annual oscillations are a result of the discrete one-year

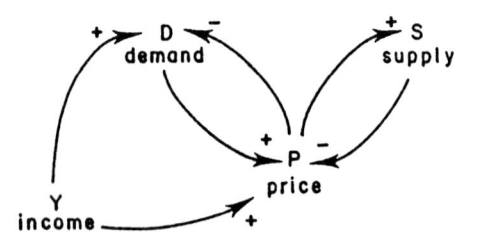

Figure 2.6 Relationships in dynamic econometric market model

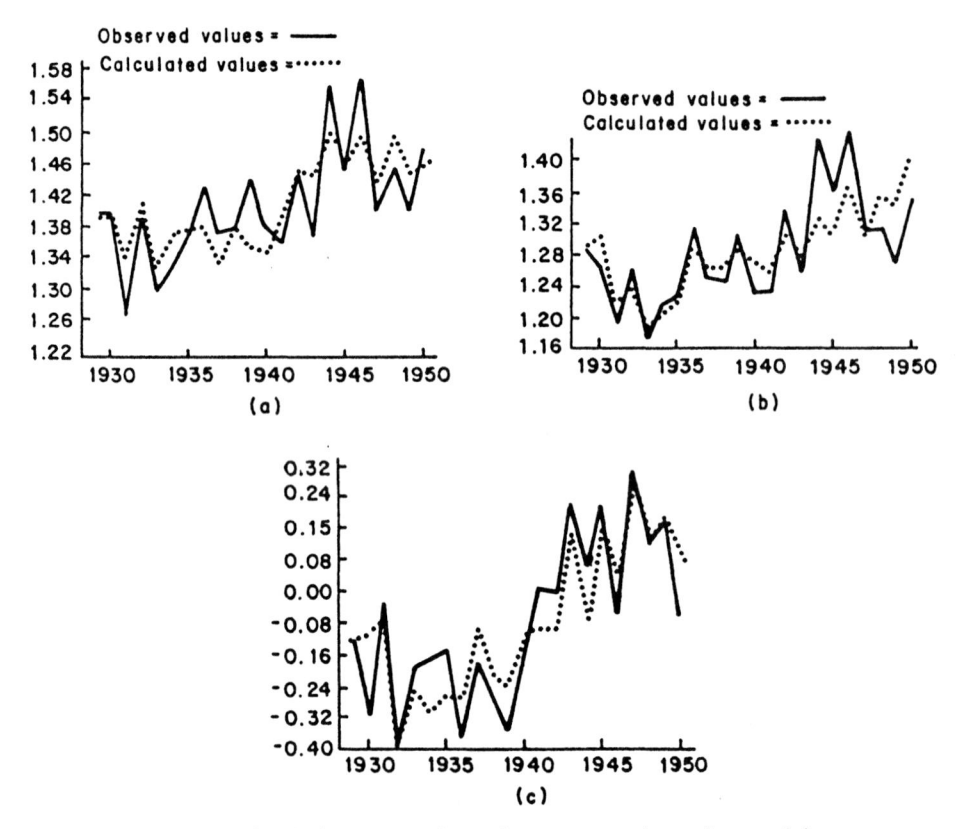

Figure 2.7 Simulation output from the econometric market model.
(a) Onion supply,
(b) Onion demand,
(c) Onion price.

Reproduced with permission from G. Stojkovic in O. A. Wold, (ed.) *Econometric Model Building*,. Amsterdam, North Holland Publishing Co., pp. 400–401, 1964

lag terms in the equations for supply and price. In this dynamic model the assumption of market equilibrium has been discarded and supply does not necessarily equal demand at every time period. There is no explicit indication in the model that unsold supply or unsatisfied demand is carried over into the next period.

Like all the sample models in this chapter, this one could be elaborated further to include more explanatory variables in the behavioral equations, to include non-linear relationships, or to make some of the exogenous variables endogenous. Econometric models of entire national economies can become quite complex, usually consisting of hundreds of equations.

c. Characteristics of econometrics

The dominating characteristic of the econometric method is its emphasis on statistical verification of model structure and model parameters. Econometricians are forced by their paradigm to tie their models firmly to quantitative observations of real-world systems. The formulation of an econometric model may be divided theoretically into two sequential phases, *specification* of structure from economic theory and *estimation* of parameters by statistical analysis from historical data. The second phase is the center of concern, occupying most of the modeler's time and attention and most of the pages in econometric textbooks and journals. To some extent, as we shall see, the mathematical and data requirements of the estimation phase influence the specification phase as well.

The information base from which an econometrician can draw his model structure is the same one underlying system dynamics or any other modeling technique—abstractions, intuitions, personal experiences, statistical data, established wisdom, experimentation, and guesswork. In practice, most econometricians are attracted to questions about economic variables. They find most of the concepts they need in traditional economic theory. They tend to make only limited use of theories from other disciplines, and when they do, their bias tends to be as much toward the social sciences as the system dynamicists' bias is toward the physical sciences.

No special distinction is made between physical and information flows in econometric models. For example, many of the common variables found in econometric models are expressed in units of unconserved monetary stocks and flows, even when they stand for conserved physical stocks and flows (examples are production, consumption, capital, investment, depreciation, and imports and exports).

The underlying economic theory from which econometrics is drawn is richer in static concepts than dynamic ones, perhaps because much of the theory was developed before computer simulation allowed dynamic analysis of complex, non-linear systems. Much attention is paid in economics to the optimum or equilibrium points in a system, comparatively little to the path of approach to equilibrium or the time required to attain it. Relatively few theorems of continuous dynamic behavior exist, but there is a collection of techniques, rules, graphs, and concepts for dealing with comparative static analysis or with dynamic progression from one equilibrium or optimum point to another.

Economic theory also leads econometric modelers to create structures that are partially open—driven by many exogenous variables rather than entirely closed into feedback loops. Economics evolved as an open-system body of theory for several reasons. Economic systems are strongly driven by forces outside the disciplinary boundary; resources come from the domain of geology, weather fluctuations from meteorology, consumer motivations from psychology and sociology, labor availability from demography. Furthermore, the relatively short-term focus of many economic problem statements means that analysts often need not take into account the closing of feedback loops with long time delays.

When two-way causation, or feedback, does appear in economic theory, it is often represented by means of simultaneous equations. The simultaneous-equation formulation is equivalent to assuming that feedback processes will be complete within one calculation interval. This assumption is justified when the calculation interval is relatively long compared to the time required to complete the equilibration process, and this condition does often hold true for econometric models, whose calculation intervals correspond to the fairly long reporting intervals (usually one year) of data-collection agencies. The simultaneous-equation formulation reinforces the tendency toward open systems in econometric models; in order to solve for, or *identify*, all structural coefficients in a simultaneous-equation model, an econometrician must include a relatively large number of exogenous variables.

Although most dynamic econometric models contain simultaneous-equation formulations, they also typically contain some feedback through lagged endogenous variables as well. These formulations are not essentially different from those in system dynamics models. The mathematical distinction between the two approaches is one of relative emphasis. Econometric models contain some feedback relationships, some of which are lagged; system dynamics models are composed almost entirely of feedback relationships, all of which are lagged.

Even within the disciplinary boundary of economics, the variables that can be included in econometric models are restricted to a subset of all conceivable elements because of the necessity for empirical validation. Each element in an econometric model must be observable, and sufficient historic observations of it must exist to permit estimation of its statistical relationship to other variables. That requirement tends to eliminate the inclusion of most of the information components of any system, especially the motivations behind human decisions. These motivational components are not absent from economic theory, which contains many inherently unobservable concepts such as marginal utility, indifference curves, and the profit motive. But none of these ideas is easily measured or contained as an explanatory variable in econometric models.

The requirement of observability is not as confining to econometricians as a system dynamicist might think. In the long run it creates pressures that are already improving and expanding data collection on economic behavior around the world. Useful but unmeasured concepts eventually can become sufficiently well defined to be calculated and included in databases. No GNP statistics were available until economists devised the concept, found it useful, and figured out how to measure it.

Econometricians can also represent an unobservable concept by means of a closely-correlated tangible substitute or proxy. Literacy may suffice as a stand-in for degree of modernization, rainfall may be a proxy for all the effects of weather on crop production, or advertising expenditures may be used to represent some of the perceived-utility assumptions underlying a consumer demand equation. In other words, an econometrician can transform a direct causal hypothesis ('in early stages of modernization people's material aspirations rise, and so they consume less and save more for investment to increase their future consumption') into an indirect hypothesis about correlated observables ('at low income levels literacy is inversely correlated with consumption and positively correlated with savings'). The use of correlated rather than direct causally-related variables allows econometricians to proceed in spite of the requirement of empirical validation, but it also reinforces that requirement because a double set of assumptions must be made. A relationship must be hypothesized not only between modernization and consumption, but also between modernization and its proxy, literacy. Both relationships must be demonstrated to have existed over the historic period from which data are taken, and to exist in the present and into any forecasting period. Since correlational relationships are tenuous and subject to change, they must be rechecked continuously against the latest available real-world data.

The principal technique used to obtain parameters for econometric models is least squares regression, a method that generates the set of numbers that best* fits a postulated general relationship to historic observations and that also provides a quantitative measure of how good that fit is. The theoretical and mathematical assumptions behind this method require that each behavioral equation be convertible to a form in which all parameters to be estimated enter linearly. As a consequence, most relationships in an econometric model are linear or log-linear. The assumed relationship between literacy and consumption is most likely to be expressed as:

$$\text{consumption} = \beta_0 + \beta_1 (\text{literacy}) + E$$

or perhaps as:

$$\log (\text{consumption}) = \beta_0 + \beta_1 (\text{literacy}) + E$$

where β_0 and β_1 are constants to be determined by fitting historical data for consumption and literacy.

To be most accurate least squares regression requires that the variation in each explanatory variable must not be linearly dependent on the variation in

---

* Where 'best' is defined as minimizing the sum of the squares of the deviations between the actual observations and those predicted by the general relationship.

any other variable and must be strictly independent from the error term. Thus if consumption were postulated to a function of both literacy and income, (consumption = $\beta_0 + \beta_1$ (literacy) + β_2 (income) + E), the statistical procedures for estimating β_0, β_1, and β_2 will be accurate only if there is no high degree of correlation between income and literacy or between either of those and any of the omitted factors that might influence the error term E.

More sophisticated estimation techniques than least squares regression are available, and when used carefully, they can partially overcome or correct for some of the most restrictive assumptions of the simple least squares technique. A practitioner who understands the real system well and who has mastered the full toolbox of statistical estimation methods does not need to distort the system specification in order to carry out empirical estimation. But *in practice* most estimations are by simple least square techniques.

The structural coefficients in an equation like the one relating literacy and consumption are estimated for the system of interest by finding observed values for all variables over some historical period or over some cross-section of subsystems (families, nations, firms, etc.) at a single time. Then the model with its estimated parameters is used to generate or simulate the values of system variables for another time period or over another cross-sectional sample. The entire procedure depends upon the assumption that the underlying causal mechanisms do not change in form, strength, or stochastic properties from the estimation period to the forecasting period or from one cross-sectional sample to another.

Econometric models tend to deal with highly aggregated quantities, even more aggregated than those in system dynamics models. Typically, the models are small compared to other kinds of models.

d. Typical uses of econometrics

As we have seen, econometric models represent systems as linear, partly open, at or near equilibrium, and centered around variables that fall within the disciplinary boundary of economics. The real-world systems that are most congruent with this paradigm deal with flows of economic goods and services, money and prices, over a fairly short time horizon. In these systems many important influences are indeed exogenous, and many relationships are constrained within ranges that are very nearly linear. Also, over the short term the numerical coefficients derived from historical observations are still likely to be valid. If adequate data are available, econometric methods can provide very precise information about such systems. Thus econometric models are most appropriately made for purposes of precise, short-term prediction of aggregate economic variables. They are at least applicable to questions of general understanding that may range across disciplines, over long time horizons, and into circumstances that have not been historically observed.

Examples of questions addressed by policy-oriented econometric studies include:

Will a change in the oil import quotas of the U.S. aggravate the shortage of domestic natural gas from 1975 to 1985, and if so, what wellhead natural gas price would alleviate the shortage?[24]

What will be the effects on U.S. economic growth from 1974 to 2000 of more or less government spending, faster or slower population growth, sustained or decreased technical progress?[25]

What will be the quarterly consumer price index for food over the next four quarters?[26]

How many acres will be planted in wheat in the U.S. next year if government acreage restrictions and loan programs are altered in various ways?[27]

How will fiscal and monetary control decisions of the Federal Reserve Board affect the U.S. macroeconomy over the next few years?[28]

Most of these questions fall within the policy design or implementation stages of decision-making.

e. Problems and limitations of econometrics

The greatest strength of the economic paradigm is its insistence on continuous, rigorous checking of theoretical hypotheses against real-world observations. This strength leads, however, to two problems. The statistical methods used for estimation interfere with the initial formulation of the model, and the data available for verification are not always sufficient.

As we have seen, the mathematical requirements of estimation, especially least squares regression, impose structural restrictions on econometric models, which cause them to represent a world quite different from either the world of economic theory or the world seen by other modeling schools. Econometric models tend to consist of linear, simultaneous relationships connecting the observable economic variables by means of coefficients derived from the historic operation of the system. Economic theory, however, recognizes that economic relationships may be non-linear, greatly delayed, dependent on unobservable goals and desires, and capable of behavior patterns not contained in the historic data. Econometric models also tend to be less comprehensive than economic theories because of a subtle psychological reaction to the mathematical necessity of avoiding co-variance of explanatory variables with each other or with the error term:

> By the very existence of a large number of intercorrelations among all economic variables we can estimate but a few partial coefficients with tolerable precision. This accounts for the contrast between economic theory and empirical research. The theory is comprehensive: if we list the determinants of, say, consumption or investment that have been discussed by economists we may easily find some ten or 20 distinct effects. But in econometric research we rarely try to estimate more than four or five coefficients.[29]

There are indeed areas where the narrow domain of econometrics overlaps the broad and complex surface of real social systems. Within these areas econometric techniques can produce accurate, informative, precise, and useful predictions. The major problem in econometric modeling is to recognize the limits of the congruent areas and to resist the temptation to push outside them. Thoughtful econometricians are aware of this problem and continuously seek to define these limits:

> What then is econometrics ... best suited for? I myself would place economic problems of the firm in the fore ... The problems confronting a firm are in general much less complex than those confronting the economy as a whole: they often are truly of a partial nature. Secondly, the number of observations of the same social system can here frequently be increased. We do not have to face the dilemma of the need for large samples in a world changing rapidly during sampling. And finally, many economic models basically assume a planning subject. In the firm it is clear who the planning subject is; while for the economy as a whole the originator of the actions described ... may be clouded behind the imprecisions of thought not necessarily excluded by the precision of the mathematics used.
> If we wish to use econometrics for macro-economic purposes—to which it first turned, perhaps because disciplines as the outflow of human perversity always first turn to the field of application least suited to them—I would think that it can well be used to test which of a large number of economic hypotheses can best explain an economic reality precisely defined as to time and place.[30]

One use that is clearly beyond the limits of econometric modeling is the exploration of conditions or policies that differ significantly from those that pertained during the historical period from which the model parameters were estimated. The quasi-causal relationships in an econometric model may resemble the real system sufficiently to indicate how the unchanged or only slightly changed system may proceed into the short-term future. But they are too rigidly tied to past behavior to represent correctly the response of the system to totally new policies.

Nearly every econometrician would list the lack of good empirical data as the most annoying and constricting problem in the field. Econometric researchers pay great attention to data problems and have developed names and categories for the most frequently occurring ones:

> Among the more important problems are that there is simply not enough data (*the degrees of freedom problem*); that the data tend to be bunched together (*the multicollinearity problem*); that because changes occur slowly over time, the data from time periods close together tend to be similar (*the serial correlation problem*); that there may be a discontinuous change in the real world so that the data refer to different populations (*the structural change problem*); and that there are many inaccuracies and biases in measuring economic variables (*the errors of measurement problem*).[31]

Econometric techniques include a number of ingenious methods for recovering from data problems and for extracting maximum possible information from real-world observations. Unfortunately, none of these methods can create more information than is already there, and a process that overcomes one data problem usually makes another one worse:

> For example, replacing annual data by quarterly data increases the number of data points but tends to aggravate both the multicollinearity and the serial correlation problems; eliminating data points referring to unusual periods, such as during war years, overcomes the structural change problem but aggravates both the degrees of freedom and the multicollinearity problems; and replacing variables by their first differences overcomes the serial correlation problem but aggravates the errors of measurement problem.[32]

Inadequate data especially limit the applicability and usefulness of econometric models for studies of non-industrialized nations, where data problems are especially discouraging:

> As the sorts of models we have been considering are being constructed for one country at a time, they have necessarily to rely on time series data. This data is generally available for only a few years, and when available is of uncertain or very low reliability. As the time series are very short and as almost all variables seem to grow or decay over the short periods for which the data about them can be assembled, every attempt to include in the equations all the independent variables that appear to be relevant on *a priori* grounds soon exhausts the degrees of freedom and is itself frustrated by the prevalence of collinearities. For this and other reasons there is every likelihood that the models and their equations are grossly under-specified or mis-specified. Moreover, in a large number of cases one can expect little help from economic theory, from mechanically applied statistical tests or from appeals to one's intuition. Any one of these objections taken individually is sufficient to dissuade one from taking these macromodels at all seriously. In combination their effect can fairly be described as devastating.[33]

Another criticism econometricians commonly voice about their own field is that econometric modeling is so often done badly. In part this may be a byproduct of widespread use of econometrics and of very convenient computer software—the same mixed blessing we have encountered in system dynamics and will encounter again when we go on to discuss the other modeling techniques. In the case of econometrics, the statistical packages that are now standard equipment at most computer centers can be used rather easily by skilled analysts, and also by those who have never understood or have entirely forgotten the assumptions and precautions underlying the regression techniques. Mechanical application of statistical techniques can easily be substituted for experience with the real-world system, for knowledge of economic theory, and for thoughtful evaluation of conclusions. Lazy, careless, or ignorant modelers can disguise poorly-conceived models with computer-aided datamassaging and spurious summary statistics. The same data can be used for both estimating parameters and assessing validity. Causation can be confused with correlation. These are not inevitable problems, they can be overcome by better training of modelers, better self-regulation of the econometric profession as a whole, and continuous questioning and review of econometric modeling efforts by modelers, clients, and sponsors.

Because econometric models are partially open, they tend to be more sensitive to parameter variation than are system dynamics models. This structural difference in sensitivity is magnified by the fact that econometricians are usually striving for more precise statements about the future than are system dynamicists. One would expect, therefore, that sensitivity analysis would be a central concern of econometricians. However, the procedures for carrying out and reporting sensitivity tests, especially for alternate forecasts of the usually numerous exogenous variables, do not seem to be formalized or regularly reported in model documentation. Testing every believable combination of values for exogenous variables would be an impossible task, and the intuitive structure-based hunches that system dynamicists use to detect sensitive points are less applicable to econometric models. Sensitivity testing, therefore, seems to be a continuing problem of the field of econometrics.

Econometricians determine the validity of their models by the use of statistical tests of model-generated data against real-world data and by the informal comparison of model results with their mental models of 'reasonable' values for economic variables. These two validity tests are probably as good as any other, when the statistical tests are done honestly and skillfully, and when the modeler has a deep understanding of the workings of real economies. A less honest, skillful, or knowledgeable modeler, however, can produce with these tests evidence of validity for almost any model. In other words, although econometrics techniques include a number of sophisticated statistical validity tests, establishing confidence in a model's output is as difficult and uncertain in this modeling school as it is in the others.

f. Summary

If system dynamicists see the world as a conglomeration of interacting feedback loops, econometricians see it as a collection of the economic variables contained in statistical databases. They tend to think in terms of simultaneous equations, linear relationships, many exogenous driving variables, and observable money flows rather than unobservable information streams. Econometricians utilize historical data rigorously to determine model parameters and to check hypotheses. Model validity is evaluated partly by summary statistics and partly by the agreement of estimated coefficients and calculated output with economic theory and intuition.

The assumptions upon which econometric models are based are most applicable to questions about systems that can be bounded by the traditional disciplinary range of economics and by conditions that do not depart greatly from observed ones. The purpose of most econometric models is precise forecasting of economic variables into the short-term future. In practice econometric modeling is limited by mathematical requirements of its estimation procedures, by the lack of adequate and accurate data, and like most other modeling schools, by unresolved questions about assessing model sensitivity and validity.

3. Input–output analysis

Economic theory seeks to explain the material aspects and operations of our society in terms of interactions among such variables as supply and demand or wages and prices. Economists have generally based their analyses on relatively simple data—such quantities as the gross national product, the interest rate, price, and wage levels. But in the real world things are not so simple. Between a shift in wages and the ultimate working out of its impact upon prices there is a complex series of transactions in which actual goods and services are exchanged among real people. These intervening steps are scarcely suggested by the classical formulation of the relationship between the two variables. It is true, of course, that the individual transactions, like individual atoms and molecules, are far too numerous for observation and description in detail. But it is possible, as with physical particles, to reduce them to some kind of order by classifying and aggregating them into groups. This is the procedure employed by input–output analysis in improving the grasp of economic theory upon the facts with which it is concerned in every real situation.[34]

a. Origin of input–output analysis

The first semblance of an input–output analysis appeared in 1758, when Francois Quesnay constructed his *Tableau Economique* representing the interdependence of various wealth-producing activities on a single farm.[35] The chain of development of this idea can be traced for nearly 200 years, through such economists as Leon Walras and Vilfredo Pareto, until it reaches Wassily Leontief, who published his original paper laying the foundation of modern input–output analysis in 1936.[36] The first official input–output table for the U.S. economy was compiled by the Bureau of Labor Statistics for the year 1947. By 1963 at least 40 countries had completed their own national input–output tables, and now at least one collection of more than 300 such tables from 80 countries has been assembled.[37] Input–output tables are widely used for national economic planning in planned economies and for forecasting and policy analysis in market economies. Although input–output techniques arose from the economic paradigm and were originally intended for analyzing inter-industry flows of money and goods, more recently the field has expanded to include flows of other quantities, such as energy and pollution.[38]

b. Sample input–output model

An input–output analysis begins with a set of data measuring the flows of money or goods among various sectors or industrial groups of an economy in a given year. These flows are summarized by an input–output table, which is nothing more than an array of the purchases made by each industry (its inputs) and the sales of each industry (its outputs) from and to each other industry in the total economy. A very simple example of a hypothetical two-sector economy is shown in Table 2.2.[39]

This matrix indicates that the agriculture sector of the economy produced 100 bushels of wheat in a given year, of which 25 bushels were used within the

Table 2.2 A simple input–output table

from \ to	Agriculture	Manufacturing	Final Demand	Total Output
Agriculture	25	20	55	100 bushels of wheat
Manufacturing	14	6	30	50 yards of cloth

agriculture sector itself, 20 bushels were sold to the manufacturing sector, and 55 bushels were sold to final consumers (households). The second horizontal row of the table shows how the output of the other sector, manufacturing, was distributed; it produced 50 yards of cloth, of which 14 were sold to the agricultural sector, six were used by the manufacturing sector itself, and 30 were sold to households. Reading down a column of the table provides a comprehensive list of the inputs to each sector. To produce its total output of 50 yards of cloth, the manufacturing sector required 20 bushels of wheat from the agricultural sector and six yards of its own cloth.

Of course a real input–output table for a national economy would contain many more sectors, perhaps several hundred. The inputs and outputs might be expressed in terms of monetary value. In that case the table would be a summary of dollar flows to and from each sector of the economy. An example of a somewhat more complex table (also for a hypothetical economy) is shown in Figure 2.8. In this economy six industries have been distinguished, labeled A–F. The flows of inputs and outputs among these six industries are shown in the upper left-hand corner, this time in units of billions of dollars. Thus industry A used $10 billion worth of its product itself, and sold $15 billion worth to industry B, $1 billion to industry C, etc. In this more detailed table, the final demand column has been disaggregated into several components (columns 7–11): additions to inventory, exports, government purchases, additions to capital plant, and households, which means final purchases by private domestic consumers. Industry A added $2 billion worth of production to its inventories, exported $5 billion worth, sold $1 billion to the government, etc.

Reading down a column gives a record of any industry's expenses for inputs. Thus industry C bought $1 billion worth of industry A's output, $7 billion from industry B, and used $8 billion worth of its own product. Industry C also depleted its inventory by $1 billion, imported $3 billion worth of materials from abroad, paid $2 billion in taxes to the government, depreciated its capital by $1 billion, and paid $7 billion to households in the form of wages.

If input–output analysis ended here, it would just be a handy way of displaying and communicating information about the complex interdependence of many subsectors in an economic system during a particular year.

Processing sector *Final demand*

Inputs↓ \ Outputs→	(1) A	(2) B	(3) C	(4) D	(5) E	(6) F	(7) Gross inventory accumulation (+)	(8) Exports to foreign countries	(9) Government purchases	(10) Gross private capital formation	(11) Households	(12) Total gross output
(1) Industry A	10	15	1	2	5	6	2	5	1	3	14	64
(2) Industry B	5	4	7	1	3	8	1	6	3	4	17	59
(3) Industry C	7	2	8	1	5	3	2	3	1	3	5	40
(4) Industry D	11	1	2	8	6	4	0	0	1	2	4	39
(5) Industry E	4	0	1	14	3	2	1	2	1	3	9	40
(6) Industry F	2	6	7	6	2	6	2	4	2	1	8	46
(7) Gross inventory depletion (−)	1	2	1	0	2	1		1	0	0	0	8
(8) Imports	2	1	3	0	3	2		0	0	0	2	13
(9) Payments to government	2	3	2	2	1	2	3	2	1	2	12	32
(10) Depreciation allowances	1	2	1	0	1	0	0	0	0	0	0	5
(11) Households	19	23	7	5	9	12	1	0	8	0	1	85
(12) Total gross outlays	64	59	40	39	40	46	12	23	18	18	72	431

Industry producing / Processing sector / Payments sector

*Sales to industries and sectors along the top of the table from the industry listed in each row at the left of the table.
†Purchases from industries and sectors at the left of the table by the industry listed at the top of each column.

Figure 2.8 A six-sector input–output table

Reproduced with permission from W. H. Miernyk, *The Elements of Input–Output Analysis*, New York, Random House, p. 9, 1967

However, an input–output table is the beginning of the analysis, not the end. The next step is to assume that the numbers in the table arise from continuous, linear relationships between the inputs and outputs of each sector. To return to the simpler two-sector example given above, the observation that 100 bushels of wheat were produced from 14 yards of cloth and 25 bushels of wheat might be generalized to say that for any level of wheat production, each bushel produced requires an input of 0.25 bushels of wheat and 0.14 yards of cloth. If that assumption can be made, the entire table can be rewritten in more general terms. The entries indicate how much input is required to produce one unit (or one dollar's worth if the table is in monetary terms) of output for any quantity of production. This rewritten table is called the *structural matrix* for the economy, and the numbers in it are referred to as the *technical coefficients* defining the linear relationships between inputs and outputs. The structural matrix for the hypothetical two-sector economy is shown in Table 2.3.

Table 2.3 Structural matrix for a two-sector economy

From \ To	Agriculture	Manufacturing
Agriculture	0.25	0.40
Manufacturing	0.14	0.12

This matrix can be used to indicate for any hypothetical output of any sector what the direct inputs to that sector must be. For instance, production of ten yards of cloth will require an input of four bushels of wheat and 1.2 yards of cloth. Because it will take some input cloth (1.2 yards) to produce the ten yards of output cloth, and also some input cloth to produce the needed four bushels of wheat ($4 \times 0.14 = 0.56$ yards), not all the ten yards of cloth produced will be available to final consumers. In fact, any time consumers demand one more yard for final consumption, more than the additional yard will have to be produced because some must go into production directly, and some must go to provide the added wheat necessary to produce the added cloth.

In order to calculate this circularity of input factors, the structural matrix is first reduced to its equivalent equations:

$$0.25W_t + 0.40C_t + W_c = W_t$$
$$0.4W_t + 0.12C_t + C_c = C_t$$

where W_t and C_t are the total amounts of wheat and cloth produced and W_c and C_c are the amounts of wheat and cloth delivered to the final consumer. These equations can be rearranged:

$$W_t - 0.25W_t - 0.40C_t = W_c$$
$$C_t - 0.14C_t - 0.12W_t = C_c$$

These are two equations with four unknowns. They are usually solved by assuming the values for W_c and C_c, the final demands for wheat and cloth to be consumed by the household sector, and solving for W_t and C_t, the total amounts of wheat and cloth that must be produced to satisfy both the household sector and the wheat and cloth industries. The solution is:

$$W_t = 1.457 W_c + 0.662 C_c$$
$$C_t = 0.232 W_c + 1.242 C_c$$

In other words, to produce one bushel of wheat for final consumption, industry must produce a total of 1.457 bushels of wheat and 0.662 yards of cloth.

For more complex input–output analyses, the procedures followed are the same as those illustrated above, but the problem of solving x equations with x unknowns is solved by using the computer to perform a matrix inversion. In our simple example, the final solution can be expressed as a matrix:

$$\begin{bmatrix} 1.457 & 0.662 \\ 0.232 & 1.242 \end{bmatrix}$$

which is simply the inverse of the matrix:

$$\begin{bmatrix} 1-0.25 & -0.40 \\ -0.14 & 1-0.12 \end{bmatrix}$$

The inverse matrix, called the *table of direct and indirect requirements*, is the primary tool of input–output analysis. Each entry in this matrix indicates the total (direct and indirect) output from the row industry that is required for one unit of production of the column industry. The table can be used to derive much useful information about the economy. It can indicate how much total production of all intermediate and final goods would be needed to satisfy any desired pattern of final demands. If final demand for some item suddenly shifts, the necessary changes in production of all supporting industries can be traced through the economy. The columns of the table can be used by individual firms for cost planning, and the rows for market analysis. Above all, since the necessary interlinking of industries is clearly represented, consistent planning and analysis on a fairly detailed scale becomes possible. Expansion of automobile production can be discussed, taking into account not only additional steel production as a direct input to the automobiles, but also additional steel production for more railroad cars to deliver the additional steel, and still more steel production to build oil refineries to provide diesel fuel to run the additional railroad cars.

c. Characteristics of input–output analysis

Input–output analysis provides a way of organizing and manipulating detailed information about interrelated flows through a social system. Since neither the system dynamics nor the econometrics paradigm can easily handle such disaggregated representation, input–output analysis is a unique tool in the collection of techniques available to modelers.

Input–output analysts, like econometricians, use directly observable economic data rather than attempting to represent underlying causal mechanisms. In fact, input–output analysis is even farther removed than econometrics from concern about why things happen; it is based entirely upon a record of what did happen. The decision rules that cause the inter-industry flows to be whatever magnitude they are do not appear in the model. The input–output table that begins any analysis is derived only from the actual performance of an economic system in a given year. No information is available about whether that performance was typical, optimal, efficient, or desirable, nor whether the system was in equilibrium. The input–output paradigm is purely descriptive, not normative or even theoretical. It is descriptive in a way that counterbalances the emphasis of much of theoretical economics, in that it directs attention to the details of actual economic activities rather than hypothetical equilibria and optima. It also tends to emphasize the actual physical flows of real goods and services.

The logical step from the input–output table (which is a summary of the operation of an actual economy in a particular year) to the structural matrix (which is a generalized model that is used for planning, forecasting, and policy testing) depends on three crucial assumptions:

1. *Linearity*. The numerical relationships between inputs and outputs in each industry must remain constant over all ranges of inputs and outputs. This is equivalent to assuming constant returns to scale. Linear relationships are mathematically necessary in order to invert the structural matrix.
2. *Continuity*. Each industrial sector must be able to expand or contract output marginally to any level while maintaining the same relationship between inputs and outputs. Thus no input or output must occur in the form of large indivisible lumps.
3. *Instantaneous adjustment*. Since there is no time dimension in an input–output table, there is no way of representing delays or bottlenecks in the availability of inputs or in the production of outputs. Using such a table to investigate the effects of changes in final demand, technological conditions, or other factors can give no information about the time necessary to achieve these changes.

The linearity and continuity assumptions are intrinsic to input–output analysis and can be weakened only at the cost of great mathematical complication. The instantaneous adjustment assumption holds for *static* input–output analysis of the sort we have discussed so far. Input–output analysis can be made *dynamic* by combining it with some other modeling method that provides a way of moving the matrix forward through time. For example, an input–output table for 1985 might be used to calculate total national production; an econometric analysis might relate national production to income and final demand (consumption) in various sectors in the following year; this relationship can be used to predict 1986 final demand. The final demand prediction can then be used with the table of direct and indirect requirements to calculate all intermediate production levels, which will add up to a prediction of 1986 national production. The process can be iterated to carry the forecast further into the future. The causal assumptions behind this dynamic analysis form a positive feedback that will generate exponential growth in national production:

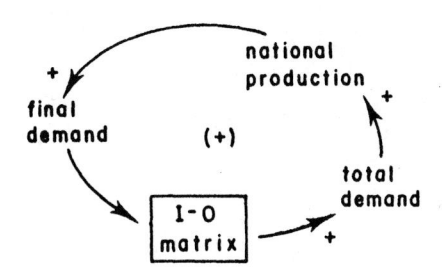

```
            _____
           /   national
      +  /    production
    final            +
    demand  (+)      \
         \          total
          \   ___    demand
           \ |I-O|___/
             |matrix|  +
```

The technical coefficients in the matrix may also be assumed to change with time as a result of exogenous technological developments or endogenous relative price shifts causing substitution. New industries may also enter the system, enlarging the structural matrix.

Any dynamic application of input–output modeling adds to the assumptions in the static analysis another set of assumptions that express the dynamic characteristics of inputs, outputs, and technical coefficients. This second set of assumptions may be simple extrapolation or exogenous driving forces derived from mental models, or it may be an adaptation of one of the dynamic modeling paradigms such as econometrics or system dynamics.

d. Typical uses of input–output analysis

Assumptions of linearity and continuity are most applicable to systems that are not greatly different from the system that generated the initial data. Thus input–output analysis is most useful for analyzing marginal changes in economic systems over the short term. Input–output models can add considerable detail to economic analysis and forecasts, and, as the following examples indicate, they can represent complex flows of dollars, goods, and even energy and water through industrial production systems. Input–output analysis has been used to provide:

A forecast for the U.S. economy, disaggregated into 90 industries, from 1965 to 1975.[40]

An analysis of water requirements by industry in the state of California (technical coefficients expressed in acre-feet of water per million dollars of output).[41]

A description of the effect over 60 industries and 19 geographic regions of a proposed shift in U.S. government spending from military to non-military procurements.[42]

A record of the energy flows within the U.S. economy (357 sectors) in 1963 and 1967, used to analyze the interindustry effects of various national energy policies.[43]

These studies illustrate the versatility of input–output analysis for detailed representation of interindustry or inter-regional flows and for short-term analysis of policy alternatives that do not include major changes or redesign the system. This method is clearly useful at the detailed implementation stage of decision-making, and to some extent at the policy design stage. Because the data requirements are significant and the construction of the initial matrix is tedious, input–output studies tend to be product-oriented; they aim to produce a single matrix that can be used for many different purposes, and more is learned from the computations made with the finished model than from the process of assembling it.

e. Problems and limitations of input–output analysis

Static input–output models are limited in scope and fixed in structure. Therefore the structural-conceptual problems of econometrics and system-dynamics are not so bothersome in input–output analysis, at least in its static form. The modeler need not spend much time wondering about the unseen mechanisms by which variables might be interrelated, he needs only assemble data on the actual measurable interrelations. This gain in conceptual simplicity is of course realized at a cost in range of applicability—many pressing policy questions cannot be addressed with an input–output model. For those questions that do fall within the range of applicability, however, structural ambiguity is not a problem.

The strength of input–output analysis and the reason for its existence is its ability to provide a disaggregated picture of a complex system. Practically, however, disaggregation has its limits. More sectors are included in an input–output table only at the cost of obtaining more data and using very much more computer time and space. Since a firm-by-firm disaggregation of a large national economy would strain any existing computer's capacity, some aggregation of productive activities is necessary.

How to aggregate is a classic problem in every kind of modeling, with no simple solutions. Should wheat producers be combined with rice producers? All grain producers with grain processors? All food producers with natural fiber producers? Natural fiber producers with synthetic fiber producers? Aggregation of entities that are actually unlike with respect to some important characteristic is always a danger.

Ultimately the aggregation decision can only be resolved by reference to the purpose of the model. Unfortunately, the construction of a major input–output model is so labor-intensive that new models are not often prepared for special purposes. Most modelers begin from some 'general purpose' model, usually made for a national economy. The degree of disaggregation in these models is decided not by purpose, but by data availability and computer capacity.

If an input–output analyst saves time in the conceptualization stage of model-making, he spends it many times over in assembling the data to fill all the entries in the input–output table. The kinds of data required are relatively straightforward—they are measurable physical or monetary flows rather than the unmeasured attitudinal variables the system dynamicist must often deal with. But extracting these numbers from actual accounting records and making them consistent is far from easy, and usually the power of a national government is required to do it.

Finding appropriate and complete industry records at the proper degree of aggregation is the first problem. For some countries or regions they simply do not exist. Even in countries with advanced systems for collecting national statistics, five to ten years are required to assemble one year's national input–output table. This delay is a great handicap for a short-term linear method whose assumptions become less acceptable as the time between database year and forecasting period increases.

Input–output tables require internal consistency. Total inputs must equal total outputs within each industry and for the system as a whole. Assembling a table is an excellent way to check on the consistency of national accounts. Unfortunately, the data are almost never actually consistent. While this is a useful lesson to learn about economic data, it threatens to stop an input–output analysis in its tracks unless the table can be 'reconciled'. Reconciliation of data relies on the modeler's judgement, intuition, and knowledge of the real system. It is a 'fudging' step that is rarely documented. Fudging of some sort occurs in all types of modeling, and it may well be that the rigorous structure of the input–output table restricts the degree of fudging freedom considerably. That conclusion would be hard to prove or disprove, however, since methods of sensitivity analysis are as primitive in input–output analysis as they are in most other modeling schools.

Input–output models focus the attention on real money or material flows through an economy, but not information flows. They allow careful computation of the real costs of production, but not of the real prices of commodities. They cannot represent the shifting exchange rates between commodities, which is to say, the dynamics of markets and prices. They shed no light on, and in fact divert attention from actual decision-making processes. And though their strong point is their representation of material flows, they do not encourage the inclusion of the ultimate sources of the economy's material and energy flows, or their ultimate sinks. (For an attempt to include resources and pollution in an input–output model, see the RfF model described in Chapter 5.)

Like econometric models, input–output models are strongly affected by mathematical requirements, especially in the central assumption of linearity. This assumption may be more unrealistic for input–output analysis than for econometrics because of the greater degree of disaggregation. Individual firms or industrial sectors may run into diminishing or increasing returns to scale, supply bottlenecks, or discontinuous, lumpy inputs before aggregated economies do. As we have already indicated, linear assumptions may be entirely acceptable in the short term; the problem is to refrain from pushing the technique beyond its range of applicability.

f. Summary

Input–output analysis is a way of representing flows of money, resources, or products among the various producers and consumers in an economy. It is based on the assumption of linear and continuous relationships between the inputs to each producing sector and its outputs. Input–output analysis can be used to trace the results of hypothetical changes throughout the economic system or to make detailed and consistent economic forecasts.

An input–output model provides only a static picture of an economic system, unless it is either driven by exogenous forecasts or combined with a dynamic modeling method. The data requirements for a detailed input–output analysis can be significant, and several years may be required to assemble the necessary information for a model at the national level. The assumptions of linearity and continuity limit the use of input–output analysis to short-term forecasts or to the exploration of marginal changes from historical conditions. Within these limitations an input–output model can provide a disaggregated, internally consistent representation of a complex, interdependent productive system.

4. Optimization

Industrial production, the flow of resources in the economy, the exertion of military effort in a war theater—all are complexes of numerous interrelated activities. Differences may exist in the goals to be achieved, the particular processes involved, and the magnitude of effort. Nevertheless, it is possible to abstract the underlying essential similarities in the management of these seemingly disparate systems. To do this entails a look at the structure and state of the system, and at the objective to be fulfilled, in order *to construct a statement of the actions to be performed, their timing, and their quantity..., which will permit the system to move from a given status toward the defined objective.*[44]

a. Origin of optimization modeling

During the Second World War the planning and coordination of U.S. military operations became so complex that several experiments were begun to attempt to compute the deployment of personnel, supplies, and maintenance activities that would best achieve wartime objectives. After the war the Air Force set up a research group for the Scientific Computation of Optimum Programs to continue working out methods for calculating optimal allocation of resources. In 1947 this group, led by G. B. Dantzig, developed the first linear programming model and the simplex method for finding optimal solutions.

Linear programming spread rapidly to many fields of application, particularly to engineering, industrial management, and economic analysis. As computers and mathematical understanding improved, extensions to non-linear optimization methods appeared, including integer programming, quadratic and geometric programming, and generalized optimization techniques.[45]

Optimization models select from a large number of possible policies or options the single set that allows maximum achievement of some objective. For example, optimization programs are used regularly in oil refineries to choose that combination of feedstocks, operating sequences and conditions, blending methods, storage locations, and shipping routes that will supply a large variety of petroleum products to a large number of widely-dispersed markets at minimal cost. Optimization is probably the computer modeling method most often used as an input to operational decision-making, especially in industry.

b. Sample optimization model

Suppose an insurance company has $100,000 to invest and a choice of two types of investment of unequal risk.[46] Investment type X pays an annual return of 5% and investment type Y yields 8%. Company policy and legal requirements stipulate that at least 25% of the available funds should be invested in type X, and that no more than 50% can be in type Y. Furthermore, the amount in Y cannot exceed 1.5 times the amount in X. Given all these considerations, how should the company invest its funds to give the maximum possible return?

There are two control variables (also called activities) open to the company: the amount of money in investment X and the amount in investment Y. These are the unknowns to be solved for in the model. The objective function is the quantity to be maximized, in this case the annual return on investment, which is

$$Z = 50X + 80Y$$

(where X and Y are expressed in units of $1000).

There are a number of constraints limiting the way the money can be invested. The most obvious is that the total amount cannot exceed $100,000 (but it could be less than $100,000).

$$X + Y \leq 100$$

Also, X must be at least 25% of the amount available and Y cannot be more than 50%

$$X \geq 25$$
$$Y \leq 50$$

Furthermore, Y can be no greater than 1.5 times X

$$Y \leq 1.5X$$

and finally negative amounts of money cannot be invested, so both X and Y

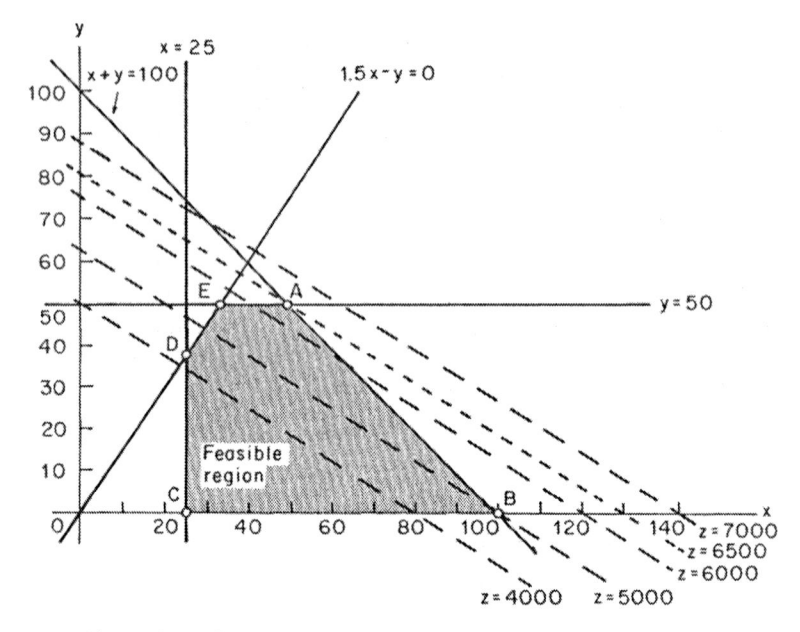

Figure 2.9 Graphical solution to linear programming problem

must be greater than zero

$X \geq 0$
$Y \geq 0$

Thus the total problem can be stated:

Maximise: $Z = 50X + 80Y$

By choosing values for: X and Y

Subject to the constraints: $X \geq 25$
$Y \leq 50$
$1.5X - Y \geq 0$
$X + Y \leq 100$
$X \geq 0$
$Y \geq 0$

This very simple problem has only two activities, X and Y, and so it can be illustrated on a two-dimensional graph as in Figure 2.9. The six constraints are plotted as straight lines, which bound the area shaded in gray. Any point within this area satisfies all the conditions of the constraints and so would represent a feasible investment policy. In this case the solution point that would yield the highest return can also be found graphically. The dashed lines indicate equal-return lines for several possible values of the objective function Z. The line through the point A is the highest-value line that still intersects the feasible region. Thus the optimal policy is to invest $50,000 in X and $50,000 in Y for a total return of $6,500 per year.

Once an optimization model is formulated, it can be used to generate more information than just an optimum point. For example, Figure 2.9 also shows which constraints are actually operative at the maximum point and which are not. One can easily explore the effects of raising or lowering various constraints. One can also work out what would happen if the objective function were different. For example, Figure 2.10 shows the optimum investment for two other objective functions, $Z_1 = 60X + 75Y$ (in which case A is still the optimum point and the return is higher) and $Z_2 = 80X + 60Y$ (in which case the optimum is at B and all funds should be invested in option X).

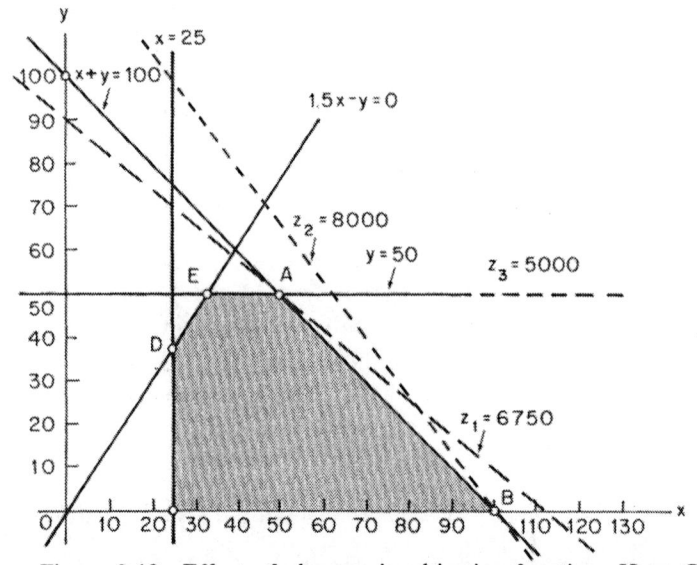

Figure 2.10 Effect of changes in objective function. Hans G. Daellenbach, Earl J. Bell, *User's Guide to Linear Programming*, © 1970, pp. 31, 32. Reprinted by permission of Prentice-Hall Inc., Englewood Cliffs, N.J.

A more realistic optimization problem might have tens or even hundreds of activities to choose from and also hundreds of constraints. In this case the problem can no longer be solved by a two-dimensional graph. The constraints bound a complex, multidimensional surface upon which the desired minimum or maximum must lie. A major part of the modeler's time, of optimization theory, and of optimization textbooks is devoted to finding efficient techniques for searching this surface to find maxima and minima and for ensuring that a discovered maximum is an absolute extreme point, not just a local one. As the dimensions and complexities of the possible surfaces increase, the mathematics can become very complicated and the search processes so tedious that they can only be done by computer.

c. Characteristics of optimization models

The optimization method requires that problems be stated in a simple and unvarying format:

>Maximize or minimize: objective function
>By manipulation of: control variables
>Subject to: constraints

The objective function is an expression either of the welfare of the system (such as profit, output, or per capita income), which is to be maximized, or of the cost to the system, to be minimized. The control variables are all the policy choices available to the decision-maker. For example, in an agricultural planning problem the objective function might be the total value of agricultural output, to be maximized. The control variables might be land area planted to each kind of crop and the amount of fertilizer and irrigation water applied to each kind of crop. The constraints express the desired or necessary relationships among the control variables. In the agricultural example, the areas allocated to each crop must be equal to or less than the total cultivable land, or the total fertilizer budget may be constrained not to exceed a certain amount.

When the problem has been stated in the proper format, it is solved by finding the extreme (maximum or minimum) point in the feasible area defined by the constraints. The mathematical difficulties of the search process are simplified if the objective function and constraints are expressed as linear equations, as they are in the example model we have described. If these conditions can be met, the problem is one of *linear programming*. The feasible area defined by the constraints is reduced to a faceted surface—in three dimensions it can be imagined as a polyhedron. Any maximum or minimum on such a surface must be at a corner, that is, at an intersection of several constraints. Thus the search procedure can be confined to a subset of points on the perimeter of the problem surface, and the location of an absolute maximum or minimum becomes much more tractable. Efficient search techniques exist for linear programming problems, and these have been incorporated into computer software packages that permit almost effortless solution to any problem, once it is stated in the linear programming format.

The conceptual paradigm of optimization, like that of input–output analysis, is rigid, yet powerful and widely useful because the limited circumstances within which it is applicable recur frequently in the decision-making process. Optimization techniques can only be used when a clear objective function can be stated, when all the control variables available to the decision-maker can be specified, and when the constraints in the system can be defined precisely. These conditions are rarely met at the general understanding or policy formulation stages of decision-making.

On the other hand, within the final stage of detailed decision-making, when a problem has been narrowed down to a choice among well-defined options to achieve a clearly-stated goal, optimization models are uniquely useful. Furthermore, at earlier stages of problem definition, the identification of objectives, policy variables, and constraints provides a powerful set of organizing concepts that may be helpful in sorting out the complexities of problems, even if they are not yet well structured enough to be thoroughly analyzed by optimization techniques. The normative view of the world imposed by the optimization paradigm encourages discussion of concrete goals, which is in itself a worthwhile exercise.

Within the relatively strict format of the optimization paradigm, an imaginative modeler has in fact a wide range of freedom. The objective function can be expressed, for example, as a minimization of cost, labor, or use of a scarce resource, or as a maximization of profit, output, productivity, or some other measure of welfare. Two objectives cannot be optimized at once, but secondary objectives can be expressed as constraints. In fact, constraints and objective functions are essentially interchangeable. For example, one may seek to maximize industrial output while insuring that energy use does not exceed a certain limit, or minimize energy use under the constraint that industrial output does not fall below a given target.

In addition to generating the best decision for achieving a given objective function, a properly constructed optimization program can provide a clear picture of the trade-offs that are implied by that decision. By strengthening or weakening various constraints slightly or by changing parameters in the objective function, the analyst can investigate how different physical conditions or social priorities might shift the optimal decision point. The model can also indicate sets of objective functions and constraints that have no mathematical solution, and rule those out as inconsistent or unrealistic problem statements.

Specification of an objective function is an obvious value statement; it is often dictated by the model's client. Specification of constraints can be a more disguised value statement, as well as a representation of the environment within which the optimization decision is made. Here the judgement and knowledge of the modeler are particularly important.

In engineering, transportation, and other physical optimization models, the constraints on the system may be numerous and complex, but they are usually conceptually straightforward expressions of physical laws, material properties, or the actual spatial arrangement of the system. The most common sort of constraint is a material balance equation, stating that the flow out of some stock cannot exceed the contents of the stock, or that the sum of the physical parts of the system cannot be greater than the whole.

The constraints amount to a static or dynamic model of the important interrelationships of the system. Linear programming and other optimization methods do not provide the basic concepts for constructing this model. In practice, therefore, the most important assumptions in optimization models are derived from some other paradigm, often from economics. For example, common constraints in social-system optimization models are requirements that supply must equal demand or that output must be a Cobb–Douglas function of capital and labor.

Optimization procedures have been combined with all three of the modeling techniques we have already described—system dynamics, econometrics, and input–output analysis. In each case the assumptions, strengths, and weaknesses of the other paradigm were dominant influences on the representation of constraints in the optimization program.[47]

Originally optimization models were linear and static—they sought the best strategy for a single decision at one moment in time, with constraints and objective function both expressed by linear, time-independent equations. Now, increasing sophistication in mathematical and computer techniques allow non-linear and dynamic programming. Constraints and objective functions can be assumed to change through time, in part as a result of an optimal decision calculated the previous time period. To some extent major yes–no decisions that cannot be expressed by a continuous linear function can also be included. However, all these improvements in realism must be bought at some price, most usually decreased transparency and tremendously increased computer time.

Optimization models tend to be highly disaggregated and to contain hundreds or even thousands of equations. A large linear program is difficult to construct, debug, adjust, and run, and so it is usually designed to be used and re-used, once it is finished, for on-going decisions. In other words, the optimization modeling process is product rather than process oriented.

d. Typical uses of optimization models

Optimization examples include models to plan lowest-cost transportation routes, to specify the least-cost sites for sewage treatment plants on rivers, to allocate electricity demand among various generating units, and to establish inventory ordering policies. These applications fit the optimization format very well; the objective function is clear, and the constraints and activities are precisely known. The objectives and constraints are so obvious that they are unlikely to be misrepresented, and if they are, mistakes are likely to be easily detectable. Virtually all these applications occur at the detailed-implementation stage of the decision-making process.

Less typical, at least in terms of use in actual policy-making, are optimization models representing more general social decision problems. Some examples within the population/resources/development subject area are:

> A determination of the allocation mechanism for all types of energy resources in the United States that would minimize the total discounted costs of meeting a projected set of final energy demands from 1970 to 2170.[48]
>
> A model to plan educational system development by selecting the optimal number

of students to enter the educational system at various times in order to meet forecasted manpower needs while minimizing costs.[49]

An economic planning model for the government of Mexico that maximizes national consumption over an 18 year period.[50]

e. Problems and limitations

Optimization models suffer from many of the same problems we have already encountered in our discussions of other modeling techniques. Linear programming search routines have been packaged into widely-available, easy-to-use software that can be misused by unskilled modelers. Data sources for optimization models are the same as those for other models, with the same uncertainties. Validation of optimization models, like all other kinds of models, is a vague and uncertain process.

Two problems especially serious for optimization modeling are computer-time limitations and sensitivity. Because of the tedious process of searching for the optimum, computer costs for optimization models are generally high, often so high that cost is the limiting factor in running and testing the model. Disaggregation into regions or subsets adds to the cost, as does stepping through time, since finding an optimum decision at each new time period for each region requires an additional search process. The trade-off between disaggregation and dynamic solution is usually severe; highly disaggregated models are typically solved for only one time period, and long-term dynamic models tend to be quite aggregated.

Unfortunately, the computer-time limitation can also interfere with one of the most important activities of the linear programmer—sensitivity analysis. Optimization models, and especially linear programming models, can be extremely sensitive to small parameter changes. The output of an optimization model is a single precise point (or series of points over time)—the minimum or maximum point of intersection of an objective function with a complex, multidimensional constraint surface. Small changes in the slope of the objective function or shifts in the constraint surface may move the optimum point long distances, to completely different policy choices. For example, dynamic linear programming models of national investment policy are known for their 'bang bang' problem: small parameter changes will shift the optimal investment pattern either (bang) all to the early years or (bang) to the late years of the projection.[51]

The mathematics of the optimization method permit partial sensitivity analyses for some parameters around the optimum point as an automatic byproduct of the optimization calculation. A single model run can thus provide some idea of the way the conclusion would change with small changes in one parameter at a time. However, a complete sensitivity analysis is as rare in optimization models as it is in other kinds of models and is much more necessary. The problem of sensitivity analysis is most serious for large social models, where there may be hundreds of sensitive parameters, where few of them can be precisely known, and where the cost of testing each one may be prohibitive.

Although the basic organizing scheme of an optimization program (objective function, activities, constraints) is an intuitive and helpful way of expressing a policy problem, the actual representation of these concepts is often highly abstract, complex, and opaque. The solution processes that lead to a model conclusion bear no resemblance to happenings in the real system (and are not intended to). Therefore it is sometimes difficult to understand intuitively why a certain conclusion comes about or how the model assumptions have shaped the conclusions. Furthermore, the models are often so big that one cannot possibly keep all the assumptions in mind. In other words, optimization models are usually black boxes.

Furthermore, as outsiders reading the optimization literature, we have rarely found clear explanations of model assumptions or behavior in non-technical language as a part of model documentation. This opacity is a necessary characteristic of complicated, detailed models for precise decision-making, and as long as the nature of the system is well understood, as it is in many engineering and industrial applications, the only problem it causes is difficulty in catching simple mistakes. For social-system models where the assumptions may be controversial or questionable, however, the impenetrability of many optimization models is more serious; it masks important assumptions and discourages criticism.

Two severe criticisms that have been leveled at the technique of optimization by one of its own practitioners have to do with the limited value of the very assumptions of its underlying paradigm. First, optimization assumes that an optimal policy path is stable long enough to be interesting.

> The structure and the parameters of problematic situations continuously change, particularly in turbulent environments. Because optimal solutions are very seldom made adaptive to such changes, their optimality is generally of short duration. They frequently become less effective than were the often more robust solutions that they replace ... Therefore, more and more so-called optimal solutions are still-born ... There is a greater need for decision-making systems that can learn and adapt quickly and effectively in rapidly changing situations than there is for systems that produce optimal solutions that deteriorate with change ... As a consequence, the application of [optimization] is increasingly restricted to those problems that are relatively insensitive to their environments. These usually involve the behavior of mechanical rather than purposeful systems and arise at the lower levels of the organization.[52]

Second, optimization assumes that there can be a clean distinction between means (activities) and ends (objective functions).

> In ... optimality the value of a means is taken to lie exclusively in its efficiency for ends: that is, the value of a means is taken to be purely *instrumental, extrinsic*. On the other hand, the value of an end is taken to lie in the satisfaction its attainment brings, to be purely *non-instrumental, intrinsic*. [Optimization] does not

acknowledge, let alone take into account, the intrinsic value of means and the extrinsic value of ends ...

Every means is also an end and every end is also a means. For example, going to school is a means of obtaining an education, an end. But obtaining an education is also a means of increasing one's income, an end. Increasing income, in turn, is a means of supporting a family, and so on ...

Non-instrumental values of means and instrumental values of ends are *aesthetic* in character, and ... aesthetic as well as ethical values should be incorporated into our theories of decision-making ... More and more people are coming to realize that optimization of all the quantities of life does not optimize the quality of life.[53]

As we have mentioned in discussing other modeling tools, the main problem is recognizing where they are and are not applicable. The narrower the range of applicability, the more difficult the match between modeling technique and policy problem, and the greater the temptation to extend the technique beyond its appropriate area of usefulness. Optimization is the most specialized and precise modeling tool we have discussed. Therefore it is the easiest to misuse. Especially in its social applications, it is often brought in to refine a specific policy when in fact there is no agreement that the policy is the right one. As Kenneth Boulding says, optimization can find 'the best way of doing something that ought not to be done at all.' (personal communication.)

f. Summary

Optimization techniques, such as linear programming, are most often used to select the final best operating decision from a set of clearly-defined alternatives at the detailed-implementation stage of decision-making. The optimization paradigm separates any policy problem into three conceptual components: the objective of the policy, the activities or options available to achieve it, and the constraints and boundaries within which those options must be used. Optimization models are normative, usually linear, static or dynamic, often disaggregated, and relevant to the day-to-day concerns of decision-makers. They tend to be product-oriented and difficult to understand intuitively. The results of optimization models are precise and may be highly sensitive to small parameter changes.

D. Composite models

A number of the models described in the next chapter do not fit neatly into any of the methodological categories we have described so far. They combine and cut across paradigms, borrowing whatever organizational concepts and mathematical devices seem helpful in solving the problem at hand. For instance, an input–output matrix might appear as part of the constraint equations in a model optimizing national investment policy. An optimization model might be used to represent farmers' investment decisions within a large-scale simulation of an agricultural economy. Econometric techniques might be used to estimate dynamic equations linking input–output tables for successive years, or to estimate parameters for a table function in a system dynamics model.

Many of these eclectic-appearing models are actually not cross-paradigm efforts at all; they are firmly founded on the philosophical principles and world view of one modeling school and have simply borrowed a few convenient concepts or software packages from another. But other modeling groups make a sincere effort to be open to all approaches and to combine paradigms. The products of such efforts are called by a number of names, ranging from eclectic models to goulash models. We will call them *composite models*.

The advantages of composite models are fairly obvious. Some of the weaknesses and rigidities of single modeling paradigms can be avoided by using combinations. In fact, the combinations that are most often formed are clues to the aspects of each method that its practitioners find most binding. For example, the composite econometric–input–output models allow input–output analysis to become dynamic and econometric models to be disaggregated and to be more closely tied to physical flows.

If composite models gain from the complementary strengths of several modeling methods, they may also suffer from combined weaknesses. Connecting a system dynamics model with an input–output model could conceivably require linearization of the system dynamics equations or greater aggregation of the input–output matrix. Using econometric estimation techniques for the constraints in a linear program could lead to the omission of some very real social or psychological constraints for which adequate data are unavailable. Interconnected chains of modeling methods may be limited like real chains by their weakest link. The combination of weaknesses is likely to dominate the complementarity of strengths, unless the linking is done very skillfully indeed.

Other problems may arise in the formulation of composite inter-paradigm models. Interfacing various model segments with different disaggregation categories, data requirements, and mathematical characteristics can be confusing. The purposes and time horizons of different parts of the model may prove to be incompatible. Most important, composite models, because of their varied capabilities and relative lack of paradigmatic limitations, tend to require less careful and bounded problem definitions. They are often attempts at general-purpose models, intended to explain everything about the system and to answer all possible questions about its future. In that case the models can become opaque and uncontrollable. As Kuhn[1] has said, paradigms may be limiting, but they are also necessary to bound and focus one's thinking. Modelers may be able to overarch and encompass all the modeling paradigms to construct their statements about the nature of the world, but they must use *some* sort of organizing concepts in the process.

As the examples in the next chapter will indicate, it is more difficult to make a useful composite model than one within a single paradigm. Combining paradigms requires skill and wisdom in more than one technical school. If the model is made by a team, the individual members must be able to communicate across paradigms, to accent the strengths and avoid the pitfalls of their own methods, and to maintain simultaneous respect and skepticism for the other methods with which they are linking. These abilities are as rare among modelers as they are among other kinds of scientists; no one receives formal training in cross-paradigm communication.

As an example of the difficulties of cross-paradigm communication, let us examine in more detail the paradigms of system dynamics and econometrics, especially as each is seen by the other. These two modeling schools are philosophically further apart than any other pair. They have a long history of generating heat rather than light when they are brought together.

E. An example of paradigm conflict: econometrics and system dynamics

System dynamics provides a theory of causal structure and its relation to dynamic behavior that is a powerful guide to model specification. Econometrics offers numerous techniques for finding empirically-based parameters and for formal comparison of model results with real-world observations. One technique is particularly applicable to long-term analysis of possible changes in historic trends. The other is best suited to short-term precise prediction in situations that do not differ from those that have occurred in the past. It would seem that use of the two methods together might produce models that combine realistic structure with precise parameters, models that could be useful at every stage of the decision-making process, particularly useful for attacking middle-term problems that are not easily analyzed by either method alone.

This logical combination of two complementary modeling tools has almost never been attempted. On the contrary, very few econometricians have bothered to learn system dynamics techniques, and those system dynamicists who have been schooled in econometrics do not regularly use its tools or concepts. Members of the two schools seem to regard each other as competitors rather than as potential collaborators and find little to praise in each others' work:

> Econometric models have intruded only slightly on the political and managerial domain of mental models ... The parameter values in the models are a consequence of mathematical manipulation and are not individually relatable to real-life human motivations. Most such models are driven by exogenous variables in such a manner that the models do not generate long-term economic behavior out of their own internal structure. The econometric methodology strongly discourages the formulation of general non-linear relationships even though many of the most important behavior models in real social systems arise because of non-linear relationships. Econometric models are limited to relationships that have held under system conditions prevailing at the time of data collection; but some of our greatest social problems arise because our social systems are operating under conditions that have not previously been encountered ... Most importantly, econometric models cannot deal with variables for which data has not been

collected. They assume that the world is described only by those variables that have been quantitatively measured. That assumption alone would exclude them from entering the realm of the mental models that dominate political and economic behavior.[54]

The methodology that was used by the M.I.T. team is that when you have a situation that you're trying to evaluate, you sit down in an armchair without any knowledge of the situation except what common sense tells you ... The point is that over the last few hundred years there has developed a methodology in scientific research ... It is customary to look at some data, to look at the experience of the countries involved. Forrester did not do that in his study ... If you ask me whether there is room for collaboration between ecologists and economists and scientists and engineers, I certainly think there is ... But if you mean, am I going to build a model in which I postulate relations without talking to knowledgeable experts, a model with one hundred equations none of which have been confirmed by an empirical study, a model in which I am seriously going to predict what will happen a hundred or two hundred years from now, I think the answer to all these questions is no.[55]

In part this hostility may be due to the personalities of the methodological founders, the natural parochialism of academics, and the inevitable jockeying for political influence and scarce funding resources. However, a closer examination of the two modeling paradigms reveals a deep philosophical gulf between them, one that is not easily bridged. The basic world views upon which the two paradigms are built are quite different, and about as easy to reconcile or even to see simultaneously as the world views of the modern graduate student and the mystical Mexican sorcerer in Carlos Casteneda's books.[56] Either paradigm, seen from the perspective of the other, looks incomprehensible, unrealistic, and misleading. Methodological conversations between econometricians and system dynamicists tend to degenerate into frustrating meaninglessness as each side misses the other's main points. Key words such as 'validation', 'sensitivity', 'data', 'equilibrium' and 'prediction' are used in different ways based on different implicit assumptions.

Thomas Kuhn is not optimistic about building bridges across paradigm gulfs:

The proponents of competing paradigms are always at least slightly at cross-purposes. Neither side will grant all the non-empirical assumptions that the other needs in order to make its case ... Though each may hope to convert the other to his way of seeing his science and its problems, neither may hope to prove his case. The competition between paradigms is not the sort of battle that can be resolved by proofs ... The proponents of competing paradigms will often disagree about the list of problems that any candidate for paradigm must resolve. Their standards or their definitions of science are not the same ... More is involved, however, than the incommensurability of standards. Since new paradigms are born from old ones, they ordinarily incorporate much of the vocabulary and apparatus ... that the traditional paradigm had previously employed. But they seldom employ these borrowed elements in quite the traditional way. Within the new paradigm, old terms, concepts, and experiments fall into new relationships one with the other ... Communication across the revolutionary divide is inevitably partial ... In a sense that I am unable to explicate further, the proponents of competing paradigms practice their trades in different worlds ... The two groups of scientists see different things when they look from the same point in the same direction ... That is why a law that cannot even be demonstrated to one group of scientists may occasionally seem intuitively obvious to another. Equally, it is why, before they can hope to communicate fully, one group or the other must experience the conversion that we have been calling a paradigm shift. Just because it is a transition between incommensurables, the transition between competing paradigms cannot be made a step at a time, forced by logic and neutral experience. Like the Gestalt switch, it must occur all at once ... or not at all.[57]

In this section we will look at econometrics and system dynamics simultaneously, switching back and forth to see each from the point of view of the other. The resulting image will necessarily be disjointed, since it will not have a constant reference point. It will also magnify the methodological division somewhat, because this description itself is an over-simplified model of reality. And, needless to say, we are not capable of giving a totally unbiased description, despite our best efforts to do so. If the following discussion does not induce mutual understanding in the 'proponents of competing paradigms', perhaps it will at least give uninvolved observers of the competition some idea of what one side is saying, and what it thinks the other side is saying.

As Kuhn says, the problem begins with the list of solvable problems. System dynamicists and econometricians are led by their paradigms to notice different problems and to strive for different kinds of insights into socioeconomic systems. For instance, a system dynamicist confronted with the patterns of city growth shown in Figure 2.11 would be struck by the dynamic similarities and wonder what universal underlying causal structure led to the growth and stagnation of all those cities. (It would take a system-dynamics perspective to draw such a figure in the first place.) An econometrician might be more likely to notice the differences and ask why St Louis peaked at a lower population than New York, or to wonder what the population of Chicago will be in 1990. Both kinds of questions are certainly legitimate, and their answers could be useful for various sorts of policy decisions. Unfortunately, each modeling school tends to regard the questions of the other not only as unimportant, but as inherently unanswerable.

Econometricians seem to feel that useful information must be precise—a picture that is not entirely in focus is not worth looking at. They would like to be able to see the future in quantitative detail. They find little substance in the ambiguous, qualitative, long-term output of system dynamics models. It does not seem very interesting just to know that the system is likely to be oscillating or growing; they would like to know exactly when the next turning point will come, or whether the growth will be at 6.5% or 7.0% per year.

To achieve as much precision as possible, econometricians work with statistical methods, which require historic databases, linear equations, and relatively open structures. They know that these methods become less and less dependable as they are applied farther into the future, and therefore econometricians have come to feel that the long term is simply inaccessible to modelers.

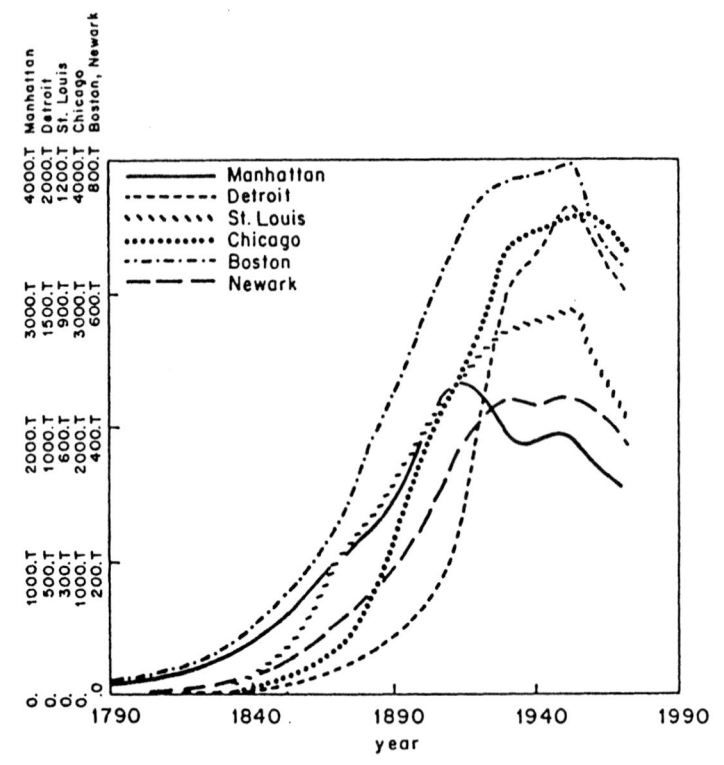

Figure 2.11 Population growth curves for older American cities. Reproduced with permission of The MIT Press from J. W. Forrester and N. J. Mass 'Urban Dynamics: a Rejoinder to Averch and Levine', in W. W. Schroeder, III, R. E. Sweeney, L. E. Alfeld, (eds.) *Readings in Urban Dynamics*, Vol. 2, Cambridge, Wright-Allen Press, p. 21, 1975

System dynamicists regard most efforts to gain precise predictions of social systems as a waste of time. They believe that human unpredictability is too dominant a factor in social systems to allow anything more than qualitative behavioral forecasts, even for aggregate systems where much unpredictability can be averaged out. Therefore they find it hard to understand the great effort econometricians go through to obtain better and better estimations or to quote their findings to six or seven significant digits. Especially when many exogenous variables must be predetermined, the whole econometric exercise looks to a system dynamicist like a transformation of one set of uncertain and unscientific guesses into a second set of equally uncertain guesses, presented with deceptive, scientific-looking precision.

System dynamicists should know from their own theorems of system behavior that most aggregate systems possess a certain momentum, and that within a short time horizon the relatively simple structural hypotheses of econometrics are usually quite appropriate. But system dynamicists tend to reject not only the possibility but the utility of working within short-time horizons. In the system dynamics world view, since the short term is already determined, unchangeable by policy, it is totally uninteresting. Furthermore, system dynamics theory says that policies designed only for short-term gain often lead to long-term loss. Therefore modelers should not reinforce their clients' interest in short-term results.

These opposing ideas about what kind of knowledge about the future might be useful arise from different basic assumptions about the nature of social systems. The econometric assumption reflects the common view of the policy-making world—that the world is essentially dualistic and open. A sharp distinction is drawn between the economy and the environment (government, weather, Arab nations, consumers, investors, or whatever). The environment delivers specific inputs, to which the system gives specific responses. Each system, input, and response may be unique, and thus particulars of different situations are more to be studied than similarities. The best strategy for policy is to foresee the next set of specific inputs and to be prepared to give optimal responses to them. This view leads to policy questions about end states, rather than paths to those states, and about particular characteristics of the system under particular conditions:

1. If the price of natural gas is deregulated this year, what will its equilibrium market price be? How much windfall profit would accrue to the gas companies?
2. How much increase in income taxes would be required to reduce the current rate of inflation by 2%? What would that tax do to the unemployment rate?
3. Given normal weather conditions, current fertilizer prices, and a subsidy of 5 cents per bushel, how much wheat will be produced in the U.S. next year? If no export embargoes are imposed, what will domestic wheat price be?

System dynamics, on the other hand, assumes that systems are primarily closed. Not only does the environment influence the economy, but the economy influences the environment. In fact, the distinction between the system and its environment is rarely clear (except for obvious exogenous factors like incoming solar energy). Attention is focused on the general system reaction to general disturbances and on the dynamic path of a response rather than its end state.

> System dynamics ... regards external forces as *there*, but beyond control and hence not worthy of primary attention ... Instead, the focus is upon examining the organization's *internal structure*; the intent being to arrive at an understanding of how this structure ... can be made more *resilient* to environmental perturbation. In adopting this approach, system dynamics is embracing the wisdom of the human body. The body, rather than forecasting—and then marshalling its forces in anticipation of—the arrival of each kind of solid and liquid input, remains continually poised in a state of *general readiness* for whatever may befall it.[58]

This view of the nature of systems leads to a very different set of policy questions:

1. How would deregulation of natural gas price affect the general depletion life-cycle pattern of U.S. natural gas reserves and the eventual transition to new types of fuels?
2. What are the dominant positive feedback loops causing inflation? How could equally effective negative loops to counterbalance them be built into the economic system without causing unemployment?
3. Why has wheat production fluctuated more in the past five years than in the preceding fifteen years? Which sort of policy—direct price supports, increased buffer stocks, or increased exports—could induce stabilization of production while not increasing consumer prices?

It would be hard to say whether these questions are more or less important than the previous ones. They do, however, reflect a clearly different attitude about how social problems arise and how to go about solving them.

After choosing different problems and dismissing the legitimacy and feasibility of each other's problem areas, econometricians and system dynamicists go on to solve their problems with totally different procedures. The differences here have deep roots in conflicting theories of knowledge. Perhaps both sides would agree that the nature of the world and human perceptions of it produce a number of happenings that humans can observe readily, resulting from an underlayer of unseen causal motivations, events and interconnections. This underlayer can be known from one's own inner experience of it, but it cannot be measured and one person's experience of it cannot be compared directly with another's. The disagreement begins in deciding which part of that double-layered world to represent in a model.

Econometrics is firmly grounded in observable reality. Econometricians may and do speculate freely about unseen psychological and physical driving machinery, drawing on substantial causal theory from their parent paradigm of economics. But their models must contain explicitly not what they experience, but only what they know, and in their paradigm one can know only what one can measure. Therefore their models tend to represent observable phenomena only, with the hypothesized causal connections implicit. There are no strong preconceived notions about the nature of those connections. They may be a web of feedback loops, a series of unrelated stochastic forces, or some combination of these. Whatever the underlying structure is, its nature and its relationship to the surface phenomena may vary randomly or shift entirely. Therefore stochastic error terms must be added to equations, and a continuous stream of new observations must be obtained to verify that the system continues to run as it has in the past. Econometricians feel a pressing need for more data, better measurements, more recent updating, better access to databases.

System dynamicists, on the other hand, feel that measurable events represent only a small fraction of what one can know. They plunge enthusiastically into the lower layer of unseen experience, armed with theories that help them relate visible dynamic variations in systems to invisible feedback-loop structure. They attempt to guess that structure, as the econometricians do, but then they include their guesses explicitly in their models. They are searching for timeless general relationships, not those that are peculiar to one system or one time period. Therefore they use information from any period and any subsystem, including, among many other sources, the same statistical data from which econometric models are derived. However, they generally prefer direct, qualitative observations of the physical processes and human decisions in the system, rather than quantitative aggregate social indices.

System dynamicists recognize a spectrum of increasingly precise information, ranging from intuitions, hunches, and anecdotal observations at one end to controlled physical measurement at the other, with social statistics somewhere in the middle. They believe that this spectrum offers far more information than is currently used, and that the real need is not for more data but for better use of the data already available. They point out that econometricians, by confining themselves to the narrow part of the spectrum consisting of social statistics, which contain no information about operating policies, goals, fears, or expectations in the system, are hopelessly restricted in learning about how social systems work.

These two approaches to the interpretation and use of various kinds of knowledge result in continuous, fruitless cross-paradigm discussions about the relative importance of structure versus parameters. Econometricians probably spend 5% of their time specifying model structure and 95% estimating parameters. System dynamicists reverse that emphasis. They find that their long-term feedback models are prone to wild excursions if even one small information link is left unclosed but are often maddeningly unresponsive to parameter changes. Having worked with such models, system dynamicists find it difficult to imagine why anyone would bother to estimate most coefficients precisely, especially when the coefficients are part of a model with what is to them an obviously open and linear structure.

The econometrician, on the other hand, may find that in his models a 6.5% growth rate produces a very different result from a 7.0% growth rate, and his client may care a great deal about that difference. To him the system dynamicists' cavalier attitude about precise data seems both irresponsible and unsettling. Furthermore, since his paradigm provides no acceptable way of finding model parameters without statistical data, he cannot imagine how a system dynamics model becomes quantified. Since the numbers are not obtained by legitimate statistical methods, they must be illegitimate, made-up, suspect.

The structure-parameter disagreement is also revealed in the complaint often voiced by econometricians that 'system dynamicists deliberately design their models to generate the results they want'. System dynamicists do habitually specify in advance the dynamic behavior they will regard as a first test of confidence in the model, and do operate with some knowledge about what kinds of structure will produce what kinds of behavior. However, the task of making a complex dynamic simulation model behave in any reasonable way is surprisingly difficult, especially with a closed structure, with a paradigm requiring every constant and variable to have a recognizable real-world meaning, and with a bias against including time-dependent driving functions. When one has worked with models like this, one begins to regard the relatively sensitive econometric model as much easier to manipulate. Therefore system dynamicists answer the econometricians' complaint this way: 'Give me an open system with five dummy variables and 40 exogenous driving functions and I *could* design my model to generate the results I want!' Both complaint and counter-complaint miss the essential point—the two kinds of models are each subject to rigid constraints of different sorts and are sensitive in different ways. A scrupulous modeler in either field will feel too bound by the characteristics of the real system to engage in conscious manipulation of results, and an unscrupulous modeler in either field can get away with outrageous fiddling. Unfortunately, neither field is sufficiently self-monitored or self-critical to reward honesty consistently or to eliminate fiddling.

Not only the inclusion or exclusion of intangibles, and the numbers and their sources are sources of disagreement. Even the basic decisions about what aspects of observable reality to include are made entirely differently in the two modeling schools. System dynamicists, as we have seen, are attuned to see and represent the stocks and flows in systems—and in fact can see nothing else, as this frustrated attempt at cross-paradigm communication indicates.

> As I see traditional economic models, they are very concerned with money flows, and especially with maintaining consistency among money flows. Supply must equal demand, sales must equal revenues, savings must equal investment, etc. These flow-equalities are the bedrock upon which economic models stand.
>
> As I see the economic world, however, it is logistically impossible to keep all flows equal at all times. A store cannot have arriving merchandise come in at the back door just as customers appear to buy it. Therefore it establishes a stock of inventory to allow its flow to be unequal. A consumer cannot arrange to receive money just at the rate he wants to spend it. Therefore he maintains several stocks, including money in his pocket, deposits in the bank, and various kinds of debts, in order to permit his spending flow to differ from his income flow. Everywhere I look in economic systems, I see stocks that exist so that flows can be unequal.
>
> When, with great excitement, I communicate this observation to my economist friends, they assure me that they already know it. When I ask them why stocks do not appear in their models, they give me three answers:
>
> 1. In economic systems, stocks are relatively invariant, therefore they cannot be important in influencing the interesting variations in flows that we want to understand.
> 2. Stocks are vanishingly small compared to flows, especially when the flows are measured over the normal economic accounting period of one year.
> 3. Anyway, it would be mathematically easy to add stocks to existing economic models, but there is not much reason for doing so because nothing would be learned from it.

Now, in my world view, the invariance of stocks is no surprise because the economy is entirely made up of *feedback systems to stabilize stocks*. Inventory holders raise prices if their inventories fall too low and lower prices if inventories rise too high. Farmers will borrow if their debt level is low but will refuse to expand further if their debt level becomes too high. Given the same income, consumers will buy at a very different rate if the condition or number of their possessions is low rather than high (as indicated by postwar consumption rates). To the extent that all these actions are effective, stocks will vary only slightly. But that doesn't mean that stocks are therefore unimportant in explaining economic variations. To the contrary, it means that *stocks are the prime determinants of nearly all economic decisions. The secondary determinants are the constraints on those decisions, which are also usually stocks.*

To represent an economic system without stocks seems to me like representing a thermostat-furnace system without the room temperature. The room temperature is exactly the signal that turns on the adjustment mechanism. If the system is effective, room temperature varies only by a few degrees. But those small fluctuations trigger great variations in the rate at which heat is flowing from the furnace. And though the stock of kilocalories in the room at any one time is very small compared to the year's accumulation of heat flow from the furnace, the room temperature is nevertheless a vital determinant of the behavior of the system.

It seems to me that economists spend a lot of time trying to find relationships between flows—between supply and demand, between consumption and income, between investment and GNP. From my viewpoint that effort is doomed to failure because *there is no unique relationship between flows*. In the thermostat example it would be impossible to establish statistically a correct relationship between the flows. Heat inflow is a function of the gap between the room temperature and the thermostat setting. Heat outflow depends on the difference between room temperature and outside temperature. Depending on the temperatures and the thermostat setting, inflow and outflow could have almost any relationship to each other at a particular moment, and that relationship would change in the next moment.

Of course, while the system is working well, and the room temperature is relatively constant, one can be under the illusion that one has established a fairly good relationship between flows. This illusion breaks down just when the system breaks down and the stock (room temperature) begins to vary, which is *just when you most need to understand the system*. Witness the sudden uselessness of every economic model in 1973 when the stock-based control systems broke down and the stocks began to change.

Therefore I must respectfully disagree that stocks can be omitted from a model because they seldom vary, or because they are small compared to a year's accumulation of flows (they would be even smaller compared to a millenium's accumulation of flows!). I must also disagree with the economists' third point, that stocks are easy to include in a model. The stocks themselves may be, but the decisions based on them are not, because we know so little about them. We know so little about them, not because they are unknowable, but because so far little attention has been paid to them.[59]

After each type of modeler has worked on an inherently unsolvable problem in the other's view, and has gone about it with entirely the wrong emphasis, the misunderstanding becomes complete when the finished models are examined for validity or credibility. Each kind of model fails to meet the other's standards. The econometrician had a hard enough time understanding where the system dynamicist's numbers came from. Now he must evaluate the result without a single R^2, t-test, or Durbin–Watson statistic to help him along. He will find it impossible to calculate these statistical summary indices for a system dynamics model, because there will be multiple covariances and colinearities and no data for many of the model's variables.

The system dynamicist, who considers summary statistics either deceptive or meaningless, looks for the intuitive reality of the individual causal relations and the total dynamic behavior of the econometric model. He finds linearities, driving exogenous variables, and worst of all, time-dependent dummy variables, which correspond to highest-order cheating in his paradigm. The few instances of feedback he finds will be predominantly positive feedback, which he knows will carry the entire model to ridiculous extremes, if forecasts are generated for more than a few years into the future.

Even sincere efforts to understand each other's evaluation techniques tend to produce muddled cross-paradigm conversations, such as the following one between a system dynamicist and two mathematical economists, all of whom seem to be trying very hard to communicate.

> *Howard:* We are used to seeing in the sciences one curve labeled 'predicted' and another labeled 'observed'. These curves allow us to make evaluations such as: 'This is good' or 'This is not so good'. Is there any reason in principle ... why you cannot take actual sales, production, and inventory data, use your model to obtain 'predicted' sales, production, and inventory figures for the corresponding period, and make a comparison?
>
> *Forrester*: Yes, there is a reason why you cannot ... Suppose you take two models, absolutely identical in structure and parameters, but both having different noise components in their decision mechanisms. If you start these models from identical initial conditions and let them run, their behaviors will diverge so quickly that there is no way of predicting what will happen on a specific day. Yet, the two models will exhibit similar quantitative performance characteristics. They will both be stable or unstable, for example ... Thus one must predict, not for the particular event, not the shape of the particular time history, but one must predict the change in the performance characteristics: profitability, employment stability, and characteristics such as these. The test you suggest of comparing a particular time history with the output of a model is not a test that you can expect to use, although it is a test that many people have been attempting for many economic models.
>
> *Howard*: But I think that you have to have some quantitative measure of how good your model is ... How can we possibly criticize you when you say, 'It has the same qualitative behavior'? We both look at the same simulated history, and I say it does not look at all like the real thing, and you say it does. You say that you cannot with your model duplicate the actual sales data because of the noise in the system. All you can do is get a signal that has the same characteristics as the actual data. I say that this statement has no content ... How can we get a quantitative agreement on what constitutes the same characteristics?
>
> *Forrester*: This is a very troublesome question in the abstract, and yet in the actual specific case it is not answered in the rigorous objective sense that you speak of; neither is it in any of our real-life activities. I think you are trying for something here that we do not have in other areas of human endeavour. We do not have it in medicine or law or engineering. You are trying for something here that is more nearly perfect, more objective than in fact we know how to do anywhere

else. I do not disagree with the desirability of it. I say we do not have it and we are not ready for it. Where we seem to have it in certain of the statistical model tests, I believe it is misleading and on an essentially unsound foundation.

Holt: It is interesting to contrast Professor Forrester's willingness in model formulation to quantify such unstructured concepts as 'integrity' with his unwillingness in model testing to accept quantitative tests of these models. Even where *quantitative* data are available for such variables as employment fluctuations both from the company and from the model, he accepts *qualitative* judgements on similarity as perfectly adequate.[60]

(Reproduced by permission of MIT from Greenberger[60] and Forrester.[8])

Can these two apparently antithetical ways of looking at and modeling social systems coexist within the mind of a single person? Can they coexist within the modeling profession? Or is it necessary, as Kuhn implies,[1] that one paradigm must come to dominate the other totally?

Some people maintain that system dynamics and econometrics can indeed be merged within one person's mind and that in practice such mergers are appearing. System dynamicists can certainly be found who use statistical techniques to determine model parameters, and econometric models increasingly seem to contain non-linearities, distributed lags, and feedback. But these examples are just borrowings from each other's techniques, not shifts in world view. If the problem addressed by a computer model reflects a basically static concern with particular responses to particular events, if the model variables are observables, if the validation procedure involves detailed matching with historic data, if stocks and flows are not carefully distinguished, then we would say the model is in the econometric paradigm, no matter what mathematical characteristics it has or what computer language it is written in. If the problem is centered on generic dynamic behavior of a mostly-closed system, if the variables include motivations and goals, if the validation includes assessment of the realism of the model structure, then it is a system dynamics model. We cannot imagine how the two basic philosophies can be mixed or merged in one model, although the operating procedures that have shaped and been shaped by these philosophies might be exchanged.

The outcome of the econometrics–system dynamics competition may be similar to the pattern of competition between species in an ecosystem. According to the competitive exclusion principle, two species struggling for the same ecological niche cannot coexist for long. One must eventually eliminate the other completely, as Kuhn says one competing scientific paradigm eventually eliminates the other from legitimate professional practice.

However, when *diverse niches* are available, one species can lose in one kind of niche and dominate in a different kind. Econometrics and system dynamics clearly fit different niches in the modeling and policy-making environment. Within the short term, a system's behavior is determined by decisions and events that have already happened and that are propogating through the delays in the system—buildings are under construction, children are growing up, orders are being filled, debts are being paid. The length of the short-term period is determined for any system by the length of the dominant delays. New policies can have little or no effect during this period, but accurate predictions can be made to help one prepare for what is coming down the pipeline. In this niche, where one can predict but not affect the system, econometrics fits well. However, in the longer term one can act to change the system, and *because* such actions are possible, accurate and unconditional prediction is impossible. Over this longer period the feedbacks are closed, one is concerned with the control or design of the system as a whole and its conditional, general response to possible changes. This is the system dynamics niche. As long as both specific short-term predictions and long-term system changes are needed, both econometrics and system dynamics can be actively pursued, probably with continued mutual hostility, at least until a better competitor comes along.

F. Conclusion

Each type of modeling brings along with it some underlying beliefs about the world that are, when they are stated bluntly, both insightful and highly questionable. Each is an oracle of a very specific type, designed for one limited way of dealing with the future. For instance, here is a summary of some of the beliefs underlying the four methods described in this chapter:

1. Systems consist of timeless underlying structure, which generates observable behavior over time. That structure is composed of physical stocks and flows, controlled by decision processes that depend on information (often biased, delayed, and incomplete) about the stocks. It is possible to know the structure and the behaviors inherent in that structure, but, because of inevitable randomness, it is not possible to predict the exact configuration of stocks and flows at a given time in the future. One should strive to configure a system's structure to increase the likelihood of desirable behaviours, not to predict or prepare for or make optimal use of inherently unknowable precise future conditions.
2. Systems consist of millions of individual decisions, the aggregate effects of which are linked through accounting identities and through behavioral relationships that may shift over time. One can never know these relationships by accumulating all the individual actions or by speculating about their motivation, but only by observing what their aggregate effects have been in the past. Statistical techniques allow one to sort out and state very precisely not only the historical relationships but also their historical degree of randomness and uncertainty. On the basis of this understanding one can make precise but short-term predictions or conditional predictions about the future.
3. Systems consist of interlocked sequences of transformational processes. Each process requires a set of inputs and results in a set of outputs; outputs of one process can be inputs to another. Ultimately all inputs come from nature and outputs go to consumers, at which points they no longer need be

accounted for. The relationship between inputs and outputs for any single transformation is alterable by technical change, which is exogenous. All inputs and outputs are physical and thus inherently measurable and knowable. With that knowledge one can explore in detail the consequences of growth in the system, with or without changed technologies, or shifts in the desired mix of final outputs.
4. For any system there is a nearly infinite set of configurations or states, and a set of constraints that rule out many of those states as infeasible. There is also a clear objective, or set of objectives, that allow system states to be ranked in terms of desirability. The possible states, the constraints, and the objectives are all inherently knowable, and stable over the time it takes to implement a policy. Policies should be chosen to move the system into that feasible state that best meets one's objective.

Every one of these methods assumes that *some* aspect of the system is inherently knowable and quantifiable. Every one also assumes some knowledge of what is good or desirable, but optimization is the only one that requires explicit statement of goals. Econometrics takes explicit account of some inherent randomness or unknowability of the system; system dynamics builds the existence of randomness into its epistemology but does not attempt to quantify it; input–output analysis and optimization take no formal notice of it. All of the methods get fuzzier and less authoritative as the boundaries and complexity of the system expand, as the time of interest goes further into the future, and as changes to be tested diverge more from what has been observed. In other words, with all methods it is easier to describe a system that exists or has existed than one that might exist. Though the methods span the range of policy interest from general understanding to detailed implementation, they are clustered, especially in their actual use, more toward implementation. Most of them *assume* a great deal of understanding and of accurate measurement of the system—in most cases they assume more than actually exists.

Each modeling school defines a particular way of looking at the world and provides a set of tools for working on particular kinds of problems. None is comprehensive enough to encompass all that might be observed about the world or to solve all problems. And of course very many observations and problems fall far outside the entire field of computer modeling. Modeling can certainly contribute greatly to human comprehension, prediction, and control of complex systems. But like any other tool, it must be used with wisdom and skill, and that means with understanding of its appropriate uses, of its limitations, and of the way it influences its users' perceptions of the world.

NOTES AND REFERENCES

1. T. S. Kuhn, *The Structure of Scientific Revolutions*, Chicago, University of Chicago Press, second edition, excerpted from pp. 46–111, 1970.

2. A. Maslow, *The Psychology of Science: a Reconnaissance*, Chicago, Henry Regnery, 1966.
3. T. S. Kuhn, *op. cit.*, pp. 64–65.
4. G. Peck, *Two Kinds of Time*, Boston, Houghton Mifflin Company, second edition, pp. 7–8, 1967.
5. E. F. Schumacher, *Small is Beautiful*, New York, Harper & Row, p. 217, 1973.
6. M. Goodman, *Study Notes in System Dynamics*, Cambridge, Mass., Wright-Allen Press, 1974.
7. J. W. Forrester, *Collected Papers of Jay W. Forrester*, Cambridge, Mass., Wright-Allen Press, p. 215, 1975.
8. See J. W. Forrester, *Industrial Dynamics*, Cambridge, Mass., MIT Press, 1961. The basic textbooks in system dynamics are J. W. Forrester, *Principles of Systems*, Cambridge, Mass., Wright-Allen Press, 1968; M. Goodman, *op. cit.*; N. Roberts, D. F. Andersen, R. M. Deal, M. S. Garet and W. A. Shaffer, *The System Dynamics Approach*, Reading, Mass., Addison-Wesley Publishing Company, 1983; G. P. Richardson and A. L. Pugh, III, *Introduction to System Dynamics Modeling with DYNAMO*, Cambridge, Mass., MIT Press, 1981.
9. See, for example, J. W. Forrester, *Urban Dynamics*, Cambridge, Mass., MIT Press, 1969; H. R. Hamilton, S. E. Goldstone, J. W. Milliman, A. L. Pugh, E. B. Roberts and A. Zellner, *Systems Simulation for Regional Analysis*, Cambridge, Mass., MIT Press, 1969; J. W. Forrester, *World Dynamics*, Cambridge, Mass., Wright-Allen Press, 1971.
10. For an example of such an elaborated model, see D. L. Meadows, *The Dynamics of Commodity Production Cycles*, Cambridge, Mass., Wright-Allen Press, 1970.
11. See A. L. Pugh, *DYNAMO II User's Manual*, Cambridge, Mass., MIT Press, 1973.
12. J. W. Forrester, *Urban Dynamics*, Cambridge, Mass., MIT Press, 1969.
13. S. B. Schantzis and W. W. Behrens, 'Population Control Mechanisms in a Primitive Agricultural Society', in D. L. Meadows and D. H. Meadows (eds.) *Toward Global Equilibrium*, Cambridge, Mass., Wright-Allen Press, 1973.
14. N. J. Mass, *Economic Cycles: an Analysis of Underlying Causes*, Cambridge, Mass., Wright-Allen Press, 1975.
15. P. M. Budzik, 'The Future of Dairy Farming in Vermont', Master's Thesis, Thayer School of Engineering, Dartmouth College, Hanover, N. H., 1975.
16. R. F. Naill, *Managing the Energy Transition*, Cambridge, Mass., Ballinger Publishing Company, 1977.
17. For examples of statistically-estimated system dynamics models, see F. H. Weymar, *Dynamics of the World Cocoa Market*, Cambridge, Mass., MIT Press, 1968, and R. F. Naill, 'Managing the Discovery Life Cycle of a Finite Resource: a Case Study of U.S. Natural Gas', M.S. thesis, MIT, 1972 (available from Resource Policy Center, Dartmouth College, Hanover, N.H.).

    For theoretical discussions of the application of statistical estimation to system dynamics models, see, N. J. Mass and P. M. Senge, 'Alternative Tests for the Selection of Model Variables', *IEEE Transactions on Systems, Man and Cybernetics*, SMC-8, no. 6, pp. 450–460, June, 1978; P. M. Senge, *The System Dynamics National Model Investment Function: a Comparison to the Neoclassical Investment Function*. Ph.D. Dissertation, MIT, 1978; and D. W. Peterson, 'Statistical Tools for System Dynamics', in J. Randers (ed.), *Elements of the System Dynamics Method*, Cambridge, Mass., The MIT Press, pp. 224–225, 1980.
18. L. R. Klein, 'The Use of Econometric Models as a Guide to Economic Policy', *Econometrica*, **15**, 2, April 1947.
19. J. Tinbergen, *An Econometric Approach to Business Cycle Problems*, Paris, Herman et Cie, 1937.
20. Many econometric textbooks are available. Some examples are: J. Johnston, *Econometric Methods*, New York, McGraw-Hill, 1963; A. S. Goldberger, *Eco-*

nometric Theory, New York, Wiley, 1964; C. F. Christ, *Econometric Models and Methods*, New York, Wiley, 1966; E. Malinvaud, *Statistical Methods of Econometrics*, Amsterdam, North Holland Pub. Co., 1966; R. S. Pindyck and D. L. Rubinfeld, *Econometric Models and Economic Forecasts*, New York, McGraw-Hill, 1981.
21. For examples of general representations of the U.S. economy, see L. R. Klein and A. S. Goldberger, *An Econometric Model of the United States 1929–1952*, Amsterdam, North Holland Publishing Co., 1955; M. K. Evans and L. R. Klein, *The Wharton Econometric Forecasting Model*, Department of Economics, Wharton School, University of Pennsylvania, 1967; and J. S. Duesenbery et al., *The Brookings Quarterly Econometric Model of the United States*, Rand-McNally & Company, Chicago, 1965.
22. The static model given here is taken from J. S. Cramer, *Empirical Econometrics*, Amsterdam, North Holland Publishing Co., p. 107, 1971.
23. From G. Stojkovic, 'Market Models for Agricultural Products' in H. O. A. Wold (ed.), *Econometric Model Building*, Amsterdam, North Holland Publishing Co., p. 388, 1964.
24. R. M. Spann and E. W. Erickson, 'Joint Costs and Separability in Oil and Gas Exploration', in M. F. Searl, (ed.), *Energy Modeling*, Washington D.C., Resources for the Future, p. 212, March 1973.
25. E. A. Hudson and D. Jorgenson, 'U.S. Economic Growth: 1973–2000' in *Long-Term Projections of the U.S. Economy*, Lexington, Mass., Data Resources Inc., p. 161, 1974.
26. T. N. Barr and H. F. Gale, 'A Quarterly Forecasting Model for the Consumer Price Index for Food', *Agricultural Economics Research*, 25, 1, January 1973.
27. R. G. Hoffman, 'Wheat—Regional Supply Analysis', in *The Wheat Situation*, Economic Research Service, U.S. Department of Agriculture, WS-225, August 1973.
28. F. Modigliani, R. Rasche, and J. P. Cooper, 'Central Bank Policy, the Money Supply, and the Short-Term Rate of Interest', *Journal of Money, Credit, and Banking*, 2, 1970; and Board of Governors of the Federal Reserve System, *Equations in the MIT-PENN-SSRC Econometric Model of the United States*, Washington, D.C., 1973.
29. J. S. Cramer, *Empirical Econometrics*, Amsterdam, North Holland Publishing Co., p. 102, 1971.
30. E. W. Streissler, *Pitfalls in Economic Forecasting*, Tonbridge, Kent, The Institute of Economic Affairs, pp. 73–74, 1970.
31. M. D. Intriligator, 'Econometrics and Economic Forecasting' in J. Morley English, (ed.), *Economics of Engineering and Social Systems*, New York, Wiley-Interscience, p. 157, 1972.
32. M. D. Intriligator, ibid., p. 157.
33. A. Shourie, *The Relevance of Econometric Models for Medium and Longer-Term Forecasts and Policy Prescription*, International Bank for Reconstruction and Development, Economics Department working paper no. 75, p. 58, May 6, 1970.
34. W. Leontief, 'Input–Output Economics', *Scientific American*, 185, no. 4, p. 15, 1951.
35. P. C. Newman, *The Development of Economic Thought*, Englewood Cliffs, N.J., Prentice-Hall, pp. 34–40, 1952.
36. W. Leontief, 'Quantitative Input–Output Relations in the Economic System of the United States', *The Review of Economics and Statistics*, 18, 105, August 1936.
37. A. Bottomley, University of Bradford, England, personal communication.
38. See, for example, W. Leontief, 'Environmental Repercussions and the Economic Structure: an Input–Output Approach', *Review of Economic Statistics*, 52, 262, August 1970.

39. This example is taken from W. Leontief, *Input–Output Economics*, New York, Oxford University Press, p. 135, 1966.
40. C. Almon, *The American Economy to 1975*, New York, Harper & Row, 1966.
41. E. M. Lofting and P. H. McGauhey, 'Economic Evaluation of Water. Part III, An Interindustry Analysis of the California Water Economy', contribution no. 67, Water Resources Center, Berkeley: University of California, January 1963.
42. W. Leontief, A. Morgan, K. Polenske, D. Simpson, and E. Tower, 'The Economic Impact—Industrial and Regional—of an Arms Cut' in W. Leontief, *Input–Output Economics*, New York, Oxford University Press, p. 184, 1966.
43. R. A. Herendeen and C. W. Bullard, III, 'Energy Cost of Goods and Services, 1963 and 1967', Center for Advanced Computation, University of Illinois, Urbana 61801, Document no. 140, November 1974.
44. G. B. Dantzig, *Linear Programming and Extensions*, Princeton: Princeton University Press, p. 1, 1963. (author's emphasis).
45. See, for example, A. O. Converse, *Optimization*, New York, Holt, Rinehart & Winston, 1970; and M. H. Mickle and T. W. Sze, *Optimization in Systems Engineering*, Scranton, Pa., Intext Educational Publishers, 1972.
46. This example is taken from H. G. Daellenbach and E. J. Bell, *User's Guide to Linear Programming*, Englewood Cliffs, N.J., Prentice-Hall, 1970.
47. See, for example, T. W. Oerlemans, et al., 'Dynamic Optimization of World 2', Project Globale Dynamics, Technische Hogeschool Eindhoven, Eindhoven, Netherlands, 1972; M. Bruno, 'A Programming Model for Israel', in I. Adelman, and E. Thorbecke (eds.), *The Theory and Design of Economic Development*, Baltimore, Johns Hopkins Press, 1966; H. B. Chenery, and A. MacEwan, 'Optimal Patterns of Growth and Aid, The Case of Pakistan', *Pakistan Development Review*, VI, (2), p. 209, Summer 1966.
48. W. D. Nordhaus, 'The Allocation of Energy Resources', in M. Okum and G. L. Perry (eds.), *Arthur Brooking's Paper on Economic Activity*, Vol. 3, Washington, D.C., The Brookings Institute, p. 529, 1973.
49. W. L. Balinsky, 'Educational Models for Manpower Development', *Technological Forecasting and Social Change*, 8, 309, 1976.
50. L. M. Goreux, and A. S. Manne, *Multi-level Planning: Case Studies in Mexico*, Amsterdam, North Holland Publishing Co., 1973.
51. D. A. Kendrick, 'Systems Problems in Economic Development' in J. Morley English, *Economics of Engineering and Social Systems*, New York, Wiley-Interscience, pp. 204–205, 1972.
52. R. L. Ackoff, 'The Future of Operational Research is Past', *Journal of the Operational Research Society*, 30, (2), 98, 1979.
53. R. L. Ackoff, *ibid.*, pp. 98–99 (author's emphasis).
54. J. W. Forrester, 'Confidence in Models of Social Behavior', M.I.T. working paper, pp. 15–17, December 10, 1973.
55. W. D. Nordhaus, interview with Willem L. Oltmans in *On Growth*, New York, Capricorn Books, pp. 120–124, 1974.
56. C. Castaneda, *The Teachings of Don Juan; A Separate Reality; Journey to Ixtlan; Tales of Power*, New York, Simon & Schuster, 1968–1974.
57. T. S. Kuhn, *The Structure of Scientific Revolutions*, op. cit., pp. 148–151.
58. B. Richmond, 'Conceptual Monograph No. 2', M.I.T. System Dynamics Working Paper, 1976, available from System Dynamics Group, MIT, Cambridge, Mass.
59. Memo from D. H. Meadows to F. Rabar, International Institute of Applied Systems Analysis, March 15, 1977.
60. M. Greenberger, (ed.), *Management and the Computer of the Future*, Cambridge, Mass., M.I.T. Press, pp. 84–86, 1962.

PART III

Nine Models

> The roads by which men arrive at their insights into celestial matters seem to me almost as worthy of wonder as those matters in themselves.
> Johannes Kepler
> *Astronomia Nova*

Here we describe in some detail the nine models in our survey. The models and their sponsoring and modeling institutions have already been listed in Part I. Table 3.1 contains a summary of each model's purpose, methodological paradigm, and time horizon. In this section, as in the table, the models will be presented in order of decreasing time horizon. Before we begin, however, a word about the process of describing and comparing diverse, complex computer models is necessary.

CHAPTER 3

How to Describe a Model?

One goal of our project was to represent all the models in a common format understandable to a non-technical audience, so that the procedures, insights, assumptions, and conclusions of each modeling effort could be compared and contrasted. There are many possible formats for describing a model, each of which accents certain model characteristics and hides others. Rather than select any one representational format, we decided to use four, one verbal and three diagrammatic, to present as complete a picture of each model as possible.

A. CHECKLIST

The primary representational form we will use is words. We will describe each model verbally according to the following outline or checklist of major points:

Institutional setting. Who are the sponsoring organizations, the client, and the modeling group? What circumstances brought them together? What tasks and deadlines were assigned to the modelers? What kinds of communications existed among sponsor, client, and modelers before, during, and after the project?

Purpose and problem focus. What was the model built to do? To what real world problems is the model addressed? What phenomena are to be explained, what policies are to be tested, or what information is to be generated?

Method. What modeling paradigm and mathematical techniques have been used in formalizing the system? What limitations are imposed on the model by the techniques used? Is the paradigm selected appropriate to the model's purpose?

Boundaries. Over what period of time does the modeler attempt to describe the system's behavior? Is this period consistent with the model's purpose? What variables have been included in the model? Which are affected by system behavior (endogenous) and which are independent of system behavior

Table 3.1

Model name (principal modelers) modeling institution	General problem focus	Intended use of the model	Specific policy questions	Time horizon	Method
1. SAHEL (Picardi) Massachusetts Institute of Technology	Famine, drought, and desertification in the West African Sahel	Ph.D. thesis. Increase general understanding of long-term effects of aid efforts.	How can the ecologically fragile pastoral system be stabilized? How can living standards of the nomads be permanently raised?	100–150 years	System dynamics
2. No model name (Ridker, et al.) Resources for the Future (RfF)	Long-term impact of population growth on resources and environment	Detailed population, economy, resource, environment forecasts as input to commission considering national population policy	What will be the relative impacts of a two-child average family vs. a three-child family under conditions of high or low economic growth?	30–50 years	Input–output analysis, technological forecasting
3. SOS (House and Williams) U.S. Environmental Protection Agency	Response of socioeconomic system to resource constraints	Eventual development of the model to test and design specific long-term policies	How will social response mechanisms allow society to adapt successfully to resource and environmental problems?	30–42 years	Simulation, based on ecology and theories of social change
4. TEMPO II (Enke, et al.) General Electric Tempo	Effect of population growth on economic development	Demonstration of beneficial effects of family planning and of quantitative long-term planning	Reductions in fertility will increase the rate of economic growth (plus country-specific policy questions)	30 years	Simulation, based on demography and economics
5. LTSM (Martos, Lin, et al.) United Nations Food and Agriculture Organization	Interaction of population and development with particular emphasis on agricultural development	Adaptation to specific countries for use in long-term policy formulation	Vary with concerns of specific countries	20–25 years	Simulation, based on demography and economics

6. BACHUE (Rodgers, Wéry, Hopkins) United Nations International Labor	Economic-demographic interactions, with particular emphasis on income distribution	Long-term policy formulation, national planning	What are the effects of education, family planning, public works, and distributional policies on general economic development, employment, and income distribution?	25 years	Simulation, input–output analysis
7. KASM (Johnson, Rossmiller, Abkin, Carroll, de Haen, *et al.*) Michigan State University	Agricultural development, systematic planning	Input to agricultural part of national five-year plan. Periodic consultation to agricultural ministry on specific policy problems	How should public funds be spent to develop the agriculture sector over the next five years? How should commodity prices, import quotas, export taxes, be determined? Where would foreign aid be most useful?	5–15 years	Simulation, input–output analysis, linear programming, econometrics
8. *Mexico V* (Beltran del Rio) Wharton Economic Forecasting Associates	Economic growth, uneven rates of development, inflation, balance of payments	Ph.D. thesis. Precise, short-term economic prediction for use by business and government planners	What effect will deflationary or expansionary policies have on economic growth rate, balance of trade, capacity utilization, employment, and rural-urban migration?	2–10 years	Econometrics
9. CHAC (Duloy, Norton, *et al.*) World Bank	Agricultural development, commodity markets	Planning tool for detailed analysis of World Bank investments and Mexican government agricultural policies	Which would be a better investment, tubewells, canal lining, or land-leveling? Which would be the most profitable crops for Mexico to export? How will farmers respond to various taxes or inducements?	1 year (5 years by 'comparative statistics')	Linear programming

(exogenous)? Are the reasons for variable inclusion/exclusion made clear? Are the included variables consistent with the purpose and time horizon?

Structure. What form does the network of variable interaction take? How does each variable tie into the system? Are model elements represented in detail or in highly aggregated form?

Data. Where did the numbers come from? Are data adequate to the requirements of the model? How have crude data been refined to meet the model's data requirements? How have 'soft' variables such as attitudes been handled? What has been done where needed data were not available?.

Conclusions. What is concluded about the system described by the model? What policies are recommended? To what extent have the modeler's conclusions been shaped by the choices of problem, technique, boundary, structure, and data? To what extent do the modelers base their conclusions on information from mental models? Were they able to answer the question they set out to answer?

Testing. How has the model been tested? What criteria were used to judge model validity? How does the model behavior respond to changes in parameters? Is it sensitive to real uncertainties? How robust are the policy conclusions?

(Note: In some modeling paradigms validity tests must precede the drawing of conclusions and in others they must follow. Therefore the above two checklist items are sometimes inverted in the model descriptions.)

Implementation history. Have the modeler's efforts been useful in formulating policy? Who, if anyone, has used the model? What successes and what problems have been encountered by people using the model?

Computer requirements. How much computer time is necessary to run the model? How much computer memory space does it require? For what computer system was it designed? In what language is it written?

Documentation. How well does the model documentation allow the above checkpoints to be assessed? Is the writing clear, organized, informative? Are equations available? Are they explained? Is it possible for the model to be run and tested by anyone other than the group that wrote it?

In attempting to answer these questions for all the models in the study, we encountered two major difficulties. The first was in locating information. Although all of the models were documented, most of them were not written up with the intent to answer all the questions we were asking. Some were described in dozens of short articles, but no comprehensive or technical description of the model was available. Few model documentations revealed the subjective milieu of beliefs, motives, and constraints that affected the model. The modelers seemed to aspire to anonymous objectivity and avoided mentioning human and institutional factors that influenced their work.

Piecing together answers for all of our questions, thus, was not a straightforward task. The information we gained from personal communication and formal documentation frequently had to be supplemented by guesswork. For example, where the model purpose was not stated, we sometimes could infer a purpose from what the model did, who paid for it, and how the modeler described the system. To minimize the dangers of guesswork we have attempted to identify our inferences in the course of discussion, and we submitted all our descriptions to the modelers for review, requesting that they correct any errors.

A second difficulty with the checklist is that verbal communication is necessarily sequential, while model characteristics such as boundaries and causal structure may be simultaneous, circular, or so complex that a verbal rendition must be either oversimplified or impossible to follow. To circumvent this problem we have supplemented our verbal description with some simple graphic presentations: boundary diagrams, causal diagrams, and comparison with a reference structure.

B. BOUNDARY DIAGRAM

The choice of boundary—what aspects of the real world to include in and exclude from the model—may be the decision that most influences the outcome of the modeling process. To understand a model or compare several models, one must have a clear picture of how that choice has been made. Figure 3.1 shows an example of a boundary diagram for a simple hypothetical food and agriculture model.

The diagram distinguishes among three sets of variables. Endogenous variables, listed in the inner circle, are determined or calculated within the model. In a system dynamics model the endogenous elements are those contained within feedback loops. In an econometric model the endogenous elements are those defined by simultaneous or time-lagged equations. Exogenous elements, in the outer circle, affect the state of the model system but are not affected by it; they are either constants or driving functions that must be specified as inputs before the model can be run.

Omitted elements are completely absent from the model and are listed outside both circles. The list that could be included in this section of the diagram is obviously endless. Only those elements most closely related to the exogenous and endogenous ones are indicated, to draw attention to the assumptions that define the model's boundary and to indicate the most fruitful areas for possible model expansion.

C. CAUSAL DIAGRAM

We have already introduced the causal notation in Chapter 1 and used it to represent some of the sample models in Chapter 2. Figure 3.2 shows a causal diagram of a simple simulation model that corresponds to the boundary diagram in Figure 3.1. The single arrows indicate causal relationships. The two exogenous elements are indicated by open arrows ($\Rightarrow$). A causal diagram of a simple econometric model is shown in Figure 3.3. This model is a mixture of

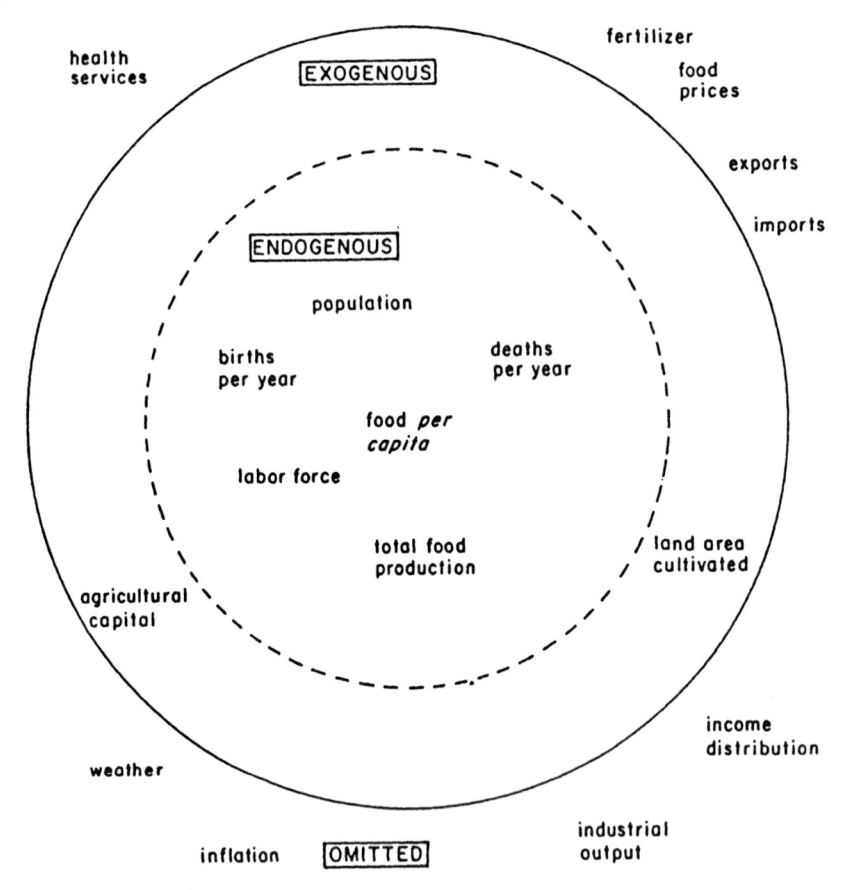

Figure 3.1 Sample boundary diagram

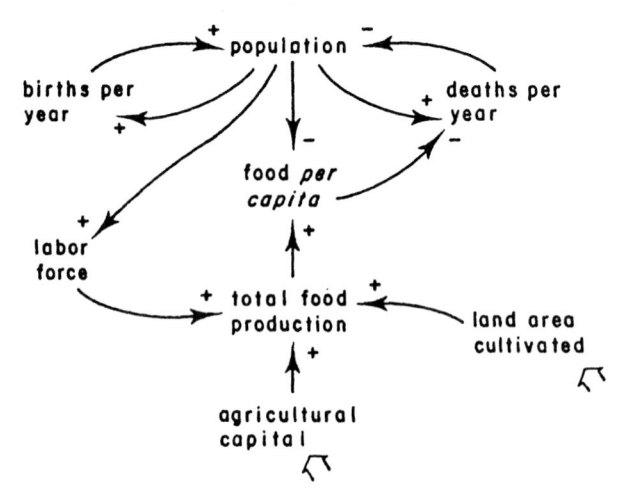

Figure 3.2 A simple causal diagram

$C = 16.8 + 0.02P + 0.23P_{-1} + 0.80(W_p + W_G)$
$I = 17.8 + 0.23P + 0.55P_{-1} - 0.15K_{-1}$
$W_p = 1.6 + 0.42Y + 0.16Y_{-1} + 0.13t$
$Y = C + I + G$
$P = Y - W_p - T$
$K = K_{-1} + I$

where

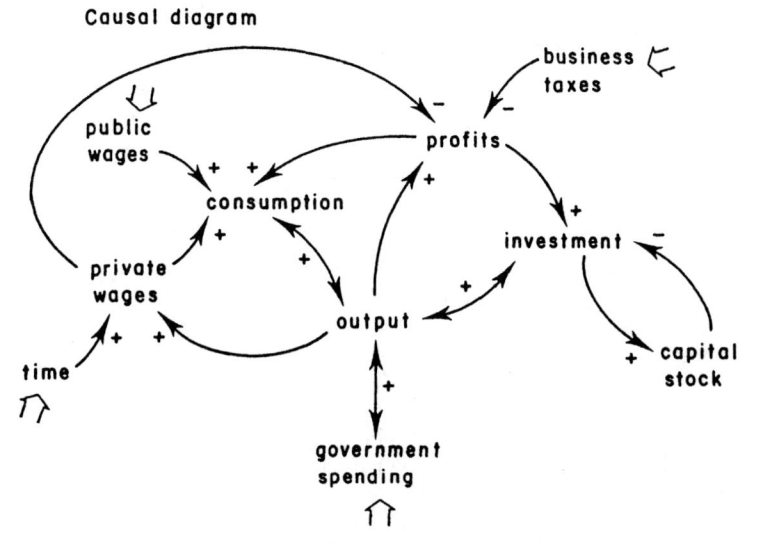

C = consumption
I = investment
W_p = private wages
Y = output
P = profits
K = capital stock
G = government spending
W_G = public wages
T = business taxes
t = time

Figure 3.3 Equations and causal diagram representation of the Klein Interwar Econometric Model

causal (behavioral) assumptions indicated with single arrows, and correlational or definitional relationships indicated with double-headed arrows ($\updownarrow$).

The main advantage of a causal diagram is that it provides a holistic summary of simultaneous, interlinked model assumptions, as a linear string of words could never do. One can learn from a glance at a causal diagram what the basic structure of the model is, whether it is open or closed, what links exist between model variables, and where important links may be missing. If the model is not too complex, one may also learn from the arrangement (or absence) of feedback loops roughly what dynamic behavior patterns the model will be capable of producing.

On the other hand, exact quantitative relationships are not pictured in a causal diagram. In order to determine whether the relationship represented by each arrow is strong or weak, linear or non-linear, instantaneous or delayed, reference must be made to the model equations. The causal diagram is only a rough sketch of the qualitative structure of the model. It may and should lead to questions about quantitative assumptions, and at that point the discussion moves from structure to parameters, and from diagrams to mathematical equations.

We encountered one problem in depicting the nine survey models in the causal diagram format; some models are so complex that a faithful translation of all their causal assumptions produces a diagram that provides about as much information as a plate of spaghetti. In some cases we have included these overcomplex diagrams in this report anyway. They communicate little about specific model assumptions, but they make a clear point about the intelligibility and manageability of the total model. In other cases we include causal diagrams of parts of a model to clarify a particular set of assumptions or to explore the reasons for the model's behavior.

D. REFERENCE STRUCTURE

The causal diagram may provide a simple representation of what is contained in a model, but it does not allow an easy comparison of the inclusions and omissions of several models. Therefore we evolved a fourth way of representing the nine models. After studying the causal diagrams of all of them, we produced a compendium of all the elements and inter-relationships that any modeler had thought important to economic–demographic systems. Of course there was a great deal of overlap; most models contained a population, a production function, and a measure of material standard of living, for instance. The areas of overlap indicated the most basic and important aspects of general population–production systems, according to a consensus of the nine different modeling groups. Figure 3.4 illustrates in a causal and very aggregated format the elements and relationships that most often appeared in the models.

The arrows of Figure 3.4 represent a number of extremely complex real-world phenomena that are included in the models in a variety of different mathematical forms. For instance, the set of arrows leading from investment to capital, energy, and the other factors of production stand for a set of investment allocation decisions that could incorporate concepts such as relative costs, marginal returns, profits, inventories, financing constraints, production delays, and many other considerations. An elaborate optimization model could be built around this small section of the system. The multiple arrows from the various factors of production to economic output could be represented by a simple Cobb–Douglas production function, by an input–output matrix, or, in the case of agricultural production, by a set of ecological and biological relationships. Other complex interactions between the physical system and human decisions occur in the allocation of output between consumption and investment, in the determination of the population's consumption habits, and in the influence of food, income, and other factors on the population growth rate.

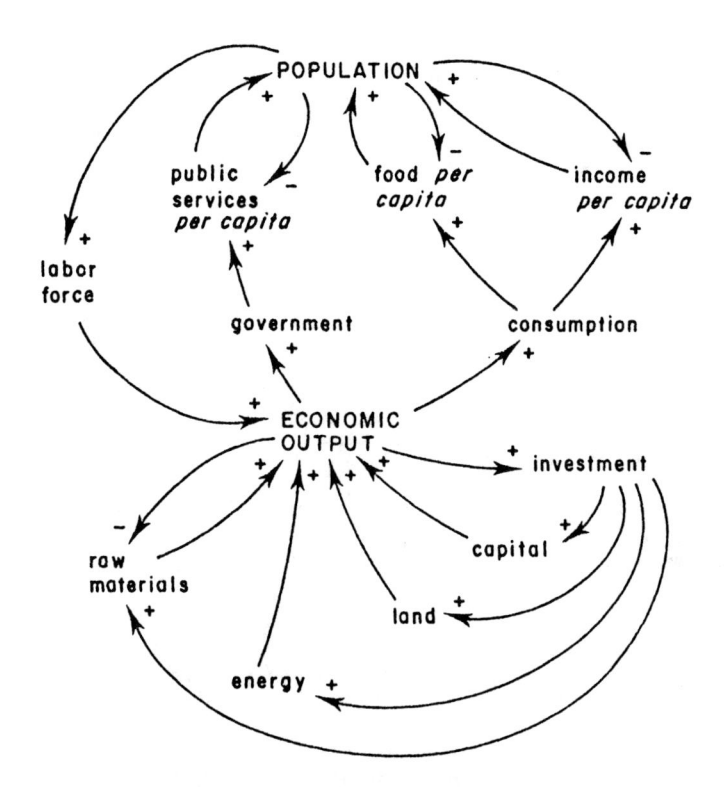

Figure 3.4 Causal diagram of common elements and relationships in economic-demographic models

If Figure 3.4 is redrawn to emphasize the social, economic, and physical factors interacting to influence human decisions, the diagram in Figure 3.5 emerges. This is not a causal diagram as used in previous figures in this report. Instead, it emphasizes the *decision points* in the system by enclosing them in ovals. Each oval could represent an extremely complex portion of a model, which in turn represents an extremely complex set of individual and institutional decisions.

Population size and income (and in a disaggregated model population characteristics and income distribution) are inputs to a set of socio-economic decisions, called 'consumption', which determine effective demands for all the priced products of the economic system. These demands, together with agricultural and industrial outputs (supply), enter a set of 'output allocation' decisions, that determine how output is divided among taxes, current consumption, research, and investment, and also how taxes, consumption, and investment are distributed over the population. *Per capita* income and services and their distribution, combined with demographic factors, influence the population growth rate through a series of 'population increase' decisions. Population determines the size of the labor force, which enters the 'production processes', along with all the non-labor factors of production such as capital

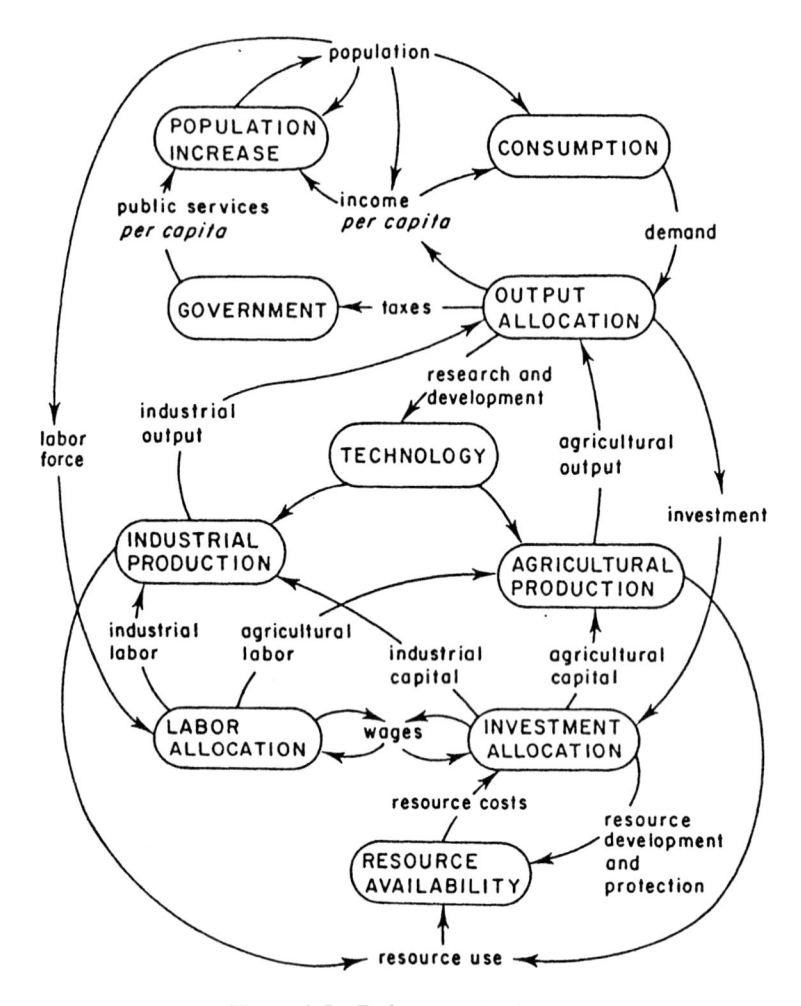

Figure 3.5 Reference structure

and technology. 'Labor allocation' decisions, including the decision to migrate, distribute labor between industry and agriculture. 'Technological' decisions affect both the industrial and agricultural production processes. 'Resource availability' represents the availability and costs of various natural factors of production such as land, minerals, water, and fossil fuels. The costs of wages, materials, and other factors are balanced against available investment funds in 'investment allocation' decisions to determine what kinds of substitutions among factors will take place and what kinds of new capital will be required.

Of course not all models contain all these elements, and each model is likely to represent them differently. For example, 'population increase' might be exogenous in one model, it might respond to food availability and family planning services in another, and in a third it might be an extremely complex function of social norms, education, female employment rates, and income distribution. We will include a few words in each oval of the reference structure diagram to indicate what sorts of factors have been included in each model as inputs to that particular set of decisions. Table 3.2 lists the sorts of factors that might be included in each decision oval.

Table 3.2 Sample factors that might be included in decision functions

Consumption	*Labor allocation*
goals and desires	wages
prices	education
advertising	migration
habits	unions
income	discrimination
credit and cash flows	housing availability
stock of household goods	perception delays
income distribution	
Output allocation	*Investment allocation*
prices	costs
tax policy	marginal returns
transfer payments	interest rates
income distribution	forecasting
interest rate	profits
social hierarchies	cash and credit flows
capital goods stock	prices
	government incentives and regulations
Technology	*Population increase*
R&D expenditures	nutrition
development delays	health care
development capital	fertility control technology
knowledge stock	status of women
perception of technical needs	education
prices	income and income distribution
	social fertility norms
	population age structure
Resource availability	*Industrial and agricultural production*
resource stock and distribution	capital
land—quantity and quality	labor—wages, skills, and availability
reclamation	technology
erosion	energy price and availability
depletion	resource price and availability
pollution	land
cartels	weather

Although the use of a reference structure is a test of model comprehensiveness, we do not mean to imply that a more comprehensive model is necessarily 'better' than one that omits part of the reference structure. Models are created to simplify the real world, which is too complex to understand in all its detail. Any model that contained all the factors in Table 3.2 and represented all the decision functions in complete detail would be incomprehensible. Since every model must omit and simplify, the omissions and simplifications of each model must be judged in the light of the model's purpose. A model intended for precise prediction of a few closely-linked variables over a short time horizon may focus on just one decision function from Table 3.2 in great detail, while treating the rest of the system as exogenous. On the other hand, a long-term model designed to explore qualitative trends may include nearly everything in the system, but represent none of it in detail. The reference structure diagram therefore can be used to represent and compare the nine models but not to judge them, at least not without reference to the purpose of each model.

E. TOLERANCE

The nine models described here have been identified as 'better than average', not only by us, but by other modelers, clients, and sponsors. We describe them here as factually as possible. We realize that no such presentation can be entirely free from the biases of the authors, nor can it be read by an audience that is free from bias.

Each model has strong and weak points. Those who are looking for flaws will certainly find them. Included in even this small sample are mismatches of methods with purposes, sloppy documentation, absurd assumptions buried in overcomplex structures, conclusions that do not even follow from model output, and project management strategies that destroy the possibility of influencing actual policy. Where we have detected these problems, we have pointed them out. There are undoubtedly others we have missed.

It would be a mistake, however, to read these models only for their faults, to associate errors exclusively with specific modelers, or to conclude that the lack of perfection precludes the usefulness of these models or of the entire practice of modeling. Finding fault can be a constructive practice if it is used for learning, so that the faults are not perpetuated. It is a waste of time if its only purpose is to assign blame or to give up. Most of the problems to be found in these models are widespread. We could have described other models with worse problems and with almost no strengths to balance them. Among those other models would be many of the mental models that might be used in the absence of these formal ones.

Furthermore, the number of mistakes a person makes is often related to the number of new things tried. Many of these models are innovations, covering totally new ground or attempting to represent systems in creative and unconventional ways. They may be experiments that did not work completely, but their own creators have undoubtedly learned from them and will avoid their mistakes in future work. The imperfections in these models are valuable to all of us, because we can also learn from them.

In short, these nine models were selected because, in one way or another, they are pioneers of the modeling field. It would be an injustice if they were to become symbols of modeling errors simply because they were included in our sample, while other models more deserving of criticism were not.

Decisions must be based on some model in any case, and no model is perfect. The proper question to ask about any of these models is not 'is it perfect?', but 'does it contribute something to the decision for which it was designed, beyond what the available mental models could contribute?'.

CHAPTER 4

SAHEL: the Tragedy of the Commons

A. INSTITUTIONAL SETTING

In June 1973 the United Nations called a meeting of its agencies and donor organizations to discuss the severe drought and famine in the African Sudano–Sahel area. The United States delegation at this meeting agreed to produce a study to 'identify the methodology, the data requirements and the possible alternatives of inquiry from physical, economic, social and cultural points of view' needed for a 'comprehensive examination of technical problems and the major alternative development possibilities' for the region.[1] The Africa Bureau of the United States Agency for International Development (USAID) took responsibility for the study. In August 1973 USAID contracted this work to the Massachusetts Institute of Technology (MIT) to be completed by September 1, 1974.[2] The Center for Policy Alternatives at MIT assembled a multi-disciplinary group to work on the Sudano-Sahel project, and each of the group members began to work on an in-depth study of some aspect of the problem.

At the time these arrangements were being made, Anthony Picardi was a doctoral candidate in civil engineering, working with the Sudano–Sahel project's principal investigator, Professor William Seifert. Picardi had studied system dynamics with Jay Forrester's group at MIT. System dynamics was viewed as one of many appropriate methods for the multidisciplinary study with which MIT was charged, and Picardi came to be included as one of the group hired under the USAID–MIT contract. His work on the project served both as his doctoral dissertation and as a report to USAID. His contribution was a small part of the total project, which included detailed studies of the economics, water resources, transportation, nutrition, health care, and social institutions of the Sahel region.

The project team of which Picardi was a part was under pressure to produce quick results, given the urgent situation in the Sahel. Less than three months elapsed between the time USAID took responsibility for the study and the time they contracted it to MIT. Two weeks after the MIT contract was signed, the study began. It was to have been completed with a deadline of one year. (The final report was actually completed 18 months after the study began.) The project was of necessity hastily conceived, and perhaps for this reason it lacked institutional grounding. The study was commissioned from the United Nations to USAID, and then through USAID to MIT, with no strong continuous working relationship between the analysts and any clients who might ultimately implement the recommendations. USAID arranged visits of the project team to Africa, heard interim presentations of results, and reviewed the final reports, but no one from USAID, the United Nations, or the Sahelian nations was directly involved in the daily planning or progress of the study.

As a graduate student working on a very large, multifaceted effort, Picardi had no clear idea who might eventually respond to his analysis or how it would fit into the total Sahel project. It was clear, however, that he needed to write an acceptable doctoral dissertation. Therefore, academic institutional requirements probably influenced his model more than did client requirements.

B. PURPOSE

The Sudano–Sahel project's stated objective was to:

> ... construct a framework—a comprehensive system of theories and concepts—that will help the Sahel–Sudan countries and international donor organizations to reach informed judgements about various alternatives for the region's long-term (20–25 years) social and economic development.[3]

After a three-week trip to Chad, Mali, and Upper Volta during which he witnessed the effects of the drought first-hand and discussed its causes with Africans, Picardi decided to limit his part of the study to the problem of desertification. He cites three reasons for this choice:

> ... it is a genuine human and ecological problem commanding worldwide concern; restoration and maintenance of the Sahel ecological resource base is a necessary (but not necessarily sufficient) step in any livestock production system in West Africa; and the problem was manageable for one person at the intended level of detail.[4]

Picardi saw three crucial things happening in the Sahel: people were starving, livestock were starving, and the range was being overgrazed and was turning to desert. He wanted to understand how the interrelationships of human population, livestock, and the grazing range in the Sahel had led to this unsatisfactory system behavior, and what changes might be necessary to reverse these trends. His questions were imprecise and general, more in the range of general understanding than of detailed decision-making.

In researching the Sahel problem, Picardi found that it could take the range more than a century to recover from serious overgrazing. Thus he increased his model's time horizon beyond the 20–25 years designated by USAID, to 150 years. Of these 150 years, the first 50 coincided with history.

C. METHOD

Picardi worked entirely within the system dynamics paradigm.[5] His modeling procedures generally followed the process outlined by Forrester in *Industrial Dynamics*:[6]

1. Establish a dynamic problem definition.
2. Formulate a hypothesis about the feedback mechanisms causing the observed problematic behavior.
3. Build a formal simulation model incorporating that hypothesis.
4. Run the model, compare its behavior with what is known about the real system, and revise the model until it is an acceptable representation.
5. Identify changes that would improve system behavior.

Picardi used the standard system dynamics tools to formulate his model. The DYNAMO compiler allowed him to write and link a series of finite difference equations and to graph the time trends they produced. DYNAMO also contained automated routines for piecewise-linear approximation and exponential smoothing with which to represent non-linear relationships and distributed time lags. The system dynamics paradigm provided a conceptual base for identifying important feedback loops in the system, and a flow diagram format to represent rates, levels, information and material flows, non-linearities and delays. The paradigm also predisposed him to seek information from many sources, including non-statistical ones, and to focus on the social, cultural, and motivational factors in the pastoral system.

Picardi was seeking general understanding of the long-term dynamic behavior of the Sahelian ecological and pastoral system as it responded to weather fluctuations. He was searching for policies that would raise the nomads' standard of living and reduce their susceptibility to drought. The system seemed to be nearly closed and dominated by feedback relationships among the people, their cattle, and the grazing range. Given this purpose, system dynamics was an appropriate method to choose. Of course, Picardi, as a system dynamicist, probably chose from the broad complex of problems in the MIT Sahel study a problem definition that fit his method, rather than vice versa.

D. BOUNDARIES

According to the system dynamics paradigm, the initial form of a model should include only those variables minimally necessary to explain the problematic behavior of the system.[7] Picardi defined the problem in the Sahel in terms of human population, livestock population, and range condition. His initial model SAHEL2, therefore, contained essentially these three variables and enough other information to explain their causal interrelationships.

Picardi was convinced, both by his preconceptions and his knowledge of specific conditions in the Sahel, that the long-term behavior of the system was largely determined by causal feedback. Accordingly he made most of his model

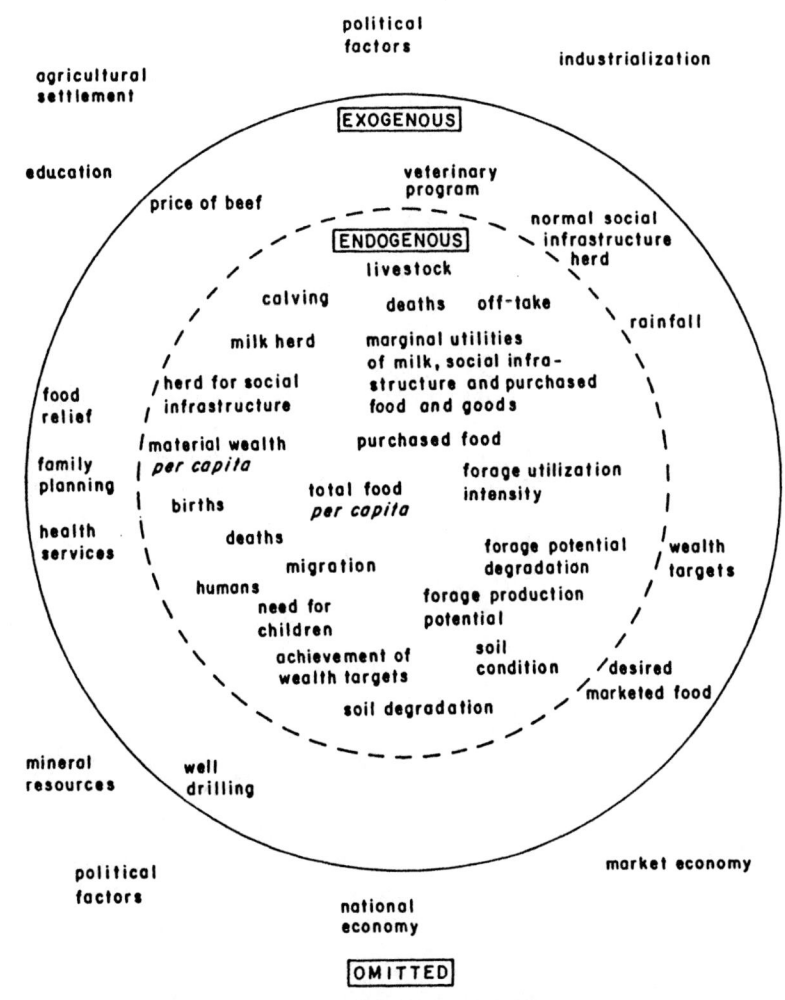

Figure 4.1 Boundaries for SOCIOMAD

variables endogenous. He did, however, include a number of exogenous variables to represent forces outside the system that had influenced or might influence the Sahel (see Figure 4.1). Principal among these exogenous forces were variable rainfall and government policies influencing human and livestock death rates such as public health services, interference with tribal warfare, and veterinary services. The literature also indicated that well-drilling in the Sahel—one of the projects humanitarian relief organizations had already implemented—caused migratory peoples to spend more time in the region. Thus Picardi included well-drilling as an exogenous policy that affected not only available water but also time spent by nomads in the Sahel.

In the course of its development, the Sahel model went through many revisions. In his thesis Picardi describes three versions of the model:

SAHEL2, ECNOMAD, and SOCIOMAD, in order of increasing complexity. In ECNOMAD and SOCIOMAD, he expanded the boundaries of SAHEL2 to include endogenous representations of the cultural factors influencing the nomads' decisions about managing the livestock herd.

The Sahel models are essentially closed, ecological models. They do not look much beyond the pastoral system of the Sahel. Elements such as industry, settled agriculture, formal education, fossil fuels, or modern market mechanisms are omitted. Government is not represented explicitly, although government programs are implied by many of the exogenous variables. As we shall see, this choice of boundaries turned out to be wide enough to encompass the problem, but too narrow to encompass those sorts of solutions that involve any permanent change in either the culture or the resource base of the nomads.

E. STRUCTURE

First we shall describe the structure of SAHEL2, the simplest model, in detail. We shall then briefly describe the structural additions made in ECNOMAD and SOCIOMAD.

SAHEL2 can conveniently be divided into three sectors—soil, livestock, and human population. The soil sector captures the dynamics of the renewable but erodable resource base that supports the human and livestock populations of the Sahel. The sector's dominant structural features are two positive feedback loops (see Figure 4.2), which are activated by high rates of forage-utilization intensity (that is, overgrazing). Under normal conditions grazing is light, the soil degradation rate is balanced by regeneration, and forage production is stable. If for some reason grazing becomes so heavy that the soil degrades, forage production will decrease. Unless the livestock herd is decreased, the remaining grass will be even more heavily grazed, degrading the soil still further, and so on. If activated, this vicious loop causes exponential

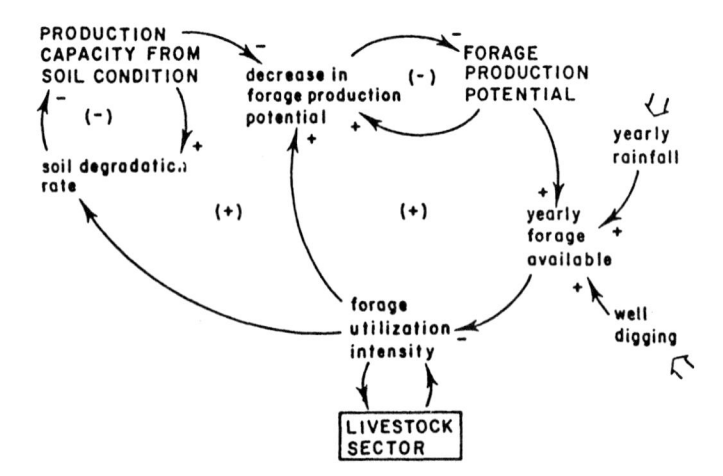

Figure 4.2 SAHEL2 soil sector (state variables in upper case)

deterioration of the soil condition and thus of the forage-production potential. If the pressure on the range is reduced, the range can regenerate by a reversal of this process.

The soil–forage deterioration loops described above are drought-sensitive. A lack of rainfall will reduce available forage. If available forage is reduced to an amount that is too low relative to the livestock population, overgrazing will occur. If this overgrazing unbalances the system to an extent that it cannot right itself—and it frequently will when drought is prolonged or extremely severe or when the stocking levels are high—overgrazing will set the soil-degradation loops into a downward spiral. If nothing is done to stop it, the downward spiral will operate until the range is converted to desert and the livestock population is destroyed.

The soil and forage resource base supports the livestock population and limits its growth. The one positive loop in the livestock sector (see Figure 4.3) is the familiar biological population growth loop. Population grows at a rate proportional to its numbers, that is, exponentially. If disease or other factors do not keep the livestock death rate as high as the birth rate, exponential growth proceeds until lack of forage or increased slaughter by the nomads (called offtake) raises the death rate and brings the population into balance. In SAHEL2 the population growth loop tends to make livestock population

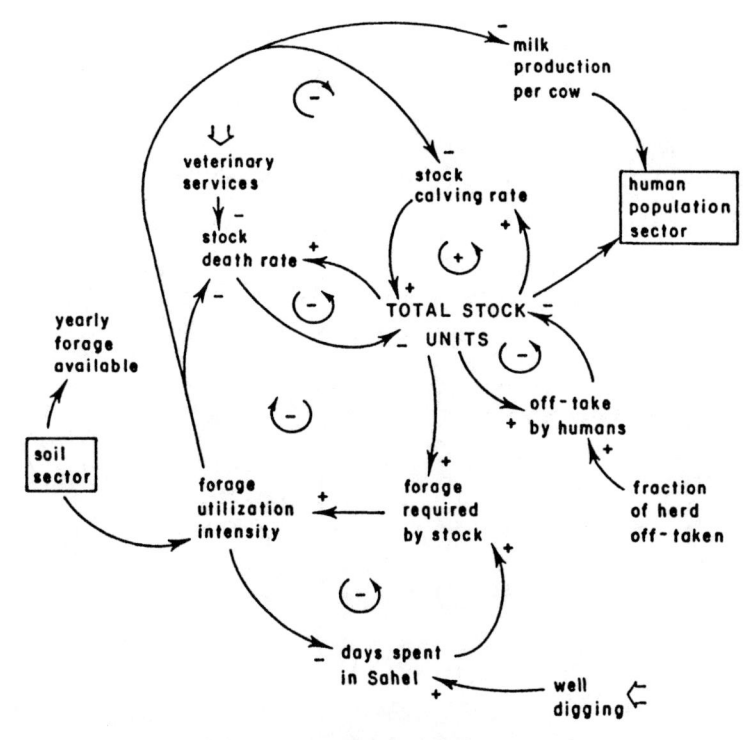

Figure 4.3 SAHEL2 livestock sector

grow to the maximum size supportable on the range, reflecting an assumption that the nomads' cultural values lead them to try to maximize their herd size (this assumption is elaborated in SOCIOMAD).

The livestock population is directly self-regulatory: livestock deaths and human offtake of livestock are proportional (but with a varying coefficient of proportionality) to the number of livestock. Also, the livestock population adjusts to limits imposed by the soil sector. This adjustment is accomplished by means of high death rates and low birth rates that reduce the livestock population when forage utilization intensity is high. In times when forage is scarce, the nomads are assumed to move livestock out of the Sahel.

Whatever resilience the system has against the downward spiral of the soil-degradation loops comes from the self-regulatory (negative) loops described above. If, when the range system is stressed, livestock population decreases faster than the soil deteriorates, the range will have an opportunity to recover. If the regulatory power of the livestock sector's negative loops is too weak, overgrazing will destroy the soil resource and drive the system to desert.

An obvious deduction from this structural hypothesis is that aid programs that decrease death rates of livestock, such as veterinary measures that reduce cattle death rates, may destabilize the system. Any measure that weakens the negative feedback loops controlling the livestock population, so that the soil degrades faster than the livestock numbers decrease, will enhance the possibility of desertification. Another such measure is well-drilling, which decreases the pastoralists' tendency to migrate away in times of drought.

The human population in SAHEL2 is limited by the amount of food the livestock sector produces, much as the livestock population is limited by the forage produced by the soil sector. The structure of SAHEL2's human population sector is very similar to that of the livestock sector (see Figure 4.4).

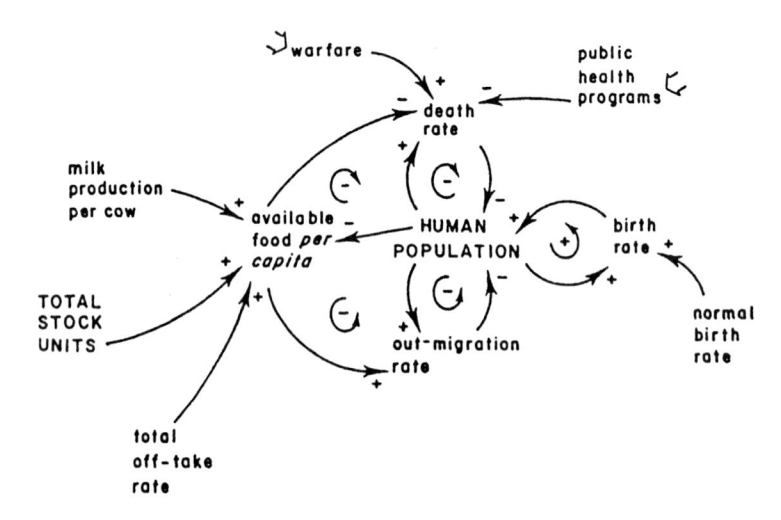

Figure 4.4 - SAHEL2 human population sector

As a high forage-utilization intensity feeds back to reduce livestock population in the livestock sector, so low food *per capita* (where the food is derived totally from the livestock) feeds back to increase the human death rate and to cause out-migration. The structure of the human population sector also includes a standard biological growth loop; more people produce more births per year, which increases the number of people. The human population sector is analogous to the stock sector in the exogenous inputs it includes. Aid-giving measures directed toward improving the human condition, such as public health programs and measures to stop inter-tribal warfare, weaken the negative feedback loops that have traditionally regulated human population.

The main differences between the livestock sector and the human population sector arise from the respective positions of the two sectors in the larger system. Livestock depend on the soil, a resource which is easy to deplete and slow to recover. Humans depend on and manage livestock, a resource which will grow quickly if forage is available. Thus excess stock will tend to bring the downfall of the whole system, while excess humans will tend merely to lower the human standard of living. Another important difference is that human decisions and values control both the human and the livestock populations, and thus the major decision variables in the model—offtake rate, human birth rate, and out-migration rate—are in the human population sector only.

After constructing SAHEL2 and trying various experiments with it, Picardi concluded that the pastoral system of the Sahel was potentially unstable, especially when modern veterinary care, health care, and other developments alter traditional system balances. He traced the instability to the lack of effective feedback between the range capacity and the human decisions that affect both human and livestock populations. The only constraints in the system to keep the livestock population from exceeding the range capacity are the traditional death rates of people and cattle and the traditional patterns of nomad movement. When these constraints are removed with no other changes, the resultant excess stock tends to drive the range towards desert.

Having identified the information available to the pastoralists' decisions as crucial to the stability of the system, Picardi constructed ECNOMAD and SOCIOMAD to elaborate on the social and economic factors that influence the nomads' decisions. He did so:

1. 'To examine the possibilities of implementing a maximum sustainable yield use of the ecosystem using conventional economic incentives'.
2. '... to examine the trade-offs ... in the sustained-yield model of behavior'.[8]

ECNOMAD postulates that the nomads allocate their herd among four functions: milk production, trade for food, trade for goods, and what Picardi terms 'social infrastructure', a function that amounts to insurance against

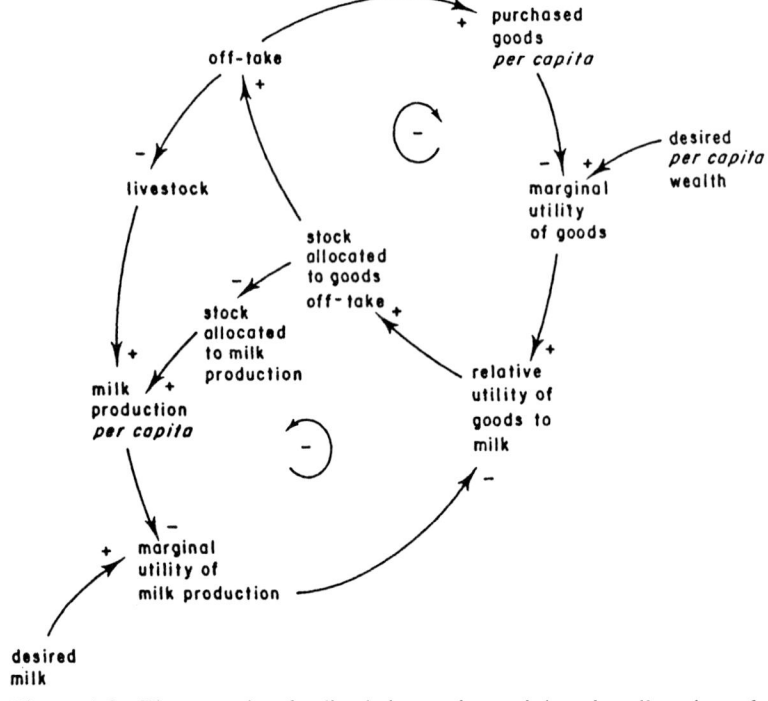

Figure 4.5 The negative feedback loops determining the allocation of stock for goods offtake.

disaster. The actual abundance of milk, purchased food and goods, and 'social infrastructure' relative to the desired abundance of each of these factors determine their relative marginal utilities, which then determine how herds will be allocated (see Figure 4.5).

With SOCIOMAD Picardi investigates the dynamics of the cultural values underlying these economic allocation decisions. While ECNOMAD contains the assumption that the desires for livestock for social infrastructure, wealth, and children are constant, SOCIOMAD assumes that they vary with both endogenous and exogenous influences. The desire for herd, for social infrastructure, is made variable by assuming that the memory of a famine, represented in the model as delayed information generated by a previous food deficit, increases the cultural value of maintaining some extra herd as a buffer against possible future famine. Desire for wealth is simulated by including an exogenous 'wealth target'. Desire for wealth will tend to rise toward that target unless the society achieves no increase in income for a number of years—in which case the desired wealth tends to slump back toward the level of wealth at which the culture has been living. Human fertility is modeled as decreasing (after a delay) in response to increases in both average lifetime and income *per capita*.

In the progression from SAHEL2 through ECNOMAD to SOCIOMAD, the Sahel models become increasingly complex. The model additions that bring on this complexity are 'soft' cultural variables, such as desires for and relative valuations of goods. The additions made in ECNOMAD and SOCIOMAD allow new policy questions to be tested, such as whether an increase in the price the herdsmen receive for cattle would lead to smaller herds. However, these elaborations do not significantly alter the model's behavior.

The total scope of the largest model, SOCIOMAD, is indicated in the causal diagram, Figure 4.6 and in the reference structure diagram, Figure 4.7.

F. DATA

Picardi modeled a system in which statistics are almost non-existent. He dealt with this problem by conducting a wide-ranging information search that encompassed ecological, demographic, and economic information at all degrees of precision. He found a small area of the Sahel, the Tahoua district in Niger, where livestock records, demographic surveys, and rainfall measurements had been made.[9] His references include ecology textbooks, anthropological reports, sociological journals, magazine articles, and the records of French colonial governments. He has been able to cite one or more references for virtually all model parameters.

Many of these citations, however, do not unambiguously state an exact numerical value for the variable they are intended to justify. For example, one estimate of how long it would take the soil to recover from serious abuse states that the ecological succession that follows overgrazing may take 'several generations'.[10] Another estimate of recovery time, this time based on observations made in the southwestern United States, states that 'at least 80 years would be needed for a significant successional change in the Sahel and subdesert'.[11] In the model, Picardi uses 80 years as a figure for the maximum time it would take soil to recover from overgrazing; this number is probably uncertain by at least 50%.

For parameters representing cultural values such as marginal utility of livestock for social infrastructure, no numbers were available. In these cases, model parameters were guessed from verbal descriptions, such as anthropologists' observations of actual allocation decisions under varying circumstances.

Picardi devotes an entire chapter to the determination of the most important numbers in the model: the potential productivity of the range, the response of the vegetation to various livestock densities, and the degree to which various technological improvements such as irrigation might increase the potential resource base. Picardi had the expertise of the other MIT team members to rely on here, including hydrological engineers and agricultural economists. The numbers in his model are probably as good a compilation of current knowledge as is possible. Current knowledge, however, especially of the cultural values and long-term ecological changes which are at the heart of the Sahel models, is not very precise.

G. CONCLUSIONS

The ten years preceding the Sahelian drought had unusually high rainfall,

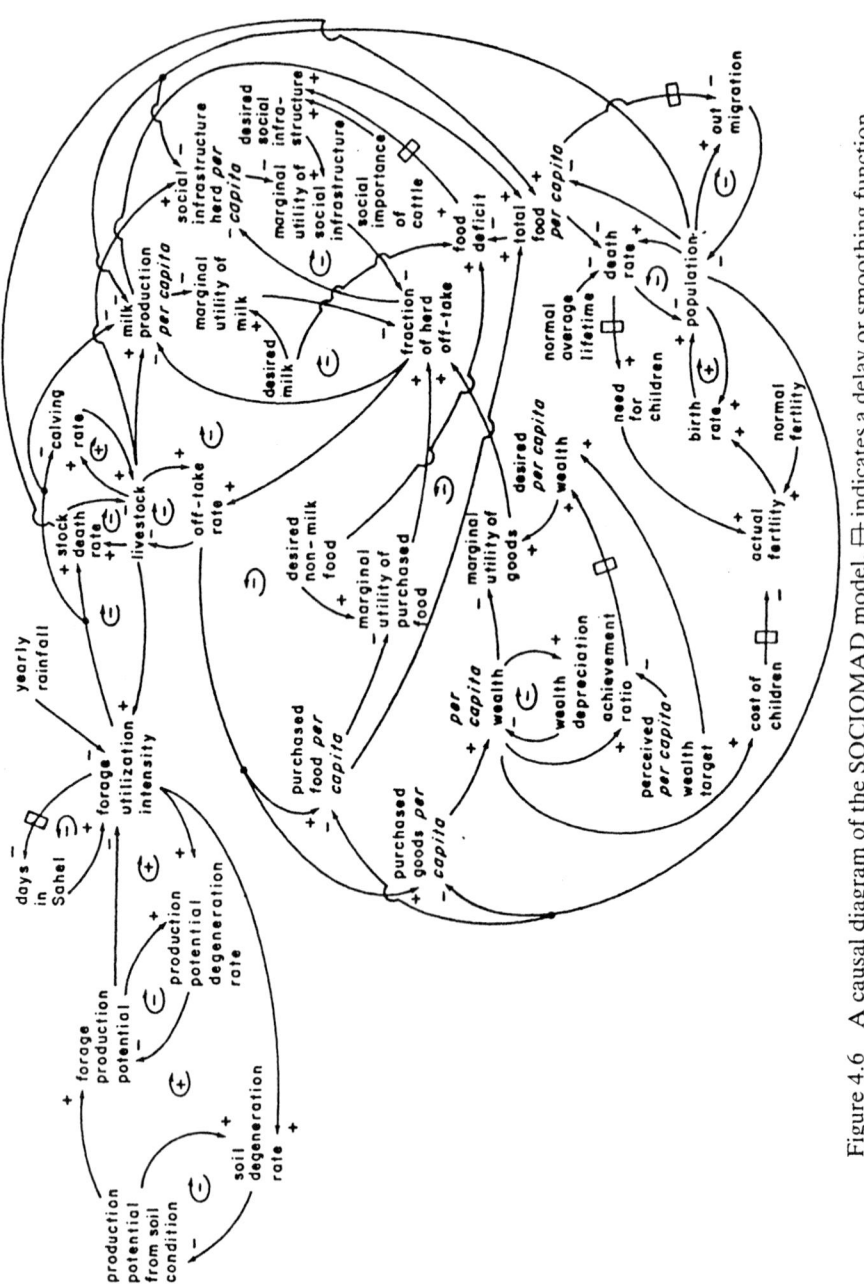

Figure 4.6 A causal diagram of the SOCIOMAD model. ▭ indicates a delay or smoothing function. Reproduced by permission of A. C. Picardi.

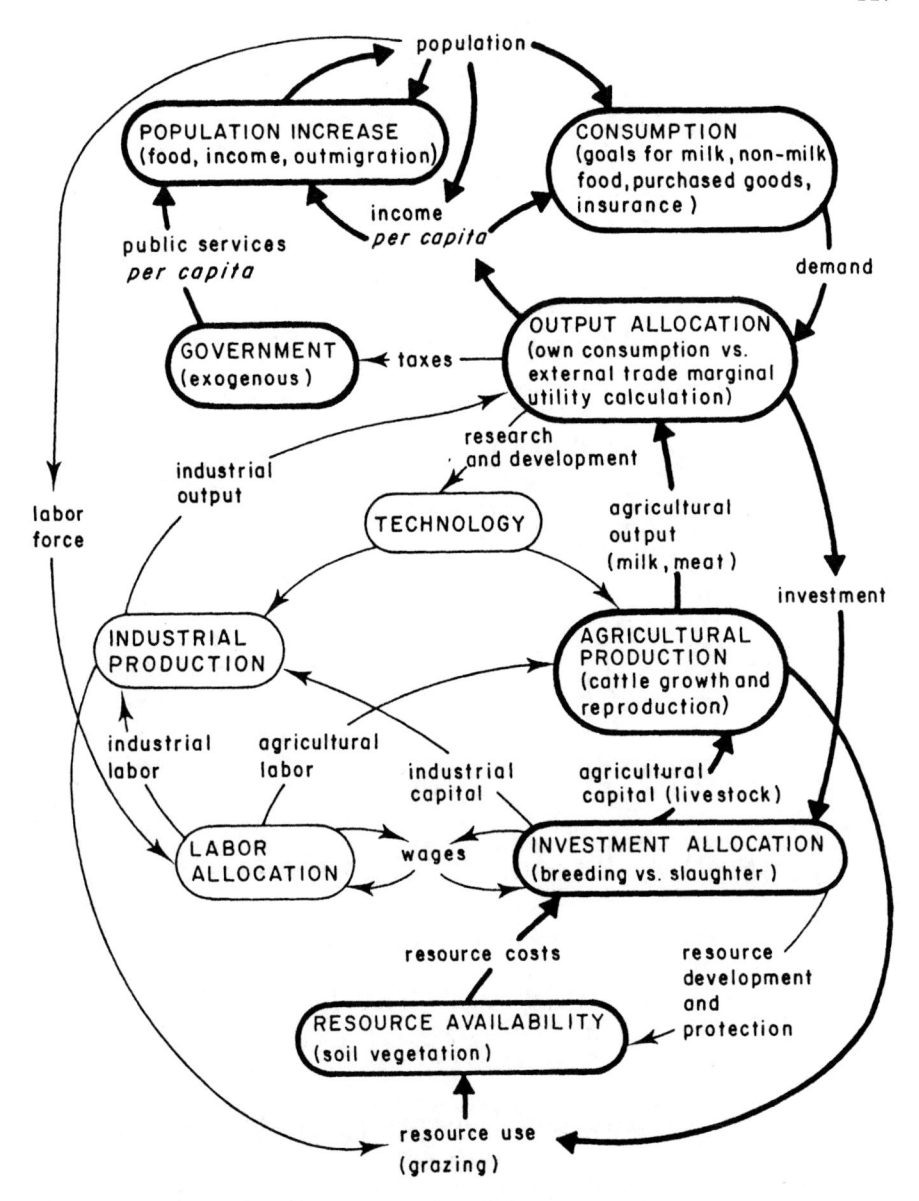

Figure 4.7 SOCIOMAD reference structure. Elements with heavy outlines are included in the model; elements with light outlines are not included.

which allowed both human and animal populations to grow to unprecedented levels. If the system is simulated without the drought, a famine occurs anyway, somewhat later and more severely, since the populations rise higher and do more damage to the range. The overstocking of the range arises naturally from the logical consequences of the nomads' value system; each herdsman benefits directly from increasing his own herd and receives no immediate reward, economic or cultural, for conserving the range. The result is called by Picardi 'the tragedy of the commons—when commonly held resources are exploited according to individual self-interest, the resources will be overexploited and destroyed by the same people who benefit from them'.[12]

Picardi concludes that the Sahel pastoral system has existed for many years on the brink of an intrinsically unstable set of human–livestock–range relationships. Under traditional conditions this instability becomes evident only during rare occurrences of severe drought. Most of the ways that aid-giving agencies attempt to help one part or another of the system, however, drive the system further toward instability, so that desertification begins to proceed even during less severe droughts. The main source of instability is the lack of effective feedback between range condition and livestock population. This conclusion was originally derived from the simple SAHEL2 model; it was strengthened by the more elaborate ECNOMAD and SOCIOMAD.

Picardi tried many policies to see if there was a way to stabilize the system through politically acceptable means. Everything he tried, including reforestation measures and private incentives, failed to bring the desired stability. Some policies had surprisingly counterproductive results. For example, raising the real price of the nomads' cattle, relative to the market goods for which they are traded, decreased the slaughter rate and allowed herds to build up faster to the point of over-grazing.

The only measures found capable of increasing system stability were:

1. Removing all outside intervention such as health services, well drilling, elimination of warfare, and veterinary services, thereby stabilizing the system by the traditional means of disease, famine, drought, and war.
2. Establishing a direct feedback link between range condition and stocking level. The feedback response cannot be too rapid, however, or the variance in stocking rate and human welfare is even greater than that induced by normal weather variations.

> What is needed is an offtake policy which does not respond to each yearly variation in the sustainable stocking rate, but which maintains the standing stock at some level based on the long-term condition of the range and the available forage. Such a policy would smooth out the fluctuation in herd size, creating a much more favorable economic environment and a more reliable source of sustenance for the human population.[13]

This policy assumes an ability to regulate livestock numbers that no one in the Sahel is known to possess and that would directly contradict the prevailing nomadic value system. Besides being difficult to implement, direct regulation of livestock numbers tends to be destabilizing in a different way. It causes intense variation in human welfare and high rates of out-migration, unless complemented with measures such as supplemental feeding in drought years.[14]

Picardi concludes that all policy objectives one might have for the Sahel cannot be achieved; that some stark choices must be made:

> The preservation of the traditional decision making structure and preservation of the ecological resource base are incompatible objectives. Increases in the health status of the population are achieved at the expense of potential improvements in material wealth ... Food shortage, either of famine proportion or chronic in nature, can be eliminated only when population growth stops and the overall level of population is low enough so that *per capita* production can result in an adequate diet.[15]

Picardi apparently assumes that such policy trade-offs are generalizable to other regions, since he concludes a summary article by raising a number of basic ethical questions:

> Is it advisable to continue traditional approaches to aid when these may have contributed to the problem? Do outside aid organizations have the moral right to intervene in a fundamental and pervasive way in a traditional society? Can any such programs be implemented without excessive violence in the form of enforcement or corruption?[16]

Picardi's conclusions are a direct result of his choice of model boundary. The nomads' economic system is limited to traditional livestock output only, and the Sahel's nomad population must remain dependent on the resource base of natural grazing lands alone. A combination of technological policies to increase the productivity of this resource base with social value changes to accommodate new technologies was not considered, except to wonder about its moral acceptability. Expanding the boundary to permit food and energy imports or industrialization of the population would certainly have altered the policy conclusions. In response to this criticism, Picardi writes:

> Please note the choice of system boundary was made after travel and extensive discussions with all manner of ministers from three West African countries ... It is patently obvious that any 'industrialization' done in West Africa must be done in the more populous Sudan zone and that long term sustained imports of food or materials to the Sahel are completely beyond the political and financial capacity of the Sahel countries. The *opportunity costs* of both of these ideas are so enormous and so obvious that they were eliminated without discussion.[17]

H. TESTING

As a system dynamicist, Picardi, denies the importance of point-prediction in assessing model validity and rests the credibility of his models on how well their structure captures real-world interconnections and how well their outputs correspond to real-world behavior trends: 'One should ask whether the simulated problem behavior arises from the same mechanisms in the models that produce the real-world problems and whether the results of policy simulations derive from a reasonable interaction of system elements ... How well these models *replicate* the real world in all its definable detail is irrelevant'.[18]

With one exception,[19] all model output is presented in the form of long-term graphs. Model sensitivity to uncertain parameters and to policy variables is demonstrated by contrasting a time-graph of the model's base run with a time-graph of the model output obtained by changing policy variables or uncertain parameters. Structural causes for sensitivity are discussed.

In the first tests, Picardi presents the uses of the SAHEL2 model to evaluate the system's sensitivity to policies commonly advocated for the Sahel—such as famine relief, well digging, and range control. In two other groups of runs, he tests model performance under various patterns of rainfall—rain being an unpredictable variable as well as one that is frequently blamed for all the failures of the system being modeled.[20] These runs show that rainfall influences the system but that the model's internal unstable structure amplifies the stochastic influence of weather uncertainty.[21] A third set of runs demonstrates that the system is somewhat sensitive to changes in cultural parameters such as the relative valuation of wealth and social infrastructure.[22] Along with these tests on cultural parameters, Picardi demonstrates that ECNOMAD is not sensitive within a broad range of variables to changes in some uncertain values.[23]

The ultimate sensitivity test of a system dynamics model is the robustness of *policy conclusions* when uncertain model parameters are varied. Picardi gives several demonstrations that the policies he tests produce the same generic effects, even under several different assumptions about, for example, future rainfall. Figure 4.8 shows the time behavior of one variable, soil condition, under four different policies, each tested with six different assumptions about rainfall patterns. Policy Set 1 (continued present policies) shows great instability and a generally declining resource base, whatever the rainfall assumptions. Policy Set 2 (direct stock control) shows improved soil condition in all cases, but still some instability. Policy Set 3 (direct stock control and supplemental feeding) and Policy Set 7 (Policy Set 3 plus veterinary services, herd management, and several economic policies) both show improvement with still less sensitivity to weather variations.

I. COMPUTER REQUIREMENTS

Picardi's models place negligible demands on any computer system. SOCIOMAD, the largest of his models, consists of 191 variables. Run costs vary from system to system, but on most standard computer systems a dollar would pay for several model runs. Picardi's models are written in DYNAMO but could be translated into general-purpose languages such as FORTRAN or BASIC.

J. IMPLEMENTATION

As discussed under 'institutional setting', the Sahel models were a minor part of a major study. The Sahel models were never seriously considered independently of the larger study, and never viewed as tools for direct policy implementation.

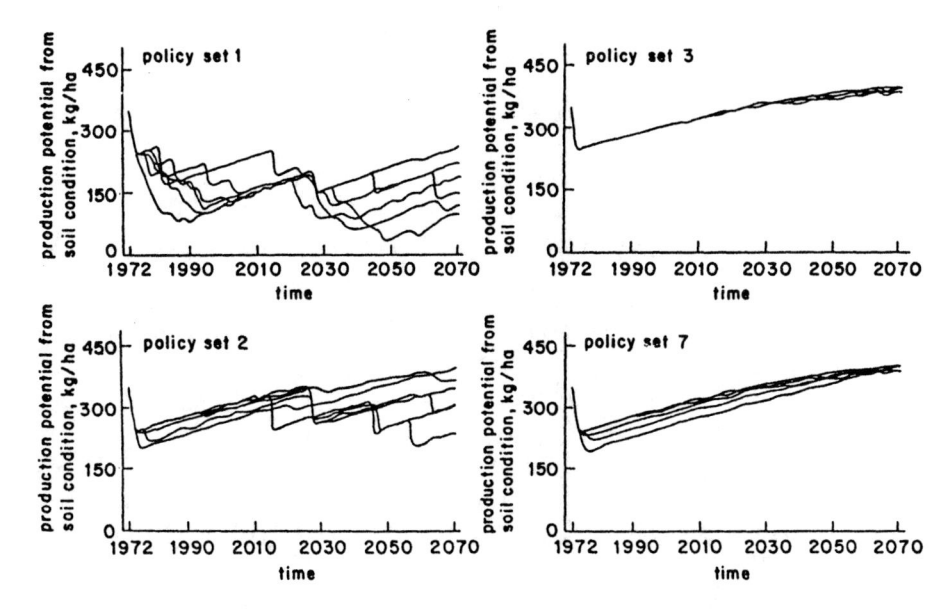

Figure 4.8 SOCIOMAD simulations with six different rainfall patterns showing characteristic soil condition behavior modes. Reproduced by permission of A. C. Picardi

The Sudano–Sahel project itself was conceived in an atmosphere of urgency, and no clear mechanism for it to relate to actual decision making, either in USAID or in the Sahel, was incorporated in its conception.

However, Picardi's conclusions certainly carried a significant policy message. He believed that the intrinsic goals of the people in the system were bound to drive their economy to the brink of ecological disaster, and that current aid programs, by helping the people to meet those goals, were hastening and intensifying the disaster. The best way to improve matters would be:

1. To withdraw current aid efforts so that the system could at least return from present-day worse to historic bad, or
2. To redirect efforts toward the goals and decision-making structures of the people, that is to alter the culture directly so that a materially-improved and less vulnerable new society could be established.

Picardi's model could have been used to provide semi-specific guidelines about where that cultural interference might have been most effectively directed, but Picardi was himself so morally uncomfortable with that choice that he did not press the model very far in that direction.

The entire MIT project report with Picardi's findings in one chapter was submitted to USAID at the end of 1974. USAID's initial response to the MIT study was decidedly cool. The agency did not publish the project report, did not provide MIT with funds to publish it, and did not actively acknowledge its existence either in communications with the public or with Congress. As a thesis, however, Picardi's model was publicly available, and MIT did reproduce and distribute about 100 copies of the final project report, some of which were requested by USAID and Sahelian national officials. Virtually everyone in the USAID Africa Bureau was at least aware of the project's existence, and many were familiar with the report's contents. In 1976 USAID developed a major new development program for the Sahel and successfully obtained Congressional funding for it. The MIT project report was used as one of many inputs to the design of that new program, and data, quotations, and figures (recaptioned) from the MIT report were used (without acknowledgement) in the funding proposal to Congress. The new program focused on increasing agricultural production and did not noticeably incorporate either of Picardi's two major policy alternatives.

As of 1979 there had been a nearly total personnel change in the USAID Africa Bureau, but the new Sahel program was still being carried out. Congressional attention had shifted first to Egypt and then to Southern Africa, and the MIT report was described as 'on the shelf'.

Picardi received his Ph.D. and joined the Cambridge firm of Development Analysis Associates, where he worked for the Saudi Arabian government on planning for water and electricity development. He used a system dynamics model for long-term demand forecasts and a dynamic integer programming model for designing supply networks. He worked directly and closely with his new clients, traveling to Saudi Arabia three or four times a year.

Picardi reports that several U.S. government agencies, dealing with issues such as fisheries and energy, have expressed interest in his Sahel paper, more in the tragedy of the commons idea than in details about the Sahel. One expression of interest has come from the International Livestock Center in Addis Ababa, Ethiopia, but Picardi lost contact with them during the Ethiopian revolution, and since then he says they have produced standard livestock models with no representation of range condition. As Picardi says, 'they kind of lost the idea'.

Picardi writes with dissappointment about his work's lack of impact. Under the heading 'Limitations to this Study', he states, 'the primary limitation of this study's usefulness to date is the almost total lack of a client'.[24] In 'Suggestions for Further Research' he says, 'further research on this ... problem will be useful only if it enlists the participation of policymakers responsible for long-term decisions in the Sahel ...'.

Picardi seems to have concluded that an academically-based general-understanding model can have impact only through the spread of insights and ideas, which may then influence decisions in ways that probably never can be traced. He has written several articles and made several speeches to communicate his general conclusions:

> I have hopes that the central theme of the study—that the Sahel is a social and cultural problem rather than one amenable to a technical 'fix'—will come across to

enough of the ... readers to add incrementally to the conviction that we should deal differently with this class of problems (the 'tragedy of the commons' problems).[25]

K. DOCUMENTATION

A clear and complete technical report on the Sahel models is presented in Picardi's Ph.D. thesis and the identical report he prepared for USAID. All computer equations, definitions of variables, and units in which variables are measured are given in an appendix.

A substantial part of the thesis is devoted to describing the culture, history, economy, and ecology of the Sahel. Model descriptions and explanations of output frequently refer back to the real-world situation. Picardi documents all his data sources in a technical appendix in his thesis.[26] In this appendix he proceeds through the computer program line by line, justifying each equation with references from the literature. Numerous sensitivity and policy test runs are shown.

NOTES AND REFERENCES

1. Final report of the Meeting of the Sudano–Sahelian Mid- and Long-Term Programme 28–29 June, 1973, Geneva, Special Sahelian Office, United Nations, New York, statement by Donald S. Brown. Cited in William W. Seifert and Nake M. Kamrany. *Summary Report: Project Objectives, Methodologies, and Major Findings*, Vol. 1, Cambridge, Mass., Center for Policy Alternatives, MIT, p. 1, December 31, 1974.
2. *Ibid.*, first page of foreword (unnumbered).
3. *Ibid.*, p. 4.
4. A. C. Picardi, *A Systems Analysis of Pastoralism in the West African Sahel*, Ph.D. dissertation, MIT, p. 311, February 1975.
5. Refer to Chapter 2 for a full description of the system dynamics paradigm.
6. Condensed from ten steps in J. W. Forrester, *Industrial Dynamics*, Cambridge, Mass., Press and John Wiley & Sons, New York, p. 13, 1961. The last of Forrester's ten steps, 'Alter the real system in the direction that model experimentation has shown will lead to improved performance' was omitted here (and in Picardi's work).
7. J. W. Forrester, *op.cit.*, p. 61.
8. A. C. Picardi, *op.cit.*, p. 109.
9. *Ibid.*, p. 36.
10. *Ibid.*, p. 277.
11. *Ibid.*, p. 277.
12. A. C. Picardi and W. W. Siefert, 'A Tragedy of the Commons in the Sahel', *Technology Review*, p. 51, May 1976. The 'Tragedy of the Commons' idea was taken from Garrett Hardin, 'The Tragedy of the Commons', *Science*, **162**. 1243, (December 1968).
13. A. C. Picardi, *op.cit.*, p. 105.
14. *Ibid.*, p. 176.
15. A. C. Picardi, 'Practical and Ethical Issues of Development in Traditional Societies: Insights from a System Dynamics Study in Pastoral West Africa', *Simulation*, **26**, Jan. 1976, p. 1.
16. Picardi and Siefert, *op.cit.*, p. 51.
17. A. C. Picardi, private communication, May 18, 1976.

18. A. C. Picardi, *A Systems Analysis of Pastoralism in the West African Sahel*, Ph.D. dissertation, MIT, p. 199, February 1975.
19. A trade-off matrix which gives static values for certain variables under eight policy sets. *Ibid.*, p. 180–181, Table 7.4-3.
20. *Ibid.*, p. 133, 210.
21. *Ibid.*, p. 206.
22. *Ibid.*, p. 212–232.
23. *Ibid.*, p. 125, 210.
24. *Ibid.*, p. 216.
25. A. C. Picardi, personal communication, May 18, 1976.
26. A. C. Picardi, *A Systems Analysis of Pastoralism in the West African Sahel,* Ph.D. dissertation, MIT, Appendix F, February 1975.

CHAPTER 5

RfF: Adding a Combine to a Tractor

A. INSTITUTIONAL SETTING

In a message to Congress dated July 18, 1969, President Nixon recommended the establishment of a Commission on Population Growth and the American Future. 'In his message (the) President ... pointed out that the population of the United States was expected to increase by 50% in the next 30 years', and further noted that: 'In the governmental sphere ... there is virtually no machinery through which we can develop a detailed understanding of demographic changes and bring that understanding to bear on public policy'.[1]

The President submitted to Congress a draft Bill. This Bill specified that the proposed Commission was to include up to 24 members, appointed by himself, that it should complete its final report two years after the legislation was passed (which would be 1972, an election year), and that it should be allocated $1.4 million. The Commission's responsibilities were to investigate:

1. The probable course of population growth, internal migration and related demographic developments between 1970 and the year 2000.
2. The resources from the public sector of the economy that will be required to deal with the anticipated growth in population.
3. The ways in which population growth may affect the activities of federal, state, and local government.
4. The impact of population growth on environmental pollution and on the depletion of natural resources.
5. 'The various means appropriate to the ethical values and principles of this society by which our Nation can achieve a population level best suited for its environmental, natural resources, and other needs'.[2]

In March 1970 the Population Bill became a law. Shortly thereafter Nixon appointed his commissioners, including two housewives, seven university professors, three foundation administrators, two senators, a corporate president, the vice-president of a large labor union, three students, and, as chairman, John D. Rockefeller, III. The group met for two or three days each month during the Commission's two-year lifetime. A staff of around 40 people (most of them part-time) did background work between Commission meetings. In its first six months of operation, the Commission defined the scope of its investigations to the point where it was ready to contract out research assignments. Thereafter it spent its time co-ordinating research activities, synthesizing research findings, and holding public hearings.

The Commission contracted about a hundred individual studies. The computer model we are considering here was the largest part of the largest single contract. It was also the Commission's dominant piece of research on economic-environment-population relationships. A computer model was not explicitly requested in the contract. The commissioners decided what specific population-environment questions they wanted answered. They further decided that Resources for the Future (henceforth referred to as RfF), a resource-orientated 'think tank' with a reputation for sober, unpartisan, and conventional analysis, would be a credible group to conduct the study. They did not, however, specify what techniques RfF was to use in its analysis. At least one person, the Commission's Executive Director, was not under the impression that RfF was going to do a mathematical model of the problem.[3]

Ronald G. Ridker, an RfF analyst, was appointed director of the Population Commission study. He had approximately one year to perform the task. He was authorized to sub-contract parts of the research, and as will subsequently be described, he did so.

B. PURPOSE

The RfF study's purpose and time horizon were defined with a precision that no other model in our case studies comes close to matching. The sponsoring body itself had a clearly designated purpose, spelled out by law. RfF was assigned to answer the fourth of the five parts of the Commission's mandate, namely to investigate the 'impact of population growth on environmental pollution and on the depletion of natural resources within the next 30 years'.[4] This purpose was even more specifically designated in the research task the Commission set for RfF. Two population growth scenarios were to be investigated: the growth patterns that would result from an average family size of two children vs. three children. The definition and means of representation of environmental pollution and natural resources were left to RfF.

C. METHOD

Observers have often noted, generally with dismay, that modelers seldom build on one another's work. The RfF model is an exception. The RfF team did not actually build a model—they revised an existing model and adapted it to their purpose. The changes made in this retrofitting process were not trivial. If one could compare the original model to a tractor, the modifications RfF made were more like transforming it into a combine than like putting up a sun umbrella. That is, the RfF additions resulted in a whole new set of processing mechanisms to accomplish a different purpose—they were not mere refinements of the existing structure. However, the basic driving unit was kept more or less intact.

RfF's original 'tractor' was Clopper Almon's inter-industry forecasting model, an input–output model* constructed in the mid-1960s to forecast behavior of the American economy from 1965 to 1975.[5] The RfF additions converted the Almon model's output, primarily dollar sales for 90 industrial sectors, into amounts of pollutants generated and quantities of resources used. The RfF team also expanded Almon's ten-year time horizon to 50 years (20 years beyond what was requested by the Commission), and by adding alternative forecasts, converted Almon's exogenous predictions of final demand from population and economic growth into scenarios dependent on family-size decisions.

Why the choice of input–output analysis as the basic technique for a long-term forecasting study? The modelers felt that detailed representation was essential for exploring the designated problem. They state:

> In this situation, aggregate analysis is of little help; indeed, it may give highly misleading results. Each sector of the economy has different resource requirements and emits different types and quantities of wastes. The effect of wastes on the environment depends on the form in which they are emitted. Moreover, the kinds of treatment possible, as well as their costs, vary between sectors and types of pollutants. Despite the fact that we are interested in an over-all assessment, disaggregation is absolutely necessary.[6]

The RfF model is indeed disaggregated. Resources are divided into nineteen mineral ores and five energy sources. Pollution is represented by one category of solid waste, seven kinds of liquid pollutants, and five kinds of gaseous emissions. The economy that generates pollutants and consumes resources is separated into 185 economic sectors.†

Almon's model, the core of the RfF model, is an attempt to use input–output analysis as a dynamic forecasting tool. There are basically two ways to convert a static input–output table to dynamic form: embed it in a dynamic simulation model, or use the table as an accounting device and drive it with a host of exogenous forecasts. Almon chose the second of these alternatives, and Ridker accepted this choice in his adaptation. Most of the RfF model's interesting and important assumptions are in its exogenous forecasts. We shall, therefore, give relatively little space here to the input–output model but instead describe at some length the method used to make exogenous forecasts.

---

* The basic characteristics of input–output analysis have been described in Chapter 2.
† We discuss here Almon's model in the 90-sector form it took when he documented it in the book, *The American Economy to 1975*. However, Almon had obtained a 185-sector input–output table by the time RfF began building on his model. Thus the RfF model, like later versions of the Almon model, contains 185 sectors.

The endogenous part of Almon's model can be described rather simply. The model's core is an input–output matrix of the United States economy disaggregated into 90 sectors. It consists of a few thousand statements noting that a change in output for any given economic sector requires a proportional change in input. All relationships between inputs and outputs are linear. There are no state variables and, consequently, no delays. The only feedback in the model comes through a set of mathematical operations that smooth out inconsistencies between exogenous forecasts. In other words, it is a typical input–output model designed to represent consistently a complicated network of interconnected flows without attempting to explain why those flows are that way, where the ultimate sources and sinks for the flows might be, or how the flows might change in response to different conditions.

To make his model move forward through time, Almon provided exogenous forecasts for population, labor productivity, employment, the technical coefficients of the production process, and a number of other such quantities. He borrowed some of his important forecasts from other models. His population forecast used the second highest of four alternative projections made by the United States Bureau of the Census. His input–output matrix was based on the one prepared by the Department of Commerce for the year 1958. Changes in the technical coefficients of this input–output matrix (i.e., predictions of the input mix required to produce a unit output) were taken from a study by Anne P. Carter and others.[7]

Almon's exogenous forecasts fall into two distinct groups. First, there are aggregate forecasts, where the thing to be predicted is one major economy-wide index. Such forecasts include average change in labor productivity, military spending, expansion of foreign trade, and percent unemployment. These forecasts are essentially derived from mental models, with little justification or reference to statistical tests. Second, there are what Almon calls 'structural forecasts', sets of technical coefficients governing each of the model's 90 sectors. Such forecasts include, for each sector, changes in consumer spending per dollar additional income, capital spending required per dollar sales expansion, labor required per dollar sales, and material required per dollar sales.

Some of these structural forecasts Almon creates for himself, accompanied by an apology 'for the limited use we have been able to make of the results of others'.[8] His forecasting techniques are diverse and flexible. As he sums it up, 'judgement, technical knowledge, and econometric research should combine in making ... forecasts. The methods needed are as various as the problem ...'.[9] Linear least-squares regressions are tried here and there, kept when they seem reasonable or when nothing better can be found, rejected when they seem unreasonable, or when something else works better.

For example, regressions were tried for factors influencing consumer demand and for determinants of investment in capital goods. For consumer demand, least-squares estimations were kept as a means of determining the effect of price, time trend, and change in price on demand, but found unsatisfactory for estimating income elasticity of demand. Here algebraic manipulation of survey (cross section) data was used to work out a weighted income elasticity. For capital goods investment, the regression results were discarded, and a complex formula was used that balances depreciation of capacity against exponential growth of technological efficiency (capacity acquired per dollar invested).[10]

To forecast changes in the labor productivity of individual sectors, Almon uses the simple technique of charting time series data for productivity onto semi-log graph paper, drawing a line through the observed data, and extending the line.[11]

Almon implies that he would like to have used approved statistical techniques throughout his analysis, but the approved techniques frequently did not produce results that satisfied his own judgement or mental model. Thus he had to piece together forecasts as best he could, balancing formal techniques with intuition until the results seemed reasonable. He is quick to point out the inadequacies in his formulations. His undertone of self-criticism, of thoughtful searching, and of hard reasoning give one the impression that he has made a well-informed, honest try and may very well have come up with the best formulations possible, given the difficulty of the task and the tools at his disposal.

In choosing to build upon this model, the RfF modelers implicitly chose the underlying assumptions of his method—an input–output core, lack of state variables or delays, absence of feedback, many exogenous driving factors, and basically linear relationships. The time horizon was expanded to 50 years, the number of sectors to 185, and some structural additions, the components of the combine, were added. The structural additions largely comprised more linear functions that converted one series of numbers into another series of numbers. For example, to determine total pollution generation, product outputs from the Almon model were multiplied by an exogenously-driven series giving pollution generation per unit output for each sector for the next 50 years.

By adapting Almon's model to a 50-year time horizon without changing its forecast-driven nature, the RfF modelers forced themselves to make an amazingly detailed series of 50-year forecasts external to the model itself and essentially based on mental models. The problems of generating these forecasts were stupendous. The coefficients for pollution generation per unit of output required forecasting thousands of technical relationships for 50 years on the basis of three to five years of sketchy data. Forecasting resource substitution (for example, substitution of polyolefins for paper and newsprint, substitution of glass fiber for steel, etc.) frequently required estimating the outcome of a process that had barely begun, or even of a process that had not yet begun.

The modelers responded to these difficulties by hiring technological forecasters to make educated guesses. RfF contracted out their studies of resource substitution and pollution generation to the International Research and Technology Corporation (henceforth IRT), a consulting company that specializes in technological forecasts. The IRT forecasters, in turn, pieced together explicit forecasts, primarily from expert mental models and known technological trends and constraints. They made systematic assumptions, such as that the best technology in 1970 will be the average by 2000,[12] and that substitution of one resource for another will follow a logistic growth trend. Statistical methods are unusable for future events about which there are no historic data. Therefore IRT shifted to estimation 'based on scattered data modified by heuristic judgement'.[13]

In choosing the method of input–output analysis buttressed by many exogenous forecasts, Ridker and the RfF team chose an efficient accounting device that gave them the detail they wanted. They also had a working model to build on, an important consideration given their one-year deadline. On the other hand, by choosing a static method, they threw the burden of the modeling work onto the exogenous 30–50 year forecasts made outside the model itself, and by insisting upon detail, they required thousands of those forecasts, each of which had to be quite precise. Ideally each forecast should be dependent upon all the others, just as the actual industrial sectors are interdependent. But the necessary consistency through time among these many forecasts depended only upon mental models; the input–output model guaranteed consistency only within each particular year of the forecast. Thus in emphasizing detail and specificity, Ridker sacrificed several other potential advantages of mathematical modeling, including internal consistency and accessibility (since the most important assumptions and modeling decisions cannot be seen in the model equations themselves). The appropriateness of this trade-off can be decided only by reference to the model purpose; it will be discussed again later in this chapter.

D. BOUNDARIES

The Population Commission presented the RfF with a sharply defined problem, and before model construction began, the study's focus was even more precisely defined. The RfF modelers were attacking a topic with almost infinite complexity, and they had but one year to produce a finished report. To meet their deadline, the modelers interpreted the problem as defined by the Commission in the narrowest possible sense.

They decided to include only such variables as are needed to link population directly to domestic pollution generation and resource usage. International aspects of the resource problem, such as the foreign sources of many fuels and minerals, were omitted.[14] Variables that might have been central to the immediate question but that, given current knowledge, were 'very difficult to link to population and economic growth in a simple and quantitative fashion',[15] were also omitted. In this latter category were, for example, fusion energy and long-lived pollutants such as nuclear wastes and heavy metals. Attitudes, political factors, over-all quality of life or quality of the environment, feedbacks and interactions among pollutants, and other such elusive factors were probably ruled out by the same criterion.

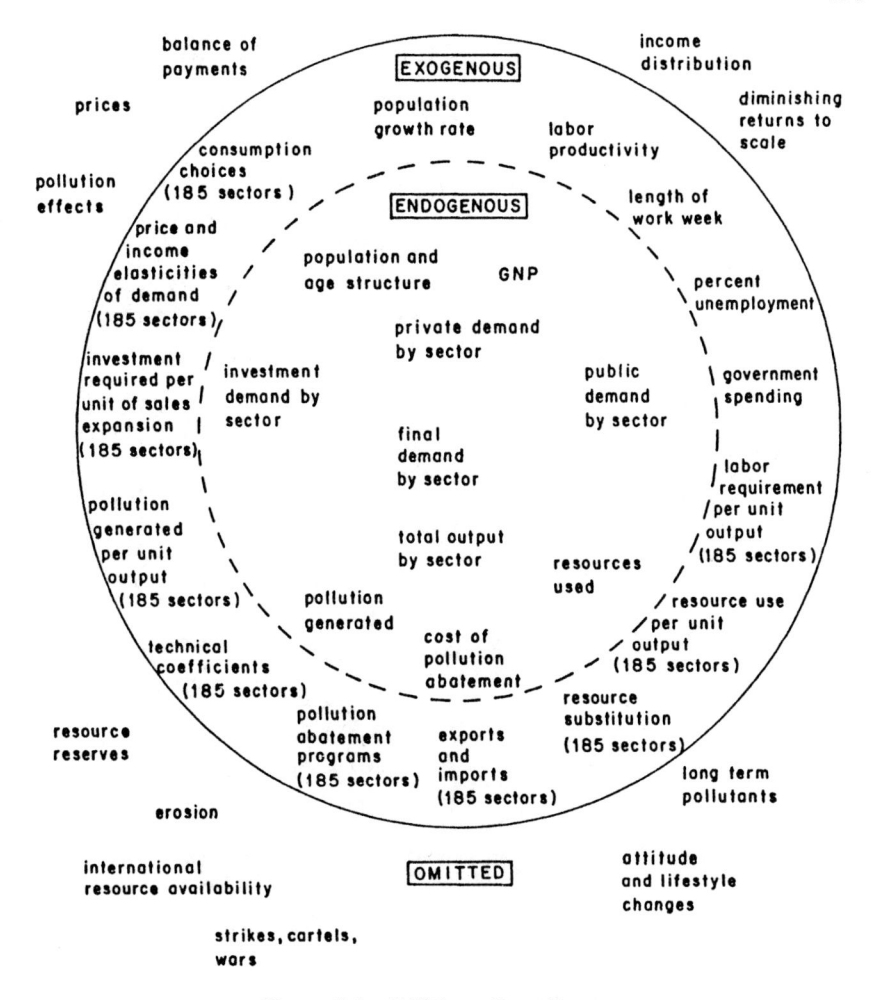

Figure 5.1 RfF boundary diagram

The model boundaries that resulted from these deliberations are shown in Figure 5.1. In order to calculate the endogenous variables, the RfF model requires forecasts of:

1. Over-all trends—population growth, economic growth, government spending.
2. How, in detail, these over-all trends will work through 185 productive sectors—time trends for consumption patterns, the ratio of resource inputs and pollution outputs per unit product outputs, and resource substitution.

Many of these forecasts entail important and hard-to-predict variables, such as the rate at which nuclear power will replace other modes of electrical generation, how automobile purchases will be related to income, and how quickly 185 industrial sectors will automate.

E. STRUCTURE

The structural elements of the Almon model—an input–output matrix combined with some heavy-duty exogenous forecasts—should by this time be clear. The calculation sequence follows a series of logical steps designed to calculate annual gross sales for each of the model's 185 industrial sectors (see Figure 5.2).

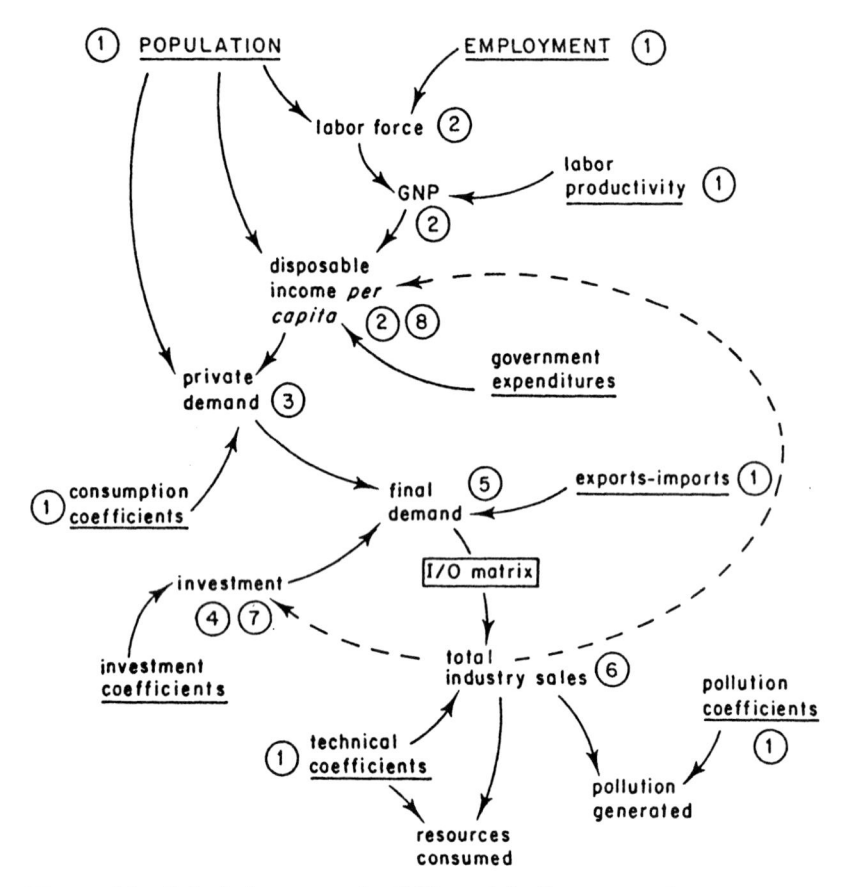

Figure 5.2 Calculation steps in RfF model. Exogenous forecasts are underlined, solid arrow (→) indicates direct calculations, dashed arrow (--→) indicates iteration to make estimates consistent

Step 1. Project the exogenous variables—population, labor productivity, government expenditures by sector, imports, exports, trends in consumption and employment, and resource, pollution, and technical coefficients—for the time horizon of the model.

Step 2. Calculate labor force from population and employment. From labor force and labor productivity, calculate GNP. GNP minus government expenditures divided by population gives disposable income *per capita*.

Step 3. From disposable income *per capita* and the structural forecast for private demand (the coefficients that relate purchases *per capita* per sector to income, time, and other variables) calculate private demand *per capita* from each industrial sector. Calculate total private demand from *per capita* demand and population.

Step 4. From a trial projection of total industry sales, calculate investment, construction spending and inventory accumulation, using coefficients from the structural forecasts. Apportion investment spending among the 185 sectors using a set of constants (Almon uses coefficients calculated in 1958 by the Bureau of Labor Statistics)[16] to get investment demand.

Step 5. Add government demand (calculated in Step 1), private demand (from Step 3) and investment, construction and inventory-related demand (from Step 4) to get final demand.

Step 6. Run final demand through the input–output matrix to get total industry sales.

Step 7. Compare the industry sales calculated in Step 6 to the trial projection of sales used to calculate investment in Step 4. If the two do not agree closely, return to and recalculate investment using the value for sales calculated in Step 6. Repeat Steps 4 through 7 until a convergent solution is reached.

Step 8. From total industry sales (Step 6) and sectoral forecasts for labor productivity (Step 1), calculate employment in various industries. Add up employment in separate industries to get total employment. If total employment agrees with the projected employment level (Step 1), calculations are complete. If not, assume government will use its power* to increase incomes in order to increase demand and thereby increase employment up to the desired level (assumed to be 4% unemployment); go back and change *per capita* income. Recalculate Steps 2–8 until employment reaches the predetermined figure.

The net result of this calculation is to convert a number of unrelated exogenous forecasts into a detailed picture of the total economic production that would necessarily result if all the forecasts actually came to be. It is an open-system accounting exercise, not a picture of the way an actual economy works. Primary attention is devoted to the way population and income shape aggregate consumer demand. It is then assumed that demand brings forth the necessary production.

The iterative procedures are mathematical devices that simply adjust investment and disposable income as residuals to make the accounting consistent for the endogenous variables. The only permissible inconsistency

---

* Presumably through taxes. No accounting is made of the costs incurred by the government in acting to increase demand.

within these variables is the difference between government expenditures and taxes (GNP minus disposable income), which is adjusted as necessary to obtain full employment, with no long-run requirement of a balanced federal budget. As Almon says: 'The concept of the full employment tax rate is something of a *deus ex machina* who appears at the end to hold the piece together'.[17]

Operationally, the RfF model is quite similar to the Almon model. It contains a few new variables—principally to render the model more sensitive to demographic influence—and requires two more steps in the model accounting sequence. Demographic sensitivity is introduced by bringing family size into the function that relates *per capita* demand to income. The two new accounting steps relate (linearly) pollution generation and resource usage to total output. Pollution generation is assumed to occur both in production and in consumption—the proportionality constant depending on the sector. Different assumptions may be made about the course of pollution generation by altering coefficients to represent abatement programs.

The addition of pollution and resources is made without inclusion of any sort of feedback. Thus it is possible for the model to use resources freely without regard to whether those resources exist. Reserves do not become depleted. Prices may rise as a result of exogenous assumptions, but not as a result of endogenous depletion. Resource substitutions may occur due to exogenously programmed changes in the technical coefficients of the input–output matrix; however, these substitutions will occur regardless of the usage of resources calculated within the model.

The reference structure diagram for the RfF model is shown in Figure 5.3. Its open structure is apparent from the diagram; as demanded by the Commission, it transforms population projections to resource-use projections through a very complex accounting procedure.

F. DATA

The 185-sector input–output matrix contains tens of thousands of technical coefficients.[18] They are derived from industry records, accounting data, and the necessary reconciliation that makes an input–output matrix internally consistent. Other numbers in the model change the input–output coefficients over time. Several sets of up to 185 coefficients each are required to break down the information that goes into the input–output matrix or convert it into desired forms as it comes out. One of these sets allocates private demand among the 185 productive sectors, another allocates government demand, a third set converts the total sales coming out of the 185 sectors into persons employed (by assuming labor productivities), a fourth determines investment in each sector from changes in output. Further numbers are required to convert production outputs into resources used and pollution generated. And, finally, there are the numbers that determine the aggregate forecasts of population growth, labor productivity, and other variables.

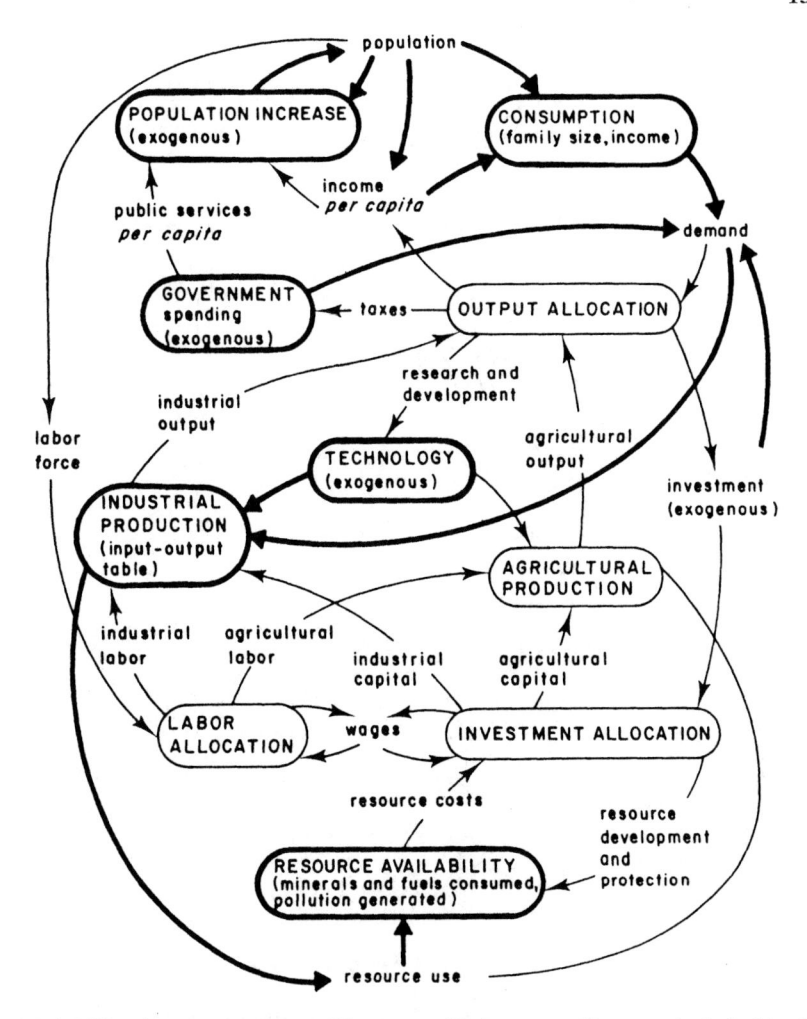

Figure 5.3 RfF reference structure. Elements with heavy outlines are included in the model; elements with light outlines are not included.

We doubt that any outside reviewer could trace the sources of all these numbers, their uncertainties, sensitivities, biases, and meanings. Some of them have a firm empirical base. The input–output coefficients were provided by the United States Bureau of Labor Statistics from actual industrial accounts from the year 1967. The time trends for the technical coefficients are much more nebulous. Almon reports spending exasperating hours trying to update a 1958 table to 1963 using his time-trend coefficients—only to find that 'time and time again the figures ... (thus obtained) failed to agree with published statistics'.[19] Though the RfF coefficients may be an improvement over Almon's, one must wonder whether they are enough of an improvement to produce reliable updates over a 30–50-year period.

The bases for other numbers are not specified and it is not clear how they were derived. For example, the coefficients that apportion export demand among sectors are not listed in either Almon's or the RfF documentation, nor are their sources identified. Pages of tables give numbers for pollutants generated in various industrial sectors and costs of pollution abatement,[20] but it is not clear which of these numbers were used to generate the project conclusions about the cost and effectiveness of pollution abatement.

In short, the processing, recording, and justification of the hundreds of thousands of numbers in the RfF model required an orderliness and effort that Ridker and his associates could not achieve within one year. Now that several years have passed since the model was last run, the modelers themselves have difficulty reconstructing the sets of numbers that were actually used, much less describing where they came from.

G. TESTING

The size of the RfF model makes testing expensive and time-consuming. The computer time required for one run of the RfF model cost $56.00 in 1972, and interpretation of a single run could easily require more than a full person-day of work.[21] Furthermore, the number of coefficients in the model presents a boundless spectrum of things to test. At one run per day, for example, it would take about six months to work through a variable-by-variable sensitivity test of just one of the many sets of 185 exogenous coefficients. The results of such tests would be incredibly difficult to interpret.

Given their time, material, and information constraints, the RfF modelers could not possibly do a complete job of model testing. An initial series of debugging tests was performed to eliminate obviously unreasonable behavior. In these tests, model output was used to locate questionable parameters. Parameters thus located were re-thought and changed if an alternative value seemed more appropriate.

No sensitivity tests were performed. Policy tests were confined to tests of the specific questions asked of RfF by the Commission, plus a few tests devoted to exploration of a pollution-abatement scenario.

The Commission's questions were explored with four scenarios:

1. High population growth—high economic growth.
2. High population growth—low economic growth.
3. Low population growth—high economic growth.
4. Low population growth—low economic growth.

'Low' population growth is equated to an average fertility of 2.1 children per woman; high population growth a total fertility of 3.1. Economic growth is varied by altering assumptions about changes in production per hour worked (labor productivity) and hours worked per laborer. High growth is equated to 2.5% gain in labor productivity each year, coupled with a reduction in hours worked of 0.24% per year. Low economic growth is represented with a 2.5% gain in labor productivity coupled with a 1% per year reduction in hours worked (resulting in a 29-hour work week by the year 2000).[22] One suspects that a *reduction* in the assumed rate of increase of labor productivity, or even a constant productivity, would have had major effects on the model's output, but this possibility was not tested.

Three pollution scenarios were tested for each of the population-growth scenarios. They were:

1. No change in the present emission levels.
2. A continuance of present trends—increasing efficiency of production leading, naturally, to reduced pollution emission levels; and
3. An active abatement policy, i.e., abatement as required to bring pollution generation down to the 1975 air and 1973 water pollution standards recommended by the Environmental Protection Agency. The model calculates the cost of such an abatement policy. However, it appears not to add that cost into the calculation of final demand or to remove it from any other consumption category.

H. CONCLUSIONS

Four types of conclusions were derived from the RfF modeling effort. First, there were the conclusions expressed by the exogenous forecasts. These conclusions were derived from technological forecasting subcontracts, expert opinion, and other mental models. They are consistently optimistic, assuming a steady, smooth substitution of more abundant resources for scarce ones, increasing abatement of pollution, and exponentially growing labor productivity. Bottlenecks, strikes, embargoes, depressions, droughts, failures of the price mechanism, and interruptions in technological advance are not included in the model or tested as possibilities.

Second, there are the conclusions literally present in the model output. These include conditional forecasts of how many resources would be used and how much pollution generated by 185 productive sectors, given the assumptions in the model's structure, the two-child, three-child scenarios, and the forecasts just described. These conclusions are occasionally problematic, if model output is taken literally. For example, under the high population growth–high economic growth assumptions, the model forecasts that the United States will have consumed 206 million tons of copper and 2.16 million tons of tungsten between 1968 and 2020. These amounts are equivalent to two-thirds of the world's 1970 known reserves of copper and over 150% of the world's 1970 known tungsten reserves (more than two-thirds of which are in the People's Republic of China).[23]

Few of the RfF model's literal conclusions are published. This is to be expected. A complete output for just one run would consist of hundreds of pages of numbers and would probably take more space than all the final RfF model documentation put together. Many of the raw output figures are almost meaningless except in the perspective of general-trend information. For example, it is of little use to know that X pounds of sulfur dioxide will be produced in 1991 under scenario 2 without knowing how that pollution production figure compares to present production or to production under another scenario.

A refined and edited version of the raw output is presented in the model documentation. This is the third set of conclusions—the conclusions that Ridker and his associates have drawn from the model by deciding what parts of the output to believe or not to believe, to report or not to report, to highlight as important or to ignore. In some cases, the modeler's conclusions originated directly from the model output. For example, model output clearly indicates that resource usage and pollution generation are more responsive to economic growth than they are to population growth. The modelers explain why this is so: 'Since a fall in population size is associated with an increase in GNP *per capita*, the effect of the decreased numbers (in the low population growth scenario) is partially offset by the greater income, and hence higher consumption'.[24] In other cases, the modelers' conclusions are explanations of why model output should not be taken literally. For example, the RfF report to the Commission notes that, according to the model, world resource reserves will not be adequate to meet needs for ten of the 19 minerals studied. The report goes on to say that 'modest price increases would bring in supplies from potential reserves, probably beyond what requirements call for ... for some minerals, while other apparent inadequacies will be met by substitution'.[25] In all, however, the report concludes 'that there is no serious reason to believe that projected standards of living cannot be met because of mineral or fuel shortages. Adjustments will be necessary, but none of them are likely to entail significant loss in material welfare during the next half century'.[26] This conclusion does not follow directly from the model but from the mental models of the modelers telling them to reject certain aspects of the computer model output.

The RfF team's major conclusion is that population growth does have a generally negative effect on the society, and therefore a slow population growth rate would be preferable to a rapid one:

> If ... we choose to have more rather than less children per family ... we commit ourselves to a particular package of problems: more rapid depletion of domestic and international resources, greater pressures on the environment, more dependence on continued rapid technological development to solve these problems, fewer social options and, perhaps, the continued postponement of the resolutions of other social problems, including those resulting from past growth ...
> If we choose to have fewer children per family, leading to a stable population within the next 50 to 75 years, we purchase time, resources, and additional options: time to overcome our ignorance and to redress the mistakes of past growth, resources to implement solutions, and additional freedom of choice in deciding how we want to live in the future.[27]

Although these same conclusions apply even more to economic growth, RfF is more reluctant to call for a slowdown in the growth of economic output:

> Similar consequences could emerge from the choice open to us with respect to alternative rates of economic growth. Indeed, the numerical analysis ... indicates that a reduction in economic growth would reduce resource consumption and pollution emissions by more than would a comparable reduction in population growth. But growth in the economy can be utilized for different ends than it is put to now. While it adds to problems that need solution, it also adds to capacity to solve problems. It is difficult to find similar offsetting advantages from additional population growth at this stage in United States history.[28]

Neither RfF nor the Population Commission chose to investigate further the ways the economy 'can be utilized for different ends than it is put to now'. Instead, the focus of the study remained on the effects of population growth. The overwhelming impression the RfF documentation gives is that the problems of population growth are not particularly urgent, threatening, or unsolvable:

> The study ... can be interpreted as saying that if some costs are paid and some adjustments made, no catastrophe is likely to result from continued growth during the next half-century. Indeed, at least as far as the United States is concerned, the results are fairly sanguine. We appear to have the resources and the know-how both to continue growing and to cope with the problems of that growth, if we are willing to adjust our lifestyles a bit. This is not to say that there will be no serious shortages during the next 50 years, but that these shortages are unlikely to arise solely as a consequence of population and economic growth.[29]

Fourth and finally, there are the conclusions that the Population Commission arrived at due to the RfF model's influence. It appears that the Commission members interpreted model results in accord with their own understanding of the population problem rather than listening carefully to the modelers' conclusions. For example, in the Commissioner's report to the President and Congress, the population-environment relationship is outlined as follows:

1. Population growth is one of the major factors affecting the demand for resources and the deterioration of the environment in the United States ...
2. From an environmental and resource point of view, there are no advantages from further growth of population beyond the level to which our past rapid growth has already committed us. Indeed, we would be considerably better off over the next 30 to 50 years if there were a prompt reduction in our population growth rate...
3. With continued growth, we commit ourselves to a particular set of problems: more rapid depletion...of resources, (and) greater pressure on the environment.[30]

The model's conclusion that economic growth pressures the environment more than does population growth is forgotten in the above statement. What is remembered is that population growth has an effect, which was indeed a model finding, but not the only one or the most significant one.

I. IMPLEMENTATION

The Commission seemed to be in a favorable position to implement policies resulting from the RfF model or any of its other contracted studies. The Commission included many powerful figures, including leaders of government, industry, labor, and academia. Moreover, the Commission was in the public eye—its findings were reported on the front page of *The New York Times*, on television, in film, and in a widely distributed paperback book.

There were, however, some problems that interfered with this seemingly favorable implementation position. The Commission on Population Growth and the American Future recommended, as one of hundreds of specific suggestions, that abortion laws be liberalized. On March 17, 1972, in the heat of the primaries for the presidential campaign, headlines across the country reported that a presidential commission had come out in favor of abortion. President Nixon thereupon went out of his way to disown and discredit the Commission. And despite the Commission's attempt to keep things in perspective, the abortion issue loomed large in the popular image of the Commission, overshadowing its many other findings.

RfF did not rely on the Commission alone to publicize the model findings. Ridker summarized the model's results in several academic articles and in Congressional testimony.[31]

The United States still has no formal population policy and no apparent interest in one, although some specific Commission recommendations have been adopted, primarily through agents other than the President (the Supreme Court in the case of abortion). Several other nations established population commissions at that time, some of them patterned directly after the U.S. one.

Ridker became fascinated with the basic question of the impact of population and economic growth on resource availability. He reasoned that the poor countries of the world might have worse resource problems than the U.S., and so he managed to stimulate and find funds for similar studies in India, Colombia, and Indonesia. He himself did not work on these studies, nor did they follow his modeling method. The *question* behind his model lives on, not the model itself.

Ridker himself was dissatisfied with the analytical shortcuts he had taken to meet the Commission's schedule. He found funding to do the whole study again at Resources for the Future with a broader scope and more time to work. He began with an even more complex model called SEAS that had been developed at the Environmental Protection Agency (partially under the direction of Peter House, one of the makers of the SOS model to be described next) and adapted it to his own purposes. The study was foundation-supported and had no specific policy client.[32]

J. DOCUMENTATION

The RfF team was hired to answer a specific question, not to develop a computer model. Although the Commission did accept the model as a means of study, it did not see the model as a piece of technical workmanship requiring detailed documentation. There is no sign that the modelers were asked for anything more than a general explanation of how the thing worked. Indeed, two basic pieces of the model's documentation[33] were published only at the request of the director of the RfF study. Moreover, the group was hard-pressed to construct and test their model in the year allotted to them to complete the study. They could not be expected to find time for detailed documentation.

Three works describing the RfF model, or parts of it, have been written. One is a description of the changes required to make the model's demand function more sensitive to family size.[34] One is a two-part report prepared by analysts at International Research and Technology Corporation describing the technological forecasting process that determined the technical coefficients of the input–output matrix and the coefficients that relate pollution to sales output.[35] The third is the general model description included in the eight-volume series published by the Commission.[36]

The former two documents are carefully detailed descriptions of substudies. The third is a broad, general description of the model that gives an impression of what is in the model but does not come close to the completeness needed for critical evaluation. By adding Almon's book to the list of documentation, one obtains a sort of co-ordinating hub from which one can begin to piece together an understanding of how the model represents the world.

The model's equations are not published in any form. The exogenous inputs used to drive the model are not systematically described, indeed some of them are never described. An impression of the model's structure cannot be gained without referring to Almon's documentation of his model. And one cannot find exactly how the RfF model differs from the model Almon documented in his book. Crucial details of model output are not presented. For example, the figures for consumption of energy resources are not printed, making it impossible to check the evidence behind the statement in the Commission's report that: 'Whether population growth will strain fuel supplies, or cause serious environmental damage in the process of acquiring and processing the necessary fuels, depends on future developments in technology'.[37]

In short, the RfF modelers managed within a year to complete a tremendously complex model and to describe it in a literate, qualitative, non-technical report. They did not manage to document the model technically, to publish its equations, or even to keep careful internal records of their work. They themselves could not now repeat the model runs upon which their conclusions were based.

NOTES AND REFERENCES

1. U.S. Code Congressional and Administrative News, *91st Congress, Second*

Session, 1970: Laws and Legislative History, St. Paul, Minn., West Publishing Company, pp. 2542–2543, 1971.
2. *Ibid.*, pp. 2540–2541.
3. Conversation with Charles Westoff, Executive Director of the Commission on Population Growth and the American Future.
4. U.S. Code Congressional and Administrative News, *op.cit.*, PL 91–213, p. 2541.
5. Described in C. Almon, Jr., *The American Economy to 1975: An Interindustry Forecast*, New York, Harper & Row, 1966.
6. U.S. Commission on Population Growth and the American Future, *Population Resources and the Environment*, R. G. Ridker, Editor, Vol. III of Commission research reports, Washington, D.C., Government Printing Office, p. 37, 1972.
7. C. Almon, *op.cit.*, pp. 110, 120.
8. *Ibid.*, p. 14.
9. *Ibid.*, p. 13.
10. *Ibid.*, pp. 55–60.
11. For full description, *Ibid.*, pp. 39–41.
12. R. G. Ridker, *op.cit*, p. 47.
13. R. U. Ayres, S. Noble and D. Overly, *Effects of Technological Change on, and Environmental Implications of an Input–Output Analysis for the United States, 1967-2020, Part 1; Technological Change as an Explicit Factor of Economic Growth*, prepared for Resources for the Future by International Research and Technology Corporation, Washington D.C., IRT-219-R/I, December 1971.
14. R. G. Ridker, personal communication.
15. R. G. Ridker, *Population, Resources and the Environment*, The Commission on Population Growth and the American Future Research Reports, No. 3, United States Government Printing Office, p. 25, 1972.
16. C. Almon, *op.cit.*, p. 16.
17. *Ibid.*, p. 17.
18. There are doubtless many zero coefficients in the matrix. The total number of technical coefficients, thus, is probably somewhat below the 34,225 required for a full 185 by 185 matrix.
19. C. Almon, *op.cit.*, p. 134.
20. L. Ayres, I. Gutmanis, and A. Shapanka, *Effects of Technological Change On, and Environmental Implications of an Input–Output Analysis for the United States, 1967-2020, Part II, Environmental Implications of Technological and Economic Change*, prepared for Resources for the Future by International Research and Technology Corporation, Washington, D.C., IRT-229-R/I, December 1970.
21. R. G. Ridker, personal communication.
22. R. G. Ridker, *op.cit.*, p. 21, pp. 47–48. Ridker points out that the assumptions about productivity and work-week could be interchanged (i.e., a constant work week but differing productivity growth rates) with no change in the model results.
23. Calculated from Tables 1 and 2 of Chapter 4, R. G. Ridker, *op.cit.*, pp. 83–85 and 87–88.
24. R. G. Ridker, *op.cit.*, p. 45.
25. *Ibid.*, p. 23.
26. *Ibid.*, p. 24.
27. *Ibid.*, p. 19.
28. *Ibid.*, p. 19.
29. R. G. Ridker, 'To Grow or not to Grow: That's not the Relevant Question', *Science*, **182**, p. 1315, 28 December 1973.
30. Commission on Population Growth and the American Future, *Population and the American Future*, New York, Signet, p. 56, 1972.
31. R. G. Ridker, 'To Grow or not to Grow: That's not the Relevant Question', *Science*, 28 December 1973, **182**, pp. 1315–1318; J. L. Fisher and R. G. Ridker,

'Population Growth, Resource Availability and Environmental Quality', *American Economic Review*, May 1973, **LXIII**, No. 2; R. G. Ridker, 'Resource and Amenity Implications of Population Changes', *Population and Economic Policy*, May 1974, **64**, No. 2; Testimony before the Subcommittee on Priorities and Economy in Government of the Joint Economic Committee, U.S. Congress, R. G. Ridker, December 20, 1973.
32. R. G. Ridker, personal communication.
33. R. U. Ayres, *et al.*, *op.cit*, L. Ayres, *et al.*, *op.cit.*
34. H. W. Herzog, Jr., A Method for Recognizing 'Demographic Specific' Family Expenditure Pattern Shifts in Long-Run Personal Consumption Functions, RfF working paper.
35. R. U. Ayres, *et al.*, *op.cit.*, L. Ayres, *et al.*, *op.cit.*
36. R. G. Ridker, 1972, *op.cit.*
37. Commission on Population Growth and the American Future, *op.cit.*, p.60.

CHAPTER 6

SOS: the Perfectly-Adjusting Society

A. INSTITUTIONAL SETTING

The State of the System model (SOS) was developed by Peter House and Edward Williams, originally under the sponsorship of the United States Environmental Protection Agency (EPA). The impetus for the model came from House, an EPA employee, who wanted to demonstrate the usefulness of computer models as policy tools and as ways to explore the linkages between environmental systems and social systems.

The EPA assigned House to develop a prototype model, and he contracted with Williams, then employed at Chase, Rosen, and Wallace (CRW), to collaborate with him. Within eight months they had produced SOS-1, which was documented as an official EPA report.[1] At that point the EPA cut back sharply on socioeconomic modeling efforts and SOS funding stopped. (However, a 'lesser-risk' model[2] SEAS, patterned after the RfF study previously described, was pursued under EPA sponsorship.)

House and Williams (who by then had left CRW and joined EPA) continued to work on the model as a low-priority staff study in addition to their regular duties. With the approval of EPA officials but without strong support, they continued to develop the model as time was available. The final report on the improved model SOS-2 was published by the two modelers as a book.[3] The manuscript of the book was prepared after both House and Williams had left EPA.

The EPA tolerated the SOS modeling effort and gave it initial support. However, it would be an exaggeration to say that the EPA was either a sponsor or a client of SOS. Neither the financial commitment implicit in the word 'sponsor' nor the recognized need for a model implicit in the word 'client' are present in the EPA–SOS relationship. SOS was a 'hobby model', analyst-generated and designed primarily to convince skeptical government agencies that modeling could be used to gain insight into problems of environmental management.

B. PURPOSE

In the foreword to the SOS book House and Williams present their view of the environmental debate. They observe that:

1. Since the day of Malthus doom has recurrently been foretold by students of the 'dismal school'.
2. The dooms foretold have not come to pass, societies have repeatedly adjusted to or overcome the problems associated with growth.
3. Malthusian ideas are again in vogue; 'suggestions are legion that we shall either suffer the fate of a wastrel in terms of one or more of our resources or we shall perish in our own waste'.[4]
4. 'Many of the efforts on limits analysis have turned out to be a mixture of pet theories, poorly tied partial conceptualizations and overly gross approximations of the total system'.[5]
5. Despite the ability of social systems to alter and evade physical limits, these limits do exist and should be taken into account in long-term planning.

The State of the System model is intended to communicate an alternate theory of the interplay between human society and physical limits, a theory that includes other adaptation mechanisms besides a deliberate slowdown of population and capital growth. House and Williams also seem to envision SOS as a conceptual base from which policy models can be built. They remark on the need for holistic planning and question whether the currently-used 'extrapolation or trend-continuance paradigm' is an adequate tool for the planner. They believe that computer simulation models would do well in cases where trend-extrapolation fails. As for their model, they speak of 'the use of a system such as this model to compare alternative scenarios of our national goal statements'. However, the SOS modelers do not assert that SOS, in its present form, is ready for use as a policy tool. They do propose that it be used as a teaching and research tool.[6]

In short, the purpose of SOS is the acquisition and communication of general understanding about economic–environmental interactions. The model is intended to demonstrate, by virtue of the insights it generates, that computer modeling is an essential tool in long-term policy-making. These are basically academic reasons for making a model, far removed from the immediate demands of any real policy client. SOS is primarily a device to satisfy the intellectual interests and personal goals of the analysts and to interest policymakers in the long-term implications of current decisions.

C. METHOD

SOS is a simulation model, strongly influenced by the basic concepts of cybernetics and general systems theory, but not adhering to any particular modeling paradigm. No statistical estimation procedures are evident, and economic elements are not represented according to classic theory. Input–output matrices and optimization procedures are not used. Although feedback relationships are present, no attempt is made to attribute model behavior to feedback processes, and little emphasis is placed on time delays or non-linearities. If any paradigm can be discerned as a guiding influence on the model, it would be that of ecology. The model documentation cites the Lotka–Volterra population growth model[7] and quotes from C. S. Holling, a prominent ecological modeler,[8] suggesting that House and Williams are familiar with the ecological modeling literature.

Perhaps it would be best to describe the model as a general, state-determined simulation model, constructed around ideas largely but not entirely derived from ecology. The method is unstereotyped. The modelers appear to have taken each process and asked 'how best could we represent this?', rather than relying on traditional formulations. As a result, each model relationship is fresh and experimental. As might be expected in such a large, innovative effort, some parts of the model are clever and insightful, others are far-fetched, awkward, or unclear.

One of the clearest influences on the model's formulation and documentation is the FORTRAN computer language. In a typical FORTRAN program, many relationships are expressed as if-then statements leading to on-off behavior, rather than gradual non-linear shifts from one type of behavior to another. FORTRAN is also a categorical language, designed to keep track of and manipulate long lists of one or two dimensions (vectors and matrices). Though nothing in FORTRAN prohibits working with aggregate variables, the language is so efficient in handling things in groups and categories that disaggregation becomes simple and natural.

SOS exemplifies both of these FORTRAN traits. If-then thinking dominates the model. The system responds to changes by switching behavior abruptly at threshold points. For instance, recycling programs or resource substitutions are suddenly turned on when a resource falls below a preprogrammed depletion point. Disaggregated categorical thinking so prevails that virtually all model variables are disaggregated and all model processes occur through multiple interactions among many variables, accomplished mathematically by manipulating matrices.

Apart from showing the marks of FORTRAN, SOS has the following mathematical properties. It includes many state variables, such as population, capital, and resource reserves, which accumulate past system changes. Many processes are regulated by constant or semi-constant coefficients (semi-constant in the sense that the coefficients remain constant until the system passes some discrete threshold, whereupon the coefficients are adjusted up or down by some constant proportion of their value). A few explicit time delays are included, and many delays are implicit in the model's state variables. There are some non-linearities in the system. Everything in the SOS-2 model is literally a function of everything else—the system is completely closed.

SOS is intended to be a perfectly general structure that could represent any nation or region, given the appropriate numerical parameters. The specific version described by House and Williams, SOS-2, is calibrated to depict the United States.

D. BOUNDARIES

The model is designed to simulate long-term events; SOS-2 runs from 1970 to the year 2000. More recent extensions allow the model to be run up to 2020.

In the SOS model the nation or region is subdivided into four conceptual sectors (hereafter referred to as 'sets'). The interactions among these sets are the focus of the model. The four sets are

1. Human population.
2. Resources.
3. Economic production.
4. Societal adjustment mechanisms.

Human population is influenced by birth, aging, death, migration, changes in occupational attributes, and various service requirements. Resources occur in the form of reserves that increase or are depleted. Some resources are replenished annually, some may be recycled, some may be replaced by substitutes. Economic production is subject to consumer demands and requires funds, capital, maintenance, new investment, resources, pollution cleanup, and imports and exports. The adjustment mechanisms sum up system attributes such as food *per capita* or air quality, compare those attributes with a standard, and try to adjust the system to bring it up to the standard.

All the variables in the model are endogenous (see Figure 6.1). The only exogenous inputs are the coefficients that specify switches and standards. For example, the minimum acceptable levels of economic output must be specified, and the various resource mixes that can be intersubstituted. These coefficients look somewhat similar to the ones required for the RfF model, but there is an important difference. In RfF the values of the coefficients were specified at the outset for 50 years into the future; these coefficients completely determined the behavior of the model system. In SOS the coefficients only indicate what resource mix or labor supply or pollution generation pattern might prevail, depending on happenings in the simulated system. Rather than stating how much copper will be needed per unit of manufactured output in the year 1990, for instance, SOS coefficients will state how much copper will be needed per unit of manufactured output in any year if the copper cost exceeds X while copper-substitute costs remain below Y.

The amount of detail included in the model can easily be adjusted by increasing or decreasing the number of entries in each set. For example, the model could accommodate ten resources or a hundred. The only difference between the two would be that the hundred-resource version would require longer lists of input data and would generate more detailed output. SOS-2, the demonstration model of the United States, provides a moderate-to-high

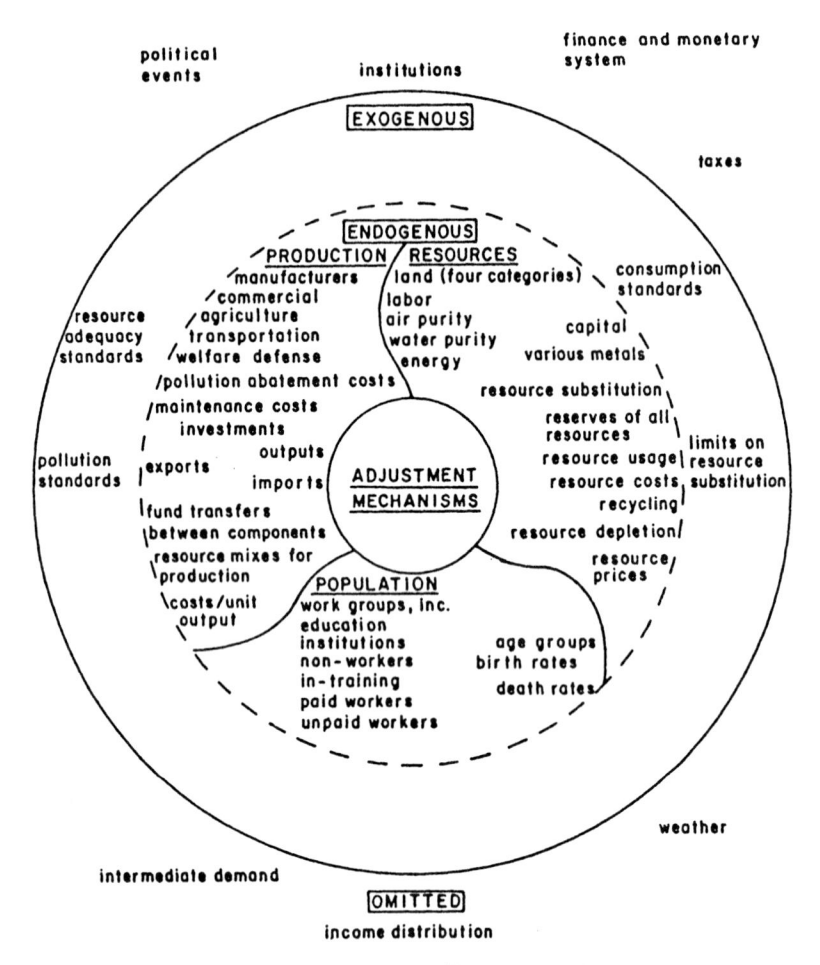

Figure 6.1 Boundary diagram for SOS

degree of detail: 18 resources, twelve production sectors, 24 population groups, and twelve demand standards are included.

Conspicuously absent from the model are any interruptions of the mechanistic system adjustments. Pollution abatement is automatic, although it may take a few years to be fully implemented. Funds are smoothly shifted between system components according to component need. There is no delay, bias or error in the system's perception of a pollution or resource problem, no political haggling, and no suboptimal adjustment for the benefit of special interest groups. The only cost associated with system adjustment is the cost of capital expansion.

Also absent from SOS-2 are destruction of renewable resources from overuse, and any influences on the system from the world outside its boundaries. Erosion, international resource depletion, war, balance-of-payments problems, and weather all are excluded. Though some index of income distribution could perhaps be derived from the model, income distribution is not included explicitly.

The geographic locations of resources are not considered in SOS-2. Resource stocks are defined without distinction between domestic resources and imports. Depending on the parameters chosen, the system may either have access to all world resources or only to its domestic resources. In either case, the question of exogenous influences on resource availability is avoided.

E. STRUCTURE

One might liken the SOS structure to the arrangement of feedback mechanisms in the human body. In the body the brain supervises by higher-level feedback a group of partially self-regulatory subsystems, the organs. In SOS the brainlike adjustment mechanism checks out the relative performance of the system's parts, and on the basis of perfect information about the entire system, directs the parts in such a way as to keep the whole in good health.

In other words, SOS's four sets are arranged in a feedback hierarchy. The three sets in the lower level of this hierarchy—population, production, and resources—are each subdivided into a number of parts and are each partially regulated by feedback within the set. The higher level of the feedback hierarchy is occupied by the adjustment mechanisms that note the relative states of the 'lower' sets and make adjustments to correct for 'undesirable' states. These lower and higher feedback sets are based on markedly different kinds of information about social systems. The three lower level sets represent relatively clear physical processes, such as production, investment, pollution generation, resource usage, and human reproduction. The adjustment set represents intangible processes such as perception, social adaptation, goal-setting, technical advance, and value change.

In reviewing the structure of SOS we shall first describe its three 'organs' and their operational rules and then describe how the model's 'brain' functions.

1. Population

Population in SOS changes through births, deaths, and migration. Each of these processes occurs at a rate proportional to the population size, thus the system includes the normal population feedback loops as shown in Figure 6.2. The proportionality coefficients that determine the rates of birth, death, and migration come from the model's brain, according to what the brain perceives about the state of the system.

Age structure is modeled by breaking the population down into age cohorts and apportioning births, deaths, and migrations among the cohorts. Within cohorts, population is further divided into consumption 'partitions', used to calculate demand for productive output. In SOS-2 these partitions include population in education, in institutions, unemployed, and in paid and unpaid labor. The population is distributed among these partitions according to linear

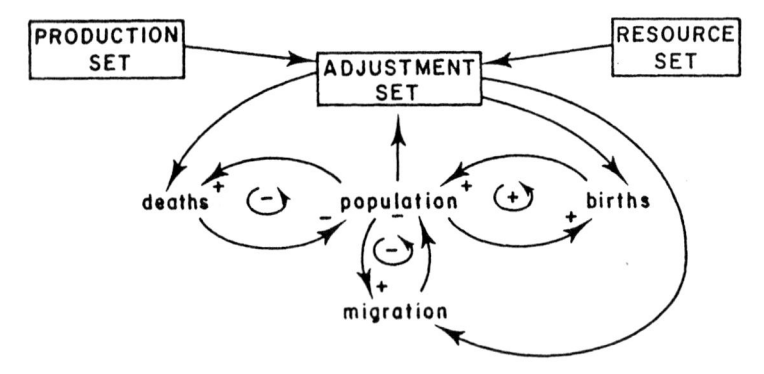

Figure 6.2 SOS population set feedback structure

functions of the previous year's outputs of the various productive sectors. Thus if the education output increases, more population can be accommodated in education; if the manufacturing outputs increase, more population is shifted to paid labor. If the number of workers in the total labor force is not sufficient to fill the total labor demand, each productive sector receives a proportionate fraction of its labor need; no productive sector has preferential access to labor.

2. Production

In SOS economic production takes place in twelve production sectors: five public sectors (education, transportation, health and welfare, public safety, and administration) and seven private sectors (agriculture, non-durable manufacturing, durable manufacturing, communication and transportation, wholesale-retail trade, services, and mining). The same mathematical structure is used to represent all twelve production sectors. Sector differences are created by tailoring data and coefficients to create variations of the basic form. For example, high resource-use coefficients would be used in the durable manufacturing sector, while relatively low coefficients would be used for education.

Each sector produces a number of output units equal to the funds spent in that sector for production, divided by cost per unit output (see Figure 6.3). Cost per unit output depends on resource usage per unit output (dependent on relative availability and substitutability, as modulated by the adjustment set) and on cost per unit resource used. 'Resources' include not only raw materials, but also capital and labor. The cost per unit of resource is calculated in the resource set, as a function of resource scarcity, which is itself determined by the effect of past production on resource reserves.

The assumptions that determine the funds available for production in each economic sector are difficult to unravel from the model documentation. The production set description is incomplete and seems to differ in the chapters describing the generalized model SOS and the specific model SOS-2. As far as

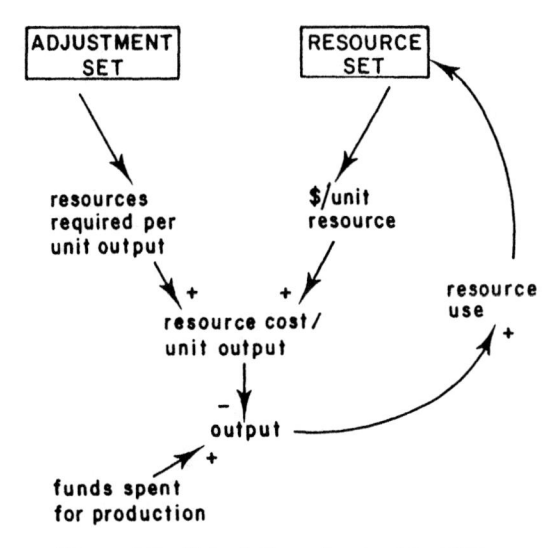

Figure 6.3 Calculation of output in SOS

we can tell, the funds available to each sector grow exponentially, with a growth rate that is dependent upon consumer demand (from the population set) and also dependent upon alterations from the adjustment set. All of the funds available to a sector cannot be used for productive output, some must be set aside for a set of activities called maintenance.

Maintenance costs are divided into three categories. One category is normal maintenance costs, calculated as a function of the capital stock in place. Another accounts for investment in expansion of production. The third is pollution cleanup costs. The costs of normal maintenance and pollution control are direct functions of output. Expansion cost is a function of *change* in output over highest previous annual output. The costs of all three processes are summed and subtracted from the funds available for production.

Thus exponential growth in output is the normal behavior assumed in SOS, but this growth can be slowed or interrupted by several events—by reduction in demand due to demographic factors, by intervention from the adjustment set (to be described later), by increased maintenance costs, or by increased resource costs, or, of course, by some combination of all these.

3. Resources

The SOS resource set keeps tabs on physical quantities (as opposed to monetary values) of things that are used in production, including land, labor, capital, mineral resources, energy resources, clean air, and clean water. In addition to accounting for resource quantities, the resource set also calculates resource costs and passes cost information on to the production set. Different dynamic processes are ascribed to resources according to whether or not they are renewable, whether they can be recycled, and whether or not they depreciate. Special attributes are assigned to labor due to its obvious dependence on population.

The general structure of the resource set describes many possible resource processes and uses zero coefficients to block out processes that do not apply to particular resources. For example, recycling mechanisms are included in the general structure. For resources such as fossil fuels that cannot be recycled, the recycling part of the program is de-activated by setting the fraction recycled always equal to zero. Renewable resources such as water are fully restored to their initial values each year; they cannot be overused or destroyed. Non-renewable resources have a zero annual restoration rate.

A much simplified diagram of the general dynamic mechanism for all resources is shown in Figure 6.4. The resource set takes in information about resource usage from the production set, calculates the effect on reserves, and passes on information about the state of resource availability to the adjustment set. This then adjusts any deficit caused by overuse through expansion of reserves, cost increases, substitution, or recycling.

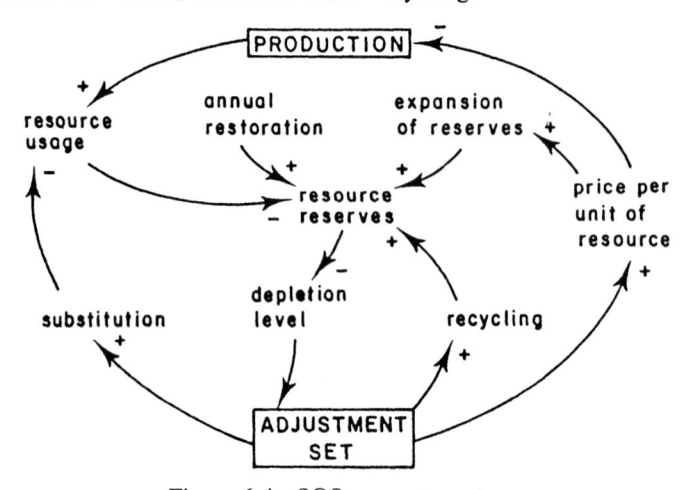

Figure 6.4 SOS resource sector

Computationally this general representation of structurally diverse resources is very efficient. Efficient communication within the computer, however, does not always lead to clarity for human beings. Trying to follow the concrete assumptions in the treatment of specific resources quite literally boggles the mind because each separate resource is buried within the coding of the general process. For example, if one wanted to learn about the model's treatment of copper, one would find that the numbers related to copper are somewhere within long data tables listing for all resources:

1. Initial reserves.
2. The possibility of substituting other resources.

3. The degree to which price increases can increase reserves.
4. The extent to which production mix modification can eliminate the need for each resource.
5. How much resource will be recycled under what circumstances.
6. The effect of depletion on price.
7. The speed at which substitution, reserve expansion, and development of recycling can progress.

All these factors are indeed reasonable to include in a resource model. But the exact numbers for how much copper can be recycled, or to what extent and at what price aluminum can be substituted for copper must be fairly important and debatable model assumptions. Checking up on the actual numbers that regulate these processes for the case of copper as opposed to petroleum or land or water requires a search through the model's unindexed and poorly-substantiated data descriptions. Even after locating the data, one would find some important structural questions unanswered. For example, the text implies that recycling and expansion of resource reserves costs something, but does not tell if and how these costs are accounted for in the model's structure.

4. Adjustment set

As we have said, SOS superimposes a higher stratum of control onto the causal mechanisms of the population, production, and resource sets. This higher-level control is qualitatively different from the feedback within sets. The feedback within sets describes gradual, automatic, ongoing processes such as growth, maintenance, and deterioration. By contrast, the higher-order feedback processes, which the authors term 'system adjustments', are discrete, non-continuous processes set off by flags and warning lights. Their operation is conditional: if resource R goes below such and such a level, adjustment number one goes into operation. If resource R drops below a second level, adjustment number two begins. If demand satisfaction for product M goes below the M threshold, then the system attempts to shift more funds to the sector that produces M.

The triggering mechanisms that activate system adjustments are of two sorts: demand satisfaction and resource depletion. The adjustments triggered by resource depletion are fairly straightforward. When a warning light goes on, signifying that reserves are low for some resource, the cost for the resource rises, the system looks for a cost-competitive substitute for the resource, and at the same time, if possible, reserves are expanded. Environmental quality standards are also included in the mechanism; clean air and water are modeled as resources that can be 'depleted' by pollution.

The adjustment triggered by unsatisfied demand is an innovative piece of modeling based on a cybernetic theory of social adjustment. If output *per capita* of some product falls below the demand standard, the system tries a series of measures designed to alleviate the problem. If any measure succeeds, system adjustments stop until the problem recurs or some other problem triggers another adjustment mechanism. The adjustment steps begin with short-term measures, such as deferring capital maintenance for a year and spending net export balances to make up the deficit. If short-term measures do not work, long-term measures are tried in the following order:

1. The resource mix used to generate a unit of output is shifted to cut costs.
2. Funds are shifted from production sectors that have surplus to the sectors that are not meeting demand.
3. If unemployment is high, out-migration is increased (or in-migration decreased).
4. If all else fails, demand standards are decreased. The demand adjustment can also work in reverse; if production overfills demand, the standards are gradually raised.

The adjustment process is represented optimistically. Production costs can be cut without a decrease in consumer satisfaction: maintenance can be deferred without a loss of productivity. Adjustments start promptly as the situation calls for them, although they may take time to complete. Previously-used resources are still available for recycling. Reductions in demand occur with no social trauma, and there is no discussion of how these reductions are distributed across the population.

The Reference Structure diagram for SOS-2 is shown in Figure 6.5. SOS covers the entire structure in one way or another, with some interesting twists. Government is represented not as a drain on output, but as a productive sector in its own right, competing for resources and attempting to meet consumption demand for public services. If the adjustment set is located anywhere on this diagram, it is in the 'output allocation' position, where it shifts funds among productive sectors, raises or lowers demand standards, and directs technology (though apparently at no cost).

Over-all the SOS structure portrays a culture with an inherent propensity to grow and consume. Positive feedback loops drive both the population and production sectors. However, as growth begins to stress resource limits, the model system adapts—first by becoming more efficient in its use of resources and by shifting its usage patterns to stress more plentiful resources, second by reducing consumption and population growth. The adjustment mechanism is modeled as an all-seeing, all-powerful central government, rather than a series of decentralized and suboptimal personal adjustment decisions. It is assumed that information is instantaneously and accurately available throughout the system; each set, including the controlling adjustment set, knows exactly and in detail what is happening elsewhere. For example, thresholds are set so that resource-conserving reactions set in when a resource is 50% depleted, but the question of how anyone might know when a resource is 50% depleted is never raised. If such a model can impart any useful message about real social systems, it must be a picture of how a perfectly controlled society would behave, if it

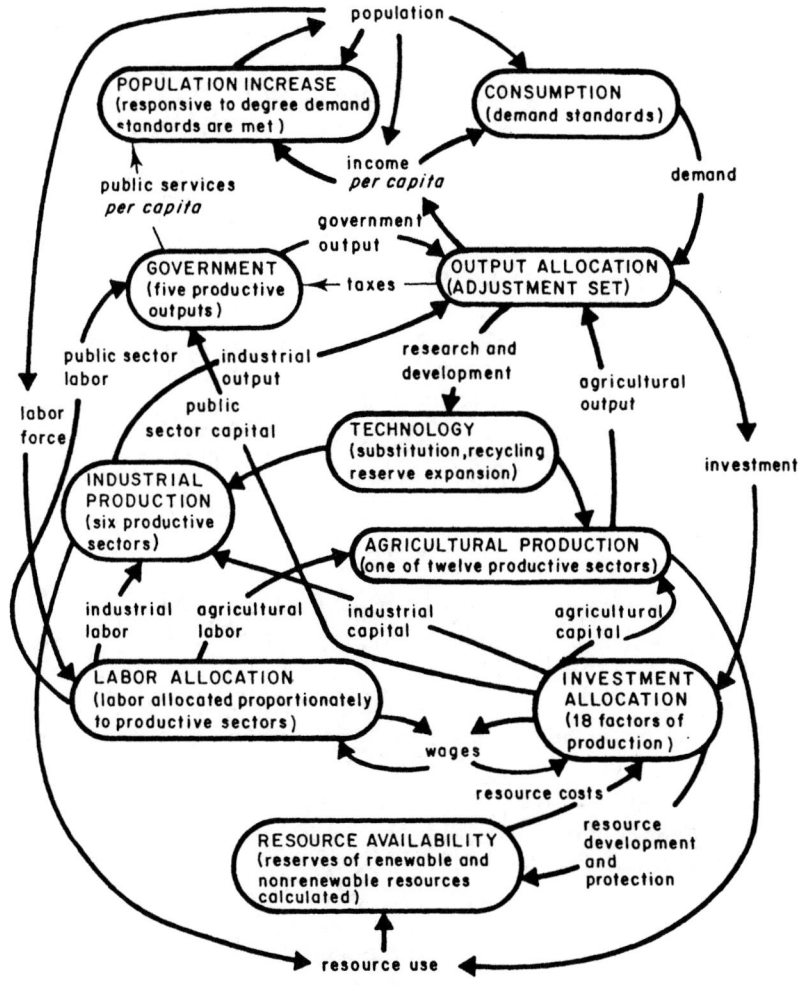

Figure 6.5 SOS reference structure

could exist. Thus the most that SOS might be expected to do is to sketch out the 'best possible' edge of the range of futures open to the region or nation represented.

F. DATA

SOS is intended as a generic structure, equally applicable to state, regional, and national levels. Data are seen as secondary considerations, to be loaded into the model as suits the user's purpose.

In the documented example, SOS-2, the model is parameterized with United States national statistics. The authors identify their data sources only by telling us that 'the data and assumptions were all taken from fairly readily available secondary source materials such as the Statistical Abstract, U.S. Department of Commerce, Survey of Current Business, the Minerals Yearbook, several Congressional or Commission reports on natural resources, and so forth'.[9] Production function and resource substitution data are said to come from EPA's SEAS system.

The inaccessibility of the SOS data is especially maddening because the authors occasionally use sweeping arguments, supposedly based on data, to justify their assumptions, as in:

> A major assumption in the model is the representation of many functions, such as the output coefficients that produce changes in consumer-need partitions, as linear or constant when even the most cursory analysis refutes this assumption when the entire range of possible data values is considered. In this experimental model, general trends in expected ranges of data are to be explored and in these ranges, small compared to the total possible ranges, much of the empirical data suggests that the assigned forms of fit are reasonable.[10]

G. TESTING

The SOS documentation offers no evidence that the model has undergone any sort of testing beyond some simple policy runs. No attempt is made to demonstrate the model's ability to replicate history. No arguments are presented to the effect that the model's response to parameter or structural changes is a reasonable replication of the way the real world responds.

SOS contains more than 2,000 numerical constants. Many of these constants, such as the degree of substitutability of one resource for another or the threshold conditions at which the system will begin looking for ways of finding substitutes, are, by necessity, guesses. Conceivably the model's behavior might be quite sensitive to one or another of these uncertain parameters. For example, the conditions under which energy shortages appear are probably highly sensitive to the parameters one uses to describe the substitutability of coal for petroleum or to the threshold point at which oil depletion is assumed to spur investment in solar energy.

The situation would seem to call for extensive sensitivity testing. But no such tests are described in SOS documentation. To make matters worse, the data used are not identified by source and the methods used to estimate parameters are not described. Therefore one lacks even the means to decide which parameters are well-substantiated and which are pure guesses.

The one testing exercise that is described is designed to show that modeler's assumptions predicate the model's conclusions. In this exercise the basic SOS structure is given six sets of parameters to represent six theories of how societies do (or should) operate, and 40-year runs are made using each of the six modified structures. These six runs are not designed to duplicate any actual region over any specific time period; they simply demonstrate the dynamic capabilities of the model system.

In the first of the six runs the basic model is simplified to simulate the result of historical exponential growth within a finite resource base, with no societal adjustment mechanisms. The productive sectors promptly run into a resource limit and collapse. Successive runs add to and expand upon this exponential growth model.

Run 2 adds a 'technological fix'; that is, the system reacts to resource depletion by instituting substitutes for depleted resources and by shifting the production mix to favor the more plentiful resources. The model shows 'modest growth with some perturbations' throughout the 40-year period, but the authors predict that a longer run would exhaust the resource base: 'Many fixes may be possible but finally the set of adjustments that are viable are exhausted and the output drops well below original output levels'.[11]

Run 3 modifies the exponential growth model to show zero population growth (ZPG). The result does not differ greatly from the Base Case.

Run 4 combines ZPG and the technological fix. The result is slower economic growth because of a reduced labor force, less 'raggedness' because of fewer technological adjustments, but still impending shortages near the end of the run.

Run 5 adds 'cultural adaption' to the 'technological fix' assumption by allowing transfer of funds between sectors and by allowing demand to fall when the system cannot meet the implied levels of demand. This flexible society is rewarded with total demand satisfaction, but shows considerable fluctuation and over-compensation in individual sectors as demand shifts.

Run 6, the 'anomic society' run, duplicates the 'cultural adaption' assumptions of Run 5 but lengthens the time required for the culture to adapt. This society is too sluggish; its reluctance to adjust causes 'all expectations to be met well for three years, then all expectations to be slightly missed for about six years and finally a collapse of the outputs in the final two years'.[12]

H. CONCLUSIONS

The conclusions from the SOS model are most fully described in a more recent House and Williams publication.[13] The model is run in a 'reference scenario', in which sectoral growth rates are set initially at those rates that pertained in the United States from 1950 to 1970. Under these conditions the system generates severe resource crises early in the next century, and the problems appear at a rate faster than the many adjustment mechanisms in the model can correct.

In the simulated year 2010, second level crisis corrections were needed for the first time as all sectors associated with goods production and transportation became increasingly deficient in meeting required demands. However, the deficiency was not great enough to decrease any of the demand levels (a third level crisis). In the year 2012, the situation became worse as material prices escalated rapidly, led by the resources of lead/zinc and petroleum. By this time, major fund transfers from government areas were occurring to provide investment and thus stimulate corrections. In 2013, as the price of lead/zinc doubled and copper jumped 20%, many demand expectations were lowered for the first time in the total scenario.

The already high depletion levels for lead/zinc, copper, and petroleum (all over 90%) suggested that correction mechanics would be too slow to save sufficient reserves for a smooth adjustment. By 2016, this proved to be the case as lead/zinc and copper resources availability collapsed. Since seven of the twelve production sectors draw on these resources, the later-year results were judged not credible.[14]

These resource problems were not solved by adding a forecasting capability to the model system. The planning addition makes 20-year linear projections of demand satisfaction patterns. If a future problem is indicated, funds are shifted *in advance* of actual need to sectors that are likely to fall short, and demand standards for those sectors are also prevented from growing. The system performs worse under these changes, because a smoother economic growth pattern over the first few decades exhausts resources even more rapidly.

Next a conservation scenario was tried, in which recycling capabilities are increased and material use is decreased for any resource that becomes more than 50% depleted, and consumer demand levels are reduced generally. This strategy avoided material shortages completely, but produced a labor shortage, slowing growth of the more labor-intensive service sectors.

> Since the cost of metals did not increase as quickly in the conservation scenario, more funds were available to produce other resources, including labor; since the labor force had been near full employment, salaries increased ... In these simulations (as often occurs in policy-making), a measure reducing one problem causes new effects to arise that are unforeseen and that occur in quite remote sectors of our modeled system.[15]

The best results were obtained by combining this conservation scenario with the forecasting capability. No crises occurred over the 50-year model run. In other words, the simulated United States socioeconomic system, with all its assumed adaptive mechanisms, did not function well on its own—the adaptations came too late and took too long. The system that avoided these problems entirely over the next 50 years required substantial government planning, forecasting, and augmenting the private sector's adjustment mechanisms. It also required value changes that reduced consumers' material goals.

It is difficult to find a clear and concise summary of the SOS findings as a whole. The primary message seems to be that the United States system as currently structured is adaptive but not quite adaptive enough. The best way to improve it would be to add a controlling, centralized, corrective overview institution, which uses mathematical models as forecasting tools.

> It should be noted that SEAS and SOS are only two of many models available and that the family of research tools includes many quantitative and qualitative techniques other than models to search further into detailed questions of interest. The major point of interest is that as the policymaker strives to provide more

complete long-term solutions to problems before they become specific crises, methods and approaches do exist that can be refined to support his efforts.[16]

The structure and parameters of SOS seem to designed to produce optimistic results. Every imaginable adjustment mechanism is included. Adjustment delays and costs are minimized and political and distributional problems are omitted. The central control mechanism runs with clock-like efficiency, and the social consequences of meeting shortages by lowering expectations are not discussed. The bias in the model is obvious and to some extent admitted by the authors in their opening statement of the purpose of the model.

However, to the extent that a model can be biased and honest, this one seems to be both. Resource limits *are* included, the adjustment mechanisms *do* impose costs on the system as a whole, and the closed boundary does not allow problems to be pushed out of the model's domain into some unaccounted real-world externality. As a result, the conclusions do not support entirely the preconceptions of the modelers. The system is quite capable of generating problems faster than it can adjust to them, even with an optimistic bias. If the assumptions are made more pessimistic (as in the 'anomic' run), the model output can indicate severe problems, and can also give some general ideas about how to prevent them.

I. IMPLEMENTATION

SOS is an unlikely candidate for direct implementation. It was developed by two people working in their private capacities and pursuing their own ideas rather than responding to any institutional needs. Even if SOS had had an official client, implementation would be unlikely. At least in its present state of development, the model does not test any concrete policies or draw any policy-directed conclusions. It is a general-understanding model, and if it supports any particular viewpoint, it is that resource problems will not necessarily solve themselves smoothly or inexpensively. The primary policy conclusion that House and Williams wanted to get across, that EPA and other government agencies should use computer models for long-term planning, was accepted, at least during Democratic administrations, but SOS was not chosen as an EPA planning model.

House and Williams were essentially their own clients, developing a model they could use as evidence in proving a point to the world. Even they seemed to lose interest eventually. House left EPA, wrote a number of books that mentioned SOS among many other models, used SOS once as a teaching tool for a university course, and went on to develop bigger and more ambitious models. Eventually House reappeared in government as director of the Office of Technology Impacts of the Department of Energy (DOE), still promoting models but now sounding more like a client, with complaints about the long development times, inadequate databases, and absence of unmeasurable qualitative factors in the models available to him. Williams says he sent out about a dozen card decks with the SOS computer program in response to requests from various users, including Battelle, but he does not know that any of them actually ran or used the model.

Williams rejoined House at DOE, working on the assembly of a massive computerized information system for energy policy modeling. House and Williams did consider dusting off SOS, beefing up its energy resource sector, and using it as a long-term complement to the 'accounting models with no feedback' the DOE uses.[17]

J. COMPUTER REQUIREMENTS

The SOS FORTRAN model contains about 1800 lines. Its run cost is about $25.00. Output from a run creates a sheaf of computer printout about three-quarters of an inch thick.[18]

K. DOCUMENTATION

The SOS FORTRAN program is listed in full, and the equations themselves are quite well documented. Comments are interspersed throughout the program, providing information about what operation is being performed in what line. The program is carefully arranged to facilitate following its logic and locating operations within the program. Should anyone ever want to check the performance of the SOS model, or to compare the program with the interpretation of it presented in the model text, he would be able to do so.

In contrast to the completeness and careful organization of the FORTRAN program, however, the model's verbal description is incomplete, unclear, and poorly organized. Language is used carelessly and imprecisely; many sentences convey no meaning at all. Documentation of test runs is sloppy, both in substance and in logic. The mathematical alterations producing the various changes in output are described only in imprecise qualitative terms. In the first group of runs, the reader is casually informed that the model producing the run output is 'slightly different' from the model described elsewhere in the text (details not offered).[19]

A similar lack of quality is manifested in other dimensions of the model documentation. The description shifts suddenly from the idealized concepts behind SOS to the actual model SOS-2, without sufficient warning to the reader that there are differences between what the authors intended to model and what they actually modeled. Composition errors, such as incorrect opposition of concepts and unexplained terminology, are common. Little concern is shown for reader convenience. Variable name definitions are presented in clusters scattered over a hundred pages of equation descriptions. Consequently, variable name definitions are hard to find, which severely hampers anyone attempting to follow the description of model equations. Trying to piece together the logic of the model is an infuriating exercise.

The SOS documentation is quite abstract, in the sense of being separated from worldly reality. Operations are discussed categorically as the interaction of sectors, components, resources, and measures. Reference to the items within categories is rare, and the real-world analogues of model processes receive almost no mention in the text. Concrete reality is subsumed by category headings, and documentation takes on the air of pure idea-play. Reading the text, one feels the vague discomfort common to laymen in the presence of dedicated computer technicians, the suspicion that these people are more at home in their mathematical creations than they are in the real world.

This blurry verbal documentation is especially disheartening because the model was built to convey general understanding. The SOS-2 model appears to be an interesting tool for exploring various assumptions about the approach of an economy to its carrying capacity, but the SOS documentation does more to fog the issue than it does to clarify it. In the course of formulating the model the modelers have had some unique and innovative structural insights. It is sad to see those insights buried in a document that is incomprehensible to anyone but a FORTRAN expert.

NOTES AND REFERENCES

1. E. R. Williams and P. W. House, *The State of the System (SOS) Model*, Office of Research and Development, U.S. Environmental Protection Agency, Washington D.C., EPA-600/5-73-013, February 1974.
2. E. R. Williams, private communication.
3. P. House and E. R. Williams, *The Carrying Capacity of a Nation*, Lexington, Mass., Lexington Books, 1976.
4. P. House and E. R. Williams, *op.cit.*, p. xiii.
5. *Ibid.*, p. xiii.
6. *Ibid.*, pp. 3–5.
7. A classic ecological model. See, for example, E. P. Odum, *Fundamentals of Ecology*, 3rd edition, Philadelphia, W. B. Saunders Co., p. 215, 1971, or any primer on population ecology.
8. See E. P. Odum, p. 291, for a description of Holling's modeling style.
9. P. House and E. R. Williams, *op.cit.*, p. 29.
10. *Ibid.*, pp. 104–5.
11. *Ibid.*, pp. 10–11.
12. *Ibid.*, p. 18.
13. P. House and E. R. Williams, *Planning and Conservation: The Emergence of the Frugal Society*, Praeger Special Studies, New York, Praeger Publishers, Inc., 1977.
14. P. House and E. R. Williams, *op.cit.*, p. 50.
15. *Ibid.*, p. 59 and p. 62.
16. *Ibid.*, p. 68.
17. P. House and E. R. Williams, personal communications.
18. From a printout of an SOS run at the OSI Bethesda Data Center.
19. P. House and E. R. Williams, 1976, *op.cit.*, p. 7.

CHAPTER 7

TEMPO: Educating the Third World

A. INSTITUTIONAL SETTING

TEMPO, General Electric's Center for Advanced Studies, was founded in 1956 in Santa Barbara, California. Population studies are headquartered in Washington, D.C. ... The population studies unit was founded by the late Stephen Enke in 1967. Unit personnel have developed economic-demographic computer models, applied the models to developing countries, produced teaching materials, and have conducted new research in the economic-demographic area ... Work to date has ... involved TEMPO personnel in over 30 countries on five continents. Most of the work has been performed under contract to the U.S. Agency for International Development. The unit currently consists of ten professionals, fifteen consultants, and three supporting staff.[1]

TEMPO is an industry-sponsored 'think tank'. In the late 1960s the Office of Population of the United States Agency for International Development (USAID) contracted the services of TEMPO's Population Unit to help developing nations analyze the economic effects of population growth. The TEMPO Population Unit constructed for this purpose an economic-demographic model, called TEMPO I, or in its later versions TEMPO II. This model was designed to be general and easily adapted to the specific economic and demographic situation in each developing country. Specialists from the TEMPO Population Unit were trained to go to different countries to teach the concepts of economic-demographic planning, using the model to help stimulate policymakers' awareness of population impacts on country development. The staff was chosen to be proficient in French and Spanish, as well as in economics, computer programming, and associated skills.

After eight years of working with economic-demographic models, the staffs of both USAID and TEMPO felt that the transfer of ideas and technology was most effective when the adaptation of the TEMPO model to a nation's individual situation was performed by analysts in that nation.[2] Therefore, the TEMPO staff shifted to advising and supporting local analysts as they applied the TEMPO model to their own nation's situation. As of 1974 the model had been adapted to represent Guatemala, Jamaica, Turkey, Chile, Brazil, India, Nigeria, Mexico, Taiwan, Tanzania, Nepal, Bolivia, Venezuela, Peru, Indonesia, and Colombia.

B. PURPOSE

TEMPO was originally requested by USAID 'to prepare materials and provide technical assistance for the analysis of the interactions between population growth and economic development'.[3] USAID's Office of Population believed that demographic variables are important but too often unrecognized factors in the development process. They wanted to demonstrate accurately, quantitatively, and convincingly to Third World planners that rapid population growth can be a deterrent to economic growth. They also felt that a computer model geared specifically to each client nation would persuade policy staffs of the benefits to be gained by using quantitative methods in the planning process.

The orginal model on which the TEMPO models are based was constructed in the late 1950s by Ansley Coale and Edgar Hoover to investigate population-development relationships in India.[4] Although the Coale–Hoover model has undergone many refinements and adaptations in its transformation into TEMPO I and TEMPO II, the fundamental assumptions and behavior (which will be discussed later) have not been greatly changed. Its structure is simple and its behavior follows clearly and understandably from its basic assumptions.

The TEMPO model has been used to generate similar and predictable forecasts for many countries, primarily for educational purposes. This exercise can be likened to the process of reconstructing a classical laboratory experiment in a chemistry class. While the outcome is known, at least by the instructor, the process of performing the chemistry experiment and interpreting its results is an effective way of getting the student to relate actively to the theory being taught, and of developing the student's skill in the process of logical inquiry.

The TEMPO Population Unit gradually expanded the original TEMPO I model to incorporate more policy levers than population growth rates and to produce a model that could be generally useful in development planning. They describe the purpose of TEMPO II as 'to investigate the long-term (e.g. 30-year) effects of different assumptions about demographic rates and government policies affecting those rates, in addition to gaining insights into other types of development planning tradeoffs'.[5] The structure of TEMPO II is still logically simple, however, and its purpose is still primarily didactic.

C. METHOD

The TEMPO model is a straightforward mathematical simulation of the dynamic changes of population and capital in a developing country. It is moved through time by algebraic statements relating the condition of the system at time t to the condition at time t + 1. There are a few non-linearities, expressed by functions such as a logarithmic Cobb–Douglas production function. However, most relationships are linear; for example, total consumption is a linear function of GNP and of population. While some parameters are statistically estimated in some specific country-adapted variants, statistical techniques are seldom mentioned in TEMPO documentation.

There is substantial dynamic feedback built into the model's structure, and the documentation occasionally refers to the concept of feedback. However, specific feedback loops from the model are never mentioned or related to model behavior. No specialized techniques, such as input–output matrices or optimization, are used anywhere in the model. All the major assumptions of the simpler model, TEMPO I, can be described by just eleven algebraic expressions. TEMPO II can be described in 34 equations.

In short, the TEMPO method is non-specialized, uncomplicated computer simulation, well-suited to the purpose of communication of one major idea about population and economic development.

D. BOUNDARIES

The TEMPO model, like its predecessor the Coale–Hoover model, focuses on the general effects of population growth on economic growth. Both TEMPO I and TEMPO II represent population as a flow of people through a series of five-year age cohorts. Entries into and exits from this stream of people are exogenously determined by age-specific birth and survival rates. On the economic side, the model calculates endogenously capital, labor force employed, gross production, consumption, savings, and investment. Labor participation rates and the rate of technological improvement are exogenous.

The later, more elaborate TEMPO II model has a larger boundary than TEMPO I. Several exogenous variables are turned into endogenous ones by the addition of:

1. An explicit government sector.
2. Feedbacks from education to labor productivity and from family planning programs to fertility.
3. Division of the economy into subsistence and modern sectors, roughly equivalent to a rural-urban disaggregation.

With these additions, such variables as subsistence-modern migration, tax payments, government deficit, and price indices (inflation) are introduced as endogenous variables, and taxation rates, allocation of government spending, and targets for education and family planning become exogenous policy variables (see boundary diagram, Figure 7.1).

In the process of adapting TEMPO II to a client nation, the TEMPO staff often adds new structures and variables to examine questions of specific interest to the client. For example, the Chilean version of TEMPO I includes a

165

EXOGENOUS

foreign trade prices
weather foreign exchange rates
  modern-sector target birth rate modern-sector mortality schedule
education goals energy
taxes technical advance in production
apportionment of government budget foreign aid and foreign investment

quality of the environment labor participation rates
political changes land
  crop yields
  attitudes

ENDOGENOUS

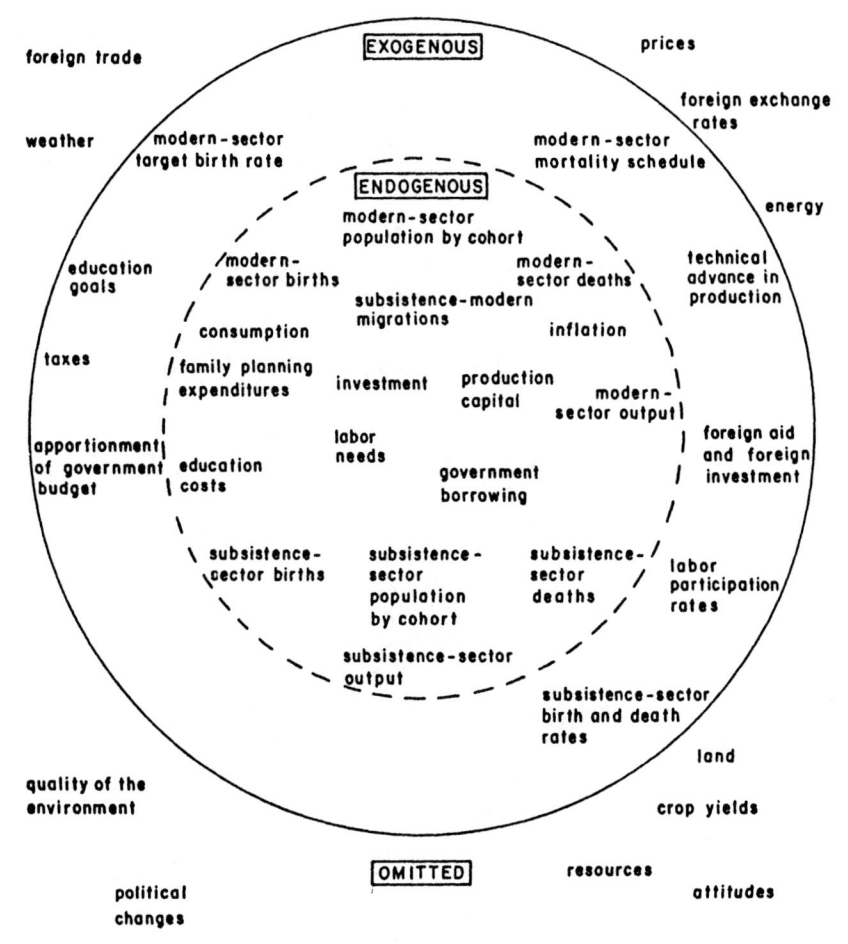

modern-sector population by cohort
modern-sector births modern-sector deaths
consumption subsistence-modern migrations inflation
family planning expenditures investment production capital modern-sector output
  labor needs
education costs government borrowing
subsistence-sector births subsistence-sector population by cohort subsistence-sector deaths
  subsistence-sector output
  subsistence-sector birth and death rates

OMITTED resources

Figure 7.1 TEMPO II boundary diagram

more elaborate treatment of health services and education than the generic form of the model.[6] The Venezuelan version of TEMPO II explicitly includes foreign investment in the petroleum industry.[7]

E. STRUCTURE

For simplicity we shall first examine the structure of TEMPO I, then TEMPO II.

TEMPO I consists of a demographic sector and an economic sector. The demographic sector is an accounting device that projects future population size and composition by subtracting deaths and adding births (both disaggregated by age and sex) to a base-year population.[8] Age-specific fertility and mortality rates are exogenous. Usually two or three fertility forecasts, including continuation of current fertility and a sharp reduction in fertility, are compared. The accounting is carried out on a five-year cohort basis to allow explicit representation of population characteristics such as labor potential and births per year, which depend on the population's age profile. Young and old cohorts are weighted less than middle-aged ones in calculating 'equivalent consumers' for the consumption function. The only feedbacks in the demographic sector come about because births are proportional to the number of women of fertile ages and because the number of deaths in a cohort is proportional to the cohort's size. There is no influence from the economic sector on either fertility or mortality rates.

> The economic model is essentially a straightforward application of a Cobb–Douglas production function. ... Output is generated by inputs to the economic process; these inputs are labor, physical capital, and technological change.[9]

Of the three inputs to production, technological change is exogenous, capital is determined by internal feedback through investment from the economic sector, and labor is determined in the population sector. Only employed labor is presumed to add to production; employment is a function of capital, and as the unemployment rate decreases, capital is substituted for labor.

The internal feedback in the economic sector is dominated by two positive feedback loops (see Figure 7.2). In the first loop output increases investment; investment increases capital; capital then increases output. In the second loop, more capital increases the need for labor, which increases employment. More employed labor generates more output, allows more investment, and further increases both capital and the capacity of the system to utilize labor productively.

Two factors can slow the expansion of TEMPO I's economic growth loops: labor scarcity can reduce production, and consumption can reduce investment. Both labor and consumption are tied to the growth of population, but the timing of their respective influences is quite different. The labor supply is increased by population growth, but only after the 15 or more years required for a new-born to enter the labor market. Consumption increases the moment a new-born appears in the model (though not by a full consumer-equivalent). Therefore, an increase in population will immediately depress the model's economic growth rate by diverting some output from investment to consumption. Fifteen years later the added population may increase the economic growth rate by relieving a labor shortage, but at the same time the consumption of these new laborers increases, as they become full consumer equivalents.

TEMPO I can be used to test the wisdom of slowing population growth to enhance economic development, but it is not detailed enough to answer the obvious follow-up questions: what government programs can affect population growth, and how can they be financed? To answer these questions, the TEMPO staff developed TEMPO I into TEMPO II, with an explicit government and financial sector, a feedback from government family planning programs to the birth rate, an education sector, and a division of the population into modern (urban) and subsistence (rural) economic activities. TEMPO II is

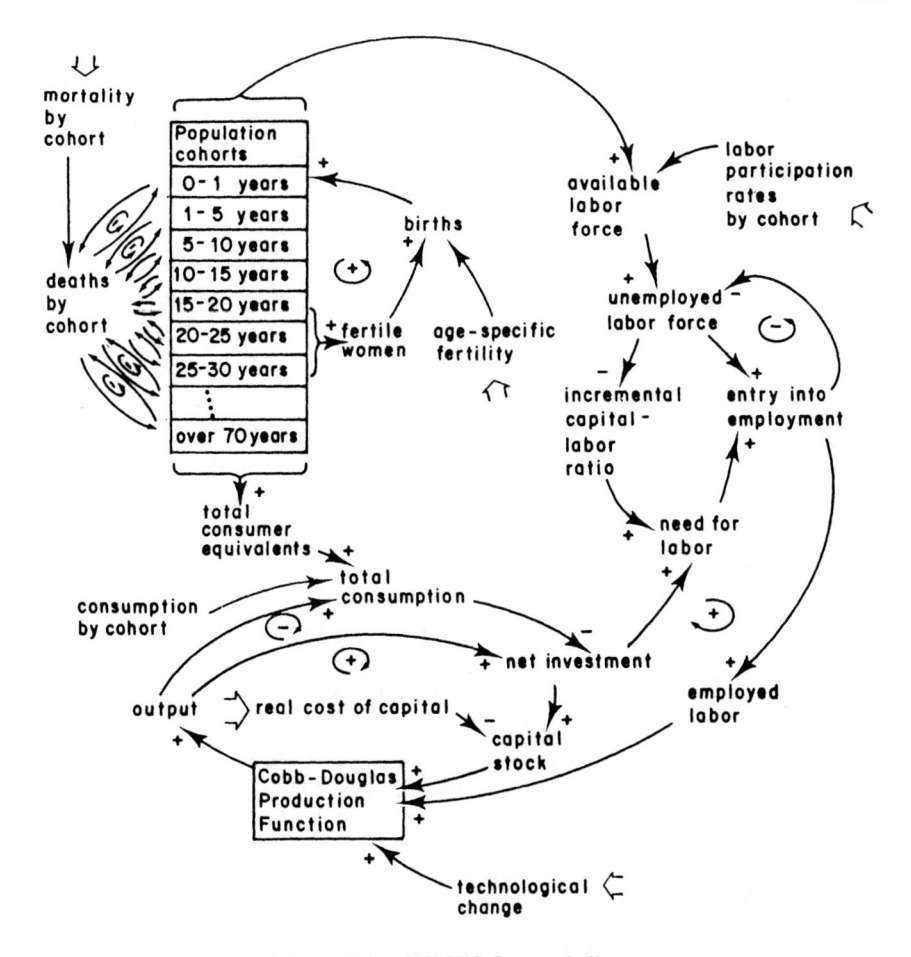

Figure 7.2 TEMPO I causal diagram

designed to explore such questions as whether it would be effective to shift some funds from education to family planning, or to finance government investment, education, or family planning programs from such sources as cuts in other programs, foreign borrowing, taxes, or inflation.

The population in the subsistence sector of TEMPO II behaves identically to the modern population (and to the population in TEMPO I) except that:

1. Subsistence population birth rates are not affected by the family planning program.
2. Subsistence population out-migrates into the modern population.

The economy associated with the subsistence population is very simple. Its output is proportional to population, subject to diminishing returns as population increases.

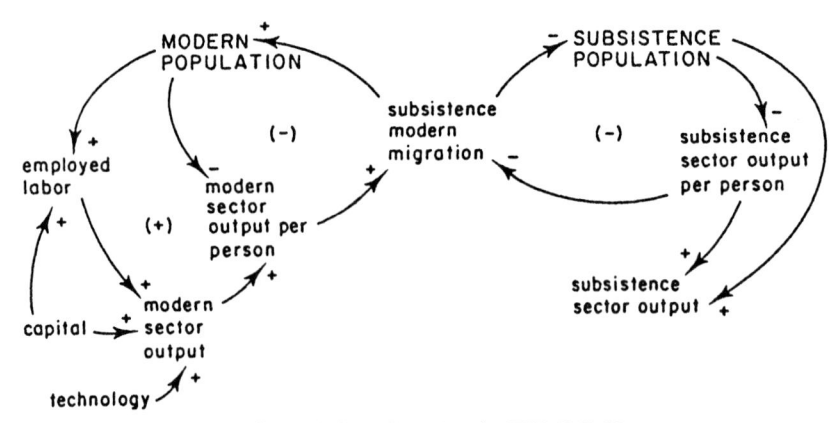

Figure 7.3 Migration in TEMPO II

Subsistence-to-modern migration proceeds at a rate proportional to the difference in production *per capita* in the two sectors. As modern sector output generally grows much faster than subsistence sector output (because of increasing returns through technology and no diminishing returns), people tend to migrate steadily from the subsistence sector to the modern sector (see Figure 7.3). This migration somewhat slows the growth rate of *per capita* income that would pertain otherwise in the modern sector and increases it in the subsistence sector. Migration into the modern sector decreases the capital–labor ratio, which increases unemployment. Unemployment, however, does not feed back directly to migration into the modern sector. Migrants from the susbsistence sector into the modern sector immediately assume modern-sector fertility, which has generally been lowered by family planning expenditures.

Production in the modern sector is a function of capital, technology, and two types of labor, educated and uneducated. As in TEMPO I, technological progress grows exogenously, allowing any given amount of capital and labor to produce an exponentially increasing amount of output. A constant fraction of the educated labor force is employed. Employment of the uneducated labor force is a fraction dependent on the capital–labor ratio.

Desired or 'preliminary' consumption in TEMPO II is the sum of three factors, preliminary private consumption, private investment, and government purchases. If these three factors add up to more than the total productive output of the economy, each is scaled down proportionately (or by weighted proportions if the user prefers). Whenever demand exceeds supply in this way, a general price index is increased to represent inflation. The three components of demand are determined as follows:

1. Preliminary private consumption is a linear function of population and disposable income (total output minus taxes plus transfer payments).
2. Preliminary private investment is equal to disposable income minus preliminary consumption minus government borrowing.

3. Preliminary government spending is a function of several exogenous policy choices, as described below.

In TEMPO's government sector an exogenously-determined portion of gross production (the sum of modern sector output and traditional sector output) is taken in as taxes and distributed among eight uses: general government spending, defense, transfer payments, health, social overhead capital, direct government investment, education, and family planning. Of these eight uses, the first four do nothing in the model other than consume output that otherwise would have been invested. By not making these four classes of government expenditure feed back into the model's causal flows, the TEMPO II model tacitly assumes:

1. That government expenditures on health do not lower death rates.
2. That general government spending and defense spending do not affect any other model variables,[10] either by diverting labor away from the private sector or by adding capital to it.

As for the latter four uses of government funds, government expenditures on social overhead capital and direct government investment increase the capital stock by an amount directly proportional to the funds spent. This capital is not distinguished from private capital, and thus the effect of these two types of government spending is to increase the economic growth rate. Expenditures on family planning are assumed to reduce births, thereby decreasing the population growth rate. Expenditures on education increase the society's cumulative level of education, which in turn increases labor productivity. Education is not assumed to have a direct effect on fertility or mortality.

For all government expenditures except family planning and education, the quantity of funds budgeted is an exogenously-determined fraction of gross production (perhaps adjusted downward if total demand exceeds total production). For family planning and education, the user supplies a target— either a fertility rate or the fraction of the population that should be educated to primary, secondary, and tertiary levels. Then the model endogenously determines the cost of attaining that goal. The cost of attaining the education target is calculated by multiplying a constant cost per student by the number in the age cohort to be educated. Similarly, the cost per family planning acceptor is multiplied by the number of women who would have to accept family planning to attain the prescribed fertility rate. Acceptance of family planning is synonymous with cessation of fertility during the period of acceptance.[11] Cost per acceptor is constant and relatively low up to a specified rate of acceptance, but increases linearly for acceptance rates beyond that point.

In the model it is possible, and even likely, that government spending will exceed the tax rate. The resulting government deficit necessitates government borrowing, which diverts funds away from investment, and this slows economic growth. At the discretion of the user, exogenous aid funds may also be assumed as additions to the government budget.

TEMPO's own causal diagram of the TEMPO II structure is shown in Figure 7.4. This diagram is partial and does not include all the internal feedbacks in the economic sector. The Reference Structure diagram for TEMPO II is shown in Figure 7.5. The relatively few equations of TEMPO II manage to capture a large number of demographic-economic interactions, primarily by keeping each assumption aggregate and including only the very most basic factors. TEMPO II is a 'broad shallow' model, interrelating many important economic variables but with simple, sweeping assumptions that do not include the detail and variability of a real economy.

The structural additions in TEMPO II do not alter the basic feedback relationships of TEMPO I or its behavior in any major way. The government sector, as it diverts funds away from investment, adds a new potential inhibition to the economic growth loops, unless government investment happens to be the only item of governement expenditure. The education sector, by adding costs proportional to the population growth in the younger cohorts, increases the economic cost of population in the short term, but decreases it as more highly skilled and productive laborers enter the work force in the long run. Disaggregation into subsistence and modern sectors removes a portion of the economy from participation in the capital-output growth loop and puts part of the population beyond the reach of the family planning program. The conceptually richer government sector of TEMPO II allows exploration of such options as increasing government debt in the short run in order to finance family planning programs, which will cut education expenditures in the long run. Or the model can simulate the results of less direct government investment in capital and more government support of education to produce more highly skilled workers. 'These decisions made over a period of years may have significant impact on the total development of the country, and consequently on the long-run availability of goods and services'.[12]

F. DATA

TEMPO I and TEMPO II are small models. They require only a few, aggregate, standard economic and demographic parameters of the sort that are likely to be available, or at least to be guessable, even for non-industrialized countries. Sensitivity testing, to be described later, plus much experience adapting the models to different national situations, have shown the population effects on the economy as indicated by the model to be quite insensitive to differences in economic parameters. Therefore data acquisition is not a major part of the TEMPO modeling effort.

GE-TEMPO does not take much trouble to document the data used in model applications. In the Chilean version, for example, neither data inputs nor data sources are listed.[13] However, suggestions for how to adapt the model by changing its parameters are given in the general description of the model.[14]

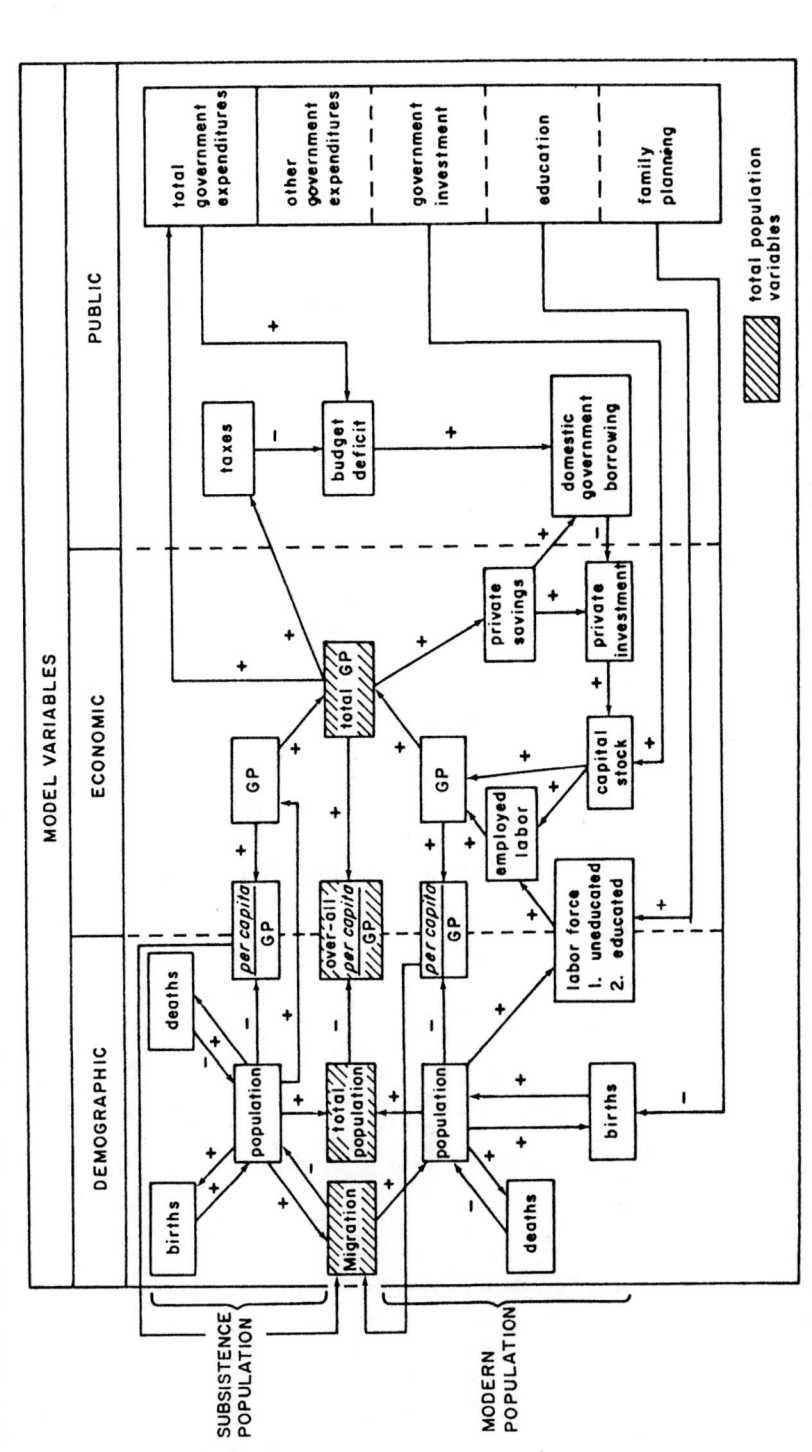

Figure 7.4 Partial causal diagram of TEMPO II. Note: The arrows indicate directions of dependency pointing from the independent variable to the dependent variable of a functional relationship. A plus sign, as from modern GP to *per capita* modern GP, indicates that a positive or negative change in the independent variable will cause a corresponding change in the dependent variable. A minus sign indicates an inverse relationship, with an increase in one variable being associated with a decrease in the other variable, and conversely. Reproduced with permission from S Enke, *Using TEMPO II: a Budget Allocation and Human Resources Model*, General Electric Company—TEMPO, Santa Barbara, California, Center for Advanced Studies, p. 10, 1973

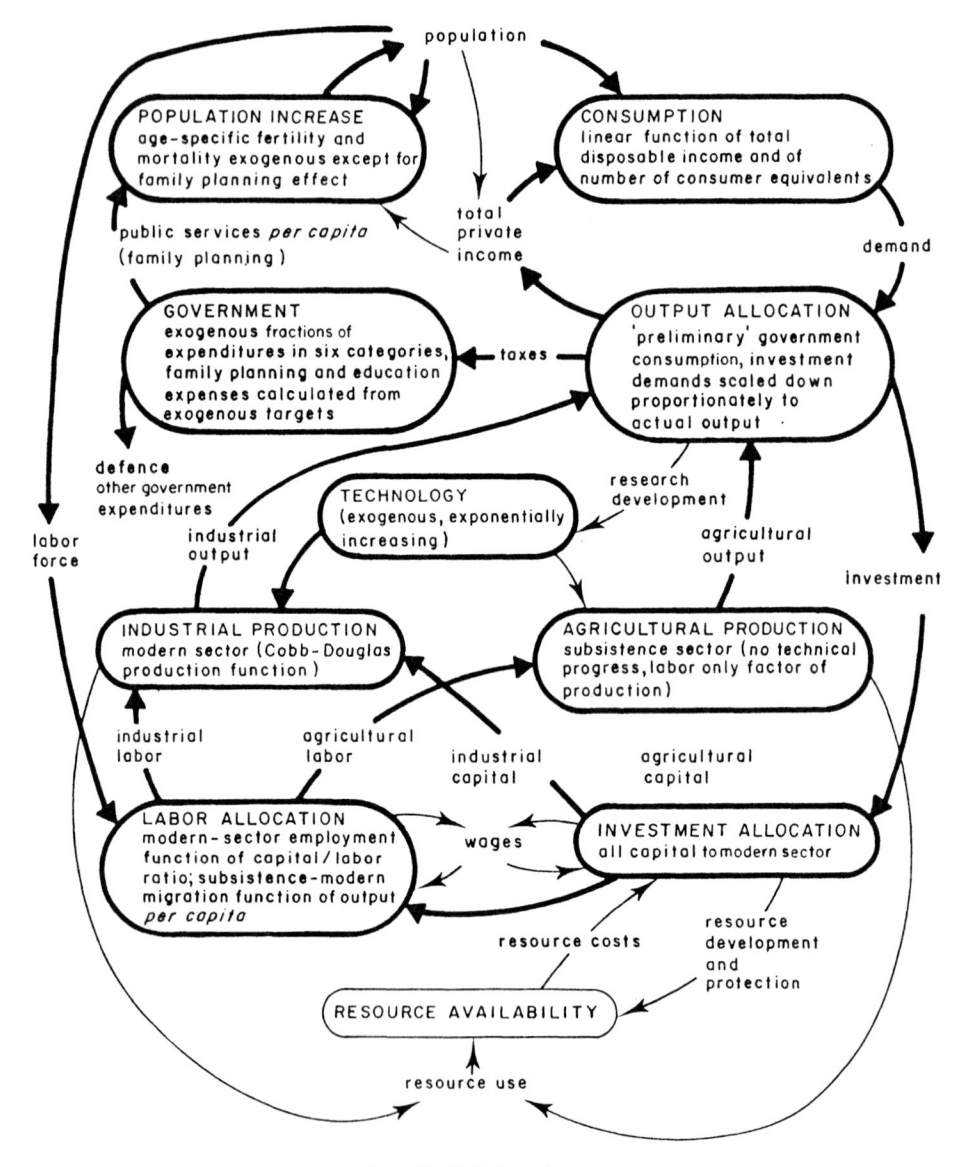

Figure 7.5 TEMPO II reference structure

These descriptions give potential users a straightforward description of where to go to find data, how to handle data that are not in the correct form for model use, and how to include new data in the computer program.

G. CONCLUSIONS

TEMPO results are always explained by following through the causal linkages in the model and translating them into clearly-understandable words and concepts related to real-world processes. For example:

> The direct impact of increased family planning services is to reduce fertility. Decreased fertility slows population growth and makes for future populations smaller than they otherwise would be. For a period of several decades, the size of the labor force is relatively insensitive to changes in fertility (since all new workers for the next 15 years are already born). Also, to the extent a smaller population leads to lower consumption, the growth of capital may be accelerated. Thus growth of *total* output remains relatively unchanged—and may be slightly higher—so that the decline in fertility increases the growth in *per capita* output. Higher *per capita* output increases tax revenues, private savings, and investment, and allows larger outlays for education. An increased stock of capital reduces unemployment and increases output per worker. The labor force becomes more educated, hence more productive, and accordingly receives higher incomes...
>
> Instead of expenditures on family planning, government might decide to invest considerably more each year on direct productive investment. The main impact would be to increase GDP. Population growth would not be slowed, however, and GDP *per capita* would increase less rapidly than if the same expenditures had been directed toward family planning programs.[15]

The TEMPO staff has provided a summary that draws together general conclusions from 19 country applications, ranging from Nepal (less than $100 GNP *per capita*) to Venezuela (nearly $1,000 GNP *per capita*). They find one result common to all the models they have made:

> Despite the wide diversity of cultures, historical experience, economic systems, languages, etc., the same fundamental economic-demographic mechanisms proved to be at work in each case. It is universally true that school-age populations, and therefore school enrollments, are very sensitive to changing fertility. Any decline in fertility consequently reduces demographic pressures on school systems, providing the opportunity for improvements in enrollment ratios and better quality education.
>
> In contrast to the school-age population, the work-age population is relatively insensitive to declining fertility for two decades or more. Largely as a result of this insensitivity of the labor force to changing fertility, projections of GNP are also relatively insensitive to fertility change over two or three decades. Thus, slower population growth, produced by declining fertility, translates directly into a more rapid growth of GNP *per capita*.
>
> This conclusion is extremely robust in the sense that it is relatively invariant under the diverse socioeconomic conditions encountered in the different countries' studies and under widely differing parameter values for the key equations in the models.[16]

This conclusion is the logical outcome of the model's structure, which counts population growth as an immediate depressant on economic growth, while its only economic benefit is the eventual increase of the labor force. Changes in model structure could alter these conclusions in many ways. For example, were other resources than land shown as limited (the land constraint is implicit in the diminishing returns to labor in the subsistence sector), the economic drag of population growth might have been magnified. On the other hand, had death rates decreased with rising standards of living or modernization, the fertility-reduction strategies could have been counterbalanced by declines in death rate. Had education been represented as decreasing fertility as readily as family planning programs, a stronger advocacy of education programs rather than family planning might have come out of the model. And if rising *per capita* GNP had been assumed to reduce fertility, more emphasis might have been put on government investments in capital rather than condoms. (The next two models in our survey explore this last assumption in detail.)

Small, broad, shallow models such as TEMPO are in one sense the highest goal of the modeling profession. Elegant simplicity, retaining the essence of the issue and removing the confusing detail, is what modeling is all about, especially when the model has an educational purpose. But the danger in making such models is that the essence of the real system may be simplified away entirely. TEMPO has been widely attacked for its simplicity, especially with regard to its omission of economic-demographic feedback (see the next two models), and to its sweeping assumption that family planning expenditures instantly and linearly prevent births. A strong argument can be made that family planning programs just provide a government-subsidized, more pleasant, and less costly substitute for widely-known folk methods already used to prevent undesired children.[17] In fairness to the TEMPO staff, the family-planning assumption in the model is an exact reflection of the assumption that pervaded the planning community, including the USAID sponsor, at the time TEMPO I was made. That assumption was gradually modified and expanded in aid institutions during the 1970s, however, while it remained unchanged in later versions of the TEMPO model. TEMPO was originally designed as a teaching model to increase the sophistication of development planners, but over the ten-year history of the model the students outgrew the teacher.

H. TESTING

The TEMPO model is among the most thoroughly and intelligently tested of all the models in our survey. In part this is because the model is small enough and clear enough that each of its uncertain parameters can be identified and varied, and the effects of the variation can be easily understood. Also, the TEMPO modelers have used an unambiguous and sensible criterion for sensitivity: a parameter is considered sensitive when its variation caused a reversal of the main *policy conclusion* of the model. That is, a change in a 'sensitive' number would cause the model system to perform better under rapid population growth than under slower population growth.

The fertility-dependent conclusions of the TEMPO II model are generally insensitive, by this definition of sensitivity, to parameter changes. Tests were conducted to ascertain the effects of differing numerical assumptions for life expectancy, technological progress, effects of labor and capital on GNP (Cobb–Douglas coefficients), increase in consumption per increase in GNP, initial ratio of capital to GNP, and initial unemployment rate. Tests were made altering parameters both singly and in combination. The combinations were chosen so as to change all parameters simultaneously in the direction that would be most favorable to high fertility and then in the direction least favorable to high fertility. As a result of their sensitivity tests, the modelers conclude that economic-demographic projections remain essentially unchanged, even when the values of parameters are subjected to substantial (10–300%) changes either individually or simultaneously.[18] This is a level of robustness very rare among model-based conclusions.

The TEMPO Population Unit does not raise the question of model validity in its documentation. No evidence of validity, such as fits with historical data or arguments for the 'reasonableness' of model behavior, is presented. TEMPO's originators make their model assumptions extremely clear; the reader is free to accept or dismiss the model on the grounds of those assumptions and the model output.

I. IMPLEMENTATION

TEMPO II is a mature, generic model. Since GE-TEMPO built their basic economic-demographic model in 1968, they have adapted it to over 30 nations. The forms taken by adapted models vary widely. A 'truncated model' that can be operated by hand calculation was developed and applied to Bolivia and Nepal. A four-sector model that explores such policy areas as foreign and government investment in industry, promotion of import substitution, and education, as well as population policy, was developed for Venezuela.

USAID and TEMPO worked together closely in deciding which countries were appropriate for use of the models and in bringing the models to the attention of government officials. The TEMPO staff worked out of USAID missions in the chosen countries. Different strategies were employed, depending on the circumstances of each area. In Peru the TEMPO team worked directly with the National Planning Ministry and developed a population plan of action. In Venezuela the best available institution was a research and training institute for government administrators, and the model was altered to include Venezuela's extensive petroleum sector. A Regional Population Center in Bogota became a place from which the models, or at least the idea of modeling, were purveyed to other Latin American nations.

As they worked in different countries, the TEMPO staff gradually modified their approach.[19] They began to sell the process of modeling more than specific models or model results. They worked with professionals in the recipient country, letting them put their own ideas into the models and make their own mistakes. The recipient-country analysts, most of whom had been trained in the universities of industrialized countries, wanted to make the models more complex and sophisticated, far beyond what the data base of the country could support. The TEMPO staff meanwhile was trying to simplify the models, to make them more transparent and easier to present in a short time to an audience of policymakers.

TEMPO models were definitely used in some form in many countries, including Peru, Colombia, Honduras, Ecuador and Venezuela. Most of these countries were the sites of extended implementation efforts, with presentations, seminars, and courses on modeling, all funded by USAID. In at least two countries, Togo and Mali, the simple TEMPO I model was taken from the literature and used as a basis for planning without the prior knowledge of either USAID or TEMPO.

According to reports of the TEMPO staff, recipient countries received the models with mild suspicion or open curiosity but not with hostility, even though the anti-natalist message was directly contradictory to the pro-natalist views of many governments. The strongest reactions against the models came from the American and European academic communities, where the TEMPO models were occasionally denounced as simplistic and propagandistic and the project participants as Malthusian imperialists. Several counter-models, including LTSM and BACHUE, were made to demonstrate that TEMPO's results had been rigged by making economic growth sensitive to population growth but not vice versa.

Relations between TEMPO and the USAID Office of Population sponsor were friendly for ten years. Then in 1977 the director of the Office was replaced and TEMPO's fortunes plummeted. For two years TEMPO received no USAID contracts at all and its staff were dispersed. TEMPO II was simplified into two new models, called DEMOS and RAPID, intended to be carried into a country on a minicomputer and to be explained to decision-makers within an hour. This work was carried out, not by TEMPO, but by other USAID contractors. A set of economic-demographic models intended for similar purposes was started by the U.S. Bureau of the Census.

Since the TEMPO models are clearly stated and have been widely distributed, they must certainly have made their point. Whether making that point was decisive in causing a shift in policy is unclear. We have found no documented examples of a policymaker being introduced to TEMPO, changing his outlook, and going off to establish a massive family-planning program. On the other hand, from 1960 to 1980 a major shift took place in the attitudes of the world's governments about population growth. In 1960 only 10% of the world's people had access to family planning programs. In 1980 90% did. The governments of 80% of the people in the developing world are now concerned about their population growth rates and are instituting some sort of population policy.[20]

Of course we shall never know to what extent TEMPO furthered this shift in world perceptions about population growth. The impact of a model designed to spread an idea is often hard to trace. Probably even the staffs of USAID and TEMPO are unaware of all the reactions to and consequences of their persuasive efforts around the world. At the least, as we shall see, TEMPO was a direct inspiration to other modelers exploring economic-demographic interactions.

J. COMPUTER REQUIREMENTS

The TEMPO models are remarkably uncomplicated and efficient. TEMPO I contains about a dozen basic equations, TEMPO II around three dozen (some of which are repeated several times to generate the different population age cohorts). Computer time, space requirements, and programming language are not described in the model documentation. Given the size of the model, however, its computer requirements must be very small. It could easily be written in FORTRAN or any other general programming language.

K. DOCUMENTATION

Over the years the staff of the TEMPO Population Unit has frequently been requested to explain the TEMPO models to both technical and non-technical audiences. Often the models have been communicated to people who are most comfortable in languages other than English. In keeping with the need for such explanations, the body of documentation that has grown around the TEMPO models is well designed for a general audience. Users' manuals, model descriptions, and more technical items, such as documentation of model sensitivity, are as plain-spoken as possible. Jargon is avoided. Equations are seldom presented without a verbal description of their conceptual import. The model documentation refers constantly to the real-world processes being represented; the reader never gets lost in abstractions.

A plain-language documentation was easier to put together for TEMPO than it would have been for many models because the TEMPO models are small and present few mathematical or conceptual complexities. Descriptions of the models concentrate on presenting the structure of the model, the rationale behind the structure used, and the output produced with various policy options. Data are cited in country applications, but not stressed. Almost no statistical analysis is presented.

In the process of describing structure, algebraic notation rather than any particular computer language is used. To our knowledge, TEMPO has not published the actual computer program for any of their models, except for the truncated versions. The TEMPO models are sufficiently simple, however, that any competent programmer could reconstruct a working computer program from the algebraic equations with little difficulty.

NOTES AND REFERENCES

1. GE-TEMPO, 'Economic Demographic Research and Studies at TEMPO' available from TEMPO Population Studies Unit, 777 14th Street, NW, Washington, D.C. 20005, undated pamphlet.

2. Personal conversations with C. Hemmer, Office of Population, USAID, October 28, 1975 and J. Palmisano, TEMPO, October 26, 1975.
3. R. A. Brown, 'Survey of TEMPO Economic-Demographic Studies', GE74TMP-19, Washington, D.C., July 1974.
4. See A. J. Coale and E. M. Hoover, *Population Growth and Economic Development in Low-Income Countries: a Case Study of India's Prospects*, Princeton, N.J., Princeton University Press, 1958.
5. W. E. McFarland, J. P. Bennett, and R. A. Brown, 'Description of the TEMPO II Budget Allocation and Human Resources Model' GE73TMP-13, April 1973. Prepared for AID Contract no. 3611, Task Order no. 4, GE-TEMPO, Santa Barbara, Calif., p. 21.
6. B. Herrick and R. Moran, 'Declining Birth Rates in Chile: their Effects on Output, Education, Health, and Housing', 71TMP-56, April 1972, prepared for USAID by GE-TEMPO, Santa Barbara, Calif., Sections 3–4.
7. R. A. Brown, *op.cit.*, p. 21.
8. B. Herrick and R. Moran, *op.cit.*, p. 8.
9. *Ibid.*, p. 12.
10. It is possible that more feedback from government spending is included in some specific country applications.
11. W. E. McFarland, J. P. Bennet, and R. Brown, *op.cit.*, p. 18.
12. *Ibid.*, p. 22.
13. B. Herrick and R. Moran, *op.cit.*
14. S. Enke *et al.*, 'Description of the Economic-Demographic Model', Revised Edition 68TMP-120, prepared for USAID by GE-TEMPO, Santa Barbara, Calif., pp. 32–75, June 1971.
15. S. Enke, 'Using TEMPO II: a Budget Allocation and Human Resources Model', GE73TMP-12, GE-TEMPO, Santa Barbara, Calif., p. 15, April 1973.
16. R. A. Brown, 'Survey of TEMPO Economic-Demographic Studies', GE74TMP-19, GE-TEMPO, Center for Advanced Studies, Santa Barbara, Calif., p. 25, July 1974.
17. For just one of many articles expressing this view, see K. Davis, 'Population Policy: Will Current Programs Succeed?' *Science*, **164**, 522, 1969.
18. W. E. McFarland *et al.*, *op.cit.*, p. 25.
19. Most of the information in this section on implementation is taken from personal conversations with H. Cole of the TEMPO staff and C. Hemmer of USAID.
20. R. M. Salas, *The State of World Population 1982*, New York, United Nations Fund for Population Activities, 1982.

CHAPTER 8

LTSM: the Race between Production and Consumption

A. INSTITUTIONAL SETTING

The Long-Term Socio-Economic Simulation Model (hereafter referred to as LTSM) was part of a project entitled 'Methodological Research and Country Case Studies on the Effects of Different Rates of Population Growth on Agricultural Development'. The project was funded by the United Nations Fund for Population Activities (UNFPA) and administered by the Policy Analysis Division of the United Nations Food and Agriculture Organization (FAO).

The FAO's intent was similar to that of TEMPO—to assist planning authorities in non-industrialized nations to describe their own nations and test policies to meet their own needs. The modeling effort was organized in three stages. The first two—constructing a general or prototype model and experimentally fitting that model to a specific nation as a demonstration—are described here. The first demonstration model was calibrated with data from Egypt. The third stage—transferring the model and responsibility for its development from the FAO to collaborating nations—was at least begun in Egypt, Pakistan, and Jordan, with the Pakistan model sufficiently well developed to be documented in draft.

Although the modeling institution (FAO), sponsor (UNFPA), and clients (member nations) are all different and widely separated geographically, they are all part of the United Nations organizational structure, and thus communication and co-ordination of efforts was possible. Enthusiasm for the modeling approach in general and LTSM in particular was high within FAO's Policy Analysis Division, and therefore the institutional environment of this model was friendly and positive.

B. PURPOSE

A primary objective of the LTSM project is:

... to assist developing countries in more fully integrating the population components into their development planning, especially in the agricultural sector.[1]

Other purposes include basic research in modeling and in understanding the process of economic development,[2] and enhancement of planning capability in participating countries via experience gained from the project.

A more specific problem statement can be found in the first published report, in which the criteria for including and excluding things from the model are listed. The model is specifically intended to be long-term, multisectoral, and suitable for planning on a national level, with special emphasis on agricultural development, as one might expect from the FAO sponsorship, and on employment, and population. The model is explicitly *not* patterned after 'purely theoretical models', short term or fully aggregated ones, or those applicable to the world as a whole or to single, specialized regions. Two lists are given in Table 8.1 of the sorts of policy problems the modelers have deliberately included and omitted from their representation.[3]

Table 8.1

Included	Omitted
population growth	political tensions and conflicts
scarcity of arable land	regional disparities
unemployment	income distribution
rural-urban migration	pollution and natural resources
backwardness in education	migration across national boundaries
economic dualism	shortage of skilled labor
capital shortage	inflation
poverty	land tenure systems
indebtedness to foreign countries	

A possible unstated purpose of the LTSM model may have been to provide a more complete alternative to the TEMPO model (described in Chapter 7). TEMPO illustrates the detrimental effect of population growth on economic growth, but does not contain any feedback effects of economic growth on population growth. The LTSM modelers carefully point out that their model is designed to represent *both* sides of the economic-demographic feedback loop. The LTSM modelers have also been in close contact with the BACHUE modeling effort (described in Chapter 9), another attempt to represent economic influences on fertility.

Purposes for the country-specific adaptations of the model were intended to be determined on an ad hoc basis, depending on the circumstances in participating nations. Problem focus was expected to differ from nation to nation. 'For example, food balance will be one of the major focuses of the Pakistan project, and rural-urban migration in the Egypt project'.[4]

C. METHOD

The purpose of LTSM limited the choice of methods to be used. The sponsor's desire for wide applicability required that very general problems be addressed with a flexible format. The fact that most potential user-nations have neither an abundance of technically-trained personnel nor sophisticated computer facilities mandated that the model be kept easy to understand and moderate in its demands on computer hardware.[5] The focus on Third World countries, which are typically data-poor, ruled out heavy reliance on data-demanding statistical techniques.

> To complain about the unavailability, uncorrectness, and inconsistency of data is too common among planners for developing ... countries. We do not want to join them and base on this any excuse for feeding large amounts of mocked-up data and uncertain assumptions into the model. We are rather inclined to sacrifice elegance and sophistication to build a model which is conceptually, structurally as simple as possible so as to minimize data requirements both in quantity and quality.

Accordingly, LTSM was written to be a non-complex simulation model, using FORTRAN, the most general and widely-available computer language. The modelers give two reasons for choosing simulation as their modeling method. First, because the model is long term, it must contain much uncertainty and many degrees of freedom. Therefore it must be possible to explore alternate assumptions about factors beyond the planners' control. Second, not only exogenous factors, but also various policy choices must be kept variable and testable, to generate a clearer picture of planning objectives and the trade-offs among them.

> The aim is not to offer a clear-cut and unambiguous program to the government of a country, but the more modest (and in our opinion more meaningful) approach to explore the possible results of different combinations of sequences of actions.[7]

Bela Martos, who constructed the original model, drew from his experiences as an economist and planner in Hungary, and particularly from the central planning models of Janos Kornai.[8] Wuu-Long Lin, who adapted the model to the specific case of Egypt, used some formulations from econometrics and economic theory. However, the model is less bound to statistical techniques than the typical econometric analysis; it contains more dynamic theory; and its time horizon (20–25 years) goes beyond the range that most econometricians would consider appropriate to their techniques. Jay Forrester, the founder of system dynamics, is also given ideological and methodological credit as an influence on the LTSM.[9] However, the study does not strictly follow the system dynamics paradigm. The LTSM modelers, although they include many feedback relationships, do not use feedback concepts to explain the dynamic behavior of their model. Moreover, they linearize far more than a system dynamicist would, they make most relationships dependent on rates of change rather than levels, and they represent time delays only insofar as they are implicit in the program's state variables.

D. BOUNDARIES

LTSM concentrates on the interactions among population, land, foreign trade, and production. Population is disaggregated into traditional (working in the family-labor sphere) and modern (working in the hired-labor sphere) sectors as well as by age and sex. Land, like population, is divided into traditional and modern acreage according to whether it is farmed with family labor or with hired labor. Seven production sectors are included: agriculture, non-capital goods, capital goods, services, construction, government services, and education. Three of these sectors, agriculture, non-capital goods, and services, are divided into traditional and modern categories. The other production sectors are treated as modern for purposes of employment calculations (to be discussed later).

The many exogenous variables of the model (see Figure 8.1) are categorized by the modelers as either *'policy target' variables*, to be varied and experimented with in the course of simulation, or *exogenous variables* that must be forecast outside the model. Examples from the exogenous category include labor participation rates, imports, and capital-output ratios. There are five policy target variables: investment allocations, exports, consumption, land reclamation, and 'population policy'. Classifying these central model variables as policy levers implies a substantial amount of government control in the LTSM society. The heavy use of exogenous functions greatly simplifies the model's structure. It also ties the model's output closely to predictions or policy choices that must come from mental models.

A model like LTSM, which is dedicated to simplicity, must omit a great deal and provide only abbreviated representations of those variables that are included. Weather, income distribution, wages, prices, soil erosion, and defense spending might all influence population and development, for example, but none are included in LTSM.

The modelers have been persistent in keeping LTSM simple and fairly uncontroversial; their rule seems to have been 'when in doubt, leave it out'. The omission of a relevant variable or relationship is usually recognized by the modelers and explained in the documentation. For example:

> These ... omissions have been made partly for keeping the model as simple as possible, partly because the problems in question only arise in a small number of countries, are rather short or medium term problems or just too hard to cope with.[10]

> The cumulative effect of the economic policy is measured (among other indicators) by foreign indebtedness. We do not restrict its level, nor do we feed it back to change the policy. Simply when choosing among the available options, the ones with excessively high and thus impossible or undesirable level of indebtedness should be rejected. We do not attempt to predict the world's willingness to lend.[11]

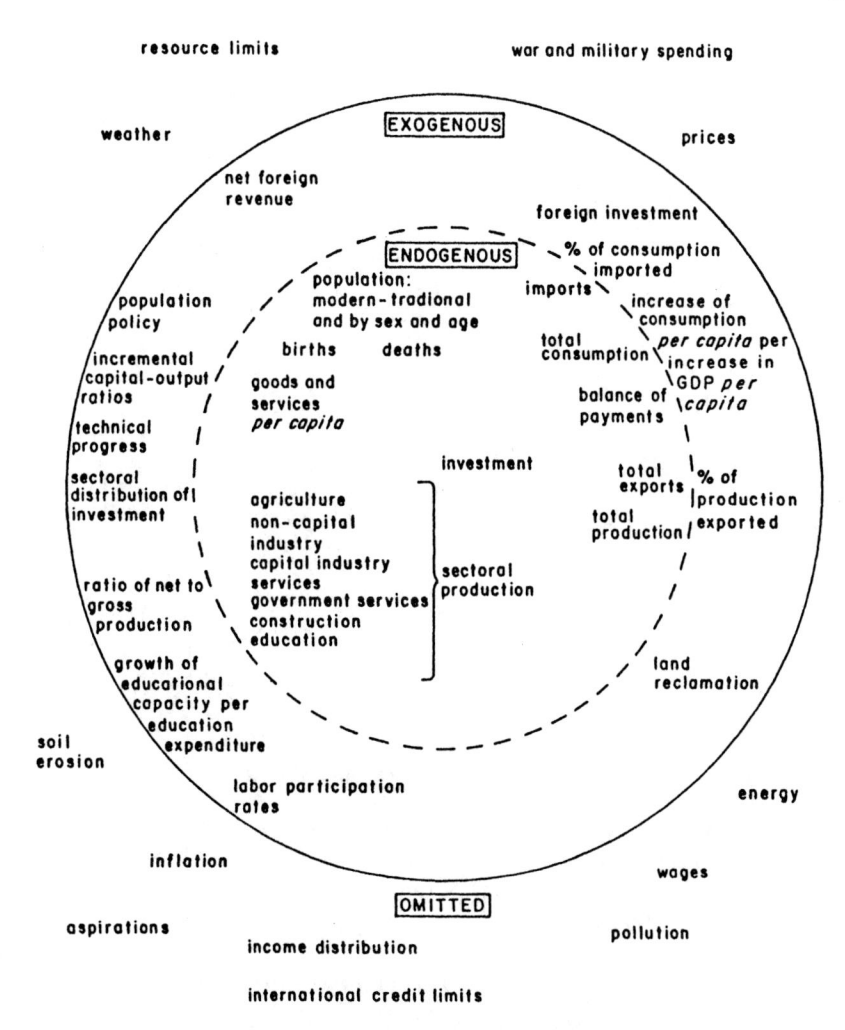

```
                    resource limits              war and military spending

        weather                                                      prices
                          ┌─────────────┐
                          │ EXOGENOUS   │
                  net foreign
                  revenue
                                          foreign investment
                          ┌─────────────┐
                          │ ENDOGENOUS  │  ╲ % of consumption
                      population:        imports ╲ imported
                      modern-tradional       ╲ increase of
          population   and by sex and age    total ╲ consumption
          policy                          consumption ╲ per capita per
         incremental   births    deaths                 ╲ increase in
         capital-output/                                   ╲ GDP per
         ratios      goods and              balance of    ╲ capita
         technical   services               payments        ╲
         progress    per capita
                                                            ╲
         sectoral                investment      total       ╲% of
         distribution of|                        exports     |production
         investment     agriculture              total       /exported
                        non-capital              production /
         ratio of net to industry                          /
         gross          capital industry    sectoral      /
         production     services            production   /
                        government services              /
         growth of      construction                    /
         educational    education                      / land
         capacity per                                 / reclamation
         education
         soil         expenditure
         erosion
                        labor participation                  energy
                        rates

            inflation                              wages
                          ┌─────────┐
                          │ OMITTED │
          aspirations                          pollution
                     income distribution

                    international credit limits
```

Figure 8.1 LTSM boundary diagram

[The] importance which we impute to education is not reflected in the model. Our representation simply connects educational investments with its effect on average education cumulated in the adult population in a very simple and rough way. Our reason for doing so is motivated by the fact that good long-term educational planning models tend to be complex exercises in themselves.[12]

E. STRUCTURE

LTSM can be understood as a competition between production and consumption. Consumption is the single most important check on economic growth in the model. That which is consumed cannot be invested, and without investment the economy does not grow.

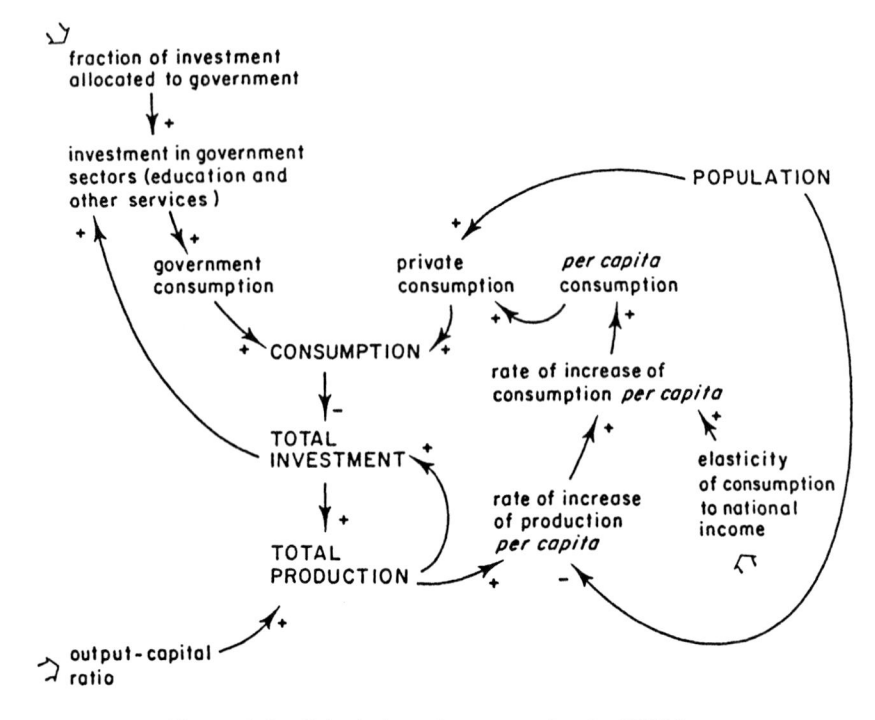

Figure 8.2 Calculation of consumption in LTSM

The way the model accounts for consumption is shown in Figure 8.2. Total consumption is defined as the sum of government consumption and private consumption. Government consumption at any time is equal to government consumption in the previous year plus the increment in government consumption. Incremental government consumption is proportional to the funds allocated for investment in education and in other government services. This allocation is an exogenously-determined policy variable.

Private consumption is the product of consumption *per capita* and population. *Per capita* consumption increases at a rate proportional to the rate of increase in total production *per capita*. Notice the rate linked to a rate here; it is not the absolute level of output *per capita* but its *rate of change* that is presumed to increase consumption. This kind of formulation is common in LTSM. Nearly every behavioral equation in the model is based on a rate of change rather than an absolute level. The elasticity of the consumption response to GNP growth rate is exogenously determined and is considered a policy variable. The elasticity is zero in the downward direction; that is, if income *per capita* should fall, consumption *per capita* will not fall.

Population, the second determinant of consumption, is a separate sector in the model, including many state variables and considerable internal feedback. The essential variables of the population sector, their internal feedback, and the inputs to the population sector from other model sectors are shown in Figure 8.3.

The population is disaggregated into four age cohorts (not indicated in the diagram) in the prototype model and 16 cohorts in the Egyptian demonstration model.

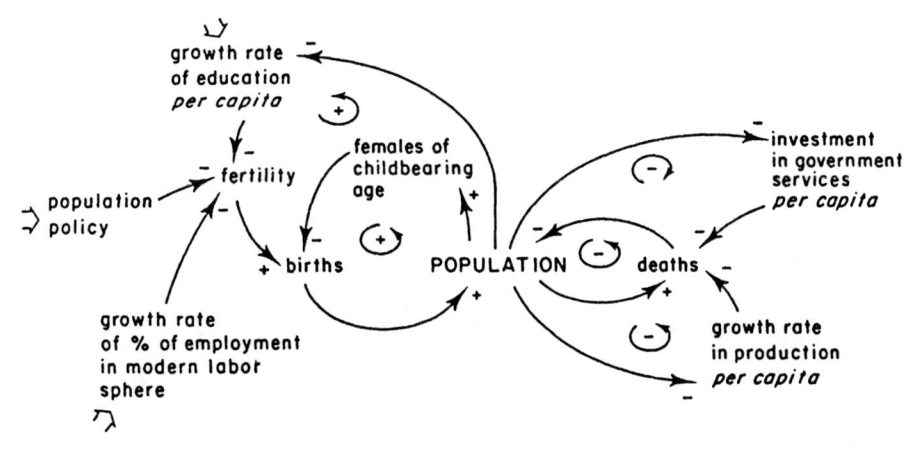

Figure 8.3 LTSM population sector

The number of births per year is a function of the number of females of childbearing age and the fraction of women in these categories giving birth (fertility). Fertility is decreased if there is a positive growth rate in the level of education, if there is growth in levels of employment in the modern production sectors relative to the size of the female population, and if the government imposes a population policy. The population policy is an exogenously-set multiplier on the educational effect on fertility—it makes education more effective in depressing the birth rate, and it is ineffective if education does not improve. No cost is assigned to the imposition of the population policy, and its exact mechanism is not specified. Note again the behavioral linkage between rates. The *rate* of decrease of fertility depends on the *rate* of increase of education, not directly on the level of educational attainment the population has reached. Thus a 10% increase in education would decrease fertility by (say) 5% regardless of what educational level or fertility level the population had reached.

This arrangement creates two positive feedback loops (see Figure 8.3). Increase in population furthers still more increase in population both through raising (after an aging delay) the number of women of childbearing age and through diluting the average growth rate of education *per capita*. Being tied to two positive feedback loops, population will grow exponentially unless some force acts to offset its structural propensity to grow, either through decreasing the birth rate or increasing the death rate (or both simultaneously).

The annual number of deaths in the model is the product of population and mortality (deaths per thousand persons per year). Mortality is decreased by investment in government services *per capita* and by the growth rate in GDP *per capita*, both of which are slowed by population increase. Thus the death rate is tied to two negative feedback loops. If GDP and government services remained constant, an increase in population would erode GDP *per capita* and government services *per capita*, thereby increasing deaths, decreasing population, and stabilizing the system.

In summary, the consumption side of the consumption-production race is dominated by exponential population growth, which can at least theoretically be offset by *per capita* production growth rates so slow that mortality rises, or by employment and education growth rates so rapid that fertility drops.

LTSM's basic production function for each productive sector states that production is equal to production in the last time period, plus the product of the capital-output ratio and investment in the last time period. Investment in each sector is equal to the total investment available (the previous year's output minus consumption) times the fraction of investment allocated to each sector (exogenous). Depreciation of capital is not modeled explicitly, but must be subsumed in the capital-output ratio. This ratio also contains an exogenously-determined technological improvement factor. The role of labor in production is omitted, under the assumption that labor is in surplus and thus never a limiting factor. The authors are careful to emphasize that the model pertains only to a labor-surplus economy.

The form of this basic production equation is replicated for production in non-capital industry, capital-producing industry, education, services, and government services. Different sectors of production have different capital-output ratios. Only the agriculture and construction sectors (as will be discussed below) vary the basic production function.

Construction output is determined as described above, but construction investment is calculated endogenously—the only investment that is not considered an exogenous policy variable. Demand for new construction is calculated as a (linear) function of the new investment scheduled for all the other economic sectors. If the construction capital is not capable of producing that much construction, the fraction allocated to construction investment is increased and all the other investment allocations are reduced proportionately. This internal balance is maintained only for construction. If other sectors require more capital than is available, the difference is made up from imports and the foreign debt level is increased.

In the agriculture sector, production is the product of land and yield per unit land (see Figure 8.4) Land may be increased by an exogenously-driven land reclamation policy variable, and it is decreased by construction activity such as road building. Yields increase with increases in investment in machinery or annual inputs (fertilizer, seeds, and pesticides) per unit land. Again the *rate* of change of yield depends on the *rate* of change of inputs. Yield response to the increase rates of both inputs and investment is linear and unbounded.

In LTSM annual agricultural input usage increases with gains in agricultural production, and agricultural production increases with higher input rates (heavily outlined inner loop in Figure 8.4). Input costs are calculated and subtracted from gross output, which could counteract this positive loop, except

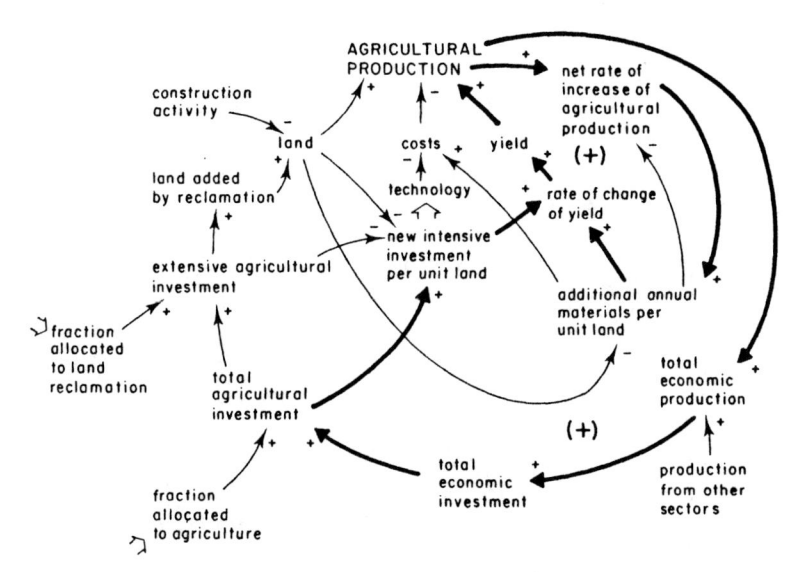

Figure 8.4   LTSM agriculture sector

that material inputs are also assumed to become more efficient as a function of time (and presumably, technology). Not only does agriculture have this internal growth loop, it is also driven by the same production-investment loop that drives the model's other sectors of production (also outlined heavily in Figure 8.4).

Since it is internally driven by a positive feedback loop, unhindered by diminishing returns and free from soil erosion or other environmental problems, production in LTSM's agriculture sector grows rapidly. The only obstacle to agricultural growth in the model seems to be agriculture's ties to the less aggressive growth structure of the total economy. Rather than coming back to agriculture directly, agricultural production is lumped into GDP. GDP growth increases investment across the board. In so doing, it increases investment in all sectors, only a fraction of which returns to agriculture. Thus the agriculture sector can expand through investment only by pulling the whole economy up with it.

In summary, economic production in LTSM is driven by positive feedback. In each productive sector production creates investable output, and investment increases production. This mutually-reinforcing growth configuration, like all positive feedback structures, will produce exponential growth. Exogenous forces directly influence the growth rate by altering:

1. Sectoral capital-output ratios.
2. The distribution of investment between sectors.
3. Sectoral ratios of gross to net production (i.e., cost margins).

Consumption can put a brake on the growth loop by decreasing the total funds available for investment.

Economic-demographic feedback appears in the model when the production and consumption sides are joined. For the most part this feedback slows economic growth. If the growth loops on the production side cause economic growth, people will have higher incomes, and (depending on exogenous policy) more government services. Both higher incomes and more government services will lower death rates and population will begin to grow, increasing consumption. Rising consumption will encroach on investment. Reduced investment will inhibit economic growth, perhaps to the point that incomes fall and the death rate rises. However, if the economic growth loops are strong enough to resist the population drag, eventually higher employment and education will decrease birth rates, permitting an economic take-off.

Education expenditure plays an important role in the model in nudging the balance between population and economic growth toward the economic side. Growth in education *per capita* lowers fertility and decreases the rate of population growth. Slower population growth means fewer children to educate and fewer mouths to feed, therefore less consumption. Less consumption leaves more funds for investment in education and in economic growth. The 'population problem' can be solved by this loop. Note, however, that if population begins to stifle economic growth, the education loop becomes a vicious circle. Instead of a launch toward economic take-off, there are more people, less education *per capita*, higher fertility, more people, less funds for education and growth, and more children to educate.

Dangling from the LTSM structure but apparently not essential to it are two population-shift processes, urban-rural migration and movement from the family labor sphere to the hired labor sphere (we shall call the latter process 'employment migration'). Labor in LTSM is not an input to production, and the urban-rural balance does not seem to affect model behavior greatly. The fertility in the family-labor sphere is higher than that in the hired-labor sphere and fertility is decreased by rapid rates of growth of employment. Therefore employment migration has some demographic consequence, apparently its only consequence. Rural-urban migration appears to have no effect on the system at all, aside from serving as an indication of policy results.

The urban-rural and family labor-hired labor shifts are modeled almost identically. To avoid redundancy we shall describe only the structure simulating employment migration. As described by the modelers, the employment function rests:

> ... on the assumption that employment growth, except for [that of] the modern agriculture [sector] is proportional to capital invested. The more rapid growth of capital will result in a more rapid growth of employment. That is, modern sectors are considered as the dynamic element whose expansion of employment depends on the process of capital formation. However, traditional sectors are assumed to absorb the residual of labor force.[13]

The causal structure of the employment function is diagrammed in Figure 8.5. Starting from the lower left side of the diagram, investment in the modern

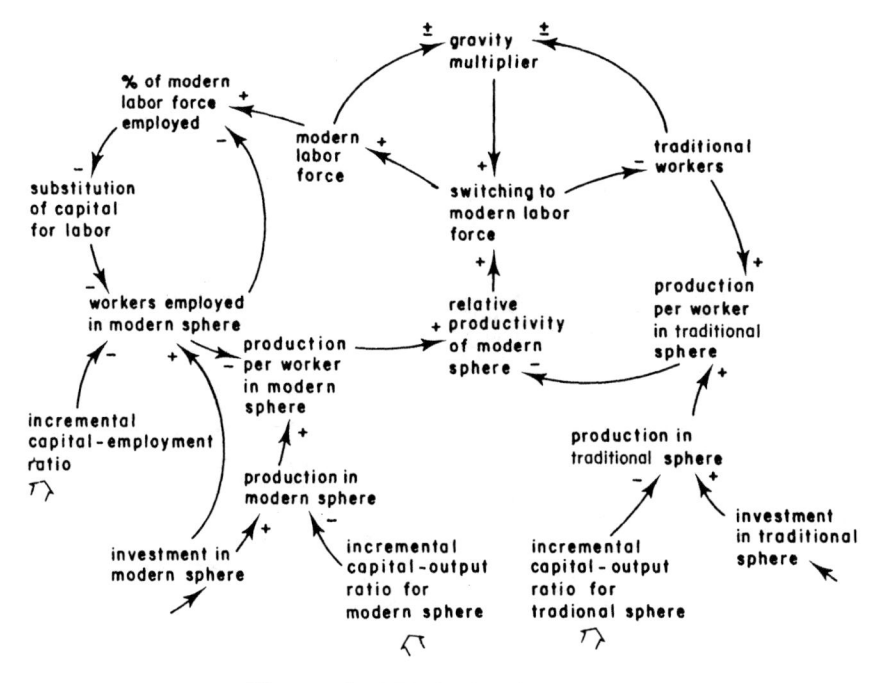

Figure 8.5 LTSM migration structure

economic sectors simultaneously increases production and employment, thereby altering production per worker. If production increases faster than employment (which will happen so long as the exogenous incremental capital-output ratio is higher than the exogenous incremental capital-labor ratio) labor productivity will rise, increasing the productivity gap between modern and traditional spheres.

As productivity in the traditional sphere falls behind, workers will move from the traditional to the modern sphere. The speed of movement is regulated by a factor termed a 'gravity multiplier'. This gravity multiplier causes motion between the sectors to be most rapid when numbers of traditional and modern workers are equal and to approach zero as the population in either sphere falls to zero. The gravity multiplier seems to be derived from a sort of diffusion theory of migration; the more workers there are in a sector, the more are likely to switch to another sector. However, in this model the flow goes only one way, from traditional to modern.

Laborers switched out of the traditional sphere become employed as further investment in the modern sector creates jobs for them. If unemployment becomes very low, the modern sector substitutes capital for labor (at no cost) and hires fewer laborers per unit of investment.

In the traditional sector, out-migration reduces the labor force but not production. Because labor productivity is defined as the ratio of production to labor force, out-migration increases labor productivity in the traditional sector,

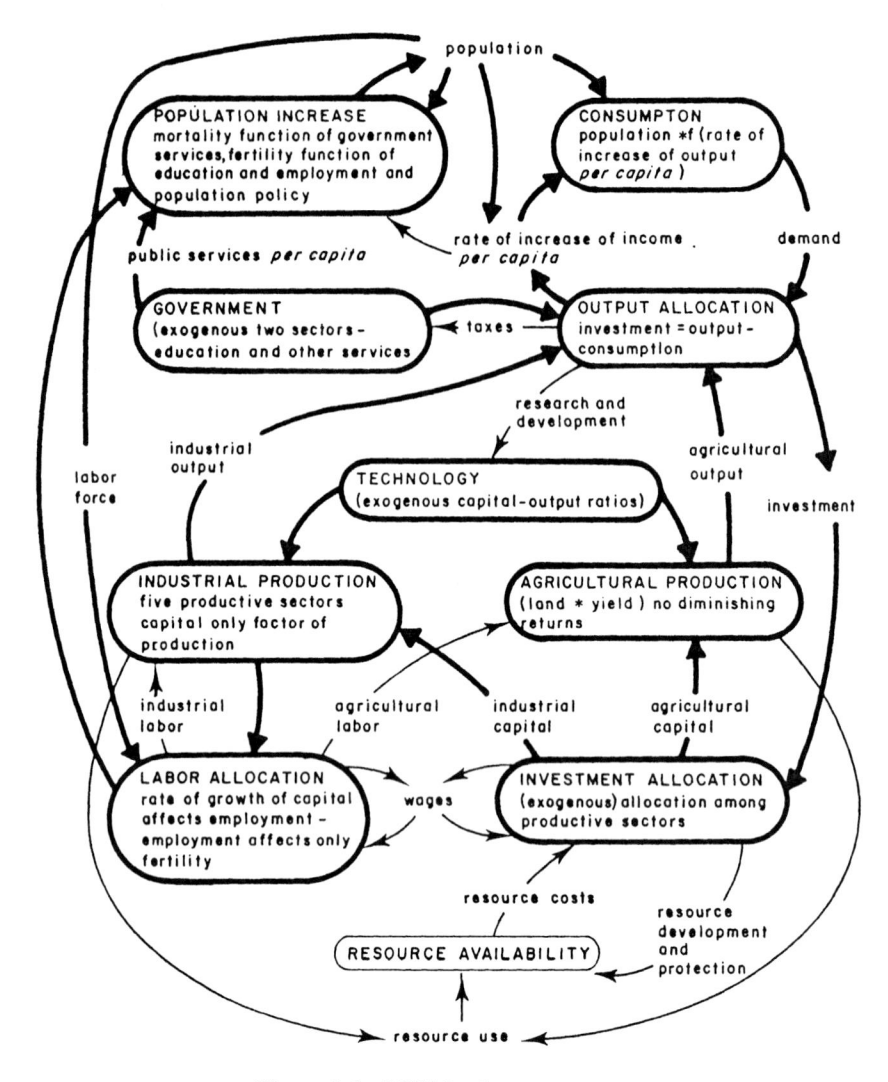

Figure 8.6 LTSM reference structure

which tends to decrease the modern-traditional labor-productivity gap. The smaller gap reduces the rate of out-migration.

The important structural elements of LTSM are shown on the Reference Structure, Figure 8.6. LTSM contains enough exogenous policy variables that anyone who understands the model's structure could adjust parameters to produce economic growth or stagnation. However, reasonable choices of parameters cannot allow population growth rates to rise above 4% per year. Since only a pessimist would make economic growth come out to less than 4%, most parameter choices will give economic growth an edge over population growth.

Expenditures on agriculture and education will tend to be very rewarding, agriculture because it contains the input-production growth loop described above, and education because expenditure on education nudges the population-economic fulcrum toward economic growth. By contrast, investment in health services, which lower death rates and thereby increase the population while simultaneously removing funds from productive investment, will tend to stifle economic growth.

Although there are many state variables in the model (such as the population levels, which are accumulations of the flows of births, deaths, and migration) the usual dynamic function of these variables in delaying and damping system changes are undercut by the nearly ubiquitous linking of rates to rates. For example, if changes in education were accumulated in an education level and fertility then made a function of that level (perhaps with a further delay assumed for perception and social change), expenditures of education would have a much smaller and slower effect in the model system. The rate–rate linking generally makes the model behavior more volatile than that of a model based on level-rate links.

F. DATA

The LTSM documentation contains a clear and useful summary of the data requirements and outputs of the model.[14] Data requirements are modest and consist primarily of initial values for such inherently measurable quantities as land under cultivation, sectoral production, outstanding foreign debt, and population by age and sex. The data for *policy* inputs are more numerous and more difficult and will be discussed further under Testing below.

The Egyptian experimental application uses data from standard sources, both from Egyptian statistical agencies and UN agencies. The model's documentation does not identify sources of individual numbers. It merely lists general sources.

A more recent adaptation of the model to Pakistan contains a lengthy appendix, listing not only data sources but tables of actual data used in determining the model parameters.[15]

G. TESTING

To verify their model's behavior, the LTSM modelers compared simulated results with historical data for the years 1964–1969. Some of the results of this test are shown in Figure 8.7. By calculating the coefficients of variation between real and simulated data, the modelers decided that model output was 'very comparable' to actual system behavior.[16] The comparability of simulated and actual data is said by the modelers to be 'the most convincing evidence found for accepting the structure of this simulation model in analyzing the Egyptian economy and accepting its predictive ability'.[17] Model projections are also compared with projections from the FAO Egyptian Country

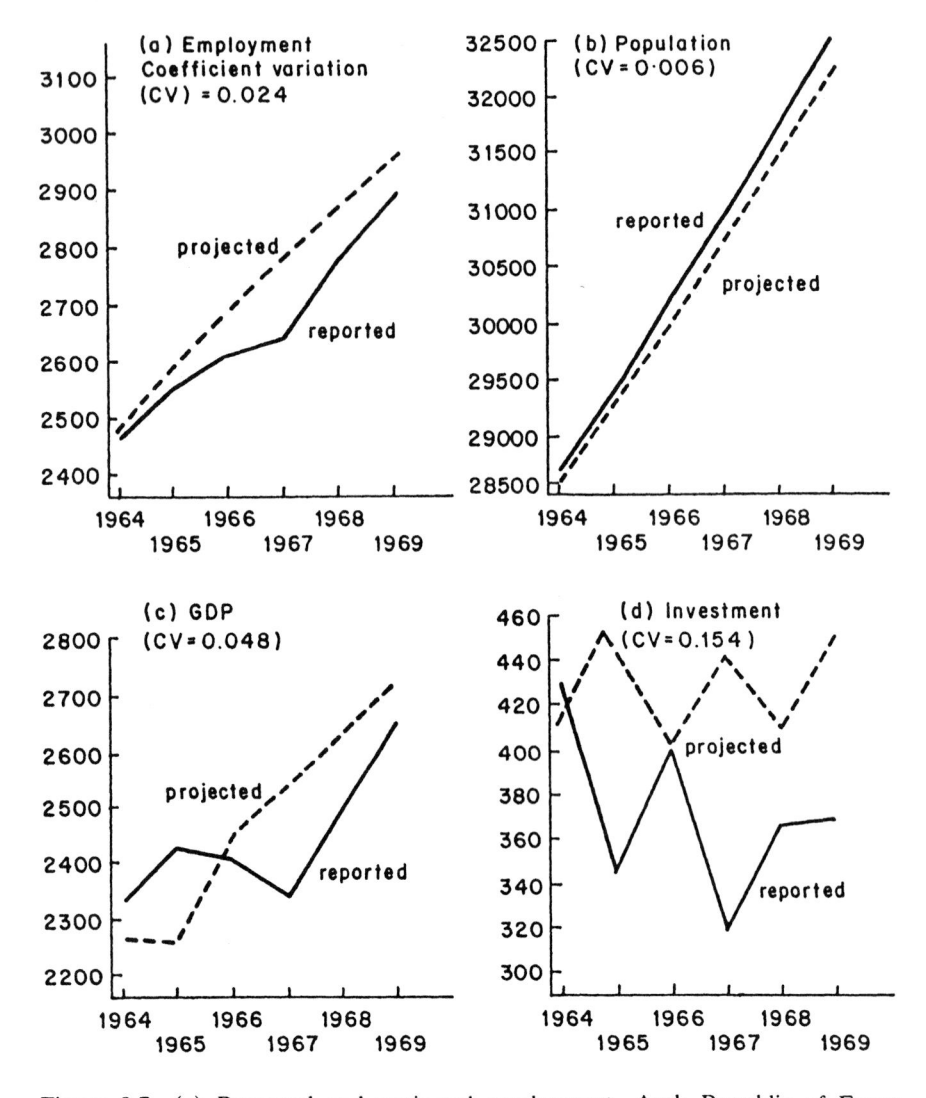

Figure 8.7 (a) Reported and projected employment, Arab Republic of Egypt, 1964–1969. (b) Reported and projected population, Arab Republic of Egypt, 1964–1969. (c) Reported and projected GDP, Arab Republic of Egypt, 1964–1969. (d) Reported and projected investment, Arab Republic of Egypt 1964–1969. Reproduced from Lin and Ottaviani-Carra, p. 45

Perspective Study as a means of demonstrating the model's validity by 'intuitive judgement'.[18] The model projections usually fall between the high and low estimates of the earlier FAO projection. No explanation is given as to how comparison with other projections demonstrates model validity, nor are the assumption behind the other projections presented.

This five-year historical tracking test is far from sufficient to demonstrate the general reasonableness of the model's behavior, even if we ignore the poor fit of the GDP and investment variables. Economic-demographic feedback can hardly become manifest over such a short period. No long-term model runs are illustrated in the documentation—in fact, the model does not seem to have been run past the simulated year 1980. The 'long term' behavior of a model named Long-Term Socioeconomic Model seems to be unexplored. (The Pakistan adaptation of the model is matched with data from 1968 to 1974 and run out to 1990.[19])

Variable sensitivity was observed by altering one at a time each policy variable of the standard model and observing the effect over the simulation period 1970–1980. A matrix is presented showing what effects changes in nine policy variables will have on 13 endogenous variables after ten years of simulation.[20] From this matrix one can, for example, find that a 100% increase (over the standard run) in agriculture's share of investment leads to at least 5% more private *per capita* consumption in 1980, and that a 100% increase in land reclamation will lead to 5% less employment in 1980. It is difficult to understand all the sensitivity results intuitively. For example, it is not clear what chain of events causes a 10% decrease in agricultural exports to produce a >5% drop in education level. The mode of presentation only allows the reader to examine how changes in exogenous parameters affect other parameters at one point of time.

H. CONCLUSIONS

Three scenarios representing different 'development alternatives' were tested in the Egyptian demonstration model for their effects over the period 1970–1980. The first (Alternative I) represents 'quasicontinuation of past trends in ... policy formation'.[21] The second, a high employment strategy (Alternative II), features investment in industry, education, and health (at the expense of investment in agriculture and other sectors) along with a population policy. The third (Alternative III) emphasizes investment in agriculture (at the expense of industry and services), increased land reclamation, and no change in education, health, and population policies.

Results of these three policy alternatives are presented (to four significant figures) and compared at length. Predictably, agriculture does best under the agricultural strategy and employment is highest with the industrial strategy. Predictably, also, given the extra growth loop in the agricultural production sector, the agricultural strategy results in faster economic growth and higher GDP. The results of the three policy tests are summarized in Table 8.2.

The authors do not emphasize the trade-offs implicit in this table, nor do they indicate whether the relationships shown there are inevitable; for example, they do not indicate whether some other policy set could be found that would produce high GNP with low population growth.

As previously discussed, the projection period used is too short to manifest much demographic feedback. The model's demographic implications would

Table 8.2 Results of LTSM policy tests[22]

Policy	GDP	Agriculture output	Employment	Population
Alternative I (continuation of present policies)	medium	medium	low	medium
Alternative II (increased total investment, 50% increase in education and health expenditure)	low	low	high	low
Alternative III (increased land reclamation and investment in agriculture)	high	high	medium	high

have come out much more clearly had model runs been sufficiently long to show the effects of today's policies on the next generation, and to cover a full population-doubling time (less than 30 years at the 2.1% to 2.6% growth rates manifested by the model). Demographic conclusions drawn from the half-generation projection contrast 41 million people for Egypt under the high-employment, low-fertility Alternative II to 43 million for Alternatives I and III. The modelers also find that more migration to cities and into the modern labor sphere occurs in Alternative II.

The modelers are careful to label their findings as tentative, to stress 'the limitations of quantitative approaches as aids in decision-making'[23] and to avoid making generalizations about the effect of one or another policy on development. Their conclusions are mostly constrained to literal reporting of model performance in forms such as: 'agricultural development is higher under development Alternative III than under Alternatives I and II'.[24]

The application of the model to Pakistan, which involved some elaboration and structural change (such as distinguishing between small and large farms and making population exogenous), was also run only under broad policy alternatives, five of them this time. The results are summarized by the authors as follows:

> Alternative I which assumes a quasi-continuation of the historical development pattern is inferior to Alternative II which places major emphasis on better income distribution, agricultural sector development and rapid fertility decline ... Development strategy aiming at industrial sector development, self-reliance and large farms (Alternative III) turns out to be substantially inferior to both Alternatives I and II as it yields lower rate of GDP growth, *per capita* consumption, food surplus and higher unemployment ... High unemployment ratio (average

20.4–21.8% in formal labor sectors) is common to Alternatives I, II, and III. This implies that unemployment is the major problem facing the Pakistan economy during the projected period. Development strategy under Alternative IV is specially designed to reduce unemployment and, at the same time, achieve better income distribution ... Alternative IV(a) combining policies of better income distribution, phased sectoral development focus, better economic management with rapid fertility decline ... results in higher overall GDP growth, *per capita* consumption and investment rate and lower unemployment ratio as compared to other Alternatives. Alternative IV(b) which adds a policy of containing consumption orientation at historical levels, yields the highest GDP growth, *per capita* consumption, investment rate and food surplus, and the lowest unemployment ratio... Differences in economic-demographic features of various development strategies imply that important policy choices exist for Pakistan economy which should make long-term perspective planning a useful exercise in national planning.[25]

I. IMPLEMENTATION

A planning group in Egypt did carry on their own adaptation of the model in their country (as opposed to the demonstration model of Egypt done in Rome). Pakistani planning experts completed and documented their country's version of the model. As of 1979, the model was no longer in use at the FAO, and the staff that worked on it were dispersed to other tasks. Whether the message from the preliminary model runs quoted above were ever heeded at the policymaking level was not determinable. The long-term institutional support and promotion that TEMPO enjoyed did not persist for LTSM. The general friendliness to the idea of modeling in FAO's Policy Analysis Division at the beginning of the LTSM project waned markedly, not so much because of any reaction to LTSM, but because of the retirement or transfer of some key institutional supporters.[26]

J. COMPUTER REQUIREMENTS

LTSM is considerably larger than TEMPO. The prototype model consists of about 140 endogenous variables, of which 74 are not repetitious.[27] The model can easily be programmed in either FORTRAN or DYNAMO following the generic equations given in the documentation. Exact computer requirements are not specified, but the data requirements are not large, and the model calculations should take very little time on any modern computer.

K. DOCUMENTATION

The FAO's intent was to build a prototype model that planning agencies in participating nations could adapt to their respective conditions and needs. Presumably the FAO modeling staff was to be available to help with these adaptations. Given this purpose, documentation had to make the model clear and usable, but need not attempt impeccable coverage of details. This is exactly the sort of documentation FAO team produced.

LTSM's documentation is straightforward, well organized, and easy to comprehend. The model has been described in a number of contexts to both technical and non-technical audiences.[28] In the original and still basic description of the model[29] generalized discussion of the study's scope and purpose leads into a description of system simulation, what it is, and why system simulation is an appropriate methodology for the study's purpose. Equations are presented and explained. Variable names are systematically defined, which makes program explanations easy to follow. Testing procedures are explained. Output is presented, in both complete and summary forms, to show the results of testing.

Bela Martos' verbal descriptions of the modeling procedure in slightly Hungarian-flavored English should be awarded a prize for honest, straightforward, unpretentious model description. Here are a few examples:

> The level of production in each productive sector is determined by its productive capacity and no possible underutilization is taken into account ... This gives the whole model a supply-oriented character. Our reasons for choosing this approach are twofold. First the studying of previous models ... convinced us that demand projections serve as the usual starting point. Thus this type of model structures is sufficiently explored and we found no reason to repeat others' approach ... We do not think that the long-term planning process consists of the application of a single model.[30]

> We are well aware that many long-term models contain an input coefficient matrix which is theoretically supposed to change in time. But when it comes to real calculations they usually replace it with a time independent matrix, not having any better choice. It is not always true that something is better than nothing and we think this is just the case when it is not.[31]

> With a fixed set of the calibrated parameters and with the initial set of policy variables we have calculated a candidate for the 'standard path' ... It need not be 'good', we shall not necessarily recommend it as one of the selection for final consideration by the policymaker. Its only role is to yield a standard with which all other paths shall be compared. The procedure is similar to that used in calibrating the parameters. It is not worth experimenting too long. The 'standard path' can be dethronized anytime during ... the simulation and replaced by another.[32]

Candid acknowledgement is made of the model's faults, as the modelers perceive them.[33] A 'Guide to the Computer Program'[34] explains how to parameterize the computer program. The language used throughout is clear and to the point. Jargon is minimized. French, Spanish, and English versions are available.

NOTES AND REFERENCES

1. H. Quaix, Policy Analysis Division, FAO, February 18, 1976.
2. The research purpose is most emphasized in the initial report on the LTSM model, B. Martos, 'Long-Term Employment Simulation Model', PA4/1 INT/73/PO2, Working Paper Series No. 1, Policy Analysis Division, FAO, Rome, May 1974.

3. *Ibid.*, p. 2.
4. H. Quaix, *op.cit.*
5. B. Martos and Wuu-Long Lin, 'Long-term Socio-economic Country Simulation', FAO Long-Term Employment Simulation Project PA4/1 INT/73/PO2 Working Paper Series No. 6. Paper presented at the Third World Congress of the Econometric Society, Toronto, August 1975. Development Research and Training Service, Policy Analysis Division, FAO, Rome, pp. 2–3, May 1975.
6. B. Martos, *op.cit.*, p. 4.
7. *Ibid.*, p. 4.
8. *Ibid.*, p. 8.
9. *Ibid.*, p. 7.
10. *Ibid.*, p. 3.
11. *Ibid.*, p. 14.
12. *Ibid.*, p. 17.
13. Wuu-Long Lin, 'A System Simulation Approach to Economic-Demographic Interaction', FAO Long-Term Employment Simulation Project PA4/1 INT/73/PO2 Working Paper Series No. 2. Development Research and Training Service, Policy Analysis Division, FAO, Rome, p. 29, September 1971.
14. Wuu-Long Lin and M. G. Ottaviani-Carra, 'A Systems Simulation Approach to Integrated Population and Economic Planning', FAO Long-Term Employment Simulation Project PA4/1 INT/73/PO2 Working Paper Series No. 7, FAO, Development Research & Training Service, Policy Analysis Division, Rome, p. 75, August 1975.
15. 'A Systems Simulation Approach to Integrated Population and Economic Planning with Special Emphasis on Agricultural Development and Employment: an Experimental Study of Pakistan', FAO/Pakistan Project on System Simulation, PA4/1 INT/73/PO2 Working Paper Series No. 11, FAO, Rome, March 1976.
16. Wuu-Long Lin and M. G. Ottaviani-Carra, *op.cit.*, p. 44.
17. *Ibid.*, p. 44.
18. *Ibid.*, p. 44.
19. 'A Systems Simulation Approach to Integrated Population and Economic Planning with Special Emphasis on Agricultural Development and Employment: An Experimental Study of Pakistan', *op.cit.*, p. 48.
20. Wuu-Long Lin and M. G. Ottaviani-Carra, *op.cit.*, p. 48.
21. *Ibid.*, p. 49.
22. Table reproduced with permission from Wuu-Long Lin and M. G. Ottaviani-Carra, *op.cit.*, p. 51.
23. Wuu-Long Lin and M. G. Ottaviani-Carra, *op.cit.*, p. 73.
24. *Ibid.*, p. 72.
25. 'A Systems Simulation Approach to Integrated Population and Economic Planning with Special Emphasis on Agricultural Development and Employment: An Experimental Study of Pakistan', *op.cit.*, p. 74.
26. M. G. Ottaviani-Carra, personal communication.
27. B. Martos and Wuu-Long Lin, *op.cit.*, p. 11.
28. For a short description plus comments from other modelers, see 'Report on the FAO/UNFPA Seminar on Methodology, Research, and Country Case Studies on Population, Employment and Productivity', FAO/UN/TF154, FAO, Rome, 1975.
29. B. Martos, *op.cit.*
30. *Ibid.*, p. 12.
31. *Ibid.*, p. 13.
32. *Ibid.*, p. 43.
33. B. Martos and Wuu-Long Lin, *op.cit.*, pp. 27–28.
34. Wuu-Long Lin and M. G. Ottaviani-Carra, *op.cit.*, pp. 89–90 Appendix II.

CHAPTER 9

BACHUE: a Twenty-Legged Robot

A. INSTITUTIONAL SETTING

BACHUE is another entrant in the on-going political debate about the role of population growth in economic development. One side of this debate argues that population growth is a serious hindrance to economic development and that fertility reduction is a necessary step toward economic growth. Opponents of this position attack it on many grounds. They claim that it ignores the positive effects of population growth on economic demand and on the labor force. It also ignores the possibility that high fertility is a result of poverty and can only be changed by eliminating poverty. Finally, advocacy of population control is sometimes attributed to a belief of wealthy people that the poor are ignorant and unthinkingly have too many children. This belief aggravates those who believe the poor are poor because the wealthy have exploited them or otherwise denied them opportunity to achieve material well-being.

Advocates of the fertility-reduction position have a number of well-established mathematical models with which to uphold their position. TEMPO, discussed previously, is one such model. Another is TEMPO's predecessor, the Coale–Hoover model.[1] Until the early 1970s, opponents of the fertility-reduction position had not produced such explicit quantitative models. In consequence, they could not debate TEMPO and its kind in the arena of quantitative analysis. Thus there was a demand for mathematical formalization of the ideological alternative to the TEMPO-type model.

One tentative response to this demand was the LTSM model of the FAO (which was also trying to make another point: that agriculture is as important as industry in development planning). A stronger response came almost simultaneously from the United Nations International Labor Organization (ILO). There Richard Blandy, then the head of the Population and Employment Project, decided to build a more sophisticated economic-demographic model than any then available. Blandy and his colleague, Réné

Wéry, built an initial model which they called BACHUE after a Colombian goddess of love, fertility, and harmony between man and nature.

BACHUE was developed under a friendly, informal management. Its initiator was head of the project, thus it tended to be administered through personal interest rather than through bureaucratic formalities. Schedules, plans, and management were flexible, and the modeling team was free to work according to the opportunities that appeared in the course of the model's progress. Over the five-year lifetime of the Population and Employment Project, the BACHUE modeling staff gradually evolved from two people finding spare moments to organize their ideas to three full-time modelers[2] plus a supporting staff working on developing the model into a usable tool for policy analysis.

B. PURPOSE

As one of the BACHUE modelers put it, the model's original purpose 'was to give a more balanced hypothesis as a response to the popular anti-natalist position shown by the Coale–Hoover and Enke–TEMPO type models'.[3] More specifically, BACHUE was constructed to bring into an economic-demographic model some factors that many professional analysts felt to be important in economic-demographic relations. Such factors include income distribution, employment, feedback from social conditions to demographic processes, and the ways in which population growth stimulates as well as slows economic growth. Thus the original purpose of the model was partly didactic and partly academic—it was an experiment in integrating theories about social change during economic development, especially theories the modelers felt had been ignored.

As BACHUE developed, its purpose became broader. The first prototype BACHUE model evolved into specific country applications, and as it did so, the antithesis to TEMPO developed into a thesis in its own right. The BACHUE team established communication with interested academics and country planners, first in the Philippines and then in other countries. They listened to the theories and problems of the specific countries and incorporated some of them in an expanded model, BACHUE-2. Gradually the modelers' initial hopes that BACHUE might eventually serve as a general planning tool began to be realized.

The model's purpose is now explained in this way:

> There are several potential uses for models in the BACHUE series, but the main rationale for their development is to provide a laboratory that can evaluate policies which affect the size and distribution of population, and policies which might create productive employment and alter the distribution of income over the longer term. At the same time, the models examine the effects of economic change on the growth, distribution, and structure of population, as well as the reverse effects of demographic change on economic development.[4]

This is a purpose so broad as to admit almost any socioeconomic theory into the model, and, as we shall see, BACHUE has turned out to be a model of enormous size. But the modelers do describe some particular angles of the industrialization puzzle they are especially interested in, and they justify their interest with one of the few value statements we encountered in any of the nine model descriptions:

> The subject focus of our work...is population, employment and income distribution, rather than population and development as a whole. This partly reflects a self-imposed limitation, an attempt to somewhat reduce the size of the subject to be covered... But it also reflects the values we bring to the subject... Underlying our work are biases towards the provision of productive employment, a more equal distribution of income and wealth and the elimination of poverty as the central objectives of development. Linked to these objectives are an appreciation of and a respect for the rights of individuals and families... While these biases are perhaps not particularly novel, nor objectionable, we prefer to make them clear since they of course influence the content and interpretation of our work.[5]

C. METHOD

BACHUE is a medium- to long-term model; it is usually run to the year 2000. It is basically a simulation model, but the BACHUE modelers are not strictly allied to one school of modeling. Literature citations in BACHUE documentation imply that prototypes for the work include system dynamics models.[6] The model builders stress the difficulty of understanding complex feedbacks with an unaided mental model. They emphasize the model as a total system, rather than specific relationships within the model. They attempt to make most important model variables endogenous, especially demographic variables, which are exogenous in TEMPO. And they adopt the system dynamics view of the world as dynamic, recursive, and dominated by lagged responses.

> In the real world, few interrelated events are truly simultaneous—they relate to each other with delays which may be a day or a month, a year or more. BACHUE-Philippines incorporates these lags by treating the process of growth as a disequilibrium one—a process of continually adjusting towards equilibria which themselves change over time.[7]

However, the BACHUE modelers also feel that system dynamics models tend to be too aggregated. They believe that the distribution of economic output and decisions at the level of individuals and households are of central importance in understanding interactions between economic growth and population growth. In defining their model, therefore, they favored representation of disaggregated networks of variables rather than aggregate indices. Population is disaggregated into a total of 152 age, sex, location, and education groups. The economy is represented as an input-output matrix with 13 production sectors. Economic output is allocated to over 40 population and employment groups. All the cross-interactions of these subdivisions add up to over 750 endogenous demographic variables and over 1000 economic ones.

Another important methodological attribute of the BACHUE modelers is their preference for statistical determination of model parameters wherever possible. In BACHUE-2, the Philippine country application (as of 1979 the only application on which documentation was available) statistical estimation techniques were used extensively both to determine model parameters and to define behavioral relationships between variables. Many regression analyses were performed, both on national data and on international cross-section data. The result is that most behavioral equations in the model are linear in the parameters and incorporate only directly measurable entities. The verbal description of the model contains many hypotheses about the goals and motivations that underlie reproductive or economic decisions, but the model itself contains only variables that are statistically accessible. For example, the modelers state that income is a poor indicator of consumer savings and that assets and permanent income would be more satisfactory to use, but in fact income is used in the model because data were not available on the other factors.[9]

The BACHUE modelers have not made statistical estimation an absolute fetish, however. Where data were not available, as in the case of price elasticities of demand, or where data were sparse, as in the case of incremental capital-output ratios, the modelers used their best judgement to fill in gaps and smooth out inconsistencies. Occasionally when the modelers had reasons to believe that the historical relationship as captured in regression analysis was likely to change, statistical findings were disregarded. For example, Philippine data showed no conclusive evidence that declines in fertility had been associated with increases in educational level or standard of living. However, analyses of international cross-sectional data indicated that such declines had occurred in other developing nations at levels of income and education somewhat higher than those that prevailed in the Philippines. The modelers therefore disregarded Philippine data and used international cross-sectional data to estimate the response of fertility to educational and economic variables.

In combining the dynamic, closed-system feedback concepts of system dynamics, the disaggregated matrix-manipulation techniques of input-output analysis, and the statistical inference tools of econometrics, the BACHUE team created a unique cross-paradigm model. The borrowings were combined thoughtfully, in a deliberate attempt to achieve the strengths and avoid the weaknesses of the individual modeling schools. The process created a horde of new conceptual, methodological, and structural difficulties. The combination of extreme disaggregation with statistical estimation resulted in staggering data requirements. The attempt to estimate formally parameters in a feedback structure violated some of the basic premises (such as absence of collinearities) of regression analysis and also required frequent linearization, violating the premises of system dynamics. And the disaggregation of a closed-loop model produced a structure of such behavioral complexity that, as we shall see, the model must be used primarily as a black box rather than as an aid to intuitive understanding.

D. BOUNDARIES

The BACHUE model is organized into three subsystems: population, economics, and income distribution. In discussing BACHUE's boundaries we shall describe the model's subsystems one after another. For each subsystem we shall enumerate the variables included, the level of aggregation at which they have been represented, and whether they are exogenous or endogenous. Variables that have been omitted will be discussed in association with subsystems within which they might have been included. The BACHUE boundaries are summarized in Figure 9.1.

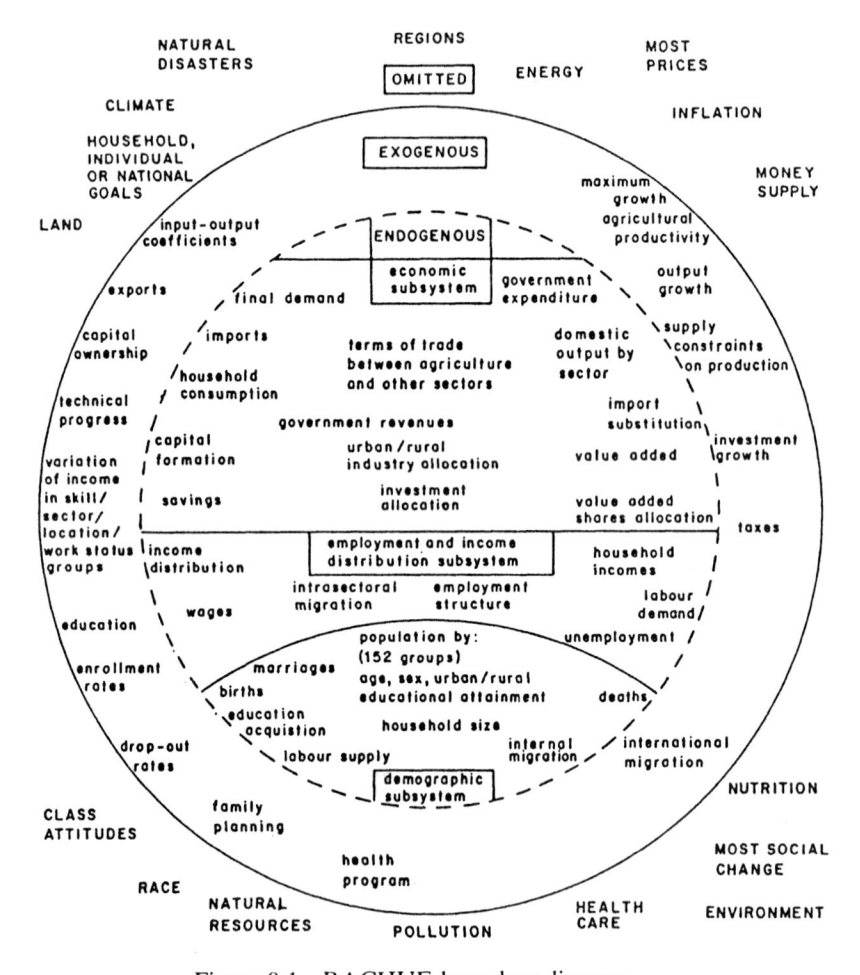

Figure 9.1 BACHUE boundary diagram

In BACHUE's demographic subsystem population is grouped by five year age cohorts, by urban or rural location, by sex, and by level of educational attainment. Marriage, marital fertility, rural-urban migration, and mortality are calculated endogenously for each age and education group. Education participation rates are introduced exogenously as a policy variable. In addition, exogenous policy controls are available for most demographic-change variables. The endogenous calculation of birth rates may be modified exogenously to represent family-planning programs; migration rates may be modified to represent restriction of migration.

Desired family size, attitudes about the economic utility of children, the status of women, nutrition, sanitation, machismo, and other hard-to-quantify variables are not explicitly included in the population susbsystem. However, in many cases they are implicit in model relationships. For example, education, a quantifiable variable that is strongly associated with attitude change, is assumed to have a significant impact on fertility, age of marriage, and migration. Likewise, income and income distribution—proxy variables that reflect sanitation conditions among other things—determine death rates.

BACHUE's economic subsystem contains 13 productive sectors, categorized according to whether they are modern or traditional and whether they are urban, rural, or split between urban and rural (Table 9.1). Private investment, exports, import substitution, input requirements per unit output, income elasticity of demand, and price elasticity of demand are exogenously determined for each sector except agriculture. Technical coefficients relating inputs to outputs are held constant. An exogenous constraint is generally placed on the growth of agricultural productivity, and an additional exogenous constraint is placed either on the rate of growth of aggregate output or on the balance of payments deficit.

Table 9.1 BACHUE-2 production sectors

	Modern	Traditional
Urban	mining modern consumer goods other manufacturers modern services and wholesale trade government	·
Split	construction transportation and public utilities	traditional consumer goods traditional services and retail trade
Rural	export crops forestry	domestic food crops livestock and fishing

From all these exogenous parameters and from information about the demographic and income distribution subsystems, the economic subsystem endogenously calculates, by economic sector, consumption demand, final demand, total output, and value-added. Only one price is calculated endogenously, the relative price index for rural versus urban products.

The economic subsystem is primarily determined by demand and by exogenous influences. Given the modelers' goal of closing the economic-demographic feedback loops, the exogenous representation of such important economic variables as investment and aggregate output seems surprising. The modelers justify this decision by the following four arguments:[10]

1. 'A realistic generation of aggregate output in the model would have required a complete disaggregated system of prices... It is very easy to think of simple ways to generate investment and output endogenously at an aggregate level, but we do not consider that a highly aggregated supply side would add significantly to the power of the model.'
2. 'The influence of demand can be underrated in production-oriented models. Demographic changes are likely to have important impacts on patterns of demand, and thus on the nature of economic growth.'
3. 'There is considerable uncertainty as to the relationships between demographic factors and output growth as a whole, particularly in relation to issues such as natural resource availability, facility of structural change, and the rate and nature of technical progress. Without substantial additional research, we considered it unwise to develop this area.'
4. 'The values of output embodied in government plans and targets are themselves valid as a framework for analysis, since it is in the context of such plans and targets that alternative policies would be designed and tested.'

Resource availability, land use, ecological variables, markets, and supply constraints from labor or capital are all omitted from the model. Socio-political and institutional forces impinging on economic behavior, such as attitudes towards risk, economic goals, and effects of uncertainty are omitted. Monetary system variables such as inflation, exchange rates, and credit structures are also omitted.

The income distribution subsystem calculates various categories of employment for each sector—rural and urban employment, skilled and unskilled employment, self-employment and wage employment, etc. From employment and values-added it calculates individual wages and non-wage incomes and translates them into household incomes. Income, income distribution, and household family size determine private consumption.

The modelers have omitted from their representation of income distribution nearly all of the variables sociologists and psychologists stress when discussing that subject, variables such as social structure, self-esteem, entrepreneurship, competitiveness, race, access to information, power relationships, and other sources of cultural diversity. Ownership of wealth is not clearly distinguished from receivership of income, although a self-employed category appears in the labor market disaggregation. The income-distribution subsystem essentially mirrors the visible and countable aspects of the existing distribution system, without representing directly the underlying forces that caused it to evolve that way or that might change it in the future.

E. STRUCTURE

Imagine the problems that would confront an engineer assigned to design a 20-legged robot that could dance the lead role in Swan Lake. The first problem would be the intrinsic clumsiness of things with many parts. How do you keep them from getting snarled up? How do you develop control mechanisms that keep the legs moving together in sensible patterns so the position of each is correct relative to the positions of the others? If the engineer were ingenious enough to perform this task, a second problem would appear. How do you program in advance the movement of 20 legs in a fashion that an audience will find intelligible, much less graceful?

The design problems the BACHUE modelers created for themselves when they opted to build a disaggregated feedback model are not unlike the problems confronting our hypothetical engineer. A feedback model is, in effect, a robot whose appendages are numbers rather than physical hardware. And as with the problem of 20 legs, the difficulties of coordinating feedbacks in a way that mimics real-world behavior increase very rapidly with the number of parts. Indeed, in some ways the robot problem is much simpler than BACHUE's disaggregated feedback problem. With the 20-leg robot one at least knows that the knee bone is connected to the thigh bone in every leg. In the interplay between 152 population groups, it may be difficult even to establish which variable is linked to which, much less whether the whole works is really being controlled by some force that has not been taken into account.

Yet despite the seeming impossibility of the task, the reasons for undertaking that task are apparent. If you have come to see the world as a series of interacting feedbacks, it is clear that realistic representation of system behavior requires attention to feedback structures. If the information stream in which you live is rich in categorical detail and you are tuned in to the importance of group differentiation, it will be hard to accept a model that excludes such detail.

In describing BACHUE's structure, we shall proceed subsystem by subsystem as we did in describing boundaries.

BACHUE's demographic component serves to keep track of the total size of the population, and to produce such information about attainments, rural-urban distribution, and age profiles as is required by other model components. The biological reality of aging and the theory of the demographic transition are the primary bases upon which the demographic sector is built.

Population moves automatically through a sex-compartmentalized age-cohort structure with the passage of time. Births are a function of (among other things) the number of women of childbearing age. A fraction of each age group, a relatively high fraction for the very old and very young, a relatively low fraction for other groups, dies each time period.

The aging module is not conceptually difficult. It is a system we all know well; it contains many repetitions of identical forms; there are few cross-flows, and most flows are uni-directional and sequential (people don't change sex, nor do they move from older to younger age groups nor from more-educated to less-educated levels). Only observable physical flows—in this case flows of people—are being accounted for.

This biological part of the population module does not deal with the most important questions about the demographic sector; namely, what determines fertility, mortality, education, and migration. The BACHUE modelers have formalized a version of the theory of demographic transition in order to deal with fertility and mortality. The theory of demographic transition holds that the process of industrialization generates a demographic shift from a high-fertility, high-mortality norm to a low-fertility, low-mortality norm, with the mortality decrease preceding the fertility decrease by several decades. Factors hypothesized to be responsible for the fertility decrease include:

1. A change in the economic and social value of children as the population becomes more urbanized and fewer people live directly from the land.
2. Changes in family structure, particularly women's roles resulting from female participation in wage labor and education-related value shifts.
3. Relaxation of the pressures to bear many children in order to ensure survival of a few.

The mortality decline is generally thought to result from improved sanitation, new medical techniques, control of infectious diseases, and improvement of nutrition and housing conditions.

The BACHUE modelers have translated the above theories into their model in rather literal terms. To simulate urbanization they have replicated the biological module twice, once for urban population, once for rural population, and then have added migration between the two. Fertility and mortality are assumed to be affected by the same factors in rural and urban locations, but the resulting demographic patterns may be very different because their determinants (such as education) are not distributed evenly in urban and rural regions.

Education is tabulated in the model for each age, sex, and location group. Education is ranked in three levels: less than primary education (illiterate), completed primary, and completed secondary education. The number in each age-sex-location group having attained each level of education is a function of exogenously-determined dropout rates and enrollment rates. Once the age group has passed through its school-age years, the number of educated people in rural and urban sectors can be changed only by rural-urban migration.

The determination of fertility has been broken down into two sub-questions: age of female marriage and age-specific fertility within marriage. Age of marriage is assumed to be a function of the educational and labor-participation characteristics of women between the ages of 15 and 29. The more educated women in that age group and the higher the proportion engaged in wage labor, the higher will be the average age of marriage. The other factor determining the birth rate, marital fertility, is assumed to decrease with increased life expectancy, with increases in the fraction of the population with more than a primary education, with increases in female labor participation, and with decreases in the fraction of the population engaged in agriculture. This formulation will produce higher fertility in rural areas than in urban areas, which contain no agricultural production, and which usually have higher education levels and higher life expectancies than rural areas. Both age of marriage and marital fertility are assumed to change instantly with changes in their determining variables.

Mortality in BACHUE is a function of income level and income distribution. The function is non-linear; as incomes increase and income distribution becomes more even, the effects on mortality become less and less strong. Health services and nutrition are not explicitly represented but are assumed to be correlated with income.

Demographers have found that the distribution of marriage, child-bearing, and mortality across the age groups of populations tends to follow regular, stable patterns. Statistical summaries of these patterns—termed life tables— are available for many populations. If one assumes that the age-specific patterns of marriage, birth, and death contained in a life table will continue, one can use a life table to transform an aggregate demographic statistic into age-disaggregate data. This is precisely what the BACHUE modelers have done to convert average age of marriage into age-specific marriage rates, marital fertility into age-specific fertility rates, and life expectancy into age-specific death rates. That is, once the life expectancy has been determined to be 42 or 67 or whatever, a table of coefficients is used to look up the mortality rates of 0–1 year olds, 1–4 year olds, etc., in typical populations with 42 (or 67) year life expectancies.

The use of life tables exemplifies a common strategy for reducing the complexity of disaggregate structures. Just as movement of a 20-leg robot could be simplified by keeping the legs moving in constant relationship with each other, the dynamics of many variables can be simplified by assuming that one kind of event, such as birth or death, is distributed among different population groups in constant proportions. The danger of such an approach, of course, is that real-system proportions may not be constant. However, this danger is probably minimized in the distribution of factors with strong biological determinants such as mortality and fertility across population age categories.

Having formulated a structure describing the internal population dynamics of urban and rural populations, the modelers next formulate the migration between the two. Here the same basic life table strategy is utilized, but in a more complex way because more variables have to be brought together and redistributed into more categories. An aggregate propensity to migrate is calculated as a function of social variables from elsewhere in the model. This propensity to migrate is then passed through a matrix of coefficients to generate not only age- and sex-specific migration rates, but also education-specific ones. These disaggregated migration rates are then further modified by a function depending on the relationship of urban population numbers to rural population numbers (different functions are used for urban-rural and rural-urban migration). The specific migration functions are described in detail in Chapter 13.

Compared with BACHUE's demographic subsystem, the economic subsystem is more a mechanical accounting sequence and less an attempt to simulate real-world processes. We will describe the economic subsystem here in (roughly) its order of calculation. This done, we shall step back and look at the structural properties inherent in this sequence.

The computational steps in the BACHUE economic subsystem are:

1. Calculation of final demand.
2. Calculation of total production needed to meet final demand.
3. Adjustment for exogenous constraints on economic growth and calculation of the amounts of demand satisfied by imports and domestic production.
4. Accounting for model elements affected by production such as capital accumulation, taxes, and balance of payments.

The basic sequence is illustrated in Figure 9.2, with the many sets of constant coefficients that regulate the computations emphasized by enclosing them in double boxes.

Final demand has four components: household consumption, government spending, investment, and exports. Export demand for each economic sector grows at an exogenously-determined rate. Aggregate investment is also exogenously determined. It is divided into three categories—housing, government, and private investment. The share of government is a policy variable. Housing investment is a function of the share of rents in household consumption. The remainder of private investment is the residual (the assumed total minus the assumed government share minus the endogenously-calculated housing share). Investment is apportioned to the various sectors according to a set of constant allocation coefficients.

Aggregate government expenditures may be calculated in several ways. They may be completely exogenous. They may be a function of population size and of GDP *per capita* (this formulation is used in BACHUE-Philippines). They may be proportional to government revenues (calculated in the last model iteration), or proportional to government revenues with added demand created by government programs simulated in the model. No matter how aggregate government demand is calculated, it is apportioned among the sectors through use of a set of constant coefficients—the assumption being that the sectoral distribution of government spending will remain constant.

The last component of final demand, household consumption (see Figure 9.2), is both the largest component and the one most tied to BACHUE's major feedbacks. Household consumption of any sector's product is determined separately for each income decile and for urban and rural populations. The same equation form is used for all groups. Variations come through differences in the constant coefficients used.

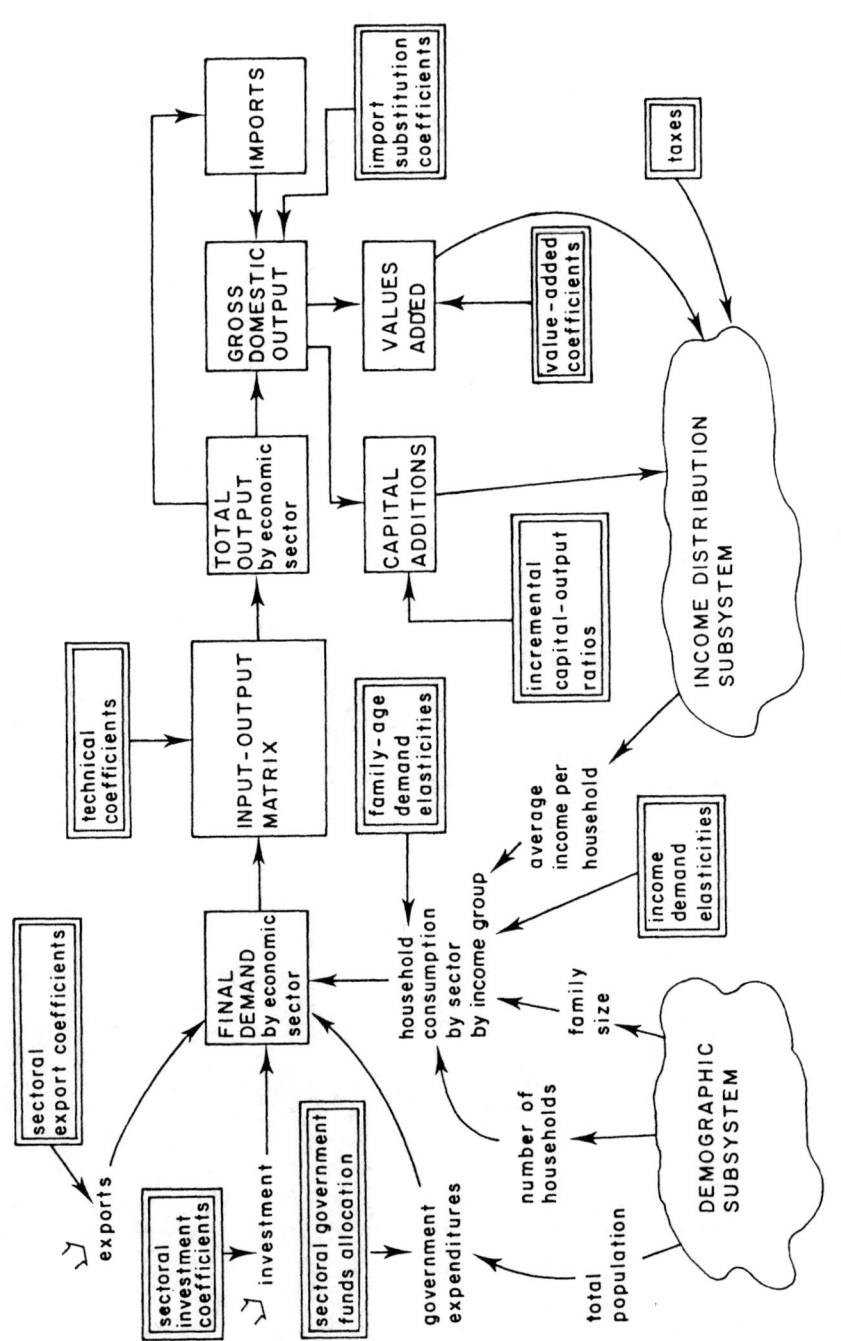

Figure 9.2 BACHUE economic sector

Household consumption is total household income minus taxes minus savings. Savings are assumed to be a linear function of the specified household income category and of family size. Total household consumption is obtained by multiplying consumption per household by the number of households in each population group. Consumption in each economic sector is then made a function of total consumption, household size, and relative price.

Once calculated, final demand is put through an input–output matrix to determine gross demand, the total production including interindustry exchanges, needed to meet final demand. Constant coefficients are used, therefore invariant linear proportions are assumed in the purchases each economic sector makes from other sectors. Gross demand is assumed to be filled by a mixture of domestic production and imports. The modelers must distinguish between the two, for they have very different effects on the system. Information on the sectoral composition of domestic production is central for determining income flows in the income-distribution subsystem. Imports, on the other hand, affect the balance of payments but do nothing to domestic income distribution. Separation of imports from domestic production is attained by controlling the fraction of demand fulfilled domestically with an exogenous set of coefficients of import substitution.

One variant of BACHUE is purely demand-driven; that is, it assumes that domestic production is automatically equal to the gross demand as calculated using the input-output matrix (with the exception of agricultural production, described below). The more commonly-used version, the version used in the Philippine model, assumes that there is a limit to how fast domestic production can expand. This limit is simulated by introducing a constraint of 7% per year on the growth of aggregate output. If the constraint is imposed and the demand-indicated production exceeds the constraint, all demand components, imports and exports, values-added and domestic production are reduced to the maximum amount the constraint will permit. The adjustment is distributed equiproportionally among model sectors.

An additional constraint is imposed in the domestic foodcrop production sector in order to represent the land constraint on agriculture and the sector's slowness to adopt structural changes. Labor productivity in the agriculture sector is constrained to grow at around 3% per year (slightly higher if agricultural prices rise). The agricultural labor force may be rising or shrinking, depending in part on labor dynamics calculated in the income-distribution subsystem and in part on rural-urban migration rates. The dynamic result of the labor productivity constraint is thus tied into complex feedback processes and is not easily predicted by intuition. One can say with certainty, however, that agricultural output will not grow in the model at more than 3% per year unless there is high migration into rural areas, which is unlikely.

This constraint on domestic food crops combined with rapid population growth, will cause domestic food production to be well below demand. The model will make up the demand shortfall partly by imports. Such a demand shortfall is also assumed to cause a shift in the relative terms of trade between rural and urban production sectors. A shortage of domestic food crop production raises prices not only for domestic food crops, but for export crops, fishing, livestock, and forestry as well. Higher prices feed back to alleviate the excessive demand situation by increasing domestic food-crop labor productivity somewhat and by reducing household demand for agricultural products. This is the only price mechanism in the model.

Once domestic output, imports, and exports have been calculated, the economic subsystem's main tasks are essentially complete. The calculation sequence then turns to information-organizing chores, manipulating the information it has produced into performance indices that will be useful to other subsystems. Values-added are distributed between urban and rural locations. Government revenues are calculated. Taxes are levied on incomes (generated in the income distribution subsystem), on imports, on output, and for some sectors on values-added (at exogenously determined rates). Government spending is then subtracted from government revenues to give an indication of Government surplus or deficit. A balance-of-payments index is tabulated from imports, exports, foreign income transfers (from the income distribution subsystem), and domestic excise taxes.

Finally, capital accumulation is calculated. Capital in any sector is equal to capital in the last time interval, plus investment, minus depreciation. To compute investment, aggregate investment (which, as previously stated, is exogenous) is broken down by sector. This formulation operates on the premise that the greater the increase in a sector's value-added and the greater its capital requirements per unit output, the greater will be its share of aggregate investment. Depreciation is assumed proportional to domestic output. Capital, it should be noted, is calculated only to generate information used in the income distribution subsystem. It has no influence on output, on input requirements for production, or on other aspects of the economic subsystem.

BACHUE's economic subsystem is strikingly different from the demographic subsystem previously described. The demographic subsystem is arranged around 152 state variables flowing into one another in orderly sequence, dictated primarily by biological laws. By contrast, BACHUE's economic subsystem does not represent the real flows of resources through various inventories and processing stages to final manufactured goods, nor the decisions governing those flows, nor the information upon which such decisions are based. The sector is dominated by exogenous parameters. The operating logic is the mathematical necessity of making certain computations so that the final result comes out roughly right, even though those computations do not match any identifiable operation in the real system.

In the demographic subsystem there is good reason to believe that the coefficients used are indeed very nearly constant in the real system. Cross-cultural and time-series examination both reveal fairly stable trends for age distribution of demographic events. In the economic subsystem there is less reason to assume the constants used will remain constant. Input-output coefficients can certainly be expected to change in a period of economic development, as can the composition of investment, exports, or government spending.

In nearly every case the modelers have admitted that the constant assumptions are regrettable, but necessary because they could not acquire sufficient data to make the relationships variable or did not want to complicate the model in order to do so.

It should be noted that the basic assumption behind the economic sector is that production follows directly from demand and is not constrained by the scarcity of any factor of production. This assumption is completely opposite from the central economic postulate of LTSM and TEMPO—that production is dependent upon capital and that population growth slows production growth by diverting output away from capital investment and into consumption. In BACHUE more rapid population growth leading to more consumption will *spur* economic growth by increasing demand and will not slow investment (which is exogenous) at all. The only factor that might drag down the economy would be a distribution of income so unequal that the masses of people are unable to consume and thus to stimulate more production.

When the economic subsystem calculations are complete for one interval of simulated time, the following information has been generated:

1. Values-added for 13 sectors, grouped as to whether they are urban or rural and whether they are modern or traditional.
2. Capital accumulation of 13 sectors.
3. Domestic output for the 13 sectors.
4. Government revenues.

The demographic subsystem, at the end of a simulated interval, has calculated the numbers of people in 152 population groups classed by education, sex, age, and location.

The problem before the income distribution subsystem is to put together the above information and come up with some indication of who gets what—of how income is distributed among different population groups. Of particular concern to the model's sponsoring organization, the International Labor Organization, are the differences between urban and rural incomes and the employment prospects for educated and uneducated workers in traditional and modern sectors.

The general strategy used in the income distribution subsystem is as follows. First the total labor supply is calculated by applying endogenous labor force participation rates to each of the demographic subsystem's age, sex, location, and education groups. These labor participation functions were formulated, like many other relationships in BACHUE, on the basis of several statistical experiments to sort out important determining factors from unimportant ones. In the case of the Philippines, the statistics indicate that important factors (included in the model) are household headship, education, income, availability of modern sector employment, and, for married females, fertility.

Given the labor supply, the model then subtracts away from each age, sex, etc. category the unemployed. Unemployment is calculated in different ways for different categories. For instance, urban educated workers tend to become more unemployed as modern sector jobs become less available and as wages slip relative to wage expectations. Urban uneducated employment, in contrast, depends only on the differential between educated and uneducated wages in the modern sector.

Now that the number of employed workers is known, the share each employment group will get of each sector's value-added is ascertained. The employed workers are allocated to each economic sector according to a complicated series of calculations involving capital, technical progress, and other factors. Wages and self-employed incomes are determined by dividing the appropriate share of the sector's value-added by the number employed. Finally, corrections are made for multiple job-holding, variation of income is accounted for, calculations are made to account for rents, taxes, and urban-rural income transfers, and information is compiled into aggregate indices of household income and income distribution for urban and rural population.

To make the above general strategy specific to various sector groups and employment categories, the modelers have had to formulate numerous hypotheses. For example, rules had to be set down for calculating, for each of the model's 13 economic sectors, the respective shares of value-added going to educated, uneducated, and self-employed persons. First non-wage shares are calculated. For each sector they are assumed to be a function of the relative contributions of urban and rural sectors to the economy's total value-added (hypothesizing a connection between degrees of urbanization and the fraction of the pie taken by the profit-earning class). What remains after non-wage shares are taken out is split between educated and uneducated wage earners. The gain in the uneducated's share is proportional to the increase in uneducated workers in the sector. What remains after the uneducated's share has been subtracted becomes the educated's share.

Further formulas establish labor mobility between sectors. Patterns of change are based on wage differences between sectors. This representation, combined with the fact that wages are the quotient in the share of value-added per employee, establishes a corrective feedback loop that will attempt to keep workers distributed in such a way that all sectors have equivalent wages.

Once wages and employment have been calculated, the subsystem must convert them into indices of household income. This final step takes into account variations in income within income groups and variations in the number of employed persons in each household. The book-keeping involved in these calculations is quite intricate. However, the structure is based exclusively on use of constant coefficients, and the step is essentially an accounting one.

Having examined the structure of BACHUE's three subsystems, we should

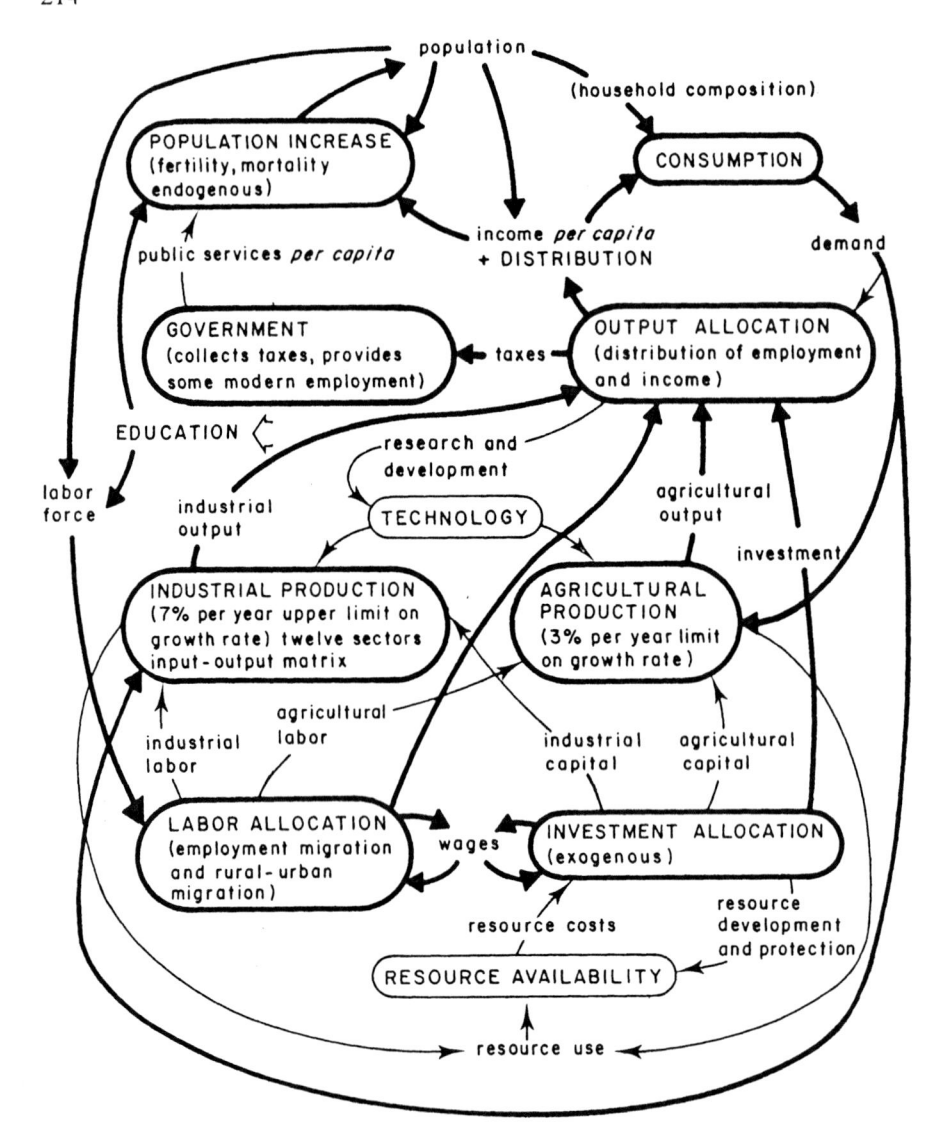

Figure 9.3 BACHUE reference structure

step back and look at the total structure that is created when these three subsystems are linked. The Reference Structure diagram is shown in Figure 9.3. The model is basically demand-driven—capital, labor, and resources do not constrain production, although there is an exogenous constraint on the rate of growth of total output. Demand is largely influenced by income and by demographic structure. Changes in income distribution and in total income will change the sectoral composition of output, as will changes in age structure and location of population. Alteration of sectoral composition has extensive ramifications in the income distribution subsystem, causing shifts in sectoral values-added, then wages, and then sectoral employment. Shifts in wages, in turn, may affect rural-urban migration patterns.

If children receive more education than did their parents, when they come of age and start making the major decisions in the system, fertility will decline, rural-urban migration will increase, and the portion of population looking for educated employment will increase. If the system's coefficients are such that economic growth has exceeded population growth (they probably are, as the constraint put on economic growth in the standard run is 7% per year—a figure that population growth cannot reasonably equal), incomes in general will rise and demand will shift away from agricultural and toward industrial commodities—presumably stimulating growth in the modern urban sectors.

Such are the general flows of causal influence implicit in BACHUE's linked subsystems. More precise identification of major feedbacks is quite difficult due to the model's complicated structure. It is possible, and even likely, that the feedbacks leading through one part of a variable set may have different behavioral characteristics from the feedbacks leading through some other part of the same set. For example, rising income could increase consumption of modern manufactures while decreasing consumption of traditional handicrafts. As a result, the feedback loop shown below would be positive for modern manufacture and negative for traditional handicrafts. A similar loop for domestic foodcrops might be positive, but being constrained by labor productivity growth (as it would be in BACHUE), it might lead to slower

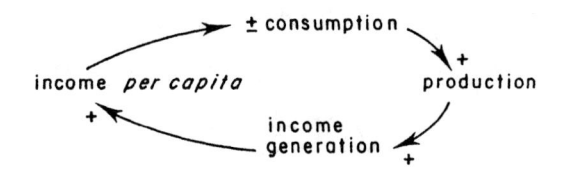

```
                    ±consumption
                 ╱              ╲
                ╱                ↘ +
   income per capita            production
                ↖                ╱
               + ╲              ╱
                    income     
                    generation +
```

growth than does the equivalent loop for modern manufactures. Thus in the course of aggregate economic growth there would be a decline or leveling of traditional handicrafts, a modest increase in domestic foodcrop production, and a spurt of growth in modern manufactures. The important element thus becomes not the feedback loop *per se*, but the respective behavior of individual elements in the sets through which the loop passes.

BACHUE's patterns of causal influences render comprehensive analysis of structural operation impossible. The best one can hope for is the gradual accumulation of a 'feel' for the model's behavior, acquired from running the model over and over and trying to generalize what sorts of changes in inputs lead to what sorts of dynamic results. This 'feel' for the model, which the ILO modelers all seem to possess, is not arrived at logically nor can it be checked by an outside observer, nor does it necessarily lead to a correct interpretation of why the model does what it does. It is distinguisable from a mental model of the real Philippine system only in that one has slightly more information about the individual relationships in the model, and one has the opportunity to observe the model system's reaction to a wider variety of inputs and over a much shorter observation time.

In short, BACHUE's structure and resulting behavior cannot be completely understood. Though the logic of the model's pieces may be quite clear, in entirety the model is a mystery that our minds cannot follow. Its output, therefore, must be assessed through black-box procedures, trying different inputs and judging the outputs according to their correspondence with those of other models, including mental models.

F. DATA

BACHUE was created in a data-rich environment. The ILO Population Employment Project, of which BACHUE was a part, included more than 60 investigations of various economic-demographic relationships, many of which were quite relevant to BACHUE's problem focus. The modelers drew freely from the data available to them.

All data sources for BACHUE are identified, and they include a wide variety of information. At the core of the model is an input–output table aggregated from a 194-sector table prepared for the 1965 Philippine economy by the National Economic Council. Labor force data came from a 1968 National Demographic Survey of the Philippines. Studies of nuptiality and migration were available from the Population Institute of the University of the Philippines. Also used were national accounts, several household expenditure surveys, foreign trade statistics, and data from government ministries on taxes, prices, and education.

The modelers characterize their information base as 'extensive but patchy, both in quality and coverage'.[11] Sufficiently long time series were not generally available, so cross-sectional data were used extensively, including international cross-sectional data to supplement Philippine data. In some cases highly refined derivatives such as standardized life tables were incorporated into the model. Almost no information was available about such dynamic factors as technological progress, import substitution, and occupational mobility, and most of these factors were made exogenous.

For each model subsystem the modelers describe at length the methods they used to formulate and parameterize the model's equations. As discussed under method, the modelers used statistical methods both to specify and to estimate their equations, but in a flexible fashion. Where data were not available for obviously important variables, such as unemployment, parameters were guessed. When statistical methods produced results that the modelers considered unreasonable, the modelers modified the results to conform to their mental models of the situation. As a general rule, however, the modelers used statistically-based equations wherever possible, and except for a few central variables they chose to omit relationships if they could not find adequate information to quantify them.

G. TESTING

As a subject for testing, BACHUE is at once intriguing and frustrating, because it contains so much to be tested. There are scores of parameters whose sensitivity should be examined. There are a like number of exogenously-forecast variables for which different time trends should be examined. And the modelers have set the model up in such a way that a large number of its behavioral relationships are subject to policy modification. Policy parameters were deliberately chosen so as to make it possible to test the major options usually discussed among development planners. Questions of the day, such as large-scale capital-intensive versus small-scale labor-intensive development, public works programs, promotion of education, family-planning programs, nationalization of industry, and more progressive income taxes, can be simulated to a considerable degree of detail. Exploring all these options thoroughly would be an enormous task.

BACHUE has the interest value of a well-designed game. Its output is a picture of the model economy with so much detail that it appears very real. The model is sufficiently complex that its behavior cannot be predicted, and it is likely to continue to produce surprises even after several hundred simulation runs. Yet at the same time the model's individual assumptions are fairly comprehensible, and upon careful examination of model output one can produce a satisfying, if not necessarily correct, explanation of which assumptions made the run come out as it did.

To encourage testing by persons other than themselves, the modelers have developed a conversational version of the model. This version operates on an interactive computer system. It automatically gives instructions to the user and makes it easy for people with no familiarity with the computer to try a wide range of policy tests.

BACHUE has been extensively tested. The modelers reject the possibility that any model can be *proved* valid, but they list the following criteria as factors that can contribute to building confidence in a model:

1. Internal consistency.
2. Quality of data base.
3. Acceptable estimation procedures.
4. Sensitivity to parameter changes that matches real-system sensitivity.
5. Insensitivity to structural changes.
6. Ability to track historical data.
7. General plausibility of model behavior.

The BACHUE team themselves assess the internal consistency of their model as good, their data base as patchy but no worse than that of other models, and their estimation procedures (ordinary least squares plus guesses) as not totally rigorous but appropriate to the quality of the data base. Their approach to assessing sensitivity to parameter changes is unusual. First they construct a 27 × 27 cross-impact matrix in which each element a_{ij} represents the three modelers' estimate of how much of the variation of variable j is explained by variable i (assuming the relationships are linear). The basis for each estimate is simply the modelers' intuitive understanding derived from experience in working with the model. Then the matrix is raised to the nth power and the rows and columns are summed to give the total forward and backward linkage effects of each variable after time period n. This analysis indicates that the model variables with most effect on other variables are birth rate, migration rate, age structure, output and employment structure, internal terms of trade, and exogenous inputs. Income distribution and employment have relatively little effect.

This elaborate procedure is based only on the modelers' hunches about the strengths of interaction between variables taken in twos. An outside observer cannot assess the accuracy of the two-by-two sensitivity estimates, much less the effect of non-linearities or the concurrent interaction of three or four variables. Although a thorough exploration by computer of the actual effect of each variable on the total behavior of the system would be impossibly time consuming, at least a few runs testing variations of some of the most obviously uncertain parameters would be helpful.

The BACHUE team has done considerable testing of structural hypotheses in areas where they or others consider the structure weak. For example, the assumption of exogenous total output has been altered to represent:

1. No constraint at all on output growth (totally demand-driven).
2. Output growth constrained by balance of payments.
3. Output determined by Cobb–Douglas production function with exogenous technological progress.
4. The same production function but with technology made an endogenous function of population growth.

All these changes except the balance-of-payments constraint slow the economic growth rate, increase fertility, mortality, and migration, and lead to deteriorating income distribution. Other tests involve changes in the formulation of technology, imports, exports, human fertility, labor force participation, and investment. In another test, the time lags in the model (nearly all one-year lags) are shortened to three months. A much more interesting test would have been to lengthen them.

These tests show that the model is sensitive to structural change (as most models are), but the alternate formulations are rejected by the modelers because in some sector of the model they produce results that are in conflict with 'conventional economic wisdom', and because each of the changed structures is still too obviously simple compared to the real system.

> So while conceding that output should be endogenous, and that our conclusions would be on firmer ground if it were, we consider that the supply side would have to be modeled in considerable detail if it is to be useful. This implies a complex sectoral output/price system, and extensive analysis of investment, money

markets, and associated institutions. We did not have the time and resources needed to develop such a system.[13]

The BACHUE team does not regard short-term tracking of historical data as a very meaningful test for a long-term simulation model; however, this test has been carried out by running the model from 1965 to 1975 with smoothed historic values for the exogenous variables. As expected, the model does not duplicate short-term fluctuations and cycles (it was not designed to), but it does follow the ten-year trend of the Philippine socio-economic system.

The final test of confidence is the ability of the model to generate believable long-term behavior. In BACHUE 'reference' runs the changes in fertility, mortality, migration, sectoral economic growth, and income distribution generally follow those observed for other countries that have industrialized in the past. Whether this future is actually believable for the Philippines depends on one's expectations about how future global conditions may differ from the past; whether, for example, international trade will break down, fusion power will become feasible, nuclear war will occur, or all nations will become sharing, altruistic, and globally-concerned. BACHUE assumes that none of these 'surprises' will occur, and therefore it generates unsurprising results; the Philippine economy industrializes smoothly and slowly along more or less typical growth curves.

H. CONCLUSIONS

The 'reference' run, reflecting continuation of current policies and attitudes in the Philippines and a 7% limit on aggregate growth rate, shows a rapid economic development. By the year 2000 the Philippines reaches a development level comparable to current Spain or Greece, or Japan of the early 1960s. The population has doubled and is still growing at 2% per year. Urban and industrial sectors grow most rapidly, but rising food demand improves the terms of trade of agriculture. Unemployment decreases and income inequality improves somewhat but the poorest 20% still have incomes well below the average Philippine income of 1965.[14]

The modelers begin their policy tests with investigations of individual policy levers—education, family planning, stimulation or inhibition of migration, changing employment conditions (wage subsidies, enhanced mobility, etc.), and public works programs. These policies are tested in various forms and intensities. The individual policy tests build toward a series of tests of integrated policy strategies. A package of 15 parameters and sets of parameters (e.g. total output growth rate and sector-specific growth of import demand) are simultaneously varied to simulate an industrialization strategy. A second such package simulates a rural development strategy, a third outlines a strategy designed to promote more equal distribution of income, and a fourth aims to simulate the policy strategy formulated for the Philippines by the 1973 ILO Comprehensive Employment Strategy Mission.

The BACHUE study's main conclusions are derived from generalization and interpretation of these individual and policy-package conclusions. These we shall paraphrase from the modelers' description of them.

First, the modelers conclude that income distribution is very stable and not easily influenced by the policies available in the model. They found that absolute income levels on the whole could be affected, as could the distribution of poverty between urban and rural areas. They also found that comprehensive policy packages tended to have more influence on income distribution than did individual policies. However, barring structural alterations that are not possible to simulate with BACHUE, the modelers conclude that poverty cannot be eliminated through conventional political means.

Second, 'demographic response to economic change is varied and often important—at least as important as economic response to demographic change, the direction of causation that is usually stressed'.[15] Fertility was found to be quite policy sensitive—but not as sensitive to a direct family-planning policy as it was to policies directed toward promotion of income equality. Slower population growth as a whole had little effect on poverty reduction, at least over the 25-year time horizon of the model.

Third, the urban-rural interface was found to be crucial. Terms of trade between agricultural and industrial sectors were found to influence incomes, demand patterns, migration, and the course of development in general. This interface was found to be policy-sensitive, often in ways that are not intuitively obvious—for example, policies to increase agricultural productivity increased poverty in rural areas but decreased it in urban areas.

Fourth, migration policies were found to be more efficient levers for influencing human welfare through the turn of the century than were fertility-reduction programs. The greater effectiveness of migration policies was attributed to the model assumptions that migration operates much more rapidly to change the characteristics of a population than does fertility.

These main policy conclusions are supported by an interesting document comparing BACHUE results with the results from a model of the Korean economy constructed by Irma Adelman at the World Bank.[16] The Korean model is in some ways the antithesis of BACHUE: it is a short-term model, population is exogenous but investment and output are endogenous, markets and prices are included in detail, with firms and households optimizing their economic responses, the monetary system is included. Despite these differences, and the differences in the Korean and Philippine economies, both models produce the basic conclusions listed above.

In broadest terms, the BACHUE conclusions began from the modelers' preconception that TEMPO is an inadequate representation of economic-demographic relationships. From this preconception came a more precise set of hypotheses about economic-demographic interactions formalized into the model. Then came specific policy conclusions based on the results of experiments performed with the model. Finally, out of specific policy conclusions evolved general conclusions about relative influences of various types of policy. Conclusions from the first two stages (which we might call input conclusions) are directly linked to conclusions in the latter two stages (which we might call output conclusions). Sometimes the linkage is so direct that it approaches a tautology. For example, the modelers conclude that feedback from economic conditions to demographic behavior—which has been omitted from TEMPO—is important. Therefore they include strong demographic-economic feedbacks in the model structure. Model output shows economic-demographic feedback is important, and the modelers confirm their original conclusion.

In other cases the interaction of input conclusions resulted in unexpected output and truly model-generated conclusions. For example, the modelers themselves appear surprised to find that increases in productivity in the agricultural sector have a pronounced tendency to lower rural incomes. Likewise, they seem not to have expected migration to play such a major role in leveling income distribution. Or, in a reverse direction, the modelers framed the model structure in such a way that education plays a large behavioral role. They report, after examining various runs featuring education policies:

> The effects of educational changes are widespread, but not particularly large up to the end of the century. This is partly because average educational levels of the population respond relatively slowly to changes in the education system.[17]

We previously expressed the opinion that BACHUE is too complex to be completely understood. That complexity prevents a total analysis of which model assumptions are primarily responsible for its conclusions, and therefore the conclusions are difficult to assess. However, unproven as it may be, BACHUE's ability to lead to unexpected results such as those described above identifies a useful tool for moving analysis out of the rutted pathways of intuition and generating fresh questions about the operation of a complex social system.

I. IMPLEMENTATION

The prototype BACHUE model was developed with hopes that Philippine nationals would adopt the model as a planning tool and that other nations would request that similar models be developed. In 1980 BACHUE-2 (the Philippine version) was housed in the Philippine National Economic and Development Authority, the body responsible for providing short, medium, and long-term plans for the country. It was providing a major input into formulating that body's long-term plans. Also, the Philippine Minister of Labor maintained close interest in the model's development.

Sinultaneously, interest spread to other nations. In collaboration with institutions and governments in the respective nations, models for Brazil, Yugoslavia, and Kenya were being constructed in 1980. Furthermore, the ILO hired eight people to be located in Latin America, Middle East, Africa, and Asia for further applications.

The BACHUE modelers' approach to implementation was deliberate and energetic. The modelers began in the Philippines in 1974 by holding a three-day workshop on the model for 50 key people in the Philippine government and academic planning community. At the workshop they presented an early version of BACHUE–Philippines, which was operating well enough to produce examinable results. Model assumptions were explained and discussed. Criticism was invited and used as a basis for later model revisions. Thereafter, a Steering Group, composed of leading academics in the population and economics fields, continued to advise and criticize during the model development.

The Steering Group served several useful functions. It operated as a quality control device; it brought into the modeling study people whose criticism, if voiced from the outside, might have been an impediment to the model's reception. And it extended the modelers' range of contacts in the international planning community. Indeed, it was through contacts of the model's Steering Group that BACHUE's Brazil and Yugoslavia models were started.

So far the modelers have had their greatest implementation success with BACHUE–Philippines—the only version of the model that was *not* developed in the country to which it is applied (BACHUE–Philippines was constructed in Geneva). The relative success of the foreign-made version was not expected. Reflecting on that point, one of the BACHUE team writes:

> I once thought this too (that involvement of analysts from the nation being modeled improved the likelihood of implementation) but am now more equivocal, since models being used in planning offices or whatever may often only be used if they back up existing government policy. Those model results that do not back up government policy may have a better chance of changing government policy if *not* developed by government analysts but developed by independent institutions—preferably in the country concerned.[18]

J. COMPUTER REQUIREMENTS

We have no information on the computer capabilities required to run BACHUE. It is obviously a large model and is not likely to be adapted, like TEMPO, for hand calculation in countries without computers. We would guess from the number of runs its makers report in the documentation that it must be somewhat less expensive to run than the largest models in this survey (RfF, KASM, and CHAC).

K. DOCUMENTATION

BACHUE's present state of documentation illustrates a recurrent conflict in model building. Getting a model into a position of influence requires a huge amount of time with public relations, administration, and (verbal) communications about the model. Of course it also involves much time and thought devoted to improvement of the model itself. But documentation is usually not necessary to impress policymakers, and so it gets done last.

It takes a versatile, tireless, and extremely talented person to work simultaneously as a modeler, a public relations man, and an author, without suffering loss of quality in any of those tasks. The BACHUE team has worked for high standards in all three aspects. They appear to have managed the work-allocation problem through close relationships among team members, with each of the project's principal workers having a hand in all aspects of model development. Regardless, it has been a very demanding task, in which everything has taken longer than expected.

A book on the BACHUE model was published in 1978.[19] It is an honest attempt to make the model, its potential, its assumptions, and its conclusions clear and examinable. The language used has the tone of experience in communicating the model to planners, economists, and demographers. Disciplinary proprieties, such as identification of data sources, and treatment and specification of the parameter changes made for a given run are carefully observed. Formats are worked out for ease of understanding—for example, a consistent and carefully chosen set of indicators is used to describe model output, and a constant presentation format is included for each of the model's three subsystems. Vocabulary, though geared to an academic audience, is kept as free from jargon and unnecessary technicalities as possible.

BACHUE's documentation starts off with general introductory statements addressing questions such as: Why model? What can models do? Why BACHUE? What can BACHUE do? Why has BACHUE used the approach it has? In other words, the introduction covers paradigm, purpose, and method. Following this is a review of the main BACHUE assumptions and conclusions. Then come detailed chapters on the Philippine economy and on the three main subsectors of the model. One chapter covers validation, and two long chapters discuss results of policy tests as single policies and as policy packages.

Given the great complexity of the model, the documentation is remarkably clear. The results of statistical tests that led to specification of the model relationships are described, and reasons for accepting or rejecting the statistical conclusions are discussed. The discussion throughout indicates an honest desire to communicate the model, a well-thought-through modeling philosophy, great care in model formulation, and considerable familiarity with the way the model runs. Unfortunately, a thorough 'feel' for a model of this size is almost impossible to translate into words. It is derived only from years of working with the model itself. The BACHUE modelers have undoubtedly learned a great deal from making the model, only a small portion of which they can capture in the verbal documentation.

NOTES AND REFERENCES

1. A. J. Coale and E. Hoover, *Population Growth and Economic Development in Low Income Countries*, Princeton, N.J., Princeton University Press, 1958.
2. Michael J. D. Hopkins, Gerald D. Rodgers, and Réne Wéry.
3. M. J. D. Hopkins, ILO, personal communication.

4. M. J. D. Hopkins, G. B. Rodgers, and R. Wéry, 'Evaluating a Basic Needs Strategy and Population Policies: The BACHUE Approach', *International Labor Review*, **114**, (3), Nov-Dec 1976.
5. G. B. Rodgers, M. J. D. Hopkins, and R Wéry, *Economic-Demographic Modeling for Development Planning: BACHUE-Philippines*, Population and Employment Working Paper No. 45, WEP2-21/WP.45, Geneva, International Labor Organization, p. I.7, December 1976.
6. *Ibid.*, p. 3 (draft).
7. *Ibid.*, p. II.1.
8. *Ibid.*, p. II.2.
9. *Ibid.*, p. IV.23.
10. *Ibid.*, pp. IV.1,2.
11. I. Adelman, M. J. Hopkins, S. Robinson, G. B. Rodgers, and R. Wéry, *The Political Economy of Egalitarian Growth*, Geneva, ILO, p. 15, 1976.
12. G. B. Rodgers, M. J. D. Hopkins, and R. Wéry, *op.cit.*, p. VII.1.
13. *Ibid.*, p. VII.36.
14. *Ibid.*, p. I.18.
15. *Ibid.*, p. I.39.
16. I. Adelman, *et al.*, *op.cit.*
17. G. B. Rodgers, M. J. D. Hopkins, and R. Wéry, *op.cit.*, pp. I.21–22.
18. Personal communication with M. J. D. Hopkins, to whose faithful correspondence we owe almost all our information on implementation.
19. G. Rodgers, M. J. D. Hopkins, and R. Wéry, *Population, Employment, and Inequality, BACHUE-Philippines*, Westmead, Farnborough, Hants, England: Saxon House, 1978.

CHAPTER 10

KASM: Not a Puree but a Stew

A. INSTITUTIONAL SETTING

In the late 1960s the Technical Assistance Bureau of the United States Agency for International Development (USAID) decided to conduct a comprehensive analysis of each economic sector of a recipient country, to obtain an overview before reaching a decision about aid programs. Sector analyses, as these comprehensive overviews are called, have since been performed for a number of economic sectors in a number of aid-recipient nations. The methods used in these analyses have varied greatly, ranging from predominantly qualitative to predominantly quantitative approaches. In several cases a computer model has been included.

The Korean Agricultural Sector Simulation Model (KASS in its first version, KASM thereafter) was begun in 1971 as part of an attempt to broaden sector analysis so that it could be useful to the analyzed nation as well as to USAID. The Korean modeling effort was done in the Agricultural Economics and Systems Science Department of Michigan State University (MSU).

KASM was the second sector analysis MSU did for USAID. The first was a non-model-based, large-scale study (35 professional man-years, $1.5 million) of the Nigerian agricultural sector. The complexities and high cost of that effort led to the suggestion by some of the MSU staff that a computer simulation model might help to co-ordinate and process information generated in sector analyses. A prototype simulation model of the Nigerian agricultural sector was worked out.[1] Civil war in Nigeria prevented further development or implementation of the modeling project, however, so the country of application was changed to South Korea. Much of the basic structure of the Nigerian model was retained, and within nine months the model had been adapted to the conditions and data base of Korea.[2]

To make this project useful to the recipient country as well as to AID, close involvement with a Korean planning institution was necessary. The institution selected was Korea's National Agricultural Economics Research Institute (NAERI), a branch of the Ministry of Agriculture and Fisheries (MAF). At the onset of the KASM project NAERI's responsibility had recently been shifted from farm-management research to national policy analysis. When the MSU team began the project, they described NAERI as in the process of transition from micro-economic, farm-level orientation to a broader national analysis and management viewpoint.

The KASM project consisted of three interrelated efforts:

1. The simulation model.
2. An American/Korean planning team in Seoul assigned to establish a modern planning system for MAF, using the model as well as other planning tools.
3. A training program, primarily conducted at MSU, in which Koreans would learn modern planning techniques, including use of the computer model.

Koreans and Americans worked together to be sure that the model could deal with the questions of concern to Korea and that Koreans could understand, use, and update the model.

Beyond the common aim of establishing systematic planning around a computer model, NAERI, USAID, and MSU each had their own institutional purpose for making the model. Presumably NAERI welcomed outside expertise at this time of expansion of its responsibilities. At any rate, it had obvious incentives to incorporate suggestions from the dispenser of United States aid funds. USAID originally commissioned the Korean study because it wanted to identify bottlenecks, constraints, and limitations hindering development in the agricultural sector, to assess the effects of different policy strategies on the agricultural sector, and to establish priority areas for aid funds.[4] And a perpetual background concern of USAID was to justify to the United States Congress, by whom the AID budget is appropriated, the expenditure of foreign aid funds. MSU, as well as wanting to meet the planning needs of USAID and Korea, undertook the study with their own institutional goals in mind. The MSU group believed in systems simulation as a policy tool. They were eager to demonstrate and disseminate systems methods in agricultural planning. The study was undertaken with specific intent to build up a library of agriculture-related computer programs to assist other institutions in expanding their analytic capability. The project also generated funds and research topics for about 30 graduate students and provided overhead funds to sustain the Agricultural Economic Department's Development Analysis Program.[5]

Thus the KASM project developed in a synergistic association of three diverse and geographically distant organizations. Communication was maintained through regular written progress reports and through periodic travel of American and Korean personnel between Seoul and Washington and East Lansing, Michigan. The project continued as MSU's responsibility for five years, and in 1977 the emphasis shifted to transferring all maintenance and further development of the model to Korea.

B. PURPOSE

According to the most specific description the modelers give, the model was constructed:

1. To be able to project the implications over a 15-year period of the Korean government's third five-year plan and two alternatives to that plan.
2. To be 'capable of handling a broad range of future policy alternatives'.[6]

These are not very distinctly defined policy goals. Rather, the MSU team sought to create a comprehensive model that could shed light on many different agricultural policies. The main guidelines that were used to limit the model's scope were the focus on the agricultural sector and the 15-year time horizon.

This is the first model we have described that is directed more toward specific decision-making than toward long-term understanding or broad policy formulation. The modeling team worked closely with agricultural planners from the beginning of the project. They listened to the problems and questions of the agricultural ministry and tried to produce a model that could answer virtually all its questions. In contrast to the models we have examined so far, the KASM model is product-oriented. It is envisioned as an on-going, continuously-revised, frequently-consulted management tool. As we shall see, this purpose required and produced a very different sort of model from the process-oriented models discussed so far.

C. METHOD

A pluralistic approach to modeling prevails in MSU's Agricultural Economics Department. The dominant attitude is 'all modeling techniques have something to offer—use each in its proper place'. Accordingly, the approach used by the KASM team was broad and eclectic. The KASM model includes every modeling technique we have discussed in this book. Simultaneous equations, regression analysis, linear programming, and input–output analysis are all incorporated within a core model that is essentially a dynamic simulation. Flexible modules for representation of repeating structural forms (such as delays, non-linear relationships, and passage of a population through a series of age cohorts) have been devised and used.

The model is divided into components, and has grown by adding new components. Each component tends to fill one functional role in the model and to be dominated by one modeling technique. For example, the Farm Resource Allocation and Production component (FRESAL) is a linear program that determines the optimal allocation of land and agricultural inputs to various crops. The National Economic component (NECON), which represents the non-agricultural economy, is based on a small (16-sector) input–output model. The Demand-Price-Trade component (DEMAND) solves sets of simultaneous equations to calculate consumption, demand, and price for farm and non-farm commodities.

Typically a component was built by one person or group, developed as an independent unit, and then linked to the full KASM model. As most components are frequently different from those used in the next, the linking of components required considerable reaggregation, redefinition, unit conversion, and other sorts of interface accounting. In one case, the grain management program (GMP), the calculation interval required to capture events of interest (two days) was so different from that of the other components (one year) that the linkage was never made. The GMP is used as a separate model.

The modeling schools combined in KASM in a way quite different from that of BACHUE, the other cross-paradigm model we have described. BACHUE uses ideas and techniques from econometrics and system dynamics in a consistent blend throughout the model. KASM is less like a puree than like a stew; large chunks of distinct model types are combined, with simulation as the surrounding gravy. This approach allows many modelers with different kinds of expertise to work on the model separately. It also allows flexibility in using the model.

> [The] components can be either run together to carry out a general sector analysis...or individual components can be decoupled and run to perform specialized analysis related to particular subsectors such as population, farm production, demand, etc.[7]

KASM thus contains sections of dynamic simulation that are intended to be literal representations of decisions and processes with the Korean agricultural system, and other sections that are 'black boxes', mathematical abstractions designed to calculate the *results* of such decisions and processes by arriving at them through a completely different logical chain than the one that pertains in the real world. The KASM modelers feel that this combination captures the advantages of both approaches:

> The 'black box' approach is based on past observations from an existing system and cannot be used in designing a new system that does not yet exist. On the other hand, in certain management problems the task at hand is to manage an existing system whose inner workings are unknowable. In this case the 'black box' approach is the only recourse. In summary then, the nature of the system will determine which of the approaches should be applied or in what combination both should be applied. Clearly, use of the two approaches together brings more information to bear on the modeling problem and will generally lead to better models than either approach alone.[8]

D. BOUNDARIES

The spectrum of information from which the KASM team has drawn is quite broad. The effort has been multi-disciplinary, with inputs from the fields of agronomy, sociology, demography, public administration, and biochemistry, as well as the obvious fields of agricultural economics and systems science. The use of data from many sources, including standard statistics, agricultural research, and expert opinion, is accepted.[9]

As will be noticeable, however, when we discuss specific variables, the model has not included (and hardly could include) all factors that significantly affect the operation of the Korean agricultural system. Rather, it has concentrated on economic factors such as output, profit, and price, from which are calculated aggregate economic welfare measures such as output *per capita*. Cultural factors such as political stability, income distribution, and social values, and ecological factors such as soil erosion, pollution, and biological diversity are omitted. The KASM authors include in their general discussions and even in their system diagrams such factors as personal freedom, equity, air and water quality, opportunity, and quality of life,[10] but no attempt is made to include them even indirectly in the model.

Those variables that are included tend to be represented in highly disaggregated form. There are, for example, 180 population groups (disaggregated by age, sex, and urban-rural location), 19 agricultural commodities, four land categories, twelve factor inputs to agricultural production, and 16 sectors in the national economy.

The boundary line between endogenous and exogenous variables has moved outward from early versions of the Korea model to later ones. The dominance of exogenous variables was so pronounced in KASS, the first Korea model, (see inner circle in Figure 10.1) that one critic of the model described it as:

> ...an accounting device where predetermined time series data for Korean agriculture 1970–85 (land yield, prices, input costs, birth rates) are translated into closely related output time series for the same period (farm income, farm expenditure, food demand, population size).[11]

The expansion of boundaries appears to have proceeded as follows. A key variable in the original model, such as land yield, was represented as exogenous, although it obviously was determined by factors operating within the Korean agricultural system. Eventually a new model component was created, with a structure that represented the variable endogenously. The new component, however, required information that was not generated by the existent model structure. Rather than create a new structure to calculate this needed information endogenously, the modelers added a new set of exogenous variables.

The above process creates new exogenous variables at least as fast as it incorporates old ones. In most cases, however, the newly-created exogenous variables are factors that are more truly exogenous to the system (such as world prices for agricultural commodities) or conceivable policy instruments for the Korean government (such as agricultural-input price subsidies, rates of taxation, and price controls). A few important variables remain, however, that are clearly endogenous in the real system but exogenous in KASM. Primary

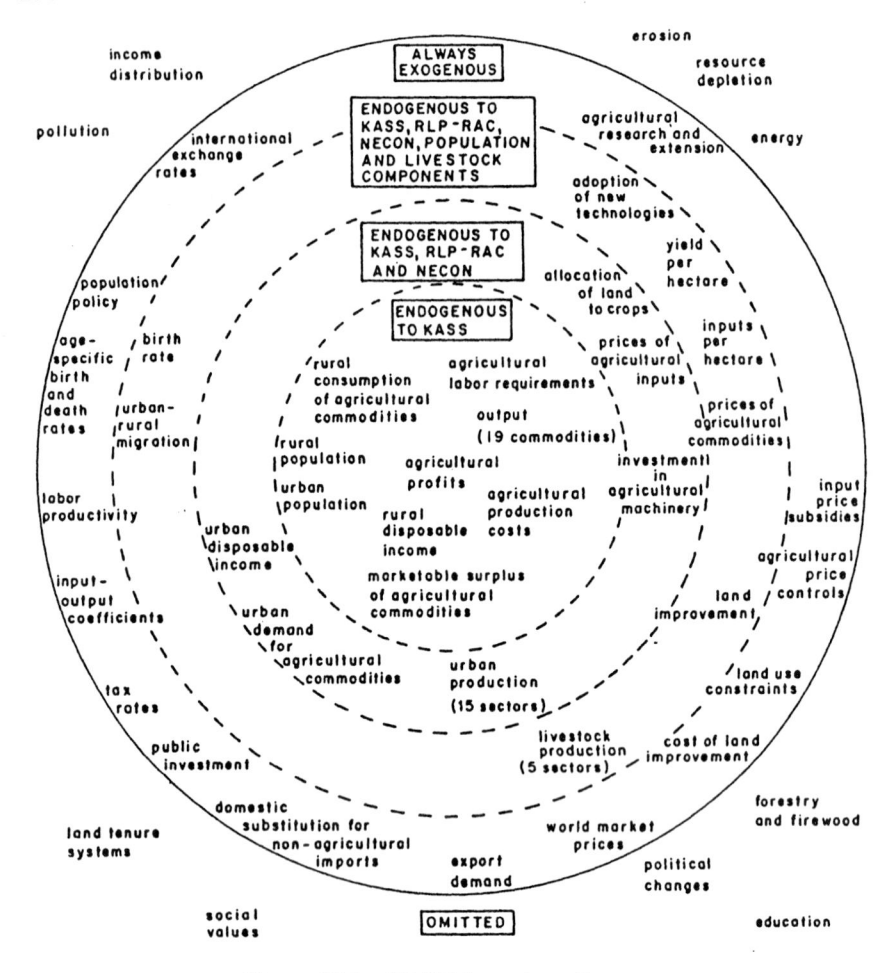

Figure 10.1 KASM boundary diagram

among these are age-specific birth and death rates, labor productivity, and input–output relationships.

E. STRUCTURE

KASM is best described not as a model but as a system of six models.[12] The models can be used separately or linked together to form one extremely complex representation of the Korean agricultural system. Each of the single models is equivalent in size to other models described in Part III.

The main connections among the six functional components of the complete KASM model are shown in Figure 10.2. The six components are:

1. Population component (POPMIG). This sector converts exogenous age-specific fertility and mortality rates (influenced by birth control and

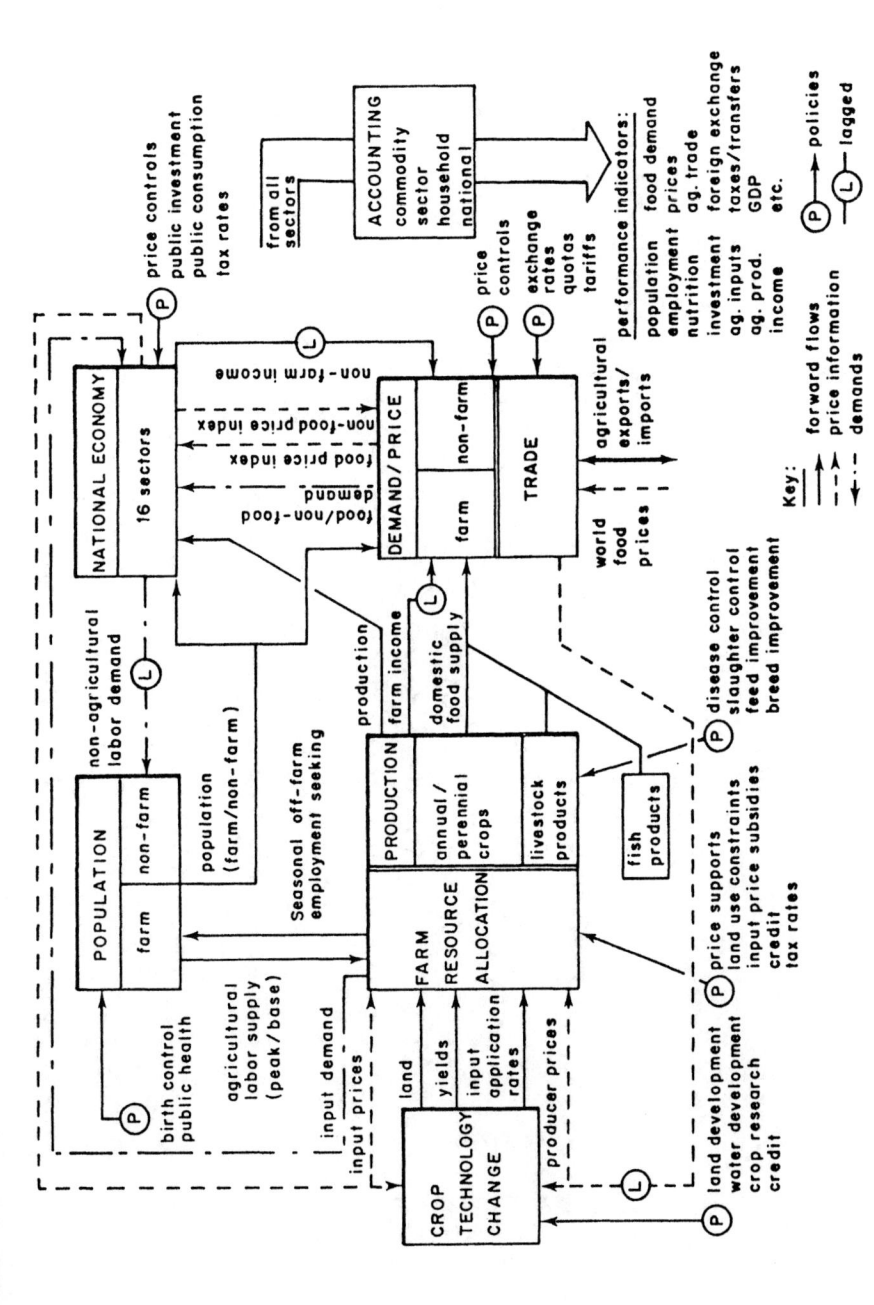

Figure 10.2 KASM system linkage diagram. Reproduced with permission from G. E. Rossmiller (ed.) *Agricultural Sector Planning*, East Lansing, Mich., Agricultural Sector Analysis and Simulation Projects. Dept. of Agricultural Economics, p. 108, 1978

public health policies) into 45 two-year age cohorts for males and females in both farm and non-farm households. Off-farm migration can be either exogenous or a function of job opportunities and living-standard differentials.[13] The population component influences the rest of the model through food demand and agricultural labor supply. This component is essentially a demographic accounting model, driven entirely by exogenous assumptions.

2. Technology Change component (CHANGE). This component takes information about input prices, product prices, and government investment in land and water resources and technology, and calculates how much arable land will be available, what input application rates will be, and what yields can be expected. CHANGE is a dynamic model of agricultural innovation. It begins with many exogenous assumptions about government investments in technological change and combines these assumptions with price information and with a geographic diffusion subcomponent to simulate the spread of new technologies over the available land area. The result is a set of production functions, which alter constraints and activities of the optimization model within the next component FRESAL.

3. The Farm Resource Allocation and Production component (FRESAL). Given land, inputs, technologies, and therefore expected yields from CHANGE, labor from POPMIG, expected producer prices from the Demand component, and expected input prices from the National Economic component, this section of the model represents the farmers' decisions about how to allocate resources among 19 possible agricultural commodities. The allocation decision is made by a recursive linear program, with an objective function of 'cautious' (highly risk-averse) maximization of expected profits. The component chooses among 61 activities such as production of twelve annual crops, five livestock commodities, and two perennial crops, capital investment, financing, importation of grain, and hiring seasonable laborers. There are 60 constraints, including four land categories, labor, machinery, and draft-animal limitations, capital stock, feed balances, and financing constraints. Once the allocation decisions have been made, this sector calculates agricultural output by crop, total input demands, and farm income. The parameters within this optimization model are continuously updated by new information from the CHANGE component.

4. The Demand-Price-Trade component (DEMAND). Agricultural output from FRESAL, effective demand from POPMIG, and government policies with regard to stockpiling and pricing are brought together to determine commodity prices. The model is run in one of three modes:
   a. Consumption is set exogenously and prices and import-export balances are calculated to clear the market.
   b. Import-export levels are set and consumption and prices vary.
   c. Prices are set and consumption and trade balance calculated.

   Substitution across commodities is taken into account. World market prices are exogeneous. This sector operates by iterative solution of simultaneous equations.

5. The National Economy component (NECON). This is a 16-sector input–output model that generates non-farm income, labor needs, and agricultural input prices. The technical coefficients are assumed constant, except for agriculture. Labor productivities are exogenous. Final demand for this sector is determined partially by input demand from FRESAL, partially by food demand from DEMAND, partially by exogenous public investment and exports, and partially by its own internal calculation of private investment and non-food demand. Private investment for each sector is assumed to be a function of profit and capacity utilization. Consumption is a function of price and GDP *per capita*.
6. Accounting component. This sector generates summary indices, such as GDP, trade balance, and nutrition levels, utilizing information from all the other components of the model.

Since each of these components was constructed separately and uses different assumptions, techniques, and degrees of aggregation, getting them to mesh involves many interface problems of the sort we have already seen in BACHUE. For example, all of the 19 crop outputs of the Resource Allocation component have to be aggregated into one of the 16 sectors of the National Economy component. Conversely, the 16 labor demand calculations from this component must be distributed over 180 population categories to determine migration flows.

It is not possible for us to go into the assumptions within each component as thoroughly as we have done for previous models in this chapter. Some important formulations such as migration, technological change, consumption, and investment will be discussed further in Chapter 13. An idea of the way the KASM sectors are interrelated can be gained from Figure 10.3, which shows in simplified form the main causal flows that influence rice output when all model components are coupled. The two three-dimensional boxes in the diagram represent optimization routines. In them resources such as land and capital are allocated simultaneously among the twelve annual crops. An analogous causal structure could be drawn from the eleven other annual crops in KASM. Were one to focus on some variable other than the output of rice (for example, earnings from the export of silk, or *per capita* protein consumption), one would see the model from a different, but equally complex perspective. The most basic interrelationships in the model are summarized in the Reference Structure diagram, Figure 10.4.

Needless to say, understanding the operation of this model system is impossible. In three years of training no Korean seems to have come close. An internal working memo suggests that even the experienced modelers at MSU had difficulty comprehending the way the model works:

> Generally, the increasing complexity of the total model, mainly indicated by the intensification of linkages between the production, supply, marketing, and demand subcomponents, makes it more and more difficult to detect the reasons for a certain model behavior. In other words, the greater complexity results in an

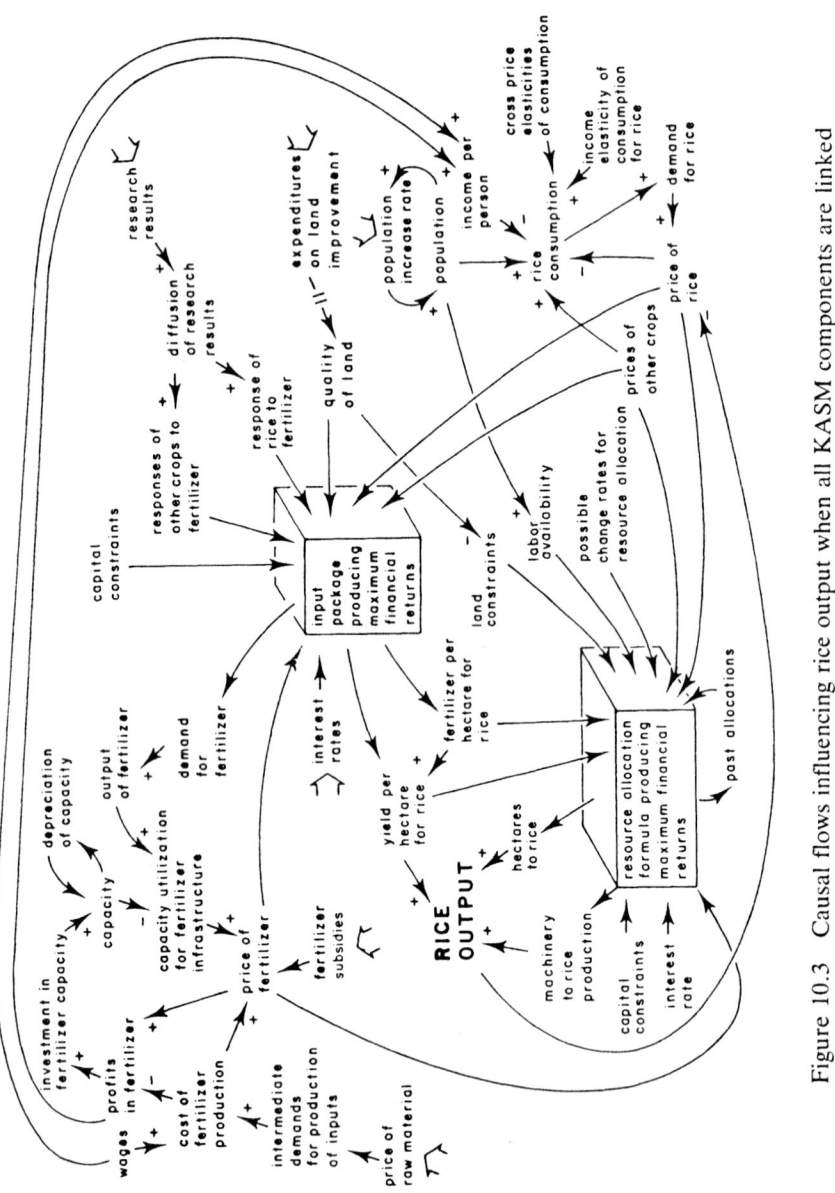

Figure 10.3　Causal flows influencing rice output when all KASM components are linked

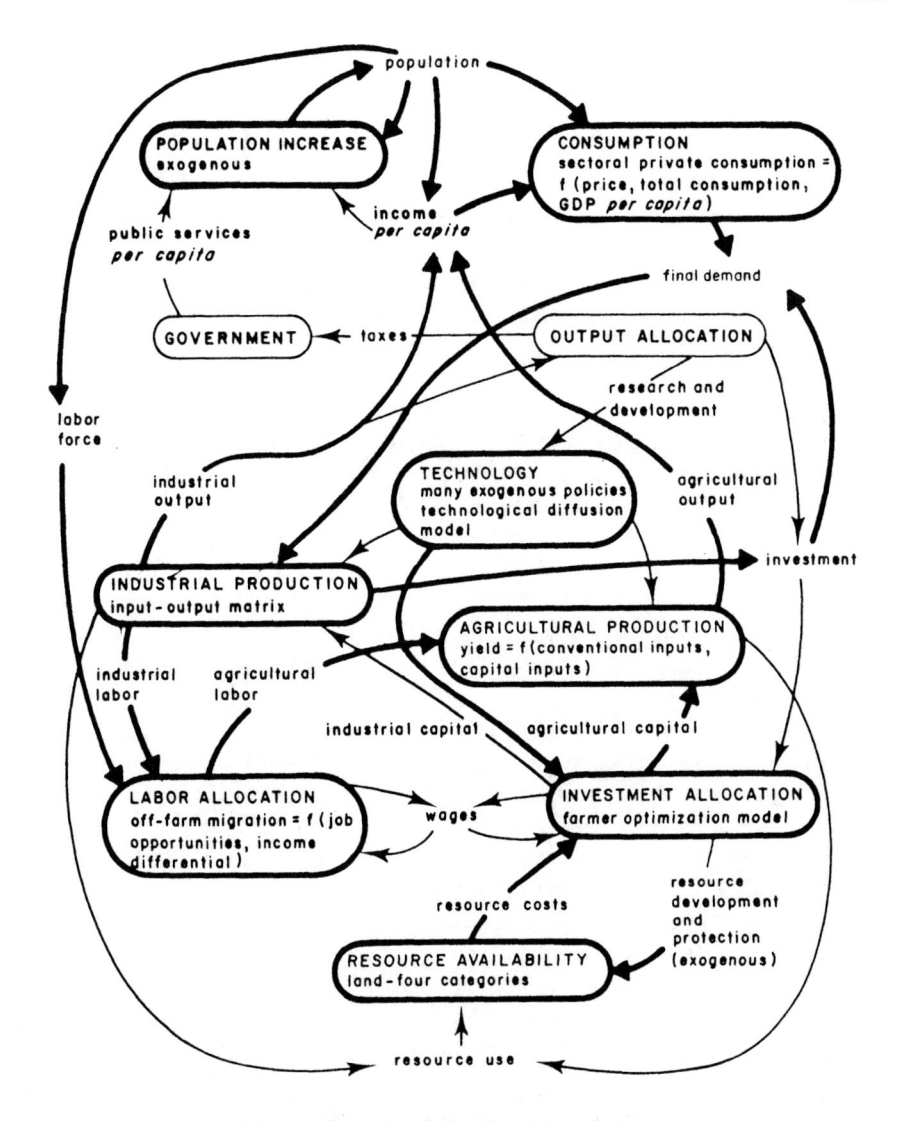

Figure 10.4 KASM reference structure

increasing number of 'surprises' in the model output. Although all this may bring the model closer to the real world situation, one should give some thought to the optimal level of detail and disaggregation the model results are supposed to contain.[14]

That is not to say that individual components of the model are not explainable. For example, the KASM team can and does explain fairly clearly how the linear program in the resource allocation component operates.[15] The difficulty arises not in understanding individual components, but in understanding the interaction of components. How does the linear program in

FRESAL reallocate capital to or from mulberry or barley production when a new high-yielding rice variety is assumed in CHANGE? How does economic information from NECON shift the rural-urban distribution of the population in POPMIG? If price elasticity of demand assumptions were changed in the Demand-Price-Trade component, how would that affect agricultural input usage rates? The KASM team members, after years of running the model, almost never offer explanations of their results in terms of interlinked assumptions from several model components. They simply describe the output and let us decide for ourselves why it might have happened that way.

The reasons why the KASM model has been taken to the point of extreme complexity compared to other models in our survey are several. First, the model was intended from the beginning to be useful at the decision-making level, with a shorter time horizon than our other models and a degree of detail congruent with the interests and responsibilities of national agricultural planners. General understanding of the system was not sought—it was assumed. The importance of foreign investment aid, the necessity for higher agricultural productivity, the insensitivity of population growth to economic events, the normal operation of the market, the ability of laborers to adjust smoothly to changing employment demand, all were taken for granted, and on the basis of these assumptions, very specific questions about investments, productivity increases, etc. were asked. Second, the time, resources, and manpower available to this project were significantly greater than they were for most other models, and so greater detail was possible. Another complicating factor may have been the close contact with Korean policymakers. This contact provided the advantages of model relevance and implementation, but the disadvantage of a continous stream of current decision-making questions, most of which the modeling team tried to accommodate in the model.

The trade-off between detail and clarity plagues all modelers and is probably never resolved to anyone's satisfaction, especially in someone else's model. Instead of expressing our own discomfort with the complexity of KASM, we will include a warning from the KASM team:

> Any formal model should be used with great caution, and KASM is no exception. KASM can be a powerful analytical tool for public agricultural decision making in Korea, where many more complex decision options can be investigated more reliably than could be done with informal or simpler formal models. Nevertheless, erroneous conclusions can easily be drawn from simulation results unless analysts and decision makers alike take care to understand, by tracing through the model's data and causal structure, what gives rise to those results. Wrong decisions can be made based on wrong explanations of projected responses to alternative decision assumptions.[16]

F. DATA

The KASM model, even in its earlier simpler forms, contains many thousands of numerical parameters. For example, simply providing initial values for the population sector of the original KASS model with its 45 age cohorts, two sexes, and separate farm and non-farm populations requires 180 numbers. Adding age-sex-specific death rates, protein requirements, caloric requirements, age-specific birth rates, age-sex-specific migration rates, etc. brings the total data requirement of this sector alone to nearly 1,000 parameters. A summary of some of the data required for other KASM components is shown in Table 10.1.

KASM documentation includes after each component description a short general discussion of the data required for that component and the sources used.[17] Time series usually begin in the mid-1960s. Sources generally are official statistics—population, housing, and agricultural censuses, government economic statistics and input–output tables, family income and expenditure surveys. KASM team members also spent considerable time in the Korean countryside checking the accuracy of the data against their own observations.[18] Some parameters were taken directly from statistics, many others were estimated through regression techniques, and quite a few came from judgement or guesses. Exogenous time series usually were taken from existing sources—world price forecasts from the World Bank, consumption trends from Korean food and nutrition specialists, with Japanese trends used as a model for stages of development beyond those that Korea had already reached.

As one might expect, the data available to the modelers were far from complete or reliable. The KASM team indicates that considerable effort was necessary to rework not only the Korean data, but the Korean data-collection system:

> In Korea, as undoubtedly in most other developing countries, there are problems with respect to reliable data for analysis. Inconsistencies and discrepancies in available data forced the modelers to rework data in order to smooth out discrepancies and bring estimates within reasonable bounds. Frustrations with available data were no doubt substantially responsible for the work the KASM team has done in re-organizing the agricultural data-collection process in Korea.
>
> During the period of forced sales of grain to the government, the planted area was underreported. After these sales were abandoned and following the government's decision to rigidly control fertilizer distribution on the basis of planted area...the planted area tended to be overreported. Reported crop yields also appear to have been influenced by various factors, such as the expectation by officials at higher levels that target average yields had been achieved.[20]

The model is initialized with data from 1970 and run to 1974 to test its tracking ability. Then, pragmatically but unscientifically, it is updated with 1974 figures before being used for projection to 1985.[21]

G. CONCLUSIONS

Since KASM was intended to be used in the middle state of the decision-making process to generate fairly detailed information about policy and implemen-

Table 10.1 Examples of types of data requirements in KASS model components Reproduced with permission from Rossmiller[7] p. 398

Component	Predetermined variables		Exogenous	Technical, institutional and behavioral parameters	Policy variables and parameters
	Lagged endogenous Within component	Outside component*			
Population (POPMIG)	Population by age, sex, and sector	Non-agricultural employment.	Urban employment.	Birth rates. Death rates. Migration rates.	Population (birth rate) control. Non-agricultural employment of farm population. Military manpower.
Crop Technology Change (CHANGE)	Crop yield. Input use. Land classes.	Prices. Crop areas. Farm income. Tree crop age composition.	Land development costs. Maximum potential land area improvement. Private non-farm capital.	Production coefficients. Diffusion rates. Input demand elasticities. Farm consumption investment ratio.	Land and water development investment. Crop improvement. Extension services. Price policies (input and output). Agricultural finance policies.

Farm Resource Allocation and Production (FRESAL)	Cropping patterns. Herd sizes. Capital stock. Farm savings.	Producer prices. Input prices. Maximum farm labor. Maximum land and water. Crop yields.	Livestock yields.	Resource requirement coefficients. Maximum credit ratio.	Agricultural finance policies. Feed grain imports (maximum).
Demand-Price-Trade-(DEMAND)	Per capita consumption. Producer prices.	Population. Agricultural supply. Agricultural income. Non-agricultural income.	Target per capita consumption. World prices.	Income elasticities. Own-price elasticities Substitution proportions.	Price policies. Food consumption policies. Exchange rates. Foreign trade.
National economy (NECON)	Unit profitability. Unit costs. Gross investment.	Non-food expenditures. Agricultural input demand.	Labor productivity. Non-agricultural exports. World prices.	Input–output coefficients. Price and income elasticities for non-food items. Profit and investment utility elasticities.	Public consumption. Public investment. Price policies. Import substitution Tax rates.

* Assumes all components are linked. If not linked, then these are exogenous variables tation decisions over a five- to 15-year period, conclusions drawn from the model tend not to be the sorts of sweeping generalizations about the development process that we have seen emerging from longer-term general-understanding models. The closest the KASM team has come to a large-scale conclusion was the summary of research results derived from the first, simple, mainly-exogenous KASS model in 1972. From that model, the researchers derived two conclusions:[22]

1. In the short term, a set of agricultural development policies would increase agricultural output, decrease rural-urban migration and enhance the rate of modernization of the agricultural sector.
2. In the long term, expanded investments in agricultural research and an effective family planning program will be needed.

Since then the expanded model KASM or pieces of it have primarily been used to draw very specific conclusions or to make short-term forecasts at the request of Korean government officials. Examples of conclusions that have emerged from KASM in this mode of operation follow:[23]

1. An over-riding objective of the Ministry of Agriculture and Fisheries (MAF) was to reduce imports of feed grains. The KASM team provided three projections; a base run without policy interventions, and two runs testing restrictions on the swine and poultry sectors. 'The alternatives thus analyzed and refined by discussions with the Livestock Bureau were combined with information from other sources to form the policy basis for policy decisions in the Fourth Five-Year Plan.'
2. In 1974 the MAF was trying to establish what commodities should be developed for export, to where, and in what quantities. The KASM team attacked this problem with the Demand-Price-Trade component's foreign trade sector, testing several alternate assumptions about future world market prices. The model proved too aggregated for this purpose; the 19 commodity groupings could not provide information about single crops. But the model results did serve as a check for conclusions the MAF had already reached.
3. After several years of trying to reduce domestic rice consumption because rice had to be imported at high prices, Korea became self-sufficient in rice in 1975. The question then arose, how could the rice-consumption restrictions best be lifted, especially so as to shift consumption to rice and away from wheat (the only grain still imported). The KASM Demand-Price-Trade component was run with several different price patterns for barley, rice, and wheat. The conclusion was that the government should keep real rice prices constant, phase out the dual price system for barley, and remove the wheat subsidy.

Detailed decision-making conclusions such as these are evanescent. They may apply to today's conditions but be completely reversed tomorrow. They require not only a correct model structure, but up-to-date parameters, since conclusions result from fine tunings of model parameters, not from patterns inherent in the model structure. Fine tuning requires a skilled modeling team on the spot, as perpetual consultants, to identify the part of the model relevant to the problem, alter and update parameters as necessary, and explain the results to the policy-makers.

H. TESTING

Each component of the KASM model was constructed separately and therefore tested separately before being linked with the rest of the model. The component tests are described only briefly in the KASM documentation.[24] The tests seem to have consisted of matches with historical data, examination for internal consistency, and some sensitivity testing. It is reported, for example, that the migration function is sensitive to assumptions about employment,[25] and that intensive 'manual' tuning of elasticities and substitution relationships in the DEMAND component was necessary.[26] In no cases are testing details given. The modelers of each component do end their descriptions of their component with a discussion of areas that are not yet satisfactory and make suggestions for further improvements. These discussions suggest that much more testing has actually been done than has been reported.

Testing of KASM as a whole is also described only vaguely. The KASM team lists four tests they consider essential to establishing their model's credibility:[27]

1. Coherence—where the model is checked for internal logical consistency, abstracted from its real-world referent.
2. Correspondence—where the behavior and structure of the model [must match that] of its real-world referent. Structure is included because it is not enough that a model be able to project; it should also explain past and projected behavior in terms of accounting and dynamic causal relationships. Time-series tracking, sensitivity tests, and decision runs all provide information for correspondence testing.
3. Clarity—where the model must be not only unambiguous...but also comprehensible to decision-makers and analysts alike.
4. Workability—where credibility...also depends on how well [the model's] prescriptions work out when implemented in the real-world.

The KASM modelers appear satisfied that their model passes these tests, but they provide very little evidence for the reader. Their description of total-model testing consists of no more than the following:

> Coherence tests take place as part of the debugging process of individual components. Correspondence testing of KASM is an iterative process wherein components are tested individually and in various combinations against knowledge of the real-world referent and then are retested continually as new knowledge is gained... The clarity and workability of KASM receive their biggest test whenever

the models are used for decision analysis. Korean decision makers and investigators understand the models more and more each time they use them. Similarly, the models become easier to use and interpret as familiarity increases. Workability tests are passed as decisions are implemented with positive results.[28]

I. IMPLEMENTATION

The KASM study was conceived and carried out from the beginning with final implementation in mind. As described in the section on model purpose, USAID commissioned the study partially to help decide what to fund in Korea and partially to institutionalize systems analysis into the planning process of the Republic of Korea government. The first goal seems to have been at least partially realized; projections from the early KASS model were used among other information in deciding upon a USAID loan to Korea for agricultural research,[29] and the MSU team was involved in negotiation of another USAID loan to finance 66 small-scale irrigation projects.[30] (This negotiation did not include any direct use of the computer model, but it relied on the expertise the team acquired in creating the computer model).

To further the second goal of modernization of the planning process, in 1973 the original KASS modeling team was supplemented by an American-Korean Agricultural Planning Project team (KAPP) to assist the Ministry of Agriculture and Fisheries in establishing a planning system, including use of the KASS models. The KAPP team acted as an interface between the modelers and the Korean ministers, helping the modelers understand the policy problems of Korean agriculture and suggesting new model components. Furthermore, a training program was instituted so that both MSU and USAID could eventually withdraw and leave Koreans in control both of planning and of further development and use of the models. This withdrawal was originally planned for June 1974 and finally took place in 1977.[31]

The KASM modelers do not seem to envisage their model as the exclusive determinant of Korean agricultural policy:

> KASM or any single model, formal or informal, must not be relied upon as the sole source of information for complex decision making. No single model can possibly provide all the information necessary—economic, social, political, military, administrative, short-term, long-term, normative, nonnormative, etc. This is equivalent to saying that every problem-oriented model for public agricultural decision analysis will of necessity be composed of multiple formal and informal models.[32]

On the other hand, they clearly do view it as an integral part of governmental decision making:

> Such a model can be a valuable analytical tool in helping decision makers in their planning, policy formulation, and program development activities... It is both broad enough and detailed enough...that in most cases relatively minor modifications and extensions allow all or parts of it to be used in specific applications to solutions of specific problems... It is used in an iterative and interactive context,

with investigators and decision makers carrying out the functions of the decision-making process.[33]

There seem to have been numerous requests from Korean planners for information generated by KASM. Several of these requests have already been mentioned in the discussion of model conclusions. However, most of the information seems to have been used for purposes of bureaucratic reports rather than for the shaping of programs and policies. Examples quoted by the KASM team as successful applications of the model include the following:[34]

1. In 1975 KASM projections were used to prepare Korea's country position paper for the United Nations World Food Conference.
2. KASM population projections have been incorporated as the official MAF projections for the Fourth Five-Year Plan.
3. The MAF Livestock Bureau has taken KASM consumption projections and:

> ...used them in the plan with some modification. On the supply side, the dynamics of the model projected turning points and cycles or declines in the herd sizes, while traditionally, planning projections are monotonically increasing. Although the Livestock Bureau did not accept the supply results for the Five-Year Plan, interest was expressed in using them at other times for policy analysis.[35]

4. The Director-General of MAF asked the KASM team to review the final draft of the Fourth Five-Year Plan before submitting it to the Minister. The team prepared a written set of recommendations for him.[36]

Dr Lee Fletcher of the Technical Assistance Bureau of USAID, who has been actively involved in evaluating the KASM project, says that the separate components of KASM and the smaller, problem-oriented models associated with the project—specifically the Grain Management Program, a short-term (three-year) simulation model of grain inventory and pricing mechanisms—appear to be more directly useful to decision-makers than the large KASM model.[37]

Some of the most important impacts of the KASM effort have come not from model-generated recommendations, but simply from the presence of systematic, analytical investigators gathering and synthesizing information about Korean agriculture. Perhaps the most notable single change the KASM team has instigated was a major revision of the process of collecting and reporting agricultural statistics, a change that was necessary to provide reliable data for the model.[38]

The permanent installation of KASM and modern planning techniques in the Korean government proved more difficult than either USAID or MSU anticipated. Training technical people to use and update the model and keeping them working on KASM-related work once they were trained was a major problem in the implementation strategy. When the KASM project started, NAERI had only three people with advanced degrees in agricultural economics, and none in systems science. Since then 45 Koreans have received some sort of technical training, 14 of whom now work in the KASM division of NAERI.[39] However, it has been found that at least doctoral-level training in systems science is necessary before a person can actively contribute to KASM model development, and no Koreans in the project have yet reached that level of skill.

Holding personnel has been difficult because there is great demand for people with technical training in Korea. Highly-trained people are likely to leave the Ministry of Agriculture and Fisheries altogether, for the wages it can pay are below the wages a technically-trained person could command in the universities or elsewhere. Even if they remain in agricultural civil service jobs, trained personnel are likely not to remain working with the model, because the Ministry does not like to concentrate its skilled manpower resources in any one field.

Further implementation problems arose because the analytical capabilities developed at NAERI were organizationally distant from the actual decision-making positions in MAF. A series of recommendations were made by the KASS/KAPP review team, both for greater exposure of MAF officials to the possible uses of their technical resources and for reorganization of MAF.[40]

In terms of meeting the stated goal of its makers and sponsors, KASM may have reached its implementation peak during the time the MSU team was tending it and enthusiastically advancing its merits. Their personal expertise was probably more valuable than their model outputs. In fact, one of the unquestionable results of the KASM project was the thorough education of a number of people at MSU in the agriculture and politics of Korea, and the education of Korean government officials in the systematic, quantitative approach to policymaking.

When the Americans left, the KASM model was housed in Korea in a newly-created research institute KREI, with a staff of MSU-trained Korean personnel who were able to run the model but not to use it creatively or to update it. KREI also requested technical assistance from MSU for installing the grain pricing model in Korea and running training sessions in its use.[41]

The KASM model has been recreated in many forms throughout the world. It has been adapted for use by the US Department of Agriculture (USDA) in analyzing US–Korean trade patterns. Members of the KASM team made similar models for the European Common Market and for the USA, and these models were linked at the International Institute for Applied Systems Analysis in a supermodel of international agricultural commodity trade.[42] MSU received inquiries about adapting the KASM model for Turkey and Thailand. George Rossmiller, the director of the KASM model, went on to serve as the U.S. agricultural attache to OECD and as an international trade policy analyst in the Foreign Agricultural Service of the USDA.

In summary, a tremendous effort was made by USAID and the KASM team to install within the government of a developing nation, within a few years, the most modern and sophisticated planning techniques, including an unusually complex computer model. If they had succeeded, Korea would have had a planning tool more comprehensive than any used for U.S. agricultural policy. It is perhaps more surprising that so much was accomplished than that the task was not 100% completed.

J. COMPUTER REQUIREMENTS

All of the components of the KASM model are written in FORTRAN. The program, relative to other models in our study, is bulky. The final KASM model requires four minutes of CPU time on a CDC Cyber 75 computer for a 15-year simulation run.[43] Disaggregation of this model into three separate geographical regions increased the run time to 35 minutes, and therefore this version of the model is no longer used.[44]

The KASM team put considerable effort into arranging computer use in Korea. NAERI has free use of the Korean National Computer Center's Univac 1108. Using this machine proved inconvenient, however. The waiting time between submitting a run and getting output allowed an average of only three to four runs a week on any line of work. To expedite runs, the team contracted to rent computer time from the Korea Institute of Science and Technology. Unsuccessful attempts were also made to implement a computer hook-up with United States facilities via satellite.[45]

K. DOCUMENTATION

The KASM effort is profusely documented. There are 84 items listed on the team's publication list for the three years July 1, 1970–June 30, 1974. The list includes working papers, Ph.D. dissertations, and miscellaneous papers, some in English, some in Korean. The multiplicity of documents, however, is not very helpful to an outsider attempting to understand the model. Most of them are either very general or very narrow and technical.

The most comprehensive single document available is a book summarizing both the model and the institutional processes of constructing and implementing it.[46] The book contains a great deal of technical information about the model but falls short of being a complete documentation for modelers—it contains few actual model equations, few tables of input data, and only vague descriptions of model output. Unfortunately, the book is also incomplete in describing the institutional and political environment of the project. More can be learned from a half-hour conversation with any member of the modeling team than from the guarded prose of the formal documentation.

In fact it is only from conversations with members of the KASM team that we have come to realize how far this model's documentation falls short of communicating the many lessons to be learned from the KASM experience. This project is one of the most sustained, ambitious, thoughtful, and costly attempts ever made to incorporate computer modeling in a governmental planning organization. Individual participants in the experiment have tried many innovative ideas both in modeling and implementation, some of which worked, many of which did not, but all of which could be educational to the entire modeling community. There are many valuable stories to tell about KASM. We hope that more of them will be told in print.

NOTES AND REFERENCES

1. T. J. Manetsch, *et al.*, *A Generalized Simulation Approach to Agricultural Sector Analysis*, Michigan State University, East Lansing, Mich., November 1971.
2. G. E. Rossmiller, *et al.*, *Korean Agricultural Analysis and Recommended Development Strategies, 1971–85*, Michigan State University, East Lansing, Michigan, 1972.
3. G. E. Rossmiller, 'Utilizing a Systems Model for Policy Analysis', presented at a seminar on the *Evaluation of the Korean Agricultural Sector Simulation Model*, Airlie House, Airlie, Virginia, p. 3, March 17–19, 1974.
4. L. Fletcher, Technical Assistance Bureau of USAID, personal communication.
5. KASM Team (unidentified authors): 'Annual Report for Period July 1, 1973–June 30, 1974 of the Project on Adaption and Testing of Agricultural Simulation Models to Sector Analysis', Contract AID/csd-2975 USAID. Ag. Sector Analysis and Simulation Projects, Dept. of Ag. Econ. Center for International Studies, MSU, East Lansing, pp. 51–59, June 30, 1974.
6. Food and Agricultural Organization of the U.N., *FAO Syllabus on Agricultural Sector Analysis, Part 3, Alternative Approaches and Models for Sector Analysis*, publication ES/MISC/73/31, FAO, Rome, p. 72, May 3, 1975.
7. G. E. Rossmiller, (ed.), *Agricultural Sector Planning*, Agricultural Sector Analysis and Simulation Projects, Department of Agricultural Economics, Michigan State University, East Lansing, Michigan, p. 104, 1978.
8. *Ibid.*, p. 77.
9. G. E. Rossmiller, 1974, *op.cit.*, p. 6.
10. G. E. Rossmiller, 1978, *op.cit.*, p. 67.
11. J. Randers, *A Review of the KASS Simulation Model*, reported to USAID/Washington. Bureau of Technical Assistance, System Dynamics Group, Sloan School of Management, MIT, p. 8, March 14, 1974.
12. This phrase and the following general summary of model structure are taken from T. W. Carroll and M. H. Abkin, *A System Simulation Model for Agricultural Development Planning and Policy Analysis: The Korean Agricultural Sector Model*, presentation at the International Conference on Cybernetics and Society, Washington, D.C., November 1–3, 1976.
13. Briefing charts on the Korean Agriculture Sector Simulation Project, p. 20.
14. H. de Haen, *Consulting Report, KASS Consulting Trip, August 25–September 19, 1975*. Unpublished draft, p. 2.
15. H. de Haen, *Preliminary User's Guide to the Recursive Linear Programming Resource Allocation Component*, KASS Working Paper 73–7/2.
16. G. E. Rossmiller, 1978, *op.cit.*, p. 248.
17. *Ibid.*, Chapters 6–10 and especially Chapter 11.
18. Several KASM modelers, personal communications.
19. G. E. Rossmiller, 1972, *op.cit.*, pp. 15–16.
20. G. E. Rossmiller, 1978, *op.cit.*, p. 222.
21. *Ibid.*, pp. 221–222.
22. G. E. Rossmiller, 1972, *op.cit.*, p. 51.
23. T. W. Carroll and M. H. Abkin, *op.cit.*, pp. 6–8.
24. G. E. Rossmiller, 1978, at ends of Chapters 6–10.

25. *Ibid.*, p. 129.
26. *Ibid.*, p. 214.
27. *Ibid.*, pp. 237–238.
28. *Ibid.*, p. 238.
29. *Report of KASS/KAPP Review Team*, based on activities of the team in Korea March 6–13, 1976, in fulfillment of contract #AID/ASIA-C-1157 (mimeographed USAID document), p. 15.
30. *Ibid.*, p. 19.
31. F. C. Jones, *Development and Implementation of a Project: Korea*, Chapter 7.
32. G. E. Rossmiller, 1978, p. 248.
33. *Ibid.*, p. 45.
34. All described in *Report of KASS/KAPP Review Team*, *op.cit.*
35. *Ibid.*, p. 17.
36. *Ibid.*, p. 18.
37. L. Fletcher, personal communication.
38. G. E. Rossmiller, personal communication.
39. *Report of KASS/KAPP Review Team*, *op.cit.*
40. *Ibid.*, p. 50.
41. G. E. Rossmiller, personal communication.
42. As of 1983 this model was not yet documented. For interim reports see publications of Food and Agriculture Program, IIASA, A-2361, Laxenburg, Austria.
43. T. W. Carroll and M. H. Abkin, *op.cit.*, p. 2.
44. G. E. Rossmiller, 1978, p. 106.
45. KASM Team 'Annual Report for Period July 1, 1973–June 30, 1974', *op.cit.*, pp. 39–42.
46. G. E. Rossmiller (ed.), *Agricultural Sector Planning*, East Lansing: Michigan State University, Dept. of Agricultural Economics, 1978.

CHAPTER 11

MexicoV: Statistical Patches

A. INSTITUTIONAL SETTING

Among the oldest and most respected names in econometrics is that of the Wharton School and its associated institutions, Wharton Economic Forecasting Associates (Wharton EFA) and the Wharton Economic Forecasting Unit (Wharton EFU). The man who is principally responsible for the Wharton School's econometric reputation is Dr Lawrence Klein, one of the founders of modern econometrics.

MexicoV is a product of the Klein-Wharton school of modeling. Abel Beltran del Rio, the model's author, constructed *MexicoV* when he was a doctoral candidate under Klein at the Wharton School. Klein's influence on the model's development is shown by regular citations of his work throughout the dissertation and by his co-authorship of a published report on the model.[1]

While constructing *MexicoV*, Beltran del Rio attracted sponsorship for the model from over 50 Mexican business and governmental agencies. This sponsorship allowed him to start a department within Wharton EFA for continued econometric study of the Mexican economy. From this base Beltran del Rio and his associates worked to refine and update the Mexican model and to communicate their findings to interested persons in Mexican businesses and government.

The connection between Beltran del Rio and his sponsors is more academic than commercial.

> Our relationship with the firms and institutions in Mexico has been and still is one of a sponsorship, rather than of commercial nature... In more than one sense their annual funding has a nature of a grant. I think this has been important, because it has allowed us to minimize the time-consuming provision of commercial 'quid pro quo'. This has meant for us almost a complete concentration on research.[2]

Beltran del Rio had been a Mexican businessman for many years before he entered the Wharton School. Unlike most of the modelers described in this study, he worked from an insider's perspective and knew his sponsors as peers. Indeed, *MexicoV* is the only example among our case studies of a citizen of a less-industrialized country modeling his own nation, funded by sources within his nation.

B. PURPOSE

MexicoV was intended to serve many purposes. It was the basis of a doctoral dissertation. It still serves as a research tool for exploring the structure of the Mexican economy. It is an economic forecasting device and an instrument for exploring the economic implications of possible government policies. Beltran del Rio and Klein also indicate that the model is intended as a demonstration of how sophisticated statistical techniques can be used to glean useful information from imperfect data, as a step toward better modeling, and as a spur to better data collection:

> Methods of dealing in modern econometrics with 'undersized' samples have been developed, and it is with these methods in mind that we have tackled the empirical task of implementing this measurement of the econometric structure of Mexico. We hope that it can set a pattern for future econometric research in the rest of Latin America.[3]

It is clear from Beltran del Rio's descriptions of the Mexican economy and from the performance indicators he selects in evaluating model output that certain economic problems are of particular concern to him. The model is to describe the behavior of the economy 'for the full period of the present Echeverria administration, 1971–76'.[4] The problems of concern center around the interrelated phenomena of income disparities, rapid population growth, unemployment, and uneven growth rates of different economic sectors. Questions that interest Beltran del Rio include, for example: Will there be enough employment for a work force expanding at 3–4% a year? Can economic growth be promoted without causing serious inflation, incurring trade deficits, and/or worsening the already troublesome disparities in income? Which economic sectors will grow and modernize most rapidly, and what might the government do to make growth rates more even?.

C. METHOD

The way Beltran del Rio used econometrics to determine the structure of *MexicoV* was unusually formal and rigorous. A considerable portion of his work went toward establishing the relationships among the model's variables. Therefore we shall discuss here at length the method by which Beltran del Rio arrived at *MexicoV*'s structure, in addition to his method of estimating parameters.

According to the philosophy evolved at the Wharton School, the task of the applied econometrician is to try to explain and link, as far as possible, all the macroeconomic accounting systems available, i.e., national accounts, input–output, flow of funds.[5]

In the Mexican case this task was not simple. While applied econometricians have generally converged on a neo-Keynesian demand-driven structure as the best econometric representation of a fully industrialized economy, basic structure is an open question for nations undergoing industrialization.

Beltran del Rio began his attempt to specify a structure for the Mexican economy with a tentative outline of which variables were to be exogenous, which were to be endogenous, and where lags were expected to appear. This list was based on economic theory and Beltran del Rio's own knowledge of the Mexican economy. From there he went on to 'a detailed empirical survey, based on the analysis of statistical material...and on work of the institutional economists'.[6] The survey resulted in a long verbal description of actual conditions in the Mexican economy as indicated by macroeconomic data, and a rough sketch of how variables were to influence each other in the model.

This rough approximation was extended by a three-front search for alternative structural hypotheses. On one front Beltran del Rio searched the theoretical literature on economic development, focusing on four theorists (Nurske, Leibenstein, Hirschman, and Lewis) who had developed explicit mathematical models of the development process.[7] On the second front he reviewed five previously-constructed econometric models of Latin American nations, paying particular attention to the modeler's treatment of inflation, capacity creation, production, income distribution, and political factors.[8] On the third front, he examined mathematical formulations of three basic theoretical models—classical, Keynesian, and Marxian. His examination of these three basic theories included both a qualitative examination of how realistically their formulations describe Mexican economic conditions and a formal, quantitative examination of how well their equations fit the Mexican data.[9]

Having generated initial structural hypotheses about the determinants of the variables to be explained, and having assembled a series of other hypotheses from the economic literature, Beltran del Rio proceeded to select the best specification for each model relationship. Ideally, he states, the choice among the alternative hypotheses 'should be resolved by trying all the alternatives and by selecting the one that agrees best with the empirical description, unless it is clearly inferior in statistical fit.[10]

As an example of how Beltran del Rio actually made his selection, we shall describe the process by which he arrived at his consumption function. The various hypothetical consumption functions included:

1. A Keynesian formulation, in which consumption *per capita* is a function of disposable income *per capita*.
2. A dynamic version of the Keynesian function, in which consumption *per*

capita is a function of the current year's disposable income *per capita* and the previous year's consumption *per capita*.
3. A Marxian version in which total private consumption is class-disaggregated and a function of income—the wage-earners consuming a high portion of their wages and the capitalists consuming a lesser fraction of their (higher) income.
4. A dynamic Marxian version in which total consumption is represented as a distributed-lag function of wages and capitalist incomes.

Beltran del Rio selected the dynamic Keynesian formulation, using the following process of elimination:

> The simple, unlagged Keynesian function fails to incorporate the dynamics of Mexican consumption. The permanent income hypothesis [on which the Keynesian equation is based] not only implies a degree of sophistication that can hardly be found in poor economies, but also produces a seemingly low estimate of long run mpc [marginal propensity to consume] of 0.79. For the United States, similar consumption functions produce estimates that range between 0.834 to 0.828. The Marxian formulation, in spite of being the one suggested by empirical analysis...for its inclusion of income distribution, was excluded because in the unlagged form, although quite acceptable in its coefficients, it fails to introduce the dynamics of Mexican consumption. The lagged form, on the other hand, gives an unacceptably high long-run propensity to consume out of wage income, 1.33. This may be due to improper measurements that could be corrected in the future by...revised figures...[11]

After deciding the nature of the model's basic structural relationships, Beltran del Rio went on to fill in the details. He disaggregated where data allowed more detailed representation (for example, inclusion of more categories of imports and exports). He performed further searches to identify exogenous political forces. In the process of refinement, the model went through five versions—hence the final model was called *MexicoV*.

The parameters of the model were estimated by ordinary least squares (OLS) regression, except for the ten equations containing distributed lags, which were estimated 'by fitting a polynomial of third degree with two end-point restrictions'.[12] The high degree of interdependence of the model variables would theoretically call for a more sophisticated statistical technique, such as two-stage least-squares (2SLS), and a 2SLS estimation of the final model was partially completed. It was not finished because of difficulties with the Mexican data and because of the high cost of the method.[13]

The mathematical model resulting from the above procedures has the following properties: it contains 143 equations, 40 of which define statistically-estimated endogenous variables, the rest of which are accounting statements (e.g., total consumption = private consumption + public consumption) or definitions (e.g., rural labor force = rural population times rural labor participation rate). All the estimated equations are linear. Ten of the estimated equations contain distributed lags of up to three years. Over a dozen one-year delays come into the model through definitional statements that include rates of change.

In some instances, both in estimated and definitional equations, a variable is defined as a lagged function of itself. For example, coffee exports are related to the previous year's coffee exports. However, only in the case of capital, which (in order to represent depreciation) is defined as 90–95% of the previous year's capital* (plus current investment), does the representation appear to be a deliberate accumulation or integration of flows.

The model contains 46 exogenous variables (not counted in the 143 equations). In almost all cases, exogenous forecasts were prepared through extensive discussions with experts. For example, government-decided variables are forecast through consultation with Mexican sources familiar with government plans. Forecasts of the many United States variables that affect the Mexican economy were made through consultation with the economists at Wharton EFA who specialize in forecasting the behavior of the United States economy.

D. BOUNDARIES

Beltran del Rio aimed to represent the following factors, which he perceived as important regardless of data availability:[14]

1. The process of creating capacity, through capital and technological imports, in the context of general capital limitations and abundance of unskilled and semi-skilled labor.
2. Internal and external sources of instability: the impact of political climate on the economy and the dependence on foreign trade; the internal and external sources of inflation.
3. The dominant role played by the federal government as infrastructure builder and entrepreneur; public finances.
4. The general unevenness in economic life, as exemplified in functional income distribution, in rural versus urban production, in federal versus non-federal taxation.
5. The rapid demographic processes resulting in high population growth, rural-urban labor force migration, and unemployment.
6. The proximity to the United States market with its effects on international labor migration, tourism, and border transactions.
7. A decision-making time horizon that is shorter than that pertaining in more industrialized countries.

This is an ambitious list, and most of the items on it are not dealt with in the model. Excluded from the above list and from the model are:

---

* 90% for private capital, 95% for public capital.

1. Physical constraints. Mining exports are not limited by resource reserves, coffee production is not constrained by acreage of potential coffee-growing land, agriculture in general is not constrained by water or land availability. (Sufficient data did not exist to permit a supply-oriented formulation of the productive sector).[15]
2. Environmental variables, such as erosion, salinization, or pollution.
3. Social factors: education, values, and social norms affecting income distribution, consumption, population dynamics, or labor productivity.

These exclusions are easily explained. All are long-term influences that are unlikely to change greatly over the five-year time horizon of the model. None could have been easily verified from available data, particularly during an era of rapid economic growth.

MexicoV's treatment of the agricultural sector is quite cursory. Specific crops that are important in trade are considered, as well as production of the sector as a whole. However, factors of production such as land, labor, water, and chemical inputs are not included.

In general, political forces, government-decided variables, and influences from other nations are exogenous. Thus the presidential election cycle, paving of roads (a determinant of tourism receipts), the international market price for cotton, and the United States hourly manufacturing wage (which affects labor exports to the United States) are all exogenous. In addition, some variables that would appear in reality to be determined by the inner workings of the Mexican economy are exogenous to the model. For example, domestic consumption and domestic production of copper, cotton, lead, and nonferrous metals are exogenous. Some of these variables may be made endogenous with the planned addition of an input–output matrix and other structural additions to later versions of the model. Beltran del Rio also states that he intends to determine the population-growth function endogenously in future versions of the model.[16]

Figure 11.1 shows the boundary diagram of the *MexicoV* model. The number and importance of exogenous variables make the modeler an important structural adjunct in *MexicoV*. In Beltran del Rio's opinion, a good economist working with a bad model can produce better forecasts than a bad economist with a good model.[17] Successful forecasts probably cannot be produced with *MexicoV* unless someone who knows Mexican politics and economics quite well is available to provide good and detailed guesses about the future of imports, exports, Presidential elections, and other exogenous variables.

E. STRUCTURE

Beltran del Rio makes no systematic attempt to trace long chains of relationships, or to relate the structure of his model to its behavior, but we shall try to do so in this description.

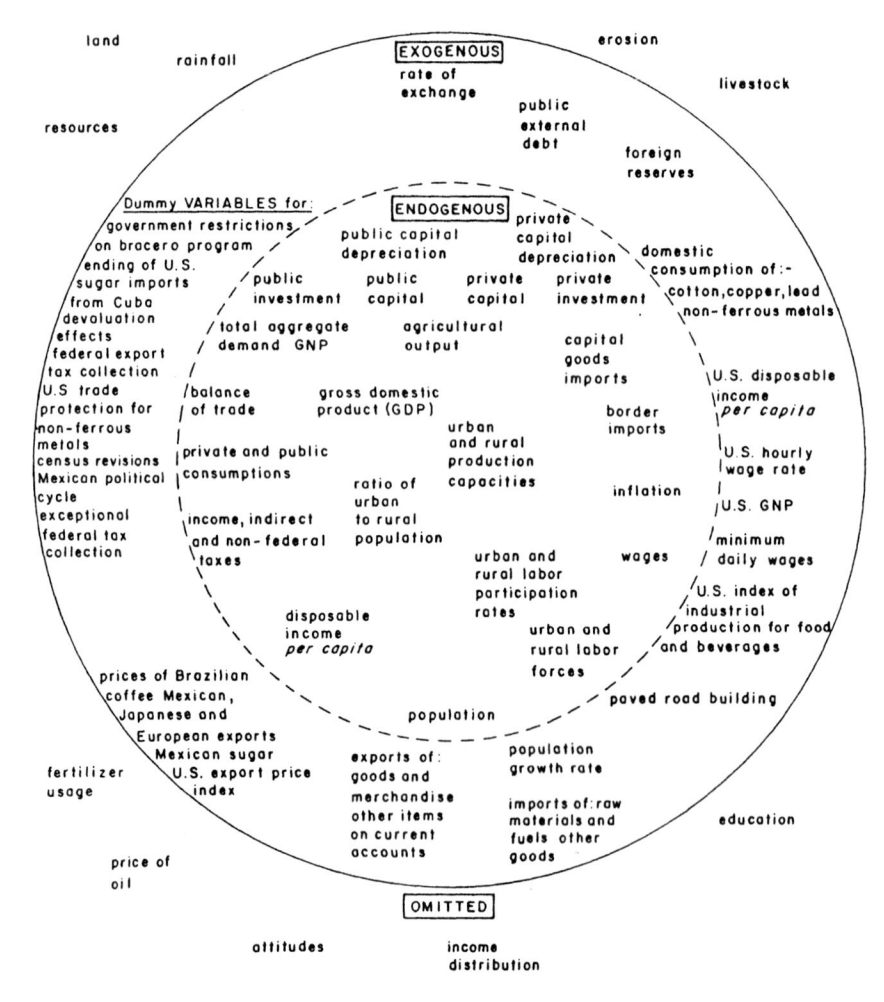

Figure 11.1 Boundaries of *MexicoV*

At the core of the *MexicoV* structure is a series of demand-driven growth loops (see Figure 11.2). Growth of private consumption (which tends to occur due to the model's exponentially-growing population) results in an increase in total aggregate demand (by definition, consumption plus investment). Higher aggregate demand means higher GNP. GNP growth results in a growth of national income and of disposable income *per capita*, if GNP has grown faster than population. Income *per capita* feeds back to increase private consumption. A similar chain of events occurs through increases in public consumption: increased public consumption creates increased aggregate demand, thereby increasing, in turn, GNP, national income, and income taxes. Income taxes are part of total taxes, which further increase public consumption.

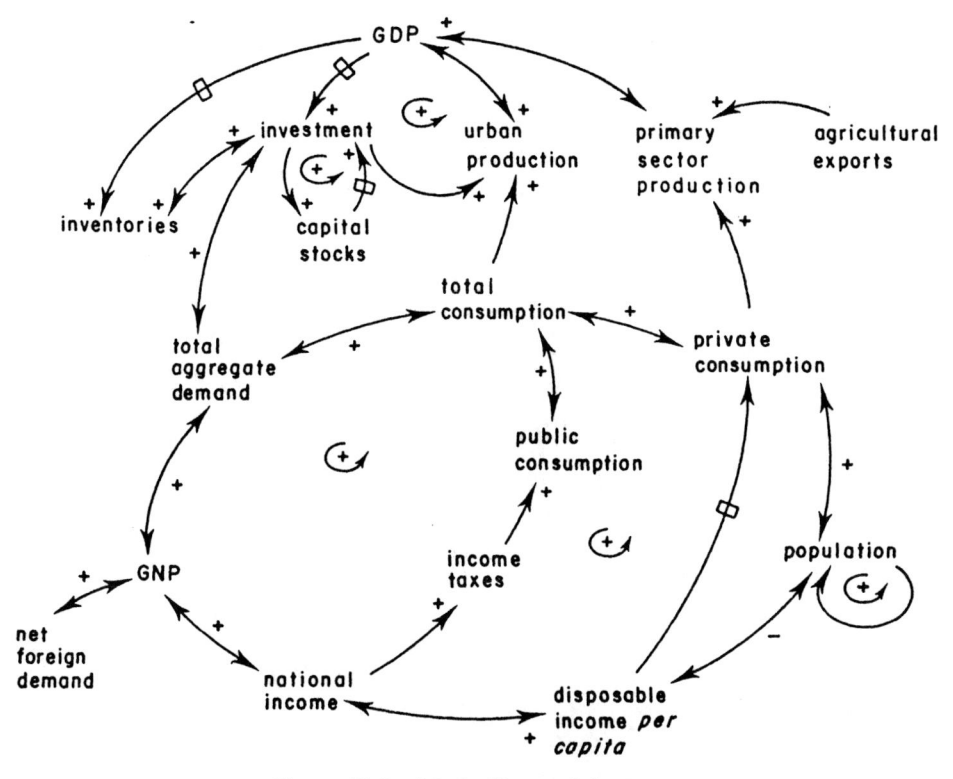

Figure 11.2 *MexicoV* growth loops

Reinforcing the linkage between consumption and economic growth, both urban (secondary- and tertiary-sector) output and primary-sector output are increased by increases in consumption. These increased outputs raise gross domestic product (GDP). Increased GDP creates higher inventories, thereby increasing investment, aggregate demand, GNP, national income, and so on. Moreover, increased investment in turn increases urban output and GDP. Investment also increases capital stocks, which feed back to boost investment still further.

Yet all is not necessarily growth in *MexicoV* (see Figure 11.3). One side effect of the growth of output is that it promotes high rates of capacity utilization which, in turn, creates rising wages.[18] Rising wages set off the inflationary wage-price spiral, which decreases real monetary values. In other words, the positive feedbacks associated with economic growth tend to enhance the positive feedback of the inflationary process which, in turn, curtails real economic growth. Economic growth also triggers inflation because rising GDP results in higher indirect taxes, which are passed on as increased prices.

Other forces that tend to restrain growth in the model include:

1. Rising population, which decreases income *per capita*.

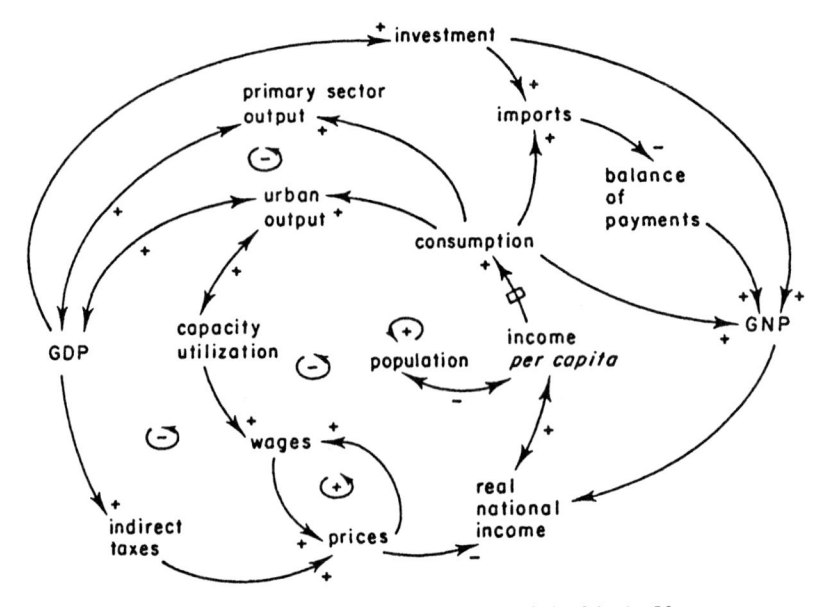

Figure 11.3 Forces countering growth in *MexicoV*

2. Rising incomes and private consumption, which lead to higher imports of consumer goods, thus worsening the balance of trade and decreasing GNP.
3. Rising investment which increases imports of capital goods, also worsening the balance of payments.

The model also contains structural elements describing unemployment, migration, imports, and exports. Imports and exports are almost completely driven by exogenous variables. They are represented in surprising detail (see Figure 11.4) considering that their only effect in the model is to modify the growth rate of GNP.

The dynamics of labor and migration, on the other hand, are driven by endogenous economic variables as shown in Figure 11.5. Economic growth results in investment and in capital formation. Urban capital is calculated from total capital using a statistically-estimated linear equation. The residual of total capital minus urban capital is assumed to be rural capital. Urban and rural capital, respectively, create urban and rural productive capacity. Capacity per worker in the labor force gives potential urban and rural labor productivities (capital per worker). The discrepancy between potential urban and rural labor productivity stimulates rural-urban migration. Migration, by reducing the number of workers in the rural sector and increasing the number in the urban sector, tends to close the gap in potential labor productivities.

Concurrently, growth of capacity tends to raise labor participation rates, and population growth tends to increase the labor force in both rural and urban sectors. (The same population growth rate is assumed in both sectors.)

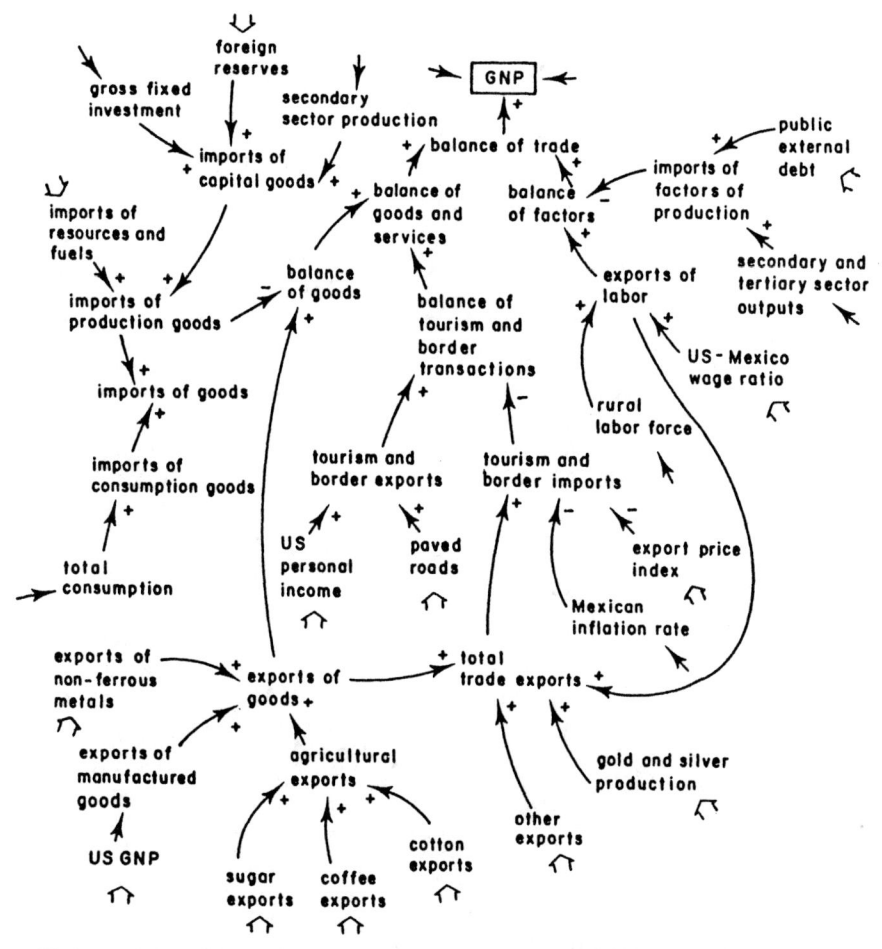

Figure 11.4 Import–export sector of *MexicoV*. Unlabeled single arrows (↑) indicate inputs calculated elsewhere in the model. Double arrows (⇑) indicate exogenous inputs

Thus the labor force tends to grow along with growth in capacity and to decrease potential labor productivities, while capital formation attempts to raise them.

Our attempt at a reference structure for *MexicoV* is shown in Figure 11.6. The reference structure concept was adequate for the simulation-based models we have described previously, but it does not 'fit' *MexicoV* very well because econometric models such as this one are not intended to make causal sense. For example, capital is calculated in the model, but it does not affect production in any way. Its only effect is on labor productivity and migration—which are calculated for informational purposes only and which also affect nothing else in the model. Output allocation is a meaningless concept in this model, since output results automatically

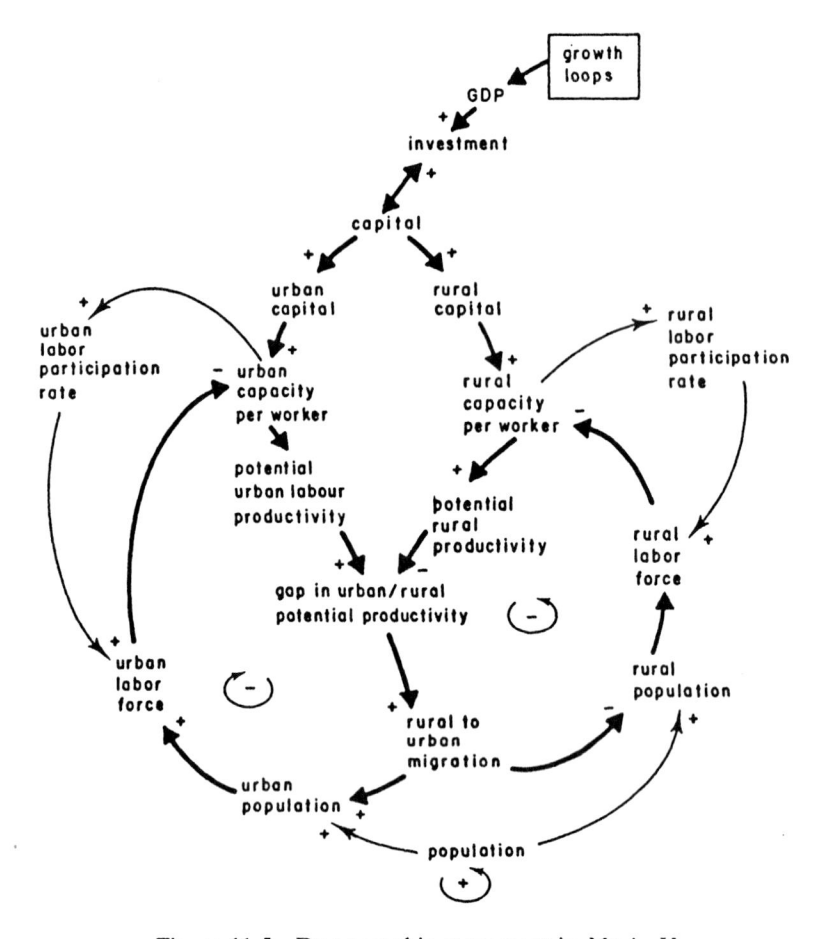

Figure 11.5 Demographic movement in *MexicoV*

from demand (consumption plus investment plus exports), and once it is produced it disappears from the system. There are two measures of output, GNP and GDP, which are determined by completely separate logical processes and never formally linked. There is no structural guarantee that GNP and GDP have any relationship to each other at all in *MexicoV*, or that output is bound in the least by capital or labor, or that energy imports should change the same way industrial production changes.

The variables in *MexicoV do* keep reasonable relationships to one another, because its many coefficients are derived from a real economy, where elements unconnected in the model are actually tightly related. From the point of view of a causal structural modeler, *MexicoV*, like other econometric models, appears to be a loose assortment of indirectly-related variables, held together by statistical patches. There are so many of these patches, however, that the final construction is fairly firm, and it probably even exhibits the same general shape

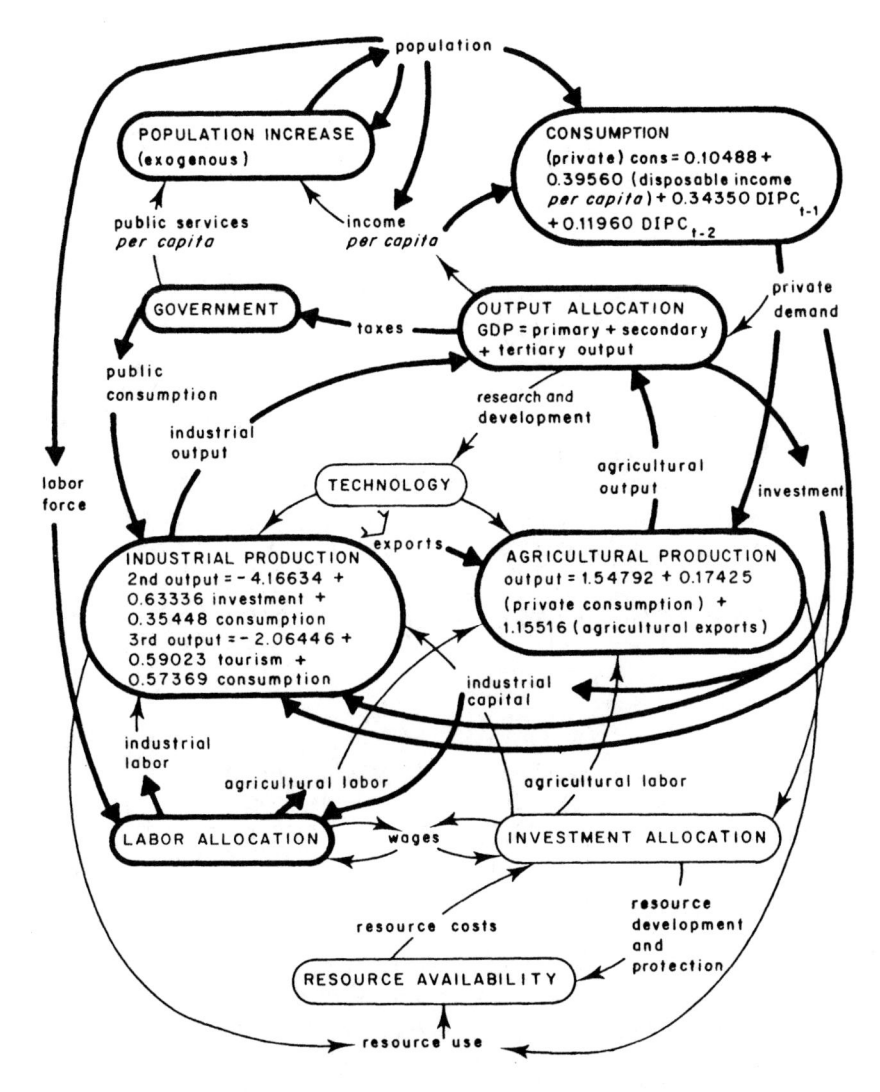

Figure 11.6 *MexicoV* reference structure

as the real system. For the short-term forecasting purposes of *MexicoV*, nothing more is required.

Insofar as we can analyze its structure, *MexicoV* appears to be dominated by positive feedback—which is to be expected from a series of relationships statistically estimated in a period of economic growth. When an economy has been growing rapidly, positive feedbacks are dominant, negative ones are overwhelmed, and regression analysis can be expected to identify a great many positive relationships. For short-term forecasts, this positive-feedback dominance is probably appropriate. If the model is constantly updated over a long period, changes in the strengths of the positive relationships will presumably be picked up in the incoming data, at least if the changes are gradual rather than sudden.

F. DATA

Beltran del Rio lists in full the database on which his model draws. The listings show that for the most part equations were estimated using data from the years 1948–1970. No verbal descriptions or source notations accompany the data tables; thus it is not possible to identify the sources of specific numbers. However, numerous official Mexican statistical documents in the bibliography of Beltran del Rio's dissertation suggest that primarily official statistics were used. Occasional references to data difficulties (such as a 1969 version of official information on private consumption, investment, and inventory change) imply that assembling data for *MexicoV* was not a straightforward task. Several comments indicate that a relationship could not be explored due to lack of data. Although Beltran del Rio and Klein state that a major objective of the modeling process was to demonstrate the use of limited data in econometric modeling,[19] no special description of data-handling techniques is given.

G. TESTING

The process by which *MexicoV* was developed was one long series of tests. Different sets of hypothetical single relationships were tested against empirical measures of Mexican conditions. The outcomes of the statistical tests were examined for congruence with the mental models of the modeler and his clients (e.g., whether the tests produced the expected signs and whether coefficient values were reasonable). The hypothetical relationships that best matched both the data and the mental models were incorporated into the model.

The full model was tested first for its ability to reproduce the behavior of variables over the period from which their coefficients were estimated (unless there are technical errors, the model should be capable of passing this test easily), and second, for its ability to reproduce historical behavior outside the period of the model's database. Variants of model structure were tried (*MexicoI* through *MexicoV*, later *Mexico VI* and *Mexico VII*). Finally, when the full model passed all these tests reasonably well, it was accepted as a forecasting tool.

The above series of formal tests was supplemented by informal testing of the model: as Beltran del Rio put it, he 'played around with it and subjected it to all kinds of crazy things to see how it reacted'.[20] That is, the model was run over long time horizons, or with extreme values for exogenous inputs. Beltran del Rio likens the process to getting to know a riding horse; testing a model, like putting a horse through its paces, makes one familiar with its 'temperament' and its quirks, thereby allowing one to 'compensate for' and 'counteract' unwanted tendencies. These informal tests are not documented, and one gets from the model description no feeling for the model's sensitivity to exogenous assumptions.

The results of the formal statistical tests are completely documented. Statistically-estimated equations are always accompanied by four summary indices of their performance. The coefficients in these equations are carried out to six or seven significant digits. An example of an equation listing in the model, complete with summary indices, is:

Exports of copper

$$\text{ECOPR} = \underset{(2.297)}{1.13451} - \underset{(-2.106)}{1.09724 \text{DUMRS}} - \underset{(-2.306)}{16.04651 \text{PRCOP}} +$$
$$\underset{(2.627)}{19.88620 \text{PRCDU}} + \underset{(1.717)}{7.69851 \text{COCOP}} - \underset{(-2.552)}{11.75707 \text{COCDU}}$$

$R^2 = 0.9088 \quad \text{S.E.} = 0.04806 \quad \text{DW} = 2.1233 \quad F(5,13) = 36.8633$

where DUMRS is a dummy expressing the United States non-ferrous metal trade protection policy (1.0 for 1958–68, 0.0 elsewhere), PRCOP is domestic copper production, PRCDU is DUMRS × PRCOP, COCOP is domestic consumption of copper, COCDU is COCOP × DUMRS, and all of these independent variables are exogenous.

Listings of eight-year (1968–1976) values for all major model variables under two policy scenarios are provided, along with the complete tabular listings of the exogenous data used in forecasts. Verbal and tabular summaries of the results of the two policy scenarios are also provided.

As two years of the forecasting period had passed by the time Beltran del Rio's dissertation was completed, it was also possible to test the model by comparing predicted to actual values. This is done briefly in a verbal descriptive summary.[21] In general the model predicted the correct direction but wrong magnitude of change of economic quantities. Some illustrative numbers are given in Table 11.1. Beltran del Rio postulates that the difference between the model-generated results and the actual behavior may stem largely from his underestimation of the 'hard shocks' the Echeverria administration gave the economy. Beltran del Rio's exogenous forecasts of the rate of change of federal capital formation were 0.96% and 10.5% for 1971 and 1972; the real values turned out to be −14.4% and +74.1%.

Table 11.1

Variable		Actual value	Model forecast
Output growth rate	1971	3.7%	5.7%
	1972	7.2%	6.8%
Inflation rate	1971	4.9%	3.7%
	1972	4.2%	4.9%

H. CONCLUSIONS

Going from the most general to the most specific, we will describe the conclusions Beltran del Rio has drawn through constructing *MexicoV* in three categories:

1. Conclusions about the modeling process.
2. Conclusions about the economic structure of the Mexican economy.
3. Conclusions about Mexican economic conditions in forthcoming years.

In the first category, Beltran del Rio's major contribution was his experimentation with formalization of classical, Keynesian, and Marxian theories in econometric models. The main conclusion from this experiment was 'that the purely theoretical effort is bound to produce a non-realistic model, and that the empirical descriptive effort should precede the theoretical'[22] None of the macro theories proved completely useful, but all had parts that coincided with empirical descriptions of the Mexican economy and that proved useful as parts of the forecasting model.

In the second category—the structure of the Mexican economy—Beltran del Rio's conclusions are, of course, manifest in the structure of *MexicoV*; that is, they are the model assumptions. Below are examples of such conclusions:

1. Details of the import-export balance must be vitally important to the development of the economy (import-export calculations account for 50 of the 143 model equations).
2. The six-year presidential term introduces regular trends into government economic behavior, and thus into the economy as a whole (a dummy variable turned on during presidential election years affects private investment).
3. Changes in inventory are a function of changes in the price index and the GDP and are not a direct function of the size of the inventory or of consumption, wages, or income distribution.
4. The fraction of population living in cities is changed only by time and by a delayed function of the urban-rural productivity gap.

Beltran del Rio clearly demarcates areas where he feels his structural understanding is weak. The final section in Beltran del Rio's dissertation begins 'In the process of finding answers to our original questions, some new ones have arisen out of the answers found and some have reappeared in clearer form, out of the incomplete attempts to answer them.'[23] He then lists a series of fundamental questions that his research has raised, questions about the Mexican monetary system and about the distribution of supply, demand, and investment among various production sectors. The dissertation closes with a brief conceptual outline of an investigation Beltran del Rio would like to make into the redistribution of wealth as a new policy approach to reducing Mexico's severe income inequalities.

In the third category of conclusions, Beltran del Rio uses the model to forecast how the economy will perform under two contrasting policy scenarios. The first scenario, the slow hypothesis:

> ...is an undiluted extension, for the full [presidential] term, of the austerity period imposed by the government since its inauguration in December 1970. Its aims are the control...of inflation and the severe deterioration of the balance on the current account. Its main tools are fiscal restraint, lower growth of internal credit and external debt, and import controls.[24]

The second scenario, the quick hypothesis:

> ...fully extends the position of high employment and growth expressed by...[the] Minister of National Wealth from 1972 onwards... The policy measures here are easier fiscal and credit policies, but continuation of price and import controls.[25]

Beltran del Rio presents detailed forecasts for these two policy alternatives in tabular form. However, his verbal descriptions of simulation results never imply that the exact figures should be taken too seriously. He always rounds off output numbers and verbally places much more emphasis on trends than on exact results. For example, the main conclusion drawn from these tests is:

> ...that it is not possible to introduce effectively the [government's] new income distribution objective via employment and fast output growth without sacrificing- ...external and internal price stability... On the other hand, the preservation of stability (with the traditional 6–7% growth) leads to deterioration of the unemployment problem, given the extremely rapid pace of labor force growth...[26]

The behavior of the model system under the two policy sets can be summarized as follows:[27]

1. For 1971 and 1972, under both scenarios, there is an economic deceleration followed by a revival and a steady improvement in the balance on current account.
2. After 1973, the two scenarios diverge. The slow hypothesis gives GDP growth of 6–6.5%, the quick hypothesis, 7–7.5%.
3. Slow growth reduces the external deficit; fast growth increases it.
4. Slow growth stops inflation; fast growth keeps it going at 1970–1971 rates.
5. Slow growth increases idle productive capacity; fast growth keeps it constant.

Neither policy set has much effect on the distribution of income or unemployment or migration.

> On the average, the urban worker will have at least 7.5–8 times more real capital to

work with than his rural counterpart in both cases. The effects of the continuation of the productive gap will be to maintain a steady migratory flow to the urban centers..., with the consequent pressure on city facilities, enlargement of the 'belts of poverty' around metropolitan areas, and growth of urban employment and underemployment.[28]

I. COMPUTER REQUIREMENTS

MexicoV is written in FORTRAN. Once its coefficients have been estimated, one six-year simulation costs approximately $3 to run.[29]

J. IMPLEMENTATION

MexicoV's forecasts are delivered regularly to its 50-odd sponsoring institutions and to the general public through publication in Mexican journals. The model's purpose is to indicate what is likely to happen in the near future, not to recommend what policies to use. Given the model's non-policy intent, it cannot be 'implemented' in the sense that we have been using that word.

As a proxy for implementation, we should consider the extent to which *MexicoV*'s prognostications are heeded, but here again we are in trouble. It is always difficult to tell who pays attention to what, and there is no means of assessing the extent to which anyone acts on the basis of *MexicoV*'s forecasts. There are, however, a few indicators that suggest that the model's impact is not negligible. First, the model's sponsors continue to give Wharton EFA's Mexico branch economic support. A few of the sponsoring institutions have been sufficiently impressed with *MexicoV* that they have begun using its forecasts as exogenous inputs to planning models of their own. Second, *MexicoV* has a virtual monopoly on forecasting the behavior of the Mexican economy. There is no directly competitive source of economic forecasts, and so it is almost unavoidable that *MexicoV* will gain a wide audience. Finally, *MexicoV* is well situated to attract the attention of decision makers in Mexico. Coming from the Mexican business community and having friends within it, Beltran del Rio is in a favorable position to gain confidence in business and government circles. Moreover, he speaks and writes with a clear-headed, practical tone that is very effective in communicating his thoughts and his model's results.

K. DOCUMENTATION

Beltran del Rio's doctoral dissertation describes *MexicoV* in depth and at length (600 pages). Although it is lengthy, Beltran del Rio's dissertation is a convenient document with which to work. Readers are greatly aided by a prevailing orderliness, which is apparent in a subject index, careful tables of contents and figures, a fully alphabetical listing of systematically-chosen variable acronyms, and carefully arranged and labelled equation listings.

In his dissertation, Beltran del Rio describes not only his model and the reasoning behind its construction, he also gives a long, perceptive verbal account of the real-world situation it represents. Relationships that *MexicoV* makes quantitative and explicit are first described qualitatively, with reference both to their histories and their present states. The real-world situation is emphasized throughout the documentation, leaving it one of the most concrete model presentations we have encountered.

MexicoV has been described in a number of places other than Beltran del Rio's dissertation.[30] Regular communiques to model sponsors update model forecasts. A paper describing the model's history of predictive success and error was prepared (in Spanish) after *MexicoV* had experienced five years of use as a predictive tool.[31]

All told, *MexicoV* is one of the best documented of our case studies, matched only by Picardi's documentation of the SAHEL models, also a Ph.D. dissertation. *MexicoV* has had the added advantage of continued sponsorship over a period of several years. (Two years elapsed between the model's first use in forecasting and completion of Beltran del Rio's dissertation.) Academic standards, ample time for preparation and revision, and an interested audience in the policy community all seem to have been factors that helped Beltran del Rio produce a high-quality description of his model.

NOTES AND REFERENCES

1. A. Beltran del Rio and L. R. Klein, 'Macroeconomic Model Building in Latin America: the Mexican Case', reprinted from *The Role of the Computer in Economic and Social Research in Latin America*, Conference Report of the National Bureau of Economic Research, New York, Columbia University Press, 1974.
2. A. Beltran del Rio, personal communication.
3. A. Beltran del Rio and L. R. Klein, *op.cit.*, p. 190.
4. A. Beltran del Rio, *A Macroeconometric Forecasting Model for Mexico: Specification and Simulations*, University of Pennsylvania Ph.D. Thesis, p. 7, 1973 (available from University Microfilms).
5. *Ibid.*, p. xxxiv.
6. *Ibid.*, p. 418.
7. *Ibid.*, pp. 29–45.
8. *Ibid.*, Chapter IV, pp. 167–190.
9. *Ibid.*, Chapter V, pp. 191–249.
10. *Ibid.*, p. 261.
11. *Ibid.*, pp. 342–343.
12. A. Beltran del Rio and L. R. Klein, *op.cit.*, p. 169.
13. A. Beltran del Rio, *op.cit.*, p. 427, and personal communication.
14. A. Beltran del Rio, *op.cit.*, pp. 281–282.
15. A. Beltran del Rio, personal communication.
16. A. Beltran del Rio, *op.cit.*, p. 358.
17. A. Beltran del Rio, personal communication.
18. This effect is partially countered by the fact that the increased GDP leads to more rapid capital formation and lower rates of capacity utilization.

19. A. Beltran del Rio and L. R. Klein, *op.cit.*, p. 190.
20. A. Beltran del Rio, personal communication.
21. A. Beltran del Rio, *op.cit.*, pp. 413–416.
22. *Ibid.*, p. 420.
23. *Ibid.*, p. 423.
24. *Ibid.*, p. 370.
25. *Ibid.*, p. 422.
26. *Ibid.*, p. 422.
27. A. Beltran del Rio and L. R. Klein, *op.cit.*, p. 183.
28. *Ibid.*, pp. 189–190.
29. A. Beltran del Rio, personal communication.
30. See, for example, A. Beltran del Rio and L. R. Klein, *op.cit.*
31. A. Beltran del Rio, *Media Decada de Proyeccion Econometrica para Mexico: Analysis de Errors de Prediccion*, Wharton EFA, Philadelphia, September 1975.

CHAPTER 12

CHAC: Optimizing Mexican Agriculture

A. INSTITUTIONAL SETTING

CHAC is part of an experiment by the World Bank and the Mexican government to explore the usefulness of multi-level linear programming as a tool for planning. The full experiment consists of three models: DINAMICO, an economy-wide model; ENERGETICOS, which simulates the energy sector; and CHAC, which covers annual crops in the agricultural sector. (CHAC is the name of a Mayan rain god.) All three are optimization-based models. DINAMICO and ENERGETICOS are dynamic; that is, they are optimized over time. CHAC is static and represents agricultural activities within a single year. The three models were to be linked hierarchically to attain a detailed representation of the interactions between the energy and agricultural sectors within the full economy. However, inconsistencies among the three models prevented the linking.

In the following discussion we shall consider only CHAC, the largest, most expensive, and 'probably the most innovative'[1] of the three models. We chose CHAC, not only because of its size and originality, but also because it has been used separately from the other two models by the World Bank and the Mexican planning authorities.

From its beginning in 1969 CHAC was a joint venture of the World Bank, the Secretaria de la Presidencia of Mexico, and the Banco de Mexico. The Mexican government and the Banco de Mexico contributed not only funding and data, but also professional assistance in constructing the model.

> The CHAC project had high-level sponsorship from within the Mexican Ministry of the Presidency, and some of the Mexican contributors at the technical level are well trained in quantitative economics... CHAC would never have been built, much less implemented, without the close professional collaboration and sponsorship of the Mexican government.[2]

CHAC was ready for full-scale experimentation by 1971; the following year a World Bank modeler joined the Mexican Ministry of the Presidency to demonstrate the use of the model and to establish it as a policy tool within the Mexican government. The government and the World Bank continued to use and improve the model through 1974, when the World Bank formally withdrew from the project. The model was left in Mexico under the care of a newly-formed commission charged with co-ordinating the policies and programs of the various agencies dealing with agricultural matters. The formation of this commission was partially inspired by CHAC, which vividly demonstrated the interdependencies of different decisions and actions within the agricultural sector.[3]

B. PURPOSE

The initial aim in constructing the agricultural model, CHAC, was to formalize the major aspects of micro-level and sectoral decision-making... The sector study has also been designed to serve both the Mexican government's interests in analytic tools for planning sectoral policies, and the World Bank's interest in the methodology of project appraisal techniques and in general policy planning models.[4]

In other words, the model had two clients. One was the Mexican government, which formulates general agricultural policies (such as public investment in irrigation or in agricultural research, pricing of agricultural products, external trade and internal land tenure constraints), and through these policies to improve the economic welfare of the country. The other client was the World Bank, which wanted to assess the impact of a potential investment in a particular project (such as a dam, tubewell, or canal lining) and compare it to the likely outcomes of other possible investments. One client was considering policies at the level of the total agricultural sector. The other was weighing specific local investment proposals. Both wanted to know the possible effects of their actions on local conditions and on the economy as a whole.

CHAC was designed to avoid the pitfalls of 'the usual approach to agricultural policy planning',[5] which involves setting individual target outputs for each commodity and then figuring out how much fertilizer, land, labor, and other inputs will be required to meet all targets. In contrast, CHAC was intended to:[6]

1. Permit sector-wide aggregation of individual commodity production processes, to assess the effects of policy not only on individual production goals, but also on total-system goals such as full employment.
2. Generate efficient resource allocation across the agriculture sector as a whole, which could require raising some product or input prices and lowering others; therefore all products and inputs should be considered at once.
3. Take account of total constraints such as balance of payments, which could require varying mixtures of domestic and imported supply of each commodity.

4. Include intercrop substitution possibilities on both the demand and supply side.

According to its authors:

> CHAC is designed to be addressed to questions of pricing policies, trade policies, employment programs, and some categories of investment allocation. It is not particularly well suited for analyzing agricultural research and extension programs, crop insurance policies, or credit policies.[7]

C. METHOD

To accomplish all these purposes and to please both the model's clients, the CHAC team had to construct a model that contained local and regional detail as well as total-sector and total-economy consistency. They went about this task by organizing the model in a geographical hierarchy. There are 20 submodels, each representing a particular climatic district in Mexico. These 20 districts are aggregated into four geographical regions which are then aggregated into the agriculture sector as a whole. The three-level model CHAC was intended to be linked to the total-economy model DINAMICO, to make a consistent representation of the system all the way from district harvesting decisions to foreign exchange balances. This final link was made only informally, however. The CHAC and DINAMICO models were run separately, and information from each was used as exogenous input to the other, with the modelers intervening.[8]

CHAC is a behavioral simulation model, describing how farmers and consumers will react to various policies, use various resources, and respond to various prices in a given year. It is a linear programming model, but the optimization procedure is not used in the usual way, in order to select that set of policy options that will maximize a precisely-defined objective function. Rather, optimization in CHAC is used as a mathematical device to represent the behavior of a competitive market.

Like all optimization models,* CHAC consists of:

1. Activities—decision variables or choices of action; the unknowns whose values the model is to determine.
2. Constraints—restrictions on the values that the activities may take.
3. An objective function—the quantity to be minimized or maximized by varying the activities within the range allowed by the constraints.

In CHAC the activities consist of farmers' production decisions, import-export decisions, domestic consumers' demand decisions, and decisions about the supply of input factors such as labor and land all for 33 different products. The constraints in the model include world market prices (which restrict import-export decisions), market clearance (for each crop domestic supply plus imports must equal or exceed domestic demand plus exports), land and

* The general characteristics of optimization models are reviewed in Chapter 2.

water limitations, availability of labor, capital and other inputs, and credit balances.

The CHAC model is very detailed and very large; there are about 1,500 constraints and 3,500 activities. The model is solved for one year only. This could be a year in the future, however, if forecasted values for model parameters are used.

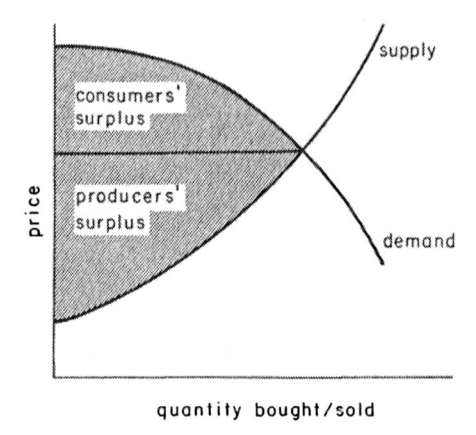

Figure 12.1 CHAC objective function

The objective function is described by the modelers as the sum of consumers' and producers' surpluses, which is to be maximized. The meaning of this quantity can best be understood by reference to Figure 12.1. This figure shows simplified supply and demand curves for one product. These curves are the aggregate result of the production and consumption decisions of millions of people in the Mexican economy, and the task of the CHAC model is to determine what these curves will be and where they will intersect. The central assumption of the model is that the producers and consumers within the system will act individually in such a way that in the aggregate they will maximize the hatched area—the sum of the producers and consumers' surplus (more accurately the sum of the areas in 33 similar and interdependent figures, one for each crop). According to the theory of competitive markets, when this area is maximized, prices will equal marginal costs, and the market will be in equilibrium.

This objective function can be altered to include monopoly behavior, or constraints can be added to represent government interference in the free market, but the model is usually run as a free market because the CHAC modelers feel this is the most accurate representation of the Mexican agricultural system.[9]

If that explanation of the objective function, which is the way the modelers explain it, is too abstract for those who do not see the world through a free market paradigm, the objective function can also be described simply as the total net revenue (receipts minus costs) of the agricultural sector, which is to be maximized (see Figure 12.2).

$$\Sigma \omega D + \Sigma \rho_e E - \Sigma \rho_m M -$$

$$\begin{bmatrix} \text{the sum over all} \\ \text{crops of price times} \\ \text{quantity demanded} \end{bmatrix} + \begin{bmatrix} \text{the sum of all} \\ \text{export prices times} \\ \text{export quantities} \end{bmatrix} - \begin{bmatrix} \text{import prices} \\ \text{times import} \\ \text{quantities} \end{bmatrix} -$$

$$\rho_l \text{SALS} - \rho_k K - \rho_l \text{CT} - \rho_c \text{CP} - 0.1 S - \Sigma 0.1 F -$$

$$\begin{bmatrix} \text{total labor} \\ \text{costs} \end{bmatrix} - \begin{bmatrix} \text{interest on long} \\ \text{and short-term} \\ \text{capital} \end{bmatrix} - \begin{bmatrix} \text{seed} \\ \text{costs} \end{bmatrix} - \begin{bmatrix} \text{fertilizer and} \\ \text{pesticide costs} \end{bmatrix} -$$

$$\Sigma \rho_a A - -\Sigma \rho_{wg} W_g - (\Delta \rho_{wg}) W_g - \Sigma \rho_{wp} W_p - (\Delta \rho_{wp}) W_p +$$

$$\begin{bmatrix} \text{draft} \\ \text{animal costs} \end{bmatrix} - \begin{bmatrix} \text{gravity water costs} \\ \text{and cost increment} \end{bmatrix} - \begin{bmatrix} \text{well water costs and} \\ \text{cost increment} \end{bmatrix} +$$

$$+\Sigma \Delta \rho_d T_d$$

$$\begin{bmatrix} \text{correction for district} \\ \text{price differentials} \end{bmatrix} \quad \text{(to be maximized)}$$

Figure 12.2 CHAC objective function. In each term the small Greek letter is a constant parameter, the capital letter is a variable

A basic requirement of any linear programming model is that the equations representing the objective function and constraints be linear. Thus CHAC's constraints all follow a linear format similar to the following, which is the general equation for the commodity balance constraint for one crop.

$$Y_1 \cdot X_1 + Y_2 \cdot X_2 + \ldots -$$

$$\begin{bmatrix} \text{yield} \\ \text{parameter,} \\ \text{production} \\ \text{method 1} \end{bmatrix} \cdot \begin{bmatrix} \text{hectares in} \\ \text{production} \\ \text{method 1} \end{bmatrix} + \begin{bmatrix} \text{yield} \\ \text{parameter,} \\ \text{production} \\ \text{method 2} \end{bmatrix} \cdot \begin{bmatrix} \text{hectares in} \\ \text{production} \\ \text{method 2} \end{bmatrix} + \begin{bmatrix} \text{similar} \\ \text{terms} \\ \text{for other} \\ \text{production} \\ \text{methods} \end{bmatrix} -$$

$$- \alpha_1 \cdot D_1 - \alpha_2 \cdot D_2 - \ldots +$$

$$- \begin{bmatrix} \text{parameter} \\ \text{indicating} \\ \text{amount of} \\ \text{crop} \\ \text{in demand} \\ \text{mix 1} \end{bmatrix} \cdot \begin{bmatrix} \text{amount of} \\ \text{demand} \\ \text{mix 1} \end{bmatrix} - \begin{bmatrix} \text{amount of} \\ \text{crop in} \\ \text{demand} \\ \text{mix 2} \end{bmatrix} \cdot \begin{bmatrix} \text{amount of} \\ \text{demand} \\ \text{mix 2} \end{bmatrix} - \begin{bmatrix} \text{similar} \\ \text{terms for} \\ \text{other} \\ \text{demand} \\ \text{mixes} \end{bmatrix} +$$

$$+ M - E + P \geq 0$$

$$+ \begin{bmatrix} \text{imports} \end{bmatrix} - \begin{bmatrix} \text{exports} \end{bmatrix} + \begin{bmatrix} \text{adjustment} \\ \text{for yield-} \\ \text{enhancing} \\ \text{technical} \\ \text{progress} \end{bmatrix}$$

This equation simply states that total domestic sales plus exports cannot exceed total production plus imports; consumers cannot buy what has not been produced or imported. According to the inequality assumption, the opposite could occur; production could exceed consumption.

While the constraint and all others are linear, the model does not depict a totally linear world. For example, there are many different production activities X_j (each with an associated yield parameter Y_j) for each crop. A farmer in one district may be able to choose among 20 different ways of growing beans, each using a different amount of land, labor, and fertilizer, and each producing a different yield. When they are all added together, the farmers' supply responses in choosing how much of each kind of cropping technology to use for each crop are in fact highly non-linear.

The requirement of linearity leads to a particularly difficult problem in the objective function, which is shown in algebraic form in Figure 12.2. The first term in this function is the sum over all crops of the price of each crop times the demand for that crop. But the modelers wanted to include the assumption that demand *depends on* price; in fact, the demand for one crop depends not only on the price for that crop but on the prices of other crops that might be substituted for it (consumer demand for wheat depends on both wheat price and corn price). If demand D is some function of price ω, then the first term of the objective function is not linear; it is a complex function of D, and linear programming search techniques cannot be used to find the maximum.

The CHAC modelers avoided this problem through the process of 'grid linearization'. Each non-linear demand curve is approximated by a series of linear segments, each of which is associated with a constant parameter indicating the price at which that level of demand will occur. Each such segment is a separate activity in the model equations, and the optimization procedure then solves for the combination of demand activities with associated prices that maximizes the objective function. The grid linearization procedure requires the creation of many long lists (vectors) of price parameters and demand activities, but it allows the essentially non-linear functioning of the market to be approximated in a linear format.

The CHAC modelers have managed by a number of such mathematical devices to make a linear programming model that represents the behavior of producers and consumers as essentially interacting and non-linear. The main reasons for going to this trouble were:

1. The modelers believed that real-world relationships are non-linear.
2. The search procedures for finding the optimal point of a linear programming model are much more efficient and convenient to use than any non-linear search procedures.

The reason for wanting to optimize in the first place was that economic theory has shown that this is one way to find the equilibrium point of a competitive market. But it is not a very usual way, nor is CHAC a very usual application of linear programming. The market is normally represented either by solving simultaneous supply and demand equations, or, if the dynamics are of interest, by simulating independently the decisions of producers and consumers. And linear programming is usually employed to find the optimal set of policies open to an identifiable policy-maker, rather than, as in CHAC, as an abstract heuristic device. One of the chief advantages of linear programming—the sharp delineation of goals, policy choices, and assumptions about constraints—is in fact not realized in CHAC, where the objective function is a mathematical artifact, the activities represent not the policy choices of government but the daily choices of farmers and consumers, and the actual policy variables are embedded within the constraint equations.

Why did the CHAC modelers choose a linear method to represent a non-linear system, an optimization method when their purpose was not to optimize, an abstract and static rather than literal and dynamic method for a purpose that required visualizing a system's response to many different kinds of policy inputs? The CHAC documentation never answers this question. We can only assume that in this project, like many others, the modeling method came before the problem. A crack team of linear programmers saw a novel way to use their technique and proceeded to do so most skillfully, without stopping to ask whether it was, in fact, the most appropriate tool for the problem at hand.

The CHAC modelers show great ingenuity in wriggling out of a number of mathematical straightjackets in order to apply their linear optimization technique to a non-linear non-optimization problem. However, each dramatic escape moves the model to a higher level of abstraction, farther removed from everyday understanding of real farmers and consumers. The final model is difficult to communicate, understand, or evaluate. What does the model really assume, implicitly and explicitly, about consumer behavior? What kinds of information and actions at what places and when would be necessary for the real market to achieve equilibrium in the way it does in the model? Would differentials in income distribution, or bottlenecks in factor supply, or stocks held over from last year make a significant difference in the system's behavior? Who in the system really sets prices, how long does it take the price-setters to act, and what information do they take into account? Are these questions even relevant ones to ask about this model?

Thus CHAC is a map of reality constructed from symbols and concepts remote from ordinary experiential knowledge. The modelers discuss it in language that refers more the formalisms of their method than to the real system they are representing:

> Notice that by the concavity of ω, no more than two of the n selling activities appear at positive intensities in an optimal solution. Through this formulation, the demand function can be transformed into a welfare function ω, and this can be approximated as closely as desired without adding additional rows to the linear program.
>
> The approach is readily extended to two or more products. For products in which the demand function is separable, there is one commodity balance and one convex combination constraint per product. For the case of product groups, there is one commodity balance per product and one convex combination constraint for the entire set of selling activities in the group.[10]

D. BOUNDARIES

CHAC calculates as endogenous variables the mix of production methods used for 33 short-cycle crops in 20 geographical districts. The crops are the leading Mexican annual crops in terms of production value; the list begins with maize, cotton, and sugar cane and ends with lima beans, garlic, and flaxseed.[11] For each crop the model calculates supply, demand, price, imports and exports (when applicable), and use of inputs. Agricultural inputs considered in the model include, on a seasonal basis, machinery, draft animals, chemical inputs, purchased seeds, and credit. Labor migration and employment are calculated from labor input usages. Various sources of labor, including farmers' own labor, hired labor, and dryland farmers hiring themselves out during slack seasons, are represented. Water is differentiated by source; canal irrigation, gravity irrigation, and reservoir irrigation are accounted separately. Prices of inptus that are available in limited quantities (land and water) are endogenously generated. Prices of inputs in 'perfectly elastic' supply (chemicals and capital) are exogenous. World market prices for traded commodities are also exogenous.

All exogenous inputs are in the form of constants in the constraint equations or objective function. There are 80,000 of these constants, most of which represent input–output relationships for the 2,345 different cropping activities. The model's constants can be grouped into three sets:

1. Policy choices.
2. Numbers that the modelers perceive as time-variant and hence update when they solve the model for a future year.
3. Numbers that the modelers see as invariant.

The set of constants representing policies is extensive. It includes factor-input pricing levels, trade policies, credit allocation, wages, and farm-size controls. Constants that are updated for future-year solutions include size of labor force, impact of technology on yields, rate of GNP growth, and ability of the export market to absorb agricultural products. The model treats as invariant such factors as spatial price differentials for crops, coefficients governing elasticities of demand, and the equivalent labor contributed by wives and children.

CHAC does not represent anything outside the agricultural sector except the demands for agricultural products and the prices of industrial inputs to agriculture. The non-agricultural portion of the Mexican economy is represented in CHAC's co-model, DINAMICO, and thus is completely omitted from CHAC. CHAC's representation of the agricultural sector is incomplete. Only short-cycle crops are represented—livestock, orchards, forestry, and fishing are not included. Population attitudes, risk, political factors, education, measures of the quality of life, degradation of the environment, and weather are all excluded. Many of these exclusions are reasonable, given the short time horizon of the model. The boundary diagram for CHAC is given in Figure 12.3.

E. STRUCTURE

The constraints in CHAC operate on three levels: the 20 agricultural districts, the four regions, and the total national agricultural sector. These levels do not

EXOGENOUS

- stocks of commodities
- industry
- forestry
- erosion
- perennial crops
- factor and product pricing policies
- trade policies
- population
- farm size
- income
- day labor wages by region
- income distribution
- farmers reservation wage
- interest rates
- possible crop yields for all technologies
- price of reservoir water
- upper bounds on credit and export
- price of fertilizer
- income elasticity of demand
- total agricultural imports
- GNP growth
- investment in land and irrigation
- spatial price differentials
- investment in research and extension
- size of labor force
- depreciation of capital
- attitudes
- pollution
- politics

ENDOGENOUS

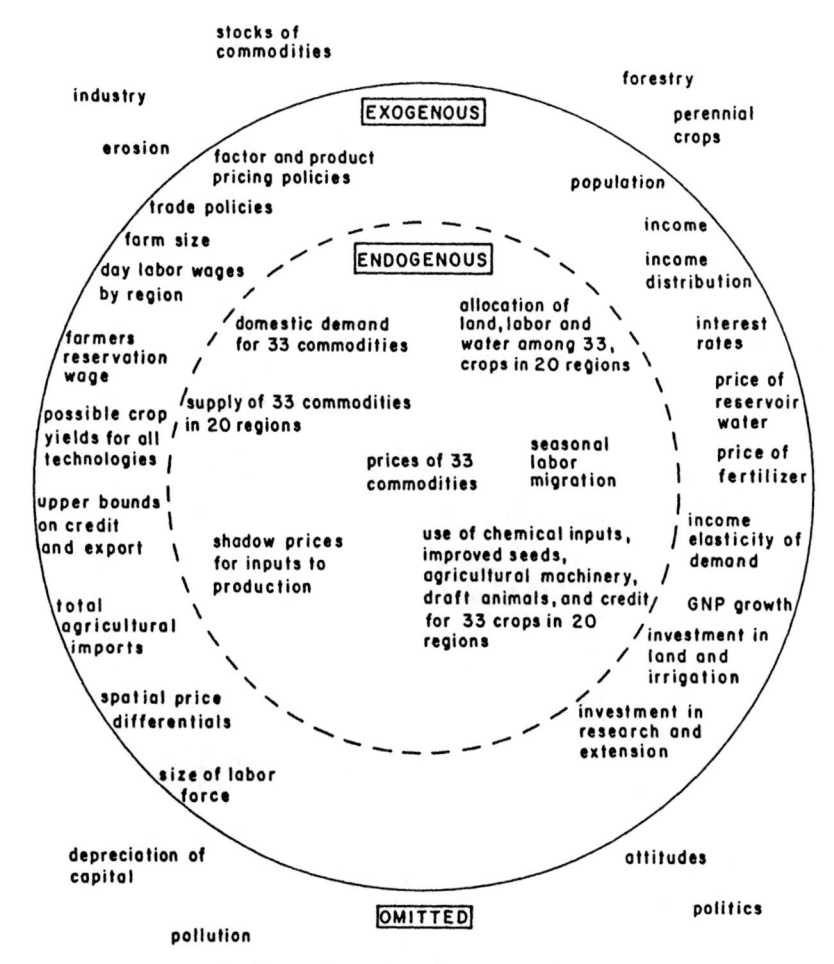

- domestic demand for 33 commodities
- allocation of land, labor and water among 33 crops in 20 regions
- supply of 33 commodities in 20 regions
- prices of 33 commodities
- seasonal labor migration
- shadow prices for inputs to production
- use of chemical inputs, improved seeds, agricultural machinery, draft animals, and credit for 33 crops in 20 regions

OMITTED

Figure 12.3 CHAC boundary diagram

operate hierarchically in the programming sense; individual optimization decisions are not made at each level. The model is optimized as a whole. The three levels serve only an organizational purpose; different constraints are enforced at each level.

At the national level the form of the market is determined (monopolistic or competitive) and commodity balances are enforced. Market demand is calculated at the national level, except for a few crops where separate regional markets are differentiated. Consumer prices are determined nationally, but producer prices are specified by district to represent transportation cost differentials. Of the 33 crops, 21 are assumed to be traded on the world market, and any export or import policies are imposed at the national level. Also at this level are the constraints on agricultural use of machinery, credit, and improved seeds.

The four regions of the model are used to specify constraints on hired labor, chemical inputs, and draft animals. The total number of landless laborers for each region is given exogeneously (landed laborers, or farmers, are specified by district). If any region demands more labor at some season than it can supply, interregional migration can result. Regional wage differentials are maintained.

Land, water, and farmer-labor constraints occur within each of the 20 districts, where the production decisions are made. Land constraints are specified monthly. Length of time land is required for a certain crop may depend on the availability of machinery to speed up the processes of plowing or harvesting. Water is available as 'gravity water' (from reservoirs, delivered through canals) or as privately supplied well water, depending on the district. In some districts, gravity water availability is subdivided into as many as four zones of varying efficiency, depending on length of canals and their state of repair.

The 2,345 production activities farmers can choose from can be thought of as 'packages' of inputs required to produce a given output. Not all activities are available to all districts; for example, tropical crops cannot be raised by farmers in the temperate districts, and in one district, called Culmaya, farmers can choose among only 16 of the model's 251 possible ways to grow corn. Two corn-production activities are shown for illustration in Table 12.1. All the production activities in the model reflect cropping techniques and yields that have actually been observed in the various districts, not necessarily the biological-maximum or the best-management choices.

One district-level model, known as BAJIO, was developed in more detail than the others in order to study investment choices and distributional effects in more detail.[12] The BAJIO model distinguishes four different farm types (large and small, irrigated and dryland) to approximate (with landless laborers) five income classes. The model also includes three different levels of farm management skill and a wider variety of cropping technologies. BAJIO can be run independently or as one of 20 districts embedded in CHAC.

Of course, it is impossible to make a causal structure diagram for a static optimization model such as CHAC. The closest we can come to a Reference Structure Diagram is shown in Figure 12.4. The model is essentially one enormous agricultural production function, with market demand as an important input. It is a narrow deep look at one aspect of a developing economy, rather than a broad, shallow depiction of the total system.

In CHAC all 3,500 activities are very literally a function of all others since they are all simultaneously determined in such a way as to maximize the objective function while staying within the constraints. To sort out what that means with respect to the implied relationship of any variable to any other is impossible. The *explicit* model assumptions, the constraints, are generally self-evident. For example, the model contains 348 equations that specify that land use within a given month and district shall be less than or equal to the total land available. The important structural assumptions are not these, but are *implicit* in the choice of the activities, the objective function, and the optimization procedure itself.

Table 12.1 Two CHAC Cropping Activities. (Note: These particular numbers do not necessarily typify the actual production statistics in the El Bajío region in any given year. The model contains many other technological choices for producing corn in El Bajío.) Table supplied by R. D. Norton.

Sample coefficients for corn production in El Bajío (all figures are on a per hectare basis).

	Rainfed Cultivation	Irrigated Cultivation
Yield (tons)	1.2	3.5
Purchased seeds (pesos)	50	55
Fertilizer (pesos)	198	615
Pesticides (pesos)	40	78
Miscellaneous costs (pesos)	44	112
February labor (man-days)	—	7.0
March labor (man-days)	—	12.5
April labor (man-days)	0.2	10.5
May labor (man-days)	0.6	16.5
June labor (man-days)	0.8	—
July labor (man-days)	4.2	—
August labor (man-days)	7.6	—
September labor (man-days)	1.5	9.0
October labor (man-days)	5.5	15.0
November labor (man-days)	3.4	—
Machinery inputs (days)	0.07	0.2
March irrigation (thous. m^3)	—	1.6
April irrigation (thous. m^3)	—	1.4
May irrigation (thous. m^3)	—	1.4
Draft animal inputs (days)	—	16.8
Short-term credit (pesos)	355	899
February land (ha)	—	1.0
March land (ha)	—	1.0
April land (ha)	0.08	1.0
May land (ha)	1.0	1.0
June land (ha)	1.0	1.0
July land (ha)	1.0	1.0
August land (ha)	1.0	1.0
September land (ha)	1.0	1.0
October land (ha)	1.0	1.0
November land (ha)	0.75	—
Management inputs	*	*

* See text of Chapter IV.4 in Goreux-Manne[1] for an explanation of management inputs and their units.

The central structural hypothesis of CHAC is that Mexican producers and consumers behave in the aggregate as competitive-market theory says they will. This theory requires a series of stringent assumptions about how the Mexican economy operates. Among these assumptions are:[13]

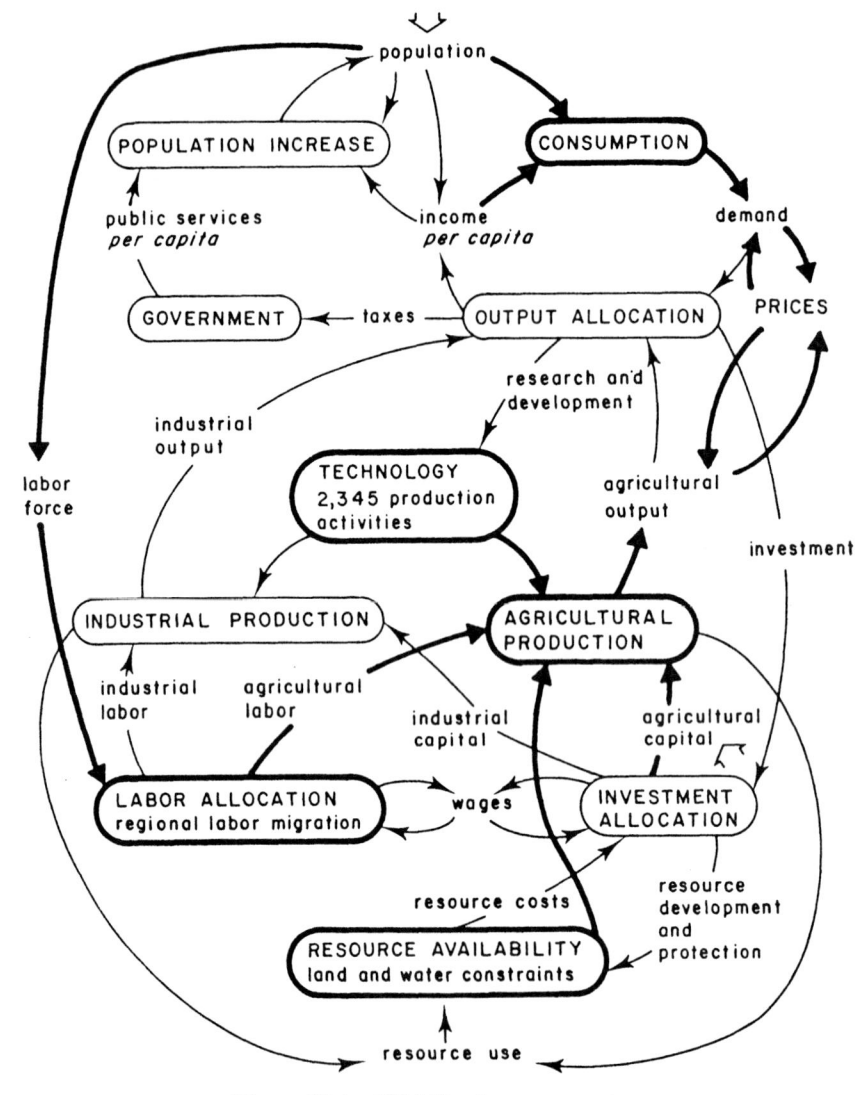

Figure 12.4 CHAC reference structure

1. The economic system operates through the interaction of producers and consumers (and government policies tested in the model)—no other set of actors has appreciable economic impact.
2. The interactions of individual producers and consumers aggregate to equate price with marginal cost (which produces Pareto-optimal utility maximization).
3. Supply and demand adjust within a year to balance each other via price mechanisms; there is no significant time lag between production, sale, and consumption of a commodity.

4. Producers and consumers operate with perfect information—producers know which production activities are available to them, what each will cost, what yield it will give, and what price it will sell for; consumers know the relative prices of all commodities and quickly adjust their buying habits to them.
5. Agricultural prices will not have a significant effect on consumer income or income distribution; demand curves will stay stable as food prices change within a given year.
6. All these conditions will continue to hold under different government policies concerning agricultural imports and exports, factor pricing, interest rates, etc.

F. DATA

One could not expect complete documentation of all data for a model with 80,000 non-zero coefficients, and the published accounts of CHAC contain only general descriptions of the ways in which all these numbers were gathered. The majority of CHAC's coefficients represent the many different cropping activities available to farmers in each district. These coefficients were partially available from official sources, especially from the Secretaria de Recursos Hidraulicos for irrigated districts and the Secretaria de Agricultura y Ganaderia for tropical and rainfed districts.[14] These statistics were only a beginning, however. The major part of the CHAC effort was filling in the holes in the official sources and making the numbers consistent:

> Collecting and verifying information on this scale is plainly a formidable task... In Mexico much of the information already existed, although not in a coherent form. Since, at its lowest level, CHAC can be regarded and used as a giant adding machine, the consistency of microeconomic information could readily be checked against macroeconomic information. For example, when coefficients of inputs of water are applied to the various crops and the areas on which they are actually grown, the total requirements should match what is known about the overall use of water. Inconsistencies were found. As a result, field trips to parts of Mexico were taken in order to check the validity of the coefficients and in some cases establish new ones, about two man-years were spent on assembling the data available, verifying them, and putting them in a format suitable for use in the model.[15]

The most difficult numbers to estimate probably were not the relatively straightforward land-yield agricultural data, but the numbers representing human choices such as the allocation of family labor, the willingness to accept risk, and consumer demand decisions. The modelers provide little explanation for how these numbers were obtained; they point them out as the most difficult and uncertain parts of the model.

G. TESTING

CHAC's nature demands that the model be subjected to extensive tests. The model's central free-market hypothesis is not proven. Thus the model should undergo validity testing to ascertain how well its behavior duplicates that of the system it is representing. Since the model contains 80,000 parameters, extensive sensitivity testing is called for, even though many of the parameters come from field observation of production processes and are probably fairly accurate. As the model was built both to demonstrate a modeling technique and to explore policy strategies, it would be appropriate for CHAC to be the subject of much methodological experimentation as well as being used for numerous policy tests.

However, CHAC is relatively expensive to test because of its size and complexity. It costs $50–100 per solution at commercial computer rates.[16] The modelers have reduced the cost to this level by devoting considerable attention to programming efficiency, and they have reduced it even further by creating smaller, more aggregated versions of the model for use in testing. For example, a model entitled PACIFICO was constructed using data from only five of the 20 production districts covered in CHAC. Another more aggregated version, CHAQUITO, includes all 20 production districts but treats input requirements on a seasonal basis, whereas CHAC uses a monthly basis. And BAJIO, as we have already mentioned, represents only one district but in even greater detail. PACIFICO has been used for methodological tests where structure is important. CHAQUITO has been used for policy tests in which it is necessary to include the whole of Mexico but not essential to have CHAC's degree of detail. Even with the use of smaller versions of the model, however, CHAC's testing remains a demanding, complicated process.

Very few testing results have been published and little has been said about the model's general validation. When the modelers mention validity, it is always with regard to some very specific result. CHAC's employment estimates are closely comparable with survey-based employment figures from Guatemala and Peru.[17] Shadow prices from the model are compared with actual factor prices to check the reasonableness of the production assumptions.

> The correspondence between the dual of BAJIO and the actual land prices in El Bajio constitutes a strong validation. It means that, at least in the aggregate, the technology set for each farm class provides an appropriate description of the process of transforming factor inputs into final outputs.[18]

Some parameter sensitivity and structural sensitivity tests have been conducted. For example, the competitive equilibrium formulation in the objective function has been changed to a monopolistic equilibrium formulation (but the concept of equilibrium has not been tested). Sensitivity of the model's most uncertain parameters, such as farmer's reservation wage and price elasticities of demand, have been tested.[19] Moreover, many methodological experiments, especially experiments with the model's computational structure, have been tried. The aim of such experiments has been to improve computational efficiency without loss in accuracy.

The bulk of CHAC's testing has been policy testing. The policy tests that have been conducted with CHAC are too numerous to describe fully here. Among the policy instruments that have been varied in model tests are interest rates, changes in foreign exchange premiums, changes in wage levels, subsidies on pesticides and fertilizer, and supply controls.[20] As many of these policy levers can be applied on a district-specific and/or crop-specific basis, the number of possible choices is astronomical. In general, the choice of tests to be conducted has been made according to specific questions asked by the two model clients.

Although an enormous amount of information is generated by each test run of CHAC, much is highly abstract and not easily translated into non-technical language. When the modelers conduct a test, they gain information about the geometry of the constraint-bound region within which the optimization takes place. Knowledge of this region's form gives them a useful general understanding about how the optimum point is likely to respond to changes in constraint parameters, and thus a 'seat of the pants' feeling for how the model works. Unfortunately, this feeling is almost impossible to communicate to others who have not shared the experience of running the model. Attempts at explanation tend to degenerate into impenetrable jargon. As a case in point, the following description of experiments designed to explore capital-labor substitution was published in a technical journal:

> ...first, the locus of equilibrium points shows a greater degree of factor substitutability than the isoprofit curve. In other words, the isoprofit curve underestimates the degree of factor response in the sector as a whole; this is the relevant point for the formulation of agricultural policy. Secondly, both curves have elasticities which vary substantially over the different segments and in some cases they are not even convex... The non-convexity rises from the fact that CHAC is a model with multiple products and multiple factors and the 'isoquants' are projections of a multi-dimensional hyperplane Euclidian two-space. The following question arises from these results: if in fact the process analysis production model is a reasonable representation of reality, how useful are substitution parameters which are estimated by a) imposing on the data a production model which includes the implicit assumption of constant elasticities of substitution; and b) utilizing a production function of two factors and one product?[21]

H. CONCLUSIONS

Although CHAC is a static model, it has been used in a quasidynamic mode by running it for two different years, 1968 and 1974. The 1968 run used actual data for that year; the 1974 run used forecasts for income growth rate and its effect on demand, for investment activities occurring within the period, for world market conditions, and for technological improvements in production. These two runs were carried out with and without policy intervention to provide at least a short-term dynamic glimpse of the response of the model system to various sorts of government policies.

The 1968 run with no policy changes already provides a wealth of interesting and detailed conclusions about the Mexican agricultural sector as represented in CHAC. Perhaps most striking are the employment estimates: taking into account seasonal fluctuations, only about 2.4 million man-years of employment are provided for an agricultural labor force of 5.2 million persons.[22]

> The seasonality may be summarized by stating that 18% of the labor force cannot find even one month's employment at a marginal productivity equal to the current wage, 44% cannot find more than three month's employment at that productivity, and only 27% are so employed on a full-time basis.[23]

The emphasis the modelers put on this result, and their apparent surprise, indicate that the extent of rural employment had not previously been measured by any other method.

Another set of 1968 results concerns comparative advantage in international trade. Table 12.2 shows the CHAC-calculated marginal gains or losses for several exported crops. The table suggests several policies with regard to export taxes and quotas; for instance, that corn exports should be strongly discouraged, and that aggregate crop exports could be taxed up to 4% without making export activities unprofitable.[24]

Comparison of 1974 results with 1968 with no government policy changes shows agricultural output growing much faster than agriculture-sector income, a behavior common to most developing countries. It also shows agricultural employment growing more slowly than the labor force; in other words, a worsening of the already astounding 46% sectoral unemployment rate.

Tests of policies to improve this situation indicate, as might be expected, that only small changes can be made over such a short time period, and that any policy that improves one part of the system makes another part worse. For example, the greatest effect on employment of all policies tested comes from a doubling of the interest rate. This change increases annual employment growth from 2.8% to 3.1%, but it also has a strongly negative effect on production and raises consumer prices. Table 12.3 gives a qualitative picture of some of the trade-offs indicated by CHAC policy tests.

The general conclusion drawn by the CHAC modelers is: 'The agricultural employment problem is fairly intractable...'.[25]

> Mexican agriculture is beginning to have to face the problem of relatively low growth rates of farm income and employment which occur in a sector constrained by the growth of domestic demand and of export demand... The problem is no longer simply how to increase production. It is, rather, how to bring about structural changes which will lead to an expansion of domestic demand. These are the real second generation problems of the Green Revolution, and Mexico will have to confront these problems before most other developing countries.[26]

This conclusion is quite similar to that of Beltran del Rio derived from the very different model *MexicoV*, and it has also been voiced by numerous analyses using mental models. And just as Picardi's model did not include the sorts of radical structural change that might have solved the Sahel nomads' problem, neither *MexicoV* nor CHAC includes the massive changes on either the

Table 12.2 Estimated profitability of selected Mexican agricultural products in international trade (1967–69). Reproduced from Goreaux and Manne[1] by permission of North-Holland Publishing Company

Crop	Tons exported in base period*	Tons exported in CHAC†	Assumed export price‡ (pesos/ton)	Marginal profits in CHAC	Marginal cost of production in CHAC (pesos/ton)
Strawberries	16,930	21,200	3,680	2,240	1,440
Sesame	8,300	16,600	3,981	2,200	1,781
Cantaloupe	45,051	45,051	2,003	1,420	583
Peanuts	4,150	8,300	2,500	1,170	1,130
Tomatoes	38,107	38,107	1,200	900	300
Watermelon	41,842	41,842	1,135	740	395
Potatoes	26	10,000	1,200	690	510
Cotton fiber	318,877	318,877	5,767	670	5,097
Cucumber	30,752	70,000	7,960	420	370
Pineapple	9,613	9,613	400	140	260
Green chile	16,700	25,100	748	130	618
Beans	66,400	99,600	1,846	100	1,746
Sugar cane§	7,967,628	7,967,682	68	20	48
Grain sorghum	2,140	—	566	−50	616
Cottonseed	—	—	416	−160	576
Oats	—	—	387	−290	677
Safflower	7,724	—	1,550	−380	1,930
Wheat	153,258	—	600	−460	1,060
Rice	137	—	750	−460	1,210
Corn	979,455	—	623	−480	1,103
Soybeans	—	—	800	−670	1,470

* Base period defined as 1967–69 average.
† Arbitrary export bounds imposed in CHAC for this solution in order to derive marginal valuations. For crops governed rigidly by international quotas, formal or informal, these bounds are set equal to the actual quantities exported.
‡ This is an average farm gate price (less than f.o.b. price). The export prices are notional in some cases, but there is sufficient information in the table to recalculate marginal profits on the basis of different prices.
§ Sugar cane exports and prices are expressed in cane equivalents, although the export product is refined sugar.

demand or supply side (in distribution of income or land, for example) that might result in productive employment for Mexico's rural labor force.

Another kind of policy test was done for CHAC's second client, the World Bank, to examine the effects of specific investment projects such as canal-lining, tubewells, and land-leveling (which increases the efficiency of irrigation water by allowing it to be applied more uniformly). These tests were run with the more detailed district-level model BAJIO (but aggregated from one-month to three-month factor availabilities; hence BAJITO) embedded in CHAQUITO.

Table 12.3 Qualitative impact of selected policy changes in CHAC. Reproduced from Goreaux and Manne[1] with permission

Target	Foreign exchange premium	Interest rate change	Wage change	Chemical subsidy	Water tax	Supply controls
			Instrument			
Producers' income	++	++	++	+	−	++
Consumers' surplus	−	=	=	++	−	=
Employment	+	+	=	=	−	−
Exports	++	−	−	+	−	++
Budget	−	n.a.	n.a.	−	+	n.a.
Production	++	=	=	++	=	−

Key: ++ strongly positive
 + positive
 = strongly negative
 − negative
 n.a. not applicable

The conclusions seem to have been surprising. Tubewells were calculated to be the most profitable investment, and the optimal allocation was to small dryland farms when wage rates were high and to large dryland farms when wages were low. Land-leveling was intermediate in profitability and canal-lining, the project that was actually being considered at the time, was lowest.[27]

Numerous other experiments were tried, and again some of the results surprised the modelers.

An apparent anomaly in the results is of some interest. This illustrates the difficulties of applying *a priori* reasoning to determine the direction of changes in a model as complex as CHAQUITO. Product prices can be no lower, and in fact increase when the premium on foreign exchange is increased from zero to 30%. Yet investment in water declines slightly when this premium increase is made... The reason for this was a switch in comparative advantage between BAJITO and another district submodel in CHAQUITO in the production of onions for export. This is a crop which happens to respond particularly well to being grown on levelled rather than on unlevelled land.[28]

I. COMPUTER REQUIREMENTS

CHAC, like all large linear programming models, is extremely demanding of computer hardware and software. Like the other short-term, detailed implementation models described here, CHAC occupies considerable computer space and takes considerable time to run. CHAC has undergone significant modification to make it operable on Mexican computer facilities. It probably would be difficult to transfer to a new system, but as CHAC is not terribly useful to people outside Mexico, non-transferability is not a serious problem. CHAC-type models are being built, however, under World Bank sponsorship for such countries as Iran, India, Tanzania, and Brazil.[29]

J. IMPLEMENTATION

CHAC has an unusually successful implementation history, according to its makers. The model began as an experiment in 1970 to test the usefulness of a method. The experiment was so successful in the view of the Mexican government, that one of the principal members of the World Bank modeling team was invited to work in the Ministry of the President to continue model development and to 'assist in making concrete applications to Mexican agricultural policy questions'.[30] While being developed under the Ministry of the Presidency, CHAC began to be used for policy analysis. Model analyses of specific issues began to appear in official policy papers, as well as in formulation of general policy plans.[31]

Over time, the model's development has become progressively more independent of World Bank technical staff support. Simultaneously, the model's institutional grounding in the Mexican government has increased. Moreover, CHAC's success has attracted the attention of international agencies outside the World Bank such as the United Nations Food and Agriculture Organization.

Within Mexico, the CHAC modelers claim to have had an influence on both specific agricultural sector policy decisions and on the policymakers' general understanding of agricultural sector operation. At the general understanding level, CHAC has fostered an awareness of the potential (or lack of potential) of various policies for stimulating employment in agriculture. Specific applications are numerous and varied. A clear-cut example of CHAC's influence on policy strategy is that of export policy. CHAC indicates that there is a great variation in the profitability of different export crops. Model conclusions on this score have had a direct influence on the Mexican government's agricultural trade strategy and have led to, among other things, stepping up exports of sesame and black beans.[32]

CHAC's implementation successes are the result of good management, fortuitous institutional circumstances, and the sort of short-term, detailed output that policymakers seek. Throughout its development CHAC has had the advantage of having 'well-trained personnel in high positions in the Mexican government who were willing to sponsor and interpret the work'.[33] The working procedure used was:

> ...based on continuous interaction between policymakers, agricultural specialists, and those working with the model. This permits better identification of problem areas and appropriate modifications of the model to address very particular problems.[34]

Having the model address questions of specific concern helped to provide a focus for policy discussion and allowed the model to 'become a flexible, vital part of the decision-making process'.[35]

K. DOCUMENTATION

CHAC was developed in an international planning agency (the World Bank) and then gradually absorbed by a national policymaking agency (the Ministry of the President). Communication channels between modelers and planners were of the sort usually found in in-house consulting situations. The modeling staff meet with planners to find out what questions they are asking. They perform the indicated analyses and report back, either verbally or through memos, reports, and other forms of internal communication. In CHAC's five years of existence it has undoubtedly generated many filing cabinets full of documentation, only a small proportion of which has been published. Much basic information is stored at the World Bank in the form of publicly accessible notebooks full of linear programming tableaus, basic assumptions, and data.[36]

The published documentation on CHAC is fragmented and, for the most part, quite technical. One book of papers on CHAC and its companion models, DINAMICO and ENERGETICOS, was published in 1973.[37] In addition, a number of papers on CHAC have appeared in technical journals.

The available papers describing CHAC deal by and large with specialized aspects of the model—its database, the decomposition algorithm used, the way the linear program was structured, application of the model to hydrological questions, etc. Many aspects of the model are not publicly documented. For example, no systematic description of CHAC's sensitivity testing is available. Moreover, non-technical summaries of basic model assumptions or plain-language description of how the model operates have not been written.

The style in which CHAC has been documented makes it somewhat accountable to the government agency within which it is used and perhaps more accountable to the technical community of linear programmers. However, outside these circles there is little to promote understanding of how the model works. The technical language used in published papers describing CHAC effectively removes the model from examination by anyone other than a linear programmer. A person who does not automatically think of the world in terms of consumers' surplus, reservation wages, shadow prices, and indifference curves must accept its basic assumptions on faith or not at all. And one wonders whether even its makers can truly envisage simultaneous interdependencies within a 3,500 by 1,500 matrix. As is the case with many detailed, short-term, implementation-oriented models, CHAC is a black box, producing impressive and useful-looking information by a process that is not quite comprehensible.

NOTES AND REFERENCES

1. L. M. Goreux and A. S. Manne, *Multi-Level Planning: Case Studies in Mexico*, Amsterdam, North Holland Publishing Co., p. 10, 1973.

2. R. D. Norton, Chief, Development Planning Division, World Bank, personal communication.
3. B. B. King, Research Advisor, World Bank, personal communication.
4. J. H. Duloy and R. D. Norton, 'CHAC, a Programming Model of Mexican Agriculture', in L. M. Goreux and A. S. Manne, *op.cit.*, p. 292.
5. L. M. Bassoco and R. D. Norton, 'A Quantitative Approach to Agricultural Policy Planning', *Annals of Economic and Social Measurement*, October-November 1975.
6. The following four points listed are adapted from L. M. Bassoco and R. D. Norton, *op.cit.*
7. J. H. Duloy and R. D. Norton, *op.cit.*, p. 292.
8. For a detailed description of this process and its results, see J. H. Duloy and R. D. Norton, 'Linking the Agricultural Model and the Economy-Wide Model', in L. M. Goreux and A. S. Manne, *op.cit.*, p. 435.
9. J. H. Duloy and R. D. Norton, *op.cit.*, p. 295.
10. *Ibid.*, p. 316.
11. *Ibid.*, p. 294.
12. The BAJIO model is described by L. M. Bassoco, J. H. Duloy, R. D. Norton and D. L. Winkelmann in L. M. Goreux and A. S. Manne, *op.cit.*, pp. 401–433.
13. This list in part paraphrases the basic assumptions of general equilibrium theory as outlined by J. Kornai in *Anti Equilibrium*, Amsterdam, North Holland Publishing Co., pp. 18–23, 1973.
14. L. M. Bassoco and T. Rendon, 'The Technology Set and Data Base for CHAC', in L. M. Goreux and A. S. Manne, *op.cit.*, p. 339.
15. B. B. King, Research Advisor, World Bank, personal communication.
16. R. D. Norton, personal communication.
17. J. H. Duloy and R. D. Norton, 'CHAC Results' in L. M. Goreux and A. S. Manne, *op.cit.*, p. 378.
18. L. M. Bassoco, J. H. Duloy, R. D. Norton and D. L. Winkelmann, *op.cit.*, p. 413.
19. J. H. Duloy and R. D. Norton, *op.cit.*, p. 381.
20. *Ibid.*, p. 374.
21. L. M. Bassoco and R. D. Norton, 'A Quantitative Approach to Agricultural Policy Planning' for publication in *Annals of Economic and Social Measurement*, October–November 1975, p. 28.
22. J. H. Duloy and R. D. Norton, *op.cit.*, p. 378.
23. *Ibid.*, p. 381.
24. *Ibid.*, p. 384.
25. *Ibid.*, p. 391. This statement is accompanied by a *caveat* that farm-size changes, which are not tested in CHAC, may have a strong effect on labor demand.
26. *Ibid.*, p. 398.
27. J. H. Duloy, G. P. Kutcher, and R. D. Norton, in L. M. Goreux and A. S. Manne, *op.cit.*, p. 417.
28. *Ibid.*, p. 426.
29. R. D. Norton, personal communication.
30. IBRD Development Research Center, 'Research Project Summary' Project No. RPO:216, p. 2, August 1974.
31. Policy analysis descriptions will be included in a forthcoming book, *Programming Studies for Agricultural Sector Policies*, to be edited by L. M. Bassoco, R. D. Norton, J. S. Silos, and M. Solis.
32. L. Barazza and L. Solis, 'Policies and the Sectoral Model' in L. M. Goreux and A. S. Manne, *op.cit.*, p. 474.
33. IBRD Development Research Center, *op.cit.*, p. 7.
34. L. Barazza and L. Solis, *op.cit.*, p. 475.
35. *Ibid.*, p. 475.
36. J. H. Duloy, R. D. Norton, in L. M. Goreux and A. S. Manne, *op.cit.*, p. 324.
37. L. M. Goreux and A. S. Manne, *op.cit.*

PART IV

The State of the Art

> If we could first know *where* we are and *whither* we are tending, we could then better judge *what* to do, and *how* to do it.
>
> Abraham Lincoln

John Maynard Keynes, writing one of the very first critiques of a computer model (one of Jan Tinbergen's first econometric models) said: 'The worst of him is that he is much more interested in getting on with the job than in spending time in deciding whether the job is worth getting on with'.[1] Is the job of computer modeling worth getting on with? Has any useful and enduring knowledge that was not otherwise attainable come out of such models? Is computer modeling a demonstrably effective means toward understanding complex social systems? Is that understanding sufficiently enduring that it can tell us something about the social systems of tomorrow as well as those of yesterday? And if there is any such understanding, has it been used deliberately, and successfully, to make the world better in any way?

In this part of the book we will be concerned with evaluating computer models; seeing how they differ from and what they can contribute to our mental models, to allow us to predict or design the systems we live in.

We will leave to Part V the question of prescription: what, if anything, should be done to improve the art of computer modeling. First, we need to make as clear a statement as possible about the state of that art.

So far we have presented the nine models one by one, with little cross-referencing or comparison one to another. To begin this evaluative section of the book we will go back and look at them as a set, cutting through them in several different ways to expose facets of their contents, different '... as the view of the interior of an orange obtained by slicing it horizontally is from the view of it obtained by slicing it vertically'.[2]

In Chapter 13 we will focus on the content of the models. We will see what the models have taught us about the process of industrialization as a whole and about five processes that accompany/cause industrialization: population growth; production and allocation of economic output; technical change; migration and labor allocation; environmental pollution and resource depletion. In Chapter 14 we will go back over the five theoretical advantages of computer models listed in Chapter 1:

1. Rigor.
2. Comprehensiveness.
3. Logic.
4. Accessibility.
5. Testability.

and see to what extent these advantages are actually realized in the nine models. In Chapter 15 we will look at the implementation of the models—have they been used, and if so how, and with what results? Is the world any different because of their existence?

NOTES AND REFERENCES

1. J. M. Keynes, 'Professor Tinbergen's Method', *The Economic Journal*, **XLIX**, (**195**), 559, September, 1939.
2. R. Ackoff, 'The Future of Operational Research is Past', *J. Opl. Res. Soc.*, **30**, 96, 1979.

CHAPTER 13

Model Content: The Process of Industrialization

The nine models, and indeed most large-scale social-system models, are all concerned with explaining some aspect of the dominant social process of this century—the transition from traditional, agricultural societies to modern, industrial ones, with all the cultural changes this transition implies. There are many possible definitions of and measurements for what is usually called 'development', but what we shall call industrialization. It is the subject of continuous research, discussion, and policy intervention. Industrialization is a complex, gradual, and all-encompassing process, far from understood, even by those societies that have experienced it most fully.

Industrialization is most often characterized by its surface attributes. It seems to be a slow evolution of a society from a pre-industrial state with properties such as:

- Technical and social change barely noticeable from generation to generation.
- Material comforts achieved primarily through human services.
- Childbearing throughout most of females' reproductive years.
- Experience of infant mortality in nearly every family.
- Geographical mobility limited to a few square kilometers; social mobility almost non-existent.
- Cultural homogeneity and cohesiveness.
- Utilization of primarily renewable sources of materials and energy; energy use rate 5,000–10,000 kilocalories per person per day.
- Local or regional self-sufficiency; political and economic decentralization.
- Information storage mainly mental: information transfer mainly verbal.

To, or at least through, an industrial state with:

- Significant change, especially in technology, within one generation.

- Material comfort achieved primarily through machine services.
- Childbearing through a minor part of female reproductive lifetime.
- Almost no experience of infant mortality.
- Geographic mobility over thousands of kilometers; some social and economic mobility.
- Cultural heterogeneity and divisiveness.
- Utilization of primarily non-renewable sources of materials and energy; energy use rate over 100,000 kilocalories per person per day.
- Local and regional interdependency; political and economic centralization.
- Information storage and transfer through print, computers, and telecommunications.

Other attributes may easily be added to this list.

Partial as it is, a list such as this raises many questions about whatever process so thoroughly transforms a society. Why does industrialization occur at all, and why does it vary so greatly in time of onset and rate of progress? Are all the attributes linked inextricably together or could some be encouraged and others discouraged? Can one society help or hinder the process of industrialization in another? Is an industrialized society sustainable over the long term or likely to evolve or collapse into some other social form? In short, how does this process start, what makes it end, what does it lead to, and how can it be controlled while it is proceeding?

Many thousands of volumes have been written presenting models, mostly verbal models, of industrialization. We cannot hope to compare the nine survey models with all the verbal, mental, and mathematical models that have preceded them, especially not comprehensively, since the models, like the real-world process, are complex and multidimensional. Instead, we shall look here at five widely-noted processes within social systems that seem to affect or be affected by industrialization. They are:

1. Population growth.
2. Production and allocation of economic output.
3. Technological change.
4. Rural-urban migration.
5. Use of natural resources.

These might be described as key indicators of industrialization; processes of the social system that seem somehow to be centrally involved or thoroughly changed in industrial development. Each interacts with all the others. Comprehension of the causes and consequences of industrialization must probably include at least some understanding of these five processes and their interactions.

Of course other processes that we will not mention here are also deeply embedded in the phenomenon of industrialization—for example, value change, international trade, the role of the family, the role of money and credit and of the government. We have limited the discussion to these five processes of an industrializing system primarily because they are included in most of our models. Value change, in contrast, is included in only two of them, and only partially. Monetary flows can be found in only one model, international trade in three, and family structure in none. Government in nearly all the models is exogenous.

We shall note how each process is represented in each of the nine models, comparing the representation to the model purpose and indicating its influence, so far as we understand it, on the model conclusions. We would like to compare the models' representations to the 'real' process, but this is not possible, since models are intended to be simplifications, not 'reality', and since we have only our mental models, not 'reality', for comparison. Thus the 'real-world' referents in this discussion can be just two things; the industrialization process as perceived by the authors and the readers of this book, and that subset of the perceived process that might be relevant to the purpose of the model. To keep these referents in mind, we shall begin each section with a brief description of our own mental models of the indicator in question, and we shall remind ourselves regularly of each model's purpose.

A. POPULATION GROWTH

1. Mental models

The size and structure of the human population respond to changes in the economic system through three basic mechanisms—births, deaths, and migrations (migrations will be discussed later). Multitudinous factors affect births and deaths—biological capability, social norms, economic pressures and opportunities, government inducements or propaganda, technologies of birth and death control, and environmental quality, to name just a few (see Figure 13.1). Industrialization affects nearly all of these factors. Better health services change biological capabilities, industrial work patterns change social norms, some kinds of economic pressures increase while others decrease. All these factors are filtered through the decision processes of individual families, and the millions of family responses add up to aggregate birth or death rates, which then change the size and attributes of the population, which then change the process of industrialization. The most general result seems to be a reduction in both birth and death rates, which has been labeled the demographic transition (see Figure 13.2).

The population size defines the level of need for various kinds of economic output, from food to education to housing. Population also provides a primary input to economic production—labor, with its various attributes of location, skills, and strength. The size, distribution, attributes, and relative power of different population subsets also affect the distribution of economic output through market demand and/or political pressure. And in general, as the population grows, the *per capita* share of everything declines.

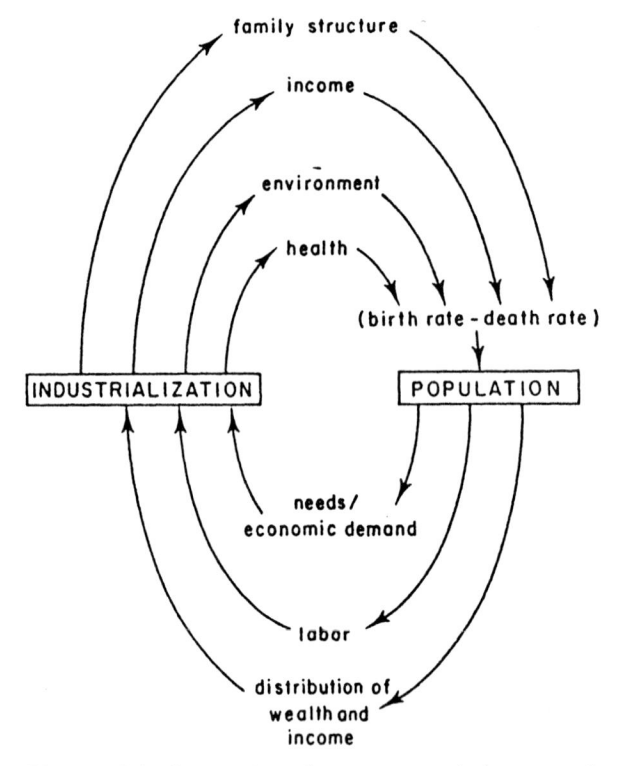

Figure 13.1 Interactions between population growth and industrialisation

Populations also exert subtle dynamic effects on societal development through biological aging. A population's size and attributes have a glacier-like inertia, gradually advancing or receding as birth cohorts steadily age together over the length of the human lifetime. Only rare events such as famine, war, or sudden mass migration can change a population's characteristics suddenly. Normally a population's size, sex ratio, abilities, health, norms, and well-being are a slowly-evolving, living record of important events in the social system over the last 80 years or so. For example, the effects of the First and Second World Wars on births, deaths, sex ratios, expectations, and physical capabilities are still discernible in the populations of most European nations. And the baby boom in the United States in the 1950s will continue to have social impact past the year 2015, when the large baby-boom cohorts reach retirement age.

Thus the population is enmeshed in the industrialization process, as partial determinant of economic demand and production, as an aggregate of actors responsive to economic conditions, and as a stabilizing, inertial element, slowing down and smoothing out the rate of change. It is not surprising that every one of the nine models incorporates population in some way, and that some of them contain very detailed and sophisticated demographic sectors.

2. Computer models

The representations of population in the nine models fall into four basic categories, as illustrated in Figure 13.3. The simplest possible way to include population in a model is to make it exogenous (either constant or exogenously driven by a constant growth rate) and to keep track of its size only, not its attributes. The two most short-term models in our survey, CHAC and *MexicoV*, do this.

CHAC uses an exogenous, aggregated population estimate in calculating consumer demand for agricultural commodities. It also uses rural population statistics for four geographic regions as labor constraints. Since CHAC is static, it does not need any population change assumptions. When CHAC is run for a hypothetical future year, population extrapolations are made exogenously. If these extrapolations are considered uncertain, alternate ones can be tested.

MexicoV, with a two to ten year time horizon, generates total population size exogenously with a fixed net growth rate:

$$N_{(t)} = NG \cdot N_{(t-1)}$$

where $N_{(t)}$ is the number of people in year t, $N_{(t-1)}$ is the number in the previous year, and NG is the constant net population growth rate. The population is not broken down into age or sex categories. Urban and rural populations are distinguished in order to calculate urban and rural labor force. The only reason for even this much detail is to generate differences in rural and urban labor productivities. Neither labor force has an effect on productive output. The total population size is used in the model only to provide a denominator for such social indices as GNP *per capita* and disposable income *per capita*.

Although these exogenous population functions are extremely simple, they are appropriate to the purposes of CHAC and *MexicoV*. Assessments of the immediate return on investment in irrigation equipment, or short-term predictions of aggregate economic variables, do not require a detailed population representation. Over the short time horizon of these models, population size can safely be considered constant or changing at a regular rate.

However, in verbal descriptions of both CHAC and *MexicoV*, the modelers express great concern about Mexico's employment problem and about excessive rural-urban migration. The modelers are unable to deal with these population-related problems, not only because of the simple population functions they use, but also because of the short-term focus of the methods they chose. The modelers limited their investigations to the immediate, population-independent questions that were of primary concern to their clients. By doing so, they gave up the opportunity to investigate the longer-term problems that they themselves clearly felt were important, perhaps not only important in themselves, but also relevant to the short-term problems the clients were trying to solve.

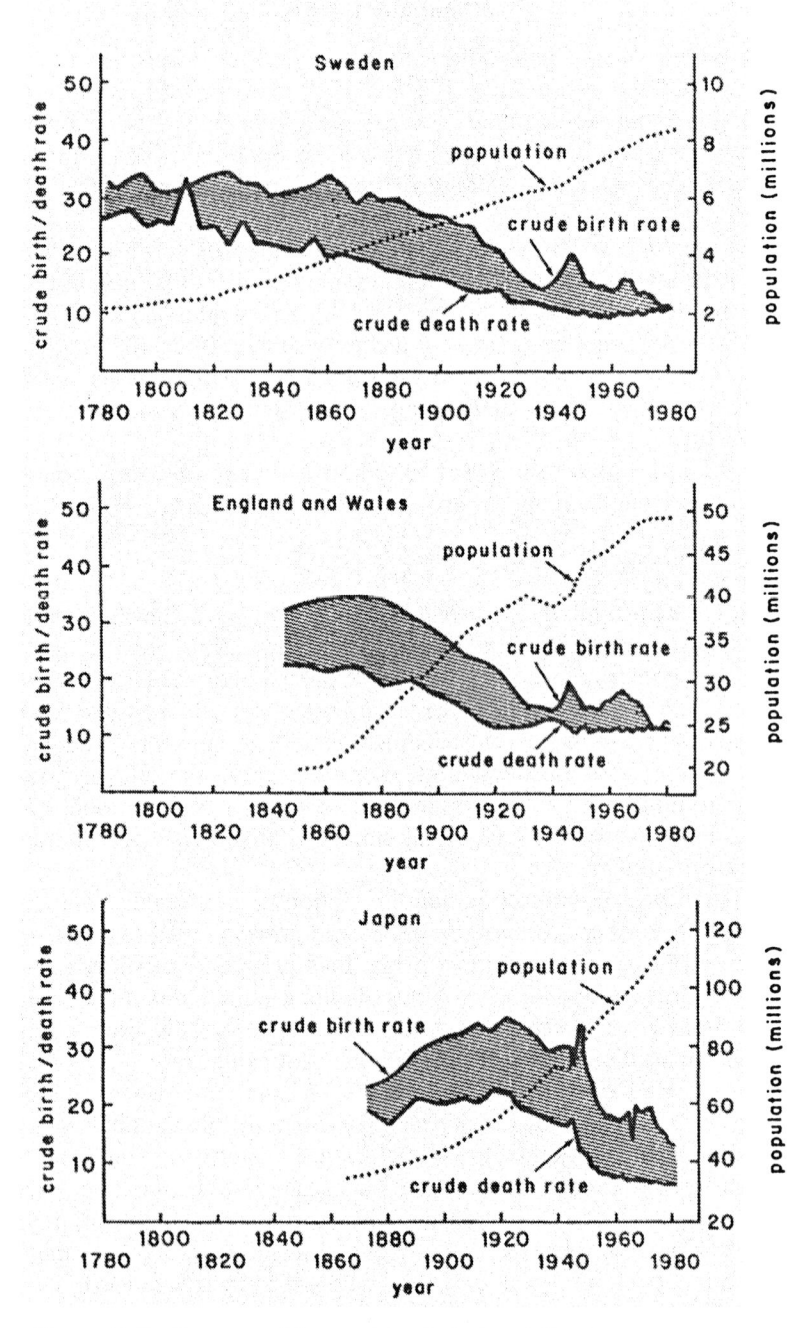

Figure 13.2 Demographic transition in industrialized and industrializing countries. Reproduced with permission from D. H. Meadows

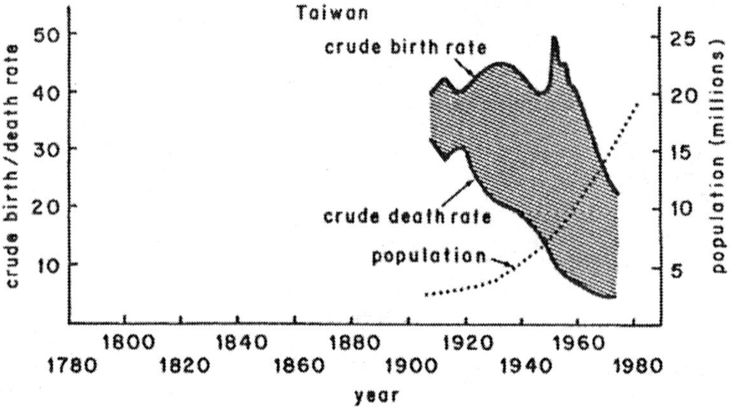
Taiwan
crude birth rate
crude death rate
population
crude birth/death rate
population (millions)
year

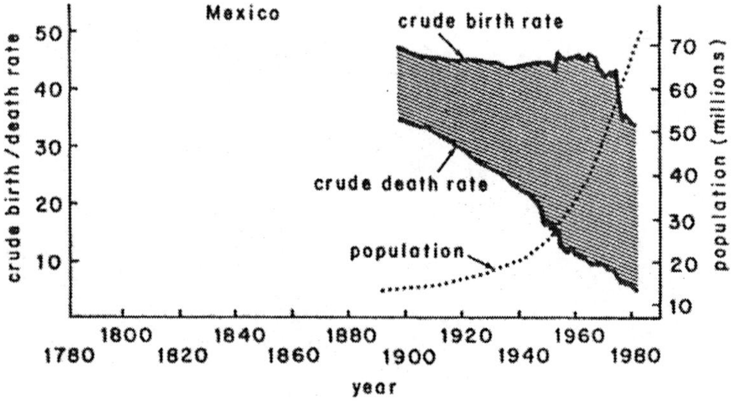
Mexico
crude birth rate
crude death rate
population
crude birth/death rate
population (millions)
year

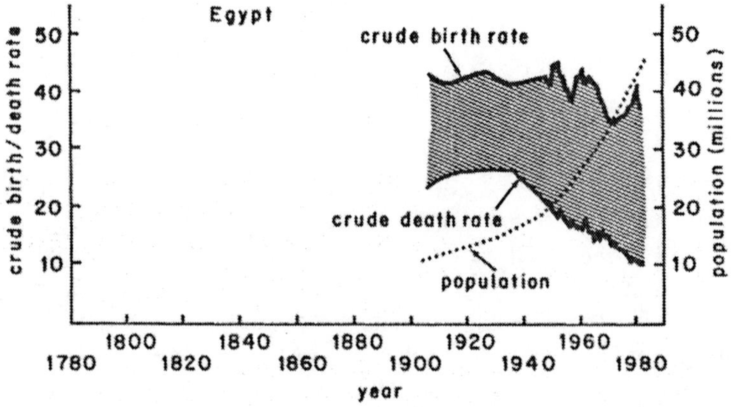
Egypt
crude birth rate
crude death rate
population
crude birth/death rate
population (millions)
year

1. EXOGENOUS AND AGGREGATED

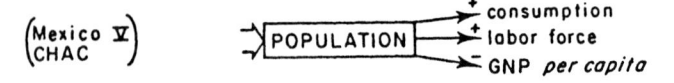

$\begin{pmatrix} \text{Mexico } \underline{\text{V}} \\ \text{CHAC} \end{pmatrix}$ → POPULATION → +consumption, +labor force, −GNP *per capita*

2. EXOGENOUS AND DISAGGREGATED

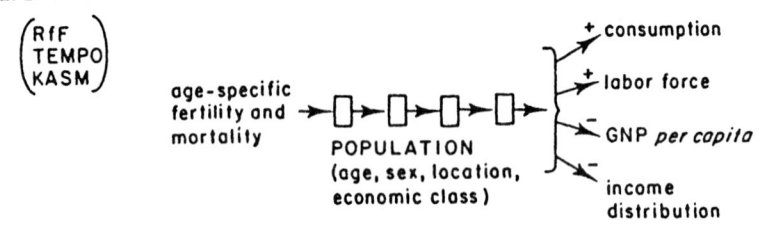

$\begin{pmatrix} \text{RfF} \\ \text{TEMPO} \\ \text{KASM} \end{pmatrix}$ age-specific fertility and mortality → POPULATION (age, sex, location, economic class) → +consumption, +labor force, −GNP *per capita*, −income distribution

3. ENDOGENOUS–DEMOGRAPHIC TRANSITION

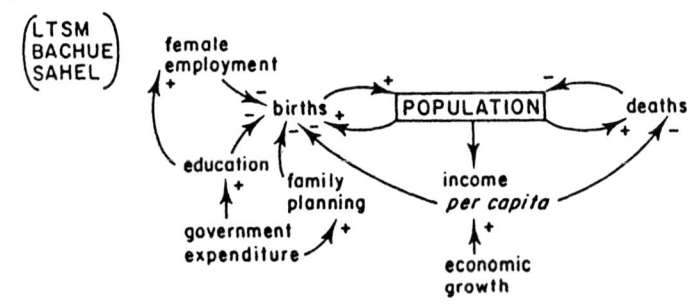

$\begin{pmatrix} \text{LTSM} \\ \text{BACHUE} \\ \text{SAHEL} \end{pmatrix}$ female employment, births, POPULATION, deaths, education, family planning, government expenditure, income *per capita*, economic growth

4. ENDOGENOUS–GOAL SEEKING

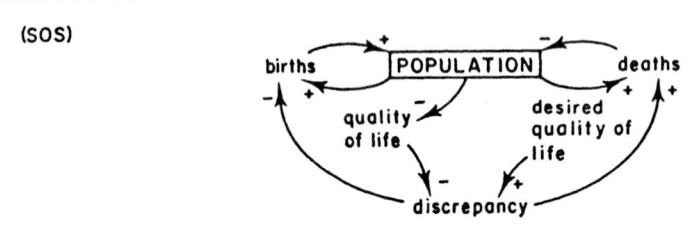

(SOS)

births, POPULATION, deaths, quality of life, desired quality of life, discrepancy

Figure 13.3 Population functions

Since the natural dynamics of populations unfold over decades, one would expect the longer-term models to represent population change processes in more detail. Three of the models, RfF, TEMPO, and KASM, take the next step upward in complexity. They keep fertility and mortality exogenous but capture the inertial effects of changing age structure through detailed age disaggregation.

In KASM the use of exogenous fertility and mortality rates most likely stems from the relatively short (five to 15 years) time horizon of the model and from an agricultural-ministry client with no jurisdiction over population matters (although this ministry might have been interested in the relationship between food sufficiency and mortality, which is not included in the model). Population in KASM influences only economic demand and agricultural labor supply. Disaggregation into 180 different age and sex groups does not seem necessary for this purpose. The population sector of the model has been used independently, however, to provide detailed population projections for Korean planning agencies. For this purpose the disaggregation is probably appropriate, but endogenous fertility and mortality assumptions might also have been appropriate.

The RfF modelers were directed by the client to explore two population-growth scenarios, the two-child and three-child families, to see whether population growth rates should be considered of national concern. Population is used in the model as one determinant of the final demand for the 185 different industrial sectors and thus indirectly to generate resource consumption and pollution. The model deals with an industrialized country, where future fertility and mortality shifts are likely to be small. Family size is the focus of the client, and it is considered manipulatable by government policy, although the mechanisms of manipulation are not explicit. Therefore the exogenous population growth assumption is probably appropriate to this model's purpose. Again, however, the detailed age and sex disaggregation does not seem necessary.

TEMPO also has a primary focus on population and was sponsored by a population-based client. It is an educational model, with the purpose of making governments worry about and take steps to reduce rapid population growth. TEMPO represents the effects of population on consumption and employment, but not the feedback of economic development on population. Fertility and mortality change internally only as a result of migration from rural areas to urban areas, where the fertility and mortality of migrants are assumed to adjust instantly. An exogenous policy can also decrease fertility by the simple process of allocating money to family-planning programs. The population is disaggregated by five-year age increments, by sex, and by modern- or subsistence-sector labor participation.

When the TEMPO model was made, its simple, one-way causal hypothesis was well-suited to the task of the model and to the state of knowledge about population dynamics. The message that new babies consume immediately but do not produce for 15–20 years was a revelation to many people who had never thought about such things before. The possibility that money spent on reducing birth rates might result in faster economic growth than money spent on capital plant was an intriguing new idea. But as a pioneering hypothesis should do, TEMPO spawned criticism, further observations, and further hypothesis that eventually went beyond the notion that population growth affects but is not affected by economic development. Partly because of TEMPO's existence and accessibility, the demographic sophistication of governments and of computer modelers developed beyond TEMPO's exogenous population assumptions.

Four of the models, LTSM, BACHUE, SOS, and SAHEL, do contain theories about how populations respond to the economy as well as about how the economy responds to the population. Three of these models, LTSM, BACHUE, and SAHEL, incorporate the theory of the demographic transition.

In its simplest form industrialization itself is assumed to cause the demographic transition. As societies industrialize (as measured, usually, by GNP *per capita*), first death rates and then birth rates decrease. More sophisticated versions of the theory attribute the demographic changes to specific aspects of industrialization such as greater labor mobility, which breaks up the extended family, or higher levels of education and rationality, or changing costs and benefits of children.[1]

In LTSM the death rate is decreased by higher *per capita* income and by exogenous government investment in services. The birth rate responds to education, to employment of women in modern economic sectors, and to an exogenous, cost-free government birth-control policy. The exact mechanisms by which these factors are supposed to impinge on families and change their health or decisions about reproductive behavior are not specified. The aggregate fertility rate responds instantly and linearly to an increase in education, employment, or population policy, but education and employment cannot be instantly generated. Education is accumulated by the aging population cohorts, depending on government service expenditures during the school-age years. Employment depends on capital plant in the modern economic sectors.

One of the motivating forces behind the LTSM model was a desire to update TEMPO by including the demographic transition theory. The result of doing so is to make this model more equivocal than TEMPO about the deleterious effects of population growth, and also to indicate the inherent slowness of any population response that has to proceed, as LTSM has assumed, through the diffusion of education and employment.

BACHUE contains a more detailed demographic transition theory. Here as in LTSM the death rate is reduced by higher income (a surrogate for better nutrition and health care). Since BACHUE keeps track of income distribution, it is the only model of the nine that can distinguish the difference between income rising only for the rich classes or primarily for the poor classes, with obviously different effect on mortality rates.

Fertility in BACHUE is a linear function of four factors: female labor participation rate (R), percentage illiteracy (I), life expectancy at birth (LE), and the percent of the population employed in agricultural activities (EA). The coefficients of the equation are derived from regressing gross reproduction rate (GRR) on these variables over a cross-sectional sample of 47 developing countries in 1969. The resulting equation is:

$$GRR(t) = 4.67 - 0.006 \times R(t-1) + 0.1063 \times I(t-1) - 0.0446 \times LE(t-1) + 0.0059 \times EA(t-1)$$

The theory behind this equation is that female participation in the labor force R increases the opportunity cost of children and thus lowers fertility. Illiteracy I and agricultural labor fraction EA are proxies for, respectively, education and the benefits of children as contributors to family-based economic enterprises. Life expectancy LE is a proxy for the assumption that parents compensate in their fertility for high risk of losing a child.

There are 150 demographic categories in BACHUE to keep account of age, sex, location, and education. The disaggregation seems justified in this case, since the model is aimed at questions of employment and income distribution. Population, with all its attributes taken into account, determines economic demand and provides both skilled and unskilled labor for modern and traditional jobs in rural and urban locations.

The BACHUE team has used the model to explore both the indirect effects of economic policies on fertility and the direct effects of fertility-reducing policies. Their conclusion is that population growth is quite sensitive to economic changes. This result should not be surprising, given the relatively strong coefficients in the fertility equation, its linear form, and the absence of any significant delays in the assumed reproductive response of the population to socioeconomic change. On the other hand, the BACHUE modelers conclude that fertility changes do not have a dramatic influence on economic conditions. With an assumed 24% decline in fertility, after 25 years total population is only 9% less than it would otherwise have been, and *per capita* income is 5% more. Fertility decline seems to make income inequalities worse for the first 30 years (due to less demand for food and a decline in agricultural terms of trade) and then increasingly better. Again, the small and slow impact is to be expected, since fertility reduction changes at first only the cohort of age 0–1. Only as this cohort and succeeding ones age will a difference be noted in the welfare of the whole system.

In modeling the Sahel population, Picardi was concerned with only one stage of industrialization. The population is uneducated, homogeneous, and locked into a simple cultural system that is not assumed to evolve into industrial complexity even over the very long time horizon of this model. Picardi represents the death rate as responsive to two factors—food *per capita* and exogenously-introduced health services. This is a Malthusian hypothesis that is probably reasonable for this population living at near-subsistence level. For his birth rate equations, Picardi combines two assumptions that sound like hypotheses about the psychological aspects of population processes, but are in fact mechanistic demographic-transition correlations similar to those in LTSM and BACHUE. 'Cost of children' rises as *per capita* wealth rises, and after a time lag, this reduces fertility. 'Need for children' is a function of the death rate; it expresses the hypothesis also seen in BACHUE that societies experiencing high infant mortality respond with high fertility, to insure that some children will survive. Picardi assumes a longer delay between mortality change and fertility response than does BACHUE.

SAHEL is the only model in our sample that is likely to produce a population decline. (The five models with exogenous populations could exhibit a decline if it were designed into the exogenous driving functions, but in no case is a decreasing population ever tested.) Pastoral families produce children (and allow their cows to produce calves) according to their own rational best interest, which is assumed to favor reproduction, given their personal economic circumstances and their perceived costs and risks of childbearing.

The aggregate consequence of these individual decisions is supported by a commonly-shared, erodable resource base, the grazing range. Since the individual reproductive decisions are taken with regard to individual needs rather than the condition of the common resource base, the range can become overloaded with people and with cattle, at which point it deteriorates, reducing both populations through enforced outmigration or starvation. Aid policies that reduce death rates through human or animal health services hasten the tragedy by allowing the nomads to achieve their reproductive goals more rapidly.

Although this model assumes the demographic transition, it also assumes the transition can be interrupted or even reversed, if resource limits become effective before it is achieved, or if economic growth does not keep pace with population growth. The long lag assumed for fertility response, the limited options for economic expansion, and the presence of erodable physical limits make a significant dynamic difference between the behavior of SAHEL and the other demographic-transition models LTSM and BACHUE.

The remaining model, SOS, pictures population growth as a goal-seeking, self-correcting process. Population growth proceeds uninterruptedly unless a significant number of consumption goals go seriously unmet for a relatively long period. In that case the birth rate falls and the death rate rises until the goals are again achieved. This population response is assumed to be a last-ditch effort, occurring only after a number of other responses such as resource substitution, shifting investment allocations, public expenditures, and even reduced material goals, are tried. This formulation amounts to a clear hypothesis about social value priorities; fertility and mortality goals are superordinate to other social goals and are changed only when material welfare falls so low that survival becomes the predominant concern. This assumption has little effect on the model behavior because under most conditions the model (with U.S. parameters and a 30-year time horizon) does not operate within the range of material dissatisfaction that would call forth population-adjustment mechanisms. In the few cases where it does, the modelers dismiss the results as 'not credible'.

3. Summary and commentary

The nine models contain statements of four basic hypotheses about population growth, each of which suggests different policy responses, and each of which is expressed vociferously in the world's policy debates:

1. Population growth takes place independently of socioeconomic events. Population is something to be predicted and adapted to, not something to be viewed as subject to social policy.
2. Population growth has a major and negative influence on economic growth and on resource use and pollution generation. Social policy should be aimed at reducing population growth rates.

3. Population growth has a minor effect on economic growth and probably a positive one. It is responsive to economic growth and will stabilize when a sufficient level of industrialization has been reached. Policy should concentrate on social welfare and economic development, not on the size or growth rate of the population.
4. Population growth is an integral part of the socioeconomy, affecting industrialization and also responding to it, with a lag and in pursuit of individual rather than social goals. Population growth can have a positive or negative effect and be stabilizing or destabilizing, depending on the response lag times and on the nature of the individual goals. Social policy should aim to incorporate population growth by changing the goals of individuals and the information upon which they base their decisions, so that they respond to total social welfare rather than short-term individual needs.

Note that these are *hypotheses*, expressed in the structure of the models, not conclusions derived from them. Each modeling group began with one of these hypotheses and then constructed a mathematical device that calculates detailed deductions that follow from the hypothesis (and from hypotheses about other indicators that will be discussed later). Note also that there is considerable evidence from the real world supporting each hypothesis; otherwise no modeling group would have found it plausible enough to include in its model. In particular, the observed pattern of the demographic transition could be viewed as perfectly consistent with all four theories. Only the fourth hypothesis is truly holistic and derived from systems theory. It is sufficiently general to encompass the previous three, and if it is not stated carefully with reference to specific, observable real-world events, it is so general that it is not falsifiable. It is the only one of the theories so conceptually complex that it probably *requires* a computer to work out its deductive consequences.

The models cannot prove or disprove any of the four competing hypotheses; they can only grind out their detailed implications. By doing so, the models do contribute considerably to understanding of population change processes. Six of the models, for example, provide an elaborate account of population aging, which permits the inertia of population change to be represented quite accurately. While demographic accounting is not a new or difficult concept, it is virtually absent from mental models, which cannot keep track of many population categories at once and which seriously underestimate the slowness of demographic change. Several of the models have emphasized that policies intended to affect total population attributes, such as education, must be maintained consistently over a period of at least 30 years before much change can be detected, a realization that is usually absent from public policy statements.

The computer has also been used to keep track of the net outcome of simultaneously-occurring but countervailing trends. For example, while the BACHUE and SAHEL models contain the assumption that falling mortality may eventually induce a decrease in fertility as parents compensate less for expected infant deaths, they also record the fact that falling mortality *immediately and certainly* raises the population growth rate. Thus unless parents overcompensate when mortality is high and undercompensate when it is low, reducing infant mortality cannot possibly reduce net population growth rate and will almost certainly raise it. Of course, mortality reduction can be defended on other grounds, but it cannot logically be defended as a population-leveling mechanism. The fact that it *is* often defended in this way[2] suggests that many mental models do not keep both the positive and negative effects of reduced mortality in focus at the same time.

The accounting capabilities of computer models can be helpful under some conditions but distracting or even misleading under others. The basic dynamics of population aging can be captured with as few as four population categories.[3] Few of the models really require the degree of precision their highly disaggregated population sectors can deliver. A model with tens or hundreds of population categories but exogenous birth and death rates is simultaneously oversimple and overcomplicated. The simplicity of birth and death rates that do not respond to happenings elsewhere in the socioeconomic system cannot justify the detail of an age–sex–location disaggregated population. At best such a model is simply confusing. At worst it contains the very sort of inconsistencies that one is trying to avoid by making a computer model in the first place. If the fertility and mortality of real populations do change continuously and significantly in response to economic and environmental happenings, and if the resulting changes in the population then further influence the economy and environment, then no exogenous forecast can properly take into account these back-and-forth relationships. Even if a very clever mental model provides the exogenous forecast and if every other assumption in the model is correct, the model behavior cannot be realistic.

Nearly all of the models remind us forcefully that as the denominator of a fraction such as GNP *per capita* or food *per capita* goes up, the value of the fraction goes down, which is useful to keep in mind. Two models give the impression that spending money on family planning will automatically, linearly, and instantaneously produce a lower birth rate. Three assume that investments in education, in employment-producing capital, and in urban development are indirect (and slow) ways to reduce fertility. Only one modeler points out that reduction of death rates too rapidly might threaten the resource base or retard development. No model suggests any use of information, examples, incentives, or ideas to affect fertility decisions, although Picardi raises the issue in his articles.

In formulating their hypotheses, the computer modelers have nearly all avoided including imprecise, uncertain, sociopsychological factors and even some quite certain but semiprecise biological factors (such as the effect of diet on mortality). Exploration of the actual human decision processes that result in aggregate shifts in fertility or mortality is limited to a vague, nearly tautological cybernetic theory (SOS).

Mental models can supply many more hypotheses about the causes and control of population growth than any of these computer models. Folklore and everyday experience are full of roughly accurate theories about attitudes toward children, about the role of social norms, about reasons for accepting or rejecting family planning, about the ways that different economic situations affect family reproductive decisions. A few governments have formed successful population policies on the basis of such mental-model theories. China and Singapore seem to have achieved lower birth rates, and Hungary has promoted and achieved a higher one, all by affecting the information, costs, and benefits perceived by families as they make their reproductive decisions.[4] The nine models in this survey are less complete (although more detailed in an accounting sense) than the verbal models used by these governments or the qualitative observations contained in any modern textbook on population.

B. PRODUCTION AND ALLOCATION

The production of goods and services and their allocation between current consumption and investment in the future are at the heart of the industrialization process, and they are also, not surprisingly, at the heart of all nine models. In fact, the central concern of economic modelers since the field began has been how to formulate mathematical functions that capture the processes of production, consumption, and investment.

We consider all three functions together here because, as we shall see, they form logically-inseparable patterns in the models. Certain types of production functions require matching investment and consumption formulations for mathematical or methodological consistency.

1. Mental models

If an unprepared observer from another planet or another century were to observe modern industrial production processes and then describe what he saw, he would almost certainly mention large mines extracting materials from the earth, enormous buildings emitting smoke or steam, high temperatures, much noise, streams of vehicles carrying materials, finished goods, and workers to and from the factory, great stockpiles of products at various stages of completion, and machines routinely performing tasks that require incredible strength or precision or co-ordination. If he described agricultural production from start to finish, he would certainly mention soil, sun, water, seeds, machines of many sorts, fertilizers, pests and pesticides, storage bins, driers, and processors, and, above all, farmers, farm communities, and families. He would conclude that production in an industrialized society is a complicated, multistep operation, each step requiring numerous factors all to be present at the right time and place. He might also notice oppressive, boring working conditions, illicit dumping of noxious wastes, and differences in living standards between workers and bosses.

Of course these are only the surface sights, sounds, and smells of the production process, and they indicate only a fraction of what is really going on. A knowledgeable businessman would speak of stock and future markets, management decisions, investments, credits, cash flows, rates of return, advertising, research and development; all inconspicuous parts of production, but constituents of an information system that is just as vital to production as materials, labor, or factories. A biologist might describe agricultural production in terms of information too—the development of the genetic potential of the seed, a gradual biochemical process of absorption of water and soil nutrients, conversion and storage of solar energy, help or hindrance at each stage from external events such as weeding, watering, and the codevelopment of insect communities. Each of these information-based descriptions would be just as involved as the first, sensory one, and still incomplete.

All of these descriptions so far have been biased by the modern assumption that production takes place in organized factories and that products go through markets where cash is paid for them. It ignores the vast unorganized productive processes of the world—bread baked in households, tools made by farmers, home gardens, owner-built houses, hand-sewn garments—which may, for all we know, actually amount to more product (especially if it is measured in human utility) than that which is officially accounted.

Production depends in part upon past investment decisions that have accumulated in present trained employees, stockpiles, technical knowledge, capital plant, and habits. The output of production is conventionally divided into two conceptual categories; consumption goods (bread, snowmobiles, novels) which are produced for their own sake, to yield satisfaction or utility or pleasure, and investment goods (seed wheat, tractors, shop manuals), which will be used for further production in the future. According to many development theories, the crux of industrialization is the decision to allocate productive output less to immediate consumption and more to investment in the means of future production. Every primitive society with the wisdom not to eat its seeds knows that more consumption in the present will reduce the rate at which output can be expanded in the future. Thus the societal decision about how much to save and how much to spend must be one of the pivotal determinants of the process of economic development.

How are consumption and investment decisions made in real economic systems? In some they are determined through centralized planning in a state controlled economy. None of the countries represented in our survey models operates entirely in that way, although in all cases the government does a sizable amount of investing, financed by enforced reductions in consumption known as taxation. In most models these public investments are represented exogenously; they are some of the most important policy decisions to be tested. In the private sector, however, consumption and investment, like population growth, are the results of millions of separate mutually-interacting decisions. Consumers look at their disposable incomes, their desires, the stocks of things they already have, their credit balances, the items for sale, prices, and advertising appeals, and somehow decide whether, when, and what to buy. Corporate leaders look at their inventories, their plant capacity utilized, their credit balances, their competitors, their sales records, and probably a hundred other things, and decide whether to defer maintenance, to maintain their capital, to expand, to go bankrupt, or to start up a whole new enterprise. Financiers presumably get as much information as possible on as many new ventures as possible, and bankroll the ones with the highest potential rate of return, or the quickest payback, or the lowest risk, or the most persuasive advocate.

Probably the greatest mystery in this process is how all these decisions affect each other. Corporate decisions about wages obviously change consumers' incomes, which influence consumption habits, which in turn alter inventories, prices, sales patterns, and bank deposits and thus come back to corporate decisions about wages. If all the orders consumers and investors decide to place add up to more steel or trucks or wheat than suppliers have on hand, there are stockouts, delivery delays, tight credit, price rises, and other means of distributing the shortage and adjusting the intentions of society to the current constraints of the economy. Just to complicate things, neither the decision to consume nor the decision to invest will necessarily result in an instant or predictable change in supply or demand at the marketplace. Consumers may stick to old habits even under new conditions or they may not have accurate information about new conditions, and they may take months to decide upon and obtain financing for major purchases such as automobiles or houses. It may take many years to construct a large modern productive installation such as a paper mill or a nuclear power plant, and when such an installation comes on-line it may not produce exactly the amount it was intended to produce at the cost it was assumed it would cost. How to make a clear, consistent model of buying and selling, investing and saving, micro- and macro-level events, is an unsolved problem for both mental modelers and computer modelers, in spite of all the mathematical sophistication of the discipline of economics.

2. Computer models

The models in our survey represent production, consumption, and investment through four basic mechanisms (see Figure 13.4)

1. *Demand-driven.* Production is determined by economic demand, which is defined as consumption plus investment. If one knows what determines consumption and investment (population, income, and interest rates, for example), then one automatically knows production.
2. *Market-driven.* Production, consumption, and investment are determined simultaneously through the price mechanism; aggregate decisions are such as to maximize profit and consumer utility within the physical and financial constraints of the system.
3. *Supply-constrained.* Production is limited by one or more scarce factors, usually capital and/or labor. Consumption is determined by population and income. Investment is whatever is left of output after consumption has been subtracted.

1. DEMAND DRIVEN (no restrictions on investment)

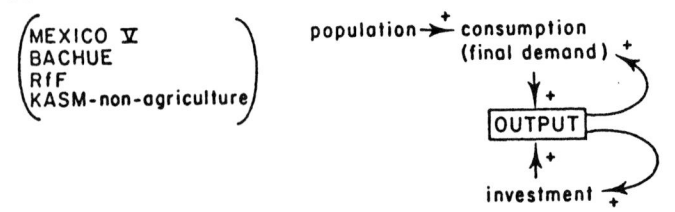

$\begin{pmatrix} \text{MEXICO V} \\ \text{BACHUE} \\ \text{RfF} \\ \text{KASM-non-agriculture} \end{pmatrix}$

2. MARKET-DRIVEN (investment to maximize profits)

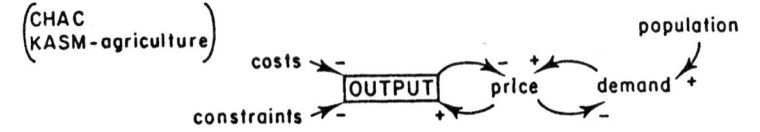

$\begin{pmatrix} \text{CHAC} \\ \text{KASM-agriculture} \end{pmatrix}$

3. SUPPLY-CONSTRAINED (investment residual)

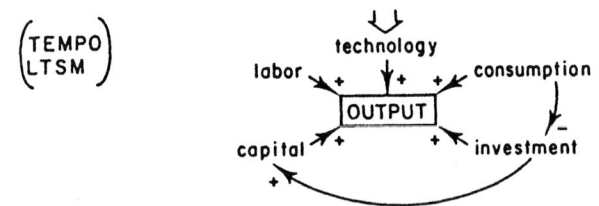

$\begin{pmatrix} \text{TEMPO} \\ \text{LTSM} \end{pmatrix}$

4. GOAL-SEEKING AND RESOURCE-CONVERTING
(investment to close gap between goal and current state)

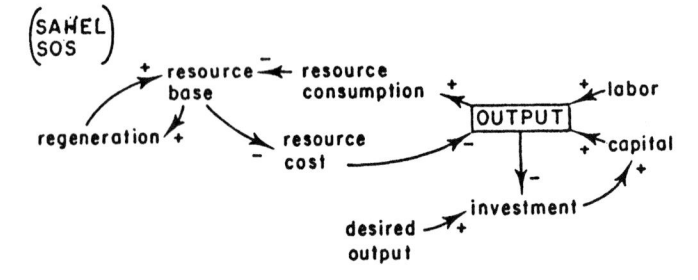

$\begin{pmatrix} \text{SAHEL} \\ \text{SOS} \end{pmatrix}$

Figure 13.4   Production functions

4. *Goal-seeking and resource-converting.* Production is the process of converting raw materials into useful goods; it is limited by resources as well as capital and labor. Consumption and investment are regulated to minimize the gap between some desired state and the actual state of the system.

The simplest approach is the one we have called 'demand-driven'. The basic assumption in these models is that economic demand is likely to be the most limiting factor in the entire production process. If market demand is present, all the factories, materials, energy, and labor to satisfy it will be forthcoming, without delay.

This formulation appears most clearly in *MexicoV*, which contains three production functions, for the primary (agriculture), secondary (manufacturing), and tertiary (service) sectors:

primary output = 1.54792 + 0.17425 (private consumption)
 + 1.15516 (agricultural exports)

secondary output = −4.16634 + 0.63336 (total investment)
 + 0.35448 (total consumption)

tertiary output = −2.06446 + 0.59023 (tourism and border exports)
 + 0.57309 (total consumption)

This model is obviously not meant to be a literal representation of the production process. If the capital stock in this system were suddenly halved, secondary output would go down by a small fraction (because investment is partially determined by capital), and the other outputs would be unaffected. An interruption in labor, energy, or material flows would have no effect. Of course, it would be illegitimate to make such changes in this model; it is designed not to investigate major discontinuities, but to predict in the short term the gross characteristics of the economic system operating in a smooth, undisturbed way. The relationships in the three equations above have been derived from the behavior of the Mexican economy over the past several years; if the underlying causes of this behavior continue to pertain for the next few years, the model is useful for its purpose.

In *MexicoV* consumption and investment are determined in four separate equations:

private consumption = f(disposable income *per capita*/lagged)
public consumption = f(taxes)
private investment = f(capital, rate of change of GDP/lagged)
public investment = f(taxes, public banking credit, rate of change of public debt)

All these functions are linear, all correlations are positive, and all coefficients are estimated from historical data. These four quantities are added to inventory changes and foreign exchange balance to determine GNP. The three output equations are added to produce GDP. No necessary connection is introduced between output, consumption, and investment, except for the connection enforced by the parameters derived from the historical values of these quantities in the real system.

Although this approach is not satisfying in that it adds little to our causal understanding of Mexican economic growth, it is at least scrupulously honest when applied as carefully as Beltran del Rio has applied it. The modeler does not pretend to know all the desires, expectations, and dissatisfactions that drive the economic system. Instead he establishes statistical relationships between measurable elements as they have existed in the past, and then assumes that those relationships will continue in the future. For short-term forecasting this is not a bad procedure. But such a model is not useful if policy changes are to be tested, particularly if the policy focus is on consumption or investment. For example, one cannot test the effect of interest rates or depreciation credits on private investment, nor the effect of oil import restrictions on production.

Three longer-term models also use a demand-driven production function but a far more complicated one. These are the three models that represent the production process with an input–output matrix—RfF, BACHUE, and the non-agricultural sector of KASM. Again the basic assumption is that final demand is the limiting factor in total output, but now both demand and output are disaggregated into many industrial sectors, with all interindustry flows taken into account. The relationships between the monetary values of inputs and outputs are constant, unless an exogenous forecast shifts them, as in RfF. But in general these models take a snapshot of the interindustry flows in the productive system as it actually operated over a database year and enlarge this picture, swelling each part proportionately as the economy grows.

Although input–output models can be used to represent accumulation of investment into capital stocks and then the influence of these stocks both on production and on further investment, none of the models in our survey do this. Thus in these models allocation questions do not arise. Output is always enough to fill both investment and consumption needs. BACHUE is a partial exception to this rule in that an upper limit of growth rate of the economy is imposed (7% per year). If desired consumption and investment increases come to more than this, both are scaled down proportionately.

The behavior pattern generated over time by a demand-driven production function depends only upon the way demand is formulated. In RfF final demand is determined by exogenous forecasts for population growth, government spending, and GNP. These forecasts are all based on steady exponential growth, and therefore the productive system dutifully produces more each year than the year before. In KASM and BACHUE final demand is a function of income, which is derived from the production of the year before. Since more demand produces more output, which generates more income, which creates more demand, this formulation also produces regular exponential growth of production. The only way economic growth could be slowed or interrupted in any of these models is by the population growing so much faster than output that *per capita* income is decreased. But in fact the parameter values in the models do not permit this to happen. None of these models could generate a business cycle or any other irregular economic behavior, unless it were deliberately included in exogenous driving functions.

The makers of BACHUE and KASM see their models as general policy tools, and RfF was supposed to provide a picture of the long-term resource situation in the United States. For these purposes, especially for depicting possible changes in resource use, energy sources, and technology over the next 30 years, less complicated but more complete representations of the production process would probably have allowed more exploration of alternative policies, and might even have produced different results. And for general planning purposes, some inclusion of the allocation process and of capacity constraints seems essential.

In two models, CHAC and the agricultural part of KASM, demand brings forth production only indirectly, through the free market. Increased demand for a good raises the price, which may cause profit-maximizing suppliers to produce more. But there are also physical constraints that may inhibit supply. Furthermore, higher prices may feed back to decrease demand. Demand in these models is a function of population and income as well as the relative prices of the commodities demanded (see Figure 13.4). Prices influence farmer's decisions about the various output activities they might participate in, and therefore, together with input costs and resource constraints, they influence supply. Demand, supply, and price are calculated simultaneously so as to be mutually consistent with each other. Both models provide an exhaustive survey of many of the physical factors needed to produce agricultural commodities (land, labor, water, fertilizer, machines, credit) and they constrain the system not to use more of any input than is actually available.

As a static model, CHAC cannot deal with long-term investment decisions; it is concerned primarily with investments in annual inputs such as fertilizers and in the effect over a one-year period of some permanent public investments such as canal linings (which are exogenous). Farmers' short-term investments come out of the simultaneous-equation solution; they are made so as to produce that amount of total supply that will balance the market at the point that maximizes producers' and consumers' surplus. CHAC's consumption function for each commodity depends upon income and price, with some possibility of substitution of one commodity for another.

KASM, as a longer-term model for an agricultural client, contains quite a detailed representation of investment in the agricultural sector. The optimization program that represents farmers' production decisions distinguishes between various forms of capital, such as machinery, buildings, livestock, and working capital. Investment decisions are made under a 'cautious profit maximization' assumption and are constrained by availability of capital and credit. Numerous government policies can affect investment through releasing credit constraints, providing new investment choices, or controlling the prices of input factors. Lags between investment and production and lags in technological diffusion are explicitly represented.

Neither of these models represents literally the human decisions by which production takes place, prices are set, and investment and consumption decisions are made. They are abstract representations of what economic theory presumes the aggregate result of many individual decisions must be. The models cannot answer the very important question of whether the real system actually operates according to this theory (or perhaps under what conditions it does and does not). They also cannot explore or even raise questions about changing the system's behavior through affecting the micro decisions that add up to macro behavior.

The remaining four models (LTSM, TEMPO, SAHEL, and SOS) are not demand-driven but supply-constrained. Production is calculated as a function of the availability of critical inputs, and then demand (investment plus consumption) adapts in some way to the available supply.

LTSM is a model for labor-surplus economies; and therefore labor is not included as a limiting factor of production. The modern production sectors in the model are represented with a Harrod-Domar production function:

output = capital/capital-output ratio

The eight capital-output ratios for the eight industrial sectors, indices of all sorts of technological and managerial factors, are specified exogenously. Each one includes an automatic technological improvement factor. In the traditional (agriculture) sectors,

output = land × yield per unit land

Yield is a function of capital and annual inputs with no diminishing returns. Input usage automatically increases as agricultural production increases and vice versa.

In TEMPO labor as well as capital is considered a potentially limiting factor. The modern sector contains a Cobb–Douglas production function:

output = f(capital, labor, technology)

with technology growing exogenously and exponentially. In the subsistence sector output is only a function of labor, and diminishing returns to this labor are assumed.

Both LTSM and TEMPO are concerned with the investment-consumption trade-off, which they represent by generating output, subtracting consumption from it, and assuming the remainder, if any, is investment, which is then added to the capital stock (a constant depreciation fraction is subtracted). In TEMPO consumption is a linear function of population and GNP, plus exogenous government spending. In LTSM consumption is the product of population and *per capita* consumption, which rises at a rate depending on the rate of increase of *per capita* national income. These simple formulations result in a tendency of capital to grow exponentially and a tendency of population growth to slow capital growth by draining output into consumption. They also capture the necessity for consumption and investment to balance output in physical terms (only in a monetary sense can one consume or invest something that hasn't yet been produced).

For broad-brush portrayals of long-term economic development as it seems to have occurred historically, these supply-constrained economic sectors are probably adequate. Depending upon their parameters, they can produce almost any behavior from economic stagnation to rapid growth. Both models are slanted toward rapid growth by their cost-free, ever-increasing technology assumptions, and LTSM is further biased by its absence of diminishing returns. These formulations sketch out only very general relationships among population growth, consumption, investment, and economic output. They are too simplified, rigid, and aggregate to provide either accurate predictions or useful policy tests.

All the production functions discussed so far measure both inputs and output of the productive process in monetary units. Only two models, SAHEL and SOS, try to express the fact that production is a physical process that transforms resources into material goods and services and that generates wastes. In these models, production can be limited not only by capital or labor, but also by the cost or availability of resources. These models also differ from the others in that they picture consumption and investment as goal-directed feedback processes, proceeding according to explicit social priorities and decision rules.

The SAHEL model depicts a simple production system with only two products: milk, which is a function of the number of living cattle and the main source of food; and beef, which is obtained by killing cattle and which is traded for other kinds of food and for material goods (called 'wealth') produced outside the pastoral system. The model is a literal simulation of the generation of soil fertility, the growth of forage, the nutrition and reproduction of cattle, and their sale or harvest by humans. The production process is biological, and the feedback-based model captures its essence, including the inherent delays in the gestation and growth of cattle. Great swings of increase or decrease in production are possible.

The trade-off between consumption and investment could scarcely be more starkly obvious than it is in this simple pastoral system. Acquisition of wealth requires killing cattle, the capital stock that produces both the daily output of milk and the increase in the stock itself. A build-up of stock for the future obviously requires deferral of consumption in the present. The social structure that governs this allocation process is traditional and tribal, and it is modeled explicitly. Four goals are specified:

1. Desired milk *per capita*.
2. Desired non-milk food *per capita*.
3. Desired wealth.
4. Desired social infrastructure (a measure of buffering capacity, or herd maintained as security against uncertain weather conditions).

The latter two goals are assumed to be variable, the former two constant. The actual amounts of milk, wealth, non-milk food, and social infrastructure are compared to the goals, and the area of greatest deficiency dominates the decision about how much of the herd to slaughter each year. This rather simple four-goal system can produce very complicated behavior patterns, as social priorities shift in response to the changing environment. And the representation of these goals and the decisions they produce requires some bold guesses about cultural preference in the Sahel nomad society.

In SOS House and Williams attempt to construct a generic production function, applicable to any production process at any time. They begin with an equation that seems to make cash flow the most limiting factor in production:

output = (funds available for output) * (cost/unit output).

Funds available for output in each productive sector are a function of past output, but with a toll taken for maintenance, for expansion, and for pollution clean-up. Because funds available for output are increased by past output, the system is capable of exponential growth in production. This growth can be interrupted, however, by the other factor, cost/unit output. This cost is defined as:

cost/unit output = (cost per unit resource) * (resource per unit output)

With this equation any factor of production can become limiting to output. Resource per unit output is a compendium of labor, land, energy, and materials associated with each productive sector. It obviously incorporates many technological assumptions. As production proceeds the resource base may become saturated (if the resource is renewable) or depleted (if the resource is non-renewable), and in either case the cost per unit resource rises. The model system adjusts for this by using less resource per unit output, but only up to a limit; SOS does not permit physical output to be manufactured from nothing. Rising resource costs can eventually stop and sometimes even reverse the exponential increase in output.

The SOS model does not express the allocation problem clearly in terms of consumption vs. investment. Instead, the operating funds available for output are divided by the adjustment-set 'brain' of the model into fractions allocated to normal production, expansion, pollution clean-up, and maintenance. The division proceeds according to prespecified social goals, thresholds, and rules for which strategies to try under what conditions. This mechanism is interesting in a design sense, for exploring the dynamic effects of different adjustment rules in a resource-constrained system. But it is difficult to relate the all-wise central allocation mechanism in the model to the primarily decentralized and uncoordinated mechanisms by which those decisions seem to be made in a real market system.

3. Summary and commentary

Each of the four basic hypotheses about production and allocation used in these models arises from a very different view of economic activity and leads naturally to a different set of policy recommendations.

The demand-driven models are propelled by the positive feedback loop of more production causing increased income causing higher consumption causing more production. If the parameters of the model are such that this loop is dominant (which is true for the four demand-driven models in our survey), the model will generate sustained exponential economic growth. Policy measures can only affect the rate of this growth. They can increase it by increasing demand, which in these models means either consumption or investment. Consumption can be increased by expanding either population or income, income usually having a larger effect. Investment can be increased most easily by public spending.

The market-driven models contain the same dominant positive feedback and therefore also generate growing economies. The growth in these models can be erratic, however, as the two negative feedbacks through price equilibrate supply and demand. These models would support the same policy conclusions as the demand-driven ones—increase demand to increase price to increase profits to increase production. But the market-driven models also suggest other places for policy inputs, including price regulation, cost controls, supply regulation through import and export policies, and government purchasing.

The supply-constrained models can also generate smooth exponential growth but through a different positive feedback loop; more production gives more output gives more investment gives more capital gives more production. This loop can be seriously weakened if consumption drains output away from investment, and so these models, at least theoretically, could also produce a stagnant or even a declining economy. The policy conclusions from these models are the reverse of the demand-driven ones. Do *not* encourage population growth or increases in demand for consumer goods; they will reduce investment and slow economic growth. Rather, strengthen the growth loop by building up capital, decreasing the capital-output ratio, encouraging investment, and discouraging consumption, especially through controlling the population.

The resource-conversion models can produce almost any economic development pattern, including cycles, steady growth, steady decline, or a growth phase when resources are abundant followed by a reversal as resources become expensive. The sorts of policies these models suggest include control of population growth, conservation of resources, monitoring of the resource base, long-term planning, and, especially, alteration of the goals, rewards, and priorities that influence individual consumption decisions. Most of these policies could not be derived from or even represented in any of the other three categories of economic models.

Active academic debates and sometimes violent political disagreements have been sustained by these different economic theories for decades. Very little effort has been put into honestly and critically *disproving* any of the theories or identifying exactly when and where one might be operational and another not. The computer models are sufficiently complicated, incommensurable, and one-sided that they do not clarify the debate. They accurately reflect the fractured state of understanding of modern economic systems; they do not suggest either strikingly new ways of looking at the system so as to clear away the clutter, or crucial tests to sort out conflicting theories.

Like the demographic models, these economic models under their complicated surfaces are surprisingly simple, even compared with most mental models of the production process. Except for the agricultural models, their production functions contain two or at most three input factors, nearly always measured in monetary units. One can obviously learn *something* about production from looking only at the money flows it engenders, but one must also miss a lot that way. Two things that are apparently easily missed are raw materials and energy, which are absent from seven of the nine production functions.

> I wonder what has happened in all these studies to material inputs. If they are omitted because of the lack of required data, we have an answer, even if to my mind a regrettable one... It seems to me that a production function is supposed to explain a productive process, such as the making of potato chips from potatoes (and other ingredients), labor, and capital. It must take some ingenuity to make potato chips without potatoes.[5]

Another input to production that is systematically omitted is the complex of information, skills, institutions, and management techniques needed to make a modern productive process run.

> The primary causes of extreme poverty are immaterial, they lie in certain deficiencies in education, organization, and discipline. Development does not start with goods; it starts with people and their education, organization, and discipline. Without these three all resources remain latent, untapped, potential... We have had plenty of opportunity to observe the primacy of the invisible factors after the war. Every country, no matter how devastated, which had a high level of education, organization, and discipline, produced an 'economic miracle'. In fact, these were miracles only for people whose attention is focused on the tip of the iceberg. The tip had been smashed to pieces, but the base, which is education, organization, and discipline, was still there.[6]

To the extent that any of the models represent such factors, it is in the form of education that reduces population growth or increases labor productivity. In general the models reflect the implicit assumption behind many development aid efforts of the past few decades; paper mills, nuclear reactors, aluminum smelters, or higher incomes, grafted onto societies such as Ethiopia, Bolivia, or Burma will not only produce as much as they would in a developed economy, but they will form the self-increasing capital base that is required for economic 'take-off'. None of the models is capable of representing, much less suggesting, policies to influence the social, technical, organizational, and entrepreneurial characteristics of the people. None of them recognizes the very existence of informal, household-based production, or represents industrialization as a shift of more and more productive functions from the household to the organized economy.

The greatest problem with the production functions of these models is not that they have omitted one or another factor of production. Including social and organizational factors, there are so many that no understandable model could include them all. Nor need they all be included, because at any time most of them are safely in excess, so that variations in them would have no effect on the production process. But it would seem to be crucial to economic planning to understand *shifts* of the productive system from one limiting factor to another, both as the industrialization process evolves and as neighbouring economies and the environment change. Demand might indeed be the most limiting factor of production at the beginning of industrialization, when potential consumers are too poor to express their wants in the market place. As the economy develops, capital may become most limiting, then, perhaps skilled labor, then inexpensive energy, and finally maybe demand again, when consumers become too nearly saturated with material goods to want more.

Economists have traditionally been concerned with one such shift, between labor and capital. The primary theories they use to explain productive-factor shifts involve optimization in a series of perfect markets. These theories need to be amended and extended, to include many factors simultaneously, to acknowledge backlogs, bottlenecks, and hiring and construction delays, to represent imperfect markets, incomplete information, and management goals more complex than minimizing cost or maximizing profits. These and other changes will begin to capture the complex productive factor shifts that are already in progress or soon will be; from manual to fossil-fuel to renewable forms of energy, from supply to demand and back again, from heavy capital to technological finesse, from productive capital to environmental-protective capital. The most adventurous models in our survey, such as SOS, have begun to try to describe these changes. In doing so they are unquestionably on the leading edge of economic theory, and well over the edge of any firm database.

The same criticism can be applied to the representations of the allocation decision. The models, for all their apparent complexity, are extreme simplifications of the allocation process. The most explicit and literal model, SAHEL, is applicable only to a society with one form of capital, four forms of consumption goods, relatively homogeneous distribution, and a rigid, tribal decision-making process. The most detailed and sophisticated allocation representations are the optimizing models, which rest entirely on the free-market, invisible-hand assumptions that are at best questionable, and at worst totally inapplicable to increasingly centralized modern productive systems. Few of the models provide any insights or even any hypotheses about the social motivations, struggles, or roadblocks that result in the accumulation and maintenance of a stock of skills, information, and productive capital or about the needs, goals, and urges that motivate people to buy things or to save for the future.

To be fair, there are few other models, mental or formal, that provide a clear picture of the social allocation process. The investment and consumption functions are the Gordian knot of economics. Some individuals, families, or firms may be able to describe accurately how they form their intentions to invest or consume, but how do these intentions become aggregated and matched against actual productive output? How do shortages get distributed, what second-choice options do investors or consumers follow if their first choice is unavailable, how long is the delay between intention and actual consumption or investment? What information is really available at the time investment and consumption decisions are made? To what extent do consumers or investors simply seize the first acceptable opportunity that comes along? The division of the problem into production, consumption, and investment may not even be a useful one, since most kinds of output, once produced, are in fact already either in the form of consumption goods or investment goods. Perhaps more attention should be paid to the role of unsold inventories and consumers' stocks of goods-in-use as determinants of production, sales, and investment.[7]

Real understanding of the allocation mechanism must involve a progression from individual decisions to aggregate expressed demands to adequacy or inadequacy of supply and back to individual actions and new decisions. This is clearly a systems-theory problem; one that requires a holistic, interdisciplinary, and quantitative approach. It does not seem to be solvable by mental models, by reductionism, or by scanning annual summations of macroeconomic money flows. Imaginative computer modeling should be able to shed some very much needed light in this area.

C. TECHNOLOGICAL CHANGE

Technology could be defined as the application of scientific knowledge to practical processes, or as the physical relationship between inputs to production and outputs, or as the general ability of a society to solve problems through readjustments in hardware, or as the continuous substitution of more abundant resources for scarce ones. However it is defined, technology is one of the most obvious factors that distinguishes an industrialized society from a non-industrialized one. Technological transfer is probably the most often-suggested and implemented form of development aid. A theory of industrialization might be expected to include an account of where technological change comes from and how it spreads.

1. Mental models

Technology is clearly a product of human ingenuity and effort, sometimes occurring by chance (as in the discovery of vulcanized rubber), but more often by a deliberate search for a solution to a specific problem (as in, for example, the development of contraceptive pills, stainless steel, or lunar landers). A successful technological development seems to require both an adequate base of general knowledge and an investment to work out the practical application of the knowledge. For example, lack of general knowledge seems to be preventing a technological cure for cancer, while sustained fusion power generation may require more design and development but perhaps no more basic scientific knowledge.

Thus the first appearance of a technological change seems to require:

1. A perceived problem.
2. A sufficient understanding of the system to suggest a technical solution.

3. Enough resources, manpower, and time to test the solution, scale it up to an appropriate size, and work out the details of its application.

At this point the further diffusion of the change depends on a number of factors such as economic cost, social acceptability, government support, marketing, the natural turnover rate of physical capital, and 'side effects'. After the societal adoption of a new technology, one would expect to see changes not only in the resource mix or input–output relationships in the problem area most directly affected, but also perhaps in physical or social relationships throughout the society. The automobile not only solved the immediate problem of personal transportation, but also affected labor relations, government expenditures, air quality, city design, political power structures, international trade dependence, and hundreds of other relationships in the socioeconomic system.

Beyond these fairly obvious generalities, mental models of technology tend to be fragmented, diverse, and intricate, because so many aspects of society have been influenced by so many different technological changes. There is also a foundation of nearly religious mystification in our mental models—technology is either the magic force that can solve all problems or the source of all evil.

Specific technological developments historically related to industrialization include the printing press, the power loom, antibiotics, radio, the computer, the transistor, nuclear power, DDT, miracle rice, offshore oil drilling, and the intercontinental ballistic missile. How can any model of industrialization ignore such vital changes, yet how can a model hope to account for future technological developments? For above all, technological change is an open-ended evolutionary process, and evolutionary processes seem to be most difficult of all to simplify, generalize, or predict. The interrelations between technology and society may be the aspect of industrialization where mental models are most inadequate.

2. Computer models

The nine models in our survey approach the representation of technology in more than nine different ways, since some of them include technological change, implicitly or explicitly, by more than one mechanism. The models can be distinguished by whether technology is included as a general concept or a series of specific changes, by whether side effects, costs, and time delays are included, and by whether future as-yet-unproven technologies are allowed. The grid in Figure 13.5 summarizes the technology representations in the models, organized by degree of aggregation and by boundary. In this discussion we will proceed across the rows of this grid, first taking up the constant-technology models, then those with technology exogenous, then those with technology endogenous.

MexicoV, as a short-term econometric model, says least about technology of any of our models, and needs to say least, given its purpose. Technology does not appear explicitly anywhere in the model; the productive process is related

	technology general and aggregated	technology specific and disaggregated
technology unchanged	MEXICO V	CHAC BACHUE-industrial KASM-industrial
technology exogenous	TEMPO LTSM	SAHEL RfF KASM-major agricultural developments
technology endogenous and implicit	BACHUE LTSM migration TEMPO	
technology endogenous and explicit	SOS	KASM-diffusion of agricultural developments

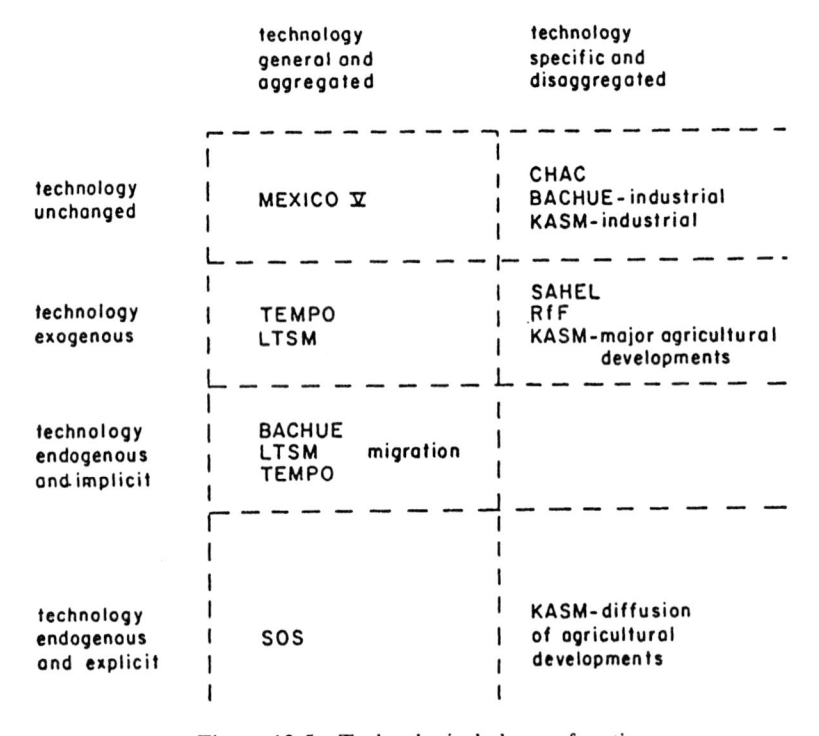

Figure 13.5 Technological change functions

to economic demand rather than technological inputs. Of course, the technological state of development of Mexico is implicitly embedded in all the parameters of the 40 behavioral equations of the model, which were derived from historical data. Therefore *MexicoV* is in a sense a technological statement, and when it is used for forecasting, it states that there will be no change in technology.

Since CHAC is a static model, it obviously does not contain any representation of long-term technological change. Yet CHAC is unquestionably the most technologically detailed model in our survey. One might summarize the entire model by stating that it is:

1. An array of the technological options currently available to Mexican farmers—2,348 such options.
2. A theory about which options will be chosen under which conditions.

CHAC is not intended to spin out a path of technological development over time, therefore it is not concerned with where those 2,348 options came from or what new ones might appear five years from now. However, the model can generate almost any set of choices from among these options for a given year, depending on economic factors and government policies. Therefore, although CHAC is a constant-technology model in terms of evolution of options over time, it does not assume that the Mexican agriculture economy will respond to policy changes with one fixed choice of technologies.

CHAC's theory of technological selection is that of free market operation, possibly overlaid with government policies. Each farmer is aware of the technological options open to him (not all 2,348—geographical district, type of land, and availability of irrigation limit the choices actually available to any one type of farmer) and of the potential costs and benefits of each. The options are selected by working through simultaneous consideration of supply and demand curves to find the point of market equilibrium. This is a theory of what the *aggregate* result of technological choices (and consumer response) will be; it does not suggest what the farmers' actual decision process is. It does imply, however, some sort of profit maximization based on accurate information at the farm level.

The two other models that assume constant technology are the industrial submodels of BACHUE and KASM. In both cases these are input–output models of interindustry flows. The technical coefficients in the input–output matrix represent what each industrial sector actually bought from and sold to each other sector in one database year. Both models hold these technical coefficients constant, implying no change in the relationship between inputs and outputs throughout the time horizon of the model. For KASM, with a 5–15 year horizon and a central interest in agriculture, where technical changes are represented in detail, the assumption of constant industrial technology is probably appropriate. For BACHUE, with a longer time horizon and a concern with general planning, it is more dubious, as the modelers themselves recognize. They justify their decision to simplify in this area as follows:

> There is considerable uncertainty as to the relationships between demographic factors and output growth as a whole, particularly in relation to issues such as natural resource availability, facility of structural change, and the rate and nature of technical progress. Without substantial additional research, we considered it unwise to develop this area.[8]

Of the models with exogenous and variable technology, TEMPO and LTSM are the most aggregated and therefore the simplest. Both contain government policies that might be considered technological, such as family planning and health care, as well as exogenous automatic technological improvement functions built into their production equations.

TEMPO's governmental technological policies include health care, family planning, and education, which can be varied at the option of the model user. Health care expenditures influence mortality in the model, family planning influences fertility, and education influences the quality and quantity (productivity and participation fraction) of the labor force. The costs of these improvements are accounted for through a government budget model. A constant cost per pupil enrolled is assumed, and also a constant cost per family-planning acceptor up to a certain total acceptance rate, above which the cost per acceptor rises linearly with the acceptance rate. The expenditures on these government services, or the setting of targets that then determine the expenditures, are up to the user.

TEMPO also contains strong assumptions about technology in its production functions. Production is disaggregated into two sectors, subsistence and modern. In the subsistence sector output is a function only of subsistence-sector population,

$$\text{GPS} = x*PS^y_{t-1}$$

(gross product, subsistence sector)   (subsistence population)

where x and y are constants and y is less than one. Thus in the subsistence sector, the tools with which labor works are relatively unimportant, technology does not change, and there are diminishing returns to labor.

In the modern sector, however, output follows a Cobb–Douglas production function:

$$\text{GPM} = Z*(1+Q)^t*K^u_{t-1} * NE^v_{t-1} * NU^w_{t-1}$$

(gross product modern sector) (technology change rate) (capital) (employed educated labor) (employed non-educated labor)

The contribution of educated labor is higher than that of non-educated labor ($v > w$). Technology in this function grows exponentially with time at the rate Q, which is set in TEMPO's 'Developa' runs at 1.5% per year. Thus any given combination of capital and labor is presumed to produce an output that increases in value by 1.5% each year, automatically and at no cost.

This aggregate, exponential technology term is quite common in macroeconomic production functions. It arises from the widespread empirical observation that ordinary Cobb–Douglas functions ($Y = zK^uL^v$) have consistently underestimated the actual growth of production over time. Output predicted by the equation has typically fallen short of real output, and the gap has increased roughly exponentially with the length of the forecast period. One could imagine several possible explanations for this observation. For example:

1. The mathematical form $Y = zK^uL^v$ may simply be inappropriate to describe the relationship between capital, labor, and output in modern economies.
2. Relative prices of inputs and outputs may change over time so that monetary measures of flows of inputs and outputs give no indication of the underlying physical relationships.
3. The equation may leave out one or more of the factors of production that are systematically being substituted for capital and/or labor.

The inclusion of an exponential technology term in the Cobb–Douglas equations is equivalent in choosing the third of these explanations and assuming that the missing factor is general 'know how', which is applied across the economy to allow more and more efficient use of capital and labor. The resulting production function seems to have good short-term predictive ability for many economies over many historical periods. But its explanatory value is less clear, and its scientific value is nil, since it is such a vague hypothesis that it is difficult to falsify. Technology is not defined in such a way that it can be independently measured. Other factors of production, such as energy, might logically be the mysterious missing factor. And other production functions can be shown to fit historical data equally well.[9]

Is the assumption of an exponentially-growing aggregate technology consistent with TEMPO's purpose? If the purpose is limited to demonstrating the effects of faster or slower population growth on an economy, simplicity is important, and this technology assumption is probably as good as any. Whether the technology growth rate Q is set at 2.5%, 0, or even -1.5%, the model's main conclusion, that slow population growth is better than rapid, would probably still hold. However, if the model's purpose is expanded to include economic planning, continued extrapolation of an exponential technology function is probably much too simple an assumption.

LTSM contains a similar combination of exogenous technology functions expressed both in policy options and in production equations. Of the five main exogenous policies in the model, three have technological implications—land reclamation (irrigation, drainage, etc.), allocation of investment among sectors, and population policies (family planning). Land reclamation is carried out at a cost to the agricultural investment allocation. Other investments have costs in terms of output, but no significant delays. The population policy is cost-free and immediately effective.

The LTSM model uses a modified Harrod–Domar production function for each of the eight non-agricultural economic sectors:

output (t) = output$(t-1)$ + investment$(t-1)$ ∗
incremental capital-output ratio(t)

The incremental capital-output ratio is an aggregate expression of the technological relationship between capital and product. It is specified exogenously and is assumed to change over time, usually incorporating a simple exponential technical progress assumption.

In the agriculture sector of LTSM technical progress is represented more explicitly. Here output is the product of land area and yield. Land area is increased by exogenous reclamation policies and decreased by construction activities. Yield is a function of investment in intensive (not land-related) capital and in material inputs (fertilizer and pesticides). Intensive capital investment comes from the exogenous investment allocation policy. The rate of increase of material inputs is a function of the rate of change of net agricultural output, which then causes a further increase in material inputs in the next period. The result of these assumptions must be a steady exponential increase in output, caused by an ever-growing amount of fertilizer and other annual inputs. Thus technological improvement in LTSM's agriculture sector is assured.

Three other models, SAHEL, RfF, and KASM, assume exogenous technology changes, but in these models the exogenous technologies are much more specific than the disembodied general production-enhancers of TEMPO and LTSM.

The nomad population of SAHEL can be given technological assistance in the form of human health care, veterinary medicine, or tubewells, at any time in the simulation, at the discretion of the model operator. The effects of these changes are to decrease human and cattle death rates and to increase the forage available and the time spent by the nomads in the Sahel. These three simple interventions seem to be sufficient to model the historical technological changes experienced by the Sahel's people. Whether they are sufficient to test all the changes that can realistically be expected in the future depends upon one's mental model. Picardi in his computer model wanted to test these particular changes alone. Therefore he made no provision for testing the impact of solar electric generators, miracle forage legumes, bovine growth hormone, or any other new technology in the Sahel region.

RfF as a 185-factor input–output model of the U.S. is as far removed from the Sahel model in method and concern for technology as a model could be. As might be expected from a model of a sophisticated society with a 30-year time horizon and a focus on resources, technology is the central issue of the RfF model. The input–output matrix expresses the actual technologies practiced in the database year (1968) as recorded in roughly 35,000 streams of purchases from each of 185 industrial groups to each other group. The technological coefficients of 1968 are then extrapolated into the future by a large number of exogenous assumptions, some general and economy-wide, and some sector-specific. Examples of general technological assumptions in the model are:

- Labor productivity will increase in all sectors at 2.5% per year (equivalent to the automatic exponential technical improvement in TEMPO and LTSM).
- The best available technology of 1968 in any area will become the average by the year 2000.
- No technical change will cause a shift in patterns of consumer demand; only population and income growth will influence final demand.
- Current technological trends will continue; there will be no dramatic breakthroughs or slowdowns.
- The historical relationship between GNP and energy use will not be changed.

In addition to these general assumptions, thousands of assumptions specific to certain industries and processes are included. For example, over the time horizon of the model polyvinylchloride pipe gradually replaces iron pipe, aluminum is widely substituted for copper, electricity is increasingly generated by nuclear reactors, and artificial sweeteners are used in place of sugar. Furthermore, the relationships between production in each sector, resource use, and pollution generated must be predicted exogenously as inputs to the model. This is done by sector by sector through equations such as the following:

$$\text{Demand}_{\text{resource } r} = \sum b^r_{jt}[X_{jt} + I_{jt}]$$

where X_{jt} is the total output of sector j in year t; I_{jt} is the total import purchase of sector j in year t; b_{jt} is the amount of resource r used per unit of output of sector j in year t.

$$\text{Pollution}_{\substack{\text{type } k \\ \text{year } t \\ \text{sector } j}} = (1 - b_t^k)\sum_j a^k_{jt} X_{jt}$$

where b_t^k is the economy-wide treatment efficiency of abatement processes for pollutant k in year t; a^k_{jt} is the amount of pollutant k generated per unit of product j in year t; X_{jt} is the total output of sector j in the year t. The coefficients in these equations can be changed to test pollution abatement or recycling policies.

Thus the RfF model draws an amazingly detailed picture of the technological development of an economy over time. The number of technological statements, all exogenous to the model, can be calculated roughly as:

```
        35,000   technical coefficients
      ×     30   years of simulation
     ──────────
     1,050,000   technical coefficients
+          185   resource-use coefficients (one for each industrial sector)
      ×     24   resources
     ──────────
         4,480
      ×     30   years of simulation
     ──────────
       134,400   resource coefficients
+          185   pollution-generation coefficients
      ×     13   pollutants
     ──────────
         2,405
      ×     30   years of simulation
     ──────────
        72,150   pollution-generation coefficients
+       72,150   pollution abatement coefficients
     ──────────
     1,328,700   exogenously-specified coefficients
```

KASM contains an entire submodel called CHANGE to represent technological change in agriculture. KASM also contains an optimization submodel, similar to but less detailed than CHAC, which generates farmers' decisions about how much land to plant in each crop each year. CHANGE produces the information needed for that submodel: the cropping technologies available from year to year, the yields they will give, the factor inputs they will require. Thus CHANGE is a crop-specific, factor-specific, dynamic model of technological development in agriculture.

The primary forces that alter agricultural technology in CHANGE are exogenous government policies. The development costs of these technologies are also exogenous. The policy instruments that can be represented and tested include the following:

1. Policies related to land and water development:
    a. Land and water improvement:
        (i) Multipurpose, large-scale, land development projects.
        (ii) Large-scale irrigation projects for paddy.
        (iii) Small-scale irrigation projects for paddy.
        (iv) Paddy consolidation projects.
        (v) Paddy drainage projects.
        (vi) Low productive paddy improvement projects.
        (vii) Upland irrigation projects.
        (viii) Upland consolidation projects.
    b. Land reclamation:
        (i) Tideland development projects.
        (ii) Upland development projects.
    c. Pastureland improvement program.
    d. Policies on agricultural land conservation.
2. Policies related to biological technology development (crop-specific):
    a. Research program.
    b. Guidance program.
3. Policies related to price controls:
    a. Product price policy (crop-specific).
    b. Factor price policy (factor-specific).
4. Agricultural finance policies:
    a. Credit program.
    b. Interest policies.

When a set of policies is chosen from this list and entered into the model, CHANGE then represents the diffusion of knowledge about each new technological option. The optimization component FRESAL then calculates its actual adoption. Since this part of the model falls into the category of explicit endogenous technology representations, we will return to it later, after discussing implicit technological change models.

In TEMPO, LTSM, and BACHUE technology changes implicitly through a process that does not at first seem to be technology-related—rural-urban migration. We will describe the assumptions that cause this migration in the next section. The result of it in these three models is to transfer laborers from a rural, traditional working environment to an urban, modern one. In other words, the models set up two different technological worlds and create a societal technological shift by moving people from one of these worlds into the other.

In TEMPO a new migrant to the city leaves a traditional-sector production function where labor is the only factor and his marginal contribution is small and diminishing. He enters (if he is hired) a modern productive system where his contribution is exponentially increasing. Furthermore, he immediately begins experiencing urban fertility and mortality rates. Even if he is not employed in the city, his absence raises marginal labor productivity in the traditional sector, and his transfer to the city decreases the birth rate.

In LTSM labor is not explicitly included in the production functions. The effect of migration into the hired-labor (urban) sphere is to remove pressure toward the acquisition of labor-saving capital. Large numbers of urban unemployed in this model depress wages and favor labor-intensive processes. Thus rural-urban migration slows down the rate at which modern industrial technology is adopted. Presumably a labor shortage would do the reverse, raise wages and encourage accumulation of capital, but LTSM represents a labor-excess society where this effect is never observed.

BACHUE contains a more disaggregated labor sector than either TEMPO or LTSM, and the distribution of workers is intricately connected with the operation of the economic system. Migration occurs not only from rural to urban areas, but among economic sectors so as to equilibrate wage differentials. Shifts in location and type of employment determine income distribution, which determines final demand, which determines output. Thus, although BACHUE assumes constant technical coefficients in its input–output matrix, its economy evolves toward a more modern technological mix by the growth of modern productive sectors at the expense of traditional ones.

Only two models contain explicit and endogenous theories about how technology changes. One theory, that in SOS, is aggregated and general; the other, in KASM, is particularized and specific.

Technology in SOS is embedded in all the decision rules by which the societal 'brain' reacts to the non-fulfillment of goals. For example, if production of copper is insufficient to meet demand, SOS contains instructions that initiate technologies to exploit new copper reserves. If these reserves also run low, the model will turn on technologies that allow aluminum to be substituted for copper, and will also specify how far that substitution can proceed in each productive sector. If pollution builds up beyond a tolerable level, resources are allocated to technologies that abate the pollution. In other words, in this model technology changes in response to perceived problems. The model assumptions include the problem threshold that will generate each technological response, the time delay, and sometimes the cost of the response, and the extent to which that response can be applied, after which, if the problem persists, a different and stronger kind of response is tried. Thus the model can generate 'future' technologies, responses that we have not yet seen to crises that have not yet occurred. Of course the general specifications of these technologies must be programmed into the model in advance, but their time and degree of application depend on events in the simulated economic system.

A general theory of adaptive technology like that in SOS is obviously suited to imaginative testing. What if we assume that any material can be substituted fully for any other or that no material can completely replace another? What if the point of adoption of recycling is raised or lowered? What if the delay times for shifting to new production methods are increased or shortened? Questions like these can be explored, at least in a general way, in the SOS model, and the logical conclusions and limitations of the technology-will-save-us theory, expressed in strong, weak, or moderate forms, can be displayed. Since this theory is a very common and controversial component of mental models, it is most helpful to have an explicit, testable version of it. Ideally such a computer model could move the discussion from an uresolvable debate over whether technology will or will not save us to a set of more operational questions about to what extent materials must be intersubstitutable or at what rate production processes will have to change in order for the productive system to avoid unpleasant futures.

We have already mentioned KASM's technology representations under two categories; the constant technical coefficients of its industrial sector, and the long list of agricultural technologies that can be tested exogenously as inputs to the CHANGE submodel. We have yet to describe KASM's major endogenous assumptions about technology; the assumptions by which the new technological options provided exogenously by the government become assimilated into the daily habits and choices of Korean farmers. Of all the models, this one is most explicit about the process of technology adoption.

A new technological possibility, such as a new type of rice with a 30% higher potential yield, is exogenously assumed, along with the factor inputs required, such as land type, fertilizer level, and labor. 'Adoption' of this particular technology is defined as acceptance of it as a factor to be entered into the farmers' decision submodel (called FRESAL). Thus adoption does not mean planting 100% of the potential land area with the new variety, but rather acceptance by 100% of the farmers of this rice variety as one to be weighed against other crops in the annual allocation of land to various crops.

The diffusion of adoption of the new rice variety is assumed to be basically sigmoid-shaped as shown in Figure 13.6. That is, any innovation is assumed to be adopted eventually, and the only questions are how quickly and over how

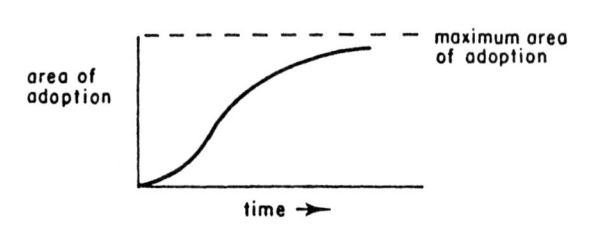

Figure 13.6

much land area. The point at which the curve levels off, the maximum area of adoption, is determined by the amount of land suitable for the new crop (for example it may only grow on irrigated paddyland) and by known regional crop specialization preferences (a region specializing in rice-growing will adopt a new rice variety over more of its suitable land than a new mulberry variety). The rate at which the adoption process approaches the maximum area is a function of public investment in promoting it (the extension budget) and of the intrinsic profitability of the new variety. Both of these factors are entered exogenously. It is assumed that the actual productivity gain at the farm level is less than at the experiment station, and that the gain drops as the area of adoption increases (because the better farms adopt first).

Thus the diffusion component of CHANGE keeps track of the extent to which any exogenously-introduced structural improvement is available to farmers in a given year. This information is then used, along with policy variables concerning credit and support prices, and input from other model sectors on product factor prices, to calculate the combination of factor inputs that will be chosen by farmers for each crop in each year. Given this combination of inputs, CHANGE uses its production function equations to calculate the expected yield of each crop in each region that year. This information is the primary output of CHANGE. It is fed to FRESAL, an optimization model, where expected yields, prices, and other information are used to determine how much land farmers will actually allocate to each crop. This decision is then recombined with the yield functions in CHANGE to compute the final production of each crop.

This complicated series of mathematical operations amounts to an extremely detailed account of technical change in agriculture. But the underlying theory is fairly understandable. Technological change is initiated by government decision and investment in various well-defined development options. The options are of two basic types:

1. Land and water resources, which become available after a delay but once available expand production permanently.
2. Biological technologies, which are represented by new input–output relationships, and which diffuse slowly (but inevitably) into the decision options of farmers. Farmers react to the various options according to rational economic optimization rules.

These farmer decisions can be further influenced by government through policies that release credit constraints or alter factor or product prices.

3. Summary and commentary

Virtually all the models in our survey represent the effects of new technology, not the causes. In only one model do technologies originate endogenously as specific responses to specific problems.

In some of the models technology is simply constant. In others it rains down magically to improve all productive processes exponentially and without cost. In most of the models specific technical changes appear suddenly from somewhere outside the system. Two models assume that new technologies are adopted and spread only as a function of their direct economic payoffs. One modeler has concluded that the effects of all technologies he has tested are bad for the system; in all the other models technologies produce only good. In only two models does technical change cost money or take time. No model explicitly relates technical change to the age structure or turnover rate of the capital plant. The representations of technological side effects, especially social and environmental ones, are minimal in all the models.

These limitations are common in mental models; in fact every person probably thinks of technology in each of these ways at different times and for different purposes. Our culture has obfuscated the word 'technology' so that its meaning is more related to faith than to hardware or human effort. Many policy decisions are made on the unspoken assumption that technology will not change, or that it will surely change so that production becomes more and more efficient, or that whatever problem turns up will eventually get solved. Technology is seen as something that happens to a society, not something a society chooses, and something that is intangible and ephemeral, not something that is embedded in the structure of machines or the education of people. Technological side effects are nearly always underestimated.

Yet each person's actual experiences with specific technical changes provide plenty of anecdotes that complicate any such simple picture. Hardware adjustments, costs, and delays are obvious, and they are crucial to any theory of technical adaptation, since they determine whether the adaptation can keep up with the rate of appearance of new problems and whether the solution of problems through technology can be afforded. Side effects, including social, psychological, and environmental ones, are also obvious and particularly important to the process of technological diffusion.

While fairly simple models of technology, constant or exponential, general or specific, costly or cost-free, may be sufficient for most everyday decisions, they are not very satisfying as bases for long-term social policy or for understanding of the process of industrialization. They provide no clue as to why the technological rain falls in some places and not in others, or why the most economically efficient technology is not uniformly adopted everywhere, or why some widely-recognized technology-related problems like hunger or cancer remain unsolved. They do not explain the observation that some societies have experienced internal technological innovation with industrialization (the U.S., most of Europe), some have exhibited innovation without industrialization (ancient China), some have industrialized rapidly with much of their technology adopted from outside (Japan, Taiwan), and some are slow to industrialize despite the availability of technology from outside (most of Africa). In fact, virtually every one of the technological hypotheses in the models can be put into one of two categories: either so vague and tautological that it is nonfalsifiable, or so easily falsified that it cannot be a useful basis for understanding or for policy.

We have no alternative theories of technology to put forward here. We can only point out that the current theories are far from adequate and thus that some startling new way of looking at technology is probably needed. For example, all the technology representations in our models are either monetary or physical; there is little to suggest that technology originates in the minds of humans. A few verbal models of technological-social-psychological interaction have been suggested. For example, E. F. Schumacher describes village-level intermediate technologies not only as improvements in the traditional productive processes, but also as inducers of new thought patterns, self-confidence, logic, and ingenuity.[10] Perhaps a theory of technology as information, combined with a theory of how the mind uses and generates new information, incorporated into a model of the physical expression of technology in capital plant, will be necessary before scientific understanding of industrialization can be achieved.

D. MIGRATION AND LABOR ALLOCATION

We have mentioned the theory that industrialization is fueled by the investment of deferred consumption into capital for expanding future production. This theory could be augmented to say that industrialization can happen only when workers leave the farm and come to the city to operate the capital that is accumulating from deferred consumption. According to this theory an optimal development process will generate rural-urban migration at just the rate the growing capital plant of the cities can absorb workers; not so slowly that the machines stay idle, and not so rapidly that unemployed migrants pile up in urban slums. Whether rural-urban migration is a cause of industrialization, an effect, or both, the two processes are certainly closely associated. Non-industrialized societies typically have a population that is 80% rural, while most industrialized countries are 80% or more urban.

A theory of rural-urban migration is usually related to a theory of labor allocation; an explanation of how workers find jobs, and especially how they shift jobs in an economy that is changing its labor needs. Shifting jobs within one location is not quite the same as moving from one location to another, especially when one place is a traditional homestead and the other is a growing city. The decisions that lead to rural-urban migration involve more than just shifting jobs, because life is more than just work. Therefore a labor allocation theory may be part of a migration theory, but it is typically not all of one. As we shall see, some of the nine models contain theories of labor allocation but not migration, some contain migration representations but not labor allocation, and some contain both.

1. Mental models

What causes people to move from one job to another and from one place to another? Sociological theories of migration usually contain three types of explanatory factors:

1. A 'push' from the place of origin due to unsatisfactory conditions like unemployment or low wages.
2. A 'pull' to the destination from some perceived attraction of the city such as better jobs or bright lights and glamor.
3. 'Intervening obstacles' that might prevent migration even in the presence of destination-pull and origin-push; such factors as separation from relatives, transportation costs, or simply fear of strange places.[11]

The concepts of push, pull, and intervening obstacles involve unmeasured values and perceptions as well as some tangible quantities such as wages, distances, or costs of living. And all three concepts can be applied to job-change decisions as well as location-change decisions.

'Push' and 'pull' must enter into the decisions of an individual to migrate or change jobs through some complex set of impressions about what the places of origin and destination are like *relative to each other*. This set of impressions has been termed 'relative attractiveness',[12] a potential migrant's mental compendium of how the perceived home village and the perceived city compare along all the dimensions of importance to him or her. It could include such factors as jobs and wages, cost of living, pleasantness of environment, personal contacts, and presence or absence of discrimination. Each person's perception of the relative attractiveness of home versus any potential destination is probably different, because each person would define attractiveness differently and would have unique perceptions of various places. Because it is based on perception, the relative attractiveness upon which a migration decision is based might change, even if neither of the places being compared actually change. For example, a radio program or personal report might provide new information to the potential migrant. Actual changes in either origin or destination will probably change most people's assessment of relative attractiveness, though perhaps only after some delay. The perception delay is probably much longer for the place of destination than for the place of origin.

The perception of a difference in relative attractiveness may not necessarily result in a decision to move, because of intervening obstacles, which might also be defined as the inverse of mobility or predisposition to migrate. This might be influenced by such factors as age, education, self-confidence, class, race, commitment to property or family, bulk of personal possessions, and ability to purchase a bus ticket or rent a moving van. Any group of people probably could be classified along a mobility spectrum; some would be willing and able to move at the slightest hint of a gap in relative attractiveness, most would have to perceive quite a gap before they would leave, and a few simply would not move, even if their home were threatened by a Mongol invasion. Both statistical studies and common sense indicate that young, educated, middle-income, or propertyless people are more mobile than old, uneducated, poor, or landowning ones.

The ideas of relative attractiveness and mobility can comprise at best only a beginning of the theory needed to explain the great wave of migration that accompanies industrialization. For one thing, they are micro-theories. They may shed light on the behavior of individuals, but they are not easily aggregated into whole populations or easily related to other aspects of the industrialization process. How do population growth and technical change affect migration rates? How does a population with primarily agricultural skills become aware of and fitted for industrial employment? Why in recent decades have migrants flooded into urban areas much faster than the rate at which jobs or even basic urban services have been provided?

Furthermore, relative attractiveness and mobility are static concepts. Even if one could measure relative attractiveness and mobility for a given population at a specified place at a certain moment and thereby explain the migration flow at that moment, one would have to go on to understand how that migration itself could in the future change the attractiveness of both origin and destination and the mobility of the population so as to affect future migration flows.

2. Computer models

The nine computer models vary greatly in the comprehensiveness and sophistication of their migration and labor allocation functions (see Figure 13.7). The simplest formulations, which we shall discuss here first, occur in SAHEL, which contains an origin-push emigration function and no labor allocation function, and in RfF and KASM, which contain exogenous migration and labor allocation functions. CHAC and the agricultural part of KASM have essentially nothing to say about migration, but contain fairly complex labor allocation mechanisms based on market equilibrium theory. SOS is also uninformative about migration, but extends the market theory to include non-equilibrium modes. *MexicoV* is not concerned with labor allocation at all, but contains a first attempt at a full, dynamic relative-attractiveness theory of rural–urban migration. And finally, the three models TEMPO, LTSM, and BACHUE have fully-linked, dynamic, non-equilibrium theories of migration and labor allocation, including many of the effects of these processes on other parts of the system, such as capital-labor substitution, income distribution, and human fertility.

The SAHEL nomad society has not evolved much division of labor, so a labor allocation process is not necessary. SAHEL represents only the origin of the migration stream and therefore contains only half of a migration theory. The nomads are assumed to move to and from the Sahel region depending upon the food supply there, relative only to the basic subsistence need of the population. It is assumed that when food *per capita* in the Sahel is higher than subsistence, there is a very slow net migration into the region. As food *per*

Migration

1. None
   - RfF
   - CHAC

2. Exogenous
   - KASM

3. Origin push
   - SAHEL
   - SOS

4. Relative attractiveness
   - Mexico V
   - TEMPO
   - LTSM
   - BACHUE

Labor Allocation

1. None
   - SAHEL
   - MEXICO V

2. Exogenous
   - RfF
   - KASM non-agriculture

3. Market allocation
   - CHAC } equilibrium
   - KASM-agriculture }
   - SOS } non-equilibrium

4. Capital-labor substitution
   - TEMPO
   - LTSM

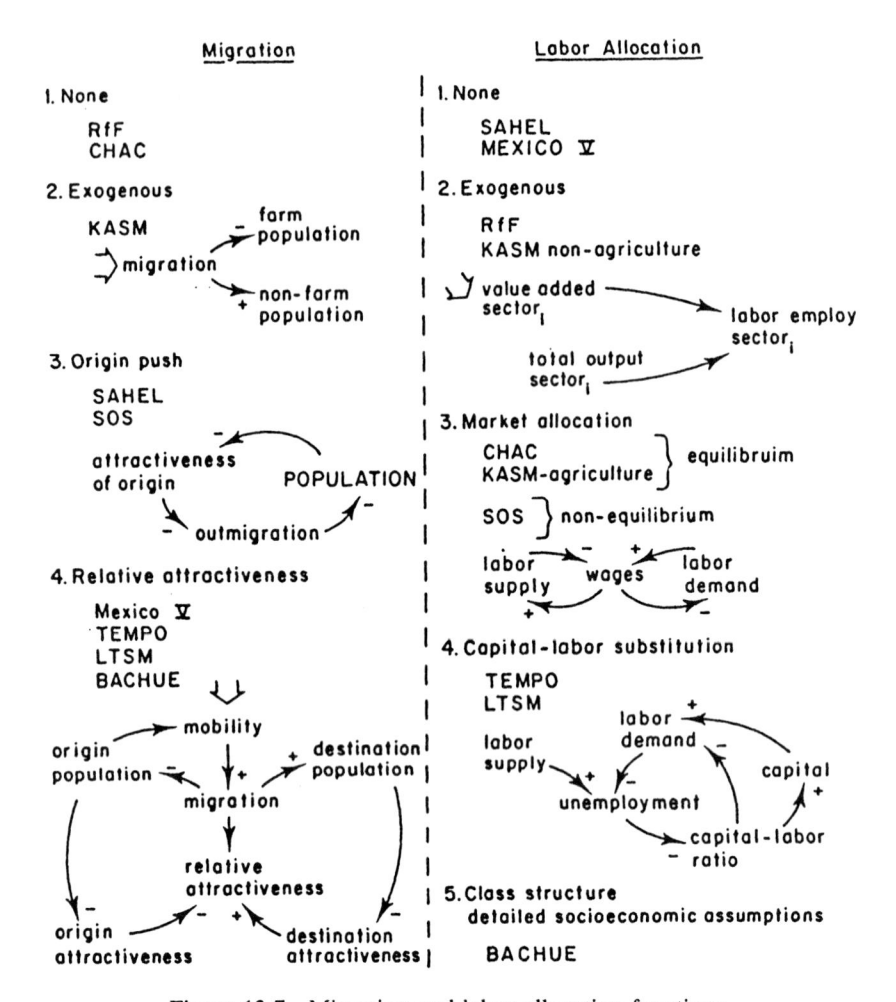

5. Class structure
   detailed socioeconomic assumptions
   - BACHUE

Figure 13.7 Migration and labor allocation functions

capita drops toward subsistence, the inmigration rate approaches zero, and if it falls below subsistence, the population begins to outmigrate at an increasingly rapid rate. The migration response is not instantaneous, but is a function of the food levels of the last three years, exponentially smoothed. This is a simple origin-push model. It says that the nomads will prefer to stay in the Sahel no matter what the conditions in neighbouring territories, and that the only conditions under which they will leave are those of desperation, when the choice is between migration or starvation. Given that choice, they will leave, regardless of whether starvation may also be awaiting them at the destination. Despite the simplicity of this hypothesis, it seems to duplicate the actual behavior of the Sahel nomads during the drought of the early 1970s. An origin-push model is probably appropriate for a society with rigid, tribal habits, low aspirations, and very little information about the outside world.

RfF is concerned with an industrialized country whose rural-urban shift is presumably completed. It does not distinguish urban and rural populations. Labor is allocated among the 185 sectors of the input–output matrix according to exogenous value-added assumptions for each sector. The economy as a whole is assumed to grow at such a rate as to maintain essentially full (96%) employment. Thus labor is allocated smoothly to where it is needed, and the economy automatically absorbs all the workers that may appear. Problems of urbanization, labor allocation, and unemployment cannot be explored at all with this model. Given that the purpose of the exercise was to advise a population commission on the economic and environmental effects of different rates of population growth, the choices of aggregation and emphasis in this model seem inept. On the one hand, the computer can print out with precision the apparent number of workers and the wage rates in any of the 185 productive sectors in any year. On the other hand, it can say nothing about the influence of population growth on job availability, on patterns of urbanization and thus distribution of pollution, or on wages and hence technical or capital-investment decisions.

In KASM three kinds of migration are distinguished. First, military service takes a significant number of 20–24 year old males out of both urban and rural labor pools. The exact number is specified exogenously. Second, net emigration out of Korea is also exogenous to the model. It is assumed to be drawn entirely from the non-farm population. Third, rural–urban migration takes place, usually exogenously, although at the option of the user it can also be made a function of the labor demand-supply gap in the non-farm economy—in other words as destination pull. In either case a total rural–urban migration figure is calculated, and then it is apportioned among age and sex categories according to weighting factors determined from historical migration patterns. For all three of these migration functions the degree of detail and the amount of data required seem unnecessary for the purpose of the model and disproportionate to the simplicity of the exogenous causal structure.

Like RfF, in its non-farm economy KASM allocates laborers to the sectors of the input–output matrix just as they are needed according to the exogenous value-added coefficients. KASM allocates farm laborers through an optimization routine simulating farmers' profit maximization decisions in a free market. Two labor constraints appear in the program, one for peak-season laborers and one for the rest of the year.

CHAC represents a country with very rapid rural–urban migration, but the model represents only the agricultural sector of the country and only for one year. Therefore rural–urban migration is omitted from the model. CHAC does calculate seasonal rural–rural migration of landless laborers and of owners of unirrigated farms during the dry season. Four regional labor pools are specified. Within each region labor is distributed and wages calculated as part of the simultaneous solution of the model's optimization equations. If there are excess laborers in one region, they can be hired into another region for a higher wage. When the model is run for some year in the future, assumptions about rural–urban migration, like other population assumptions, must be made off-line to set up the labor constraints for that year. CHAC provides a detailed account of the shocking rate of rural unemployment in Mexico, but it offers no information about its causes or cures.

The labor allocation by optimization in both KASM and CHAC differs sharply from the input–output allocation in RfF, in that labor can be a limiting factor to production or, alternatively, labor can be unemployed if other factors are limiting. Farmers are assumed to shift their planting schemes in response to labor shortage (as well as shortage of other factors) to make most profitable use of the workers available. In KASM, where the optimization model is embedded in a dynamic simulation model, further adjustments can be made in subsequent years—wages can rise or fall, or investment in machinery can substitute capital for labor where there is economic benefit in doing so.

SOS, like RfF, the other model of the United States, is not concerned with rural–urban distribution and is not disaggregated along rural–urban lines. It does contain a theory of net immigration or emigration into or out of the country, however. Under 'normal' conditions, when the U.S. employment rate is 95% or more, it is assumed that there will be a net immigration of 0.2% of the U.S. population every year. If the employment rate drops, the immigration rate decreases until, at 90% or lower, it becomes net outmigration. This formulation is equivalent to the origin-push assumption of SAHEL, except that unemployment rather than starvation is the source of the push.

SOS contains quite a detailed theory of labor allocation among the industrial sectors; it is, as one might expect, a cybernetic, feedback-based theory. The SOS population is divided into four age cohorts: 1–17 (immature), 18–24 (young adults), 25–64 (working adults), and 65+ (retired). Each of these cohorts is further divided into six functional partitions:

1. In education.
2. In institutions.
3. Non-workers.
4. In training.
5. Paid workers.
6. Unpaid workers (housewives).

These 24 population groups must be allocated to satisfy the labor demands of twelve productive sectors. Each sector contains a technical matrix specifying for 20 different factors of production how much of each factor is required per unit of output of that sector. Labor is factor 18. Each year the desired output of each sector is calculated, which, when multiplied by the matrix, gives the total requirement for each factor, including labor. If the total labor available is not sufficient for the demand, production is reduced in that year. In the next year corrective measures begin to take effect; wages in the sector rise, and as a result labor is transferred from other sectors or from the unpaid labor population, or some other more abundant factor of production is substituted for labor, or demand for the product of that sector is reduced. The corrective measures may take some time, and they may not be sufficient. This formulation differs from the one in RfF and KASM-non-farm, in that labor does not automatically and instantaneously appear where it is needed. It is similar to CHAC and KASM-farm in that it contains the same three basic adjustment mechanisms that they do: a shortage of labor can bring about:

1. More labor supply.
2. Less labor demand through production cutback.
3. Less labor demand through substitution of some other factor.

The difference is that in SOS the adjustments are not instantaneous or optimal. The labor market in SOS need not ever be in equilibrium.

MexicoV is too aggregated to need a labor allocation function. It does not specify different economic sectors, nor does it represent labor as a factor of production. It does, however, have a rural–urban migration function, primarily because Beltran-del-Rio perceived migration to be a dominant trend in Mexico, one that he wanted to explain. He mentions as facts of concern to him that urban labor productivity is five times rural, that a Mexican urban worker has eight times as much capital to work with as does his rural counterpart, and that the population shifted from 43% urban in 1950 to 58% in 1968. The rural–urban distribution does not affect anything else in the model, except itself, through a feedback to be described in a moment, and, partially and indirectly, the inflation rate.

According to *MexicoV* the fraction of population in urban areas can be forecast by the equation:

ratio of urban to total population = $a + b*\text{time} + c*(\text{gap between urban and rural productivity})$ distributed lag

The lag is distributed over three years. The gap between urban and rural productivity is defined as the urban productive capacity per urban person minus the rural productive capacity per rural person, where productive capacity in each place is a linear function of the capital stock. Note the use of time as a driving factor in this equation and also the fact that migrants respond to potential productivity, not the actual capacity utilized or the actual employment rates.

This migration formulation amounts to two negative feedback loops (Figure 13.8). Over a long enough time span they should operate in the model to equalize urban and rural productivity (or perhaps to keep urban productivity lower than rural because of the 'time' term in the migration equation). The real system, however, seems to be behaving in the opposite way—the productivity gap is widening in favor of the urban population. According to the *MexicoV* hypothesis, this can occur only if urban capital is growing at a rate faster than migration can occur.

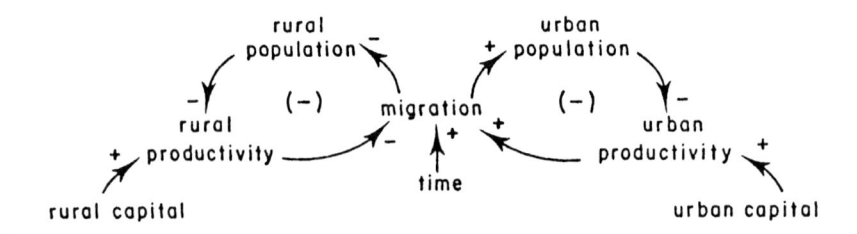

Figure 13.8 Migration in *MexicoV*

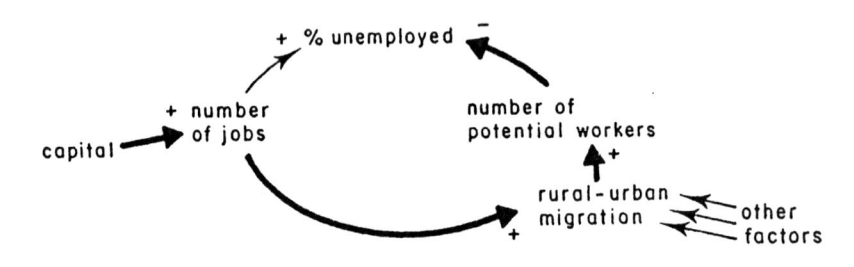

Figure 13.9 Causation vs correlation in migration

Beltran del Rio also includes in his labor participation equations an implicit hypothesis about the demographic attributes of migrants. The urban participation rate (% of eligible workers actually working) in the model *decreases* as urban capital *increases* and as idle capacity *decreases*. In other words, more jobs are correlated with a lower percentage of the labor force working. The reasoning given for this surprising correlation is that more urban capital and higher capacity utilization stimulate the flow of rural-urban migrants, who are the poorest families with the lowest ratios of workers to dependents. As these migrants come to the city, the ratio of workers to the total population falls.[13] Beltran del Rio came to this conclusion after reviewing the historical evidence; from 1950 to 1968 in Mexico, during the period of rapid capital growth, urban labor participation fell from 31.9% to 27.3%, while the rural labor participation rate rose from 31.6% to 37.1%.

The problem here is a classic confusion between correlation and causation. What probably happens is that the number of jobs increases employment directly, as it logically should, but because migration is influenced by more factors than jobs alone, in-migration overbalances this effect and increases the labor pool even faster (Figure 13.9). A model derived from historical data will catch only the net effect, outlined by the heavy arrows in the diagram above, which indicates that capital decreases employment. But in Mexico migration has proceeded quite independently from urban job availability and must be responding primarily to some other factors. These factors could be overpopulation, poverty, and desperate lack of opportunity in rural areas.

The remaining three models, TEMPO, LTSM, and BACHUE, contain interlinked theories of labor allocation and migration, with explicit consideration of the characteristics of both origin and destination and of the mobility of potential migrants. We will discuss them in order of increasing complexity, starting with TEMPO.

The net rural–urban migration flow in TEMPO is a function of the ratio of income of the uneducated modern population to the income of the subsistence population. The equation is:

$$\text{migration} = m_1 * R^{m_2} * \text{subsistence population}$$

where

$$R = \frac{W * \text{modern gross product}}{\text{uneducated modern population}} \bigg/ \frac{\text{subsistence gross product}}{\text{subsistence population}}$$

In this equation W is the wage income share of the uneducated modern labor force (the exponent of uneducated labor in the Cobb–Douglas production function), m_1 is an initialization constant, and m_2 expresses the sensitivity of the subsistence population to changes in the modern/subsistence income ratio. Thus m_2 summarizes in one constant value mobility and perception factors such as cost of migration, cost of living, cultural preferences, etc. If $m_2 = 0$, net migration is simply a constant proportion (m_1) of the subsistence population, regardless of conditions in either origin or destination. If $m_2 = 1$, the proportion migrating varies directly with the income ratio. Typically in the model m_2 lies between 0 and 1. Total migration calculated from this equation is then distributed across age and sex groups by exogenous weighting factors as in KASM.

This formulation causes migration to increase if the subsistence population increases, or as the modern sector output increases from some other factor such as technology. Migration decreases if the subsistence sector output increases, or if unemployment in the modern sector increases. Relative attractiveness is summarized by the single index of average income differential. Mobility is capsulated in the constant m_2 and the age-sex weightings. Migration responds without delay to income changes, and migrants instantly adopt the fertility and productivity of the urban uneducated population.

The feedback structure of this migration hypothesis is similar to but more explicit than that of *MexicoV* (see Figure 13.10). As rural–urban migration proceeds, it begins to choke itself off by diluting the wage income of the urban sector and raising the relative income of the remaining rural population. These two inner negative loops should work as in *MexicoV* to equalize incomes in the two sectors, at which point migration stops.

The two outer positive loops of Figure 13.10 are not in *MexicoV*. They express the positive contribution of the population to *per capita* income through labor. Since in TEMPO labor in the subsistence sector is subject to diminishing returns and uneducated labor in the modern sector has relatively

[Figure: diagram showing relationships between rural population, urban population, subsistence sector income, rural-urban migration, modern sector income, subsistence sector production, modern/subsistence income gap, modern sector production, technology, and capital]

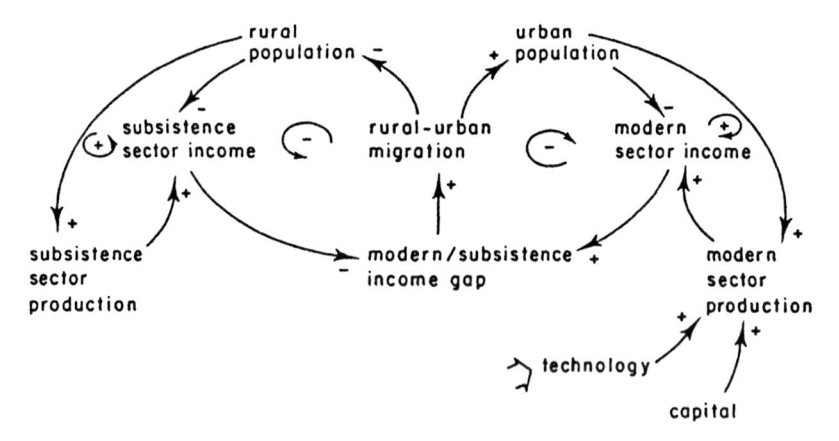

Figure 13.10 Migration in TEMPO

low productivity, these outer positive loops are not very strong. The entire migration structure is dragged along by technology and capital increases in the modern sector, which exponentially raise incomes and thus spur rural–urban migration.

Labor allocation in TEMPO is fairly simple, since there are only two productive sectors, subsistence and modern, and three types of labor, subsistence, uneducated modern, and educated modern. The primary allocation is the migration formulation just discussed, which shifts uneducated workers between subsistence and modern employment. The educated modern labor pool is determined by government educational spending as it accumulates in the age structure of the population. Labor participation rates by age, sex, and educational status are constant and exogenous. Educated labor force employment is assumed to be a constant fraction of the educated labor force available. The fraction of the uneducated labor force actually employed depends on the capital–labor ratio. As the amount of capital per laborer increases, the fraction of laborers employed increases asymptotically up to some maximum employment level. The incremental capital–labor ratio depends on the amount of unemployment, so that in a tight labor market capital additions create fewer jobs than in a period of high unemployment. This is a shortcut method for representing the effect of wages on labor-replacing capital without actually bothering to represent wages.

LTSM contains migration and labor allocation functions somewhat similar to those in TEMPO. The major difference is in the greater disaggregation (ten economic sectors, seven in the hired-labor sphere, and three in the family-labor sphere). The LTSM rural–urban migration equation is:

$$\text{migration}_t = \text{migration}_{t-1} * \frac{\text{rural population}_t}{\text{rural population}_{t-1}} * \frac{\text{gravity multiplier}_t}{\text{gravity multiplier}_{t-1}} * \text{productivity differential multiplier}$$

The gravity multiplier occurs again in BACHUE (in fact the LTSM modelers adapted it from BACHUE). It expresses the idea that migration between two places is more likely to occur when the populations of both places are about equal than when either one place or the other has a great excess of people. The gravity multiplier is:

$$\frac{(\text{rural population}) \times (\text{urban population})}{\text{total population}^2}$$

It attains its highest value (0.25) when the two populations are equal and is zero if the population is totally rural or urban.

The productivity differential multiplier in LTSM's migration equation is a function of the rate of change of net product per laborer in the hired-labor sector compared to that in the family-labor sector. The concept of relative attractiveness therefore is, as in TEMPO, dependent upon output per person (not per employed laborer). LTSM's migration theory is different from TEMPO's only by the addition of the gravity multiplier and by the formulation of all relationships in terms of rates of change.

LTSM is a model of a labor-surplus economy, and therefore the labor allocation problem is not so much how to distribute workers where they are needed as how to distribute unemployment among workers of various sectors. The change in employment in the seven hired-labor economic sectors each year is proportional to the change in the amount of capital in each sector. The proportionality factor, called the incremental employment–capital ratio, may decline if the unemployment rate declines; that is, if labor ceases to be abundant and cheap, capital will become less labor intensive. The change does not occur in the reverse direction; high unemployment does not cause the substitution of labor for capital. In the modern agriculture sector the employment–capital ratio may be negative. Within the urban and rural areas it is assumed that labor instantly becomes available to whatever economic sector needs it; across the rural–urban boundary migration has to take place first. In the family-labor sectors employment is not calculated; it is assumed that all available labor is absorbed, and therefore labor productivity is relatively low.

LTSM thus raises the interesting question of why in areas of chronic labor surplus economies still proceed inexorably in the direction of increasing capital intensity instead of labor intensity. Unfortunately, instead of attempting to explain this puzzling behavior, LTSM simply assumes it.

As might be expected of a model made by and for the International Labor Organization, labor allocation and migration are central components of BACHUE. The theories behind these components are rich in detail. Migration is calculated both from rural to urban areas and vice versa and is disaggregated by age, sex, education, and marital status. A series of exogenous mobility assumptions determines the propensity to migrate in each direction for individuals in each class. Educated people are highly likely to move from rural to urban areas but not the reverse, single persons are more mobile than married in both directions, etc. These migration propensities are then multiplied by a relative attractiveness indicator, the ratio of destination to origin income for jobs of the skill level that matches each education category. The entire migration function is then multiplied by a gravity multiplier as explained under LTSM. Thus BACHUE contains three sorts of inputs to migration: a detailed series of micro-level mobility assumptions, a macro-level assumption that relative attractiveness is determined by income, and the gravity multiplier.

BACHUE's intricate labor-allocation mechanism distributes laborers among five urban production categories and four rural ones. It begins by calculating labor participation, that part of the population in rural and urban areas that are willing to be employed. Labor participation is not exogenous as it is in many of the models, nor does it depend solely on economic variables such as wages. The BACHUE modelers believe that labor force participation is primarily sociologically determined and that anyone who really needs a job will get one, although it may be in a relatively unproductive traditional sector. Virtually all male household heads are assumed to work. Other family members tend to work more if they are educated, more if the family is in a lower income decile, more if modern-sector employment is available, more if the household head is operating a traditional, family-based enterprise, and more if there are not many children to be cared for.

The labor force calculated according to all these factors is then allocated to economic sectors by a three-step process. First the total valued added (labor cost) of each sector is calculated in the economic part of the model. The shares of value added that go to the entrepreneur/profit receiver class, the skilled workers, and the unskilled workers are also determined—they are assumed to follow the historical patterns of other countries at different stages of industrialization. These calculations result essentially in a money pool to be divided up in the second step among the workers in each class (which has already been determined in the labor participation calculation). The division gives the mean income sector by sector for each group. In the third step intercategory labor migration and rural–urban migration proceed in response to income differentials and in directions that tend to equalize them. An exogenously specified elasticity indicates how much labor movement will occur for given wage differentials between each pair of categories. These elasticities contain numerous socioeconomic assumptions: it is easier to move from modern to traditional sectors than vice versa, it is difficult to move into the self-employment profit-sharing class, it is easy to move from one area of skilled employment to another. Because of the different elasticities, the delays in the migration flows, and assumed standard and accepted wage differentials between various categories of jobs, labor migration flows never come close to equalizing incomes. As in SOS, the system is always moving in the direction of equilibrium but never achieving it.

3. Summary and commentary

More than half the modelers in our survey mention unemployment and migration as major forces and major problems in the countries they are modeling. Five of the models, however, contain no representation of migration or labor shifts, or make them exogenous, thereby leaving the theorizing to mental models. Others allocate labor smoothly according to the needs of an input–output table or an optimizing program. These models record the fact that labor re-allocation takes place, but they offer no clear reasons why it takes place, nor can they deal with any of the problems associated with delays or insufficiencies in the response of human workers to the changing needs of the productive system, or vice versa. One model represents a delayed, imperfect, problematic response of labor force to shifting economic needs. Three models attempt to capture management decisions about labor-capital substitutions. No model deals explicitly with household decisions about labor–leisure substitutions, although BACHUE does so implicitly.

The concept of relative attractiveness is contained in four of the nine models, but only one aspect of relative attractiveness, income or its surrogate labor productivity, is taken into account. No model contains an explicit hypothesis about the information people have access to before deciding whether to migrate, especially the imperfections in that information. In several cases the coefficient relating relative income to migration flow is inelastic, allowing a large income gap between city and country to persist. But no account is given of *why* it is inelastic.

The representations of migration and labor allocation in TEMPO, LTSM, and especially BACHUE are fairly complex and probably come about as far as social understanding of this interface between economic structure and family decision-making has progressed. Few of the models can explain or even reproduce some of the greatest mysteries of the labor allocation process; why migrants continue to come to the city when unemployment is high, why the urban–rural income gap persists in the face of this high unemployment, why the migration and labor absorption process seems to have proceeded relatively smoothly in the history of the now-industrialized nations but is going so roughly in the now-industrializing ones.[14] The only policy advice one could deduce for governments concerned about too-rapid urbanization would be to raise incomes or install capital in rural areas, a conclusion most people can reach via mental models.

On the positive side, several of the models recognize the importance of migration as a subtle influence on other aspects of a developing economy. Migration is a rapid, effective, individual response to economic problems or opportunities. It is usually more obvious and promising, and therefore more often elected, than other possible responses, such as changing one's personal habits or values, or attempting to improve the environment at the place of origin. When this individual response is aggregated into significant migration flows, it has multiple effects on the place of origin, the place of destination, and on the migrants themselves. Some of these effects can be surprising. Migration can dilute or confound regional development policies, transferring costs and benefits to regions or types of people quite different from the ones for whom they were intended.

The models in the survey, especially BACHUE, have fulfilled a valuable function in identifying migration as an integral and insufficiently understood process in industrialization, a process that can divert apparently straightforward policy efforts and produce unexpected results. Insofar as modeling is a progressive field, this discovery should inspire further experimentation, observation, and hypotheses about the role of rural–urban migration in industrializing economies.

E. ENVIRONMENT AND NATURAL RESOURCES

An industrialized society is built not only from capital, labor, and technology, but also from petroleum, iron, soil, water, sunlight, and the services of natural processes that recycle nutrients and carry away wastes. Healthy, functioning natural systems are a form of real economic wealth, although not a form that is easily measured in monetary terms.

Industrialization in the past did not seem to be related to resources or the environment in any simple way. Abundant coal and iron reserves were obviously instrumental in the mechanization of Britain. The United States certainly based its industrial growth on virgin forests, prime soils, and plentiful mineral deposits. Current industrialization in Venezuela and Saudi Arabia is clearly related to petroleum. But other countries like Japan, Switzerland, and Hungary industrialized without great domestic resource endowments, and resource-rich countries like Brazil and India have been late to develop industrially. So the availability of cheap, nearby resources seems neither a necessary nor a sufficient condition for the earliest stages of industrialization.

However, the maintenance of an industrial society once it has developed certainly requires immense, continuous flows of resources. And the cost of maintaining a 'natural capital stock' that yields a steady output of resource goods and environmental services can become a significant fraction of the expense of running an industrial system. In other words, a growing industrial society puts an increased burden on its natural support systems, and there are diminishing returns to the utilization of those systems. At some point natural resources rather than capital or labor can become limiting factors of production.

1. Mental models

Economists tend to see an industrial society as a circular and complex flow of money, rather like the circulation of the blood through the many branches and capillaries of the human cardiovascular system. If resources are in this picture at all, they are coupled to and driven by the flow of money. Faster money streams will induce larger resource streams. The physical origins of these resources, and the environmental sinks to which they flow once they are used are not really very much in focus.

Ecologists are more likely to see a process akin to the digestive system; an open-ended transformation of energy and materials from low-entropy concentrated deposits in the earth, through refining processes, into manufactured goods, and finally into scattered, high-entropy waste deposits, with a continuous dispersal of respiratory by-products at every step along the way. This one-way flow of materials through the human society is linked to all the great circular flows of materials through nature; the hydrologic cycle that moves fresh water from the sea through rain onto the land and back to the sea, the nitrogen cycle that restores soluble nitrogen as a nutrient for plants in the soil, and all the other cycles, driven by solar energy, that move and regenerate the materials necessary for life. If one views the human society as a pipe, attached to the finely tuned cyclical natural system, removing materials in virgin form at the one end and spewing them forth degraded and sometimes poisonous at the other, one asks quite different questions and worries about different problems than does one who sees the environment as an inert, infinite background that yields up resources in response to the circulation of money.

Clearly both the economic and ecological views are partially correct. Economic activity may not create resources that were not already there, but only scientific knowledge and labor and human-produced capital can make resources like undersea petroleum or enriched uranium accessible and useful. Intensive farming may deplete the nutrients in soil, but it also may replenish them. Increasing use of fossil fuels may make more minerals or fresh water accessible, and it may, at the same time, create acid rain or CO_2-induced climate change. An industrializing economy and its natural environment interact with each other in thousands of different ways; the economy may exhaust or enrich the environment, the environment may support or limit the economy. Because of the immensity of the environmental system and the technical changeability of the economic one, decades or even centuries may pass before the consequences of their mutual interactions are revealed.

2. Computer models

A complete representation of the role of natural resources in the process of industrialization would require a model of the entire ecological system as well as the economic one. Such a model would be hopelessly complex, even if knowledge of both systems were sufficient for it to be made. The modelers in our survey have handled this difficult area in four basic ways (see Figure 13.11).

1. Three models simply do not include resources or the environment.
2. Three models represent the impact of some resource constraints on the economic system, but not the impact of the economy on the resource base.
3. One model contains assumptions about the impact of the economic system on the resource base, but not the reverse.
4. Two models attempt to close the feedback loop and represent both the effect of the economy on the environment and vice versa.

1. NONE - beyond general diminishing returns

$$\begin{pmatrix} \text{MEXICO V} \\ \text{BACHUE} \\ \text{TEMPO} \end{pmatrix}$$

2. RESOURCE CONSTRAINT ON PRODUCTION

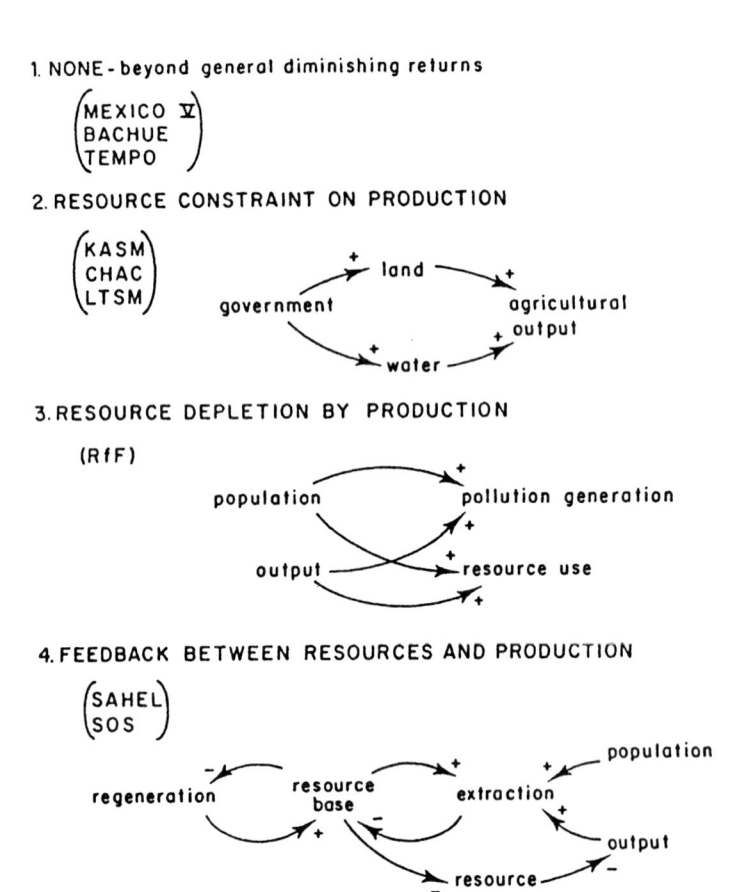

$$\begin{pmatrix} \text{KASM} \\ \text{CHAC} \\ \text{LTSM} \end{pmatrix}$$

3. RESOURCE DEPLETION BY PRODUCTION

(RfF)

4. FEEDBACK BETWEEN RESOURCES AND PRODUCTION

$$\begin{pmatrix} \text{SAHEL} \\ \text{SOS} \end{pmatrix}$$

Figure 13.11 Resource and environment functions

MexicoV contains no hint of environmental factors, and resources do not appear in any form in its production equations. Monetary values of exports of lead, copper, gold, silver, and zinc are calculated in the foreign exchange sector, but all of these are determined exogenously. It is implicitly assumed that no environmental or resource factor, including land, water, or domestic supplies of exported metals, will significantly affect the Mexican economy over the time horizon of the model. Since the time horizon is so short, this assumption is probably appropriate.

BACHUE and TEMPO also contain no explicit representation of any environmental factor. They do contain implicit recognition of resource limitations, however. In the subsistence sector of TEMPO the production function exhibits diminishing returns to labor, which is an indirect way to represent the effect of a fixed supply of land. Presumably the rate at which labor productivity diminishes could be adjusted for countries with more or fewer land resources. BACHUE also recognizes land limitations in its labor productivity assumption. It sets an upper bound of 2% per year on the rate of growth of labor productivity in agriculture. This limitation is much less strict than TEMPO's; it is not an absolute limit but a statement that the combined effects of land development and yield increases can gradually overcome natural limits but cannot double the limits more than once in 35 years.

The three models that represent resource limitations to production explicitly (but not the effects of production on resources) are all agricultural: KASM, CHAC, and LTSM. In KASM and CHAC agricultural resources are represented in detail, land of various types in various geographical locations, water from natural rainfall, tubewells, and canals. These constraints are assumed to be increased at a cost, by exogenous investment in land reclamation, irrigation networks, etc. They are not decreased by anything. Erosion, water pollution, disintegration of irrigation facilities, and salting of soils through improper drainage are not included. CHAC is sufficiently short-term that mechanisms of environmental degradation can safely be ignored. KASM with a 15-year time horizon is on the borderline.

LTSM assumes no water constraint but does include land in the agricultural production function. Land under cultivation can be increased by government reclamation (apparently at no cost) and reduced by construction activity. Land is not really an effective limiting factor, however, because yield per unit of land is exponentially and automatically increased without limit by material inputs (fertilizer).

None of these models represents plant genetics, insect communities, soil quality, or the use of solar or fossil-fuel energy in agricultural processes. KASM and CHAC include fertilizers, insecticides, and machinery as factors of production, but do not follow the effects of fertilizer run-off, insecticide resistance, or machinery-induced soil compaction. The dependence of modern agriculture on petroleum, both directly through machinery and indirectly through fertilizers and other petrochemicals, is also absent.

The RfF model is the only one of the nine that attempts to calculate in great detail what resources are used by industrial production and what pollutants are generated. The output of each of 185 industrial sectors is translated by exogenous coefficients into usage rates for 19 minerals and 13 types of pollution. The mineral use coefficients are derived from 1976 data relating resource quantities consumed to dollar values of output for each industrial sector. Coefficients for future years are altered by exogenous technical change assumptions that we have already discussed.

Only short-lived pollutants, such as sulfur oxides and airborne particulates (as opposed to long-lived pollutants such as heavy metals and some pesticides, industrial chemicals, and radioisotopes) are considered. Therefore pollutants do not accumulate in the model; the amount present at any time is assumed equal to the amount generated in that year.

Each pollutant is discharged, by another set of coefficients, to the three receiving media, water, air, and land, and the total national pollution load in each medium is further broken down into geographic regions; water pollution into 22 water resource regions, and air pollution into 95 metropolitan areas. A wealth of different pollution abatement policies can be tested and their costs compiled. There is also no representation of the long-term dynamics of the receiving media; no toxic build-up in groundwater, no acid rain, no climate change, no soil erosion.

All these calculations of resource use and pollution generation are based on the basic input–output model that recursively generates dollar flows in the 185 industrial sectors over time. They are tacked on after each year's economic activities have been calculated, and they have no effect on any future year's activities. If resources become depleted, the economy goes on using them anyway. Pollution abatement costs are made a function of the amount of pollution generated, but these costs do not affect labor productivity, or capital investment, or final demand for various kinds of industrial output. Resource substitution and improved abatement technologies are assumed, but these are programmed before each model run begins. Thus aluminum may be assumed to be gradually substituted for steel, but the extent and rate of substitution are not related to the cumulative amount of aluminum or iron consumed or to prices of aluminum and iron or to the rate of turnover of capital stock. Air pollution may be assumed to be reduced by the use of catalytic converters on automobiles, and the use of platinum may also be assumed to be increased by the manufacture of the converters, but the abatement coefficient cannot be made a reactive function of the amount of air pollution actually present in the nation's cities, and the shift in platinum consumption will proceed regardless of the availability of platinum. Furthermore, the increase in abatement is not necessarily related to the increase of platinum use; the two exogenous assumptions are completely independent and nothing but the watchfulness of the person who makes them guarantees that they will be consistent with each other, or with the other million or so such exogenous assumptions.

At the other extreme, the human population in the SAHEL model is assumed to live on just one resource, cattle. The cattle in turn live on one resource, the forage plants of the Sahelian region, and the plants live on the nutrients of the Sahelian soil. All three resources in this chain are constantly renewed, but not necessarily at the rate the nomads choose to use them. The SAHEL model contains an explicit representation of the level of each resource and the rates at which it is renewed or depleted.

The cattle level is increased by calf births and decreased by natural deaths and by slaughter for tribal economic purposes. As cattle increase, they increase the rate of forage utilization. Forage is measured not in absolute units, kilograms of biomass, but in units of production potential, the number of kilograms that can be produced per hectare per year. Thus forage production potential represents seeds, roots, buds, and other regenerative plant parts that are present on the range, modified by amounts of rainfall (exogenous). If the forage utilization rate exceeds the production potential, the production potential falls (seeds and roots are being consumed). If the production potential exceeds the utilization rate, the production potential rises until it reaches the maximum potential allowed by the range soil.

The condition of the soil is also measured in units of potential production (kg/ha-year). As long as forage utilization does not exceed the potential forage production rate, soil condition increases until it reaches its maximum. If forage utilization becomes excessive, soil condition deteriorates at a rate that increases more rapidly the higher the forage utilization intensity gets. A lower soil production potential (nutrients and soil structure) decreases the forage production potential (seeds, roots, and buds), which further unbalances the ratio between forage consumption and forage regeneration, unless cattle are removed from the range.

As long as consumption exceeds the potential of the biomass to regenerate, the system erodes through three feedback mechanisms, which occur at different rates: the potential of the soil to support plants decreases, the potential of the plants to regenerate themselves decreases, and the stock death rate increases. The third of these mechanisms, stock deaths, if it occurs rapidly and strongly enough, can halt the erosion by removing the consumption pressure on the system. The behavior of the model depends on the balance between these three feedbacks: if the third one is weakened through human intervention, so that veterinarians or feeding programs prevent the sudden decrease of the cattle population, the whole system can enter a destructive behavior mode that takes decades to unfold.

Scientifically this is an important, and clear hypothesis. The model is rich enough to suggest leading indicators, parallel systems that have already run their course, and other detailed observations that might allow it to be tested.

SOS also contains links in both directions between the human economy and the natural ecosystem. In contrast to the simple SAHEL system, here the economy is a complex, fully-industrialized one, and the resources are accounted for in relatively great detail. In fact this model is the only one in our survey that takes on the task of quantifying the carrying capacity of a modern industrialized society. Carrying capacity is defined by ecologists as the level of population that can be sustained indefinitely by the environment at a given living standard and set of technologies. The SOS modelers have attempted to capture all the intricacy of that concept. For example:

1. At any time the carrying capacity is determined by the *most limiting* factor needed to sustain the population. For instance, it would make no difference how abundant food might be, if oil were scarce, or vice versa. Adding more nitrogen to the soil would not increase yields if in fact calcium were the most limiting factor.
2. The carrying capacity is *dynamic*. The levels of the various environmental resources, relative to the population's need for them, change constantly. Therefore the most limiting factor may shift from resource to resource over time. One that is safely in excess today may become the critical determinant of the carrying capacity tomorrow. The relative abundance of

food vs. oil may depend on weather fluctuations; the relative abundance of nitrogen vs. calcium may depend on the type of crop grown.
3. The shifts in relative abundance of the many resources that define the carrying capacity are complicated by the fact that their availability may depend on *each other* (oil is needed to grow food; nitrogen availability in the soil may be linked chemically with the calcium concentration) and on the *response of the population* to its perception of relative abundance (food and oil may be substituted for each other by shifting the balance between labor and capital; the demand for nitrogen-requiring crops may be increased and the demand for calcium-requiring crops may be decreased, or vice versa).

In spite of the complexity of these ideas, the SOS simulation of the dynamic interaction between the population and its carrying capacity is conceptually rather simple. Twenty different resources necessary to production are accounted for. Some of them, such as petroleum, are non-renewable; their levels steadily decline as the model economy uses them, but larger pools are assumed available at progressively higher costs. Other resources, such as wood, are assumed renewable; their stocks are increased each year by regeneration rates, which may or may not balance their consumption rates. Still other resources, such as clean air and water, are not modeled as stocks; instead their levels of pollution are accumulated as outputs of the productive processes and, simultaneously but not necessarily equally, reduced by expenditures on pollution control.

Each productive sector is presumed to operate by a formula indicating the inputs of each resource needed to produce one unit of output. If any of the 20 resources is inadequate for desired production, the output of that sector is temporarily cut back to the amount permitted by the most limiting resource. Then various adjustment mechanisms are called upon to bring the economic demand and the resource capacity into agreement. The production formula may be shifted so as to use less of the scarce resource. New, higher-cost reserves of the resource may be tapped. Recycling may be instituted, if possible. Demand of the population for that product may be reduced by out-migration or deaths. None of these processes is presumed to occur immediately, and each is assigned a cost.

Although the basic idea of adjustment through feedback in this model is straightforward, its actual representation requires a heroic set of detailed assumptions. For each productive sector one must specify not only a starting recipe for its inputs, but also the range over which that recipe may vary; to what extent any resources may be substituted for any other, if the need should arise. For each resource, the modeler must enter a complete list of how much of it is available at successively higher cost levels, at what rate it is naturally renewed, and to what extent it can be recycled. For the whole society, the preference function for adjustment mechnisms must be postulated; how much substitution will be tried before recycling begins, what cost will be paid before demand is decreased, to what extent production goals will be sought at the expense of pollution-control goals.

Given all these data requirements, it is not surprising that the SOS modelers simplified their model relationships as much as possible. They maintained linear relationships between inputs and outputs and between degree of adjustment and costs of adjustment, although they knew that the real relationships were not linear.[15] They also ignored the interrelationships among resources; the possible dependence, for example, of fish or wood renewal rates on the cleanliness of air or water, or the necessity of energy resources for the refining of mineral resources. And of course many kinds of resources and pollution were simply not included.

3. Summary and commentary

Simplified though it is, SOS is by far the most comprehensive of the nine models in its treatment of resources, which is to say that none is very comprehensive. Although fertilizer is represented as an agricultural input in five of the models, not one of them suggests that fertilizer does anything more in the environment than increase crop yields. Fertilizer is spread on the earth by the millions of tons annually, but none of these models represents where it comes from or where it goes. Not one of the nine models recognizes energy as an economic input with significantly different properties from materials or capital or cash. None accounts for the buildup of solid waste in an economy or the cost of dealing with that waste, none keeps track of the flow of organic nutrients from soil to produce to sewage to water bodies, only one mentions that land can erode, only two that mines or oil wells can be depleted. Only two of the models even come close to recognizing the most generally-accepted physical law of the universe, that matter and energy are conserved, that they cannot appear out of nothing or disappear into nothing.

We can imagine three excusable reasons for the uniformly cursory treatment of environmental systems in these models. The first is that the purposes of the models did not require anything more; resources and environmental services were simply irrelevant to the question being asked by the modeler. *MexicoV* and CHAC are probably the only models with such a limited time horizon and purpose.

A second reason might be that the modelers were so dedicated to simplicity and transparency that they deliberately chose extremely crude environmental representations in order to keep their models understandable. This explanation might suffice for TEMPO, but otherwise the simplest environmental assumptions occur in the most complex models (like BACHUE, KASM, and CHAC), whereas the general-understanding models that are most intended to be transparent (like SOS and SAHEL) in fact go farthest in representing natural systems.

A third reason for omitting the environment from socioeconomic models, a reason less excusable but at least understandable, might be a deficiency of theories or data about natural systems. One cannot put into a model what one does not know. However, currently available information about environmental systems, while far from perfect, is certainly more empirically grounded, more comprehensive, and more precise than information about social systems. The fields of ecology, hydrology, geochemistry and agronomy contain a wealth of information about the matters that intersect human economic activities, and much of that information is carefully quantified and even computer coded.[16] The imbalance between ecological and socioeconomic hypotheses in these models must be due to some other reason than an imbalance between ecological and socioeconomic knowledge.

If there is no excusable reason for the underrepresentation of the environment in the models, we can imagine several inexcusable reasons. However, in defense of the computer modelers, we must remember that the sophistication of mental models about environmental matters is also very limited, and that until very recently concepts of resources and environmental services were almost never apparent or even welcome in public policy. Some of these computer models have clearly gone beyond mental models, in keeping track of several environmental constraints simultaneously (KASM, CHAC), in attempting a detailed account of the environmental impact of a modern economy (RfF, SOS), and in exploring the very long-term effects of current policies on ecological stability. (SAHEL).

F. CONCLUSION: LESSONS ABOUT INDUSTRIALIZATION

In Table 13.1 we summarize what we believe to be the broad and total hypotheses about industrialization, the combinations of all the specific ones contained within each model. We also list the major conclusions or deductions that result from those hypotheses.

Before we go on to discuss the usefulness and scientific quality of these nine messages about industrialization, we should make some disclaimers about Table 13.1. It contains only our own rather baldly-stated summaries of the outstanding model assumptions and conclusions as they have entered and informed our own mental models. The statements we most readily picked out are, of course, those most consistent with or opposed to our own paradigm. The model makers themselves might perhaps choose other statements as most memorable, and they would certainly express them with more detail and precision. It is also likely that the modelers learned more from constructing and testing their models than they communicated in their documentation, and that we absorbed. General lessons are more easily derived from the longer-term, more transparent models such as SAHEL and TEMPO than from the shorter-term, more detailed models such as KASM and CHAC. We may have seriously perverted the purposes of the latter models in seeking to gain basic understanding from them, since they were primarily intended to provide specific, situation- and parameter-dependent advice, rather than lasting knowledge.

However limited the list in Table 13.1 may be, it is an honest compilation of the primary messages about industrialization that the nine modeling groups were able to communicate to two interested colleagues. Therefore it is some indication of the scientific content of the models.

To begin with the hypotheses, they constitute a remarkably diverse list. These models put forth a number of interesting ways of looking at the development process explored to a depth and detail far beyond what mental models could do. In some cases the major theory of one model directly supports or contradicts the major theory of another, but generally they are such different views of the world that they are impossible to compare, contrast, or even discuss using the same kinds of words or measures. Like the various modeling paradigms they employ (and partly because of them), these models focus on incongruent aspects of the world. Only a few of them can be used to shed light on each other or to suggest real-world tests that could resolve the policy arguments implied by their conclusions. The TEMPO-LTSM-BACHUE series can be discussed as a comparable set and perhaps SAHEL and SOS can as well. The others stand alone. Anyone who attempts to draw together all the models, to summarize their main areas of disagreement, or to suggest general tests to distinguish their validity finds the task frustratingly unstructurable. One cannot even find a common set of concepts or symbols with which to work.

Perhaps because of this incommensurability, the modelers themselves have made very few attempts to assess their theories in the context of other possible theories, whether formalized as mathematical models or not. Only Martos and Beltran del Rio have seriously discussed the possibility that there might be other ways of looking at the world besides the ones represented in their models. Martos justifies his choice of a capital-constrained economic hypothesis as a contrast to the demand-constrained one he sees in most other models. Beltran del Rio statistically tests several major competing hypotheses about macroeconomic structure. The TEMPO-LTSM-BACHUE modelers are very conscious of their contrasting demographic hypotheses, but have built their economic theories and chosen modeling techniques in such different ways that even their demographic hypotheses cannot be compared. The other modelers have simply thrown their theories into the wind, as if there were no other theories already there.

In spite of this diversity and incomparability, the range of hypotheses represented in these nine models is in some ways very narrow. With few exceptions, they assume that industrialization will and should proceed everywhere as it has in the West, that the important policies are those carried out at the level of national government, that the important variables to keep track of are measurable in monetary terms. They view governmental action as an external plan or a one-time event, rather than as a *process* that is itself an integral part of the system. They deal mainly with the concrete, objective, physical, or monetary aspects of an industrializing society, not with information, ideas, goals, motivations, institutions, politics, power, oppression, or subjective perceptions.

Little formal use of information theory or of disciplines other than economics and demography is evident. There are surprisingly few applications of cybernetics or systems theory, few overt attempts to relate system behavior

Table 13.1

Model	Major hypotheses	Major conclusions
SAHEL	Human economic and reproductive decisions are closely interlinked with the resource base that sustains human activity. Human decisions are based on material and cultural goals and on short-term information about the constraints of the resource base.	A lack of information about the long-term state of the resource base will cause instability or even destruction. Policies that are sincerely designed to aid the system may make it worse by making individual destabilizing decisions more effective.
RfF	The pollution generated and resources used by an industrial economy are linear functions of the monetary value of the output of that economy. The monetary value of economic output is a result of economic demand. Economic demand is generated by past output, moderated by variations in the population and formation of families.	Economic growth in an industrial society places more of a burden on the resource base than does population growth. Reduced population growth may help conserve resources, but its effect is partially countered by the fact that each person then has a higher income and thus demands more resources.
SOS	A growing industrial system has numerous material goals arranged hierarchically. If a goal is not met, there are numerous adaptive responses, both technical and social, to correct the situation. These adaptive responses take time, cost something, and have partial limitations.	Because of the delays, costs, and limitations of its adaptive mechanisms, the industrial system will not achieve its goals smoothly or optimally. Long-term planning and reduction of material desires improve the behavior of the system.
TEMPO	The output of the economy can be allocated either to investment or to consumption. A growing population forces the allocation more toward consumption.	Rapid population growth can reduce the rate of economic growth. Investment in family planning can have as positive an influence on material living standards as investment in the economy.
LTSM	Same basic assumptions as TEMPO, with the addition of feedback from rapid economic growth to reduce population growth. Also strong assumptions about possible productivity increases in agriculture.	Investment in agriculture can be even more effective in raising living standards and employing a labor surplus than investment in industry. To some extent there is a trade-off among the goals of raising industrial output, raising agricultural output, reducing unemployment, and reducing population growth. Single policies to achieve one goal may interfere with the achievement of the others.

Model	Major hypotheses	Major conclusions
BACHUE	A society's aggregate behavior arises from the detailed responses of various income classes to economic conditions. Fertility, migration, labor participation, and productivity all depend on the education, income, and opportunities available to different classes.	Poverty, unemployment, and income inequities are deeply persistent problems, solvable only by determined, major efforts applied consistently over long periods. Policies intended to aid one economic or geographic sector may in fact aid another by diverting streams of migrants or workers in unexpected ways.
KASM	The agricultural economy is largely driven by exogenous population growth and distribution, industrial factor prices, and government-initiated investments and new technologies. Farmers make cropping and allocation decisions by optimization. New technologies diffuse smoothly and sigmoidally. Markets operate essentially freely.	Active government policies and new technologies can increase agricultural output and smooth commodity price fluctuation, but the correct policy to produce a given result is usually not intuitively obvious and may have unintended side effects.
MexicoV	The macroeconomy is best represented by annual accumulations of various sorts of money flows. The relationships among these flows will continue to be in the near future exactly what they have been in the past. The main determinant of economic output is economic demand.	The Mexican economic system does not behave either like a pure free-market or a pure Marxist model. Central macroeconomic policies can enhance total economic growth, but only by increasing national debt and inflation. These central policies have almost no effect on the endemic problems of rural poverty and too-rapid urbanization.
CHAC	Market prices, supply, and demand are determined simultaneously so as to maximize the sum of producers' and consumers' surplus. Farmers make decisions by a process of risk-avoiding optimization. The agricultural economy is essentially independent from the industrial economy.	Seasonal unemployment in agriculture is much greater than aggregate data would indicate and not easily countered. The most effective investments in agricultural capital and most profitable crops to raise for export are not those that government, aid, or market institutions have intuitively selected.

to structural assumptions. Holistic conclusions seem to have appeared in spite of, rather than because of the efforts of the modelers. The variables, categories, and ways of describing the system are traditional and familiar, shaped more by standard disciplinary thinking than by the particular purpose of each model. One gets the impression that these modelers believe that human socioeconomic activities *actually exist* in traditional, separable, physically-distinct categories (production, investment, consumption—employment, labor participation, labor productivity—marginal returns to labor, to capital, to technology), rather than as a magnificent, throbbing, incredibly diverse but integrated whole that could be logically divided in many different ways to obtain many different insights.

So there is a general lack of creativity, and a predominant use of safe, conventional limited theories. But within that arena these models bring together a lot of ideas and keep track of an amazing number of interactions. Surprising and thought-provoking results can emerge, as can be seen in the list of model conclusions in Table 13.1. All these major conclusions seem to us plausible, useful, and probably generalizable. Few of them can be said to be widely-shared knowledge, regularly used as a basis for policy. Many are statements of uncertainty or impossibility: the system is so complex that it does not behave in the way we would expect; the reasons for its behavior are deeply imbedded in the system's own structure and are not changeable quickly or by minor readjustments of current policies; it is difficult to find policies that will satisfy all goals simultaneously. Few of these major conclusions arise from any one of the industrial indicators we have discussed—population, production, and the like. Rather they result from the assumptions that have been made about how each indicator is linked to all the others. They are truly holistic conclusions, unlikely to be perceived by looking at any part of an industrializing system in isolation. These models do illustrate the potential of systematic modeling as a practice that can direct one's attention to the interconnections within complex systems and to the meaning and importance of those interconnections.

NOTES AND REFERENCES

1. For some example textbooks, see C. B. Nam and S. O. Gustavus, *Population: The Dynamics of Demographic Change*, Boston, Houghton Mifflin Company, 1976, and R. Thomlinson, *Population Dynamics*, New York, Random House, 1976.
2. See for example, H. Fredericksen, 'Feedbacks in Economic and Demographic transition', *Science*, **166**, 837, 1969; D. M. Heer and D. O. Smith, *Demography*, **5**, 104, 1968.
3. D. H. Meadows, 'Population Sector', in D. L. Meadows, W. W. Behrens, D. H. Meadows, R. F. Naill, J. Randers, and E. K. O. Zahn, *Dynamics of Growth in a Finite World*, Cambridge, Mass., MIT Press, 1974.
4. See the chapter on Hungary by A. Klinger in B. Berelson (ed.), *Population Policy in Developed Countries*, New York, McGraw-Hill, 1974. For an interesting summary of the situation in Singapore, see *Coevolution Quarterly*, Fall 1983.

5. E. D. Domar, quoted in P. Rao and R. L. Miller, *Applied Econometrics*, Belmont, Calif., Wadsworth Publishing Co., p. 41, 1971.
6. E. F. Schumacher, *Small is Beautiful*, New York, Harper & Row, p. 159, 1973.
7. See, for example, N. J. Mass, 'Stock and Flow Variables and the Dynamics of Supply and Demand', in J. Randers (ed.), *Elements of the System Dynamics Method*,Cambridge, Mass., MIT Press, 1980.
8. G. B. Rodgers, M. J. D. Hopkins, and R. Wery, *Economic-Demographic Modelling for Development Planning: BACHUE-Philippines*, Population and Employment Working Paper No. 45, International Labor Organization, Geneva, p. IV-2, 1976.
9. H. Millendorfer and C. Gaspari, 'Immaterielle und Materielle Faktoren der Entwicklung: Ansatze auf einer Allgemeinen Produktionsfunktion', *Zeitschrift fur Nat. Okonomie*, **31**, pp. 81–120, 1971.
10. E. F. Schumacher, *op.cit.*
11. For a very clear summary of classic migration theories, see D. L. Bogue, *Principles of Demography*, New York, John Wiley and Sons, pp. 752–283, 1969.
12. J. W. Forrester, *Urban Dynamics*, Cambridge, Mass., Wright-Allen Press, 1969.
13. A. Beltran del Rio, *A Macroeconometric Forecasting Model for Mexico: Specification and Simulations*, Ann Arbor, University Microfilms, pp. 359–360, 1973.
14. For the generic difference between historic urbanization patterns and those now occurring in non-industrialized nations, see K. Davis, 'The Urbanization of the Human Population', *Scientific American*, September 1965.
15. House and Williams manuscript, unpublished.
16. For examples, see any professional ecological journal, or C. A. S. Hall and J. W. Day (eds), *Ecosystem Modeling in Theory and Practice*, New York, John Wiley & Sons, 1977; D. Daetz and R. H. Pantell (eds), *Environmental Modeling*, Stroudsburg, Pa., Dowden, Hutchinson & Ross, Inc., 1974; C. S. Russell (ed.), *Ecological Modeling*, Washington, D.C., Resources for the Future, Inc., Working Paper QE-1, 1975.

CHAPTER 14

Model quality: Advantages of Computer Models

So far we have looked at the *contents* of the nine models—what hypotheses they contain and lessons they lead to about distinct aspects of industrialization such as population and production. We have found a few truly creative hypotheses and some attempts to use the computer to test hypotheses against real-world data. Primarily, however, we have found familiar, and quite simple ideas, not very different from the ones in mental models. The primary contribution of the models has been in *linking* those formulations, in calculating the details of their combined workings, and perhaps in making clearer which aspects of social systems are, and which are not, well understood.

No one has ever claimed that computers are sources of brand-new knowledge or that computer modelers have been trained to be bold innovators or critics of the social order. Everything that goes into a computer model must, after all, come from a mental model. Instead of looking at the *substance* of these computer models and expecting to see something new, perhaps we should look at the modeling exercises as *processes* and see how they have contributed to the precision, communication and testing of old ideas. If computer models simply expose and clarify mental models and force them to be more explicit and more complete, they will contribute immensely to the quality of public debate and the process of decision-making.

We will proceed one by one through the five advantages we cited earlier for computer models. They were rigor, comprehensiveness, logic, accessibility, and testability. To what extent do these models actually illustrate these advantages? Can they be said to excel or supplement mental models along these dimensions?

A. RIGOR

The first potential advantage we claimed for computer models over mental models was that *computer models must be rigorous, organized, and precise.*

Computers are notoriously unforgiving. Before any results at all can be produced, every item in a model must be defined exactly. No item can be defined twice. Each computational rule must be specified. A single minor mistake can either prevent the model from running at all or cause it to produce obvious nonsense, such as a negative population or an income growth rate of 10,000% per year. The indisputable fact that each of the nine models has actually been run on a computer means that each meets the computer's high mechanical standards for precision and consistency. A precise and internally-consistent statement about society should certainly be superior to the vague, inconsistent ones in people's minds.

In some senses computer models clearly do excel in rigor and consistency. A mental model can easily put together a plan that depends on using 150% of the available agricultural land or three times the earth's known oil reserves, without detecting any problem. A properly written constraint in a linear program would prevent this from happening. Even if planners do remember that producing more fertilizer will require more fertilizer plants, more petroleum, more trucks to haul the petroleum, more refineries, and therefore more steel, they are unlikely to be able to calculate *how much* more steel with anything approaching the thoroughness of an input–output matrix. Inherent in the various modeling paradigms are practices and mathematical devices that enforce certain kinds of consistencies almost automatically, and these consistencies reflect real-world certainties that are vitally important in determining how social systems work.

The models described here illustrate many times over the valuable contribution enforced orderliness can bring to the understanding of social systems. The KASM team, trying to collect Korean data with which to construct a model, almost immediately uncovered a faulty data-reporting process that local and international statisticians had previously either ignored or been unaware of. The same team produced a set of consistent demographic forecasts superior to any others available at that time. In fact nearly all of the models described here contain detailed and useful demographic components. It is a trivial task for a computer to remember how many nine-year olds there were last year and to move them into the ten-year old category this year, removing those who died or migrated away. It is not so trivial for a person to keep mental track of 80 or so age categories.

Another example of rigorousness and consistency is CHAC, which contains a fascinating catalog of 2,340 ways Mexican farmers actually grow crops, and which can generate various combinations of these cropping activities, all of which are guaranteed not to require in the aggregate more land, labor, water, fertilizer, or machinery than can be found in Mexico. Picardi's SAHEL model also performs some useful consistency-maintaining functions. It does not allow the nomad's cattle stock to increase faster than the normal fertility of cattle would permit, it does not allow the herd to grow past the size the grazing land can support, it keeps track of the fact that more cattle will eat more forage and thus reduce the supportive capacity of the land, and so forth. Similarly, the RfF model reminds us of a set of interlinked factors that tend to be forgotten in verbal debates; a slower rate of population growth will reduce resource demand because there will be fewer consumers, but this effect may be offset by increased resource demand because each consumer is likely to have a higher income.

However, organization, precision, and rigorousness can be deceptive. Every modeler knows that the computer's ability to produce numbers with six to twelve digit precision should not be taken as a sign that one really knows anything about the system that precisely. But the temptation to produce such apparent scientific certainty is almost impossible to resist. For example, Beltran del Rio is under no illusions about the availability or accuracy of data on Mexico's economy. Yet he applies sophisticated statistical techniques to fit his structural hypotheses to observed data, and he enters the results into his model like this:

$$\begin{pmatrix} \text{urban labor} \\ \text{participation} \\ \text{rate} \end{pmatrix} = 0.68591 - 0.12852 \begin{pmatrix} \text{potential} \\ \text{urban labor} \\ \text{productivity} \end{pmatrix} + 0.00301 \begin{pmatrix} \text{urban} \\ \text{idle} \\ \text{capacity} \end{pmatrix}$$

To his credit, Beltran del Rio does not read his model *output* to the sixth significant digit; the conclusions he draws are strictly qualitative.

Spurious precision model input, which is neither required nor utilized in model output, is a common tendency, to be observed to some extent in RfF, LTSM, BACHUE, and particularly in KASM, *MexicoV*, and CHAC. The outputs of these models are generally described in qualitative terms with many disclaimers about taking precise quantitative values too seriously. Yet great care is taken to estimate input parameters as exactly as possible—probably even more exactly than possible.

Over-emphasis on precision is not only time wasting, it can be misleading. It can disguise the shaky knowledge base upon which the model is built. One can start with a series of guesses about the 50 year future of population growth, economic growth, and technical advance, as the RfF model does, and then use a 185 × 185 matrix of uncertain coefficients to produce a detailed, internally consistent, extremely precise picture of a future economy. The wealth of detail can distract one's attention from the fact that the entire structure depends on the unrigorous, imprecise mental model that generated the initial exogenous forecasts.

This sort of unbalanced rigor is commonplace in our survey models, many of which combine some detailed, organized, accurate representation with some astonishingly simplified guesses or omissions. KASM has 180 population groups and 19 agricultural commodities, but no feedback from nutritional sufficiency to death rates, or from urban conditions to migration rates, or from industrialization to birth rates. The RfF model keeps track of inter-industry flows through 185 industrial sectors but does not alter those flows when resource reserves become depleted. BACHUE distributes the output of 13 economic sectors over 40 income groups but relies on mental models to forecast investment. CHAC combines an immensely sophisticated description of farmers' cropping activities with simplistic assumptions about perfect competition, perfect information, and society-wide market balances. It is very easy for clients and even modelers to be seduced by the elaborate output graphs from these models and to forget the controversial theories and imprecise guesses upon which they are based.

If the drive toward precision had no effect other than to waste modelers' time, it would be a tolerable quirk of the profession. If it did nothing more than deceive model clients about what modelers really know, a bit of client education could reestablish a proper degree of skepticism. But the quest for precision generates a worse problem than either of these, the problem that has most hampered the contribution of modeling to new knowledge in the social sciences. The need for the appearance of rigor fosters uncritical use of the neatly catalogued data in standard statistical sources, and discourages utilization of less precise but perhaps more pertinent sources of information about the way systems function. A modeler can easily find age and sex data for a population in an official census, so considerable time is spent constructing a population model disaggregated into 180 age and sex categories, even though the original purpose of the model does not require such information. The model purpose *may* require a representation of the long-term response of the population's fertility and mortality to economic or environmental changes, but the modeler finds no official data on such things, especially not for all 180 age and sex categories. Professional colleagues will be scornful of any hypotheses that are not backed by statistical fits to data. Therefore the modeler is likely to leave important factors of the system out of the model or to make them exogenous.

The complaint we have put forth in the last few paragraphs should not be taken to imply that rigor is *not* a major advantage of computer modeling. We believe that it is one of the main advantages, but one that accrues primarily to the mental model of the modeler alone. We have found that the frustrating exercise of setting down what we think we know about a system in precise and internally-consistent language has two marvelous effects. First, it forces us to clarify our thinking enormously. Second, it makes us very humble about how much we actually know. We wish every policy-maker could be put through the exercise.

But we find that model-induced clarity and humility very hard to transfer to anyone else. The best lessons of rigor remain with the modelers, with the thoughtful ones anyway. And that result—learning on the part of those who build the models—falls far short of the claim that the modelers can deliver precision and rigor to the policy process. And, as another critic of modeling has said, there is no guarantee that the exercise of modeling educates even the modeler:

> There is a popular illusion that confronting a computer with one's ideas enforces rigor and discipline, thereby encouraging the researcher to reject or clarify fuzzy

ideas. In the very narrow sense that the human must behave exactly like a machine in order to communicate with it, this is true. But in a more useful sense, the effect is the opposite; it is all too easy to become immersed in the trivial details of working with a problem on the computer, rather than think it through rationally. The effort of making the computer understand is then mistaken for intellectual activity and creative problem solving.[1]

In summary, computer models do tend to be more rigorous, organized, and precise than mental models, and this rigor is useful, especially for the modelers' own learning. But often the apparent rigorousness is simply an elaborate accounting structure built upon an uncertain mental model. And nearly always the drive for scientific-looking precision leads to misallocation of modeling effort and omission of some important aspects of real social systems.

B. COMPREHENSIVENESS

Computer models can contain and process more information than mental models can. They can combine many mental models, cross disciplines, and provide a more complete view of the world.

All these computer models, even the simplest, keep track of a number of items far beyond the capability of the human mind. Several of the models served as research hubs, bringing together interdisciplinary teams of people who combined insights about many different aspects of social systems. A formal model, within which different assumptions can be expressed in a neutral language, can be a key integrating factor in cross-disciplinary conversations. KASM utilized agricultural economists, macroeconomists, demographers, and agronomists from both Korea and the USA. CHAC brought together a similar team of Mexicans and Americans, and BACHUE and LTSM intended to create interdisciplinary research efforts in several different countries. The SAHEL, BACHUE, and SOS models truly transcend disciplines, trying to provide holistic, systematic descriptions of self-contained systems and creating new theory as well as data-accounting. KASM and BACHUE also combine several different modeling paradigms.

Most of the models provide some meeting ground for two fields, economics and demography, that are not very often contained simultaneously within single mental models. Two models represent the effects of various population-growth scenarios on the economy (TEMPO and RfF). Four others take the greater step of closing the economic-demographic feedback loop by including the effects of economic change on the population growth rate (SAHEL, SOS, LTSM, and BACHUE). Although the theories used to close this loop in the models are extremely simple, any attempt to keep in focus both sides of this feedback process is a concrete step toward understanding the process of economic development. Verbal arguments in the field of politics too often favor only one or the other side of the economic-demographic feedback ('If those people had fewer children they would be better off' vs. 'If those people were better off they would have fewer children'). In this respect the computer models are certainly more comprehensive than many mental models.

While the capacity of a computer to hold and synthesize information favors comprehensiveness, it is still a finite capacity, and the mental capacity of the people who must program, check, and interpret computer models is even more limited. Modelers understandably strive for mathematical simplicity, which sometimes can get in the way of model comprehensiveness. Most of us visualize relationships in our social systems as diffuse, non-linear, delayed, and often sharply discontinuous. But these nine models are predominantly linear, instantaneously adjusting, and continuous (especially RfF, *MexicoV*, CHAC, and parts of BACHUE and KASM).

This oversimplicity is not strictly necessary; many mathematical tools are available to deal with non-linearities or discontinuities. But simple equations are especially necessary if a model is intended to be very detailed. Linear matrices can be inverted, no matter how huge, and linear constraint spaces are more easily optimized than non-linear ones. Thus mathematical convenience forces a trade-off between *comprehensiveness* (inclusion of much mental-model knowledge) and *complicatedness* (inclusion of lots of categories of population or output or resources). In order to preserve complicatedness, comprehensiveness is usually sacrificed.

Human minds are full of information about how people make decisions and how constraints, goals, expectations, fears, hopes, hates, and loves influence the workings of the social system. But little of that information is contained in computer models. Of the nine in our sample, only SAHEL, SOS, and BACHUE make a concerted attempt to represent 'soft' social processes. The BACHUE modelers gave up that attempt when they ran across data deficiencies. The SAHEL and SOS modelers lost considerable credibility by going ahead without the data.

Thus these computer models are not truly comprehensive; they are strangely silent about aspects of social systems that everyone knows to be important, but that no one has yet included in data banks.

In short, computer models are in some senses more complicated and detailed than mental models, but they are rarely as complete and comprehensive. Qualitative, motivational factors tend to be systematically omitted, as are physical factors for which there are few standardized data (pollution, erosion, energy, household production). The theories underlying the models are unsophisticated, and individual relationships are often simplified for mathematical convenience. Though the models can and do link together more factors than mental models can, there are mathematical and scientific biases limiting what actually gets linked.

C. LOGIC

We have claimed that computer models can draw error-free conclusions from their assumptions, a feat that mental models are generally incapable of performing, especially when there are many assumptions.

Probably the only way of ascertaining whether this is true of the nine models would be to check every individual equation and to perform numerous computer tests. Only four of the modeling groups have published their equations, although program tapes could probably be obtained from four others. But a program with 80,000 parameters or 1,500 main equations is inherently uncheckable. The probability of a mistyped decimal point or algebraic sign, of an accidentally inverted ratio or of garbled numerical digits, must be very high for the massive programs in our sample. And the probability of detecting such a mistake is nearly zero. Of the nine models, probably only TEMPO and SAHEL are transparent and intuitive enough to be thoroughly checked for mechanical mistakes.

The problem of mechanical mistakes is compounded by the ingenious way modelers can rationalize them. We once personally demonstrated this ability with a relatively small model of about 200 equations. One erroneously-typed decimal point escaped our attention for several months. During that period the model output showed some significant wobbles that had no effect on the general model conclusions (fortunately), but that showed up clearly on the output graphs. With great ease we were able to explain how these wobbles were generated by a particular combination of the model's assumptions. Our explanation was entirely specious but very plausible. It took a critic from outside our group to find the typing error; we never suspected that there was one.[2]

This example illustrates a difficulty that is harder to deal with than just the probability of typographical errors. Not only may there be errors in the process of *translation* from verbal assumptions to mathematical equations to typed-in symbols stored in the computer's memory; there may also be errors in the *interpretation* of the symbols that come out the other end of this process. The computer does not deliver a sweeping conclusion, summarizing the accumulated wisdom inherent in the model assumptions. Rather it produces a stack of paper, sometimes several inches thick, covered with numbers. These numbers must be examined, organized, compared, and digested before any meaning can be extracted from them, and this process is conducted by people using fallible, biased, and illogical mental models.

There may be several errors of interpretation in our sample of nine models that we as critics did not catch because our own mental models are similar to those of the modelers. One we did catch, because of a bias opposing that of the modelers, was RfF's conclusion that further population and economic growth could be supported in the United States by the known resource base. In fact the model results indicated severe problems. The high-growth scenarios seriously depleted not only domestic but world reserves of most resources over the next 30 years, in spite of the model's sanguine assumptions about technological development. The modelers interpreted their results with an optimism derived from their mental models, not their computer model. The Population Commission sponsor further warped the message by advocating slower population growth with no mention of economic growth, although the model had indicated that economic growth placed much more of a burden on resources than population growth. Even if all the assumptions in this model were reasonable and correctly entered into the computer, which is doubtful, the conclusions drawn from it were not error-free.

We should mention some good examples under this category, because good examples certainly do exist. There are several cases of real learning from the computer models, cases where the modelers expected one output, received another, and after careful rechecking of both mental model and computer model, decided that the mental model had been in error.

Picardi probably did not expect to find that aid programs in the Sahel were counterproductive, and probably did expect to discover with his model some relatively simple policies that would permanently improve the lot of the Sahel nomads. He can now explain his results with a fairly compelling logic based on intuitively-understandable interlinkages in the Sahel system. This explanation is derived from a mental model that has been 'educated' by working with a relatively transparent computer model.

Similarly, House and Williams deliberately designed the SOS model to demonstrate all the effective adaptation mechanisms of modern society, but the resultant model system did not adapt effectively. The system's response delays, and the costs of the adaptive responses, were what their mental modelers had not adequately accounted for. (Jay Forrester says that most people underestimate system response delays by a factor of about three.) House and Williams conclude by recommending significant changes in the system, which reflect an understanding quite different from the 'nothing to worry about' attitude with which they started.

The BACHUE modelers received several surprises from their model. Projects designed to help rural areas in fact distort migration streams and end up helping urban areas instead. Education proves to be a much less effective change agent than had been expected. Income distribution is distressingly resistant to change.

We do not mean to imply that all these unexpected conclusions are necessarily correct simply because they were unexpected, nor that conclusions that are expected are likely to be wrong. The correctness of any conclusion depends upon the accuracy of the assumptions that went into it and the reliability of the translation process that communicated it to and from the computer. We have already indicated that there are several problems at each of these stages. But these examples do indicate the potential of computer modeling to enhance the limited reasoning power of the human mind and to strengthen the logical chain from assumptions to conclusions.

Thus computer models are definitely capable of proceeding in a logical, error-free fashion from assumptions to conclusions and of generating information that is unlikely to come from mental models. However, errors can easily be introduced either in the process of translating the assumptions into computer language or in the process of interpreting numerical output. The probability of such errors multiplies rapidly as models become more detailed and complex.

D. ACCESSIBILITY

Computer models are explicit and open to criticism in a way that mental models can never be. They can be examined, revised, and corrected; each assumption can be tested against the real-world.

As outsiders who have attempted to understand the nine models on the basis of their written documentation, we should be in a good position to assess this claim. From our personal experience with these models, we must conclude that the record is decidedly mixed.

To begin with the good examples, SAHEL is clearly documented, and we felt we could understand it thoroughly. Part of this accessibility may have been due to the fact that we share the paradigm of this model, but its structure is so simple and its documentation so non-technical that we suspect anyone could review it rather easily. Another excellent example is TEMPO, a small model with a simple structure, carefully described in both words and algebraic equations. This model is so clear that it *has* drawn criticism; both LTSM and BACHUE were made to correct and expand it. In fact these three models, and the Coale–Hoover model that preceded them, provide a fine demonstration of modeling as a progressive science. Each set of modelers commented upon, criticized, and elaborated the model that came before. The entire chain of four models is notable for the efforts of the modelers to document their work clearly and honestly.

Four of the nine models (SAHEL, SOS, TEMPO, *MexicoV*) present easily-available technical documentation sufficient to permit the model to be reproduced and run on virtually any computer. Two models (SAHEL, TEMPO) are simple enough and described clearly enough that a non-technical reader can understand most of their assumptions and the logical flow that leads to their conclusions. Three models (LTSM, *MexicoV*, SOS) are sufficiently simple in concept that their major assumptions can be assessed one by one, although it is difficult to see the over-all structure. The verbal documentation of SOS manages to make a relatively straightforward set of assumptions seem unnecessarily complicated. Four of the models (RfF, BACHUE, KASM, and CHAC) can only be described as mind-boggling, despite significant efforts by the BACHUE and KASM teams to provide clear documentation.

A look at the characteristics of these four inaccessible models will reveal some reasons why the computer models are not always as explicit as they should be. First, all of these models are detail-rich to the point where the forest is almost totally obscured by the trees. The modelers themselves cannot comprehend all the interactions that must have led to a certain result, and therefore even those who have invested considerable effort in documentation have not been able to make themselves clear. It is extremely doubtful that any member of these modeling teams really understands what the model does and why, and therefore it is not surprising that the documentation does not convey a clear picture.

When a very complicated model is combined with a tight deadline, and no particular emphasis on documentation, as in the RfF case, the result is complete inaccessibility. The modelers cannot explain how the model produced a given output, nor can they repeat their own experiments on the computer. This model is no more explicit or accessible than a mental model. Probably it is less so.

CHAC, RfF, *MexicoV*, and parts of KASM and BACHUE suffer from another problem that hinders model accessibility. None of these models attempts to simulate real-world happenings directly. Each is instead a mathematical abstraction designed to produce a certain result that is assumed to be typical of the real system, but that result is achieved through a mechanism totally different from the one operating in the real system. The modelers do not believe in a great optimizing program in the Mexican sky, nor do they think the US economy presents a vector of final demands which gets cranked through a matrix to produce economic output. These non-behavioral models are impossible to understand intuitively, because they do not operate in the same way our intuition tells us the real system does. One must either be able to reason through the abstract mathematical properties of the model system under a variety of circumstances and then compare those properties with the real system's, or else one must take these models as black boxes. The simulation models (SAHEL, TEMPO, SOS, LTSM, parts of BACHUE, and KASM) attempt to replicate decisions, stocks, and flows in roughly the same way that most people represent them in their mental models, and thus they are intrinsically more open to investigation and criticism.

A final obstacle to critical understanding in nearly all these models is that their most important assumptions are implicit. Problem definition, choice of method, boundary, and selective omission of facts about the system being modeled are the most essential assumptions of any model. These assumptions are almost never documented, not because modelers wish to hide them, but because they are largely unconscious of them. As we have discovered in compiling this book, considerable training and effort are required to ferret them out. There are undoubtedly crucial implicit assumptions within each of the nine models that we have not yet discovered, in spite of the fact that we were actively looking for them.

In other words, computer models are indeed more accessible to criticism than mental models. But important parts of all these models are in fact not explicitly stated. In some cases the modelers themselves do not understand even the explicit parts of the models and are unable to explain them to others. The problem of model communication is most difficult when the model is complicated and when its structure is not causal or behavioral. Most of these models are accessible to thorough criticism, if at all, only by a limited and specially trained group of people.

E. TESTABILITY

The claim was that computer models can easily be tested, to explore their sensitivity and validity, to probe alternate assumptions, to try out policies that would be difficult to try in the real world.

We should distinguish in this discussion between two kinds of testing, methodological testing and policy testing. Methodological testing is undertaken to learn something about the model: where it is sensitive, whether it can replicate historical developments, how it reacts to certain kinds of pushes and pokes, what causes it to go beserk. This kind of testing is designed to explore the strengths and weaknesses of the model as an analogy of the real world, thereby giving the modeler some idea of how much confidence to place in the model results. Ideally, after thorough methodological testing has provided understanding of the range of the model's credibility, policy testing then begins. The model system is subjected to different exogenous policy inputs to see how it will respond, or the internal structure of the model is altered to see how a differently-designed system would behave.

The two doctoral-thesis models, *MexicoV* and SAHEL, provide the best examples of methodological testing. Picardi, aided by a software package that makes experimentation cheap, quick, and easy, did extensive sensitivity testing, varying all the uncertain parameters in the model as well as the unpredictable exogenous variables such as rainfall. He also explored the model's behavior under varying time horizons and extreme conditions. Beltran del Rio took the rare and painstaking step of testing different structural theories. Real structural testing of this sort may have been tried with other models, but if so, it was not reported.

Comparison of these two models with the others in our sample leads to the conclusion that graduate students are held to much higher standards of methodological testing than full professors or professional modelers. Most of the models received (or reported) only desultory and unimaginative testing. TEMPO and LTSM should have been relatively easy to test, but the experiments actually reported are minimal. This is especially surprising, given that each of them contains highly uncertain assumptions, for example those about the effects of exogenous family planning programs on fertility.

SOS was run under a variety of different assumptions (zero population growth, slower response to scarcity, etc.) but only as a generic system with hypothetical parameters—no attempt was made to relate the results to the behavior of any real system. CHAC, RfF, and KASM received very little methodological testing. These three models approach the size where testing becomes prohibitively expensive, which is unfortunate because models of this size also contain an especially large number of assumptions that should be tested. RfF is driven by uncertain exogenous forecasts, which should be varied both singly and in combination. Even if this model could be run inexpensively and its output interpreted easily, it would take years to test its robustness to all its exogenous inputs. But since running the model was not cheap, interpreting one run took several days, and there was a client deadline of one year, methodological testing was foregone almost entirely.

Eight of the nine models pass the validity test of fitting historical data or behavior to some extent (SOS never tried). None of the modelers seemed to derive much confidence from this test alone. We suspect that most models can pass it so easily that modelers have come to regard it as a ceremonially necessary but far from sufficient reason to believe in a model. Other arguments for model validity vary widely; an appeal for the intuitive reasonability of each individual assumption (Picardi), comparison with the results of other models (BACHUE), formal summary statistics (*MexicoV*), and examination of the dual variables generated in the solution of a linear program (CHAC). From their discussion of model results, one has the impression that the modelers have all developed a feeling in their bones about how literally to believe what parts of their models, but these feelings are communicated only indirectly, by the fact that some results are discarded while others are made much of. There is no objective, quantitative, or agreed-upon method for establishing confidence in a model or for reporting on the degree of confidence the modeler himself feels.

When it comes to policy testing, the best examples are models made in close collaboration with an interested client. CHAC and KASM were run through a variety of interesting policy variations, both as complete models and as various combinations of components (although they were given little methodological testing). The more academic or pedagogic models SOS, SAHEL, TEMPO, and RfF were not really subjected to the pressure of providing answers to practical policy questions.

When the policy tests were dictated by actual clients, they almost all involved watching an existing system react to exogenous inputs (What would be the effect of a two-child or three-child family? What happens if we line canals in Bajıo Province? Suppose we shift the support price of rice relative to that of wheat?). Policy clients, not surprisingly, seemed much more interested in modifying parameters than in exploring redesigns of system structure. Only the (academic) SAHEL model was used to simulate the effects of change in the structure of the internal decision system. (What if the herd size were adjusted in response to the condition of the range?).

The ways that policies are represented and tested are some of the best clues to the biases of the modelers and clients. Favored policies are represented with wondrous efficiency. In LTSM investments in agriculture produce immediate, significant output increases with no diminishing returns. In TEMPO family planning expenditures bring down birth rates promptly and linearly. Policy tests are also revealingly asymmetrical. More rapid technical change is tested, not slower technical change. More investment in agricultural research and extension, not less. Various positive rates of exponential economic growth, not zero or negative rates. More fertilizer, not less. More labor productivity, not less. More government, not less.

In summary, it seems that computer models are flexible in theory, but in practice they are seldom subjected to thorough testing and experimentation.

Tests tend to be weak, marginal, unsymmetrical, and very biased. In part this is due to oversized models whose complete testing would be impossibly expensive and tedious. It is also due to a general lack of imagination, motivation, training, client pressure, and agreed-upon methods for testing.

F. CONCLUSION: ROOM FOR IMPROVEMENT

We have had several good things and many bad things to say about computer models as inputs to human decision-making. Although computer models certainly could surpass mental models along at least the five dimensions we have discussed, they do not always do it. The models typically hide extremely simple theories under heaps of numerical gadgetry. Their methodological paradigms constrain creativity and limit comprehensiveness as often as they lead to insight. Computer models are hobbled by their very bigness and impenetrability. By limiting themselves to things for which numerical data are available, they ignore much of the real-world. There are exceptions to these sweeping judgements, of course. The achievements of these nine models are substantial enough to illustrate the exciting potential of the field. But at the same time they are disappointing enough to make us wonder why the field is falling so short of its potential.

Since we have been fairly critical in this chapter, we should take some time to defend the claim that the models *do* have value. To see that value, we should remember what we are left with if we choose to reject computer modeling altogether. The alternative to computer modeling is not absolute truth, but mental modeling. Like the schools of formal modeling, mental models are useful for some purposes and unsuited for others. They are most applicable to short-term personal decisions, where a single person's base of experience is most relevant. They contain much information about subjective human factors, values, goals, aesthetics, motivations. They are superbly handy; they operate quickly and cheaply, and they will always be used for urgent decisions and those that do not justify a major expenditure of time or resources. However, mental models are incapable of analyzing truly complex interactions, they are often willfully resistant to testing or change, they are unexaminable, and logically fallible. In many instances, mental models are just plain wrong, and not notably open to improvement.

The sorts of problems mental models are best at solving are probably less and less important in the world—because mental models are solving them. The problems that persist tell us where mental models consistently fail, and where formal models, perhaps improved over any we know about now, are the only hope. These are problems that span more than one person's expertise, problems that involve many interlinked factors, problems that concern complex non-linear aggregations of people and things. Russell Ackoff has termed such problems 'messes'.[3] Examples of messes are poverty and hunger, ecological destruction, the nuclear arms race, international interdependencies, and the processes of urbanization and industrialization.

Each of the modeling efforts we have described here has contributed something to understanding such messes.

1. SAHEL is a crisp, uncomplicated, and fresh conceptualization of an urgent short-term problem with long-term intractable causes. It demonstrates the interconnections between an ecological system and the values of a human culture. It resulted in a clear and unexpected policy message.
2. RfF coupled population growth, pollution generation, and resource use in a detailed, quantitative way for the first time. It also spawned an extremely comprehensive side study on technological forecasting. The question it raised and addressed is vital and was legitimized by the very fact of being computerized.
3. SOS is full of original hypotheses that raise important questions about societal control mechanisms. Of all the models, it is the one that most shakes up old patterns of thinking and forces one to take a long-term holistic look at industrial systems.
4. TEMPO broke new ground at the time of its conception by integrating demographic and economic concepts. It also was transparent enough to convey a clean and powerful message, and to serve as the foundation of several succeeding models.
5. The LTSM modelers set an excellent precedent in candidness of model documentation. They also closed the economic-demographic feedback while preserving the essential simplicity and comprehensibility of their model.
6. BACHUE is the only one of our models to incorporate a dynamic theory of income distribution or even to focus attention on the vital issues of labor, wages, and distribution. It is also one of the few models in the survey to attempt to include both the numerical precision of statistical inference techniques and the concepts of causality and feedback.
7. KASM is based on both extensive fieldwork and regular contact with the policy world. It has probably gone farther than any of the other modeling efforts in melding academic theory with pragmatic policy concerns. The KASM modelers also coupled several different modeling approaches in a creative way, and took on the pioneering task of institutionalizing a model within a Third-World government.
8. *MexicoV* provides our best example of systematic and open-minded theory testing, one of the clearest model documentations, and a pure application of a single modeling technique to exactly the sort of problem it is best able to handle.
9. CHAC gives us not only a meticulous assembly of field studies on Mexican cropping techniques—an assembly that could be useful for numerous other models and purposes—but also an example of a modeling technique pushed to its maximum through a series of ingenious mathematical innovations.

But the rigor, comprehensiveness, logic, accessibility, and testability with which these things might have been accomplished has fallen short of the potential that is intrinsic to the tools of computer modeling. The tools do have their faults, as the nine models occasionally illustrate. But the main problems come from the way human beings, embedded in social structures, are using the tools. We will have considerably more to say about that in the prescriptive part of the book. First, we need to take on one last evaluative task—to assess whether and how the models were actually used to solve problems in the real world.

NOTES AND REFERENCES

1. D. B. Lee, Jr., 'Requiem for Large-Scale Models', *AIP Journal*, **39**, (3), 163, May 1973.
2. D. H. Meadows and D. L. Meadows, 'Typographical Errors and Technological Solutions', *Nature*, **247**, 98, 1974.
3. R. L. Ackoff, *Redesigning the Future*, New York, John Wiley & Sons, 1974.

CHAPTER 15

Implementation: Changing the World

A tremendous amount of time, money and ingenuity was expended in creating the nine models described in this book. What was the return on that investment? Have the models in our survey changed anything in the world? Beyond employing modelers and using computer time and producing thick reports, did the use of the modeling process have any effect on reality? If there was an effect, was it an intended, deliberate one, or an accident? Did it make things better or worse? And most important, can either modelers or clients do anything to improve not only the quality of computer models, but the effectiveness of their impact? Can whatever nuggets of truth that do come out of computer modeling be implemented more usefully in the prediction, design, or management of complex systems?

We will begin here with a quick summary of the implementation record of the nine models, after a digression on the difficulty of reviewing implementation records. We will discover that we do not know and can never find out the total effects of these models on the world. The effects we can discover cannot easily be judged either good or bad. However, we can see just enough of what happened in these nine modeler–client–world systems to draw some tentative conclusions.

The main conclusion is that few of the models produced exactly the results they were intended to produce, but they did create some unintended and sometimes surprising side effects. That is, modeling clearly has an impact on the operation of social systems, but not an impact that is controlled or especially intended by anyone, modeler, sponsor, or client. We will then raise the question of why the process of modeling is apparently so difficult to aim. We will provide some tentative answers, which will be developed into prescriptions in the last part of this book.

A. THE EVALUATION OF MODELS AND OF POLICY: A NECESSARY DIGRESSION

The literature is full of judgements about the usefulness of computer modeling. The judgements seem to be of two types. On the one hand many people observe an increasing number of solemn-looking, sharp-talking modelers present near the seats of power; some ex-modelers have even moved into the seats of power. Books and articles about models appear and, occasionally, are widely read. Models are cited to prove a point, modelers are called to testify in congresses and courts, and newspapers interview modelers for pronouncements on this or that current event. Millions of dollars flow from clients to modeling institutions. Those who view modeling through these surface clues are likely to conclude that all those busy modelers must be having a huge impact on policy, and this is generally viewed with alarm. Among the viewers-with-alarm are many modelers, who are quite convinced that all *other* modelers are insinuating themselves successfully into the policy process, and who are not heartened by this trend.

On the other hand an even greater number of people, including some modelers and most policymakers, agree that the surface bustle is there and increasing, but believe that the modeling process has little actual effect on the way important decisions are made. Very few modelers claim that their *own* models have had significant impact, except when they are writing funding proposals or posturing before other modelers. Clients say that modelers are mildly tolerated, used as ways of postponing decisions, hired to reinforce a conclusion already reached, or viewed as diverting court jesters, but they rarely shape or influence an actual policy. These people agree that modeling has had little or no effect, and they disagree about whether that is bad or good.

These judgements are based on an intuitive feel for the situation, usually based on a small sample of actual modeling projects and a large desire to believe that modeling is or is not important in the world. Like most judgements people make in evaluating most social change efforts, they are formed quickly and easily, and they reveal more about the judge than about what is being judged. Evaluation of any political process, food stamps, zero-base-budgeting, promotion of nuclear power, or commissioning a computer model, is a slippery, tricky task. Before we attempt to do it for these nine models, we would like to look at the task itself—to consider what things we would really need to know about a model to assess its impact accurately.

Here is an idealized list of what we should include in a complete assessment of a model's effect on reality.

1. The modelers' and clients' and evaluators' goals

Evaluation by definition involves comparison of actual results to some standard or goal. However, there are so many goals floating around in any human endeavour that no single one presents itself as the obvious measure by which to judge a model. Confusion of goals is one of the chief causes of disagreement in policy evaluation. Each person in a modeling project has at least one goal for it; the goals of different people need not (seldom do) agree. The modeler, the sponsor, and the client may be trying to achieve disparate and even conflicting purposes. Is a model a failure if it serves the modelers' and sponsors' goals but not the clients'? Or the clients' and not the modelers'?

To complicate things further, most people have more than one goal. For example there may be:

1. *The stated goals*—the ones listed in the research contract or the model documentation; the ones mentioned when the model is described to outsiders. (To make a planning tool for ministry X, to increase general understanding of problem X, to reduce the cost of program X.)
2. *The personal or institutional goals*—rarely stated, but very important; the immediate close-to-home results that each person is expecting from the project. (To write a PhD thesis, to support one's graduate students, to appease a boss who wants some action on the issue, to justify a budget increase.) These goals are rarely stated, but with a little empathy one can infer many of them.
3. *The wild hopes and fears*—the creeping thoughts in the back of one's mind that form one's dreams and nightmares, not seriously believed, but subtly influential in shaping how the project is done. (To be summoned to give a personal briefing to the head of state, to avoid being the laughing-stock of one's profession because of a stupid mathematical error, to work out a methodology that will be used by everyone, to avoid giving advice that turns out to be dead wrong, to win a Nobel Prize.) Wild hopes and fears are seldom verbalized, even to oneself, and are hard to guess, but they are there.
4. *The life goals*—the very basic, deep ideals and hopes about where one is going, how one can make a difference, how this project is integrated with one's values, one's loyalties and one's worldview. (To raise everyone's awareness of the importance of population growth, to demonstrate that a woman can be rational and hardheaded, to destroy class distinctions, to show how a political scientist can contribute to economic analysis, to gain some legitimacy for system dynamics.)

Of course only the stated goals are directly accessible to an outside evaluator (and sometimes, as we have discovered, not even those—some models have no clearly stated goals). The others must be inferred, and if this were not enough of a tangle, the evaluator must also be aware of his or her *own* goals in all these categories and how *they* affect the evaluation. For example, in our own view the world has major problems, the present situation is intolerable, and great changes are welcome and necessary. Therefore we automatically approve of models that shake things up and suggest major changes, and we are less interested in modelers who are only aiming at minor adjustments. Notice that our bias leads us to compare the model's effect on the world to *our* standard, not to the modelers'. Watch for that throughout this chapter (we have tried to restrain it until the end of the book, where we let it go full force and with due warning).

2. The extent to which goals were reached

For those models with stated goals, this should be ascertainable. The SAHEL study was to provide an input to aid policy to the Sahel. Did such a policy appear and did it reflect the findings of the model? KASM was built as an on-line planning tool for the Korean government. Was it ever used that way? Did the World Bank follow CHAC's advice about whether to fund canal linings or tubewells? These questions can be answered, at least qualitatively, by looking at some process, person, law, or institution.

Quantitative assessment of the extent to which the model achieved stated goals is far more difficult. How much of an input to a decision must a model make to justify its creation? Is a useful planning tool one that is consulted daily, yearly, or just once? Is a model used regularly for very small decisions more successful than a model used once to shed some light on a major policy?

The extent to which *unstated* goals were reached is a matter of pure speculation, since we cannot even be sure of the goals. We can see the effects of the modeling projects, however, on the careers and institutions of modelers and clients and therefore infer something about personal and institutional goals.

3. The cost of reaching whatever goals were reached

Direct costs in terms of money, human effort, computer time, and travel are measurable, though seldom mentioned in model documentation. Much more difficult are opportunity costs and the possible costs of reaching the same goal another way. What would have happened if the money and professional hours spent on modeling had been devoted to some other purpose? How would the decision or policy process have gone if there had been no formal modeling? What results could have been obtained in two hours with a hand calculator? Most of these questions of the 'what if?' sort can be answered only by indulging in wild speculation or entrenched preconceptions.

4. The unintended, unforeseen impacts

As we shall see, this is a big category, containing both positive and negative items. The positive side effects of a study are sometimes easy to see, especially since modelers are eager to point them out. Scattered information can be gathered and organized in a way that is useful to others beside the original client. Data collection procedures can be improved. Related studies can be stimulated, to copy, correct, or extend the initial one. A striking new idea can percolate through a society, eventually transforming many decision processes.

Modelers can become recognized for their astuteness and knowledge of the system and put into policymaking positions themselves (modelers regard this as a positive outcome).

On the negative side, impacts can be more subtle and hard to trace. A model may dwell on accepted theories and available data and draw attention away from crucial matters that do not fit conventional ways of looking. Successful implementation of a short-term model may enhance a policymaker's tendency toward short-term thinking, when only a long-term approach would be effective. The existence of a modeling study may delay a decision that should be made promptly, or may reinforce a decision that is totally wrong. The results of the study or the way it is done may offend someone and create personal enemies for the modeler or client, or for the field of modeling.

The task before us in assessing the impact of the nine models is something like assessing, five years after they were written, the effect of Adam Smith's *The Wealth of Nations* or Marx's *Communist Manifesto* or, perhaps more accurately, some work of equal ambition that has now disappeared without a trace. What we need is the ability to follow a social system for 20 or 100 years with complete omniscience and with an understanding of how the system would have gone without the modeling project. What we have, of course is far short of that.

We are two people looking from one moment in time. We can see a few results, both intended and unintended, of the models, but many have occurred, if they did occur at all, in countries, cultures, and institutions far away from us, both geographically and culturally. Where it looks like nothing happened, we may not have waited long enough or looked in the right place.

Even the positive evidence we can find about what a model accomplished is usually second- or third-hand, reported to us almost invariably by a source with an axe to grind. We have had much more rapport with and co-operation from modelers than from clients, and so our evidence is biased in the modelers' favor. Our dependence on reports of others sometimes leaves us with apparently simple 'facts' that are so contradictory we cannot know what to believe. Consider, for example, the following descriptions of the SAHEL study in Africa:

> Sandy Rotival, the UNDP representative in Niger, calls the study an 'insult' to the Nigerois and says, 'At the same time that this country was fighting for its survival, MIT was carrying out a $2 million planning exercise and telling them how to organize themselves. The government officials resented it, but considered it part of the price they would have to pay for American aid. The graduate students MIT sent to Niger know almost nothing about the country, and since they could not speak French very well, they knew little more by the time they left. American AID personnel, for whose benefit and enlightenment the study was supposedly being written, had to take them around and interpret for them'.
>
> Laura MacPherson, one of those AID employees, says that 'A lot of bright-eyed, overpaid graduate students and young professors came to Niger to learn about the drought from people—us—who had only arrived in the country a few months earlier. We had to waste a tremendous amount of time talking to them and

interpreting for them ... '.

The head of AID's agriculture program in Niger, Jim Livingston, says, 'The project must have been a vehicle for a graduate thesis. It did not come close to fulfilling the contract, and at least a dozen glaring errors rendered it useless. AID instructed me to throw away the preliminary report and not to consult it.'

The MIT contract with AID was $1 million, not $2 million ... Most of the government officials we interviewed were cognizant of organizational and jurisdictional problems, and government officials in the seven departments we interviewed in Niger were receptive to our efforts and welcomed the chance to discuss the long-term prospects of their development plans.

Niger was visited by MIT's principal investigator and several other senior staff members. Niger was visited after six months of intensive study, including briefings in Washington, New York, Paris, and several field trips to countries including Chad, Mali, Mauritania, Upper Volta, and Senegal ... Four of the five MIT people who visited Niger spoke French fluently. At no time did any AID personnel interpret for members of the MIT project.

The comments of Jim Livingston betray the underlying problem. The fact that Mr Livingston made no effort to read the final report says little enough for his initiative as head of AID's agriculture program in Niger.

The hallmark of a good bureaucrat is to do what he is told. In fact, Mr Livingston was ... an unwitting dupe of an unofficial AID policy to discredit the MIT project in order to bury the final report so that it could be later used in bits and pieces to AID's advantage.[2]

We are underlining the difficulties of evaluating model implementation not to provide an excuse for ending this chapter abruptly here (though we seriously considered doing so), but to establish a sufficiently humble and skeptical mood for the job we are about to do. Past judgements about the effects of any social interference, including computer models, have been too quickly and firmly made. So little is understood about social policy, so few of the necessary facts about any policy process can be assembled, so many information sources are subjective and self-serving, that no perturbation of the social system, whether computer-generated or not, can be fully traced and evaluated. It is because social systems are so bewilderingly complex that mathematical models are turned to in the first place.

B. THE IMPLEMENTATION RECORD – AS WE SEE IT

The nine models that are the subject of this book are a sample taken from the leading edge of social-system modeling. They are not standard shipping-route optimization models used daily in the operations department of a large industry, nor are they trouble-shooting models taken on by a consulting firm to solve some nagging organizational problem.[3] These models are addressing the long-term problems of the economic development of entire nations, or they are trying to provide short-term predictions and guidance for decision-making at the national level. They take on issues in the arena of the public sector and of high-level politics. No decision-making arena needs a systems viewpoint more than this one, but no arena contains more obstacles to admitting such a viewpoint. These models have been tested in the toughest of all possible implementation environments.

In Part III we included the implementation history, insofar as we know it, of each model. Rather than repeat these histories, we recommend that the reader go back over just those sections of Part III. Here we will confine ourselves to sweeping generalizations.

The nine models certainly support the contention that model-making has an effect in the world. Like the expanding circle of ripples from a stone thrown into a pond, waves of influence have radiated out from each modeling project, changing people's ideas, decisions, occupations, and reputations. Some of the waves damped down sooner than others, some expanded beyond our range of vision, others cut across each other in complicated patterns. TEMPO spawned LTSM and BACHUE. Ridker borrowed a model from Almon and then another from House. A Nigerian model became a Korean model and then inspired a Common Market model and an international trade model. Each of the nine models was prominent enough in the worlds of policy or modeling to come to our attention and to provide lessons about modeling for this book.

Three of the models, KASM, *MexicoV*, and CHAC, were used by policy clients roughly as their makers intended them to be used, at least for a short time. These are the models in our survey with the most limited stated purposes and the shortest time horizons. Their stated goals are directed toward the detailed-implementation end of the policy spectrum. They are based on the operating paradigms and criteria for success already familiar in the policy world. The modelers were in relatively close contact with the clients throughout the development of the model, and they put significant attention to communicating, promoting, and institutionalizing their work. However, KASM and CHAC never were embraced as general planning tools used in an on-going way, as their makers had hoped, and as far as we can tell, when their makers and promoters left, they fell into disuse.

TEMPO pleased its USAID sponsor very much, but its effect on its Third World clients is a subject of controversy. This model is an instrument for conveying a strong view from one culture to another. The implementation task is inherently very difficult. The TEMPO staff put much more effort into simplifying the message and transmitting it effectively than into the formation of the model itself, and according to at least some onlookers, what they did worked.

LTSM and BACHUE were received with some indifference by their clients. They are policy-formulation models, containing a few revolutionary new messages hidden within the concepts and methods of conventional wisdom. They were made in one place for implementation in another and much more effort went into modeling than into communication. (That is more true of LTSM than of BACHUE, but for BACHUE there is much more to communicate.) These models may have changed some minds, certainly educated the people who made them, but they were not actively or regularly consulted at high levels of government, as their modelers had hoped.

The three longest-term models, SAHEL, RfF, and SOS, produced messages that questioned current policy and suggested whole new ways of looking at things. They were also made at some distance from the intended point of implementation (in the case of SOS there was no intended point), and the clients were not at all involved in the modeling process. The clients actively dumped these models and in the case of SAHEL and RfF tried to suppress communication of their findings. In all three cases the modelers finally came to view the general public as their clients and wrote articles and editorials to communicate their findings.

Looking just at the *stated goals* and the direct effects of the models, we could label KASM, *MexicoV*, CHAC, and TEMPO as partial implementation successes and all the others as failures. If we then try to find the simple, universal formula that accounts for these successes and failures we will have a difficult time.

Documentation, for example, is vital for scientific purposes but seems to have little to do with implementation. CHAC was used roughly as it was intended, but it was never adequately documented. *MexicoV* was documented beautifully and also well used. KASM was described in writing only after its period of greatest impact; SAHEL was always clear and accessible and never used.

Models made in academic institutions were both effective (*MexicoV*, KASM) and ineffective (SAHEL) in accomplishing their stated goals, and the same can be said for in-house models (effective—CHAC, ineffective—SOS) or models made by professional consultants (effective—TEMPO, ineffective—RfF). Both complex and simple models have found favor (complex—CHAC, simple—TEMPO) and disfavor (complex—BACHUE, simple—SAHEL). No particular modeling technique seems to bring an inherent advantage in implementation, nor does any particular size of budget or type of client.

One would think that promptness would be important, since the policy world moves at a distinctly faster pace than the world of scholars and analysts. But Ridker and Picardi both met rigid one-year deadlines with indifferent implementation success, while the TEMPO and KASM models dragged on for years with at least partial success. CHAC was done rather quickly and implemented, BACHUE took years and was not implemented.

But our judgement so far is based only on success in *stated goals*, which is a narrow, rigid definition of success. The tasks the modelers chose vary enormously in difficulty. It was one thing to convince the World Bank that tubewells are a more profitable investment than canal linings, using the bank's own assumptions about how economic systems work and its standard criteria for profitability. It would have been an achievement of a different order of magnitude to get USAID officials to extend their time horizon to 200 years, think in feedback loops, adopt ecological stability as a dominant value, and admit that their past aid expenditures in the Sahel had been counterproductive.

Picardi would have had to do more than adopt the tactics of the CHAC team to have achieved his goal.

If we expand our view to include personal and institutional goals, all of the modelers and most clients did very well indeed. Beltran del Rio and Picardi got their doctorates. MSU paid its graduate students and its overhead expenses. USAID justified an expanded Sahel budget. CHAC was awarded a prestigious prize in the field of operations research. The Korean Ministry of Agriculture and Fisheries improved its database and analytical capabilities. MIT kept many people employed for a year, the Presidential Commission received a thick, authoritative report, the Bank of Mexico got some forecasts that were probably as good as any others available.

All the modelers are still professionally active, indeed thriving. Most have moved up to bigger projects with better funding, and some have even entered the hallowed halls of policymaking. They claim that their understanding and subsequent analyses have benefitted from lessons learned in doing these nine models. Nearly all the models sired living progeny, similar studies carrying on a method, a part of a model, or a central question. Analysts in many different parts of the world talk about 'a CHAC-type model', or 'updating TEMPO'.

Each model generated, on the average, a set of written materials stacked one foot high, not counting computer output. Hundreds, perhaps thousands, of briefings, testimonies, conference papers, and workshops were given to spread the ideas and the findings from the models. None of the models generated an earth-shaking new idea, but many of them picked up new ideas in the air, made them precise, consistent, and concrete, and weighted them with the authority of computer code and prestigious institutions. Who knows how many minds were struck by TEMPO's message that population growth can inhibit economic growth? Surely many people read and heeded Picardi's analysis of the Sahel commons, or the U.S. Population Commission's statement that resources will be adequate and pollution controllable, or the BACHUE team's plea for economic equity. All the models pointed out the interconnectedness of apparently separate things, and reminded society of how partial everyday understanding is.

On the other hand, none of the modelers appears to have succeeded very well in achieving what we might infer were life goals. There is still plenty of misery, poverty, and industrial chaos in the world. None of the systems with which the models deal (Sahelian nomads, the U.S. economy, the nations of Egypt, the Philippines, Mexico, etc.) seem to be working with notable smoothness or efficiency, by anyone's standards. Korean agriculture is thriving, but probably not because of KASM. It would be difficult to argue that any of the systems addressed by the models are behaving measurably differently than they would have behaved had the models never been made. None of the modelers has won a Nobel Prize or been asked to take the helm of any major political entity. None of their names is a household word.

In summary, there seem to be several grand conclusions that leap out at us as two evaluators, writing from our own point of view at this time in history.

1. The models had many different effects that we can see and probably even more that we cannot see.
2. The effects that we can see correspond only occasionally and partially to the stated goals of the modelers, sponsors, and clients.
3. The personal and institutional goals, so far as we can guess them, seem to have been met—at least no person or institution seems to have been hurt by association with the modeling projects.
4. Wild hopes and fears probably did not materialize—nothing very wild happened at all.
5. The models improved or changed the visible functioning of the world, only marginally, if at all, even the functioning of the parts of the world the models were directed toward.
6. The main impact was on a vital but unmeasurable part of the system: the world of ideas. The models legitimated, publicized, opposed, or made concrete some major old or new ways of thinking about the systems we live in. They enhanced the mental models of the modelers. They were clear reminders that the world is complex. They contributed to the debate; they did not end it.

C. SOME HYPOTHESES

Theories about why models do not regularly or predictably achieve the stated goals of their makers, much less change the world, are easy to find. The modeling literature, classroom lectures, conference workshops, and professional gossip are full of them. If we ignore the subtleties of the discussion and look for the essence, we can find six basic hypotheses. We state them here in their most extreme and blunt form, to clarify them and to keep everyone awake.

1. Policymakers as boors

Making models for politicians is casting pearls before swine. The policy world is irrational or even systematically corrupt. Clients just want to hear what they already think; if you tell them anything else, they will force you to distort it or else fire you. Even well-meaning bureaucrats are locked into an overwhelming system of non-functional subdivisions and short-term parochial interests. There is no room in that system for a long-term, cross-disciplinary, whole system viewpoint. The tool is terrific, but the world is not ready for it.

Advice to modelers: You have three options:
1. Prostitute yourself.
2. Avoid the politicians, make the general public your audience and learn to exist on very little money.

3. Go into a more promising profession.

Advice to clients: Be a hero, fight the system, defend modeling and create new niches for it. If this causes you to lose your job, that job was not worth having. Go into a more promising profession.

2. Modelers as clowns

Modelers are ignored because they deserve to be. They are starry-eyed idealists with no understanding of how the world really works. They create mathematical monsters that require continuous feeding with zillions of senseless numbers and large flows of money. They never address vital issues. Modelers talk a fancy language that makes everyone else feel inferior, but when you press them for a translation, they never tell you anything you did not already know. By the time they finish studying something, no one else cares about it any more. The tool is awkward and useless, an expensive toy but not a serious policy instrument.

Advice to modelers: Speak plainly, listen to someone else now and then, spend some time in the policy world so you learn how things really are. Meet deadlines. Work on your client's problems, not your own. Stop being so pretentious. If you cannot do those things, go into a more promising profession.

Advice to clients: If you must deal with modelers, treat them like children. Do not expect much of them, and keep them firmly in line. Tell them exactly what is expected of them, make them report back regularly, be sure they're working on *your* problem, cancel the contract if a deadline is missed or a word of jargon is spoken. Audit their accounts carefully.

3. Supermodeler

It takes a remarkable set of scientific and technical abilities just to make a good model. It takes a different set of skills, in communication and interpersonal relations, to sell that model and see that it is used properly. Only very extraordinary people are born with all these skills. If you are not born with them, you can never acquire them. The tool is just too tricky to be used by ordinary people.

Advice to modelers: Be honest: Do you have what it takes? Are you a supermodeler? If not, go into a more promising profession. Or, if you have some of the qualities necessary for excellent modeling, team up with people whose abilities compliment yours.

Advice to clients: Hire only supermodelers or superteams.

4. The two cultures

Modelers and clients live in totally different worlds, see different things, respond to different pressures. In each world are basically honest and gifted people trying to do a good job. Each side has useful insights into policy; each can benefit from working with the other. The main problem is learning to communicate from each world to the other. We are not talking about a tool, we are talking about a subtle process of human communication.

Advice to both modelers and clients: Be patient. Listen carefully. Empathize with the other side and respect its needs and problems. Have a beer together. Go back and forth between the two worlds so you can experience both. Educate policymakers in modeling techniques, or hire modelers to in-house policy positions, or find a good translator who can interpret each side to the other.

5. The learning curve

Computers have been around for only 40 years, and social-system modeling has been seriously attempted for only a decade or so. Modelers have all they can do to work out the technical and scientific side of their job. Clients have not yet learned to use this powerful tool. Both sides are learning quickly, but a revolutionary social technology like this one cannot be expected to develop instantly or smoothly. After all, medicine was practiced for hundreds of years before its cure–kill ratio began to exceed 1.0. Especially if modeling is a subtle process of human interaction, not a tool, it will take time to develop.

Advice to modelers and clients: Be patient. Keep trying. Learn from your mistakes and communicate your knowledge to others. Look for little tricks and techniques that will hasten the learning process. Be bold. Nothing ventured, nothing learned.

6. No problem

The only trouble with modeling is that most people lie about why it is being done. The grand statements about revising policy and improving understanding are just smokescreens to gain public acceptance and funding. The real objectives are the personal and institutional goals of the participants, and those goals are being achieved brilliantly. Modelers get to play with their equations, clients bask in the scientific aura of the computer. Everyone enjoys the game. In the few cases where modelers and clients have been truly intent on solving a policy problem, the problem has been solved and the solution implemented. The methods, communications, abilities of modelers, intelligence of clients are all capable of doing the job. Both modelers and clients can get whatever they want from the modeling process. So far, all they have wanted was to make a model.

Advice to both modelers and clients: You're doing fine. Be sure you express your real goals clearly, at least to yourselves, because those goals, even if only subconscious, are the ones that will be realized. The rest of the world would benefit if you could bend those goals more in the direction of solving social problems.

Following normal-science procedures, we would now muster evidence to *prove* any or all of the above hypotheses. That would not be difficult to do. Each of them captures part of the truth. The nine case-study models illustrate all of them to some extent. There *are* boorish clients in the world, and clownish modelers. There are gulfs between the two worlds, and lessons to be learned. Probably every person in the field views it from each of these hypotheses at different times and in different situations.

If we examine these theories with an eye to *disproof*, we find them all close to unfalsifiable. We have no independent way to measure a modeler's superman qualities, or the intrinsic corruptness of a client, or the modeler/client system's real intent. We can easily blame an implementation failure on insufficient learning or weak wills or the modeler/client communication gap, and thereby explain everything and nothing. In fact, these theories are not scientific hypotheses at all; they are selective filterings of the truth, put forward to justify past results.

A more fruitful path would be to ask not which hypothesis is *true*, but which is *potent* in the sense of producing desired results. Social systems, unlike natural systems, are affected by hypotheses—the hypotheses are themselves a part of the system. These six ways of looking at the modeling/policy system are not only explanations but also to some extent causes, shapers of reality, self-fulfilling prophecies. Some of them can be immediately dismissed as barren and unhelpful.

Consider, for instance, the intrinsic unworkability of a relationship between a modeler operating with hypothesis 1 (clients are boors) and a client with hypothesis 2 (modelers are clowns). If a modeling project even got started, it might go something like this:

Modeler	*Client*
Here I am, ready to bring the light of systems analysis to the beclouded, dismal world of policy.	Here comes another one of those pointy-headed modelers.
I am going to make a model to show you why policy X is best.	I already like policy X. Maybe you could make a model to sell policy X to agency Y. They're always blocking me, and they like this computer stuff.

This guy is a jerk, but I really need a contract to keep my staff together.	I need all the help I can get pushing policy X.
I will need a staff of 20, 6,000 hours of CPU time, and $100,000 for travel and overhead.	Well, at least that will justify my budget increase request. Can you spend it all in this coming year?
Now I am going off to make the model. You won't understand this part, so I'll just deliver the report in January.	Good, don't bother me until then.
(time passes)	
Sorry for the delay—we had software problems, and we had to wait for the new quarterly economic accounts, and to tell the truth, the model didn't compile until last Thursday.	What did you say your name was?
Notice that in this case it has been necessary to impose restrictions on the market response, which has forced the aggregate value of production to differ significantly from its full equilibrium level along the unrestricted response surface.	Getting plain language from a modeler is like getting blood from a turnip.
The upshot of it all is that policy X is not as beneficial as we thought. In fact, it's counterproductive.	Garbage in, garbage out.
If they were going to ignore us, why did they hire us in the first place?	I knew this would never work. Why did I hire them in the first place?
Policymakers are impossible boors.	Modelers are irresponsible clowns.

And so both initial hypotheses are strengthened. The only result of the whole effort is that both modeler and client get to be right about each other's deficiencies.

'Policymakers are boors' and 'modelers are clowns' can be eliminated as fruitful hypotheses. The 'supermodeler' theory is also basically nihilistic and unconstructive. It feeds elitism, it fails to specify any selection mechanism for identifying supermodelers, and it leaves no room for improvement—no hope for merely mortal modelers to become super.

So we are left with three hypotheses—'learning curve', 'two cultures', and 'no problem'. The 'learning curve' and 'two cultures' theories (which are not very different from one another) suggest that there are techniques and guidelines one might look for to hasten the learning process and to bridge the worlds of policy and modeling. (We will list some of these guidelines in the next section.) The 'no problem' analysis is cynical as we have stated it—everyone is just trying to satisfy narrow, personal goals. But it can be inverted into a positive hypothesis—modeling can already be used effectively to help complex systems perform better. Modelers and clients can achieve just about any goal they choose. The main trouble so far has been the *expectation* that modeling cannot be very useful in solving real problems.

Most important, all three theories remind us that useful modeling, like useful policymaking and, indeed, any other creative and serviceable human activity, is an on-going, ever-changing experimental process, which can always be improved.

So now it is time to talk about improvement.

NOTES AND REFERENCES

1. T. Clarke, *The Last Caravan*, New York, G. P. Putnam's Sons, p. 182, 1977.
2. A. C. Picardi, letter to T. Clarke, May 4, 1978.
3. For examples of the successes and failures of operations-level modeling, see M. Greenberger, M. D. Crenson, and B. L. Crissey, *Models in the Policy Process*, New York, Russell Sage Foundation, 1976.

PART V

Prescriptions

> The most important problem does not lie in understanding the laws of the objective world and thus being able to explain it, but in applying the knowledge of these laws actively to change the world.
>
> Mao Tse Tung
> *On Practice*

When a field that occupies hundreds of highly-trained individuals, that disburses millions of dollars of public money, and that delivers authoritative statements about matters of political concern operates for years below its potential, people notice. Furthermore, people begin to come up with all sorts of advice about how to improve matters. The advice ranges from 'forget the whole effort' to 'fund and support this promising effort so that it can demonstrate its real potential'. Here we collect, sort through, organize, and comment on the many prescriptions the field of social-system analysis has accumulated for itself.

Chapter 16 is a compendium of the suggestions for improvement that the analysts themselves have come up with. It contains a good deal of excellent advice, which, if the analysts would actually take it, would probably transform the usefulness, efficiency, accuracy, insight, and implementation success of the field. Unfortunately, the striking characteristic of the practices advocated in this chapter is that modelers say them, but rarely do them.

In Chapter 17 we look more deeply into this interesting phenomenon of excellent advice that nobody follows. We probe the philosophical base of the very idea of social-system modeling in order to see what deep social beliefs and self-images hold social-system modeling in such a relatively impotent state. What we uncover raises questions not only about society's shared beliefs about computers and modeling, but also beliefs about science, social science, and policymaking—and therefore about society itself.

Any examination of the paradigmatic base of a profession, much less a whole society, is a dangerous exercise. Exactly to the extent that it is successful in touching and questioning the unexamined base of a society's self-image, it can generate bewilderment, resistance, outrage, and rejection. These reactions have to be evoked and withstood if any real change is to take place, either in the practice of a profession or in the progress of a society. We are strengthened in our attempt to get to the very bottom of the social system of modeling by the fact that others are searching there too—many of whom we quote in Chapter 17. The awakening profession of social-system modeling is already undertaking its own self-examination and is, we think, strong enough to use whatever it discovers not for its own invalidation, but for its own transformation.

CHAPTER 16

An Inventory of Suggestions for Improvement

Modelers know very well that the current state of modeling could be better. Dozens of them have written cogent articles and books deploring various practices and making constructive suggestions for change. We have compiled here a list of the major complaints and suggestions that we have been able to glean from the voluminous literature of model criticism. We shall embellish the list with numerous direct quotations, because the modelers' own words express better than our paraphrasing could the frustration, uncertainty, and urgency many of them feel. Where we could not resist, we have added our own comments to the list (identified by parentheses around them). The list is rather long, so we will use little space justifying each item on it. Most items have been amply illustrated by the nine models that are the focus of this book.

For organizational clarity we have aggregated the complaints and suggestions about modeling into three categories:

1. *Knowledge problems*—difficulties with the theories, data, and concepts that computer modelers have to work with.
2. *Institutional problems* that arise from the way modeling is funded, housed, and received by the outside world.
3. *Practice problems* generated by the everyday activities of the modelers themselves.

Many of the items in this inventory are controversial and some are contradictory. We have tried to indicate the places where there is clear disagreement within the profession. We expect that the list itself would generate heated discussion within any group of modelers about the worth and priority of each suggestion. We ourselves do not endorse all the suggestions, as we will make clear later. The purpose of including this list at all is not to put forth a manifesto of what should be done, but to indicate the state of thinking within the field of modeling about how modeling practice can be improved.

A. KNOWLEDGE PROBLEMS

Complaint: Data are inadequate

> As more complex systems are addressed and as the time dimension of decision-making is extended into the future, data become a major limiting factor.[1]

> Problems presented by both census and operational data are that models demand higher levels of accuracy than one has come to expect from census data, and that operational data are rarely collected in standard units, for comparable areas, at comparable times, etc., even within the same city, to say nothing of between cities.[2]

Suggestions for improvement:
1. Governments, businesses, universities, or research institutes should assemble bigger, more standardized data bases.

   > 'Data, data everywhere but not an item to trust.' Under the pressure of wanting to know more and more about our society and because of the seeming ability of our science and scientists to absorb the information and translate it into usable form, data collection activities have increased steadily for decades. The problem with these mounds of data is that they often cannot be used together since they are not calibrated or even documented. Until standards are set in the data collection area, this issue will continue.[3]

   But on the other side:

   > Funding of data banks should be carefully evaluated in light of the United States' experience which indicates that exhaustive data gathering without a specific problem or objective in mind is largely inefficient.[4]

2. Model funders and modelers should recognize the necessity of allocating more resources to data gathering within each modeling effort.

   > One outstanding feature which runs throughout all [large-scale modeling] efforts is the level of resources typically devoted to the collection of data and preparation of this data for use in analysis. It has been the experience of this consultant, for example, that a minimum of 20% of the cost of applying land use models will be directly associated with data collection, while in the case of standard travel analyses 45% to 50% of the cost is likely to be incurred before any real analytical efforts can be made. The nature of these data requirements severely limits the range of situations to which models may be applied. Only when a major study is undertaken or when there is clearly an on-going need for analytical capability, will the level of resources available be adequate to support an application of models requiring large input data bases.[5]

3. Modelers, social scientists, or mathematicians should invent new methods for signalling or recovering from data insufficiencies.

> I (believe) that the fact that some social mechanism is difficult to model is no valid excuse for ignoring it altogether, because this amounts to introducing the assumption that the mechanism has no influence whatsoever. Almost any educated conjecture about such a mechanism seems to be better than ignoring it. However, this does not necessarily mean that the best procedure is to hide such a conjecture away in a computer model algorithm and to act as if the uncertainties no longer exist ...
> As one possibility I would suggest the use of flags to signal unusual conditions during simulations ... During the model construction phase, one would not attempt to make any model of hard-to-quantify, unquantifiable, or ill-known interrelations, but only to specify under what conditions these might come into play, thus specifying appropriate *flags* instead of dubious *causal interrelations*. During subsequent simulations, if, and only if, a flag is to be waved, the situation and the circumstances will have to be studied more closely in a variety of ways unrestricted by the paradigm of quantitative modeling.[6]

4. Modelers should use sampling and surveying techniques especially designed for the purpose of each model.

> Sampling enables data to be collected with a particular problem in mind, while still maintaining a desired level of precision. In fact, some authorities believe that the 'only known technique for gathering data at reasonable cost is a scientifically designed and executed sample survey'.[7]

5. Modelers should document more carefully data used within each model, so that they can at least build on each other's data accumulation efforts.

> Problems with data are bad enough without having to reinvent the wheel. We should not only support each other by sharing what data we have unearthed, we should also perhaps clarify where we have rejected unacceptable data or searched to no avail, to save each other some digging.[88]

6. Modelers should use whatever information is available, including qualitative and intuitive information.

> If, in order to provide answers for the future, we require information about the past that is not directly available, an informed guess concerning the past is still likely to improve our perception of the future. Hence the absence of formal data about any element in a system should not lead to omission of an estimate for that element or to the abandonment of the system. Such a negative approach, carried to its logical conclusions, would lead to the abandonment of most— some might say all—social science research. This is not to understate the problem of inadequate and inaccurate data that plagues social scientists. But it is hardly a reason for ceasing to try to organize what information we have into a coherent framework.[9]

7. Modelers should use models to test sensitivity to variations in uncertain parameters, in order find out which data are most critically needed.

With respect to lack of data and/or knowledge of relations, the essential point is to admit that, with or without models, every society has to take decisions involving these factors. In this sense, besides experts' judgements for defining plausible relations, it is important to study deeply the model sensitivity with regard to these variables and to present a spectrum of runs under different hypotheses, covering the range of their variation.[10]

Complaint: Social theories are inadequate

We assumed that demographers would have developed a causal model to account for temporal changes in age-specific birth rates, economists would have developed models explaining business cycles, transportation engineering would have models to account for energy consumption per person per year ... , and epidemiologists would have developed models to account for age-specific mortality rates as functions of pollutant concentrations ... We expected that the only tasks facing systems modelers would be to discover these models as off-the-shelf immediately usable items ... We discovered that the submodels we needed from the specialist disciplines were simply not available ... [11]

Suggestions for improvement
Modelers should be sources of theory, not mechanical assemblers of other people's theories.

If modelers are forced to wait for theory to be developed by other scientists, the time required for model development will increase. This problem may be resolved by encouraging modelers to stimulate and guide other groups in the scientific community to develop the theory necessary for model development. This is all the more appropriate since the ability of the model development process to identify gaps in theoretical knowledge is a widely recognized one which could be better exploited.[12]

Complaint: Modeling tools and methods are inadequate

An attack on the problems of air pollution, urban renewal, vocational rehabilitation, or criminal justice involves investigating a 'system' that has grown without conscious design, the goals of which may be obscure and conflicting, and doing this in a situation in which authority may be diffuse, overlapping, and possessing different sets of goals. Data collection is difficult; the act of investigation may even bias the data. Linear programming, queueing theory, statistics, and the computer are still enormously useful here, but this is usually true for segments of the problem and not for the central question.[13]

Suggestions for improvement
Modelers should think more and wield tools less.

In disciplines with a long intellectual tradition, the introduction of new tools usually opens up lines of research that were previously inaccessible. In newer fields, on the other hand, we often witness the phenomenon of "new toolism", a disease to which operations researchers and systems analysts seem to be particularly predisposed. Those affected by this disease "come possessed of and by new tools ... and they look earnestly for a problem to which one of these tools might conceivably apply."[14]

B. INSTITUTIONAL PROBLEMS

Complaint: Funding for modeling is inadequate and misapplied. It is too irregular, too tied to short-term political needs, trying to buy too much for too little. The expectations of funders are inflated.

> Typically, respectable but hopelessly inadequate amounts of money (in relation to the goals of the project) are awarded to conduct a large-scale, totally innovative research program of great complexity on a strictly 'crash' basis, with the further proviso that public policy should be demonstrably and positively affected by the time that grant is terminated or soon thereafter ... Those staff members who do reveal themselves as having the capability to be productive in such an environment will soon be confronted with tremendous incentives to leave because of the uncertainty of future funding and because of the great demand for their services in other, more stable institutional settings.[15]

Suggestions for improvement

1. Governments, businesses, and foundations should increase their total budgets for modeling, and especially for building up a sustained effort to accumulate, house, and update models.

   > There must be support for sustained modeling endeavours so that, over a period of time, there are maintained and available a number of well-understood, well-respected models that can be applied solely or in combination to a wide variety of policy issues. We would not have these models housed and cared for in a government-controlled model shop, but in universities, research centers, and especially mediating institutions that form bridges between the research and political worlds. The models would be alive and continuing in the sense that they would be used repeatedly, kept up-to-date, and modelified as needed. In effect, they would become institutionalized.[16]

2. Model funders should emphasize basic, not applied, research.

   > Basic research and knowledge is lacking. The majority of the MSGs (models, simulations, and games) sampled are living off a very slender intellectual investment in fundamental knowledge ... The 'image' of research needs refurbishment among funders and builders in the professional community. Research appears to be so stigmatized that one can scarcely acknowledge sponsorship of a pure research project without bracing for criticism. The need for basic research is so critical that if no other funding were available, we would favor a plan to reduce by a significant proportion all current expenditures for MSGs and to use the saving for basic research.[17]

3. Policymakers should educate themselves about modeling and have more realistic expectations.

   > Policymakers need to become better informed about models and more realistic

about what models can and cannot do. They must be more willing to accept their own part of the responsibility for the disappointments, and they must take the lead in seeing to it that a healthier environment for policy modeling is created.[18]

4. Modelers should make models that require less support.

> Instead of having large teams working on a 'crash' basis, over a very few years, with a rented computer, on very complex data-rich models, without a permanent organization, without long-term funding, and without adequate budgets for publicizing research findings, we should have small teams (of about four persons) working on a steady basis, over many years, with a purchased computer, on simple process-oriented models (with minimum data banks), with a permanent organization, with long-term funding, and with most of the budget devoted to communicating research findings to policymakers and the public in language they will understand.[19]

Complaint: Academic structures discriminate against systems analysis and interdisciplinary problem-oriented research.

> An adequate reward and accountability system for faculty engaged in interdisciplinary work has not been devised by most universities, and most faculty participate (in such work) at the risk of professional advancement.[20]

Suggestions for improvement
Universities and agencies that fund academic research should establish reward structures and departments for interdisciplinary research and teaching in systems analysis.

> (Recommendations to the National Academy of Sciences and the National Academy of Engineering.) A study should be undertaken to determine how the university reward system can be made more conducive to interdisciplinary and applications-oriented research. The issues of academic advancement and monetary and professional compensation for the risks associated with such activities should be examined. Institutional mechanisms to encourage interdisciplinary and applied research should be formulated.[21]

C. PRACTICE PROBLEMS

Complaint: Models are overcomplicated

> Although there are dangers in oversimplifying the model, it generally pays to be simple. Complicated formulas, or relationships so involved that it is impractical to reduce them to a single expression, are likely to convey no meaning at all, while a simple relationship may be understood. A major error may invalidate the more complicated expression, and yet, in the general complexity of the formulation, pass unnoticed. In uncomplicated expressions, serious error is apt to become obvious long before the computation is complete, because the relationships may be simple enough to reveal whether or not the behavior of the model is going to be reasonably in accord with the intuition. The most convincing analysis is one which the non-technician can think through.[22]

It is a trait of modelers and nonmodelers alike to throw in everything at once when they do not understand a problem; odds are that somewhere in the jumble are the parts to the explanation. The trouble is, nothing is learned from such an exercise, and future problems receive the same treatment.[23]

The evident preference for large, all-machine models and simulations is questionable on several grounds ... Large models are usually complicated, expensive to build and use, take extended periods to operate and interpret, and are the least scientifically defensible. They quickly begin to suffer from the disorganization created by changes in purpose and personnel, bad documentation, gaps in logic, and problems of database preparation, maintenance, and validation.[24]

Suggestions for improvement
1. Funders should resist financing large models.

   We recommend that standards for approving the construction of large-scale MSGs be much more stringent than for smaller projects. We believe that large-scale MSGs tend to lack the capability of handling scenarios and other hard-to-quantify elements. Funds would be better spent on the basic research to acquire that capability than on the premature construction of large programs.[25]

2. Modelers should define carefully the exact problem they are studying and use that problem definition to simplify the model.

   It is a serious pitfall to attempt to set up a model that treats every aspect of a complex problem simultaneously. What can happen is that the analyst finds himself criticized because the model he has selected has left out various facets of the situation being investigated. He is vulnerable to these criticisms if he doesn't realize (that) ... the question being asked, as well as the process being represented, must determine the model. Without attention to the question, he has no rule for guidance as to what to accept or reject; he has no real goals in view and no way to decide what is important and relevant. He can answer criticism only by making the model bigger and more complicated.[26]

   We have found the following study process to be effective ... A substantial fraction (up to ¼) of the project period is spent in defining the problem on the presumption that no matter how good the analysis, the results will be of little importance if the problem is irrelevant. The decisive choice of problem focus should not be made haphazardly prior to the study, but be an important part of the project.[27]

3. Modelers should approach complex problems from the top down, rather than assembling pieces from the bottom up.

   Often the top-down approach is a good way to start simple. The top-down process starts with representations of the market, company operations, and so forth, joined together in a very rough aggregate, the kind of broad-brush picture seen from the top of the company. Later, if more detail is required, some variables can be disaggregated and the description enriched. By using this approach, the planner has a working model at all points—a great advantage. The reverse—the bottom-up approach—requires tedious acquisition of data and modeling by product line, division, market area, and so on ... and ultimately combining these to reflect the corporate picture. But the working model emerges quite slowly; it frequently ends up being difficult to debug and too detailed for the purposes intended.[28]

The predominant modeling strategy is to decompose the problem into a set of subsystems, and further reduce each subsystem into its components until each component is recognized as a segment of some discipline that can be understood by an individual. Once all segments are understood by their respective disciplines, the pieces of the model can be integrated upward and the total model used for analysis. The decomposition strategy has a tendency not to address the primary issue, since 'adequate understanding' is never achieved and models never are integrated.[29]

Complaint: Models do not correspond sufficiently with the real world. Modelers omit many important real-world factors.

Contrary to being an instrument of innovation, the systems approach is essentially reactionary. By defining problems in terms accessible to the tools, systems analysis has encouraged systematic neglect of facets and variables which could be crucial in both their generation and amelioration. In most social problems, even those attributable in large part to technology, aspects amenable to technical treatment are likely to be less important than those which are culture-bound, value-laden, and honeycombed with a political power network.[30]

Suggestions for improvement
1. Modelers should focus more on the problem and what is relevant to it than on what is measurable or what can be accommodated within any particular technique.

    It is easy for an analyst to become more interested in the model than in the problem itself ... A great pitfall of quantitative analysis is to quantify and model what we can, *not* what is relevant.[31]

2. Modelers should be wary of inappropriate substitutions of measured quantities for difficult to measure ones.

    Ultimate goals tend to be obscure and intangible. The most common pitfall is to substitute something that can be measured, no matter how appropriate. Thus we find cost used to measure effectiveness (expenditures per pupil, for example, used to measure the effectiveness of public school education), the response time used to measure the effectiveness of ambulance service for health care, and the rise in the price of narcotics to measure effectiveness of ways to reduce flow of narcotics.[32]

3. Modelers should be open to a variety of structural hypotheses. They should test not only alternate parameters, but alternate model structures.

    The modelers can best contribute to the task of 'getting the problem right' if he is prepared to work with many alternative models rather than with a single model and a set of 'data'. Insistence on a plurality of model structures should *not* be regarded as a demand for a preliminary phase in the modeling process which will later be replaced by a 'correct' model structure. Structural pluralism must be an *essential feature* of any modeling exercise which claims to improve our ability to deal with real-world problems ... However closely a forecasting model seems to reproduce a historical situation, however obvious the assumptions embodied within the model, and however necessary those assumptions seem to be to both the users and the constructors of a model, its adequacy as a basis for forecasting can be asserted only after it has been confronted with alternative models.[33]

Complaint: Modelers do not build on each other's work. There is no scientific accumulation of experience and wisdom because such experience is not recorded or transferred to others or subjected to open criticism.

The lack of documentation in the two cases is shocking. In large part documentation of the projects was ignored in the headlong rush to get an 'operational' model. Progress is unnecessarily impeded by the lax or non-existent account of the problem-solving process. How many times must we reinvent the wheel?[34]

Documentation is one of the most neglected aspects of modeling and simulation, partly because it is largely non-creative and therefore uninteresting ... Most workers find documentation distasteful because it is part of the cleanup operation.[35]

Professional standards for model building are non-existent. The documentation of models and source data is in an unbelievably primitive state. This goes even (and sometimes especially) for models actively consulted by policymakers.[36]

Suggestions for improvement
1. Funders should enforce documentation standards.

> If ... a sizable portion of payment for a contract were to be withheld until documentation standards had been met, think what might happen: more, better, and more useful documentation; more carefully executed models; a written testimony of the problem-solving process in many locales; better communication and education; and in time, perhaps, models that can be understood and eventually put to use.[37]

> Before undertaking model development, the modeler and user should agree upon the definition of the problem to be modeled, as well as the scope of the project in terms of available resources. The modeler and user should also define an acceptable level of model validity and precision. Finally, documentation standards or guidelines should be established ... To ensure the process of model development as described, funding should be made contingent upon the satisfactory completion of each phase of model building.[38]

2. Modelers should plan to allocate half the resources for any modeling effort for documentation and communication.

> For the sake of discussion, let's say that as much money should be spent on documentation as on the model itself; this is a rule of thumb that many computer software producers currently employ. If one concedes that the process of problem-solving is more important than any one product, doesn't it then follow

that as many resources should be devoted to recording the process as to developing the product? ... In any future expenditure of public funds for computer-based research, at least one half of the total expenditures should be earmarked for documentation.[39]

3. Journals should enforce documentation standards and should ensure that the equations for all published results are accessible, so the results can be duplicated by any interested researcher.

   Only those models accompanied by evidence of adequate validation and documentation should be published. This evidence should be available for professional review and user evaluation.[40]

4. Governments or professional societies or universities should establish a library or clearing house for models, programs, and subprograms.

   The idea of a 'clearing house' for modeling information is such a natural one that it has been suggested by many simulationists and others ... For instance, services could range from simply cataloging model names and sources for further information to completely checking out, documenting, and certifying models. Methods could vary from card files to computer storage and retrieval, while the cost might be borne by the users or granting agencies.[41]

   Most respondents favored the idea of developing more standardized routines and procedures for modeling. They saw this as a means of cutting costs and development time, and possibly as a means of increasing standardization and compatibility across models ... Principal points in the arguments against such development were:
   It is unnecessary, because such routines are already being produced ...
   The diversity of models means that general routines need much modification to apply them. The variety of computer equipment would require multiple versions of routines ... Changes in the state-of-the-art ... would require continuous updating.
   Packaged routines would tend to limit the flexibility of models, and might inhibit the creativity of model developers.[42]

   (Our own reaction to the idea of maintaining libraries of model pieces to be picked up and assembled by other modelers is that it will enhance all the problems of mechanicalness, overcomplexity, irrelevance, and rigidity that have been discussed here. It would be equivalent to maintaining libraries of prefabricated images for painters or paragraphs for writers.)

5. Funding agencies should allocate funds for communication among modelers.

   Several alternative actions by a funding agency could stimulate communication:
   a) Require that any newly funded project have the principal investigators spend several days at each of several existing projects to identify common areas of interaction.
   b) Identify major topics that are central to most regional environmental modeling efforts and fund semi-annual workshops to maintain interaction among researchers.

c) Increase communication of new Ph.Ds working in this field by holding special workshops for this group, since they appear to be the major forces in most modeling efforts.[43]

Complaint: Models are poorly tested and seldom evaluated.

Many capabilities built into these devices have not been subjected to validation. Not only is their empirical basis dubious or admitted to be lacking, but few efforts are being made to collect missing or questionable input data or to execute sensitivity analyses according to an appropriate experimental design. The lack of sensitivity analysis is related to deficiencies in estimating the validity of input parameters. Neither of these matters seems to be taken seriously. There is a less than 50/50 chance that a sensitivity test will be done, and when it is done, there is frequently no record of the outcome.[44]

Suggestions for improvement
1. Governments or funders should establish clear standards for model validation and evaluation.

> Validation standards were seen, on the positive side, as a means of avoiding or discarding bad models and enhancing the credibility of good ones. The main advantage ... would be the greater uniformity of criteria, and thus perhaps more even and comparable results.
> But validation standards also brought forth the strongest arguments against 'government intervention in scientific matters'. The need for uniformity in such standards would make them either too vague to be effective, or inapplicable across all models. Further, they might inhibit good developments that would conflict with the standards, and possibly curtail support for exploratory efforts. Finally, it was argued that a model should only be as good as its use requires, and that only the user can determine appropriate standards.[45]

2. Modelers or funders should give models to an independent evaluation agency for testing.

> What we ... propose ... is the development of a new breed of researcher/pragmatist—the model analyzer—a highly skilled professional and astute practitioner of the art and science of third-party model analysis. Such analysis would be directed toward making sensitivity studies, identifying critical points, probing questionable assumptions, tracing policy conclusions, comprehending the effects of simulated policy changes, and simplifying complex models without distorting their key behavioral characteristics.[46]

> A modeling review process including independent modelers, users, and individuals with experience in interdisciplinary research should be required.[47]

> To appraise a system and discover its value, good analysts obligate themselves to consult people with an adverse opinion of the worth of the system, largely because they know how hard it is to get a scientist or engineer to display much ingenuity in tearing down a technically brilliant design he has been working on for years.[48]

3. Modelers should test *each part* of the model against the world, not just the summary output.

> The most rigorous method of validation is detailed comparison of model outputs against historical or experimentally measured outputs of the real system when the model is presented with the same inputs as occurred in the real system. To be effective this method must be applied to small sections of each model or submodel, rather than to the model as a whole. Otherwise, when it comes to correcting the discrepancies that are sure to be present at first, it will be difficult to know which equation or numerical value, amongst a bewildering array, requires amendment. If the model is validated by comparing the behavior of each small section with the behavior of each corresponding section of the real system, then there will be no possibility of juggling the model of one part to overcome what is really a deficiency in the model of some other part.[49]

4. Modelers should test their results against the real world, rather than against a set of artificial rules or formulas.

> If a model or mathematical formula were used to indicate which proposal to select, the proposers' emphasis would soon focus on how to make his design look good in terms of this analytic definition, not on how to make it look good against reality—a much harder problem.
>
> C. J. Hitch, while Assistant Secretary of Defense, made this last point with an analogy. Another kind of problem that might be encountered with an analytically based contract would be 'rule beating'. An analogy can be found in the case of some of the handicap rules drawn up by yachting organizations. The intent of these rules is to allow the owners of often greatly dissimilar sailing yachts, basically designed for cruising, to compete against each other on an equitable basis. The rules are generally empirical in nature, and take into account such factors as the dimensions of the hull, the amount of sail area, and so on ... However, once such a rule is established, the serious competitor has a considerable incentive to study it very carefully when he is considering a new yacht ... There have appeared some fairly unconventional yachts, designed not in the usual way, but in a way specifically tailored to beat the rules. From a practical point of view, these yachts are freaks; nobody would have designed such a thing or wanted to own one save for the existence of the rule.[50]

5. Governments or professional organizations should certify not models, but modelers.

> Consider an analogy with the doctor, who is certified and must take responsibility for all events of consequence to his patients. A master-modeler qualification might be made to assume similar stature and symbolic meaning. At a minimum, attention would be redirected to the execution and appraisal phases of the sequence. There is something quite chilling about the present practice of allowing inexperienced or substantively unqualified persons to write computer programs that ostensibly will help make public policy.[51]

This very long menu of modelers' own proposals for ways to improve modeling is simultaneously encouraging and exasperating. On the encouraging side, it contains some sincere self-criticism and some clear calls for increased responsibility on the part of modelers as well as everyone else. On the exasperating side, most non-modelers will quickly spot the self-serving items on the list, as well as the absence of any totally cynical comments of the sort occasionally heard from outsiders.

Knowledge problems would be an ideal excuse for modelers to pass the blame for poor modeling onto other scientific fields. Yet a surprising number of the specific suggestions within this category dealt with things modelers should do to improve the knowledge base or to work effectively within its constraints. While nearly every modeler grumbles about the quality of the data at times, and very real data problems do exist, we suspect that few modelers would identify available information as the *main* limitation to the development of modeling as a field (though they might see it as the main problem with their current models). Computer modelers have yet to utilize fully all the information, theories, and tools that are already available. The knowledge base is the new material with which modeling must be done. If the modelers stop blaming it and develop creative strategies to deal with it as it is, they will expand and improve it, in the very process of working around its deficiencies. Virtually all of them know that, and they are already working to overcome knowledge problems.

Institutional problems, like knowledge problems, are safe conversational territory because they seem to be beyond the modelers' own areas of responsibility. There are real problems here, some of them totally independent of modelers' own actions, and some of them at least partly traceable to the early history of interactions between modelers and the institutions that have surrounded them. Whatever their causes, modelers seem to realize that institutional problems, like knowledge problems, are for the short term unchangeable. Their list of suggestions includes challenges for modelers to work as constructively as possible within institutional constraints, thereby building up a record of co-operation and productivity that can bring about a more friendly environment for modeling in the future.

No modeler, of course, has suggested that modelers may not be trying to be helpful at all but may only be interested in money, power, or personal advancement. Or that the tools of modeling are inherently elitist, mystical, and dehumanizing, bound to corrupt anyone who touches them. Or that the whole exercise is so mathematically constrained and artificial that it can never be of real use. Modelers are unlikely to think that way. But in several decades of social experience with these quantitative tools, very few other people have reached such cynical conclusions either. Most everyone senses a potential to be released, and most prescriptions are for improvement, rather than for discarding tools altogether.

D. GUIDELINES, FOR WHAT THEY ARE WORTH

Since this book is based on the assumption that the field can be improved, primarily from inside and by its own practitioners, let us pass quickly on to some positive guidelines for that improvement. These guidelines can be viewed as an enhanced summary of the long preceding list, ordered a bit more logically, reshaped to keep the complete modeler/client system in focus, and, of course, structured to emphasize the aspects of practice that we, the authors of the book, see as most pivotal to realizing the full potential of the art of modeling. If there is any accumulated wisdom in the field, this is it.

Having a list of guidelines is about as useful as having a sign saying 'think' on the wall. It cannot force one to think, or tell one *how* to think or sound an alarm when one has stopped thinking. At best it can wake one up occasionally and remind one of what to check or question when a model is going wrong.

It is important to emphasize that the list is of *guidelines*, not rules. Making a model and putting it to work in the world is a matter not only of mathematics—it is far more than exercise in human relations. There seem to be very few absolute rules about hunan relations. But we can think of four statements that seem to be basic enough to be cast as rules (the more tentative guidelines are coming in a minute):

1. *Do what is appropriate.* No guideline is equally applicable in all situations, and the practices most useful in one modeling task may not be useful in the next one. Any excellent human endeavour is done from an awareness of the current situation, not from a formula. The most important task is to stay awake.
2. *Plan the implementation along with the model.* Successful implementation is rarely, if ever, laid on the end of the technical job. It should be designed into the project from the beginning, and, of course, altered appropriately as the modeling adds to system understanding. The *use* of the model should be the focus of attention all through the project.
3. *Respect all parties to the relationship.* Anyone in a position to commission a model or to make one can be assumed to have enough intelligence, sincerity, and survival skills to be worthy of respect. Respect can rarely be summoned out of nothing; if one gives it a fair chance to develop and it does not, a model may be completed, but it will not be implemented as planned, at least not by *that* client, and no other client owns it. If either client or modeler treats the other more as an object than as a person, the project probably cannot be effective.
4. *Support the needs of all parties.* Modelers and clients exist in a buzzing world of short-term needs and pressures, jobs, families, bosses, students, budgets, secretaries, degrees, publications, and telephone bills. If each party has some understanding of and sympathy for the personal and institutional needs of the other, the project can be designed to meet, or at least not to increase, those needs, while still achieving the central task that is the point of the exercise. These 'overhead' considerations are not luxuries that add to the expense of the project. As we have seen, they will be achieved in any case. They are necessary costs of doing business. Every corporation has discovered that. Designing the project so the modeler can get a publication

and a secretary out of it, while the client can get a travel budget and a stellar presentation for the boss, will guarantee enthusiasm, attention, and maybe even a job well done. If there are no personal rewards or if there is a significant threat of personal risk, the job is not likely to be done at all.

The guidelines listed below are applicable in varying degrees to different kinds of modeling tasks. They are more useful where there is a clear problem and an obvious client than where the job involves spreading a totally new idea to many people. Where there is no clear client, the modeler's job is much more difficult. He or she must summon the personal energy to step out of the modeler's perspective and assume the guiding, critical role that these guidelines assume the client can fill—or adopt a wise, knowledgeable person or group to fill in the gaps left by the absence of a real client.

The guidelines have been compiled from the preceding list, from our own personal experience, from conversations with all sorts of modelers, and from what seems to have worked in the nine case studies. It deals not only with the primarily scientific suggestions in the previous compendium, but also with the bureaucratic reality within which models must be implemented. Guidelines are listed for both modelers and clients; obviously the system works best when both sides are working in the same direction. All guidelines should be freely used or discarded, as warranted by the situation.

Guidelines for effective modeling

1. *Modeler*: Don't be hungry.
   Client/Sponsor: Avoid hungry modelers, and do not keep modelers hungry.

Modelers who have arranged their lives and their groups to depend on the 'contract at any cost' are simply not free to follow the rest of these guidelines with attention and care. Unworkability in the modeler/client relationship often begins with the necessity to keep a group together and pay the rent, which results in hurriedness that rules out negotiating or carrying out the modeling process properly. There are many institutional reforms and thoughtful gestures from clients that could help modelers relax from insecurity about future funds. There are also many ways that modelers could manage their work and their needs to use funds more efficiently.

2. *Modeler*: Work only for the person who can actually implement results.
   Client/Sponsor: Never hire a modeler for someone else's problems.

Many excellent models fail to be implemented because the person who could really use them never sees them. Many others fail when their personal benefactor loses power or is transferred suddenly to Botswana. Modelers should beware of very mobile clients and of powerless ones. Clients should refrain from undertaking a study directed at policy levers they do not control.

They should not start a project if they do not expect to be around at its conclusion, and they should involve enough people from their own organization to guarantee continuity, should an unforeseen bureaucratic rearrangement arise.

3. *Modeler*: State your own biases openly and be aware of the client's biases.
   Client/Sponsor: State your own biases openly and be aware of the modeler's biases.

Biases are inevitable and they are most troublesome when they are hidden. It is probably a good situation when client's and modeler's biases do not match, because each can check the other, as long as both are more interested in learning about the world than they are in being right about their biases. Both parties need to see differences of opinion as opportunities for learning, rather than arenas for winning. Client/modeler relationships based on both sides trying to prove the same point are dangerous—they are likely to result only in propaganda, not analysis.

4. *Modeler*: Take time to define the job precisely and completely.
   Client/Sponsor: Take time to define the job precisely and completely.

During the period when the problem is being defined and operational procedures are being worked out, there is strong pressure to begin modeling, to show something is being accomplished. Resist this pressure. All aspects of the project should be specified as clearly as possible beforehand, from the problem definition (see below) to the budget, the deadlines, the documentation standards, and the institutional goals and constraints of both modeler and client. Patience and openness are essential here—expectations of the modeler/client relationship are formed at this stage and shape the progress of the rest of the project.

5. *Modeler*: Insist on a clear and significant problem definition.
   Client/Sponsor: Deliver a clear problem definition for a problem that is worth solving.

Probably the single most important cause of modeling failure is the temptation to model the whole system, instead of one specific problem. General purpose models are never finished and rarely useful. Keep talking and probing until the *real* problem becomes clear—a problem whose solution would make a significant difference to the client. Just as it is easy to model too much, it is also seductively easy to choose a trivial, easily-modeled problem instead of the one the client really has. For the continuing application of interest and support, the problem must be worth solving. The exercise must count, or it will not be done well.

Problem definition takes longer than almost anyone has patience for. Many modelers say a quarter of the project effort is required for clear definition of the exact question being asked, its measurement, its boundaries, and the policy levers of interest.

> 6. *Modeler*: When stuck, look again at the problem definition.
> *Client/Sponsor*: Keep the modeler's sight on the defined problem.

Modeling efforts often succumb to a slow, creeping drift, away from simplicity and toward complication, away from what is important and toward what is mathematically tractable, away from unconventional viewpoints and toward established wisdom. At each little decision point—whether to include a variable, to disaggregate, to update the parameter estimation—the guiding question should be 'would it help solve the *problem*?' Problem definitions may need to evolve and be altered as the investigation proceeds and learning takes place. But the criterion for decision should always be what will most help real-world decisions, not what the modeler will find easy or fun or what the client will find harmless or uncontroversial.

> 7. *Modeler*: Match the method to the problem, not vice versa.
> *Client/Sponsor*: Hire a modeler whose method matches your problem. Do not let the modeler warp the problem because of mathematical necessity.

Entirely too many modeling projects become irreversibly derailed by the wrong method. Most modelers go around fitting the world to their favorite kind of matrix, optimization routine, or spaghetti diagram. Modeling techniques used appropriately, are powerful conceptual aids. Misapplied, they can be more distorting than fun-house mirrors. The modeler must be aware of and open about his or her methodological filters. It would help if the client were also aware of the inherent biases and limitations of different methods.

> 8. *Modeler*: Expect the problem to be solved and commit yourself to doing whatever it takes to solve it, including taking risks.
> *Client/Sponsor*: Expect the problem to be solved, and let the modeler do whatever it takes to solve it, including making mistakes. Be committed yourself to the problem's solution, and be ready to take your own risks.

If either modeler or client feels doubtful about the project, it should not be started. Expectations of this sort are too likely to be self-fulfilling. On the other hand, false starts, experiments, and revisions *should* be expected, as an inevitable part of the learning process. The mysterious human quality called commitment cannot be summoned at will, but its presence or absence can easily be detected. The commitment will be easier to find if guideline 5 has been followed and a truly significant problem has been chosen.

9. *Modeler*: Experience the system.
   Client/Sponsor: Share your experience of the system.

The client usually knows more about the system than the modeler and can arrange site visits, data availability, interviews with key personnel, and the time of in-house staff. The modeler should participate in as much of the system as possible to build up a base of information, empathy, and understanding. Watch the real decisions being made in the system, and notice what information is available at decision points. Get a physical hands-on sense of how things work. Talk to people. Listen to the client, who usually has a good sense of what is connected to what. (We have known modelers to tend warehouses, mine coal, milk cows, take heroin, and join logging crews in order to learn about the systems being modeled.)

10. *Modeler*: Include the client in the modeling process.
    Client/Sponsor: Allocate your own time and that of your staff to following and participating in the modeling process.

This recommendation not only enhances implementation by building the client's understanding and ownership of the model results, it also helps keep the model on target and ensures that it includes the client's knowledge of the system. A client who is not willing to commit institutional time and attention to the modeling process is not sufficiently interested in the problem to make it worth modeling. Experienced consultants state that the most important guarantee of modeling success is the interested participation of the client in the modeling process.

11. *Modeler*: Have a rough model operating quickly (within one month).
    Client/Sponsor: Insist on a rough model operating quickly.

The initial model can be very crude, with little detail and with parameters that are only guessed. It should be only a basic sketch to show how the pieces will fit together. The purpose of a rough prototype model is to sketch out the scope of the problem and to provide a discussion instrument for the comments of the client and other reviewers. It assures that what the modeler plans is what the client wants and expects. It also requires keeping the model simple and adding complexity only slowly, with the client's understanding and agreement.

12. *Modeler*: Use a level of detail just necessary to capture the problem and to communicate to the client, no more.
    Client/Sponsor: Do not insist upon detail just because you are used to seeing it.

Many clients, perhaps because they know the system details intimately, ask for detail-rich models. Many modelers are good at disaggregating and are pleased to respond to client pressure. And many models end up so full of detail that they are untestable, undocumentable, incomprehensible, and useless. Avoid unnecessary clutter. The appropriate degree of detail *for the problem* may not be the one that the client, the modeler, or the data-collectors have ever thought of before.

The traditional categories through which a system is viewed may obscure rather than illuminate a problem solution. Logically cutting through the system a new way may simplify the model and suggest new solutions (though it may also complicate data-gathering).

13. *Modeler*: Design the model to generate the *client's* usual criteria for system performance and validity.
    Client/Sponsor: Make very clear your usual criteria for measuring system performance and model validity.

The client may be more interested in profitability or budget balance or general trends in market share than in 95% confidence levels or quality of life or achieved χ-square ratings. In some cases the cause of the problem may be wrong criteria, in which case the uselessness of the old criteria still needs to be demonstrated. Model design should respond to client concern and to the most real, direct, and measurable indices possible of system performance.

14. *Modeler*: Describe the model in terms the client can understand.
    Client/Sponsor: Insist on model descriptions you can understand.

A sure sign that a modeler does not understand his own work is his inability to communicate it. Clients, trying to appear sophisticated, are too often reluctant to keep questioning until they really understand, and so they tolerate muddy explanations. A model that cannot be described is very rarely implemented. Modelers, speak clearly. Client, do not accept work you do not understand.

15. *Modeler*: Document your model with scientific precision and completeness.
    Client/Sponsor: Understand, support, and finance the modeler's obligation to document the work.

For proprietary information, urgent or in-house work, or very specific trouble-shooting this guideline is obviously inapplicable. For large public issues, and for long-term, generic or exploratory work, however, it is essential. All results should be replicable, by the original modeling group and all others. Lessons learned, mistakes made, and tasks unfinished should also be mentioned. Just as sponsors of scientific work accept unquestioningly the obligations of supporting not only the performance of the experiments but also their publication, so should the sponsors of social-system modeling. The resources required for proper documentation are usually underestimated—they often are equal to the time and money required to make the model in the first place.

16. *Modeler*: Design policy recommendations with a clear understanding of real-world constraints and possibilities.
    Client/Sponsor: Do not underestimate the real possibilities for change.

Things are easier to change in models than in organizations. As effective policies emerge from the model, they will be met by institutional resistance to change—probably the more effective they are, the more threatening they will appear. The modeler must remain aware of the difference in difficulty of firing someone in his model versus actually firing someone. The client should be able to envision acceptable ways of carrying out changes that really will improve the performance of the system. More can be changed, more easily, than most people's mental models will admit.

17. *Modeler*: Test the model carefully and completely.
    Client/Sponsor: Ask hard questions of the model and support its testing, even though mistakes are revealed.

Modelers, better to find problems yourself than have them revealed by critics or, worse, by the real system not behaving the way you said it would. Do whatever you can to cause the model to break down or explode. Set different initial conditions, double and halve all parameters, push exogenous variables to extremes—not because these conditions are realistic, but because they will reveal faults in the model. Make all policy tests symmetrical—if you test the effects of more of something, also try less of it. Give the model to a relentless ideological critic for testing, if you really want to find its weaknesses. Clients, be patient with all this testing—*not* doing it is ultimately likely to cost more than doing it.

18. *Modeler*: Stay with the project long enough to assist attainment of results.
    Client/Sponsor: Use the model and modeler as aids to promote change.

Bringing about change is hard work; it requires patient, persistent, repetitive explanation. And as model findings are explained, new questions will arise and new tests will be thought of. The modeler should remain available, if the need arises, to explain results, to test options, or to find out why the real situation is not behaving as predicted.

Nearly every experienced modeler knows guidelines like these and probably could add to the list. Most modelers also have a good inner sense of which ones apply when—and they know that most of them apply most of the time. But very, very few modelers actually do find themselves practicing all that they preach, even though the preaching is totally sincere. The modeling literature has contained lectures about documentation for years, but the state of documentation is still atrocious, and pressure from funding agencies seems to work only sporadically. Every standard econometrics textbook warns against taking R^2 or other summary statistics too seriously as a measure of model validity. But practicing statisticians still spend more time juggling summary statistics than they do devising more imaginative ways of judging their models. Modelers declare the goals of simplicity and transparency at virtually every professional gathering. Then those same modelers give incomprehensible presentations of their own gargantuan models, expressing pride in how many more factors are represented than are in the models of their competitors. Modelers intone to themselves over and over that the client should be involved in the modeling process, but they really prefer to have technical conversations with each other. And very seldom in practicing or teaching modeling do analysts investigate seriously the question of which methods are best applied to which types of problems. The nine models described in this book illustrate clearly the degree to which the guidelines are put into practice.

If people consistently give themselves good advice and systematically ignore it, something is wrong at a deeper level than can be touched by simple guidelines, resolutions to reform, or pressure from funders. The vast majority of the problems of modeling are embedded firmly within the rational, well-meaning, regularly reinforced habits of modelers. All the suggestions for change that have been expressed clearly and compellingly, in some cases over many years, have had no effect for very good structural reasons.

Like all complex social entities, the system of systems analysis will not be changed through one simple technical fix, or through exhortation, guilt, good resolutions, or new and better ways of doing the same old things. The system will only improve by radical redesign, primarily redesign of the goals, rewards, punishments, values, and self-images of those within it. To discuss that, we need a whole new chapter.

NOTES AND REFERENCES

1. Holcomb Research Institute, *Environmental Modeling and Decision Making*, New York, Praeger Publishers, pp. 21–22, 1976.
2. G. D. Brewer, *Politicians, Bureaucrats, and the Consultant*, New York, Basic Books, p. 239, 1973.
3. P. W. House, 'The Developing Forecast Hoax', *Simulation*, p. 140, November 1977.
4. Holcomb Research Institute, *op.cit.*, p. xxiii.
5. A. M. Voorhees 1973, quoted in P. W. House and J. McLeod, *Large-Scale Models for Policy Evaluation*, New York, John Wiley & Sons, p. 37.
6. O. Rademaker, in D. Meadows, J. Richardson, and G. Bruckmann, *Groping in the Dark*, Chichester, John Wiley & Sons, pp. 207–208, 1983.
7. Holcomb Research Institute, *op.cit.*, p. 22.
8. D. Meadows, *et.al.*, *op.cit.*, p. 282.
9. G. B. Rodgers, R. Wéry, and M. J. D. Hopkins, 'The Myth of the Cavern Revisited: are Large-Scale Behavioral Models Useful?', *Population and Development Review*, 2, 395, 1976.

10. H. Scolnik, in D. Meadows, *et.al.*, *op.cit.*, p. 149.
11. K. F. Watt, 'Why Won't Anyone Believe Us?', *Simulation*, p. 1, January 1977.
12. Holcomb Research Institute, *op.cit.*, p. 21.
13. E. S. Quade, *Analysis for Public Decisions*, New York, Elsevier Science Publishing Co., Inc., p. 154, 1982.
14. G. Majone, 'Pitfalls of Analysis and the Analysis of Pitfalls', *Urban Analysis*, **4**, 235, 1977.
15. K. F. Watt, *op.cit.*, p. 3.
16. M. Greenberger, M. A. Crenson, and B. L. Crissey, *Models in the Policy Process*, New York, Russell Sage Foundation, p. 327, 1976.
17. M. Shubik and G. D. Brewer, *Models, Simulations, and Games—A Survey*, Rand R-1060-ARPA/RC, pp. 69–70, May 1972.
18. M. Greenberger, M. A. Crenson, and B. L. Crissey, *op.cit.*, p. 338.
19. K. F. Watt, *op.cit.*, p. 3.
20. B. W. Mar, 'Problems Encountered in Multidisciplinary Resources and Environmental Simulation Models Development', *Journal of Environmental Management*, **2**, 83, p. 91, 1974.
21. Holcomb Research Institute, *op.cit.*
22. Quade, *op.cit.*, pp. 329–330.
23. D. B. Lee, 'Requiem for Large-Scale Models', *American Institute of Planners Journal*, **39**, 3, p. 175, May 1973.
24. M. Shubik and G. D. Brewer, *op.cit.*, p. 61.
25. *Ibid.*, p. 70.
26. E. S. Quade, *op.cit.*, p. 330.
27. J. Randers, 'The Potential in Simulation of Macro-Social Processes', Oslo, Gruppen for Ressorsstudier, 1977.
28. J. S. Hammond, 'Dos and Don'ts of Computer Models for Planning', *Harvard Business Review*, **52**, 117, March–April 1974.
29. B. W. Mar, *op.cit.*, p. 90.
30. I. R. Hoos, *Systems Analysis in Public Policy*, Berkeley, University of California Press, 1972.
31. E. S. Quade, *op.cit.*, p. 322.
32. E. S. Quade and W. I. Boucher (eds), *Systems Analysis and Policy Planning*, New York, American Elsevier Publishing Co., 1968.
33. M. McClean in H. A. Linstone and W. H. C. Simmonds, (eds), *Futures Research*, Reading, Mass, Addison-Wesley, p. 148, 1977.
34. G. D. Brewer, *op.cit.*, p. 237.
35. House and McLeod, *op.cit.*, p. 76.
36. M. Greenberger, M. A. Crenson, and B. L. Crissey, *op.cit.*, p. 338.
37. G. D. Brewer, *op.cit.*, p. 241.
38. Holcomb Research Institute, *op.cit.*, p. xxii.
39. G. D. Brewer, 1973, p. 238.
40. Holcomb Research Institute, 1976, p. xxiii.
41. House and McLeod, *op.cit.*, p. 101.
42. G. Fromm, W. L. Hamilton, and D. E. Hamilton, *Federally Supported Mathematical Models: Survey and Analysis*, Washington D.C., National Science Foundation, p. 38, 1975.
43. B. W. Mar, *op.cit.*, p. 96.
44. M. Shubik and G. D. Brewer, *op.cit.*, p. 62.
45. Fromm, *et.al.*, *op.cit.*, 1975.
46. M. Greenberger, M. A. Crenson, and B. L. Crissey, *op.cit.*, p. 339.
47. Holcomb Research Institute, 1976, p. xxii.
48. E. S. Quade and W. I. Boucher, *op.cit.*, p. 352.

49. A. G. Biggs and A. R. Cawthorns, 1962, quoted in House and McLeod, *op.cit.*, p. 73
50. E. S. Quade, *op.cit.*, pp. 338–339.
51. G. D. Brewer, *op.cit.*, p. 241.

CHAPTER 17

The Transformation of Modeling

Unfortunately, the polite guidelines of the previous chapter will not suffice. They probably would, if this were a discussion of a normal academic field gone slightly astray while the real-world system is thriving. But the field of social-system analysis is not normal and not yet even very academic. It is far astray. And the systems it studies and tries to serve—large-scale complex social systems—are in deep trouble.

The Sahelian nomads Picardi modeled are threatened not only with individual starvation, but with ecological degradation and cultural extinction. The Mexico of CHAC and *MexicoV* has 40% rural unemployment, a population growth rate that is still above 2% per year, massive poverty, severe water shortage in its arid zones, and, in spite of its petroleum resource (perhaps because of it) one of the greatest foreign debts of any nation. The United States, the subject of the RfF and SOS analyses, is facing serious erosion on 40% of its arable land, toxic-waste pollution of its groundwater, and acid rain in its eastern ecosystems. Meanwhile it is adding to an arsenal of tens of thousands of nuclear weapons, while 14% of its people live below the poverty level and 3 million have no housing.

On the earth as a whole, 28 people die each minute of starvation, 21 of them children. In that same minute, $1 million are spent on armaments, and 40 acres of tropical forest are leveled. At least one species of life becomes extinct every day. The net annual production rates of nine of the twelve great ocean fisheries have collapsed to a small fraction of their original potential. Enough nuclear weapons have been accumulated to release the explosive power of 5,000 Second World Wars all at once.

All of these system problems, and more, are persistent. They go on in spite of the most sophisticated scientific establishments, communications systems, satellites, models, and databases the world has ever known. And at the same time, a field that has real promise of raising the global level of understanding and of giving human beings a perspective from which they might be able to untangle their self-tied knots, that field itself is persisting in its own perverse behavior:

- It concentrates on easily-quantifiable parts of the system, not important parts.
- It devotes tremendous labor, both in data-gathering and computation, to achieving small increases in precision, meanwhile doing little effective testing for general accuracy.
- It assumes and reinforces the social structure that is the cause of the destructive behaviors, rather than raising questions of long-term goals, meaningful social indicators, or system redesign.
- It produces complicated black boxes that outsiders must take on faith—it does not share its learning effectively with users—in fact it is condescending to users.
- It proceeds from the paradigm that the future happens and at best can be foreseen, rather than from the paradigm that the future can be chosen and designed.
- It rarely sets its sights high enough to demonstrate its most unique contribution—its ability to focus attention on systems as wholes and on long-term evolution.
- Many of its efforts are not credible, not used, and not even documented so that others can learn from mistakes.

If a system is behaving badly, consistently, over a long time, and in spite of many variations in surrounding conditions, then something more than marginal tinkering is required to bring about improvement. Something within the system itself must change, to a new structure that brings forth a new behavior.

Computer modelers often reach that conclusion about the industrial, social, and economic systems that they model. It is interesting that they have been less able to see it within their own system; the system of institutions, tools, and individuals that produces computer models. We have pointed out many ways in which that system underperforms. The modelers themselves recognize and complain about underperformance. They describe the better ways they could all behave, to be more effective. Then they don't behave that way. Clearly there are systematic, structural reasons why they do not. But there the conversation stops.

In human systems talk of change nearly always generates resistance. Few people in a system, no matter how much they complain about it, welcome any real change in it—it is so much more pleasant to put up with the faults one is habituated to, than to try something new and lose the comfort of old habits. Even the complaining is habitual and comfortable.

So computer modelers, like all people, are reluctant even to contemplate deep structural change in their own system; change that can produce whole new kinds of behavior; change that goes far beyond better documentation or clearer problem definition. In this chapter we are going to contemplate such deep and thorough structural change. We will use the word *transformation* to refer to it, to emphasize that we are talking about something different from what most people mean by the word 'change'.

By transformation we do not mean a massive effort that forces a lot of people to do difficult things against their very nature. We do not mean a list of tasks to be carried out, new job descriptions, or people to be hired or fired. A transformation, as opposed to a change, is not even a process that can be charted in advance, or laid out in foreseeable operational steps. Transformation is such a subtle restructuring of the system that the guidelines of the previous chapter, and other constructive behavior we may not even have thought of, will flow forth naturally, as that which is appropriate and easy to do. A transformation is a release of possibilities and capabilities already within the system. It evolves effortlessly from the system itself; it is not imposed from outside and it does not follow a plan made in advance.

One of the problems of talking about system transformation is that the very concept of it is foreign to western industrial culture, and particularly to the more scientific side of that culture. Though most people have experienced some sort of transformation in some area of life, few of them have recognized and acknowledged it or formed a category in their minds in which to store the experience. Everyday conversation does not point out or reinforce its existence. Transformation does not fit well into the modern paradigm; and so its possibility is generally denied. Social change, if it is even viewed as possible, is envisioned as effortful, violent, painful, or carried out according to a plan enforced by some people on other people. If that is the only concept of how things can change, it is no wonder that change is resisted.

The central thesis of this chapter is that what we allow ourselves to think of as real and possible shapes our language, our expectations, and our behavior, which then brings forth the structure of our social systems. Transformation begins with thinking differently, thinking in such a way that new expectations, behavior, and system structure naturally follow. If computer modelers can think of transformation as a possibility, if they can learn the principles of creating it, and if they can bring about a transformation of their own profession, they will have done more than reform social systems analysis. They will have found and demonstrated a key, maybe the key, to solving the problems of social systems.

In this chapter we will present and expand on that central thesis: the system of systems analysis performs the way it does because of the deep paradigmatic assumptions society and the modelers themselves make about that system. The system can only be changed if the assumptions are changed. Then we will look at what some of those assumptions are. In particular, we will examine the three prevailing social assumptions about computer modelers that we think actively hold in place much of the perverse behavior that the modelers themselves complain about. The assumptions are:

1. Computer modelers are and ought to be much like scientists.

2. Computer modelers are and ought to be something like policymakers.
3. Computer modelers are not and ought not to be quite fully human beings.

Investigating these assumptions and their consequences will, of course, lead us into society's assumptions about scientists, policymakers, and human beings.

We are about to enter dangerous territory here. Trying to see clearly the paradigmatic base of the society we ourselves belong to is, as the Buddhists say, like trying to see the lenses of one's own eyes, or like trying to bite one's own teeth. We may not succeed in removing our self-identities from the exercise sufficiently to carry it out fully—but we think we can at least begin.

To the extent we succeed, we face a larger danger, which is that societies never appreciate having their foundation assumptions laid out for examination. What we suggest here, if it is really on target, will be easy to dismiss as unreal, impractical, simplistic, or subversive. The best measure of its success will be the mental discomfort it induces in the reader, especially if the reader is a computer modeler. If there is no negative reaction to the ideas put forth here, then we have not gone deep enough.

So now that everyone has been duly warned, let us proceed.

A. THE ULTIMATE SOURCE OF SYSTEM STRUCTURE

As far as science can tell so far, things in the physical world are what they are and do what they do, whatever people happen to think about them. The behaviors of physical objects are objectively dictated by the laws of science. Human opinions, beliefs, hopes or prayers about them have absolutely no influence. People once had to struggle and die for that idea, but now it is so commonplace that we think it without even being quite aware that we think it. It is part of the shared social paradigm of the industrialized world. Like many paradigmatic assumptions, because it is so deeply grounded within us, we tend almost unconsciously to apply it not just to the part of the world for which it seems to hold—physical objects—but also to human beings and to social systems.

The behavior of human beings, in contrast to physical objects, depends to a very great degree upon what they themselves and those around them think. And the structure of social systems depends to an equally great degree on what the mass of human beings in the system have been thinking, about themselves, about nature, about the meaning and purpose of individual and societal life, about what is possible and what is not. A society preoccupied with death, grounded in mysticism, and believing that inequality is the natural order of things produces pyramids and priests, pharaohs and slaves. A society that defines the good in material terms, that is grounded in rationality, and that believes in individual merit with equal opportunity produces factories and scientists, elections and supermarkets. The human-produced physical system, the industrial plant, the technologies, the institutions and hierarchies, all are the historical accumulation of whatever the shared social mindset, tempered by the laws of physical possibility, has brought forth.

The importance of social paradigms in shaping system structure is not a new idea, but it is certainly not commonly agreed upon. It is a subject of controversy, and the argument covers many different points of a spectrum. At one extreme is the belief that people and societies are as deterministically propelled by the known physical laws as billiard balls. At the other extreme is the notion that even the second law of thermodynamics will capitulate to a sufficiently powerful individual or group application of mind and intention. It is not hard to find people running their lives contentedly and fairly effectively from almost any point on the spectrum.

We are not writing this chapter from either extreme, but we are much closer to the side believing in the formative and transformative power of shared mental concepts than is popularly accepted in our own society. We happen to be firm believers in the second law of thermodynamics. But we cannot ignore our own direct experience of system transformation, brought about by thinking about something in a completely different way. Examples of such transformation on the individual level include alcoholic treatment programs, techniques of the best athletic coaches, and teachings of the Zen masters. Examples on the social level include, in the United States, such extensive social transformations as the American revolution, the end of slavery, and the achievement of basic civil rights by blacks and women.

Social systems evolve from a shared mindset, and are constrained or altered by the nature of the physical world. A system cannot be changed unless minds are changed, a system cannot be destroyed unless ways of thinking are destroyed, and if ways of thinking do change, nothing can keep the physical and social system from changing to be more consistent with the new shared 'reality'.

Here are some others who have expressed the same thought in different ways:

> To tear down a factory or to revolt against a government ... is to attack effects rather than causes; and as long as the attack is upon effects only, no change is possible. The true system, the real system, is our present construction of systematic thought itself, rationality itself, and if a factory is torn down but the rationality which produced it is left standing, then that rationality will simply produce another factory. If a revolution destroys a systematic government, but the systematic patterns of thought that produced that government are left intact, then those patterns will repeat themselves in the succeeding government. There's so much talk about the system. And so little understanding.[1]

> It is important to keep in mind that the objectivity of the institutional world, however massive it may appear to the individual, is a humanly produced, constructed objectivity ... The objectivity of the social world means that it confronts man as something outside of himself. The decisive question is whether he still retains the awareness that, however objectivated, the social world was made by men—and therefore can be remade by them ... Typically, the real relationship between man and his world is reversed in consciousness. Man, the producer of a world, is apprehended as its product ... Human meanings are no longer understood as world-producing but as being, in their turn, products of the 'nature of things'.[2]

If the system of computer modeling is consistently producing results that are too complicated, poorly explained, unimaginative, irrelevant, or unused, there must be something in the way participants in that system construct their 'reality' that leads them to go on behaving in that way. So the task is to discover how computer modelers think of themselves and how the world thinks of them. How does that thinking produce the sorts of behavior that we have described in this book? And what other ways of thinking might produce different behavior?

B. COMPUTER MODELERS AS SCIENTISTS

The most obvious image society has of computer modelers and computer modelers have of themselves is that they are, or should be, scientists. Modelers of social systems, like most social scientists (note the very name social *scientists*) appropriate as much as they can of the trappings of the established physical sciences. They aim for precision to many decimal points, for specialized jargon, for complicated-looking journal articles, for statistical 'proof' of validity, for mathematical rather than verbal languages. Their main tool is the computer with its mystique of all-knowingness. They have picked up nearly every surface characteristic of the physical scientist except the white coat.

> The references to science that figure so prominently, for instance, in the official definitions of operations research are not so much methodological indications as they are ideological props. They attempt to increase the collective confidence of a group of new disciplines striving for academic and social recognition.[3]

But real science is not a set of techniques, journals, formulas, or anything else detectable by the senses. Those things are the physical attributes generated by the *mindset* of real science, and that is what science, like every human institution, primarily is—a mindset, a way of thinking. When practiced by a master, it is a tremendously powerful method of fixing one's attention on the physical world and asking questions framed so precisely and cleverly that a useful answer is bound to emerge. Science is, quite simply, the scientific method, the relentless iteration of induction and deduction, of precise hypothesis-formation and careful experimentation.

The aspect of science that computer modelers have almost totally failed to adopt is the scientific method. There is some question whether they should, given that they are dealing with social as well as physical systems. Later in this chapter we will qualify and amend any impression we may leave here that the scientific method is the only key to modeling success. But we do think that elements of the critical thinking required for scientific investigation would greatly further social-system modeling. It is worth looking a bit deeper into what practicing real science means, to see what difference it might make if computer modelers thought of themselves as people who use the scientific method, instead of people who act on the surface like scientists.

The scientific method starts with a very directed question. The question depends on the accumulation of answers so far, on a very clear appreciation of what is known and not known. The success of the whole investigation depends on questions poised exactly on the boundary of the unknown, and on the clarity and pointedness of those questions.

Computer modelers, as we have seen, are particularly bad at asking clear, single questions. Many of the models described here are the equivalent of the biologist entering the laboratory and asking 'what is life?'. There is an implicit attempt, probably stemming somehow from the image of the computer as omniscient, to be able to answer all questions at once. The infant science of social-systems analysis attempts to be, and is expected by its clients to be, instantly authoritative and comprehensive, as scientists are believed to be. But the best of real scientists do not pretend to be experts at everything. They are content to ask one question at a time, and to be extremely clear about what the limits of their knowledge are.

After meticulous selection of a pointed question that is consistent with the actual degree of understanding, two other attributes of the scientific method are:

1. The generation of multiple hypotheses.
2. The design of experiments to *disprove* hypotheses.

In an excellent article, directed toward physical scientists, who themselves often forget to practice science, John Platt describes these two attributes:

> Our trouble is that when we make a single hypothesis, we become attached to it ... The conflict and exclusion of alternatives that is necessary to sharp inductive inference has been all too often a conflict between men, each with his single Ruling Theory. But whenever each man begins to have multiple working hypotheses, it becomes purely a conflict between ideas ... In fact, when there are multiple hypotheses which are not anyone's 'personal property' and when there are crucial experiments to test them, the daily life in the laboratory takes on an interest and excitement it never had, and the students can hardly wait to get to work to see how the detective story will come out.[4]

Platt describes the dangers of failing to focus on disproof of hypotheses with the story of a theoretical chemist, who explains to his class:

> 'And thus we see that the C–Cl bond is longer in the first compound than in the second because the percent of ionic character is smaller.'
>
> A voice from the back of the room said, 'But Professor X, according to the table, the C–Cl bond is shorter in the first compound.'
>
> 'Oh, is it?' said the professor. 'Well, that's still easy to understand. It's because the double-bond character is higher in that compound.'
>
> To the extent that this kind of story is accurate, a 'theory' of this sort is not a theory at all, because it does not exclude anything. It predicts everything, and therefore does not predict anything. It becomes simply a verbal formula which the graduate students repeat and believe because the professor has said it so often. This is not science, but faith; not theory, but theology. Whether it is hand-waving or

number-waving, a theory is not a theory unless it can be disproved ...

In chemistry the resonance theorists will of course suppose that I am criticizing *them*, while the molecular orbital theorists will suppose I am criticizing *them*. But their actions ... speak for themselves. *A failure to agree for 30 years is public advertisement of a failure to disprove.*[5]

Computer modeling, like most of social science, is imbued with single hypotheses with which individuals and even whole nations are identified. When one's self or nation is deeply identified with any hypothesis, there can be no serious attempt at disproof, and, as Platt says, disagreements can go on forever. The Malthusian hypothesis is still a source of controversy after 200 years. The hypotheses of Karl Marx, of Adam Smith, of John Stuart Mill have generated 100 years of conflict with no convergence in sight, and now these hypotheses are built into social-system models.

A final characteristic of the physical sciences that computer modeling has yet to adopt is the sense of community and of the shared endeavor to build accumulated understanding of the world. Instead of viewing themselves as Lone Rangers, striding forth to bring knowledge to the world single-handed, scientists absorb almost unconsciously a sense of themselves as contributors to a long-term, slow, communal endeavor. Most of them are content to add one or two small bricks to the mighty edifice of scientific understanding. Among many constructive behaviors that this communal view induces are two that are notably absent from computer modeling:

1. Painstaking documentation, so that the whole community can share in every advance.
2. Community self-policing with stringent rules for replicability, criticism, testing, and evidence.

A common excuse for the absence of rigorous testing in the social sciences in general, and computer modeling in particular, is that there is no opportunity for experiment in social systems. Aside from the fact that only one of the several characteristics of science listed above involves experimentation, the physical sciences themselves have not all depended upon a laboratory for their success:

It is frequently said that economics is not penetrable by rigorous scientific analysis, because one cannot experiment freely. One should remember that the natural sciences originated with astronomy, where the mathematical method was first applied with overwhelming success ...

It is also frequently said that in economics one can never get a statistical sample large enough to build on. Instead, time series are interrupted, altered by gradual or abrupt changes of conditions, etc. However, if one analyzes this carefully, one realizes that in scientific research as well, there is always some heterogeneity in the material and that one can never be quite sure whether this heterogeneity is essential. The decisive insights in astronomy were actually derived from a very small sample: the known planets, the sun, and the moon ...

The chances are that methods in economic science are quite good, and no worse than they were in other fields. But we will still require a great deal of research to develop the essential concepts—the really usable ideas. I think it is in the lack of quite sharply defined concepts that the main difficulty lies, and not in any intrinsic difference between the fields of economics and other sciences.[6]

What would computer modeling be like if its practitioners sought sharply defined concepts, pointed questions, multiple hypotheses, disproof, and gradual communal accumulation of knowledge—that is, if they chose to identify themselves with the disciplines and responsibilities of science, rather than just its authority and privileges? That is hard to tell, but most likely, of course, it would resemble the world of the physical sciences at an earlier stage. By no means does every physical scientist practice these disciplines and responsibilities, but a sufficient number do, with sufficient community dedication to rewarding real excellence, and with clear enough standards of excellence, that there is undisputed forward progress.

As just one example of computer modeling in a scientific context, we would like to tell the story of a modeler hired to join an interdisciplinary team of chemists, biologists, and engineers, who were engaged in an aquaculture project. (We would like to supply a similar story of a purely social-system application, but we do not know of any). The team was using dozens of upright, cylindrical tanks full of algae and a single species of algae-eating fish, and trying to discover a feeding and management program to produce rapid fish growth at low cost. Policy variables included stocking densities, feeding programs, aeration and mixing, and cleaning schedules—far too many options to test in all possible combinations in the real system.

The modeler began simply by creating, with the team, a diagram of the interactions in the entire system. This diagram was a first sketch, very incomplete, but it already was a useful vehicle for communication among the scientists. The chemists could point to the importance of nitrogen compounds in the water, the biologists could include the various bacteria that colonized the detritus in the tanks, and all could see how their particular interests interacted in the system with all the others and, most important, with the growth rate of the fish. This discussion, before anything was computerized, already raised new questions and suggested new experiments.

A simple computer model was up and running quickly. As it took shape, it began producing results that surprised everyone. Many of those results were wrong. They arose from the combined incompleteness of the mental models of the project team, and they could easily be disproved by data from the real tanks. Each time this happened, everything had to be rethought, and usually new things had to be measured that were previously thought unimportant. The bacteria in the tanks emerged as an important factor in controlling the water chemistry. The algae as a food source came to be viewed as less important. Whole new experiments rarely had to be initiated, but on-going experiments had to be monitored in entirely different ways as understanding increased.

Over a period of two years the model suggested new observations to be made in the real system, which led to corrections in the model, which then produced new results, more measurements, more corrections. All the time the computer model of the system was evolving, the mental models of the team were also becoming more complete, encompassing more aspects of the system, and greatly raising the level of communication across disciplines. Eventually the model was at a level that everyone trusted and understood. It duplicated observations in the real tanks in an impressive way. At this point the model could finally be used to suggest effective management techniques for increasing the growth rate of fish.

This was a system with only a few interacting species (fish, algae and several bacteria), with only incoming sunlight and the chemistry of oxygen, carbon, and nitrogen to monitor, and with a large but finite number of management possibilities. The desired outcome was measurable and non-controversial. The final model was about as big as the intermediate-size models in this book. It took two years of tight coupling back and forth between observations of the system and observations of the model before enough convergence was obtained for the model to become credible, useful, and used. During this time the yield in the fish tanks steadily went up. Everyone involved in the process considered it a great success.

If there is any lesson in this example for social-system modeling, it should be to make everyone more humble in aspiring to a high degree of understanding of entire economic systems coupled with entire ecosystems, where there are multiple goals, some of them conflicting, some of them unmeasurable. Another lesson is in the position of modeler-as-scientist in this endeavor. He was not in the objective stance of an experimenter in a laboratory, not caring how the experiment comes out. He had a clear goal for the system. He was learning about the system and trying to influence it simultaneously and he was totally embedded in the process, not above or outside it. He used the model to draw multiple hypotheses from the disciplinary experts, to integrate them, and to suggest what observations to make on the system to disprove them. He was subjected to the discipline of comparing his model results, in detail, with real-system behavior almost daily.

The process described here uses the tools of critical scientific thinking, but it is not value-neutral science. In the aquaculture example, and in social system modeling, the system is being interfered with to produce a desired outcome while the modeling proceeds. The process is not a distant wielding of expertise with no involvement in the situation. It is, rather, what Donald Schön calls 'reflection-in-action':

> The practitioners' moves also function as exploratory probes of their situation. Their moves stimulate the situation's backtalk, which causes them to appreciate things in the situation that go beyond their intial perceptions of the design ... The exploratory experiment consists in the practitioner's conversation with the situation, in the back-talk which he elicits and appreciates ...
>
> The inquirer's relation to this situation is *transactional*. He shapes the situation,

but in conversation with it, so that his own models and appreciations are also shaped by the situation. The phenomena that he seeks to understand are partly of his own making; he is *in* the situation that he seeks to understand.[7]

Or, to take a more prosaic analogy, not from the world of science, but the world of craftsmanship:

Sometime look at the novice workman or a bad workman and compare his expression with that of a craftsman whose work you know is excellent and you'll see the difference. The craftsman isn't ever following a single line of instruction. He's making decisions as he goes along. For that reason he'll be absorbed and attentive to what he's doing even though he doesn't deliberately contrive this. His motions and the machine are in a kind of harmony. He isn't following any set of written instructions because the nature of the material at hand determines his thoughts and motions, which simultaneously change the nature of the material at hand. The material and his thoughts are changing together in a progression of changes until his mind's at rest at the same time the material's right.[8]

The mindset of physical science that would transform computer modeling is not the mindset of precision and certainty, or of distance and uninvolvement. Rather, it is the intellectual discipline of question-posing, hypothesis generation, and searching for disproof, and the recognition that one is part of a community of seekers and experimenters, all practiced from the position of 'reflection-in-action', involvement with the social system, and caring about its evolution. That way of thinking would make modelers more scientific, in that they would make more rigorous use of the scientific method, and less scientific, in that they would allow themselves to be subjective actors within the system, expressing values and working for their chosen results.

But social-system modeling is poised between two worlds—that of science and that of policy. The current view of computer modeling contains images not only of scientists, but also of policymakers. These images also bring forth their resultant actions and behaviors, and they too need to be examined.

C. COMPUTER MODELERS AS POLICYMAKERS

Most social-system models are not much used for policy, at least in the way they were intended to be used. But even if these models were made in a way that caused them to be more welcomed and used by policymakers, we are afraid they would not make much difference. Computer models of social systems, the ones described in this book and most others as well[9] are made and interpreted well within the confines of conventional political wisdom. For example:

- They reinforce the idea that the important decisions in the world are made at the national level. By making national policies exogenous, they imply that national policymakers (only) are free from the rest of the system, above it, and able to do what they want. They rarely depict the ways that

national policy is itself embedded in and driven by the system, or the possibility that national-level policy levers have little effect on anything.
- They depict the populace as lumpish raw material, the source of labor and consumption, partially moldable by policy, never initiating anything, or exhibiting any creativity or will, or exerting any power.
- They continue to generate, display, and thereby legitimate as social indicators standard money-flow measures, rather than focusing on physical stocks or distributional equity or basic human needs or any non-monetary and non-material measure of welfare.
- They accept implicitly the West's definition of 'development'. They assume the world will and should evolve along the paths the industrial cultures have taken, rather than questioning the desirability, feasibility, or sustainability of those paths. They never picture societies where jobs do not have to be 'created', where work enhances human dignity, where environments are whole and pleasing, where people have roles other than consumption, where human variability is appreciated and encouraged.
- They concur with the economists in calling some results of industrial activity 'products' and others 'externalities'. They draw conventional boundaries that bypass questions about where natural resources come from or where pollutants and discards go. They do not attempt to represent the costs of production to the wholeness of human communities, to individual identities, to ecosystems, or to the stability of the international order.
- Above all, computer modelers endorse the cynicism of their culture, the idea that human nature is basically flawed, that people will never act sensibly, that society must be founded on the assumption of immorality. They treasure up selective evidence of unworkability, not noticing that they are surrounded at every moment by people who are decent, caring, co-operative, and contributing.

The primary offering that the analysis of complex systems could bring to policymaking—a questioning, total-system, long-term perspective on things—is least demonstrated by the field so far. Instead of questioning the present policymaking mindset, computer modeling has in general adopted that mindset and legitimated it. (There are exceptions, of course, including a few of the models in this book.)

There are many assumptions within the world of social policy that need to be challenged, some of which computer modeling is especially suited to take on—such as the assumption that focusing on the short term will also serve the long term, or the assumption that maximizing the welfare of particular parts of a society will benefit the whole society. The reason that computer modeling is used more often to promote such assumptions than to test them probably stems from another very deep belief. It is the assumption, which also can be traced to the physical sciences, that social systems are ordered, knowable, and controllable, and that political leaders must be able to order, know, and control them.

The political leader, as depicted by the media, by history books, by myths and legends, and by every other means with which society describes itself, knows the answers. Leaders are expected to be firm, to act unswervingly, and to be right. It is not acceptable for a policymaker to admit not knowing, to try experiments, or to decide that the appropriate solution yesterday is no longer appropriate today. The political belief system does not admit the possibility of problems without knowable and permanent answers. And yet much of the world, at least the social world, is made up of exactly such problems:

> The physical sciences and mathematics are concerned exclusively with *convergent* problems ... When they have been solved, the solution can be written down and passed on to others, who can apply it without needing to reproduce the mental effort necessary to find it ... The true problems of living—in politics, economics, education, marriage, etc.—are always problems of overcoming or reconciling opposites. They are *divergent* problems and have no solution in the ordinary sense of the word. They demand of man not merely the employment of his reasoning powers, but the commitment of his whole personality. Naturally, spurious solutions, by way of a clever formula, are always being put forward; but they never work for long because they invariably neglect one of the two opposites, and thus lose the very quality of human life. In economics, the solution offered may provide for freedom but not for planning, or vice versa. In industrial organisation, it may provide for discipline but not for workers' participation in management, or vice versa. In politics, it might provide for leadership without democracy, or again, for democracy without leadership.[10]

Donald Michael has speculated on the source of the idea that the world is knowable and controllable, and on some of its consequences:

> As the beliefs of the Age of Enlightenment were promulgated and disseminated, ascribing to science and technology unlimited ameliorative power to free humankind from its constraints, males were most exposed to these beliefs through their activities in industry, business, and government, under circumstances that demonstrated their utility and, hence, their validity ... Males came to embody these beliefs, practicing them when they could and affirming them always. In such a heady atmosphere of successful efforts to control (in part 'successful' because those who were victims rather than beneficiaries of technological control were routinely ignored or discounted), there was every reason to suppose that the same worldview and definition of competence would hold true under any and all societal circumstances: a competent person could, through information, gain the knowledge needed to discover the causes and effects of the human condition and to control them.
>
> Under such norms errors became failures and these are evidence of incompetence: they demonstrate a failure to apply correct knowledge and through it to exercise control ... Operating by this definition of competence, one's self-image is closely tied to and tested by successfully exercising control. Besides seeking to demonstrate ability to control it is also very important to deny to one's self and surely to others evidence that one is not in control ...
>
> In today's world information increasingly demonstrates that things aren't going as intended. The result is ... (that) there is retrenchment by those who would control, an effort to deny their impotency by more intense efforts to control.[11]

The image of the oracle, which knows the future, though its origins are pre-scientific, is still dominant in the modern social world-view. The oracle's knowledge is no longer ascribed to gods and spirits, but to science, rationality, and the computer. There is still no doubt that such knowledge is possible, and that leaders are to be judged by the extent to which they possess and act on it.

Computer modelers have unthinkingly absorbed this view of policymakers as unerring controllers. By their very presence they reinforce that view. They either bring with them into the association with clients, or adopt from the clients, the self-image of competence through certainty. And if you must appear knowledgeable to be credible, you must have all-inclusive, complicated models, you must deliver numerical answers with many significant digits, and you will not be eager to test your model very openly or thoroughly. You will leap into the detailed implementation stage of management when in fact you have almost no general understanding. You will certainly not challenge the conventional way of seeing things, because your own image of certainty depends upon the degree to which you uphold your client's image of certainty.

Donald Schön characterizes this way of thinking as the 'Model I' theory of action.

> An individual who conforms to Model I behaves according to characteristic values and strategies of action. His values include the following:
> —Achieve the task as I define it.
> —In win/lose interactions with others, try to win and avoid losing.
> —Avoid negative feelings, such as anger or resentment.
> —Be rational, in the sense of 'Keep cool, be persuasive, use rational argument'.
>
> Among the strategies by which he tries to satisfy these values, there are the following:
> —Control the task unilaterally.
> —Protect yourself unilaterally, without testing to see whether you need to do so.
> —Protect the other unilaterally, without testing to see whether he wishes to be protected.
>
> When the several parties to an interaction behave according to Model I, there are predictable consequences. The behavioral world—the world of experienced interpersonal interaction—tends to be win/lose. The participants in it act defensively and are perceived as doing so ... And individuals tend to employ strategies of mystery and mastery, seeking to master the situation while keeping their own thoughts and feelings mysterious.[12]

Mystery and mastery, win/lose, knowledge and control, the claim to have found convergent solutions to divergent problems—all these are attributes of the social image of policymaking, and all have been absorbed into the self-image of computer modelers, like any advisors to the policy-making process.

Another way of thinking, one that would transform not only modeling, but also social policy, begins with letting go of the main assumption—that social systems are basically known and can be controlled. A simple admission of society's actual degree of ignorance about itself may produce at first a somewhat sickening dizziness, with the loss of foundation of certainty upon which social self-identity rests. But it takes only a short time to begin to see the course of action that then becomes possible. It is a shift from certain, forceful leadership to honest, experimental redesign.

> At present, the tendency is to hold out hope that a specific project ... will provide *the* much-desired *answer*. A more productive strategy might be to devise questions, techniques, and procedures that shift the focus of attention away from particular solutions and over to the difficulty of the problem itself ... Redefining innovation efforts as *experiments* ... removes the onus of having to produce *the* answer, and frees us to focus attention on appraisal of the current experiment. A distinction between *trapped* and *experimental* administrators drawn by Donald Campbell illustrates the point. The former 'have so committed themselves in advance to the efficacy of the reform that they cannot afford honest evaluation' and the latter 'have justified the reform on the basis of the importance of the problem, not the certainty of their answer, and are committed to going on to other potential solutions if the one just tried fails'.[13]
>
> What if uncertainty were accepted and shared as our common condition and acknowledged by leaders rather than being denied by them in order to sustain the belief that certainty is attainable through their vision and judgement? Surely we can tolerate much more uncertainty when we have others to share it with ...
>
> Neither we ourselves nor our associates, nor the publics that need to be involved if they are to learn to make responsible demands, can learn what is going on and might go on if we act as if we really had the facts, were really certain about all the issues, knew exactly what the outcome should/could be, and were really certain that we were attaining the most preferred outcomes. Moreover, when addressing complex social issues, acting as if we knew what we were doing simply decreases our credibility ... Distrust of institutions and authority figures is increasing. The very act of acknowledging uncertainty could help greatly to reverse this worsening trend ...
>
> Actions intended to affect something would be based on shared and acknowledged ignorance that must accompany any body of knowledge. And it would reduce the need to act over-cautiously and conservatively out of fear of being caught-out in a mistake, of being unable to control. Accepting this ignorance and its associated vulnerability would reduce the need for those defensive, self-protecting, interpersonal and political posturings that make it so hard to act responsibly and compassionately.[14]

If modelers, instead of seeing themselves as scientific adjuncts to the policy process, could shift to seeing themselves as experimental, and even compassionate, their practice would be turned inside out. They would be free of having to make complicated models in order to stave off the worst possible criticism, that of not knowing. They would no longer be boxed into personal and institutional situations where they dare not be wrong. They could participate in experiments, publicize and learn from their mistakes, work closely and honestly with people, communicate clearly.

To us the saddest result of the 'Model I' pattern of knowing and controlling is that the technique of computer modeling becomes distorted, with great effort, into a tool for the impossible tasks of predicting, optimizing, and prescribing, rather than being used for what it actually can do best. Modelers are bold to the point of hubris about their abilities to do what in fact they cannot do, while being humble to the point of blindness about their truly great potential as contributors to the processes of social experimentation and design. Models could be used to develop social visions far more internally consistent than those generated by mental models alone. They could point the way to critical, decisive experiments, and actively test social theories at far less cost than the costs of imposing those theories in ignorance and arrogance upon the whole society. They could be used to search for imprecise policies that are robust against uncertainties rather than precise policies that try to optimize something that is not understood. Perhaps most important, they could simply serve as communication devices in which different, partial, mental models of the social system could be expressed and integrated.

The self-image that can replace the idea of the policymaker as omniscient controller is that of the policymaker as an interactive, responsive social designer, where the designing is an experimental and democratic process.

> We have in our hands the potential to create a blossoming of human culture—an Eden on earth and in the minds of men. Will we be able to do it? Can we find the will to do it? For me, this is a design problem ...
> 'Design', as used here, implies not only beauty, well formed for use, but includes also the factor of human shaping for positive ends. Good design is one of the most critical needs at this point in human history—good design not only by those who call themselves designers, which will not suffice, but also by society at large. We need a general awareness of the need of good design in all elements of life and the encouragement to all people to take part. The finest design for society will not be one worked up by specialists, but one designed by the people themselves to fit their needs. Planners and designers are needed, but only to help, not to pre-empt the work of creating a new society.[15]

Seeing computer modeling as an aid to social exploration and design rather than certainty and control is perfectly consistent with seeing computer modeling as a tool for the practice of the scientific method. But we believe that even these two ways of seeing are not enough. The focus of the modeling profession needs to be shifted from technical and rational abilities (which are still very much necessary) to another set of abilities. Some of them have already been named in the discussion so far: compassion, humility, vulnerability, honesty. All of them are simple human abilities. They are barely visible in the old self-image of the computer modeler, but they are critical to the new one.

D. COMPUTER MODELERS AS HUMAN BEINGS

The published accounts of computer modeling, including this book so far, contain almost no recognition of the individual, personal, quirky humanity of computer modelers. The modelers' own self-descriptions of their work, and our presentation of the models in Part III, which is written in traditional mode, talk about everything except the personalities of the modelers. The avoidance of this issue is striking when you begin to notice it. We would find it hard to talk about the work of a painter or a novelist without some sense of the cultural context and personal idiosyncracies of the person behind the work. It would be important to know about his or her health, relationship with parents or spouse, age at the time of the work, degree of integration or rebellion with society, psychological stability. But it is taboo to want to know these things about computer modelers (or scientists, or, to a lesser degree, policymakers).

And yet, even in our outsiders' descriptions here of the modeling work and in the short technical quotations from the modeling groups, some sense of who the modelers are as people does manage to come through. We submit that the unacceptable topic of the humanity of modelers is, in fact, always being addressed in an implicit way, and that we all know it is of utmost importance. People who make computer models of social systems are part of that very powerful group who define society to itself. Their activities within the system affect the system. To be responsible for the fact that their models are at least partially reality-shaping and legitimating, modelers have to be, in addition to good scientists, good people. They have to be open, wise, empathetic, and self-insightful, all traits for which they have received no training and for which they have not been selected.

> Now to be the kind of person who truly accepts his responsibility as that of creating certain kinds of temporary realities requires knowledge of and access to self far beyond that possessed by most people in this society. It requires such knowledge and access because being a creator and participator in temporary myths in a turbulent world lays very heavy personal demands on the systems person and the planner. I will mention two requirements: living with uncertainty and embracing error.
>
> The experience of uncertainty, as I am using the word, is not that dealt with in economics or decision theory. I mean psychological uncertainty: the uncertainty that arises when you know that you do not know; when you know that there is no honest way to put a number on something, no subjective probability to be assigned. It is the uncertainty that comes when you realize that you do not understand your situation well enough to be in control of it. All one can do is live in it and learn from it and try to create possibilities and see what happens to them as one goes along, whether they add to one's life and the lives of others or they do not. But living this way, especially as a professional using the systems approach ... calls for a special sense of self-worthiness.
>
> Error-embracing is *the* condition for learning. It means seeking and using—and sharing—information about what went wrong with what you expected or hoped would go right. Both error embracing and living with high levels of uncertainty emphasize our personal as well as societal vulnerability. Typically we hide our vulnerabilities from ourselves as well as from others. But if we are going to create and live in temporary myths, we must understand our repressed fears and anxieties about being vulnerable and learn to live with them and use them creatively.[16]

The myth that prevents being the sort of person described above is the myth of analysts as objective and impersonal. The myth, or way of looking, that will bring forth a new behavior is the self-image of analysts as individual human beings who know how to use rational tools, but also know their non-rational selves.

No human activity, including science, including computer modeling, is truly objective. Far more than modelers are willing to recognize, their personalities are interwoven with every phase of their modeling activity, from the choice of method and research question, through the writing of equations, to the mode of interacting with the client and presenting the results. Each model is a subtle reflection not only of the insights, experiences, and technical expertise of its makers, but also of their biases and worldviews, fears, repressions, loves and hates. Computer modeling, like science, policymaking, and business, is a very human drama.

That fact is a cause for dismay only if one fails to recognize it, and only if one needs to hold to the view of social systems as objectively knowable and controllable. By recognizing their humanity instead of denying it, computer modelers can release their energy from trying to produce something that is not possible—objective, comprehensive understanding—and turn instead to what can be produced—a human sharing of perceptions that can lead to deeper insight about why people do what they do, value what they value, and resist what they resist.

To explore that territory requires venturing far beyond the boundaries of what science has labelled as legitimate. It requires treading into two areas where scientists have been trained to be most skeptical and uncomfortable. One is the soft and slippery fields of psychology, psychotherapy, religion, philosophy, and the 'consciousness' or 'human potential' movements. The other is self-examination, being willing to watch one's own experience more carefully and to feel one's own intuitions and emotions more fully. Nothing could be more difficult for a well-trained scientist. And yet these processes, which are viewed as antithetical to physical science, are absolutely necessary to social science, where the investigator is not and can never be fully distinct from the system under investigation. To make the tool of the scientific method applicable to social systems, the scientist must release it from the unexamined beliefs and unrecognized emotions in which it is embedded.

Modelers are human, not detached, machine-like, infallible, or unfeeling objects. They make mistakes, from which they learn and change. They do not always work with quality, but they can recognize quality when they see it. They create, innovate, seek to overcome their limitations, and cling desperately to their old habits. Each one has moments of brilliant insight and apathetic dullness, selfish distrust and loving contribution. To the extent that modelers can recognize their own miraculous complexity, they will be able to recognize it in others, including their clients and the masses who make up the systems they model. To that extent modeling will become more accurate, more useful, and more used.

Modelers are themselves in the system, as is everyone. Their models reflect and feed back the paradigms they themselves were raised and trained in. They are constrained by the limits of their own experience, mental categories, and imaginations. Modelers influence each other, sensing each others' approval or disapproval, responding to their system's information streams, rewards, and punishments. They can transcend the system's structure only by seeing clearly how the system includes and influences them.

Modelers need each other, as all people need each other, to sort out particular, partially correct viewpoints from whatever globally enduring truths there may be, and to pool very different talents, disciplines, and methods. The models themselves emphasize the fact that no individual or economic sector or company or nation can succeed through the failure of others, but each can blossom through the support of others.

And above all, modelers, like all human beings, care. The currently accepted ways for modern human beings to look at themselves do not make it easy to acknowledge or express their actual deep interest in the welfare of the planet and of all who live on it. But the caring is there. We have perceived it in all the modelers described in this book; indeed in all the modelers we have known. It is hard to imagine why anyone would enter such a demanding and often tedious field in the first place, if not propelled by some vision of a world that is very much better, by some commitment to that vision, and by a belief that computer modeling can help to achieve it.

The job is to balance a more rigorous scientific self-image with a more permissive human one. It is a classic divergent problem—a problem of reconciling what our culture usually views as incompatible opposites. Holding onto both opposites at the same time can strengthen each of them, as Eastern thinkers, who practice the art of balancing dualities, know. For Westerners, Robert M. Pirsig has expressed the possibility and the potential of blending the human capabilities of rational thinking and of caring. The following compilation of his words is slightly paraphrased so that the discussion is about modeling instead of motorcycle mechanics:

> In the past our common universe of reason has been in the process of escaping, rejecting the romantic, irrational world of prehistoric man. It's been necessary since before the time of Socrates to reject the passions, the emotions, in order to free the rational mind for an understanding of nature's order. Now it's time to further an understanding of nature's order by reassimilating those passions. The passions, the emotions, the affective domain of man's consciousness, are a part of nature's order too.
>
> The difference between a good modeler and a bad one is precisely the ability to *select* the good facts from the bad ones on the basis of quality. He has to *care!* This is an ability about which formal traditional scientific method has nothing to say. To put it in more concrete terms: If you want to build a model or fix a motorcycle or set a nation right, then classical, structural, dualistic subject-object knowledge, although necessary, isn't enough. You have to have some feeling for the quality of the work. You have to have a sense of what's good. *That* is what carries you forward.
>
> We think that if we are going to reform the world and make it a better place to live in, the way to do it is not with talk about relationships of a political nature, which are inevitably dualistic, full of subjects and objects and their relationship to one another; or with programs full of things for other people to do. We think that kind of approach starts at the end and presumes the end is the beginning. Programs of a political nature are important *end products* of social quality that can be effective only if the underlying structure of social values is right. The social values

are right only if the individual values are right. The place to improve the world is first in one's own heart and head and hands, and then work outward from there.[17]

Modelers can see themselves as well-meaning but basically powerless pawns in the system of political shoving, at the mercy of clients and funders who are bent on trivial purposes and who are not likely to follow any advice that is different from what they already thought. They can see themselves as removed, objective, purified by the truth as revealed within social statistics and high R^2 values. They can believe themselves to be more knowledgeable about the system than anyone else, and regard knowledge as necessary for action and mistakes as proof of incompetence. They can consider that their major contributions to society are their quantitative tools and the precise-appearing numbers they generate. It is not hard to imagine what kind of structure and behavior are bound to emerge from this way of seeing—it is the field of system analysis depicted in this book.

Or modelers can see themselves as responsible not to parochial, short-term interests, but to all humankind. They can see themselves as simplifiers, clarifiers, and fellow-explorers. They can listen more than they talk, ask the questions people really want asked, draw forth visions, designs, and experiments. They can be comfortable with the fact that they have glands, hearts, values, beliefs, moral stands, and blind spots. They can be willing to be wrong, vulnerable, caring, and idealistic. They can hold the highest intellectual standards of scientific hypothesis-formation and disproof, along with the highest human standards of integrity, compassion, and truthfulness. We can imagine what kind of system of modeling such a self-image might bring forth. It would be a transformation.

NOTES AND REFERENCES

1. R. M. Pirsig, *Zen and the Art of Motorcycle Maintenance*, Toronto, Bantam Books, p. 94, 1975.
2. P. L. Berger and T. Luckman, *The Social Construction of Reality*, New York, Anchor Books, pp. 60 and 89, 1967.
3. G. Majone, 'Pitfalls of Analysis and the Analysis of Pitfalls', *Urban Analysis*, **4**, 249, 1977.
4. J. Platt, 'Strong Inference', *Science*, **146 (3642)**, 347, October 16, 1954.
5. J. Platt, *op.cit.* Our italics.
6. J. von Neumann, *Collected Works*, London, Pergamon Press, Vol. VI, p. 101, 1963.
7. D. A. Schön, *The Reflective Practitioner*, New York, Basic Books, pp. 148 and 150–151, 1983.
8. R. M. Pirsig, *op.cit.*, pp. 160–161.
9. See for example, the seven global models described in D. Meadows, J. Richardson, and G. Bruckmann, *Groping in the Dark*, Chichester, John Wiley & Sons, 1982.
10. E. F. Schumacher, *Small is Beautiful*, New York, Harper & Row, pp. 97–99, 1973.
11. Donald N. Michael, 'Competence and Compassion in an Age of Uncertainty', *World Future Society Bulletin*, January/February 1983.
12. D. A. Schön, *op.cit.*, pp. 226–227.

13. G. Brewer, *Politicians, Bureaucrats and the Consultant*, New York, Basic Books, p. 234, 1973.
14. D. Michael, *op.cit.*
15. W. S. Cowperthwaite, 'Society by Design', *Manas*, **XXXVI**, **50**, 1, December 14, 1983.
16. D. Michael, in H. A. Linstone and W. H. C. Simmonds (eds), *Futures Research*, Reading, Mass., Addison-Wesley, pp. 98–99, 1977.
17. Paraphrased from several scattered excerpts from R. M. Pirsig, *op.cit.*

Epilogue

The computer as oracle is a natural image, a modern twist of an ancient thread, an expression of the continuing desire to know the future as a way of making wise decisions in the present. But even in the earliest forms of human society there were sources of wisdom very different from the oracles. There were sages and masters, much less flashy, less popular at court, who denied both the possibility and the utility of knowing the future. They focused attention not on the crystal-ball but on the being who gazed into it. Instead of predicting, they:

- Questioned how it is we know what we think we know.
- Exposed false assumptions.
- Put daily affairs in a larger perspective.
- Showed the interconnectedness of all things.
- Pointed to the wisdom each person can find within.

The oracles gave down-to-earth, practical-sounding messages that seemed compelling at the time. Most of them are forgotten now, and the few that are remembered are not notable for their accuracy or usefulness. But the sages, who talked more about the present than the future, and more about acceptance than about manipulation, gave messages that are still quoted, pondered, and used, even thousands of years later. For example:

> To every thing there is a season, and a time to every purpose under the heaven. A time to be born and a time to die, a time to plant and a time to pluck up that which is planted. A time to kill and a time to heal, a time to break down and a time to build up. A time to cast away stones and a time to gather stones together, a time to embrace and a time to refrain from embracing.
> Ecclesiastes

> All actions take place in time by the interweaving of the forces of nature, but the man lost in selfish delusion thinks that he himself is the actor. But the man who knows the relation between the forces of nature and actions, sees how some forces of nature work upon other forces of nature, and becomes not their slave.
> Bhagavad Gita

> Disputation is a proof of not seeing clearly.
> Chuang Tzu

Any path is only a path, and there is no affront, to oneself or to others, in dropping it if that is what your heart tells you ... Look at every path closely and deliberately. Try it as many times as you think necessary. Then ask yourself, and yourself alone, one question ... Does this path have a heart? If it does, the path is good; if it doesn't it is of no use.

Don Juan in Carlos Castaneda,
The Teachings of Don Juan

I am not at all concerned with appearing to be consistent. In my pursuit after truth I have discarded many ideas and learnt many new things ... What I am concerned with is my readiness to obey the call of truth.

The opinions I have formed and the conclusions I have arrived at are not final. I may change them tomorrow ... All I have done is to try experiments ... on as vast a scale as I could do.

Gandhi

The more laws and restriction there are,
The poorer people become.
The sharper men's weapons,
The more trouble in the land.
The more ingenious and clever men are,
The more strange things happen.
The more rules and regulations,
The more thieves and robbers.
Therefore the sage says:
    I take no action and people are reformed.
    I enjoy peace and people become honest.
    I do nothing and people become rich.
    I have no desires and people return to the good and simple life.

Lao Tzu,
Tao Teh Ching

Man is describing himself when he thinks that he is describing others ...

When he says: 'This teaching is sublime,' he means: 'This appears to suit me.' But we might have wanted to know something about the teaching, not how he thinks it influences him.

In order to know the nature of the teaching, we would have to know the nature of the person upon whom it has acted. The ordinary person cannot know this: all he can know is what that person assumes to be an effect upon himself—and he has no coherent picture of what 'himself' is ...

While this situation still obtains, there will generally be an equal number of people saying; 'This is marvelous,' as are saying: 'This is ridiculous'. This is ridiculous really means: 'This is ridiculous to me,' and this is marvelous means: 'This is marvelous to me'.

Would you like to be able to test what is really ridiculous or marvelous, or anything in between?

You can do it, but not ... in the midst of being quite uncertain as to what it is you are and why you like or dislike anything.

When you have found yourself, you can have knowledge. Until then you can only have opinions.

You have not met yourself yet. The only advantage of meeting others in the meantime is that one of them may present you to yourself ...

When you do meet yourself, you come into a permanent endowment and bequest of knowledge that is like no other experience on earth.

Tariqavi retold by Idries Shah[1]

We have been in the process of writing this book for a long time. It took so long because we chose to let our other activities take up much of our time. Most of those activities were in the modeling world—teaching about models, making them, working with clients successfully and unsuccessfully, attending conferences in which modelers talked about their work with varying degrees of honesty, watching how policymakers used, did not use, or misused models.

Our own perceptions about modeling have developed considerably over this period, necessitating the rewriting of sections of this book we thought we had finished. The primary shift we have experienced is, as the sages have always advised, a decreasing interest in the hardware, the techniques, the data and apparatus of modeling, and an increasing interest in the persons using the apparatus.

While we were learning and changing, the field of modeling was also developing. The stories of the nine models are still unfolding, especially their effects on the world. And in the process those modelers, and most others we have encountered, have been developing as persons. The rewriting we have had to do has primarily been to excise our most cynical and hopeless sentences.

We have seen many modelers become less mechanical and more human, less intellectually rigid and more open, less apparently omniscient and more willing to discuss humbly what they do and do not know. The literature reflects this change, with interesting new articles about the philosophy of knowledge, about human relations, about ethics and paradigms.[2] Modelers are beginning to view themselves less as objective technicians and more as well-meaning but very fallible participants in a social system where everyone is fallible in some way or another, but also where everyone has something unique to contribute.

We believe that this trend toward humanization of modeling is not an accident, but is an inevitable consequence of the process of modeling itself. The computer is not and will never be a reliable oracle. But it can be an unrelenting, merciless guru. It demands complete precision, consistency, and explicitness, and it delivers back the logical results of one's statements about the world with no tactful allowance for what the modeler might have expected or hoped. Modeling forces the modeler to look at interconnections and to see that the separations of disciplines and politics are artifacts of the human mind, not characteristics of the real world. The clash of modeling paradigms awakens one's interest in the very existence of paradigms and alerts one to how mental models shape the world. Any modeler wrestling with the representation of a social system in the demanding language of the computer must come to terms with uncertainty, with the inadequacy of social data, and with the annoying tendency of interconnected elements not to behave in the way he or she thought they would. Modelers may enter their profession in hopes of becoming oracles, of knowing all there is to know and of seeing clearly into the future. But if they let it do so, the profession itself will nudge them in the direction of becoming sages, questioning conventional wisdom, examining the ultimate purposes that should guide decisions, and shaping the future rather than predicting it.

We have said that computer modeling can add five important qualities to human understanding beyond what can be achieved by the mind alone:

1. Precision.
2. Comprehensiveness.
3. Logic.
4. Explicitness.
5. Flexibility.

The great problems that threaten modern social systems—poverty and hunger, armaments and terrorism, environmental destruction and resource depletion—certainly would be helped if these five qualities became regular elements in human decision-making. But we have also said that these qualities cannot be realized unless modelers become compassionate, humble, open-minded, responsible, self-insightful, and committed. If *those* qualities became regular elements in human decision-making, the problems of the globe would certainly be solved.

NOTES AND REFERENCES

1. Idries Shah, *Wisdom of the Idiots*, New York, E. P. Dutton, 1971.
2. For a set of excellent examples, see H. A. Linstone and W. H. C. Simmonds, *Futures Research*, Reading, Mass, Addison-Wesley, 1977; D. A. Schön, *The Reflective Practitioner*, New York, Basic Books, 1983; and for a similar trend in the world of business, see T. J. Peters and R. H. Waterman, *In Search of Excellence*, New York, Harper and Row, 1982.

Index

accuracy
  definition, 12
activities
  in optimization modeling, 65, 68
Adelman, Irma, 220
aggregation of models
  in input–output analysis, 62–63
  in optimization models, 70
  in system dynamics, 39
agricultural output, 305–318
  in the CHAC model, 275–279
  in the KASM model, 232–233
  in the LTSM model, 186–187
  possible determining factors, 103
Almon, Clopper, 127–129, 132, 134–136, 141, 379

BACHUE model, 9, 94, 176, 180, 228, 353, 355, 365, 371
  boundary, 202–204
  comprehensiveness of, 362, 363
  computer requirements, 222
  conclusions, 219–221
  data, 216
  documentation, 222–223, 366, 367
  implementation, 221–222
  institutional setting, 198–199
  method, 200–201
  migration in, 333, 334, 339, 341–342, 343, 344
  population growth in, 298, 299–303
  production, consumption, and investment in, 308, 310
  purpose, 199–200
  resources and environment in, 346–347, 351
  rigor of, 360
  structure, 205–216
  technology in, 320, 321, 327
  testing, 217–219, 369
Banco de Mexico, 9, 267, 381
Barney, Gerald O., v, xv
behavioral equations
  in econometric models, 43
Beltran del Rio, Abel, 9, 95, 248–253, 260–265, 282, 309, 338, 353, 360, 368, 381
biases
  of modelers and clients, 406
  of the authors of this book, 13–15, 27, 364
'black box' models, 14, 228
  see also simplicity
Blandy, Richard, 198
boundary of model, 93–97
  definition of diagram, 98
  diagram of BACHUE model, 202
  of CHAC model, 275
  of KASM model, 230
  of LTSM model, 183
  of *MexicoV* model, 254
  of RfF model, 131
  of SAHEL model, 109
  of SOS model, 148
  of TEMPO model, 165

causality
  definition and representation, 11
  diagram of, 97–100
  in system dynamics, 34
CHAC model, 9, 94, 222, 352, 355, 371, 414

boundary, 273–274
comprehensiveness of, 362, 363
computer requirements, 284–285
conclusions, 281–284
data, 279
documentation, 286, 366, 367
implementation, 285–286
institutional setting, 267–268
method, 269–273
migration in, 333, 334, 335–336
population growth in, 295, 298
production, consumption, and investment in, 308, 311
purpose, 268–269
resources and environment in, 346, 347, 351, 352
rigor of, 359, 360, 361
structure, 274–279
technology in, 320, 321
testing, 279–281, 368, 369
checklist for model description, 93–96
clients for models
definition, 13
for the nine study models, 9
relationship with modelers, 385
system dynamics and, 41–42
Coale–Hoover model, 163–164, 198, 199
Cobb–Douglas production function, 100, 166, 218, 312, 322–323, 339
Commission on Population Growth and the American Future, 9. 125, 130, 139–141, 381
complexity in models, *see* simplicity
composite models, 73–75, 201
constraints
in optimization modeling, 65, 68, 69
consumption, 305–318
in the BACHUE model, 209–210
in the LTSM model, 184
in the TEMPO model, 168
possible determining factors, 103
correlation
definition and representation, 12
in econometrics, 49

Dantzig, George, B., 64
data, 392–393
in econometric models, 52–53, 80, 81
in input–output models, 60, 63
in system dynamics models, 80–81
in the BACHUE model, 216
in the CHAC model, 279
in the KASM model, 236–237
in the LTSM model, 191

in the *MexicoV* model, 260
in the RfF model, 135
in the SAHEL model, 115
in the SOS model, 155–156
in the TEMPO model, 170, 172
decisionmakers, *see* clients
delays, *see* time lags
demographic transition, 293, 296–297, 298–302
desertification, 107, 112, 118
detailed-implementation models, 25, 51, 62, 69, 70
documentation of models, 366–367, 393, 399–400, 409–410
in optimization, 72
in system dynamics, 38
DOE
see US Department of Energy
Duloy, Jacques, 9, 95
DYNAMO computer language, 29, 37, 39, 40, 108, 120, 195
sample model, 30

Econometrica, 43
econometrics, 42–54
characteristics, 47–50
in the *MexicoV* model, 249–252
origin, 43
paradigm, as opposed to system dynamics, 75–86
problems and limitations, 51–54
sample models, 43–47
typical uses, 50–51
endogenous
definition, 12
Enke, Stephen, 9, 94, 162
environment, *see* resources
EPA, *see* US Environmental Protection Agency
error term
in econometric equations, 43, 50
estimation, *see* parameters
exogenous
definition, 12
variables in econometrics, 48
expectations, inclusion in models, *see* 'soft' variables

feedback
behavior of negative loops, 36
behavior of positive loops, 36
definition, 12
importance in system dynamics, 34
presence in econometrics, 48

forecasting, *see* prediction
FORTRAN computer language, 37, 146, 160, 161, 177, 181, 195, 245, 264
Forrester, Jay W., 27, 38, 76, 84–85, 108, 181, 365

general understanding models, 24, 38
Global 2000 study, xiii, 13
guidelines for modeling, 403–411

Harrod–Domar production function, 312, 323
Holling, C. S., 146
Hopkins, Michael J. D., 9, 95
House, Peter W., 9, 94, 140, 144–147, 157, 159–160, 365, 379

implementation, 373–387, 404, 405
 hypotheses about ineffectiveness, 382–385
 of the BACHUE model, 221–222, 379, 380, 381
 of the CHAC model, 285–286, 379, 380, 381
 of the KASM model, 242–245, 379, 380, 381
 of the LTSM model, 195, 379
 of the *MexicoV* model, 264, 379, 380
 of the RfF model 140, 380
 of the SAHEL model, 120–123, 377–378, 380
 of the SOS model, 159–160, 380
 of the TEMPO model, 175–177, 379, 380, 381
income distribution, *see* output allocation
industrial output, 305–318
 in the LTSM model, 186
 in the SOS model, 150–151
 in the TEMPO model, 168
 possible determining factors, 103
industrialization, 291–293, 352–356
input–output analysis
 as demand-driven production function, 310
 characteristics, 59–61
 in RfF model, 127–130, 132–134
 origin, 55
 problems and limitations, 62–64
 sample model, 55–59
 typical uses, 61–62
International Bank for Reconstruction and Development (IBRD), *see* World Bank
International Institute for Applied Systems Analysis (IIASA), xiii
International Research and Technology Corporation (IRT), 129–130
investment allocation, 305–318
 possible determining factors, 103

KASM model, 9, 94, 222, 352, 355, 371
 boundary, 228–230
 comprehensiveness of, 362, 363
 computer requirements, 245
 conclusions, 241
 data, 236–237
 documentation, 245–246, 366, 367
 implementation, 242–245
 institutional setting, 225–227
 method, 227–228
 migration in, 333, 334, 335, 336, 337
 population growth in, 298–299
 production, consumption, and investment in, 308, 310–311
 purpose, 227
 resources and environment in, 346, 347, 351, 352
 rigor of, 359, 360
 structure, 230–236
 technology in, 320, 321, 325–329
 testing, 241–242, 368, 369
Keynes, John Maynard, 250–251, 289
Klein, Lawrence, 248
Klein Interwar Economic Model, 99
Korean Ministry of Agriculture and Fisheries (MAF), 226, 240, 243–244, 381
Korean National Agricultural Economics Research Institute (NAERI), 226, 244
Kornai, Janos, 181

labor allocation
 possible determining factors, 103
 see also migration
least-squares regression, 49, 251
 in Almon input–output model, 128–129
Leontief, Wassily, 55
levels (state variables)
 in system dynamics, 34–35
Limits to Growth study, 13
Lin, Wuu-Long, 9, 94, 181
linear programming
 see optimization
linearity
 in econometrics, 49
 in input–output analysis, 58, 60, 63–64
 in optimization, 68, 70
 see also nonlinearity

Lotka–Volterra model, 146
LTSM model, 9, 94, 176, 198, 212, 353, 354, 371
 boundary, 182–183
 comprehensiveness of, 362
 computer requirements, 195
 conclusions, 193–195
 data, 191
 documentation, 195–196, 366, 367
 implementation, 195
 institutional setting, 179
 method, 181–182
 migration in, 188–190, 333, 334, 339, 340–341, 342,343
 population growth in, 298, 299–300
 production consumption, and investment in, 308, 312
 purpose, 179–180
 resources and environment in, 346, 347
 rigor of, 360
 structure, 183–191
 technology in, 320, 321, 323–324, 326–327
 testing, 191–193, 368, 369

Malthusian theory, 13, 145, 176
market system
 in input–output analysis, 63
 representation in the CHAC model, 270, 274–279, 311
  in the KASM model, 311
 sample dynamic econometric model, 45–47
 sample static econometric model, 43–45
 sample system dynamics model, 29–33
Martos, Bela, 9, 94, 181, 196, 353
MexicoV model, 9, 94, 282, 355, 371, 414
 boundaries, 252–253
 comprehensiveness of, 363
 computer requirements, 264
 conclusions, 262–264
 data, 260
 documentation, 264–265, 366, 367
 implementation, 264
 institutional setting, 248–249
 method, 249–252
 migration in, 333, 334, 337–338, 339
 population growth in, 295, 298
 production, consumption, and investment in, 308, 309
 purpose, 249
 resources and environment in, 346, 351
 rigor of, 360

 structure, 253–260
 technology in, 319–320
 testing, 260–261, 368, 369
Michael, Donald, 426
Michigan State University (MSU), 225–227, 242–244, 381
migration, 331–344
 in the BACHUE model, 333, 334, 339, 341–342, 343, 344
 in the CHAC model, 333, 334, 335–336
 in the KASM model, 333, 334, 335, 336, 337
 in the LTSM model, 188–190, 333, 334, 339, 340–341, 342, 343
 in the *MexicoV* model, 333, 334, 337–338, 339
 in the RfF model, 333, 334, 335, 336, 337
 in the SAHEL model, 333–334
 in the SOS model, 333, 334, 336–337
 in the TEMPO model, 168, 333, 334, 339–340, 343
Miser, Hugh J., v, xiii, xv
Models, computer
 advantages of, 6, 14, 15
 dangers of, 14, 15
 definition, 5
 for detailed implementation, 25
 for general understanding, 24
 for policy design, 24–25
 illustrative uses of, 5
Models, general
 definition, 2, 11
Models, mathematical, 5
Models, mental
 definition, 2, 11
motivations, human, *see* 'soft' variables

Nixon, President Richard M., 125, 140
nonlinearity
 importance in system dynamics, 37
 representation in system dynamics, 30, 31
Norton, Roger, 9, 94

objective function
 in optimization modeling, 65, 68, 69
 of the CHAC model, 270–271
optimization
 characteristics, 68–70
 in CHAC model, 269–273
 origin, 64
 problems and limitations, 71–73
 sample model, 65–68

typical uses, 70–71
oracle at Delphi, 1, 3, 14
output allocation
   in the BACHUE model, 212–213
   possible determining factors, 103
overgrazing, 110–111

paradigm, 19–20, 26, 417–419
   combinations of, 74–75, 85
   conflict between econometrics and system dynamics, 75–86
   definition, 19
   gulfs between, 76–77
   of computer modeling, 21–22
   of econometrics, 47–50
   of input–output analysis, 59–61
   of optimization, 68–70, 72–73
   of systems dynamics, 28, 34–38, 108
   ways of classifying modeling paradigms, 22–25
parameters of a model, 32
   definition, 12
   estimation of
     in BACHUE model, 201
     in econometrics, 47, 51–53, 81
     in system dynamics, 40, 81
Pareto, Vilfredo, 55
perceptions, inclusion in models, *see* 'soft' variables
Picardi, Anthony, 9, 94, 106–109, 113–115, 118–123, 282, 324, 365, 368, 379, 380, 414
Pirsig, Robert M., 432
policy-design models, 24–25, 38, 43, 51
population growth, 293–305
   as a deterrent to economic growth, 163, 173, 198
   in the BACHUE model, 205–208, 298, 299–303
   in the CHAC model, 295, 298
   in the KASM model, 298–299
   in the LTSM model, 185–186, 298, 299–302
   in the *MexicoV* model, 295, 298
   in the RfF model, 138–139, 298, 299
   in the SAHEL model, 112–113, 298, 301–303
   in the SOS model, 149–150, 298, 299, 302, 304
   in the TEMPO model, 298–300
   possible determining factors, 103
precision
   definition, 12

importance of, in econometrics and system dynamics, 77–78
prediction (forecasting)
   in econometrics, 43
   possibility of, 21–22, 75–76, 77–79
problem definition
   in econometrics and system dynamics, 77

Quesnay, François, 55

rates
   in system dynamics, 35
reference structure diagram
   definition of, 100–104
   for the BACHUE model, 214
   for the CHAC model, 278
   for the KASM model, 235
   for the LTSM model, 190
   for the *MexicoV* model, 259
   for the RfF model, 135
   for the SAHEL model, 117
   for the SOS model, 155
   for the TEMPO model, 172
resource and environment, 344–352
   in production functions, 313–314, 316
   in the BACHUE model, 346–347, 351
   in the CHAC model, 346, 347, 351, 352
   in the KASM model, 346, 347, 351, 352
   in the LTSM model, 346, 347
   in the *MexicoV* model, 346, 351
   in the RfF model, 127, 129, 130, 138, 346, 347–348, 352
   in the SAHEL model, 346, 348–349, 351, 352
   in the SOS model, 151–153, 346, 349–351, 352
   in the TEMPO model, 346–347, 351
   possible determining factors, 103
Resources for the future, 126
RfF model, 9, 94, 144, 222, 354, 359–360, 371, 414
   boundaries, 130–132
   comprehensiveness of, 362, 363
   conclusions, 137–140, 364
   data, 134–136
   documentation, 141, 366, 367
   implementation, 140
   institutional setting, 125–126
   method, 126–130
   migration in, 333, 334, 335, 336, 337
   population growth in, 298, 299
   production, consumption, and investment in, 308, 310

purpose, 126
reference structure, 135
resources and environment in, 127, 129, 130, 138, 346, 347–348, 352
rigor of, 360
structure, 132–134
technology in, 320, 324–325
testing, 136–137, 368, 369
Ridker, Ronald, 9, 94, 126, 130, 136, 140, 379, 380
Rockefeller, John D., III, 125
Rodgers, Gerald D., 9, 95

Sahel
drought in, 106–107
development policies for, 109, 112, 121–122
development policies for, 109, 112, 121–122
SAHEL model, 9, 94, 352, 354, 359, 364, 371
boundary, 108–110
comprehensiveness of, 362–363
computer requirements, 120
conclusions, 115–119
data, 115
documentation, 123, 366, 367
implementation, 120–123
institutional setting, 106–107
method, 108
migration in, 333–334
population growth in, 298, 299, 301–303
production, consumption, and investment in, 308, 313, 317
purpose, 107
reference structure, 117
resources and environment in, 346, 348–349, 351, 352
rigor of, 359
structure, 110–115
technology in, 320, 324
testing, 119–120, 368, 369
Schon, Donald, 423, 427
Schumacher, E. F., 331
scientific method, 419–420
SEAS model, 140, 144, 156, 158
Seifert, William, 106
sensitivity of models
in econometrics, 54
in optimization, 71–72
in system dynamics, 40–41
sensitivity testing, 368–369, 393–394
in the BACHUE model, 217–218

in the CHAC model, 280
in the LTSM model, 193
in the RfF model, 136
in the SAHEL model, 120
in the SOS model, 156
in the TEMPO model, 174–175
simplicity in models, 14, 74, 362–363, 396–398
in system dynamics, 39
simulation modeling, 28
simultaneous equations
in econometrics, 48
'soft' variables, 363
inclusion of, in econometrics, 48–49
in system dynamics, 38
in the SAHEL model, 114
SOS model, 9, 94, 353, 354, 365, 371, 414
boundary, 147–149
comprehensiveness of, 362, 363
computer requirements, 160
conclusions, 157–159
data, 155–156
documentation, 160–161, 366, 367
implementation, 159–160
institutional setting, 144
method, 145–147
migration in, 333, 334, 336–337
population growth in, 298, 299, 302, 304
production, consumption, and investment in, 308, 313–314, 317
purpose, 145
resources and environment in, 151–153, 346, 349–351, 352
structure, 149–155
technology in, 320, 327–328
testing, 156–157, 368, 369
state variables, *see* levels
structural coefficients
in econometric models, 43–50
structural matrix
in input–output analysis, 58
structure of a model, 32
definition, 12
relation to behavior, 37
system
definition, 11
system dynamics, 13, 27–42, 106, 200
characteristics, 34
origin, 27
paradigm, as opposed to econometrics, 75–86
problems and limitations, 39
sample model, 29

typical uses, 38
use in SAHEL model, 108

table of direct and indirect requirements in input–output analysis, 59
technical coefficients
  in input–output analysis, 58, 61
  in RfF model, 128–130
technology, 319–331
  possible determining factors, 103
  in the BACHUE model, 320, 321, 326–327
  in the CHAC model, 320–321, 325
  in the KASM model, 320, 321, 324–326, 327–329
  in the LTSM model, 320, 321, 323–324, 326–327
  in the *MexicoV* model, 319–320
  in the RfF model, 320, 324–325
  in the SAHEL model, 320, 324
  in the SOS model, 320, 327–328
  in the TEMPO model, 320, 321–323, 326–327
TEMPO model, 9, 94, 180, 195, 198, 199, 200, 212, 221, 222, 353, 354, 364, 371
  boundary, 164–165
  comprehensiveness, 362
  computer requirements, 177
  conclusions, 172–177
  data, 170–172
  documentation, 177, 366, 367
  institutional setting, 162–163
  method, 163–164
  migration in, 168, 333, 334, 339–340, 343
  population growth in, 298, 299–300
  production, consumption, and investment in, 308, 312
  purpose, 163
  resources and environment in, 346–347, 351

  structure, 165–170
  technology in, 320, 321–323, 326–327
  testing, 174–175, 368, 369
time lags
  in econometrics, 48
  in input–output analysis, 60
  in system dynamics, 34–35, 37
Tinbergen, Jan, 43, 289
tragedy of the commons, 118, 122, 123
transformation, 414–443
  definition, 416
transparency in models, *see* simplicity

UN Food and Agriculture Organization (FAO), 9, 179, 195, 198
UN Fund for Population Activities (UNFPA), 9, 179
UN International Labor Organization (ILO), 9, 198, 216, 219, 221
US Agency for International Development (USAID), 9, 106, 107, 121–123, 162–163, 174–176, 225–226, 242–244, 377–378, 379, 380, 381
US Department of Energy (DOE), 159–160
US Environmental Protection Agency (EPA), 9, 144, 159

validity of models, 368–369, 401–402
  in econometrics, 54, 83–84
  in system dynamics, 41, 83–84

Walras, Leon, 55
Wery, Rene, 9, 95, 199
Wharton Economic Forecasting Associates (Wharton EFA), 248, 252, 264
Williams, Edward, 9, 94, 144–147, 157, 159–160, 365
World Bank, 9, 220, 237, 267–268, 283, 285–286, 380